**Collins** **éHow™**

# HOW TO DO
## just about
# every-
# thing

HarperCollins Publishers
Westerhill Road, Glasgow G64 2QT
www.collins.co.uk

**UK Edition**
Produced by Grant Laing Partnership
**Editors:** Jane Simmonds, Helen Ridge and Terry Burrows
**Designer:** Christine Lacey

**eHow, Inc.**
**Editor-in-Chief:** William R. Marken
**Book Editor:** Sharon Rose Beaulaurier
**Editors:** Dale Conour, Julie Jares, Jason Jensen,
Roberta Kramer, Deborah McCaskey, Jill Metzler,
Sonya Mukherjee, Mimi Towle
**Editorial Assistants:** Shawn Asim, Linette Kim,
Alison Goldberg, Matt Holohan
**Creative Director:** Patrick Barrett

**Founder:** Courtney Rosen
**CFO:** Mark Murray
**VP of Engineering:** Gladys Barnes
**Director of Business Development:** Jose Guerrero
**General Counsel:** James M. Hackett
**VP of Commerce:** Josh Prince
**VP of Marketing:** Kristen Sager
**VP of Operations:** Jeff Tinker
**VP of Product Strategy:** Joseph A. Vause
**VP of Sales:** Kevin Walsh

Courtney Rosen and other contributors to this book
appear on behalf of eHow, Inc.

**.com press**
**CEO:** John Owen
**President:** Terry Newell
**COO:** Larry Partington
**VP, International Sales:** Stuart Laurence
**VP, Publisher:** Roger Shaw
**Creative Director:** Gaye Allen

**Managing Editor:** Janet Goldenberg
**Art Director:** Diane Dempsey
**Series Manager:** Brynn Breuner
**Production & Layout:** Joan Olson, Lorna Strutt
**Production Director:** Chris Hemesath

**Project Coordinators:** Margaret Garrou, Lorna Strutt
**Contributing Edictors:** Mandy Erickson, Norman Kolpas
**Copy Chief:** Elissa Rabellino
**Copy Editors:** Linda Bouchard, Claire Breen,
Kathy Kaiser, Gail Nelson, Cynthia Rubin,
David Sweet
**Proofreader:** Ruth Jacobson
**Indexer:** Ken DellaPenta

●com|**press**
Designed and produced by .com press
.com press is a division of Weldon Owen Inc.,
814 Montgomery Street, San Francisco,
California 94133

Printed and bound in Dubai by Oriental Press

10 9 8 7 6 5 4 3

A catalogue record for this book is available from
the British Library.

ISBN 0-00768776-1

**Collins** **éHow™**

# HOW TO DO
## just about
# every-
# thing

**Courtney Rosen & the eHow Editors**

## TED SMART

# Contents

# PERSONAL FINANCE, BUSINESS AND PROPERTY

# Contents

## HOME MAINTENANCE AND IMPROVEMENT

### Plumbing

### Electrical

### Upkeep and Repair

### Security

### Remodeling

# Contents

## FOOD

## FUN ACTIVITIES

# Contents

# PETS

## Acquiring a Dog or Cat

## Dog and Cat Care

## Behaviour and Training

## Health and Safety

## Other Pets

## Coping With Loss

# Contents

**SPORTS AND RECREATION**

# Contents

# Contents

# TRAVEL

# A NOTE TO READERS

When attempting any of the described activities in this book, please note the following:

Risky activities  Certain activities described in this book are inherently dangerous or risky. Before attempting any new activity, make sure you are aware of your own limitations and consider all applicable risks (whether listed or not).

Professional advice  While we strive to provide complete and accurate information, it is not intended as a substitute for professional advice. You should always consult a professional whenever appropriate, or if you have any questions or concerns regarding medical, legal or financial advice.

Physical or health-related activities  Be sure to consult your GP before attempting any health- or diet-related activity, or any activity involving physical exertion, particularly if you have any condition that could impair or limit your ability to engage in such an activity.

Adult supervision  The activities described in this book are intended for adults only, and they should not be performed by children without responsible adult supervision.

Breaking the law  The information provided in this book should not be used to break any applicable law or regulation.

All of the information in this book is obtained from sources that we believe are accurate and reliable. However, we make no warranty, express or implied, that the information is sufficient or appropriate for every individual, situation or purpose. Further, the information may become out of date over time. You assume the risk and full responsibility for all your actions, and eHow, Inc. and the publishers will not be liable for any loss or damage of any sort, whether consequential, incidental, special or otherwise, that may result from the information presented. The descriptions of third-party products and services in this book are for information only and are not intended as an endorsement by eHow, Inc. of any particular product or service.

# Foreword

We created eHow with one clear and ambitious goal: to help people discover how to do just about everything. It's a concept that stemmed from my own personal experience.

It all began when I found myself surfing the web for hours one afternoon, trying to find out how to rotate the wheels on my inline skates. No site could give me the information I needed. *What if?* I wondered. What if there were one place on the web where I could look up just about anything I wanted to do – and get easy, step-by-step instructions?

Less than a year later, we launched eHow.com – the world's most useful website – which now provides millions of people, including me, with more than 15,000 concise sets of instructions (or "eHows", as we call them). For this book we have selected 1,001 of our favourite and most requested eHows to help you tackle life's basics during those times when you aren't online. Like our site, they provide the essential steps along with useful tips and warnings. Skill-level icons – ⌐ – indicate the ease or difficulty of each undertaking on a scale of one to five, with one being the easiest. In the last few pages you'll also find a keyword index to help you locate instructions for every task quickly.

Keep this book handy so you can refer to it whenever you need to accomplish things like removing red wine from your carpet, jump-starting your car or arranging fresh flowers. Or enjoy browsing through these pages just for fun. Who knows? One day you may need to know how to buy a property abroad, deal with foxes in your garden or cope with an au pair – and you'll find the instructions right here.

This book and the eHow.com site were made possible by the knowledge and hard work of our talented writers and editors. Our team has created answers to more than 90 per cent of the questions eHow's visitors ask day after day. Thanks to these fabulous individuals, I at last know the proper way to change a tyre, boil an egg, load a backpack, fix a toilet, and much more. I hope you'll find this knowledge as useful and rewarding as I do.

Have fun getting things done!

Courtney Rosen
Founder

## 1  Help Your Child Prepare for the First Day of School

**Is it that time again already? Follow these simple steps to help your child face those first-day fears.**

### ⊙ Steps

1  Begin preparing your child a few weeks before the big day – sooner, if this is his first school experience or a new school. If your household has relaxed bedtime and morning routines over the summer months, start to wake your child a little earlier each morning, and move bedtime up 15 minutes every few nights to re-establish "school hours".

2  Plan a back-to-school shopping day with each child individually, and make it a special event. Leave room in your budget for one or two small treats (for example, re-use last term's backpack, but buy this year's hottest cartoon-character notebook).

3  Before the big clothes-shopping trip, spend some time with each child sorting through last year's things and deciding together what goes into one of three piles marked: "to keep"; "hand-me-down"; "charity". Insist that your child try on everything being kept.

4  For a new year in a new school, try to arrange a visit a week or so before the first day. Walk through the buildings, locating the classrooms, the toilets and the canteen.

5  If your child will be going to school by bus, find out the route he will take and drive it together a few times. If he likes walking, plan the route and walk it together both ways.

6  Help your child deal with first-day jitters by focusing on some special advantage of being in a new school year. Perhaps if your child is just starting secondary school he or she is now old enough to carry a house key, or deserves an increase in pocket money.

7  Celebrate the big day. Go out for dinner, plan a special meal the night before, or present your child with a small gift.

### ✳ Tips

Unless your child's school sends out a detailed list of required supplies for his or her year, make only general purchases in August. Some secondary schools may provide lists of items your child will need for each subject a few days into the school year.

Don't wait too long to make that back-to-school shopping trip. By the middle of August, local stores may have sold out of the most popular items.

Review important safety rules with your child, such as using established walking routes to and from school, what to do if approached by a stranger, and what to do if your child misses the bus or loses the house key.

## 2  Help Your Child Make Friends at a New School

**It's hard to be the new kid, but here's how you can help your child survive and thrive in a new school.**

### ⊙ Steps

1  Contact teaching staff at the new school as soon as you know your child will be attending. Ask for whatever suggestions or support the staff can offer to help your child connect with classmates.

2  Address your child's practical concerns with specifics. Talk through ways to handle particular situations, such as who to sit with on the bus, who to eat lunch with and how to remember all those new names.

3  With a younger child, rehearse conversations she might have with a potential new friend. Suggest that your child approach a potential friend with a question or remark that will engage the person in an ongoing dialogue, which might lead to a conversation about a shared interest.

### ✳ Tip

Encourage your child to keep in touch with friends from his or her old school or neighbourhood by supplying her with stationery and stamps or – even better – an e-mail account.

4   Encourage your child to join clubs, teams or other groups that relate to his or her interests.

5   Emphasise that making friends takes time. Celebrate small successes, such as learning the names of all the girls in chemistry class or getting invited to a birthday party.

6   Be a good role model. Share with your child your own feelings about the family's recent move and how you are going about making your own new friends.

7   Be a good friend. Recognise that your child will need extra support and understanding from you to make a successful transition.

⚠ **Warning**

Most new friendships take time to develop. If, however, your child seems to have made no progress toward establishing new relationships after a few months, consider talking to a family counsellor.

---

## Reinforce Your Child's Learning at Home    3

Show your child that learning can be fun. Here are a few ways to do it.

### ⊙ Steps

1   Teach reading and writing by using holidays as a learning experience. Get younger children to read road signs, and encourage older children to keep a travel diary.

2   Enlist your child's help in writing postcards during holidays.

3   Ask your child to read for at least 30 minutes a day, and encourage him to keep a daily diary or journal.

4   Sharpen your child's skills at mental arithmetic while you shop – teach him to compare values and to add up prices.

5   If your child enjoys football or other sports teach him about league tables and other statistics.

6   Bring your child into the kitchen and ask for help in measuring ingredients for cooking.

7   Use items around the house – tins, boxes, books – to teach younger children about geometry.

8   Expand your child's horizons with history. You could construct a family tree, using your ancestors to show how history connects us with the past. Read about historical events in an encyclopedia or on a computer CD-ROM.

9   To teach geography, give your child a jigsaw puzzle map of the world to work on at home, or get him to follow a map on family trips.

10  Introduce your child to the world of science by getting him to observe and record details about the environment, such as the variety of plants and insects in the front garden, and by buying science kits.

11  Take your child to a science museum, especially one that offers lots of hands-on activities.

12  Get your child to observe the properties of water: freezing, melting, boiling, evaporating and condensing.

**✹ Tip**

Stimulating a child's curiosity and love of learning can help to develop critical mental habits that will last a lifetime.

**Things You'll Need**

❏ books

❏ notebooks

❏ encyclopedia

❏ educational puzzles

## 4   Get your Child into the Right School

A child's school days are critical to their development, both academically and socially. So choosing the right school may be one of the most important decisions you ever make.

### ⊙ Steps

1. Start thinking seriously about your child's schooling when they reach the age of three. You have to register which school you want your child to attend during the year prior to attendance, so leave yourself plenty of time to weigh up the possibilities.

2. Get a list of local state schools from your Local Education Authority (LEA) or library. Begin by looking at those in your immediate geographic vicinity. Consider the distance and routes between the school and home.

3. Make a shortlist of suitable candidates and call each one, asking for brochures or literature. The manner in which a school deals with such a simple request may give you a clue as to its desirability.

4. Visit the OFSTED web page (www.ofsted.gov.uk) and check out the government's official report on each of your possible schools.

5. Arrange to visit the school and talk to the headteacher, or other senior member of staff. Always visit during term time: this will give you a more accurate picture of day-to-day life in the school. Pay attention to the general "vibe" of the surroundings: an overly noisy atmosphere and hostile children – not to mention harassed staff – may be warning signs.

6. It's a good idea to apply to more than one school – each one will give you details of its application process.

### ✱ Tips

Sometimes the school you choose for your child will be over-subscribed. Local Education Authorities usually give precedence to those applicants with siblings already attending the school, or those who live in close proximity. If your child is refused entry because of over-subscription you have the right of appeal to your LEA.

When visiting, always look for signs of success within the confines of the National Curriculum.

## 5   Learn to Type

Mastering a computer keyboard isn't that difficult if you go about it methodically and practice a little every day. Here are some basic steps to get you started.

### ⊙ Steps

1. Put your fingers on the "home row": left fourth finger on *a,* left third finger finger on *s,* left middle finger on *d,* and left index finger on *f.* For the right hand, put the fourth finger on the semicolon, the third finger on *l,* the middle finger on *k,* and the index finger on *j.*

2. Type the following letters – looking anywhere but the keyboard – saying the names of the letters out loud and using either thumb to hit the space bar: *f f space j j space d d space k k space s s space l l space a a space semicolon semicolon space.*

3. Repeat this as many times as you need to in order to feel that you're getting an intuitive sense of these letters.

4. Bring in *g* and *h* by reaching with the appropriate index finger.

### ✱ Tips

Consider taking a a typing class or using instructional software if you feel you would learn better from a structured course.

Some find the number keys too far away to type accurately. If you experience this, watch these keys as you type, since errors with numbers can be costly.

If you use a word-processing program, check the reference manual or Help menu to learn about formatting techniques, such as changing the type style and setting new margins.

5 Use this same talking-out-loud technique to learn the rows above and below the home row: the left little finger for *q* and *z*; the right little finger for *p* and the slash. Again, the index fingers do double duty: *r, t, v* and *b* for the left index finger; *u, y, m* and *n* for the right index finger.

6 Use your little fingers for the shift key: the left when the right hand is typing the letter and vice versa.

7 Learn the numbers: left little finger for *1,* left index finger for *4* and *5,* right little finger for *0,* and right index finger for *6* and *7.*

8 Move to actual texts as soon as you can, since they'll make your learning real.

9 Master other keys as you see fit – such as the Control key and the arrow keys – but be aware that these differ from keyboard to keyboard and may not be worth learning.

10 Practice for at least 15 to 30 minutes every day.

### ⚠ Warnings

However tempting it may be, avoid looking at the keyboard – it really is the only way to learn to type.

Although the letters always remain the same, some of the other character keys may vary slightly on different models of computer keyboard.

## Study for the GCSEs
6

Success with GCSEs is dependent on two factors: building the foundations through two years of diligent classroom work, and good preparation for the exams.

### ⊙ Steps

1 Make sure that you understand *everything* you are taught in class – ask questions if you don't.

2 Take notes during classes. Make sure they are legible – they will form the basis for your exam revision. Supplement your classroom notes by looking through the syllabus and textbooks for extra information.

3 If you understand the subject, homework should be easy; if you find it too hard this could be a warning sign that you need assistance.

4 YOU CAN NEVER BEGIN REVISING TOO EARLY. Work out how much time you have before the exam and – using the syllabus – *what* you need to revise. Draw up a revision timetable.

5 Revise in a quiet, distraction-free room, taking breaks every 20 to 30 minutes.

6 Try to revise each topic at least three times before the exams – build this into your timetable. The more you revise the more you will remember. Working through past exam papers can prove helpful; use examiners' reports to read what they see as ideal answers.

6 When you begin the exam, concentrate and read the questions through several times before you begin your answer. If applicable, see how the marks are allocated among the questions: don't devote 50 per cent of the exam time to a question that is worth 20 per cent of the marks.

7 Don't simply recite your knowledge, but apply what you have learned to the question. Be detailed and concise, and – particularly in science subjects – show how you worked out your answers.

8 Always check your answers before the end of the exam.

### ✳ Tips

When you create your revision timetable try to leave two weeks blank before the exam in case you get behind.

When revising, put the subjects you like least near the front of your timetable.

### ⚠ Warning

Don't put off your revision – tomorrow never comes!

Don't believe your friends when they tell you they haven't been revising – every student revises, but some don't like to admit it.

## 7    Choose a University

Take care when choosing where you want to study – it's where you will be spending at least the next three years of your life.

### ⊙ Steps

1   You won't be spending every minute of your college life engaged in study, so your choice should be geared towards your own personality and what you *want* to get out of the university experience. Think beyond the academic: do you want to spend the next three or more years living on a self-contained student campus, or as a part of a "real" community? Do you want to remain within easy reach of your home town? These are the kinds of questions you should ask yourself.

2   The universities of Oxford and Cambridge are held in such high regard that sufficiently capable A-level students are often encouraged to apply to them, even if a course more appropriate to their own needs exists elsewhere. Keep an open mind.

3   Some newspapers print an annual league table of universities. *The Times* also publishes league tables for each main subject, including the employment prospects for graduates. Such tables are more rigorous than they used to be, but it is important also to consult university prospectuses and websites.

4   Most universities have open days to which A-level students are invited to visit. These will provide a good feel for the environment. They may also give an opportunity to question staff and students.

5   Even if eventually you – like many of the UK's movers and shakers – plan to base yourself in London, it may not be the best place to study. The cost of living may be up to 50 per cent higher than in some other parts of the country, meaning that without parental support or a scholarship you may have to work your way through college.

### ✱ Tips

In real terms, the cost of being a student have risen considerably over the past two decades. As a consequence, students are increasingly choosing to study at local universities, enabling them to reduce costs by continuing to live with their parents. Although you may end up with less of a student loan to pay off, you may also miss out on a valuable experience – for many, student life provides a first real taste of life as an independent adult.

### ⚠ Warning

Think carefully before making a decision based wholly on where your best friend, girlfriend or boyfriend wants to study: relationships can be volatile during college years.

## 8    Decide What to Study at University

The course you choose doesn't necessarily set the path for the rest of your life, but it's an important starting point. For those who have already decided on a career – medicine or law, for example – it's the first stage of the training process; for others it's an opportunity to follow interests and see where they lead.

### ⊙ Steps

1   By the time you consider college courses you will already have made your first set of choices when you selected the subjects to study for A-level. For many, university is a continuation of this process: if you enjoy and excel in one or more of your A-level subjects, university gives you the opportunity to take your study to a higher level.

### ✱ Tips

As more and more students are forced to work to finance the completion of their studies, universities are increasingly sympathetic towards requests to take breaks between academic years. Check on faculty policy beforehand if you think this may apply to you.

2 When you have decided the areas in which you want to study, find out which universities run your chosen course. Go to the UCAS (Universities and Colleges Admissions Service) web page (www.ucas.com) for a complete list.

3 Get hold of a prospectus for each university running a course in your chosen subject. You can find these in most public libraries, or order free copies direct from the university. You should be able to get the same sort of information from the university's own web page.

4 Make a shortlist of courses that interest you.

5 Discuss your shortlist with your career's guidance officer. Ask teachers in associated subject for their views.

6 Find out what the course is like in practice. What is the ratio of lectures to personal tuition? How many other students will attend seminars? Will the course be marked by continuous assessment, annual exams, or "finals" at the very end? Which system suits you best?

7 Ask yourself if the course gives you the right degree of specialisation or breadth

8 Does the course give the right qualification to fit in with your long-term aims? Will it be recognised by employers when you hit the job market..

9 Finally, ask yourself if you honestly believe you'll enjoy the course. Think again if you're not absolutely certain.

If your entry qualifications are insufficient to get you onto the course of your choice, consider first taking a lower qualification that can later be used to satisfy requirements.

## Take Lecture Notes                                                9

There are many ways to take lecture notes. The "trigger" method shown here is time-tested and widely practised.

### ⊙ Steps

1 Write down the date.

2 Draw a vertical line down the lined portion of the page, about one-third of the way over from the left margin.

3 Write down categories and questions on the left side of the line as the lecture proceeds.

4 Put specifics and answers on the right side of the line.

5 Use abbreviations to keep up with your lecturer. Simple symbols include an up arrow (↑) for "increase" and a right arrow (→) for "leads to" or "results in".

6 Note anything you're unclear about at the top of the page, and ask about it during the question period.

### ✳ Tips

Number your lists for easier structuring and recall.

Review your lecture notes during the evening of the day you took them. This should help the knowledge stick in your mind.

Consider studying for exams by covering the right side of your notes and using the left side as a trigger to help you recall details.

## 10 | Research a Subject on the Internet

If you know where to look and what sources to trust, the internet can be a great tool for conducting research.

### ⊙ Steps

1 Begin your search with a web search engine. Enter keywords or phrases related to the subject matter that interests you, and click Search.

2 In the results list, click on a site's name to go to it. Even if the site doesn't have what you're looking for, check to see if it has links to other sites that might be more useful. Use the Back button on your browser to return to the original results list.

3 If the first list had too many or too few results, tinker with your keywords to produce more focused search results.

4 Go to some of the many online encyclopedias for information about your subject. You'll find them under the Reference heading at a subject-indexed search site such as Yahoo!. From the encyclopedia's search page, enter keywords and phrases related to your subject.

5 Go to sites that specialise in internet research. These sites offer links to research materials and will sometimes do your research for you.

6 Look for online library catalogues. Some provide online access to the full text of certain articles and books.

7 Check out internet newsgroups on your subject. You can even post a request for information.

8 Visit chat rooms that are related to your subject matter.

### ✳ Tips

Use multiple search engines to get a variety of search results: the same keywords can yield very different answers.

### ⚠ Warning

Always consider the source of information: university web pages and government sources tend to be more reliable than those belonging to individuals or businesses with vested interests.

## 11 | Research a Subject in the Library

The library is an excellent place to begin researching a subject. Works are catalogued either in a computer database or – in older libraries – on cards in drawers.

### ⊙ Steps

1 Check the computer database, if your library has one. Go to a computer terminal and enter a keyword or phrase from the subject matter you wish to research. Most systems will allow you to enter a specific author, title or subject. If you are searching for newspaper, magazine or journal articles, look in an online periodical index. Note that there are indexes for specialised subject areas, such as medicine.

2 Make a note of the item's unique code: this will indicate where the book, magazine or microfilm can be found, as well as its availability status (whether or not it's checked out). At some libraries you can print or e-mail this information.

3 Alternatively, find your library's card catalogue. This is a stack of drawers containing an enormous number of note cards stored in alphabetical order. Every item in the library should have three note cards: an author

### ✳ Tips

When you find an item in the non-fiction stacks, it will usually be surrounded by many other works on the same subject. Browse the surrounding works for extra research material.

Most modern libraries offer not only books and periodicals but also microfilm, videos, audio resources and possibly internet connections. Ask your librarian for details.

card, a title card and a subject-heading card. These are often filed in separate sets of drawers. For newspaper, magazine and journal articles – especially older ones that may not be indexed in computer databases – ask a librarian to recommend the appropriate periodical index to use. Older periodical indexes are usually in book form. When you find the appropriate item, look for its code number.

4  Make a list of as many code numbers on your topic as you can find before taking them along to the bookshelves. Try rephrasing your keywords and subjects to find a broad range of books that you can narrow down after some browsing. To make life easier when searching the bookshelves, make note of the codes on your list that are close to each other.

5  Find the section in the library that corresponds to the code number of your item. Some books and periodicals may be in storage and may have to be ordered in advance.

6  Remember that librarians are paid to help library users. If you need help, ask someone.

Most libraries have photocopiers. Rather than check out a large number of books, make copies of just the pages with the material you need. Note which books they're from.

If your library doesn't have the material you need, ask a librarian about arranging for an inter-library loan.

## Create Your Own Reading List    12

So little time, so much to read. Making a list of books to read for pleasure is a lifelong process.

### ⊙ Steps

1  Buy a journal, notebook or electronic assistant and use it for your list.

2  Join the public library, even if you go there just to browse.

3  Subscribe to book-review magazines or newsletters. Scan them for books and authors that interest you.

4  Read the best-seller lists to glean even more suggestions.

5  Investigate award-winning authors and books. Prestigious awards such as the Nobel Prize in Literature, the Pulitzer Prize and the Booker Prize signify worthy literary accomplishments.

6  Read up on favourite topics and peruse the books' bibliographies (usually found in non-fiction works), adding titles to your list.

7  Discover your favourite authors and note their other works.

8  Join a book group and get referrals from other readers.

9  Take an evening class or visit an internet chat room or newsgroup. All can offer good pointers to worthwhile reading.

### ✳ Tips

You will find out about more books than you can possibly read in one lifetime, so focus your list from time to time, according to your interests.

Going on a trip? Read guide-books, historical novels, cook-books or whatever interests you most about your destination.

Take suggestions from people whose opinions and taste you trust.

## 13 | Read Quickly and Effectively

Sail through the barrage of information out there by using some key reading and skimming skills.

### ⊙ Steps

1   Read different materials at different speeds: skim or speed-read less important items, and save critical or difficult works for when you are most alert and have time.

2   Pick out the main ideas of a book by reading its cover flaps or scanning the table of contents. Use the index to locate key words quickly.

3   Survey the layout of your reading material. Look at the title and section headings and piece together its logical flow. This framework will guide you in reading the piece more carefully.

4   If you need to skim, try reading the first sentence of each paragraph (which is usually a topic sentence) to get a general idea of its content.

5   Practise reading more quickly by moving your index finger down a row of text at a speed slightly faster than your normal reading speed.

6   Underline sparingly so the truly useful information doesn't get lost.

7   Jot down quick notes, questions or thoughts that will make it easier to refer to the material later. Taking notes also makes for active reading and better retention of important points (see 14 "Take Reading Notes").

### ✳ Tips

Increasing your vocabulary will help you to improve your reading speed.

Take a speed-reading course – there are many available.

## 14 | Take Reading Notes

Remembering what you read will help your schoolwork, and taking good reading notes will help you retain what you've read.

### ⊙ Steps

1   Budget enough time for taking notes. The time you spend now will pay off with less review time and increased retention.

2   Date your notes, and write full bibliographic information next to the date, including author, title, publication, date of publication, city, publisher, and volume number for journal articles.

3   Take notes in outline form to structure the material, and break it into related sections and sub-sections.

4   Use the structure of the book (or article) as the structure of your notes. For instance, chapters correspond to major headings, chapter sections to sub-headings.

5   Note anything that is pertinent to the author's argument; try to avoid trivial minutiae. Important points tend to be contained in introductory and concluding paragraphs.

6   Distinguish facts from opinions, and quotations from summaries, in a way that will make it clear which is which when you review your notes.

7   Review your reading notes the next day, and do it again a few days later. This is a time-efficient way of retaining the material.

### ✳ Tips

Consider using index cards if you're taking notes for a research paper. Be sure that you list the bibliographic information on a separate, numbered card.

One way of deciding what is relevant is to "cheat" by reading the conclusion first so that you'll know what's important as soon as you come across it in the text.

Use abbreviations in your notes: for instance, an up arrow (↑) for "increase" and a delta (Δ) for "change".

## Outline a Paper                                        **15**

An outline helps you organise a paper's content in a logical and sequential way. Here is a basic guide.

### ⊙ Steps

1  Write your composition's working title at the top of a blank sheet of paper. It does not need to be the one you use for your final paper.

2  Beneath the working title, write a few lines about the purpose of the paper and the steps you will take to achieve that goal. For example: "In this paper, I will show the secrets of a successful and happy life, using scholarly journals from psychologists and veterinarians."

3  Follow the summary with a statement of your paper's thesis: for example, "Owning a dog can make one's life healthier and happier".

4  Begin to lay down the basic framework for your paper by dividing its content into sections.

5  Start by writing either an Arabic or Roman numeral 1 – depending on your style of outline – followed by a period, then the title of the section (a "section heading"). In an informal outline use Arabic numerals; in a formal outline use Roman numerals.

6  Follow this with a few lines describing what you wish to accomplish in the section.

7  Use sub-sections to list specific examples or topics that you wish to discuss under each heading. Mark them with a lowercase letter (*a, b, c* and so on).

8  Follow this format for each section heading, then put the sections in the following general order: introduction, body, conclusion.

### ✱ Tips

You may find it helpful to write each section heading on a separate sheet of paper to allow yourself room to take notes and brainstorm.

Remember that the outline is merely a tool in the writing process – it does not bind you to anything. Feel free to change its format to suit your needs.

As you write your paper, refer back to your outline to make sure you're on track.

## Write a Paper                                          **16**

Writing a good research paper can be a tough challenge, but breaking it down into smaller pieces helps a lot.

### ⊙ Steps

1  Choose a topic that is broad enough to be interesting but narrow enough to be manageable.

2  Find your sources. Start with three or four, check their bibliographies for additional sources, and repeat the process until you have sufficient material with which to work.

3  Reserve one index card for each of your sources. Record the bibliographic information for the source on its index card, and number each card for ease of future reference.

4  Take reading notes on index cards, writing down only the material that is most relevant to your project. Write the source number on each card.

5  Organise your index cards by topic and sub-topic.

6  Use the cards as a basis for an outline (see 15 "Outline a Paper").

### ✱ Tips

Avoid letting the size of a project daunt you. Stay focused on each task, and remember that if you do those well, you'll end up with an excellent research paper.

Use bibliography software to help manage your sources. Consult a style guide for details on citation of sources.

Consider taking a class on writing research papers.

Don't leave such a difficult task to the last minute. Start early, and work gradually.

7  Write an introduction that grabs the reader and plots out the trajectory of your argument.

8  Write the body of the paper, following the structure you created in your outline. Be sure to cite sources.

9  Write the conclusion, reviewing how you've made your points.

10  Come up with a title after you've written the paper, not before: you don't want the content of the paper to be hamstrung by an inappropriate title.

11  Read your paper at least twice to be sure your argument makes sense and is presented logically.

12  Proofread carefully; academics hate typographical errors. Use your word processor's spelling checker, but don't rely on it wholly.

## ⚠ Warning

Be sure to cite your sources whenever you make use of an idea from someone else.

## 17   Write a Bibliography

A bibliography or reference section is necessary for any research paper. Here is the standard method of writing one.

### ◉ Steps

1  List, alphabetically by author, each source used in writing the paper. Write the last name of the author, followed by a comma, and then his or her first name, followed by a full stop.

2  Include the full title of the work, if it is a book. Underline the title and follow it with a full stop.

3  Name the city where the work was published, followed by a colon.

4  Include the name of the publisher, followed by a comma.

5  Conclude the entry with the date of publication, followed by a full stop.

6  If you are citing an article from a periodical, list the author's name as you would when citing a book. Begin with the article's name enclosed in quotation marks, followed by a full stop. Then write and underline the name of the journal or magazine from which it came. Include the date of publication, followed by a colon and the relevant page numbers; close the entry with a full stop. Volume and issue numbers are not included for newspapers and magazines. For trade or academic journals, include the volume and issue number after the underlined journal title. Follow with the date of the publication enclosed in brackets, then a colon and the relevant page numbers.

### ✳ Tips

Buy a good writers handbook that gives examples of research writing for your area of study.

Cite material from the web by giving the author's name; the title of the document (in quotation marks); the title of the periodical, or web page (underlined); the names of the editors, if given; the name and location of the institution or organisation; the date of access of the source; and the full web page URL in angle brackets <like this>.

## 18   Improve Your Memory

Scores of books, videos, web sites and seminars are devoted to memory enhancement. The steps below summarise the main points of most techniques.

### ◉ Steps

1  Make sure you're alert and attentive before trying to memorise anything.

### ✳ Tips

Review the things you have memorised right before going to sleep; this might help you recall it better in the morning.

2   Understand the material rather than merely memorising it, if it's the type that requires deeper comprehension.

3   Look for larger patterns or ideas, and organise pieces of information into meaningful groups.

4   Link newly acquired knowledge with what you already know. Place what you learn into context with the rest of your knowledge, looking out for relationships between ideas.

5   Engage your visual and auditory senses by using drawings, charts or music to aid memory. Creating a memorable mental picture can also help.

6   Use mnemonics – devices such as formulas or rhymes that serve as memory aids. For example, use the acronym "HOMES" to memorise America's Great Lakes (Huron, Ontario, Michigan, Erie and Superior).

7   Repeat and review what you've learned as many times as you can. Apply it or use it in conversation, as continual practice is the key to remembering things in the long term.

Things that interest you are easier to remember. Try to develop an interest in what you're memorising.

Your memory and thinking will function much better if you're in good health, well-rested and properly hydrated.

Try writing down or reciting aloud what you've memorised – this can help etch it in your mind.

## Cram for a Test                                    19

While not an ideal style of study, cramming is an inevitable part of student life. Focus on general concepts, memory techniques and relaxation.

### ◉ Steps

1   Compose yourself. Relax and take several deep breaths to clear your mind of clutter and stress.

2   Cover the most difficult information first.

3   Review the main points, general ideas and broad, sweeping concepts. These are essential to understanding the more detailed points on which you will be tested.

4   Skim lecture notes and assigned reading materials (see 13 "Read Quickly and Effectively").

5   Take breaks to stretch, relax, eat or exercise. As a general rule, you should take a break for 10 minutes out of every hour.

6   Review the main points and concepts one more time and then get some sleep before the big exam.

### ✳ Tips

Go easy on the caffeine and sugar. The initial boost from these substances will inevitably be followed by a crash.

Nourish yourself. Eat a good meal with a balanced ratio of carbohydrates to proteins. Avoid overeating, which tends to cause sluggishness.

### ⚠ Warning

Avoid staying up all night before a test. Depriving yourself of sleep may hurt more than it helps.

## Break the Procrastination Habit              20

There's an old joke that the members of Procrastinators Anonymous plan to meet ... but keep putting it off.

### ◉ Steps

1   Think about why you procrastinate: Are you afraid of failing at the task? Are you a perfectionist and only willing to begin working after every little element is in place? Are you easily distracted?

### ✳ Tip

Remember that progress, not perfection, is your goal.

2  Break up a large, difficult project into several smaller pieces.

3  Set deadlines for completion. Try assigning yourself small-scale deadlines: for example, commit to reading a certain number of pages in the next hour.

4  Work in small blocks of time instead of in long stretches. Try studying in one- to two-hour spurts, allowing yourself a small break after each stint.

5  Start with the easiest aspect of a large, complex project. For example, if you're writing an academic paper and find that the introduction is turning out to be difficult to write, start with the paper's body instead.

6  Enlist others to help. Make a bet with your family, friends or co-workers that you will finish a particular project by a specified time, or find other ways to make yourself accountable.

7  Eliminate distractions or move to a place where you can concentrate. Turn off the television, the phone ringer, the radio and anything else that might keep you from your task.

## 21 | Find Out Your IQ

Though IQ (intelligence quotient) has come under scrutiny as a measure of intelligence, finding out your IQ can help you join certain organisations and can open other doors for you.

### ⊙ Steps

1  Find an appropriate IQ test – there are a great many out there. On the web, consider visiting www.iqtest.com to take an IQ test and to get general information about the process.

2  Take the test and score it.

3  Take several more tests and average the scores, dropping the lowest and highest. The result will give a good approximation of your IQ.

4  Understand the results. Generally, an IQ of 100 places you in the 50th percentile (exactly average); 110 puts you in the 75th percentile; 120 in the 93rd; and 130 in the 98th, which is high enough to join Mensa.

5  Remember that no single number can measure something as complex as intelligence. Instead, IQ is intended to measure your chances of academic success in schools.

### ✱ Tip

Be aware that high-IQ societies such as Mensa usually accept the results of only certain IQ tests. Contact individual societies to find out its requirements (see 22 "Join Mensa").

### ⚠ Warning

Bear in mind that there are many important human "intelligences" that standard IQ tests can't measure, such as musical or artistic talent, social ability, physical coordination, ambition and sense of humour.

## 22 | Join Mensa

Mensa is an international organisation of people in the top two per cent of the intelligence range. Founded in England in 1946, it now has more than 100,000 members. Here's how to join.

### ⊙ Steps

1  Bear in mind that testing in the top two per cent on an accepted IQ test or standardised test is the only membership criterion.

### ✱ Tips

Visit Mensa's website to get more detailed information for your specific situation.

2   Visit the Mensa website (www.mensa.org.uk) to get the information you'll need to complete the steps below. Alternatively, call (01902) 772771 or send a letter to British Mensa Limited, St John's House, St John's Square, Wolverhampton, WV2 4AH.

3   Find out if Mensa will accept the results of an intelligence test you've already taken. Mensa also accepts scores from approximately 200 standardised tests (such as the LSAT or GMAT).

4   Order official test results from the appropriate testing company and send them to Mensa.

5   Contact your nearest Mensa office to take the official Mensa test, if you haven't qualified through another test.

6   Be prepared to pay annual fees if you're admitted.

As a Mensa member, you'll be able to interact with other Mensa members at social events, through publications and during various activities.

# Get a Job                                                    23

Good timing plays a role in finding a job, but that's only part of the picture. Here's how to find the job you want.

## ◎Steps

1   Assess your skills, experience and goals, and look into appropriate employment fields that interest you.

2   Spread the word. Tell everyone you know and meet that you are looking for a job – you will be surprised at the number of opportunities you may discover this way.

3   Network, network, network. Attend professional-association meetings in your industry, scour the associations' membership directories for contacts, and schedule informational interviews with people in the field. Always try to get more names of people to contact at the end of the informational interview. Volunteer for something.

4   For resources and leads, contact your local employment office or your school/university careers advisor.

5   Get out and about. The most direct way to learn about job openings is to contact employers themselves. Target an area, dress the part, and stop in at every appropriate business establishment, including employment agencies, to fill out an application.

6   Remember that many job openings are not listed in the newspaper job section. However, internet job boards are often used by employers for their ease and immediacy.

7   Pick up the telephone. It may be scary – and you will hear "No" a lot – but you may only need to hear "Yes" a few times to land a job.

8   Follow up on written contacts. Send out CVs and fill out applications, but understand that these alone won't land you a job. Follow up with a phone call within five to seven days of every written communication.

9   Ask for interviews. If you find yourself being interviewed for a position that's not right for you (or with an interviewer who doesn't think you're right for the opening), request interviews with other department heads

## ✱ Tips

When you're interviewing, make it a dialogue. Asking questions will make you appear knowledgeable and eager, as well as help to calm your nerves.

Review the Sunday job section to get a feel for the hiring marketplace.

Drop in on your local chamber of commerce breakfast or after-dinner meeting. These are usually open to non-members for a small fee and offer the opportunity to make valuable contacts.

See 27 "Speed Up a Job Hunt" for additional pointers.

## ⚠ Warning

Avoid making the mistake of turning down additional interviews once you've had a good one. Keep your job search in high gear right up until your first day on the new job.

**www.ehow.com**

for resources and leads, or even with other companies that the interviewer may know are recruiting.

10  Prepare. Do some research on the hiring company and its industry so that you'll have a stock of relevant questions to ask the person across the desk.

11  Give the impression that you're ready to be part of the team.

12  Send a thank-you note after the interview. E-mail is acceptable.

13  Call your interviewer three days later and ask if there is any further information you can provide.

---

## 24  Find a Job Online

The internet is rewriting the rules of the job-search game. Make sure that you know all the ways to find a job online.

### ⊙ Steps

1  Peruse the websites of any companies that may interest you. Most companies will post job openings on their sites.

2  Go to a website specifically geared towards finding jobs. You can search for jobs on these sites by career field, location and even potential salary.

3  If you're a student, your school or university may have a careers advice web page with job listings, guidance for writing CVs and advice on being interviewed.

4  Visit an online newspaper and search the classifieds section for job adverts and job opportunities. Many newspapers – national and local – have web pages.

5  Check out search engines, as these also feature classified sections. Browse according to your location and interests.

### ✳ Tips

Search frequently: new job listings are posted every day.

Many sites offer services that will allow you to e-mail your cv directly to a potential employer.

### ⚠ Warning

Some sites designed specifically for finding jobs may require a membership fee. Read the small print before signing up.

---

## 25  Network Effectively

Networking can help you to get a job or otherwise expand your business horizons. The key to successful networking is taking the initiative – and refining your conversational skills.

### ⊙ Steps

1  Talk to people you don't know, everywhere you go. Cocktail parties and weddings are just the tip of the iceberg; don't forget about aeroplanes, supermarket queues, sports events, festivals, bookshops and so on.

2  Learn to ask "What do you do?" with comfort, sincerity and interest.

3  Become a better listener. Ask a question and then be quiet until you hear the answer.

### ✳ Tips

Make news so that you can get your name out there. Be the dog walker who gets on the evening news for organising the Doggy Olympics.

Stay in touch with people you like and respect even if they can't help you immediately. You don't want to go to someone only when you are desperate.

4    Practise the way you present your own skills. Learn more than one approach, whether frank or subtle.

5    Keep a great updated brochure, business card or some other form of information about yourself on you at all times. Get comfortable with handing out your card.

6    Take classes to improve your public speaking, body language and writing skills.

7    Join every networking club and association in your field.

8    Follow up on any lead, no matter how minor.

## Prepare a Basic CV 26

**There are as many kinds of CV as there are jobs. Use a style that matches your personality and career objectives.**

### ⊙ Steps

1    Choose one or two fonts at most, and avoid underlined, boldfaced and italic text. Some companies use automated recruiting systems that have difficulty with special formatting.

2    Opt for the active voice rather than the passive voice (say "met the goal" rather than "the goal was met").

3    Provide contact information such as your home address, telephone number and e-mail address at the top of your CV.

4    Include an objectives statement, in which you use clear, simple language to indicate what kind of job you're looking for. This should appear below your contact information.

5    List your most recent and relevant experience first. Include time frames, company names and job titles, followed by major responsibilities.

6    In a second section, outline your education, awards, accomplishments and anything else you wish prospective employers to know about you.

7    Hire a proofreader or ask someone you trust to proofread your CV. Mistakes in spelling, grammar or syntax can land it in the bin.

8    Limit your CV to one page unless it is scientific or highly technical. Less is definitely more when it comes to CVs.

9    Write a cover letter to submit with your CV (see 29 "Write an Effective Cover Letter").

### ✱ Tips

Refrain from using "I" in your CV.

Leave out personal information, particularly as it relates to your age, race, religious background and sexual orientation.

Avoid obscure fonts, clip art and other unnecessary visuals.

### ✓ 27 Speed Up a Job Hunt

When you're looking for a job, it's all too easy to let yourself be lulled by the familiar rhythms of home or work life. Before you know it, another month has gone by and you're still out of work or unhappily employed. Here are some ways to jump-start your job search and get your career in gear.

checklist

#### Know yourself

- ☐ Make a list of your skills. Note which ones you're most interested in using, and which are most likely to interest employers.

- ☐ Identify the skills that you haven't had the chance to use in your current or most recent job. Which ones are of greatest importance to you?

- ☐ Think about how you can use your favourite skills in a new job. Set specific short-term and long-term goals to guide your job search.

- ☐ Decide which of your short-term goals are negotiable and which are not.

- ☐ Write a two-minute speech describing your experience, skills and goals. Rehearse it.

#### Get organised

- ☐ Make a list of leads: people you know, people they've referred you to and companies that interest you.

- ☐ Set goals – for example, to send out ten CVs this week, make five cold calls or conduct two informational interviews.

- ☐ Make weekly and daily to-do lists, and check off each item as it's completed.

- ☐ Keep files or notebooks with details of everyone you've written to, called or who has interviewed you, and anything you want to remember. Include job listings and contacts' business cards.

- ☐ Keep your filing system handy and well-organised so you can refer to it quickly in case of a phone call.

#### Brush up job-seeking skills

- ☐ Hire a proofreader to catch any errors in your CV.

- ☐ Ask a friend or colleague to grill you about your experience so you can practise your answers.

- ☐ Videotape yourself in a mock interview to see how you come across.

- ☐ Hire a consultant to look at your CV and teach you some interview techniques.

- ☐ Make sure you have clean, wrinkle-free professional attire ready to wear for job interviews.

#### Research and target employers

- ☐ Read trade publications to learn about companies in your field and determine which ones may be hiring.

- ☐ Talk to friends or acquaintances in the field for the inside scoop on companies.

- ☐ Set up informational interviews or ask to spend a day with someone who has the type of job you're seeking.

- ☐ Aim your cover letters to individuals who may be in a position to hire you – send a copy to the personnel department as well.

- ☐ After scheduling an interview, search the web for more facts about the company.

- ☐ Ask the company for a press kit or annual report if it's not available on the web.

- ☐ Make a list of questions that show your knowledge and interest in the company.

## Write a CV When Changing Careers  `28`

Your CV should change along with your career goals. Here are some ways to restructure and polish your CV as you move towards a new profession or career.

### ⊙ Steps

1 Read up on the skills and requirements for the new career or job you are seeking. Look at job listings in the newspaper or online to get an idea of what skills you'll need to break in.

2 Make a list of the skills and requirements you discovered in step 1. Your new CV will need to focus on them.

3 Compare the skills and requirements on that list with those listed on your current CV, underlining the qualifications both have in common. These are the skills that will carry over to your new CV.

4 Rewrite the CV to highlight the skills that apply to your new career. Focus on your strengths, experience and education in these areas.

5 Change the focus of your CV. If you are a pharmacologist trying to break into pharmaceutical sales, for example, focus on your experience with different vendors and other tasks that relate to sales.

6 Think of any other experiences relevant to the skills on your list – this may include volunteer work, internships, hobbies and travel. Work all of these experiences into your CV.

### ✳ Tips

Consider volunteering, interning or taking a second job within your new area of interest to gain practical experience.

If you don't feel you can write an effective CV, specialised services can do it for you. Look on the internet under "CV service".

### ⚠ Warning

You may have to settle for a lower-paying job until you can build up your experience – and hence your CV – when changing careers.

## Write an Effective Cover Letter  `29`

A CV is an essential tool for any job search, but it's not the only tool. Your cover letter is equally important.

### ⊙ Steps

1 Find a job posting, job tip or advertisement that interests you, and make sure you are truly qualified for the position. Busy employers sometimes receive hundreds of letters, so don't waste their time or yours.

2 Match the letterhead style and paper you will use for your cover letter to that of your CV. This helps to establish a solid first impression.

3 Don't bother with the salutation if you do not know the name of the person who will be reviewing your CV. It's best to address the letter to a specific person; call the company and see if the receptionist can give you a name and title.

4 Grab the reader's attention right away – make him or her want to keep reading. You need to distinguish yourself early from the rest of the pack.

5 Mention in the first paragraph where you learned about this particular job opportunity and why you're interested.

6 Establish a professional image in the second and third paragraphs by highlighting your most significant accomplishments and qualifications. Be careful not to quote your CV verbatim.

### ✳ Tips

Before writing your cover letter, research the company to which you're applying. Then your letter can refer to specifics about the employer's business as reasons for your interest in working there.

Keep it short. Most cover letters are one page and use a standard business-letter format (see 36 "Write a Formal Business Letter").

Consider using bullet points in your middle paragraphs to further highlight accomplishments.

Avoid getting too personal or wordy. Save stories and relevant anecdotes for the interview.

Avoid bragging. Confidence is important, but don't overdo it.

7   Clarify what you can contribute to the employer's organisation rather than what you hope to gain from this potential relationship. You can discuss the latter in the interview.

8   In the last paragraph, remind the reader that your CV will explain your qualifications, experience and education. Request a personal interview, and indicate the times you will be available.

9   Close your letter by telling the reader that you look forward to hearing from the company, and restate your enthusiasm for learning more about the opportunity.

10  Double-check your document for spelling and grammar; refer to a style-book if necessary. Carelessness makes a bad impression on employers.

11  Print your letter using a good ink-jet or laser printer.

⚠ **Warning**

Never send a photocopied letter or use a form letter. This tells the prospective employer that you are not interested enough to write an original letter.

---

## 30 | Succeed at a Job Interview

**Most interviewers form their opinion of you in the first few minutes of a meeting. Here's how to make a good impression.**

### ⊙ Steps

1   In the days before your interview, talk to people who have worked at the company. If it's practical, hang around outside the building while employees are arriving and note how they dress and behave.

2   Learn the name and title of the person you'll be meeting. Arrive at least ten minutes early to collect your thoughts.

3   Take time to greet and acknowledge the secretary or administrative assistant; it's good old-fashioned courtesy, and besides, this person may have a lot of influence.

4   Bring along an extra copy of your CV or letters of recommendation in case the interviewer doesn't have them handy.

5   Be open and upbeat. Face your interviewer with arms and legs uncrossed, head up, and hands and face at ease. Smile and look the interviewer in the eye.

6   Know the company's business, target clients, market and direction.

7   Walk in prepared with a few relevant questions and listen carefully.

8   Subtly give the impression that you're already part of the team by using "we" when asking how something is done. For example, say, "How do we deal with the press?"

9   Conclude with a positive statement and a quick, firm handshake. Ask when you might follow up, and get a business card from the interviewer.

10  Send a thank-you note.

✱ **Tip**

Avoid asking about money at the start of the interview.

## Request a Reference From a Former Employer 31

A good employment reference can seal that job offer that you've worked hard to win.

### ⊙ Steps

1  Get references before you need them. Managers make job changes, too, and time can erase the memory of even the most outstanding employee.

2  Offer to write the reference letter for your former employer to review and sign. This saves him or her valuable time, and it allows you to highlight the accomplishments you consider most valuable to future employers.

3  Contact former employers and other referees before offering their names to potential employers. Beyond simple courtesy, this gives you the chance to supply these people with important information such as who might be calling, the type of job you're applying for, and which of your skills you would like your referee to emphasise.

4  Acknowledge a referee with a thank-you note, even if you didn't get the job. If you did, offer a celebratory lunch.

### ✱ Tips

If you encounter an unhelpful policy, such as one that restricts managers from giving reference information beyond confirming job title and relevant dates of employment, ask the manager if he or she will give you a personal (rather than professional) reference.

Consider colleagues with whom you've interacted – they can be good referees, too.

---

## Negotiate an Employment Contract 32

Be confident and careful when negotiating a new contract.

### ⊙ Steps

1  Research your market value before your first interview: Talk to friends and acquaintances in the business, contact headhunters, and consult career web pages that include information such as salary ranges and benefits packages.

2  Assess the company's approach, noting whether it invites negotiations or makes an offer first.

3  Listen to the way an offer is presented. A negotiation-minded manager will ask what figure you had in mind to get the process moving.

4  Delineate the different aspects of the job offer: money, benefits, stock options, responsibilities, schedules.

5  If the offer appears set, be creative in negotiating for alternative perks such as time off, relocation expenses or a travel allowance.

6  Repeat the offer out loud after you hear it, then don't say anything until the employer does. Your silence may be misinterpreted as hesitation and the employer will sweeten the pot.

7  Speak your mind if you have any concerns.

### ✱ Tips

Clearly demonstrate your sincere excitement and interest in the job as well as in the compensation.

Focus on being an ally – not an adversary – throughout the negotiations. This will keep things amiable and show that you are a team player.

## 33 | Work Efficiently

We'll keep this short so you can get back to work.

### ⊙ Steps

1 Keep your desk and your files organised to avoid wasting time shuffling through piles of paper.

2 Go through your inbox at the beginning of each workday. Either throw away, file or follow up on each item.

3 Prioritise a list of the tasks you need to accomplish that day.

4 Delegate tasks to co-workers and assistants if possible.

5 Finish one task before you go on to the next.

6 Reduce paperwork by storing important information on your computer or electronic organiser.

7 Communicate effectively and plan carefully to make sure a job is done properly the first time around.

8 Schedule time when you'll be available and let colleagues know, to avoid constant interruptions. Close the door if you need to.

9 Take breaks. A short walk or quick lunch away from the office will increase your overall productivity.

10 Before leaving for the day, tidy up your desk and make a short list of projects you will need to do the next day.

11 Try not to take work home. You need the break.

### ✳ Tips

Recognise when you have the most energy in a day and do the important or harder tasks then.

Note that certain days – usually Monday or Friday – are more hectic, and schedule accordingly.

Have someone else answer your telephone if possible. Give instructions about calls you wish to take and those that can be returned later.

### ⚠ Warnings

Avoid regularly going out for long business lunches – heavy meals make for unproductive afternoons.

Avoid procrastination (see 20 "Break the Procrastination Habit").

## 34 | Make a To-Do List

Invest just a little time planning your day, and accomplish more things smoothly.

### ⊙ Steps

1 Set aside 10 to 15 minutes before you go to bed or as soon as you wake up in the morning to jot down a to-do list for the day.

2 Use any format that is comfortable for you – try writing in your daily planner. Make sure your list is on one page and can be carried with you wherever you go.

3 Try assigning tasks to hourly time slots, even if exact timing isn't crucial.

4 Fill in preset, mandatory appointments such as business meetings or child-pickup times.

5 Prioritise tasks in order of urgency, and write those down before less important ones.

6 Figure out when, during the day, you are most productive and alert. Schedule the more demanding tasks during these times.

7 Schedule an easy job after a difficult one or a long task after a short one to keep yourself stimulated.

### ✳ Tips

Schedule things comfortably, allowing time for unexpected delays or mishaps; avoid an impossibly tight timetable.

Be sure to list everything you need to accomplish – the more you can account for, the more smoothly your day will run and the less you need to remember.

Break down large projects into specific tasks before writing them down on your list.

Feel free to revise your list as necessary, as the day goes on.

8 Indicate time for breaks and time to spend with family and friends.

9 In addition to your daily schedule, keep an ongoing list of projects that you need to accomplish but haven't pencilled into your daily list – things to fix around the house, bills to mail, people to call. Update this list at least once a week.

10 Keep a list of long-term goals. For example, you might be planning to remodel your home or return to school for an advanced degree.

11 Make a running list for leisure or entertainment goals – books to read, films to rent, restaurants/bars/clubs to try. Write down names as you hear or read about them.

## Delegate Responsibility | 35

**Many people delegate less than they should. Divide your assignments and hand out tasks for others to do – this will increase your overall productivity and efficiency.**

### ⊙Steps

1 Decide whether you want to delegate.

2 Decide to whom you want to delegate responsibility. Does this person have the necessary skills and background knowledge? How quickly will your helper learn?

3 Brief the person on the task: Define exactly what he is responsible for. Explain how the task fits into the larger project. Clarify objectives and decide on deadlines.

4 Encourage your delegate to act independently and to make his own decisions by emphasising the results. Say, "I want to see such-and-such. Don't tell me the details."

5 Allow the person to perform the task. Offer help as needed, but don't be intrusive – if he has a different way of doing things than you, be flexible and open-minded about it.

6 Periodically check the standard of work. Provide helpful feedback.

7 Recognise the person who does the job – give him credit for it. Public recognition for a job well done will encourage effort in the future.

### ✳ Tips

Delegate tasks at times when productivity is likely to be high – try earlier in the week as opposed to Friday.

Be available to answer questions and discuss progress.

Be generous with praise for jobs that are well-executed.

### ⚠ Warnings

Avoid thinking that it is too much trouble to delegate responsibility – delegating will pay off over time, especially if the task needs to be done again and again.

Delegating a task doesn't mean you are no longer responsible for seeing that it's completed.

## Write a Formal Business Letter | 36

**The business-letter format is very important for communicating formally with a company. These steps describe the "full block" format, in which all lines start at the left.**

### ⊙Steps

1 Type the letter using word-processing software. Formal letters should not be written by hand.

### ✳ Tips

Some people prefer to centre the date and closing section instead of aligning them at the left.

2   Use your own letterhead. If you don't have a letterhead, use formal A4 stationery with a matching envelope. Avoid shop-bought note cards.

3   If you don't have a preprinted letterhead, type your name, title and return address four to six lines down from the top of the page.

4   Type the date two to six lines down from the letterhead or return address. Three lines below is the standard.

5   Choose your alignment: left aligned or justified on both sides.

6   Skip two lines and type the recipient's full name, business title and address, aligned at the left margin. Precede the name with Mr, Mrs, Ms or Dr, as appropriate.

7   Skip two to four lines and follow with your greeting, again using the formal name and closing with a colon – "Dear Mr Jones:" for example.

8   Skip two more lines and begin your letter. Introduce yourself in the first paragraph, if the recipient does not already know you. Examples: "We recently met at a seminar at the Royal Academy of Music" or "I recently purchased an insurance plan from your company".

9   Continue with the body of the letter, stating your main purpose for writing. This may be to lodge a complaint, compliment the business on its products or services, or request information. Be as brief and concise as possible.

10   Skip two lines and conclude the letter with "Yours sincerely", "Thank you" or "Best wishes", followed by a comma.

11   Leave at least four blank lines for your signature, then type your name and title. Sign the letter in ink in the space created.

Try to keep the letter to one page. Generally, a short letter will get a quicker response than a long, rambling composition that takes several pages to come to the point.

Make certain your punctuation, spelling and grammar are letter-perfect. Use your computer's spelling-check program and proofread the letter before you send it.

## ⚠ Warning

No matter how upset you are with the recipient, try not to show your anger in your letter. You are much more likely to get the response you desire if you remain courteous.

---

## 37  Write a Speech

Composing a speech shares many of the most important aspects of preparing a paper.

### ⊙ Steps

1   Assess how much time your speech should take. If you don't have a time limit, try to keep your speech brief yet informative.

2   Think about your audience and let your perception of the audience shape the tone of your speech as you write it.

3   Begin with an introduction establishing who you are, what your purpose is, what you'll be talking about and how long you're going to take. You may want to include a joke, anecdote or interesting fact to grab the audience's attention.

4   Organise your information into three to seven main points and prioritise them according to importance and effectiveness.

5   Delete points that aren't crucial to your speech if you have too many for your time frame.

6   Start with your most important point, then go to your least important point and move slowly back towards the most important. For example, if

### ✱ Tips

The introduction should make up between 10 and 15 per cent of the total speech. The conclusion should make up 5 to 10 per cent.

When preparing your speech, make your notes easy to read by writing or printing them in large, clear letters.

Rehearse and time your speech before delivering it. Prune it if necessary.

If you are presenting a great deal of information, consider using handouts or visual aids to help your audience remember your most important points.

you have five points, with the fifth being the most important and the first being the least important, your presentation order should be 5, 1, 2, 3, 4.

7   Add support to each point using statistics, facts, examples, anecdotes, quotations or other supporting material.

8   Link your introduction, points and conclusions with smooth transitions.

9   Write a conclusion that summarises each of your points, restates your main purpose and leaves the audience with a lasting impression.

## Deliver a Speech 38

Mastering your tone and body language is the formula for a successful delivery.

### ⊙Steps

1   Approach the podium confidently and put your notes in a place where you can see them easily.

2   Stand up straight with your feet shoulder-width apart. Look at your audience, pause and begin speaking. If there is no microphone, project from your diaphragm, not your throat.

3   Set the tone in your introduction with appropriate facial expressions and diction, and a specific mood.

4   Make eye contact with people in different parts of the audience, including the back row.

5   Pause briefly after you state key points to allow the audience time to absorb the information. Also, use natural and relaxed hand gestures and facial expressions to emphasise certain points.

6   Pronounce your words clearly and vary your rate, pitch and volume to keep the delivery lively.

7   Refresh your memory by periodically glancing at your notes, but avoid reading from your notes directly unless you are reading a long quotation.

8   Close your speech by thanking the audience and then confidently leaving the stage.

### ✴ Tips

Success come with practice. Video yourself watching out for distracting habits such saying "er" and "um" too often, or making nervous gestures.

During your speech, if you stumble on a word, it's a sign you should slow down.

## Lead Effective Business Meetings 39

Too many business meetings are ill-directed, digressive and drawn out. Call a meeting only when it's absolutely critical, and structure it firmly so that it achieves its purpose.

### ⊙Steps

1   Decide whether you really need to call a meeting. Can the issue be resolved by an individual or a conference call?

2   Determine who needs to attend. Try keeping the number of attendees small, as large meetings get unwieldy. Suggest that people attend only

### ✴ Tips

To prevent a meeting from going on too long, schedule it before lunch, at the end of the day or immediately before another one.

the parts of the meeting that involve them. This way you can keep the discussion more focused.

3 Set definite starting and stopping times.

4 Prepare an agenda. Explain the goal of the meeting; if there are many goals, decide which ones command priority and make this clear.

5 Circulate the agenda in advance to allow attendees to prepare.

6 Assemble visual aids, such as charts, handouts or slides.

7 Start the meeting at the designated time, regardless of whether everyone is present. Avoid taking too much time to summarise for latecomers.

8 Start off the meeting with straightforward, easily resolved issues before heading into thornier ones.

9 Allocate a specific amount of time for each issue. Move through issues, allowing for discussion but discouraging digression or repetition. Use a timer to help monitor the time.

10 Postpone discussion until the end of the meeting if debate on an issue runs overtime. Make sure to cover the other issues on the agenda.

11 Follow up: Circulate copies of the minutes after the meeting to remind everyone of conclusions and action plans.

Try removing the chairs from the meeting room and conducting a stand-up meeting to make it shorter and more efficient.

## Things You'll Need

☐ written agenda

☐ visual aids (optional)

☐ timer

---

## 40 Take Minutes at a Business Meeting

Business meetings may be conducted formally or informally, depending on the company and the circumstances. These guidelines are based on Robert's Rules of Order.

### ☀ Tips

You do not need to record topics irrelevant to the business at hand. Taking minutes is not the same as taking dictation.

Consult only the chairperson, not the attendees, if you have questions.

The person taking minutes does not participate in the meeting.

Write in a concise, accurate manner, taking care not to include subjective opinion.

No matter what type of minutes you take, focus on capturing and communicating all the important actions that took place.

### ⊙ Steps

#### Taking Minutes

1 Obtain the meeting agenda, minutes from the last meeting, and any background documents to be discussed. Consider using a tape recorder to ensure accuracy.

2 Sit beside the chairperson for convenient clarification or help as the meeting proceeds.

3 Write "Minutes of the meeting of [name of committee or association]".

4 Record the date, time and place of the meeting.

5 Circulate a sheet of paper for attendees to sign. (This sheet can also help identify speakers by seating arrangement later in the meeting.) If the meeting is an open one, write down only the names of the attendees who have voting rights.

6 Note who arrives late or leaves early so that these people can be briefed on what they missed.

7 Write down items in the order in which they are discussed. If item 8 on the agenda is discussed before item 2, keep the old item number but write item 8 in second place.

8 Record the motions made and the names of people who originate them.

9   Record whether motions are adopted or rejected, how any vote is taken (by show of hands, voice or other method) and whether such a vote is unanimous. For small meetings, write the names of the attendees who approve, oppose and abstain from each motion.

10  Focus on recording actions taken by the group. Avoid writing down the details of each discussion.

## Transcribing Minutes

1   Transcribe minutes soon after the meeting, when your memory is fresh.

2   Follow the format used in previous minutes.

3   Preface resolutions with "RESOLVED, THAT...".

4   Consider attaching long resolutions, reports or other supplementary material to the minutes as an appendix.

5   Write "Submitted by" and then sign your name and the date.

6   Place minutes chronologically in a record book.

## Negotiate an Agreement                                      `41`

Whether you are negotiating a business contract or the use of a cubicle, it takes tact and understanding to reach an agreement. Here are some ways to take the sting out of negotiating.

### ☉ Steps

1   Ask questions to learn what the other side wants. Try to step into the other person's shoes to see the problem from his or her point of view.

2   Communicate what you want. When you speak, make a point instead of just arguing. Focus on understanding and addressing everyone's needs.

3   Summarise conflicts of interest and obstacles to solutions.

4   Break down what you want into specific details so you can search for areas of agreement.

5   Keep talking until you find a solution that meets your mutual interests.

6   If you reach an impasse, end the meeting and reschedule it for another time. A few days of rest might spark some new ideas.

**✱ Tips**

See yourself and the other person as two team members searching for a solution, rather than as opponents.

Stay calm. Nothing is negotiated successfully when both parties are agitated.

**⚠ Warning**

Avoid taking things personally. When someone is attacking you, he or she is usually just attacking your position.

## Resolve Conflicts at Work                                   `42`

Friction at work can be stressful and counterproductive for everyone involved. Learn to approach the person with whom you are struggling and resolve the situation.

### ☉ Steps

1   Decide whether you want to confront the person who is bothering you. It is usually better to air grievances in the open than to let them fester.

**✱ Tips**

Deal with any personality clashes by trying to understand what motivates their behaviour, and then tailoring your actions to

2   Speak to the other person calmly, politely and rationally. Focus on the situation and facts, avoiding gossip and personal attacks.

3   Be careful not to express hostility in your posture, facial expression or tone. Be assertive without being aggressive.

4   Listen to the other person carefully: What is she trying to say? Be sure you understand her position.

5   Express interest in what the other person is saying. It's possible to acknowledge her ideas without necessarily agreeing or submitting. Saying "I understand that you feel this way. Here's how I feel..." acknowledges both positions.

6   Communicate clearly what you want, offering positive suggestions and recommendations. Be willing to be flexible.

7   Speak to your supervisor if a problem with a difficult co-worker seriously threatens your work, but avoid whining.

work with the personality type. Once you grasp why people behave as they do, you will be able to interact with them more effectively.

For example, be firm with bullies at work – don't let them pressure you into doing anything unwanted. Be forceful in your opinions, but act with a bit of caution.

Around complainers, avoid acting too sympathetically if you feel their complaints are ill-founded – it's better to ask them what sorts of actions they plan to take to change the situation. Squarely ask them what they want.

## 43   Give a Negative Employee Reference

While it is easy to provide a glowing reference to a former top-notch employee, it is much more challenging to give a negative reference. Here are some simple steps to guide you.

### ⊙ Steps

1   Confirm to the employer who contacts you that the job candidate worked for your company.

2   State the time period during which the person in question was employed, and his or her job title. Let your personnel department confirm the former employee's salary.

3   Offer no additional information. Derogatory remarks could land you in a costly and lengthy lawsuit.

4   Give the ex-employee a written letter stating the dates of employment and his or her pay level at the time of discharge. This could be presented to prospective employers instead of their having to call you.

5   Inform the ex-employee – if he or she wants to know what you have said – that as a matter of policy you only provide confirmation of employment dates, job title and pay levels.

6   Tell your former employee exactly what you said, if he or she asks you.

### ✳ Tip

If the person enquiring about the ex-employee is your close friend, you might be willing to risk making a few general comments about the ex-employee's merits or performance on the job.

### ⚠ Warning

Remember that anything you say to a prospective employer – even a close friend – could get back to the employee and land you in court.

## Get Promoted 44

Promotion is about more than just doing a good job and hoping that your boss notices your huge potential.

### ⊙ Steps

1 Your biggest clue is in the word "promote". In the workplace, make sure that your strengths and potential are well advertised to colleagues and senior staff.

2 Feel confident that you know every aspect of your current position.

3 Be aware of vacant jobs within your organisation – at the very least, this will show your interest and commitment to the company. Find out as much as you can about any position that interests you.

4 Be seen as smart, punctual and reliable, and willing to take on extra tasks if necessary.

5 Be prepared to work beyond your normal hours if necessary – why would anyone want to promote a "clockwatcher"?

6 Carry out your day-to-day tasks with enthusiasm. It's much easier to get on if you're liked by those around you.

7 Use meetings, conferences and appraisals as opportunities to shine.

### ✳ Tip

Take any training opportunities you are offered – it shows that you want to get on. Seek others out for yourself.

### ⚠ Warning

There's a delicate line between "selling" yourself and outright bragging. Tread that line with care – you don't want to come across as an arrogant git!

---

## Ask for a Pay Rise 45

Consider whether you merit a pay rise and whether your company is in a position to give you one. Then choose your moment and your methods carefully.

### ⊙ Steps

1 Evaluate your worth. List your achievements, skills and contributions.

2 Arm yourself with information. Know what a normal rise is for someone of your experience and occupation.

3 Assess your superior's mood and outlook. Do you think he or she is ready to consider your request?

4 Choose an appropriate time of day. Make an appointment or ask if there are a few minutes to spare. Plan for an end-of-business-day meeting.

5 Consider asking for a specific amount that's a little higher than you want. Say "eight per cent" when you would be happy with six.

6 Be realistic. If your company is going through tough times but you still feel deserving, decide how you'll respond if a lower amount is offered.

7 Be flexible. Would you consider a supplement in perks, time off, flexible time or holiday time in lieu of a rise? Negotiate.

8 If your superior turns you down, have a back-up plan ready.

### ✳ Tip

If you can, print out an outline showing that you're paid less than others in your position – but are producing more and better results.

### ⚠ Warning

Avoid losing your temper or your sense of humour.

## 46 | Resign From a Job

Regardless of your reasons for leaving a job, you should do so in a professional manner.

### ⊙ Steps

1 Consider all your options before resigning. Could your employer offer you something that would make you want to stay? Perhaps you should discuss with your employer your dissatisfaction or the better offer that you have received before making a permanent decision.

2 Write a letter of resignation and sign your name. If you were unhappy at the time of leaving, the letter might be a simple sentence conveying the effective date of your resignation. If you were genuinely happy, it could express your regret at leaving and the fact that you'll miss everyone.

3 Refrain from explaining in detail why you are resigning, where you will be working or how much more money you will be making. Do say that you are willing to help with the transition that your resignation will cause.

4 Request a formal meeting with your manager, ideally at the end of the day, so that you can deliver the news in person in addition to giving in the letter. Be sure to close the door.

5 Remember that you can be specific or vague if your supervisor asks for a reason. It's best not to use this time as a venting session.

6 Stick with the "better opportunity" angle if your tenure was unhappy. If you feel you must tell the truth, try not to be too personal. For example, "I would have preferred more training" is better than "You were terrible at training me".

7 Keep in mind that you may have to get a recommendation from your supervisor, so don't burn your bridges.

### ✳ Tips

If you would like a letter of recommendation, request one. Have it posted to you.

If you prefer not to say where you're going, a simple "taking time off" will do.

In most cases, a period of notice is expected. This is usually stated in your contract of employment.

Your employer may be angry that you are leaving. Try not to become involved in a dispute about the situation.

### ⚠ Warning

Be as positive as possible. You might return, or you may later need to ask for a reference. Keep your departure neutral.

## 47 | Survive Redundancy

Losing your job is one of life's most stressful experiences. As more and more companies get "lean and mean", you may find yourself laid off – but you will survive.

### ⊙ Steps

1 Leave your place of work immediately. Even if you saw it coming, you are likely to be too upset to answer questions from colleagues. You can come back later for your coffee mug.

2 Discuss your situation with your spouse and other family members who will be affected. Will your partner have to work overtime for a while? Can your son or daughter get a part-time job to help with college tuition fees?

3 Review your financial situation. You may have set aside what seemed like a reasonable amount for a "rainy day", but if your unemployment goes beyond a month or two, you may need to make some serious lifestyle adjustments.

### ✳ Tips

Get references in writing from your supervisor or personnel manager. Be sure that any "official" documentation states clearly that your termination was due to a workforce reduction.

Be sure that when you leave the office you have all the paperwork necessary for you to claim any statutory benefits.

4   Request a meeting with the company's personnel representative. Find out what redundancy package is being offered, ensure that you are paid for unused holiday, and request details of other relevant aspects, such as dealing with an employment pension or company car.

5   Take advantage of any outplacement services your employer offers. Many companies now provide career assessment and counselling as well as use of company facilities, such as personal computers, copiers and fax machines, to aid redundant employees in their job searches.

6   In most cases, redundancy will entitle you to immediate social security allowances. This may be a blow to your self-esteem, but you and your family are entitled to such benefits, and meeting basic needs must come before pride.

## ⚠ Warning

Losing a job – even if through no fault of your own – can be devastating. If your feelings of anger, sadness or helplessness persist beyond a few weeks, consider getting short-term therapy for depression.

## Become a TV Presenter                                        48

The emergence of digital television has meant a proliferation of new cable and satellite channels. This means there are plenty of opportunities to be discovered for would-be TV presenters.

### ⊙ Steps

1   A fundamental requirement of a television presenter is the ability to project his or her personality in front of a camera. Although there is no substitute for real broadcast experience, domestic video equipment can help you to get used to being in the camera's gaze. Frequent video taping will also help you to assess your own performance.

2   What kind of TV presenter do you want to be? Someone fronting a music programme will usually have different skills to someone presenting a current affairs show. Watch a wide range of different programmes – on both terrestrial and cable/satellite – to see which areas interest you the most.

3   Are you an expert in anything? The chance to present a TV show often comes from fame in a specific field. Many sports presenters, for example, will previously have enjoyed successful sporting careers. As an expert in your field, send your CV to as many TV production companies, producers, researchers and media freelancers as you can.

4   Many successful presenters began life as TV journalists. Another common route is to work your way up within a TV production company – typically as a runner or researcher.

5   Which TV presenter would you choose as a role model? If someone already has your dream job, research how he or she got to that position. Try to identify what skills or qualities he or she possesses, and attempt to acquire them yourself. You might even try to contact him or her directly – you'll be surprised how many celebrities are flattered to be asked for their advice.

6   Plum jobs are rarely advertised: staff are often "head-hunted" or simply in the right place at the right time. Those with the best connections are usually first in line for the top positions.

## ✳ Tips

Consider attending one of the many short courses available teaching simple techniques for on-camera behaviour. These are usually aimed at businessmen or executives who make periodic media appearances, but include lessons that any fledgling TV presenter will find useful.

## ⚠ Warning

Whatever a university prospectus may claim, a degree courses in Media Studies or Broadcasting is unlikely – in itself – to lead to a job as a TV presenter.

## 49 | Become a Vet

Although an eternally popular dream career for many young animal lovers, only students with the highest grades will have a chance of even getting an interview for vet school.

### ⊙ Steps

1 By law, to work as a veterinary surgeon in the UK you must first be registered with the Royal College of Veterinary Surgeons (RCVS).

2 To join the RCVS you need a veterinary degree from one of the UK's six RCVS-approved vet schools. They are based at the universities of Bristol, Cambridge, Edinburgh, Glasgow, Liverpool and London.

3 This career is only open to the most academically able. Degree course entry qualifications are high – usually three grade-A A-levels. (Chemistry is mandatory; the other two subjects must include biology, physics or maths.)

4 Entrants will be expected to have gained practical experience at handling animals, usually at a veterinary practice.

5 Make sure you can finance your studies. Veterinary degrees take five years (six at Cambridge), and the nature of the study is such that taking a part-time job outside of college or during holidays won't be possible.

### ✱ Tips

For every undergraduate place at vet school there are up to 20 applications. Since qualifications and work experience will be of a similar high standard, your acceptance may hinge on how well you perform at the entrance interview. It's therefore critical that you are well-prepared. Try to ask a recently qualified vet for tips on what to expect. Or get student views from a university vet school web page.

### ⚠ Warnings

You will often be on call during non-working hours, just like a medical doctor.

## 50 | Become a Film Director

There are many paths to a career in directing films.

### ⊙ Steps

1 Brainstorm to come up with any potential contacts in the film industry. Work as an apprentice under anyone currently directing student films, TV commercials, music videos or feature films.

2 Consider applying to film school to gain both knowledge and industry contacts.

3 Apply for work on film sets, in entry-level jobs such as production assistant – or as anyone's assistant. If you work hard and make friends, you can move up the ladder.

4 Target jobs directing TV commercials or music videos, where many film directors get their start.

5 Develop a reel (a tape of the work you've directed).

6 Make self-financed films of your own; to start with, they can be short (10 minutes long) and shot on easily accessible and affordable DV video equipment. If necessary, cast and write your films yourself to build your experience and CV.

7 Send postcards and updates regularly to industry contacts you have made, including directors, producers and actors. Constant networking leads to opportunities.

### ✱ Tips

Be creative and persistent, and understand that there isn't one right way to become a film director.

Read *The Hollywood Reporter* and *Variety* to find out about upcoming productions and possible job openings.

Network, network, network.

### ⚠ Warning

As with most jobs in the field of entertainment, directors work long and irregular hours.

## Become a Photographer

To be successful in this satisfying career, you need an artistic eye, technical skills, a knack for marketing yourself and a passion for your work.

### ⊙ Steps

1 Take pictures for your school magazine or student newspaper after you have studied the basics. You will get an idea of how deep your passion is for the medium.

2 Decide which type of photography – such as news, advertising or fine-art photography – best suits your interests and talents.

3 A degree in photography may help you get your foot in the door of some more prestigious employers. In general, though, practical experience is far more marketable than any academic achievement.

4 Develop an outstanding portfolio. Include excellent photographs you have taken on your own – in particular, those focusing on your own specialised themes.

5 Be willing to work as a photographer's assistant once you have some experience. You are unlikely to be competing with experienced photographers for a while.

6 Realise that more than half of all photographers work on a freelance basis. Many magazines and organisations that use photographers do not keep them on staff.

7 Attend workshops and seminars to remain up-to-date about new technical advances in photography.

**✳ Tips**

Use the best camera equipment you can afford.

Take classes in business and public relations if you eventually want to set up your own studio.

Volunteer your services as an assistant to a local studio photographer. It's good on-the-job training and may result in a full-time position.

Consider using stock photo agencies to sell your photos.

**⚠ Warning**

If you become a photojournalist you must be willing to travel at a moment's notice, and also be prepared to work irregular hours.

## Become an Interior Designer

Professionals in this field design and furnish the interiors of commercial, industrial and residential buildings. They have to combine artistic flourish with a working knowledge of statutory building regulations.

### ⊙ Steps

1 Understand that as an interior designer you will need to know more than how to decorate a space. For example, you will need to fully understand building regulations, be able to easily read a blueprint and know how to communicate with engineers, architects and clients.

2 Unlike the fields of architecture or medicine, there is no legislation or industry body which requires qualified membership as a necessity to work. But although anyone could theoretically set up as an interior designer, most working in the field have some sort higher education – HND or BA degree – most commonly from an art school.

3 When choosing a design course at art school or university, make sure that it includes a module on computer-aided design (CAD). As a modern designer you will be expected to know how to use a computer to create either two- or three-dimensional designs.

**✳ Tip**

Subscribe to interior design and architecture magazines to learn about the latest trends.

**⚠ Warning**

Designers often work irregular hours, at the convenience of their clients.

4   Some interior design degree courses incorporate periods of industrial placement, which give students the opportunity to obtain genuine work experience in a design or architecture practice – if, usually, in a low-paid junior capacity. Following graduation, students with practical experience are generally the most sought-after – some are even offered full-time jobs with their placement employers.

5   Most experienced interior designers working in Britain operate either within small business partnerships or freelance. With less security than those in full-time employment, this lifestyle is not to everyone's liking.

---

## 53 | Become a Private Investigator

Private detectives are used by lawyers and solicitors, insurance companies, businesses and individual members of the public. They are usually self-employed.

### ◎ Steps

1   Forget the mysterious world-weary characters from Raymond Chandler novels: most people working as private detectives are experienced professionals from a military or law enforcement background.

2   If you don't have an investigative background you may need to acquire certain skills to help with your work, such as learning how to fingerprint, conduct an interview, take samples of evidence or write reports.

3   Polish your writing skills. This is one of the most important things you can do to ensure success. You'll need to write reports frequently, and they must be of professional quality.

4   Become proficient at using credit checks and computer searching resources.

5   You do not need any form of government licence to operate as a private investigator. However you may reach a wider client base if you are a member of the Association of British Investigators (10 Bonner Hill Road, Kingston Upon Thames, Surrey, KT1 3EP), or the Institute of Professional Investigators, Burnhill Business Centre, provident House, Burrell Row, High Street, Beckenham, Kent, BR3 1AT.

### ✱ Tips

Honestly assess how well equipped you are for such a career. You need to be mature, assertive, persistent and logical.

### ⚠ Warning

Be prepared for long, irregular, solitary work hours, especially during surveillance work.

If it's the "glamour" of the TV and cinema private eye that attracts you to this career, think again. Most of your time will be spent in fairly mundane pursuits such as checking out credit ratings. And while it may not be a job for the weak-hearted, British gun legislation means that it's unlikely that you'll ever find yourself in the middle of a shoot-out.

---

## 54 | Become a Chef

A chef is a highly skilled and inventive cook who can turn a delicious meal into an artistic presentation. It usually takes years to become accomplished and known in this field.

### ◎ Steps

1   Work in a restaurant while still a student for the experience, even if it is in a non-cooking position. You will learn what it is like to be on your feet for long hours.

2   Ask your careers guidance advisor if there is a local catering college, or suitable college/university courses in this area.

### ✱ Tips

Be certain that this is the career to which you want to devote your time. Initially, consider taking a short course at a culinary school while working in a restaurant kitchen.

---

3 Decide what type of cooking you would like to do and in what type of kitchen you would like to work.

4 Although dedicated college courses will teach you valuable skills, it is more likely to be practical experience in a commercial environment that impresses potential employers.

5 Be aware that an apprenticeship will almost certainly require you to work at first in the least-skilled jobs in the kitchen. As you develop, you can advance up the culinary ladder in a larger restaurant by becoming a line chef, sous-chef, head chef, executive chef and, finally, master chef. Pastry chefs follow their own distinct ladder.

6 The restaurant business in the UK is more conscious of trends in food than in most other countries, with influence usually coming from the hippest of London's eating establishments. A poorly paid apprenticeship served at a Michelin-rated restaurant is a path trodden by many of today's most noted celebrity chefs.

7 If you think you would like to open your own restaurant, take a business course that specialises in catering. Look for one that places equal emphasis on health and safety legislation and aspects of business finance – getting a loan, hiring staff, dealing with taxation, pension and national insurance issues.

Stay up-to-date on food trends and kitchen equipment. Read as many culinary magazines and journals as possible.

Choose an area of specialisation if you want to work in up-market restaurants.

## ⚠ Warning

If the head chef leaves, his or her entire staff may be asked to (or choose to) do the same.

## Become a Radio Disc Jockey                                    55

You need confidence, a pleasant speaking voice and excellent communication skills for this job. On the air, you may introduce music, conduct interviews, and read commercials or even the news and weather forecast.

### ⊙ Steps

1 Take public speaking and drama courses at school or university. Make tapes of your speaking voice and ask your speech and drama teachers for their opinion of your vocal projection.

2 Consider taking any relevant part-time unpaid work while still at school or college. Working as a mobile disc jockey at friends' parties will also provide useful experience – especially if you have the opportunity to work with an experienced professional.

3 Ask your career's guidance officer for a list of colleges and universities that offer an education in broadcasting.

4 Be aware, however, that although many universities now offer degrees in broadcasting, this may not be the best way to a broadcasting career. For example, the majority of successful "talking heads" in the areas of news and current affairs are more likely to have crossed over from a background in political journalism.

5 Gain experience at your college radio station by doing any work that will teach you about the practical side of radio broadcasting, a station's equipment and the problems associated with airtime. Offer to be the DJ or radio announcer at the station during unusual hours. Then make a tape of the show and include the experience on your CV.

### ✱ Tips

Become an expert on a variety of interesting topics. Prepare a demo CD that demonstrate your knowledge and your excellent speaking voice.

Time management during a show and the ability to connect with your audience are key skills to have in this field.

### ⚠ Warning

Be prepared for the possibility of unusual working hours if you become a DJ.

6   While you are a student, try to get part-time work in local radio or as hospital radio volunteer. At first you will more than likely be doing dull office work rather than talking into a microphone or running the board. But the experience will be valuable.

7   If the opportunity presents itself, consider a job in local radio after you have completed your education. You're almost certain to begin with an entry-level position aimed at showing you the ropes, but – if you're ambitious – your chances of getting airtime in the near future will be far greater than on a larger station. Most national radio positions will require you to have had several years of on-air experience.

## 56  Become a Model

With supermodel salaries matching those of pop stars, it's no surprise that so many are attracted to a career in modelling.

### ◉ Steps

1   Be aware that only the tiniest percentage of wannabe models actually succeed. If you are rejected it WILL be for reasons that may be deeply hurtful to you.

2   To work as a model you need representation by an agency. You won't even get a look-in if you fail to meet certain physical criteria. For a woman, you must be: at least 1.7 m (5 ft 7 in) tall; 81–89-cm (32–35-in) bust; 56–64-cm (22-25-in) waist; 84–91-cm (33-36-in) hips; clear skin; healthy hair; immaculately straight white teeth. Male models need to be at least 1.8 m (6 ft) tall.

3   Many of the household names were "discovered" by agencies in very ordinary settings. They can spot potential – however well masked – walking down any high street. Some of the most famous models didn't even have ambitions in this area until approached by an agency.

4   If you are trying to get your first break you need some photographs. Get as many pictures taken as possible, and then choose the best five images to be blown up to 25 x 20 cm (10 x 8 in) format. Have three sets made: mount the first on black A4 card and slot them in an A4 display folder (this is the start of your portfolio); keep the second set safe, along with the negatives; keep the third set to send to your first agency contact.

5   Get a list of modelling agencies: go to a public library and look in the Yellow Pages – the vast majority of major modelling agencies will be based in the Central London area.

7   Telephone your target agencies. Tell them you have some photographs and would like to get some opinions of your potential.

8   If asked for photographs, send them in a hard-backed envelope, along with a typed covering letter detailing your measurements. If you haven't heard anything in seven days, call again to check that your pack arrived safely. If the agency shows no interest, get another set of prints made and contact another agency.

9   Don't be disheartened by a few rejections. If, however, a dozen or more agencies turn you down, then you must assume that you just don't have the look they are currently after.

### ✱ Tips

Have your portfolio photographs shot on a white background. Include some close-ups of your head and shoulders (both with and without makeup). Take a mixture of colour and black and white images. Include some swimwear shots – although avoid anything that even vaguely resembles soft porn.

### ⚠ Warning

There is no point in using your photographs to hide physical shortcomings. These will become apparent as soon as you meet agency staff, and will only waste everyone's time.

## Become a Celebrity                                    57

What makes a celebrity? Something indefinable that makes we mere mortals think beyond a person's ability, to wanting to know every last detail of their lives.

### ⊙ Steps

1   An obvious starting point for most is to become exceptionally good or successful in a sphere of work. But that's not the only way.

2   If you have no discernible talent, an alternative is to appear on a "Reality TV" show, such as *Big Brother*. Beware, however, that celebrity without the talent to back it up is usually short-lived.

3   Behave in a way that keeps your name on the front pages of the tabloid newspapers. A romantic liaison with another celebrity is usually a good guarantee of coverage.

4   Hire public relations staff – their job is to keep you in the headlines. (You'll need a seven-figure bank account if you want to engage a top PR company for any length of time.)

5   Invite celebrity magazines such as *OK* and *Hello* to photograph you and your loved ones in the glamourous surroundings of your home.

6   Appear on as many chat shows as you can. If the opportunity arises, do something shocking that will get reported in the following day's press.

7   Make sure you know – and can get into – the hippest joints in town. Make sure there is someone there to photograph you as you enter and when you leave – preferably arm-in-arm with another celebrity.

**❋ Tip**

Hire a society party planner to organise your gatherings. They will be able to guarantee a high celebrity count in attendance … for a fee, of course.

## Become Prime Minister                                58

There is no standard career path to holding the highest-profile job in Britain. But somebody's got to do it, so why not you?

### ⊙ Steps

1   The prime minister is the leader of a democratically elected political party. As politics since World War II has been dominated by three parties, that means first becoming leader of the Labour party, Conservative party or Liberal Democrats (although the latter has not yet managed to provide a premier).

2   Before you become party leader you must be an elected member of parliament. You are also likely to have first served as a cabinet minister (or shadow cabinet minister).

3   To become an MP you must be chosen to represent your party at an election. Most MPs will have participated in politics from their teenage years – often in the youth wings of their parties – and become party activists concurrent with their studies and subsequent careers.

4   Most MPs switch from a different career once they have been elected to parliament. The combative oratory nature of parliamentary politics means that some of the most successful politicians were once lawyers.

**❋ Tips**

Many successful parliamentary MPs have started in politics as local government councillors. The Trades Union movement has also provided a number of leading politicians.

## 59 | Buy a Computer

Buying a computer means investigating its different features: RAM (random-access memory), processor speed, graphics capability, hard disk space and so on. Here's how to start.

### ⊙ Steps

1   Before you start shopping, decide which features you'll need based on what you're planning to do with the computer. For example, if you're going to be creating graphics, sound and video, you'll want plenty of RAM. If you're going to be doing heavy computational tasks (searching large databases, watching video), you'll want a faster processor.

2   Decide which "platform" you want to use: the most common two are PC and Apple Macintosh.

3   Decide if you want a laptop computer, which you can carry around with you, or a desktop model.

4   Choose a computer brand based on quality, price and technical support.

5   Figure out the core configuration you need, including processor and speed, amount of RAM and hard disk capacity.

6   Determine which additional types of drive you need, such as CD-ROM, DVD-ROM, CD/DVD recorder or Zip.

7   Select any necessary peripheral hardware devices, such as printer, scanner, modem, sound cards, video cards and speakers, and decide how many extra internal card slots and disk-drive bays you'll need in order to allow room for future expansion.

8   Determine any pre-installed software you may need. For example, an operating system – Windows or the Mac OS – an anti-virus program and software for word processing, spreadsheets and databases.

9   Choose the warranty or service coverage appropriate to your needs.

10  Buy from a computer specialist, retail chain, consumer electronics shop, discount chain, or mail-order/online retailer. Buy when you need to buy. No matter how long you wait for the best deal, the same – or better – configuration will cost less in a few months.

### ✱ Tips

Keep abreast of the latest technology by reading the new-product reviews in magazines and on the web.

Find out which hardware and software are included with the models you're considering, and use that as a basis for comparing prices. Ask "What's the catch?" if a price seems too low.

Understand that RAM is where your computer temporarily stores data to be processed. Although more RAM is better, you don't necessarily need much if you restrict your computer use to simple tasks such as sending e-mails or word processing. Games, however, can require lots of RAM; graphics and sound are other space hogs.

The processors found on most modern computers are usually fast enough for all but the most demanding applications, such as streaming video.

## 60 | Install RAM

If your computer slows down when you're working with large files, try adding extra RAM. These instructions will work for most machines built since the mid-1990s.

### ⊙ Steps

1   Determine what kind of RAM you need – and whether your computer has enough open slots to hold it. The new RAM should match the existing RAM's specifications and configuration.

2   Shut down the computer, unplug it from the mains, and disconnect the monitor, keyboard and all other peripherals.

### ✱ Tips

Your computer will accept either SIMMs or DIMMs. Check your manual to find out which.

If you have an older machine, you may need to adjust DIP switches or jumpers. Consult your manual.

3    Remove the computer cover.

4    Ground yourself to the computer with professional grounding equipment, or by touching a metal part of the chassis.

5    Remove any cards or internal components necessary to give yourself unobstructed access to RAM sockets.

6    Pick up your SIMM (single in-line memory module) or DIMM (dual in-line memory module) by the ends without touching pins or chips.

7    If adding a SIMM, find the notched end and turn the SIMM so that it is parallel to the existing RAM card(s). Insert the SIMM into the socket at a 30-degree angle. If adding a DIMM, insert the DIMM straight in so that it is perpendicular to the motherboard.

8    Use slight pressure to keep a SIMM from backing out while rotating the module to an upright position perpendicular to the motherboard.

9    Make sure the small holes on each side of a SIMM fit into holders.

10   Feel or hear retaining clips lock a SIMM into the socket; close the side clips on a DIMM.

11   Gently try to pull the module out to ensure that it is locked in position.

12   Replace all internal components.

13   Leave the cover off and reconnect the monitor, keyboard and mouse.

14   Turn on the computer.

15   Check the amount of RAM by right-clicking the My Computer icon in Windows and choosing Properties. On a Mac, use the About This Macintosh command in the Apple menu.

16   If the right amount of RAM is not indicated, it probably means that it has not been correctly installed; turn off the computer, remove and replace the RAM, and reboot. If it still doesn't work, the RAM may be faulty; return it to the vendor or call a technician.

17   If all is well, shut down the computer, disconnect the peripherals once again so that you can replace the cover, and then reconnect peripherals.

## ⚠ Warnings

Stand on uncarpeted flooring to reduce static electricity. Touch as little as possible inside your machine and especially avoid touching chips. Static damage, and even oil from fingertips, may cause a failure months later.

Label any cards or internal components that are removed to access RAM sockets so that you'll replace them in the correct positions when you are finished.

Some "stub-chassis" computers built by Compaq, Hewlett-Packard and others have little or no work space inside. Some units require the removal of the hard drive and power supply to access the RAM. You should only attempt this for yourself if you are an experienced computer technician.

If your computer is under the manufacturer's warranty, any modification of the product may void that warranty.

Apple Macintosh G3 and G4 "towers" are designed to allow internal access without the removal of the case or hardware peripherals. However, a tower must still be disconnected from the mains.

## Back Up a Hard Drive                                             61

It's important to make frequent back ups of critical files. The following explains how to run Microsoft's built-in Backup utility in the Windows operating system (from Windows 95 onwards).

### ◉ Steps

1    Connect a drive (such as a Zip drive or other removable media, a tape drive or a second hard disk drive) that can hold the information you want to back up.

2    Open the Start menu and select Programs.

3    In the submenu that appears, click Accessories, then System Tools.

4    Click Backup to run Microsoft's Backup program.

### ✳ Tips

If you don't have a large-capacity backup drive, it may be more convenient to save a limited number of critical files, not your entire hard disk. You can also back up files to a network drive.

To restore a disk from a back up, open the Tools menu in the Backup utility. Select Restore Wizard.

5  For the easiest back up, answer the questions presented to you by the Backup Wizard. (The wizard will ask you what you want to back up, where you want to store the back up, if you want the data to be verified and/or compressed, and what you want to name the back up.)

6  Click Next after you answer each question.

7  Click Start to commence the back up.

---

## 62 Buy Peripherals for a Computer

**You need a monitor, keyboard and mouse to use a computer. What other peripherals are worth considering?**

### ⊙ Steps

1  You will need a printer – unless you have access to one at work or plan to use your computer only to surf the internet. Ink-jet printers cost less and can print colours. Laser printers are more expensive (only very expensive ones can print in colour) but have better text quality and are more likely to print industry-standard PostScript fonts. Laser printers cost less per use, as ink-jet cartridges run out quickly and are expensive. (See 66 "Buy a Laser Printer" and 67 "Buy an Ink-Jet Printer").

2  Buy a scanner if you want to "photocopy" text, documents or pictures into your computer (see 68 "Buy a Scanner").

3  Buy a back up storage device, such as an external hard drive, Zip drive or CD-RW drive, if you need to back up large amounts of data and your computer doesn't have a suitable built-in drives.

4  If your system came with unpowered speakers, buy a pair of powered stand-alone speakers for better sound quality and higher output .

5  Buy a microphone to record your own sounds, or to use computer telephony, voice activation and various educational programs.

6  A digital camera is the easiest way of transferring photographs into your computer (see 64 "Choose a Digital Camera").

7  Buy other peripherals to meet specific wants and needs. For example, buy a joystick to increase your speed and flexibility when playing action games, or a digital video camera for teleconferencing (see 65 "Choose a web Camera").

### ✱ Tip

Manufacturers introduce new types of peripherals all the time. Something not even invented when you buy your computer might well increase its capability later on.

### ⚠ Warning

Ensure that your computer is capable of meeting the minimum system requirements of any peripherals you buy.

---

## 63 Buy a Computer Monitor

**The main criteria for selecting a monitor are size and resolution (the ability to render detail). If you work with graphics or play computer games, you'll need a monitor with higher resolution.**

### ⊙ Steps

1  Determine how big a monitor will fit on your desk. If desk space is limited, consider buying a flat-screen monitor.

### ✱ Tips

For gaming or graphics, look for a refresh rate of at least 75 Hz at 1,024 by 768 resolution.

2  Even if ultimately you buy from a mail-order or web retailer, visit a local computer store to check out different monitors in person.

3  Compare features such as anti-glare coating, digital controls, built-in microphone, built-in speakers or speaker mounts, USB ports and ease of adjustment.

4  Compare limited warranties.

5  Make your buying decision based on display clarity in the size you want, for the price you want to pay.

Ensure that your graphics card meets the monitor's maximum specs for refresh rate and resolution.

## ⚠ Warning

The tube size and viewable area of a monitor are not the same. Read system specs carefully.

---

## Choose a Digital Camera                                64

Digital cameras offer the convenience of immediate viewing, multiple-image storage and computer connectivity – and there's no film to develop.

### ◎ Steps

1  Buy the camera with the highest resolution you can afford. At least 3 megapixels (3 million pixels) are needed for professional results.

2  Look for a 100-per cent glass lens as opposed to a plastic one.

3  Most digital cameras store images on removable RAM cards, such as the SmartMedia format; the larger the capacity, the less frequently you'll need to download or erase your photographs.

4  Expect zoom to be the feature you will use most. Compare optical, as opposed to digital, zoom capabilities.

5  Compare the different flash modes.

6  Investigate viewfinders: Look for an optical (through-the-lens) viewfinder as well as an LCD display.

7  Consider autofocus and macro features, shutter-release lag times, and bundled software.

8  Compare additional features you might want, such as interchangeable lenses, steady-shot, burst mode, auto exposure, variable shutter speeds, automatic white balance, voice memo, manual focus and self-timer.

9  Compare removable media of various types (if you need more storage space for your photographs).

10  Investigate batteries, chargers and AC adaptor units.

11  Look for additional features, such as USB or FireWire connectivity (to connect the camera to your computer) or a battery-status indicator. As well as video connections for looking at your pictures on a TV screen.

### ✱ Tips

If you will only output pictures to a computer monitor (for viewing, web-page use or e-mail), an inexpensive digital camera with a 640-by-480-pixel resolution will provide satisfactory results.

If you plan to print photographs on a good (at least 720 dots per inch) colour printer, look for a high-resolution camera.

A 2-megapixel camera will be able to provide photo-quality output for 13- by 18-cm (5- by 7-in) prints.

### ⚠ Warnings

Watch out for high-resolution cameras at bargain prices. The resolution claimed may only apply to software interpolation, rather than true optical resolution.

If you do buy a cheap camera, make sure that it has a charge-coupled device (CCD).

## 65 | Choose a Web Camera

Web cameras (webcams) stream live video or frequently changing still images onto web pages. The most commonly used type
– a videoconferencing camera – is discussed here.

### ⊙Steps

1   Try to get the highest frame-per-second rate, highest resolution and best
fidelity you can.

2   Compare lens types and focus controls.

3   Consider camera sizes and mounting options. Most cameras will sit on
top of a monitor, but not all rotate both horizontally and vertically.

4   Compare bundled software and the manufacturers' limited warranties
(most run for one year).

5   Check for additional features, such as a zoom or telephoto lens, video
still-capture quality and a built-in microphone.

### ✳ Tips

You can also use a digital still
camera or a digital camcorder
to set up a webcam.

Make sure your computer has an
appropriate port for connecting
the camera. USB is the most
common interface standard.

### ⚠ Warning

Windows NT does not support
USB.

## 66 | Buy a Laser Printer

For most uses, laser printers provide better quality than ink-jet
printers. However, they also cost more. Consider print quality,
speed, reliability and price.

### ⊙Steps

1   Decide what types of documents you want to print – text, graphics,
non-standard paper sizes, for example.

2   List specific needs, such as the ability to handle large files, printing on
different types of media (labels, envelopes) without jamming, the number
of paper trays, and compatibility with specific software.

3   Compare the print quality of different printers. Compare the resolution,
or dpi (dots per inch). Use a magnifying glass if print quality is critical.

4   Compare speed specifications. Although you may not achieve the rated
speed in a domestic setting, it is useful for comparing printers.

5   Learn how much RAM the printers have, and whether it's expandable.

6   Understand that the printer's paper path needs to be no sharper than
90 degrees to consistently handle envelopes, labels, transparencies or
card stock. If you plan to use special media often, avoid printers with
180-degree U-turn paper paths.

7   Compare prices of consumable items such as toner cartridges and
replacement drums.

8   Compare warranties and service contracts.

### ✳ Tips

Look for at least 600-by-600 dpi
(dots per inch) resolution.

If you want to print PostScript
fonts or graphics, you'll need a
PostScript printer. Many –
although not all – laser printers
can cope with PostScript; most
ink-jet printers can't.

Printer RAM will affect the speed
of the printer and its ability to
handle large files. If the printer
includes many built-in fonts, that
may also improve speed.

You may need to purchase the
printer cable separately.

### ⚠ Warning

Be wary of "laser-class" printers.
These inexpensive printers use
toner cartridges, but use LEDs
instead of lasers and produce
inferior text quality.

## Buy an Ink-Jet Printer

While ink-jet printers are widely viewed as cheap substitutes for laser printers, in certain cases they may be better for particular functions, such as printing colour photographs.

### ⊙ Steps

1 Prioritise according to price, versatility, print quality, speed and reliability.

2 Add specific capabilities such as photographic reproduction, printing onto CDs, compatibility with operating systems other than Windows, ease of use, cost of use, ability to handle large files quickly, USB connectivity and the capability of printing on various media without jamming.

3 Choose a specialised photo printer if you plan to print a lot of photos.

4 If you want to print presentation-quality text, graphics and photos, choose a higher-end model with a small dot size (and thus a higher resolution).

5 Choose a printer whose paper path is no sharper than 90 degrees if you want to print on envelopes, labels, transparencies or card stock.

6 Spend £200 or less unless speed is the most important consideration.

### ✳ Tips

For quality, buy a model with at least 600-by-600-dpi resolution.

Avoid single-cartridge printers – those that only come with a colour cartridge: they can't print "true" colour.

Most ink-jet printers are not PostScript-compatible. If you need to print PostScript graphics or fonts, consider a laser printer.

Colour ink-jet cartridges can be expensive, offsetting the low cost of the printer. Special coated papers can also add to the cost of colour printing.

## Buy a Scanner

Use a scanner to transfer printed materials – photos, drawings, even text – onto your computer's hard disk.

### ⊙ Steps

1 Only buy a low-resolution scanner if you just want to scan text.

2 If you don't plan to scan from books or magazines, consider a sheet-fed unit, which takes up far less desk space than a flatbed scanner.

3 Purchase a low-resolution or medium-resolution scanner if you plan to scan photographs to use on the internet, as the resolution of web graphics is low anyway.

4 Buy a high-resolution scanner if you plan to scan photographs to print and you have a high-resolution printer (greater than 600-by-600 dots per inch, or dpi).

5 If you plan to scan photographs or colour graphics, look for a model with 36-bit colour depth.

6 Purchase a parallel-port scanner if you don't expect to use the scanner often or work with large files.

7 Remember that even scanners costing less than £100 will provide a decent picture – 600-by-1,200-dpi resolution. Scanners priced above £150 usually provide at least 1,200-by-1,200-dpi resolution.

8 Speed is the biggest factor in pricing. For PCs, parallel-port scanners, which connect to the existing printer ports, are the cheapest, but also the slowest. For PCs and Macs, USB or FireWire scanners are much faster, however they cost more and also require that your computer has compatible ports.

### ✳ Tips

Most computers will need at least 64 MB of RAM to scan.

Don't buy a scanner that has greater resolution than your printer or display device. The extra money will be wasted.

Make sure the scanner includes scanning software. You may also require an image-editing program and an OCR (optical character recognition) program to translate scanned writing into text you can edit on screen.

### ⚠ Warnings

Some manufacturers mislead consumers with resolution claims. Optical resolution is the primary determining factor of quality.

Beware of small flatbed scanners using a contact image sensor (CIS) instead of a charge-coupled device (CCD). These produce inferior image quality and colour.

## 69 | Use a Computer Scanner Efficiently

Here are a few tricks to help you make the best possible scans.

### ⊙ Steps

1 Pre-scan; then drag diagonally to select the area for the final scan.

2 Avoid scanning anything at a greater resolution than you can display or print.

3 Adjust scanning software settings to match the type of document: text document, line art, black-and-white photograph or colour photograph.

4 If you are scanning photographs or documents to use on the Web, scan at 72 dpi (dots per inch) – there is benefit in using a higher resolution, and images will take up less space.

5 If you are scanning text documents or documents to archive, scan at no more than 200 dpi.

6 Scan at the scanner's maximum optical resolution if you are scanning photographs to print on a high-resolution printer (greater than 600 dpi).

**✳ Tips**

Images scanned at a lower resolution produce smaller files, which load faster, are easier to edit and conserve disk space.

Scanning software designed to improve the resolution of your scanner may be useful where graphics and photographs are lacking detail.

## 70 | Update Any Device Driver

The driver software tells a computer how to work with peripheral devices, such as scanners and printers. Upgrading to a new operating system or other software may cause conflicts with existing drivers. Sometimes device manufacturers upgrade drivers, which can fix known problems when installed.

### ⊙ Steps

1 Begin by working out which driver version you currently have in use. For PCs running Windows, right-click My Computer and click Properties; select the Device Manager tab. Click the plus sign to the left of a specific device to find the currently installed drivers. For Macs running System X, this information is shown in the Print Centre application stored in Applications/Utilities; for pre-System X Macs, use the Apple System Profiler program.

2 Find out whether a newer driver exists by visiting the manufacturer's website. A newer driver will have a later creation date than the one you have installed.

3 Follow instructions to download a newer driver.

4 Make sure you have the original drivers. If there are problems with the new driver, you should be able to restore the old one.

5 Double-click the icon for the downloaded driver.

6 Follow installation instructions that appear; look for a file named readme.txt or readme.doc.

7 If the installation failed to remove the old driver, remove it manually. On a

**✳ Tip**

If upgrading the driver doesn't solve problems with the device, replace the device or remove the new software from your system.

**⚠ Warnings**

Attempting to change video drivers may make your computer inoperable. Get professional help if you need it.

These instructions are intended for Windows 95/98 and do not necessarily apply to Windows NT or Windows 2000.

Windows computer, right-click the driver in the Device Manager and select Remove. On a pre-System X Mac, drag the old driver file out of the Extensions folder in your System Folder, and either save it elsewhere or delete it. (This step should not be necessary for System X Macs.)

8    Restart the computer.

## Buy a Laptop Computer     **71**

A laptop computer is no real substitute for a desktop computer, but a good laptop can be a solid and convenient supplement to a desktop model.

### ⊙ Steps

1   Check out the periodic surveys in leading computer and technology magazines for comprehensive information on the reliability of specific laptop brands. (Customer satisfaction ratings are a good indicator.) Make your choice based on quality, price and limited warranty.

2   Determine the core configuration you need, including processor and speed, amount of RAM, and hard disk size.

3   Decide on the type of display. Choose a dual-scan display if your budget is extremely limited. Select an active-matrix display for the quickest response and best visual quality, though at the cost of shorter battery life. Choose an HPA (High-Performance Addressing) display if your budget rules out an active-matrix display but you need to use the laptop under difficult lighting and wish to maximise battery life.

4   Compare weights of units you're considering. Think about how often and how far you'll need to carry the computer and its peripherals.

5   Determine the size of display you want. Remember that bigger screens add to the unit's price, weight and bulk.

6   Choose an ultraportable unit if weight is more important than price, reliability, battery life and ease of use.

7   Buy a unit with built-in CD-ROM or other drives if convenience is more important than portability or reliability. Consider a model with removable drives for the most flexibility.

8   Test the comfort and feel of the input device and keyboard. Choose between a touch pad, used by most manufacturers, and the pointing stick (also called the "command point") used by IBM and Toshiba.

9   Make sure the laptop comes with a lithium-ion battery. Be sceptical of manufacturers' battery-life claims.

10   Decide what pre-installed software you want or need.

11   Choose the length of warranty or service coverage you need.

### ✳ Tips

Touch pads are more reliable than pointing sticks.

Get a laptop with a DVD-ROM drive if you would like to watch films while travelling.

Consider leasing a computer if you need to upgrade often or spread out payments over two or more years. Keep in mind, however, that leasing is always more expensive than buying.

## 2 Get the Best Battery Life From a Laptop Computer

A rechargeable battery will last an average of two years. You can, however, take steps to get a better total battery life and longer battery life per charge.

### Steps

1 Charge the battery for 12 hours before use.

2 Let the battery drain completely before recharging if you have a nickel-cadmium (NiCad) battery. Upgrade to a nickel-metal-hydride (NiMH) battery – or better, a lithium-ion battery – if one is made for your machine.

3 Let the battery drain as much as possible before recharging if you have an NiMH battery.

4 Recharge an NiMH battery between long periods of inactivity.

5 Travel with an extra battery. Use the two batteries equally.

6 If you can, avoid running floppy, Zip, CD or DVD drives off the battery.

7 Reduce the display's brightness when possible.

### ✳ Tips

As time goes by, you will need to recharge any rechargeable battery more frequently. When the battery life is less than 25 per cent of its original level, it's probably time to get a new battery. (With normal use, expect about half the per-charge life claimed by the manufacturer.)

Only use power-management software in those instances when you can sacrifice performance for battery life.

If you're buying a laptop, get one with a lithium-ion battery.

## 3 Travel With a Laptop

Protecting your laptop from theft and damage, and ensuring that it can be used in foreign countries, requires preparation and care.

### Steps

1 Get a heavily padded carrying case that will hold the peripherals and accessories you need to carry.

2 To deter theft, use a case that isn't obviously for a laptop.

3 Take the components, peripherals and accessories you might need, but leave the CD-ROM drive or other parts you won't. Take an extra fully charged battery if you intend using the laptop on a long journey.

4 Remove disks from disk drives.

5 Ensure that you have any power and telephone adaptors necessary for use abroad. Find out the power requirements and plug shapes for your destination before you leave.

6 Find out what communication facilities will be available. Learn in advance how you can connect to your ISP if necessary.

7 Back up all important documents before you leave.

8 Check your insurance and warranty cover.

9 Make sure your laptop has enough battery power to boot if required by customs or security personnel.

10 Avoid leaving your computer unattended in the airport.

### ✳ Tip

An airport X-ray machine won't erase your data, but a metal detector can.

### ⚠ Warning

Do not plug your laptop directly into a foreign outlet, even if you have an adaptor plug – or you may fry your computer. Always use a power converter that claims it can handle the voltage at your destination. (Make sure it can handle your computer's current draw as well.)

### Things You'll Need

☐ carrying case

☐ extra battery (optional)

☐ adaptor plug(s) and power converter (optional)

☐ telephone adaptors (optional)

11  Deter theft and breakage by monitoring your laptop closely as it travels through the x-ray machine. Better yet, ask for a manual inspection.

12  Keep your laptop out of overhead bins and in plain sight when flying.

13  Once you arrive, change the date and time settings and – if necessary – the modem settings.

## Exit a "Frozen" Windows Program      74

When a program freezes, you can't work in it or exit from it. You're trapped! But not if you follow these instructions, which work for Windows 95/98.

### ⊙ Steps

1  Use the keyboard command Control+Alt+Delete, pressing the keys simultaneously. A box labelled Close Programs appears.

2  Scroll through the list of open programs until you come to the one that has frozen.

3  Select the frozen program.

4  Click on End Task.

5  A message will appear saying, "Program is not responding. End task?" Click on End Task. The program will shut down, and you'll be able to reopen it in the usual way.

### ✳ Tips

Using the command Control-Alt-Delete twice in a row will shut down the computer.

If your programs keep freezing, restart the computer.

### ⚠ Warning

When a program freezes, any unsaved material may be lost. Some applications may allow you to recover some material lost in a crash.

## Uninstall a Windows Program Safely      75

When you install a program, it usually includes additional files scattered throughout your Windows folder. To remove a program completely, use the Add/Remove Programs utility.

### ⊙ Steps

1  Check your documentation to see if the application has its own custom uninstall program, and use it if it's available.

2  If not, open the Start menu and select Settings, then Control Panel.

3  Double-click on Add/Remove Programs.

4  Find the program you want, then click Add/Remove.

5  In the box that appears, confirm to remove the program and click through the Wizard that follows.

6  Consider using a third-party utility, such as Clean Sweep or Norton Utilities, to uninstall remnants of programs from your system.

### ✳ Tips

The Add/Remove Programs utility will normally alert you to the presence of shared programs and allow you to leave them on your system.

Only delete an application folder as a last resort. The program could have added programs or files to additional folders. To be safe, rename the application folder and reboot your PC. If it restarts without a problem, delete the folder. If it does not, rename the folder with its original name and do not delete it.

## 76 | Troubleshoot a Computer

Is your computer functioning strangely or – worse still – not at all? Before paying for technical support, look at your system. A little common sense may help you solve simple problems.

### ⊙ Steps

1 Restart the computer. Some software problems will correct themselves when you do this.

2 Check your cables. Keyboard not working? Make sure it's plugged in. Mouse not responding? Make sure it's plugged in.

3 Check the electric power. Test the outlet by plugging a lamp into the same power source as your computer.

4 Disconnect peripheral devices (such as a printer or external drive) and restart the computer.

5 Consider the possibility of a computer virus. Run an anti-virus program (see 85 "Protect a Computer From Viruses").

6 Run a utility program (such as Norton Disk Doctor) to defragment your hard drive or to identify and fix certain problems.

### ✳ Tips

If you do decide to call technical support, write down the exact problem and what you were doing when it occurred. Also note any error messages.

Be as specific as possible when talking to the support person.

Computers tend to crash or hang when their hard disks become too full. Try to free up space by deleting any unnecessary files and emptying the Trash or Recycle Bin.

## 77 | Start Your Windows Computer in DOS

Installation instructions for some older DOS games and other applications require you to boot to MS-DOS. Troubleshooting in Windows may also require this.

### ⊙ Steps

1 Click Start.

2 Click Shut Down.

3 In the box that appears, click Restart in MS-DOS mode.

4 Click OK.

### ✳ Tips

Type "exit" and press Enter to return to Windows from MS-DOS.

DOS can also be opened in the Start menu and selecting Programs, then MS-DOS Prompt.

## 78 | Change Your Default Printer

You can change the default printer to any other printer that is connected to your computer. These instructions are for the Windows 95/98/NT operating systems.

### ⊙ Steps

1 Click on the Start menu and click on Settings, then Printers.

2 A window will appear showing the icons of all the printers that are installed on your system. Right-click on the icon for the printer you want to use as the default. A menu will appear.

### ✳ Tip

Once you have set a printer as the default, you can still print from other installed printers. The Print dialog box offers you a selection each time you print, but the default printer will be the one that appears automatically.

3   Click on Set as Default.

4   To make sure the correct printer is now set as the default, right-click on the printer icon again. When the menu opens, a check mark should appear before Set as Default.

## Find a File on Your PC's Hard Drive                         79

Use your computer's Find function when you have forgotten the name or location of a file. These instructions are for Windows 95/98/NT.

### ⊙Steps

1   Click on the Start menu, then on Find, and then on Files or Folders.

2   Enter the filename in the box labelled Named. If you remember only key words or phrases used in the document, enter them in the box labelled Containing Text. Try to choose a unique word or phrase to help narrow the search.

3   If you have an idea where the file is stored, use the Browse function to start the search in a particular folder.

4   Tick the box labelled Include Subfolders.

5   Click on Find Now. Within a few moments, you will receive a list of every file in the folder or drive that you selected whose name (or contents) includes the words you typed. (For example, if you entered "apples", you would get files called "Red apples" and "Golden delicious apples" in addition to "Apples".)

6   Double-click on the file to open it, or note the location so you can open the file later.

**✳ Tips**

Click on the Date tab to search for a file created or last used within a certain time frame.

Click on the Advanced tab to search for files created by a certain application.

You can also carry out file searches from within many software applications, such as Microsoft Word.

## Find a File on a Mac                                         80

Mac OS 8.5 onwards (including OS X) feature the powerful Sherlock search program.

### ⊙Steps

1   For pre-System X Macs, click on the Apple menu and select Sherlock. OS X users can click on the Sherlock icon in the Dock. Alternatively – for both systems – from the Finder, press the keys Command-F.

2   Choose your search criteria. You can search by one or more attributes of the file (name, size, type, date modified, creator and so forth).

3   Choose a location to search. You can search locally or on a network.

4   To search the contents of a file for specific phrases, click on the Find by Content tab, then specify the phrase and a location in which to search. If the Find button is dimmed, click Index Volumes first.

5   Search the internet by keyword by selecting the Search internet tab.

6   Click Find to run the search.

**✳ Tips**

When you search by name, the search finds all filenames that include the phrase you typed. So a search for "apple" would find files named "Aunt Mary's apple pie recipe" and "Apple Computer stock prices".

In the Sherlock results list, if you click once on the icon of a file, Sherlock will give its location, no matter how embedded within folders it may be. If you double-click on the icon, the application will launch.

## 31 | Use Mac Files on a Windows Computer

If you save Mac files on a PC-formatted disk, you can open them on a PC, but you may lose some formatting. Here are tips for saving your Mac files so they transfer as well as possible.

### ⊙Steps

1  If you can, save the file on your Mac using the same program (such as Microsoft Word or Excel, or WordPerfect) as you'll be using on the PC. Make sure to add the three-letter file extension (such as ".doc") when saving the file. You should then be able to open the file on a PC just by double-clicking it, and your formatting should be retained.

2  If you don't have the same program in Mac and PC versions, try saving your file in a common format, such as Rich Text Format (RTF), which most word processors can read, or JPEG, if saving images. To open these, you might need to open the program you want on the PC, then use the Open command in the File menu.

3  If the first two options don't work, buy a conversion program for your PC to translate Mac file formats.

**✳ Tip**

You can save any text document as Plain Text; you'll lose all the document's formatting, but the file will be guaranteed to open in any word processor.

## 32 | Use Windows Files and Disks on a Mac

Any Macintosh built since the mid-1990s will be capable of reading any removable media formatted for a PC. The operating system contains translators that can open Windows documents if you have the same application type on your Mac.

### ⊙Steps

1  Make sure Automatic Document Translation is turned on in the Macintosh Easy Open or File Exchange control panel.

2  Put the PC disk in the Macintosh disk drive.

3  Double-click the PC disk icon.

4  Double-click the icon of the document you wish to open.

5  If the document doesn't open immediately, the Mac's Easy Open or File Exchange control panel may give you a list of applications to try. Choose the same type of application (graphics, word processing, spreadsheet) as the document.

6  If this method doesn't work, open the Mac version of the PC application that created the document. (For example, if it is a Microsoft Word for Windows file, open Word on the Macintosh.) If you lack that application, try a similar one (for example, the word processor in AppleWorks). Open the File menu and choose Open, then browse your disks for the PC file. If the file you are looking for doesn't appear in the Open box, make sure that All Files is selected, if possible, in the File Type menu. If that doesn't work, try another program.

**✳ Tips**

If your system software includes the PC Exchange control panel, make sure it is turned on.

If you can't open the file, or if its formatting is messed up, ask the person who created the document to save it again, this time in a translatable format, such as RTF (Rich Text Format).

Programs such as Word can also save files in the formats of earlier versions of the software.

**⚠ Warning**

You can't run or install Windows application programs on a Mac (unless, that is, you have installed Windows emulation software); you can only open documents.

## Increase the Memory for a Macintosh Application 83

If you work with large documents, you may see a message complaining about insufficient memory (RAM). A document might not even open, or a program might run very slowly. You can assign more RAM to the application to see if that helps.

### ⊙ Steps

1 Single-click the icon for the application to which you want to allocate more memory. Be sure to exit the application first.

2 From the File menu choose Get Info, or press the keys Command-I.

3 In OS 8.5 and later versions, select Memory from the Show menu in the box that appears.

4 Type a new value into the Preferred Size box, perhaps 1.5 or 2 times the suggested size shown. You can decrease the memory in the same way.

5 Click the close box. Your change will take effect the next time you launch the application.

**✳ Tip**

If you attempt to increase the minimum size to a value larger than the preferred size, you will get an error message.

## Format a PC Disk on a Mac 84

If you want to use Mac files on a PC, you need to make sure you use PC-formatted disks to transfer the files. (Macs read PC disks, but PCs don't read Mac disks.) But even if you have Mac disks, you can reformat them as PC disks using your Mac.

### ⊙ Steps

1 Insert a floppy disk (with write protection off) or Zip disk into its drive.

2 If a dialog box appears, telling you the disk is unreadable, you can format it by clicking on the appropriate button.

3 If a dialog box doesn't appear, select the disk by clicking on it, click on the Special menu option, and select Erase Disk.

4 Select the format you want from the menu in the dialog box that appears. Your Mac will format the disk and tell you when it's finished.

**✳ Tip**

Make sure there is nothing you want to keep on the disk before formatting it.

## Protect a Computer From Viruses 85

If you think your computer may be infected, take all necessary steps to clear your system and avoid infecting other computers.

### ⊙ Steps

1 Be cautious about what disks and files you accept from other people. Don't reuse disks that have been in other computers, don't download files from insecure sites, and don't open e-mail attachments unless you are expecting them. Be wary of messages and attachments, even from

**✳ Tips**

Keep up-to-date on virus alerts and install any patches released by software publishers.

people you know, with vague subject lines and contents, such as "CHECK THIS" or "SEE THESE PICS!!!".

2 Obtain an anti-virus program to share disks more safely, download files from the internet and open e-mail attachments.

3 If your system gets a virus, visit your virus-scan software manufacturer's website and install any virus updates that are available. Then run the software. The software may not be able to delete the virus, but it may be able to identify it.

4 Search the web for information regarding your specific virus by typing the name of the virus or its associated file into a search engine, followed by the word "virus". For example, "Melissa virus", "BubbleBoy virus", and so on.

5 Download and install any software patches or other programs that will help you eliminate the virus. Or follow any instructions you find on deleting the virus manually.

6 Run another virus scan to make sure the virus was dealt with properly.

7 Employ extra caution when you receive attachments that end in the commonly used PC extensions .doc, .exe, .com, .xls or .ppt. Never open attachments that end in .vbs or .js, since a typical PC user would never have a reason to open such types of file.

If you think your computer has been infected with an e-mail virus that mails itself to people in your e-mail address book, phone those people and tell them not to open messages or attachments. Avoid sending out any messages until you have properly eliminated the virus.

Some viruses attach themselves to outgoing messages without your knowledge.

Generally, deleting the file that caused the virus isn't sufficient to eliminate the problem, since some viruses can create new files or corrupt existing files.

---

## 86   Get the Best Price on Computer Software

Price variations on software from retail stores and internet retailers are small, but you can get legal programs free, or find other ways to save. Here are some options to explore.

### ⊙ Steps

1 Use internet search engines that find the best price on specific products.

2 Get software free from your employer. Many businesses purchase multi-computer licences and are only too happy to have you work from home.

3 If you will be using the software for a home-based business, ask a large retailer for a business price.

4 Buy a "works" program (one program with various functions) or an office suite (a set of related programs) instead of individual word processing, spreadsheet and database programs if you plan on using most or all of the programs.

5 Buy the upgrade version of Microsoft Office instead of the full version if you already have any of these programs: all office suites, Microsoft Works, WordPerfect, Lotus 1-2-3 or any Microsoft program included in the version of Office you want.

6 If you don't need sophisticated features, consider shareware or freeware programs or buy a basic program instead of a professional version. Search the internet for programs of the type you want.

7 If you don't need new features, you can usually buy older versions of a program at a hugely discounted price after an update has been released. If you change your mind, you can often upgrade inexpensively.

### ✳ Tips

Be aware that most software manufacturers offer upgrade prices to users of competing software.

Most chain retailers will give you a price adjustment (usually between 100 and 150 per cent of the difference) if the price on a product is reduced (by that store or a local competitor) within a week or two of purchase.

### ⚠ Warning

Remember to add shipping costs when comparing prices from internet and other mail-order retailers.

## Play Music CDs on the Computer 87

The Windows operating system has in-built software for playing compact discs.

### ⊙ Steps

1 With the computer turned on, put a music CD – label side up – in the CD-ROM drive. Close the drive.

2 If auto play is enabled, the CD will start playing the first track. If this is the case, go directly to step 6.

3 If the CD does not start playing automatically, open the Start menu. Choose Programs, then Accessories, then Entertainment.

4 Click CD Player.

5 Click the Play button on the CD Player window (a single right-pointing arrow in the top row).

6 Use the Pause, Stop, Skip to Next Track, and Go Back to Last Track buttons to control what you listen to.

7 Choose Edit Playlist from the Disc menu to program a particular sequence of tracks

8 Minimise the CD Player window if you plan to listen to the entire CD while working.

### ✳ Tips

Sound cards usually come with a more sophisticated CD program.

Adjust volume by clicking on the speaker icon on your desktop.

### ⚠ Warning

Some new CDs – mostly big-name artists on major labels – have in-built copy-protection to prevent duplicate CDs being made. Where incorporated, this system prevents CDs being played on the hard drive of a computer. Read the back of the CD jacket before purchasing.

## Use a Computer to Transfer Cassettes to CDs 88

You can use a CD burner to make a complete transition from tape to CD, or to make compilation CDs. You'll need a sound card with a Line In jack (other than a microphone jack).

### ⊙ Steps

1 Plug in your tape deck or portable player near your computer.

2 Connect the tape deck or player to the Line In jack on the sound card.

3 Use the jacks labelled Tape Out, Line Out or Playback on the deck, or use a headphone jack.

4 If you're using a tape deck with a Tape Out, Line Out, or Playback jack, connect a cable with two RCA plugs on one end to the back of the deck. Connect the stereo miniplug on the other end to your computer's sound card.

5 If you're using a deck with a headphone jack, connect a cable with a 6-mm (¼-in) plug on one end to the headphone jack. Connect the stereo miniplug on the other end to the sound card.

6 If you're using a portable player, connect a cable with stereo miniplugs on each end from the unit to the sound card.

7 Open your CD recorder application.

8 Select Line In as the source or input.

### ✳ Tips

If you are planning to play your recorded CD on an old CD player, select the Close the Session option before you start recording the CD. Some old CD players will not read recorded CDs unless the session is closed.

### ⚠ Warnings

Any computer activities during recording can interfere with the process. Prevent your modem or screen saver from activating during recording.

Note that it may be illegal to duplicate copyrighted materials without permission from the copyright owner – especially if used for commercial purposes.

9   Open the File menu and select New (or whatever command your chosen software uses for beginning a recording).

10  Sample a track to set a recording level. Set the level to peak at 0 dB, 80 VU, or as high as possible without going into the red portion of the meter display.

11  Put the tape deck in "play/pause" mode before starting the track. If your source unit lacks a pause button, press play a few seconds before the end of the preceding track.

12  Look for the command that begins recording: probably Record, Save or Extract to File. Start the recording process just before the song starts.

13  Click Stop when you want to end the recording.

14  Save the recording as a WAV file to the desktop. Save individual tracks as separate WAV files, or save the entire side of the tape if your software allows it. (The Macintosh equivalent will save files in the AIFF format.)

15  Open the file in your CD-burning program (in some applications you can drag it into the CD-R window).

16  Select the recording speed (8x, 16x, etc.).

17  Choose the command that will record the file to CD: probably Record, Create or Save.

## Things You'll Need

☐ tape player

☐ CD burner

☐ recordable CDs

☐ cables

☐ sound card (Macs are readily equipped with suitable hardware)

---

## 89 | Use a Computer to Transfer LPs to CDs

**You can use your CD burner to archive your record collection or to make compilation CDs. You will need a sound card with a Line In jack (other than a microphone jack).**

### ⊙ Steps

1   Clean the LP and the stylus.

2   Plug in your turntable and pre-amplifier or receiver near your computer.

3   Connect the pre-amp or receiver to the Line In jack on the sound card. Use jacks labelled Preamp Out or Tape Out or a headphone jack. Use a cable with two RCA plugs on one end and a stereo miniplug on the other end. (Use a 6-mm/¼-in plug-to-miniplug adaptor for a headphone jack.)

4   Switch the pre-amp or receiver to Phono.

5   Open your CD recorder application.

6   Select Line In as the source or input.

7   Open the File menu and select New or whatever command is used for beginning a recording.

8   Sample a track to set a recording level. Set the level to peak at 0 dB, 80 VU, or as high as possible without going into the red portion of the meter display.

9   Lower the stylus to the beginning of the LP to record the entire side. Or start a few seconds before the end of the preceding track.

### ✳ Tips

If you hear a hum, try grounding the turntable or preamp to the computer by connecting a wire to screws on the chassis of each component.

Many programs for cleaning up LP noise are available. Before burning the CD, use software to remove noise before and after songs, clicks and pops, and unwanted songs or excerpts.

### ⚠ Warnings

Do not expect the CD to sound as good as the LP.

Your pre-amplifier or receiver must have a Phono section.

10  Look for the command that starts the recording process: probably Record, Save or Extract to File. Begin recording before the song starts.

11  Click Stop at the end of the track or side.

12  Save the recorded file to the desktop as a WAV file. Save individual tracks as separate WAV files, or save the entire LP side if your software allows. (Mac users save as AIFF files.)

13  Open the file in the CD recorder software (in some applications you can drag it into the CD-R window).

14  Select the burning speed.

15  Look for the command that will record the file to a CD: probably Record, Create or Save.

Any computer activities during recording can interfere with the process. Prevent your modem or screen saver from activating during recording.

Note that it may be illegal to duplicate copyrighted materials without permission from the copyright owner – especially if used for commercial purposes.

## Get Internet Access                                    90

The following steps describe how to access the internet using an internet service provider (ISP) and a computer modem. Many new computers include software that lets you set up an ISP account and connect to the internet immediately.

### ◉ Steps

1  Buy a computer that has a modem or add a modem to your existing computer. Most internet service providers require at least an Intel 386 processor (or a Macintosh of any vintage) and a modem capable of at least 28.8 Kbps. New computers more than satisfy these requirements.

2  Make sure your modem is properly installed, and connect it to your nearest telephone socket.

3  Look on your computer's desktop for an icon that bears the name of an internet service provider. If you find one, double-click on the icon and follow instructions to install the software and activate your account.

4  If you can't find an icon and you are using Windows, open the Start menu and choose Settings, then Control Panel. In the window that appears, double-click the internet Options control panel. Click the Connections tab, then click the Setup button at the top of the window.

5  On a Mac, look for the Internet Setup Assistant in the Apple menu.

6  If your computer doesn't come with internet software, buy a computer or internet magazine and look for the names of ISPs in the back pages.

7  Look for special offers from large, commercial ISPs on television, in newspapers and in the mail.

8  Contact a provider and request installation software.

9  Once you've received the software, follow the installation instructions and set up your account.

### ✳ Tips

Fast access to the internet requires an ADSL "Broadband" connection.

Read your terms-of-service agreement carefully before signing on.

Consider rates and fees, e-mail and other features, technical support and system requirements when choosing an ISP.

Popular internet software can often be obtained free of charge on the "freebie" CD-ROMs that accompany computer and internet magazines.

## 91 Evaluate Free Internet Service Providers

Some ISPs don't charge a monthly account fee. Before you sign up, make sure that there are no hidden costs – either in terms of quality or cash.

### ⊙ Steps

1 Find out what features the ISP offers. At a bare minimum, these should include e-mail and access to the World Wide Web. Other good features include access to newsgroups, instant messaging, chat and web hosting services.

2 Ask the same questions you would of other ISPs: What modem speeds does the ISP support? What operating systems? How many users per ISP modem? Is technical support available by phone?

3 Make sure the ISP is actually free. Read the fine print to see if there are any hidden charges that may show up later.

4 Determine how the company supports itself. Many free ISPs depend on advertising and end up bombarding customers with e-mail adverts.

5 Look for reviews to get a feel for user satisfaction and service.

6 Carefully review the ISP's terms of service and other fine print, keeping an eye out for any deceptive wording or other traps.

### ✳ Tip

There's nothing to lose if you sign up for a free ISP and end up not being satisfied – you haven't paid anything.

### ⚠ Warnings

Just because you don't have to pay a monthly fee, it might not be the cheapest way to connect to the internet. With all "free" ISP accounts you have to pay for your dial-up connection as if it were a telephone call. Most ISPs also offer "unmetered" access, meaning that for a monthly fee you have unlimited online access and your connection calls are not charged. This may provide huge savings in the long run.

## 92 Choose Broadband Internet Access

High-speed internet access is becoming more available. Depending on where you live, you may be able to get a Broadband (ADSL) connection.

### ⊙ Steps

1 Find out what services are available in your area. Although all Broadband lines are ultimately owned by British Telecom, BT is not the only provider. Contact your current ISP to see if it offers a Broadband upgrade, and also check computer periodicals and the web. If your local BT exchange is not equipped to provide Broadband services the only real option is a satellite installation. These are VERY expensive.

2 High-speed internet connections are also offered by most of the major cable companies.

3 Compare prices and speeds for various services.

4 Compare all hardware and installation costs.

5 After completing your basic research, decide whether the extra cost of increased speed is worth it. If you regularly send and receive large files or download MP3s or video clips from the internet, then a Broadband connection will make life a good deal easier. However, you may choose to wait until competition drives down prices.

### ✳ Tips

Telephone and cable companies often provide free or subsidised hardware and installation. A service-term contract is required with these deals.

If Broadband is not available in your area you should register your interest with the British Telecom website, www.bt.com. BT set targets for each exchange; once that level is reached the exchange will be upgraded.

Regardless of whether you select your telephone company to be your ISP, you will be dependent on it for ADSL service.

6   However your connection is rated, expect actual ADSL speeds to vary according to your location, neighbourhood and usage at any given moment. You should be aware that your connection may not ever achieve the maximum speed advertised by the provider.

7   Before choosing your current telephone or cable company as your ISP, consider your level of satisfaction with its current service.

8   Find out how many other users will ultimately share access to your line – this will affect your connection speed.

9   Compare extras offered by high-speed ISPs, such as multiple accounts, domain aliasing and extra web space, if you'll use them.

## Choose a Good Computer Password    93

Whether it's for e-mail or for online banking, a good password should be easy to remember and difficult for others to figure out

### ⊙ Steps

1   Use numbers as well as letters. If possible, use symbols such as % and *.

2   Randomly capitalize letters if the password is case-sensitive.

3   Use as many characters as possible – and a minimum of six.

4   Choose a string of characters that can be typed quickly without looking at the keyboard.

5   Avoid using your username, personal name, the personal names of friends or family members, your birthday or other things that people may know about you.

6   Avoid using an actual word from any language. If someone is serious about cracking your password, he or she will be able to run dictionaries from multiple languages against your account. However common, the word "password" is an obvious no-no.

7   Find an easy way to remember your password, but avoid writing it down.

8   Change your password every three to six months, especially if your account gives you access to restricted information.

9   If you have different accounts, it's wise to use a different password for each one, as long as you can remember them.

### ✳ Tips

Acronyms for a phrase work well because they're much easier to remember – for example, "MNIJS" for "My name is John Smith.

For a more effective password, add a number or symbol at some point within the acronym. For example, "IMMNS?" for "Is my mother's name Susan?"

## Avoid Giving Personal Information to Websites    94

Protect your privacy and security and minimize junk mail by using caution when browsing the web.

### ⊙ Steps

1   Avoid giving your credit card number to anyone online for any reason unless you are certain that the site is trustworthy and the browser connection is secure.

2  When shopping online, make sure the site is secure before providing your name and address.

3  Be selective when registering with websites. Take care that you read the company's privacy policy before providing personal information. Look for a little box somewhere in the registration form that allows the company to send you mail or – even worse – sell your personal information. This box is often pre-ticked. Remove the tick if you do not wish to receive mail from the site.

4  If you don't see any privacy information in the registration process, look for a statement somewhere on the site that describes the company's policy. If you don't find one, send e-mail to the site's webmaster. Ask that your information not be used.

5  If you get e-mail from a site where you registered or shopped, and you didn't request it, look for a way to "unsubscribe" – this is usually described at the bottom of the e-mail message. If you don't find one, write back to the e-mail address and ask to be taken off the mailing list.

6  When posting to a web-based discussion board, use a false name. Avoid providing any contact information other than your e-mail address and the URL of your web page.

7  Try setting your browser to reject "cookies" – small files that load into your browser and enable a site to know that you've been there before. (Note: some site features won't work without cookies.)

**✳ Tips**

It's possible to configure most browsers only to accept cookies from specific websites.

---

## 95  Find Free Stuff on the Web

**It's often said that nothing in life is free – but in many cases the internet may be an exception to this rule.**

**⊙ Steps**

1  Enter whatever you're looking for, preceded by the word "free", into a web search engine. (If you're looking for free downloads in general, a good search string is "free stuff".)

2  Once you've found a site that offers what you're looking for, follow the instructions on how to download.

3  Check software manufacturers' websites for free trial versions of their software. Sometimes you can get a complete program to try; it will expire after a certain date. The trial program may have limited features.

4  Visit the websites for your favourite products to see if the sites give away free samples.

**✳ Tips**

Some "free stuff" may have a catch: you might have to view ads while using a free ISP, for example. Always investigate first.

Free stuff includes screen savers, clip art, computer "wallpaper", and simple software.

**⚠ Warning**

Computer "shareware" can be downloaded for free, but you generally have to pay later on to keep using it.

## Download Files `96`

Downloading files may open up your hard disk to computer viruses. Avoid downloading from websites that you think might be dangerous or insecure.

### ⊙ Steps

1  Visit the web page that has the link to the file you wish to download.

2  Click on the download link (usually a link that says "Download" or the name of the file).

3  Indicate which language and operating system you use, if necessary.

4  Select the download site nearest to you geographically, if given a choice. A window will pop up asking whether you wish to open the file or save it to disk.

5  Select "Save To Disk" to retain the file for future use. If you want to use it only once, select Open.

0  If you selected "Save To Disk", choose where you want the file to go on your hard disk. Most browsers then open a window indicating download progress – usually percentage downloaded and time remaining.

### ✱ Tips

Many browsers offer the option of downloading multiple files simultaneously. Be aware that this generally takes just as long as downloading the files one at a time.

You can still browse the web while your file is downloading. Just click on the original browser window.

Larger files are often compressed, typically as Zip files. To open them up, you'll need access to file compression/decompression software.

## Conduct an Advanced Internet Search `97`

To conduct an advanced search on the internet, use Boolean operators, such as "AND" and "OR", to make your search as specific as possible.

### ⊙ Steps

1  Go to a web search engine.

2  To find documents containing an exact phrase, type the complete phrase, surrounded by quotation marks, into the search field. If, for example, you type in "fish sticks" (with the quotation marks) you will get a list of documents that contain the phrase "fish sticks", but NOT web pages that contain only the words "fish" or "sticks".

3  To find documents containing a pair of words, but not necessarily together, type those words separated by the word "AND" in capital letters. For example, typing "fish AND sticks" (without the quotation marks) will return web pages that contain "fish", "sticks" and "fish sticks".

4  To find documents containing either one word or the other, type those words separated by the word "OR" in capital letters. For example, typing "fish OR sticks" (without the quotation marks) will return documents that contain "fish" or "sticks", or both.

5  To exclude a word from your search, type the word you wish to exclude into the search field, preceded by the word "NOT" in capital letters. For example, typing "fish NOT salmon" (without the quotation marks) will return only documents that contain the word "fish" but DON'T contain the word "salmon".

### ✱ Tips

Check the directions for the search engine you're using. Some require very specific syntax.

Some search engines allow the following symbolic substitutions for Boolean words: & for AND, | for OR, ! for NOT, and ~ for NEAR. (Not all searches allow this, so if your query comes up blank, try using the words instead.)

Some search engines will not support the Boolean words "NEAR" or "NOT".

6   To find documents that contain two words separated by 10 to 25 words, type the two words separated by the word "NEAR" in capital letters, into the search field.

7   If your search expression is lengthy or complicated, use round brackets to separate the different parts. For example, typing "fish OR sticks NOT (salmon OR trout)" will generate entries that have the words "fish" or "sticks" or both, but do not have the words "salmon" or "trout".

## 98 | Shop Online

You can now buy just about anything online. If you haven't yet tried e-shopping, here's a general outline.

### ☉ Steps

1   If you don't know specifically which site to visit, use a search engine to find the product you're seeking. Or try a product-comparison site to check different prices or product reviews.

2   Visit several sites to find the best products and prices.

3   Most sites use a "shopping cart" system. As you browse the site and find items you want, click Add to Cart (or a similar button).

4   Specify a quantity and other relevant specifics (colour, size and so on) when you add an item to your shopping cart.

5   Click Continue Shopping (or a similar button) to keep browsing. Otherwise, click Proceed to Checkout (or something similar) to finalise your order.

6   For any kind of shopping site, provide your name, address, e-mail address, phone number and payment information when prompted during checkout. Once you've entered this information, you should be presented with an order-confirmation page, including all your items, the total price, and the address and other information you've entered.

7   Make sure your order is accurate and then confirm it.

### ✻ Tips

Most traditional mail order catalogue retailers now have websites.

Only shop from sites that use a secure server. If you're uneasy about providing your credit card details online, look for a contact number and pay over the phone.

In most cases, the online store will send you an e-mail message to confirm the details of your order. Many online stores send e-mail updates if any problems occur with your order.

### ⚠ Warning

If you buy in Europe from sites based in the US you may well be charged customs duty on receipt of the goods.

## 99 | Bid at Online Auctions

Online auctions can be a great way to get deals on goods, from computers and electronics to antiques and collectibles.

### ☉ Steps

1   Register as a bidder. This usually entails giving your name, address and e-mail address (and in some cases credit card details), and setting up a unique username and password.

2   Search categories to find things you want to bid on.

3   Select an item; enter your username, your password and the bid amount.

### ✻ Tips

Before bidding, ask the seller questions about how the item was stored or cared for and whether it has a certificate of authenticity. Check out the specifications to ensure that you know EXACTLY what you're purchasing.

4   Enter a bid that is within your budget but higher than the current high bid. High bids are displayed along with the description of the item.

5   Click the Submit Bid button to go to the website's confirmation page. The site will advise you immediately on the status of your bid (whether you've been outbid or currently have the highest bid).

6   Look for a Current Winner message on the page showing that your bid is currently the highest. If no one outbids you before the auction period ends, you "win" the auction.

7   Check your e-mail (or the auction website) regularly during the auction. You will receive an e-mail message if you are outbid. Place another bid if you wish to bid higher.

8   Work out payment and shipping details directly with the seller. (The seller will most likely contact you via e-mail.) On some auction sites, you can submit payment through the site or a third party. Payment is usually accomplished with a credit card, money order or personal cheque. Some sellers also accept internet "cash" such as PayPal.

If you encounter problems with a seller, complain to the auction site. There is usually a forum for posting negative feedback about a seller, so you can warn others who might have similar problems in the future. Be a good buyer as well, as you may be rated by the seller.

## ⚠ Warning

Just because something's up for auction doesn't mean it's a good deal. Shop carefully – you could end up paying more money than in a traditional store – especially if you buy from overseas where there may be hidden costs to be paid, such as customs duty.

## Watch Video Clips on the Web                    `100`

You can watch anything from music videos to political debates on the web, as long as you have the appropriate web browser plug-ins and viewing software. With "streaming" video, you can watch the clip as it downloads; otherwise, the complete file needs to be downloaded first.

### ◉ Steps

1   Visit the website that hosts the video clip you wish to view. The clip will probably have several different links according to viewing format – such as QuickTime or RealPlayer – and modem speed.

2   Select the link that matches your connection speed and offers a format that your software supports.

3   Try a different format if you cannot view the clip you chose and another is offered (not all sites offer a choice of formats and connection speeds).

4   Download and install the appropriate viewing software or plug-in if you cannot view the clip in any format. Many sites that host video clips also provide links to sites where you can download such software for free.

5   Technology in this area is advancing quickly, so ensure that your player is updated frequently.

### ✱ Tips

PCs come equipped with the Windows Media Player; Macs come with the QuickTime MoviePlayer. Use a search engine to find and download other alternatives.

If the clip is choppy or refuses to play, try defragmenting your hard disk; also see if the site provides minimum requirements to view the video.

### ⚠ Warning

Video quality is often barely watchable on connections slower than 56 Kbps.

## 101 | Use the Internet to Locate People

Put the internet to work to find your best friend from infant school, a long-lost relative or the flat-mate who left without paying the phone bill.

### ⊙ Steps

1. The person you're looking for may have a personal home page. To find out, simply type the person's first and last names into a web search engine and view the results.

2. To find old school or university chums, try the Friends Reunited website – www.friendsreunited.co.uk. (This is especially good if you want to find out what old friends are up to without having to make direct contact!)

3. If the person you're looking for is a college student, he or she may have an e-mail account through the university's website.

4. The person may have an e-mail account through his or her job. If you know where the person works, visit the company's website and use its directory. If the site has no directory, try sending an e-mail message to the person at firstname.lastname@company.com.

5. If none of the above suggestions work, try an online directory website.

### ✳ Tips

Some online search services find e-mail addresses, some find phone numbers and postal addresses, and some find both.

## 102 | Make Phone Calls Over the Internet

Using the internet as an alternative to traditional telephone calls can be less expensive – if slightly more complicated.

### ⊙ Steps

1. Make sure you can connect to the internet at a minimum speed of 56 Kbps. Higher connection speeds will allow clearer conversations.

2. Make sure your computer is equipped with a sound card of at least 16 bits. The sound card should also allow recording.

3. Purchase compatible speakers and a microphone if you don't already have these components.

4. Buy (or download) internet telephony software and install it on your computer. The software you choose must be the same as, or compatible with, the software of the people you wish to call.

5. Make arrangements with the person you wish to call establishing that you will be online at a specific time.

6. Follow the instructions of your specific telephony software for making a call. This usually involves accessing a server and selecting a name from a list of users who are currently online.

### ✳ Tips

In general, online telephone calls can only be made between two people who have computers, internet access and compatible software.

For optimal clarity, you should use a full-duplex sound card.

Instant-messaging software will give you instant messages, but without the voice effects.

## Create Your First Website

These simple guidelines are for entry-level web programmers. Better options are available for more sophisticated users.

### ⊙ Steps

#### Getting Started

1 Choose an ISP or other web hosting service to host your site.

2 Investigate several hosting services, considering maximum space, accessibility, reputation and terms of service.

3 Choose a suitable web-page editor. A number of simple editors are available for free download. This software lets you see what your site will look like as you build it, so you won't have to learn HTML or any other programming languages. Newer word processors, spreadsheets and other applications can also generate HTML files.

4 Your web-page editor will give you specific instructions about options such as naming your site, creating different sections, creating backgrounds, adding links and inserting images.

#### Using Images

5 Create images for your site using a computer graphics program or by scanning photographs and other hard-copy images. You can also take photographs with a digital camera.

6 If you find an image on another web page that you'd like to use, send an e-mail to the page's owner or administrator and request permission to download and post it. Download an image from a website by right-clicking on it (or on a Mac, click and hold down the mouse ) and select Save Picture.

#### Publishing Your Site

7 Your web host ISP may have its own system for uploading pages. Otherwise, obtain a File Transfer Protocol (FTP) program. Any will do.

8 Open your FTP program and log in to your host server by entering your login name and password.

9 Access the directory where your home page belongs. (Your web ISP will give you this information.) The directory address is usually in the form of /pub/username, /pub/www/username, or /pub/username/www. Your FTP program and host server will have specific instructions on how to access your directory.

10 Upload each page and graphic of your site according to the specific instructions of the FTP program and your host server.

### ✱ Tips

Many web hosts let you use your own "domain name" (such as www.me.com) if you have one, or will assign you a name.

Many graphics programs come with clip art – simple images in various categories – that you can use on your site.

Clip art CD-ROMs can be bought from software retailers.

You may want to limit the size of the images you include; larger images can make your page take a long time to view.

Your FTP program may give you a choice between ASCII and binary mode when uploading. Use ASCII mode for uploading pages, because pages are text files. Use binary mode for image files.

The steps shown are a general strategy for uploading your site. Your FTP program and web-page ISP will have more specific instructions.

### ⚠ Warning

To use content from another website, you need permission from the creator – unless it specifically states that text or images can be reused.

## 104 | Choose a Domain Name for a Website

A domain name reflects your business or personal identity.
Choose wisely.

### ⊙ Steps

1   Write down the name of your business. Remembering that short and
    sweet domain names are the easiest to remember, create a possible list
    using your business name (for example, smithauto.com, smauto.com,
    smitheys.com).

2   Create a list of services your business provides and a list of possible
    names from those services (for example, autorepair.com, fixcar.com,
    brokedown.com).

3   Use catchphrases from your brochure and other promotional materials to
    create additional possibilities.

4   For personal domain names, you could use your name, your pet's name,
    your hobbies, your surname or even your child's name.

5   Visit the Whois website (www.whois.org). Using Whois, you can type in
    your favourite names and see if they're already taken and by whom. If
    they are taken, keep trying with alternative choices.

6   If the popular ".com" name is taken, use other suffixes, such as ".co.uk",
    ".net" or ".org". Since users randomly searching for your site may be
    directed to the ".com" site first, ".net" and ".org" suffixes are best for
    personal rather than business domain names.

7   If you're really set on using a domain name that has already been taken,
    contact the owner of that domain name by checking the Administrative
    Contact section on the Whois site. Domain-name owners sometimes sell
    domain names they don't use.

### ✱ Tip

Ask your family, friends and
associates for their opinions of
your choices. What seems funny
to you may be incomprehensible
to someone else.

### ⚠ Warning

Don't use the name of a well-
known company or product, or
any variation of that name, in the
hope of attracting people to your
site. It may subject you to legal
action.

## 105 | Register a Domain Name

Setting up a website with your own domain name (www.me.com)
is a straightforward process, though finding a name you like
may prove difficult. Registration usually gives you exclusive use
of a domain name for a period of two years.

### ⊙ Steps

1   Go to a website offering domain name registration, such as www.123-
    reg.co.uk.

2   Enter the name or phrase of the domain name you would like to register.
    Follow the rules regarding name length and format.

3   Search for the name.

4   If the name has already been registered, enter a new name and search
    again until you find one that is still available. If you first tried ".com" as a
    suffix, try ".co.uk", ".org" or ".net" instead.

### ✱ Tips

Have a list of possible names
ready when you visit the site.

The more unusual the name, the
more likely it will be available.
Most common or well-known
corporate names are taken.

If the domain name is already
taken and you desperately want
it, you may contact the owner
and offer to buy it.

5 Register the domain name.

6 Pay the filing fee online or through the mail, following the instructions on the website.

Once you have the domain name, contact your ISP to see about using it as your website or e-mail address.

## Learn HTML 106

HTML, which stands for Hypertext Markup Language, is the formatting language used to create most web pages.

### ⊙Steps

1 Call your local college or university. Many adult education centres also give courses on HTML and web design. Search the internet for online courses – many of which will be free of charge.

2 Purchase a book on HTML design. Book/CD-ROM combinations offer hands-on learning and web development tools.

3 Go to the HTML Writers Guild website (www.hwg.org) and sign up for the trial membership. The HTML Writers Guild offers classes in HTML, web design and web graphics for members.

4 Learn HTML on your own by looking at a page's source code. With your browser, open a simple, easy-to-read page. Open the View menu, then select Source or Page Source, depending on your browser. Study how the source code translates into the page you see in the browser.

5 Purchase an HTML reference manual to help you decipher the tags and their roles. You can even copy a page's source code and insert your own elements to see what happens.

6 Visit the World Wide Web Consortium at www.w3c.org to find an HTML tutorial and learn more about HTML's history.

7 Ask a web-page designer to teach you HTML as he or she designs a page for you. It costs a little more, but you will learn as you go and be able to update your own page.

**✳ Tip**

It is best to learn HTML before you use an HTML "assistant" or specific web design application. You can use HTML code to make changes that some programs won't allow you to make.

**⚠ Warning**

Use another's source code only to learn. Using parts of someone else's web page as your own is copyright infringement. Once you have learned HTML, you can then create your own pages.

## Learn About Java 107

Java is a programming language created for the internet. You can use Java to create scripts, animated text and other visually interesting objects.

### ⊙Steps

1 Call your local college or university. Many adult education centres also give courses on Java and web design. Search the internet for online courses – many of which will be free of charge.

2 Log on to the website of Sun Microsystems, the company that created Java, to find tutorials and examples of Java programming.

3 Purchase a comprehensive book about Java. It should include an outline of Java history, an explanation of how the software works, examples and worksheets; some even come with interactive CD-ROMs.

**✳ Tips**

Java applets are applications written in Java. They are typically attached to web pages.

One of Java's strengths is that it is platform-independent. Java programs can run on various operating systems, as long as the computer has a Java virtual machine installed to interpret the Java code into commands that will run on that system.

4   Sign up for an online Java course. The HTML Writer's Guild (www.hwg.org) is one potential source.

5   Search the internet for some of the many useful user groups, forums and websites dedicated to Java.

6   Consider learning JavaScript, which is used in web browsers. Unrelated to Java, JavaScript is an "interpreted" language. JavaScript is easier to learn but more limited than Java.

7   If you're serious about programming, read up on general skills such as developing algorithms and designing data structures.

## 108 | Publicise Your Website

**Get the word out! Help people from all over the world find your website.**

### ◎ Steps

1   Register your site with your favourite internet search engines. Most search-engine sites have links (towards the bottom of the engine's home page) that say "Add a site" or "Add URL". Click on these links and follow the instructions.

2   Visit websites such as Submit It (www.submit-it.com), which help you submit your URL to multiple search engines simultaneously.

3   Visit sites that are related to or similar to your own, or maintained by your friends, and suggest linking to each other's pages.

4   Join a web ring, a group of websites on a particular topic that link to each other in a chain. Or start your own web ring. Visit the webring site (www.webring.org) for information.

5   Pay to place banner ads on well-trafficked websites; contact individual sites for their rates. Or join a free banner exchange, such as LinkExchange (www.linkexchange.com).

### ✱ Tip

Use META tags in your HTML pages to help your website come up in more search-engine results. To learn more about META tags, visit web developer sites, such as WebDeveloper.com or internetDay.com. For other tips about search-engine results, go to Search Engine Watch (www.searchenginewatch.com).

## 109 | Get a Free E-mail Account

**Free e-mail is typically web-based. It may not have as many features as ISP or work-based e-mail, but it does mean that you can access your mail anywhere in the world via the web.**

### ◎ Steps

1   Decide what type of e-mail service would be best for you. Consider factors such as the volume of outgoing and incoming mail, message storing, the ability to send and receive attachments, frequency of use and security.

2   Do a search for "free e-mail" or "web mail" using a web search engine.

### ✱ Tips

If you travel a lot or often use other people's computers, a web-based e-mail service – such as Microsoft's HotMail – will probably be best for you.

3   Visit various sites that offer free e-mail. Review their respective plans, features and terms of service.

4   Once you've found a free service that suits your e-mail needs, follow the site's instructions on how to set up your account.

Free e-mail services sometimes function by inundating customers with advertising e-mail messages from their sponsors; others make you view ads on the screen.

## Send an E-mail Attachment                                  110

These instructions will give you the basics of how to send an e-mail attachment no matter which program you are using.

### ⊙ Steps

1   Go to your e-mail program.

2   Click the New Mail, Write Message or similar button, depending on your application, to create a new e-mail message.

3   Enter the address of the recipient in the To field.

4   Type a subject in the Subject field.

5   Add a message to the body of the e-mail as usual.

6   Click the Attachments button (many programs show this as a paperclip icon). Also look for an Insert File or Insert Attachment option in the File menu.

7   Browse your files to find the attachment you want to send. You may need to click on a Browse or Find button to see your directory.

8   Click on the filename. If your program allows you to attach more than one file at once, hold down the Control key (or Shift key on a Mac) as you select another one.

9   Click the Attach Insert or Open button, depending on your e-mail program.

10  To send another file located in a different area of the hard disk, click the Attachments button again and repeat the previous steps.

11  Click the Send button when you're done.

### ✳ Tips

Change picture attachments to the JPEG format. They'll take up less space and may be sent faster in that format.

Make sure the recipient can read your attachment. Most word processors can read RTF (Rich Text Format). Web browsers can invariably open JPEG and GIF image files.

If you're sending files to a person who uses a modem, be careful about sending large files (300K or more) – they can take a long time to download.

Consider compressing your files with a utility such as WinZip or StuffIt. Your recipient may need to have the same compression software as you, although some programs are able to create "self-extracting" files that decompress automatically.

## Create Your Own E-mail Mailing List                        111

By creating your own e-mail mailing list, you can easily send copies of a single message to a group of recipients.

### ⊙ Steps

1   Collect the e-mail addresses of your recipients.

2   Open your e-mail program and save these names as a group. Look for a function that is called something like Address Book, Contacts or Nicknames. Name the group and enter your recipients' e-mail addresses separated by commas or semicolons. Click Save. Note that many e-mail programs require that you enter all of the individual addresses to your Address Book before you can add them to a group.

### ✳ Tips

Using the BCC field instead of the CC field allows the messages to be sent without showing each recipient the e-mail addresses of the other recipients. However, not all e-mail programs support the BCC feature.

3    Open a new message and address it to yourself.

4    Add the subject and body of the message.

5    Put the group e-mail addresses in the field marked BCC (blind carbon copy). Your e-mail software should allow you to do this automatically from the Address Book or from the Nickname function. If it doesn't, copy the list and paste it in the BCC field of your message.

6    Click Send. The original message will be sent to you, as you entered your own address in the To field.

7    Each member of the group will receive a copy of the message.

If you have a large mailing list (hundreds or thousands), you may want to consider buying specially designed bulk e-mail software. To avoid being accused of spamming, include only the addresses of people who have already agreed to receive your messages.

---

## 112 | Stop Unwanted E-mail

As anyone who's ever had an inbox cluttered with unwanted advertisements knows, spam, or unsolicited commercial e-mail, can be a big problem.

### ⦿ Steps

1    Contact your ISP and complain. ISPs don't like spam any more than you do; the mail clogs their servers. The ISP may be able to filter out mail from a suspected spammer address.

2    Avoid displaying your e-mail address in internet chat rooms and only give out your e-mail address on secure sites.

3    Avoid including your e-mail address when you post to newsgroups.

4    Send a complaint message to the postmaster at the spammer's ISP, if you can figure it out. Many spammers forge return addresses, but you can sometimes figure out the ISP from the full e-mail header. In some e-mail programs you can right-click on the e-mail message and choose Options or Properties to see this information.

5    Be careful when selecting a free ISP or e-mail account. Some of these services make their money by letting "sponsors" send e-mail messages to their subscribers.

6    If your e-mail provider doesn't have a built-in spam filter, search the web for e-mail filters and other anti-spam software. Many of these programs are free and can be easily installed.

**✳ Tip**

To reduce spam in your e-mail account, open a second, free e-mail account which you use exclusively for web registrations, chat rooms and mailing lists (see 109 "Get a Free E-mail Account").

**⚠ Warning**

Don't reply to spam unless the message includes specific instructions for removing yourself from a mailing list. In most cases, responding only verifies that your e-mail address is active. Sometimes the spammer will have forged a return address, so by responding you're actually bothering an innocent person.

---

## 113 | Read a Newsgroup on the Internet

Internet newsgroups are a great way to share information online. Once you have a news reader set up on your computer, reading and posting to newsgroups is relatively simple.

### ⦿ Steps

1    Get your news server name from your ISP or network administrator.

**✳ Tips**

Your ISP may not subscribe to all your chosen newsgroups. If possible, use a separate reader to

2   Determine whether your current ISP software, e-mail program or web browser includes a newsreader – most of them do. If not, download and install one.

3   Configure your newsreader by inputting your news server address and any other information it requests (it might ask for an e-mail address and mail server as well).

4   Use your reader to call up a list of available newsgroups. This list will probably pop up during setup the first time you use your reader.

5   Look through the hierarchical list of newsgroups to find any that sound interesting. Let the prefixes of each group (such as "comp" for computer-related topics and "rec" for recreational topics) guide your search. The other words in the name go from general to more specific keywords.

6   Subscribe to whichever newsgroups you want to read or post to. (Note that some readers allow you to read newsgroup messages without your having to subscribe.)

7   Select the newsgroup you want to read.

8   Select a message by double-clicking on the subject. (Note that different readers may have different ways of reading messages.)

maximise your access to the internet. Newsgroups that begin with "alt" (denoting "alternative" topics) may be especially hard to find on some ISPs.

If you come across a newsgroup message that appears to be gibberish, it may be a message encrypted into "Rot13". This is a simple encryption code that replaces each letter with the letter that is 13 spots ahead of it in the alphabet. This coding is used mainly to protect people from possibly offensive postings. You can decode these messages by hand, or your reader may have a Rot13 decoding utility.

# Use Online Forums 114

Online forums – also called discussion boards – function in a similar way to newsgroups, except that they are available through ISPs and individual websites.

## ⊙ Steps

1   Explore some of the forums and special-interest groups on your ISP or online service.

2   Use a search engine and look for websites that focus on your interests. Many of these will have forums or chats.

3   Begin by reading the "posts" (messages) and follow the current "threads" (comments related to a single topic) for several days. See if the group has a FAQ (frequently asked questions) document.

4   Write a post of your own. Be prepared for a mixed response.

5   Explain yourself if someone takes exception to your comments, but do not get into a heated argument via posts.

6   Determine whether your forum companions get together for online chat sessions. Join in if they do.

7   Send e-mail to your new friends and develop new relationships.

## ✳ Tips

Keep your initial posts short and noncontroversial.

Befriend a veteran or two and ask about the group's taboos.

Represent yourself accurately; you may want to meet the forum regulars one day.

## ⚠ Warning

Generally, forums are open to all. That means you may run into angry, combative people who will "flame" you for posting ideas that run counter to their own. If you handle the attacks calmly without retaliating, others will respect you.

## 115 | Find an Internet Chat Room

Use these guidelines to communicate in real time with people all over the world.

### ⊙ Steps

1   Check for any chat utilities offered by your ISP, if you use one. Most large commercial ISPs offer a variety of chat rooms categorised by topic and demographic segment, as well as general chat rooms with no specific focus.

2   Find out about chat functions offered by any instant-message programs you use. Many of these programs let users participate in public chat rooms as well as create their own.

3   Search the web, either directly or through a chat room database, for web-based chat rooms on specific topics.

4   Check out IRC, or Internet Relay Chat, which requires IRC downloadable software and involves a set of networks and channels.

### ✳ Tips

Many web-based chat rooms require you to download and install plug-in software before they can be accessed.

Many chat services let users preview a room by reading the profiles of any users who are currently in the room.

## 116 | Practise Chat Room Etiquette

Many chat rooms have sets of rules and guidelines – often unofficial – by which users are expected to abide.

### ⊙ Steps

1   Find out whether a particular chat room has its own FAQ (frequently asked questions) section before you enter. If it does, review the FAQ section for specific etiquette guidelines.

2   Introduce yourself when you enter a room by typing your age and gender. In some rooms, it is also appropriate to mention your geographical location.

3   If you want to address an individual in the room without sending an instant message, introduce your statement or question with the person's screen name and a colon or hyphen (for example, "SportsFan: What's your favourite football team?").

4   Avoid referring to users by their real names.

5   Allow all users to make comments and ask questions. Don't try to take control of the room by flooding it with your own entries.

6   Avoid direct confrontations with rude users. Report disruptive users to the chat host if a host is available. Otherwise, leave the chat room.

7   Don't harass other users with threats, unwanted sexual comments or anything else that might make them uncomfortable.

### ✳ Tips

Some chat rooms offer the option of blocking out messages from specific users. This is a good alternative to abandoning the room or getting the chat host involved.

To get a feel for how a chat room operates, begin by "lurking" – observing the activities in the room without joining in – for a while before offering your own comments.

### ⚠ Warning

Don't type the same sentence, word or phrase into the chat room over and over again. This is called "scrolling" and is heavily frowned on by users and hosts.

## Decide Whether to Repair an Electronics Product

While manufacturing quality may have declined over the years, performance and functionality have improved. Weigh up the pros and cons before deciding whether to replace or repair a formerly reliable product.

### ⊙ Steps

1 Find out if the product is still covered by the manufacturer's warranty or an extended service agreement.

2 Research the cost of a replacement product.

3 Get a free estimate on repair, If shops in your area will provide one. Otherwise, find out the hourly labour charge. (Expect to pay from £30 to £50 per hour depending on how specialised the work.)

4 Find out how long the repair is guaranteed. Most shops gurantee repairs for 60 to 90 days.

5 Consider the resale value of the product if it is repaired.

6 Consider the portability of the broken product and how far you'll have to haul it to the repair shop.

7 Remember that you might have to spend time learning how to use a new product.

8 Ask a repair technician if any additional components are likoly to nood replacement in the near future.

9 Look into features on current products that your product lacks.

10 If applicable, make sure your software will work on new hardware before abandoning the broken product.

11 Repair the product if it no longer exists in the same form (such as a Betamax VCR or eight-track tape player).

12 Replace the product if you feel you will benefit from upgrading to newer technology (such as from a VCR to a DVD player).

13 In addition to the manufacturer's warranty, you have statutory rights of repair or replacement on faulty new products.

### ✱ Tips

Expect a repair shop to take several weeks to repair your product.

Manufacturers can be slow to send proprietary parts or may no longer stock them.

CD players are among the most common electrical products to go wrong. Unless it is a "top-end" model, it is rarely worth the cost of repair – a replacement model of the same cost is certain to be an improved model.

If your video recorder goes wrong, do you roally need to replace it? Consider upgrading to newer technology such as recordable DVD.

If you choose to replace the product, try to find a way to dispose of the old product that is kind to the environment.

## Set Up a Hi-Fi System

While these instructions are based around a simple stereo amplifier or receiver, the connection process is essentially the same for more complex arrangements, such as those found in home cinema surround systems.

### ⊙ Steps

#### Connect CD Player to Amplifier

1 Connect the phono (RCA) cables to the Output sockets of the CD player. Connect the red plug to the socket marked "Right", and the black plug to the socket marked "Left".

### ✱ Tips

Phono cables (sometimes called RCA cables) are usually supplied with mass-market components, but less commonly with top-end components.

2    Connect the other ends of the cables to the sockets labelled "CD" or "CD Player" on the back of the amplifier. Ensure that the red plug goes into the socket labelled "Right", and the black plug goes in the socket marked "Left".

3    If both components have digital connections you will get a superior sound by using a SPDIF or other digital cable.

## Connect Cassette Deck (or MiniDisc) to Amplifier

1    Connect one pair of phono (RCA) cables to the Output sockets on the cassette deck: the red plug goes in the socket marked "Right"; the black plug goes in the socket labelled "Left".

2    Connect a second pair of phono (RCA) cables to the Input sockets on the back of the cassette deck in the same way.

3    Connect the two output cables from the cassette deck into the sockets on the amplifier labelled "Tape In" or "Tape Play". The red plug goes in the socket marked "Right"; the black plug in the socket labelled "Left".

4    Connect the two input cables from the cassette deck into the sockets on the amplifier labelled "Tape Out" or "Record Out". Again, the red plug goes in the socket marked "Right"; the black plug goes in the socket labelled "Left".

## Connect Amplifier to Speakers

1    If your amplifier or speakers have "bare wire" connectors, strip the ends of the speaker wire with wire cutters, then twist the exposed ends. If your receiver or speakers accept connectors such as spades or banana plugs, add connectors to the speaker wire as needed.

2    Connect one pair of wires for the left speaker (meaning the speaker that is to your left as you face the speakers).

3    Connect the positive terminals of the receiver to the positive terminals of the speaker, and connect the negative terminals of the receiver to the negative terminals of the speaker. Speaker wire is labelled "+" or "–", or each lead is a different colour or has a colour-coding strip. Outputs on the receiver and inputs on the speakers are labelled "+" and "–".

4    Securely tighten the lugs or binding posts on the receiver and speakers.

5    Install the wires for the right speaker the same way.

6    Position the speakers. Place the two speakers away from the walls, at the corners of an equilateral triangle (with your listening position as the third corner). For an average size room, start with the speakers 2 to 3 metres apart and angled to face each other slightly. Experiment to achieve the ideal positioning.

Any line-level component can be connected to any line-level input on an amplifier – this generally means anything not labelled "Phono". These sockets are of a different impedance, and should only be used with turntables.

Equipment kitted out with digital connections will work better with digital cables.

Always buy specially made speaker cable: the difference in sound quality – especially in the treble end – can be astonishing.

Surround-sound systems are becoming increasingly popular. These require multiple speakers (at least six) and a multi-channel AV amplifier. However, the same rules of connection apply as to a regular stereo system.

## ⚠ Warnings

Most audio components need ventilation. Leave "breathing room" around vents.

You must have an input labelled "Phono" for your turntable to work. Otherwise, you will need to buy a phono pre-amplifier.

## Things You'll Need

❑ screwdriver

❑ wire cutters

## Improve AM Reception 119

AM radio reception can be noisy as a result of distance from the transmitter, interference from other stations, the quality of your radio or conditions in your home.

### ⊙ Steps

1 Gradually rotate the radio 360 degrees. Leave it in the position where it sounds best.

2 Reverse the AC plug if it isn't polarized. (If you can flip the plug over, then it's non-polarized.)

3 Plug the radio into a different AC outlet.

4 Move the radio closer to a window.

5 Experiment to learn if appliances and powered products in your home are causing interference: computer monitor, television, electric blanket, light dimmer, fluorescent light, hair dryer, air conditioner, smoke detector. If possible, turn off the offending item. Otherwise, move the radio to another room.

6 Upgrade to an external aerial if your receiver, tuner or radio has a place to connect one.

7 Buy a passive AM aerial that doesn't need to be connected to a radio or receiver.

**✳ Tip**

A passive aerial – those not AC- or battery-powered – cannot boost the signal as much as a powered aerial. However, powered aerials may boost noise along with signal.

## Improve FM Reception 120

Poor FM reception may be caused by the quality of your radio, the distance from the transmitter, interference from other stations or signal blockage.

### ⊙ Steps

1 If you have a radio with a telescopic antenna, extend it fully and rotate it to different angles.

2 If you live in a big city or mountainous area, move the radio to the place in your home that has the fewest large obstacles between you and the radio station's transmitter.

3 Switch from stereo to mono.

4 With a receiver or tuner, connect a wire-loop or T-shaped FM aerial to the back of your unit. Move the aerial until you get the cleanest signal. Use a signal-strength meter or display to gauge signal strength if your unit has one.

5 Alternatively, upgrade to a third-party passive or powered aerial.

6 Install a rotatable roof aerial for the best possible reception. Connect your unit to an existing television roof aerial for the next-best alternative.

**✳ Tips**

If your unit didn't come with an aerial and you don't wish to buy one, run wires from the aerial terminals to the outside of your home.

Passive aerials don't boost signal as much as powered aerials. However, powered aerials boost noise along with signal. If you live near the station, a passive aerial may provide better results; if you live far from the station, a powered aerial is likely to prove more successful.

## 121 | Get the Best Price on Music CDs

CDs that sell at retail shops can often be found for up to 40 per cent less on the internet.

### ⊙ Steps

#### Individual CDs

1 Use internet search engines called shopping bots, which find the lowest prices on specific products. You can find these by typing "shopping bots" in one or more internet search engines.

2 Avoid CD merchants in shopping centres, as these have higher prices.

3 Find CDs at consumer electronics stores for 15 per cent to 25 per cent less than at CD shops.

4 Check general-merchandise discount stores for popular titles.

5 Ask if a shop offers loyalty schemes (for example, buy 10, get 1 free).

6 Check specialist CD stores for unadvertised sales, usually covering all titles on specific labels.

7 Consider used CDs. Ask the shop if you can listen before you buy.

#### CD Clubs

1 Consider a "CD of the Month" club only if you plan to limit your buying to popular titles from major artists.

2 Expect to pay up to pay up to £2 per CD for shipping and handling – including "free" selections.

3 Be prepared to make your selections and rejections (some such clubs automatically send you a CD every month unless you instruct them not to) within the required periods.

4 Check the CD club's FAQ web page for suggestions about getting the best value from CD club membership.

5 If a club offers wholesale prices, and you will buy enough CDs to justify the dues, membership may be a good deal.

### ✱ Tips

Remember to add shipping charges before comparing prices from internet and other mail-order retailers.

Check several internet price-comparison sites before making a decision.

A club is a good value if you can find enough "free" selections you would buy anyway.

The average price of a CD is vastly less in the US than in Europe, so it may be possible to obtain bargains by buying from US websites. Be aware, however, that you might well be charged customs duty on your purchase.

## 122 | Buy Recordable CDs

Recordable CDs are a great way to archive your LP collection, make compilation albums and put your computer's audio software to good use.

### ⊙ Steps

1 Buy CD-R discs for your audio deck unless the manufacturer specifically claims the audio deck will recognise and record CD-RW discs.

2 Buy blank discs that can be used at your drive's fastest speed(s).

3 Only buy computer CD-R discs for your CD-R drive.

### ✱ Tips

Check whether the blank discs can record and play as fast as your equipment can.

Check your owner's manual for recommendations of disc brands.

4 Buy CD-RW discs for your CD-RW drive to back up your hard drive.

5 Buy CD-R discs for your CD-RW drive for archival use or for permanent recording of music.

6 Compare block error rates (BLER) of different discs to find the highest-quality discs.

7 Buy blank CDs in jewel boxes unless you use another type of protective case.

8 Ask about manufacturer's discounts before buying a large quantity of CDs.

9 Make sure you test a brand carefully before you buy a lot of discs – some brands of recorders, burners and players have problems reading some brands of recordable discs.

If you experience problems when using a disc on other playback units, try re-recording at a different speed.

It may be possible to alter an audio CD recorder so that it can use cheaper CD-Rs designed for computer drives. There will be no difference in sound quality.

Media sold on spindles may be scratched and unusable.

## Repair Scratched CDs 123

For the cost of one CD, you can repair many with a CD-repair kit – these can work on audio CDs, CD-ROM discs and DVDs.

### ☉ Steps

1 Buy a fluid-based CD scratch-repair kit.

2 Get a soft, lint-free cloth, such as one made for cleaning eyeglasses, if your kit doesn't come with cloths or swabs.

3 Follow the manufacturer's instructions. Wipe across the CD, working from the inside out in straight lines. Never wipe in a circular pattern.

4 Repeat the process, if necessary.

### ✳ Tips

Use a cleaner rather than a repair kit if the scratches are minor but cause skipping or stopping.

Avoid using alcohol, abrasive cleaners, petroleum-based products, ammonia, commercial plastic cleaners or toothpaste, and avoid scrubbing, polishing or buffing.

## Troubleshoot a CD Player 124

Although you will rarely be able to repair your own CD player, you may be able to diagnose problems. This may help you decide whether to have it repaired.

### ☉ Steps

1 Check all connections – CD player-to-amplifier, amplifier-to-speaker, and so on. Check and clean contacts on phono cables and try a different input on the amplifier.

2 Clean the lens. Use only a special CD lens cleaner and follow the instructions carefully.

3 Check the traverse assembly (the metal rod that the laser travels along and the gear that drives it) if CDs are not recognised or won't play, frequent skipping occurs at random, CDs randomly get stuck in one spot, the player can't find tracks correctly, or cleaning the lens doesn't work. Dust and fluff may be interrupting its function.

### ✳ Tips

Check the CD manufacturer's website for a troubleshooting FAQ or a way to e-mail questions. Make a note of the serial number on your CD player before you contact the manufacturer.

### ⚠ Warning

Indications that you have removed screws or handled any internal components will void a manufacturer's warranty.

4   Have the laser-head assembly checked by a repair person if the traverse assembly seems intact and free of debris.

5   Check for a stuck CD if the drawer won't open or close or will only partially open or close. If there isn't one, have gears and belts replaced.

6   Lubricate the gears if the CD player will only play certain tracks or up to a particular point on a disc.

7   Look for broken plastic parts, such as gears and clips.

8   Look for loose or broken internal connections.

9   Have the power supply replaced if your CD player overheats.

10   If your player won't recognise a disc, make sure the CD is properly loaded and not scratched, and that the lens is clean.

Once you open the chassis, you may cause additional damage that increases the cost of repairs.

Avoid CD-cleaning discs with brushes attached. Some can damage the lens-suspension system.

## 125   Buy a Video Recorder

Video recorders offer a variety of features. Do your homework thoroughly before buying so you avoid paying for options you aren't going to use.

### ⊙ Steps

1   Decide how you're going to use the machine. Will you use it just to run rented videos or do you intend to tape television programmes? If the former, a DVD player may be a better investment.

2   Determine if you would like automated features such as auto-start, which turns on the VCR whenever a tape is inserted; auto-rewind, which automatically rewinds a tape once it gets to the end; auto-shutoff, which shuts off the VCR automatically; or auto-eject, which ejects the cassette when the VCR shuts off.

3   Decide if you want index search, which marks the tape each time you record so that you can return to the exact spot either by number or by scanning forward or backward. Another feature, jog shuttle, lets you scan at various speeds, from frame by frame to warp speed.

4   Think about different playback options, such as still picture, frame-by-frame playback, slow motion, reverse slow motion, variable-speed search and reverse-motion playback.

5   Figure out if you want special features such as digital effects, including picture in picture, which lets you see two programs simultaneously; or a flying erase head, which is used to edit tapes. Other features include manual tracking, editing from a camcorder, editing to or from another VCR and audio dubbing.

### ✱ Tips

If you ever tape programmes, think about index search or high-speed searching methods.

If you watch or tape sports events and like to deconstruct the action, consider advanced playback options.

## Program a Video Recorder 126

Programming a video recorder is a notoriously complicated task. Here are some general strategies to try out.

### ⊙ Steps

1   Read the instructions thoroughly. If you have lost the manual, contact the manufacturer to order a new one. You may be charged a small fee.

2   Make sure your TV and video are connected properly to each other and to your cable system or aerial.

3   Bear in mind that if you have a cable or satellite box, you may need to tune a dedicated channel on the video and then select the desired channel on the cable or satellite box.

4   You'll need to provide aerial reception for the video if you don't have a cable or satellite system in place. Usually the video and TV can share an aerial, but you may need a separate antenna for the video.

5   Check that the date and time (including the AM/PM settings) are set correctly on the video recorder before you program it.

6   Put a blank tape into the video. If you are reusing an old tape, wind it back to the beginning and check that the erasure-prevention tab is still present. If it's been broken off, you can't record.

7   Schedule recording to start and end a few minutes before and after the show, just in case your video's clock is a few minutes off. If it's a sports event that might run into overtime, program even more time at the end.

### ✳ Tips

Most video recorders require a remote control for programming. If yours is lost or broken, and a universal remote won't work with your model, contact the video manufacturer or search the web for sites that specialise in replacing remote controls. Be ready to provide the make and model number of your video recorder.

Try to keep abreast of evolving technology. There are personal television services that may let you record programs directly onto a dedicated hard disk without the need for video tape.

## Buy a DVD Player for Video 127

A DVD, or digital versatile disc, is a compact disc that holds movies instead of music. Because the format is digital, the picture and sound quality can rival that of a cinema.

### ⊙ Steps

1   Consider your budget. DVD players are generally more expensive than video players – and DVDs certainly cost more than pre-recorded VHS video tapes.

2   Read audio-video magazines to investigate reviews and features.

3   Check your television to determine what kind of video and audio inputs it has so that you can choose a DVD player that is compatible.

4   Choose a player that has a minimal number of controls on its face. A few players have a lot of buttons, switches and dials, which can make things confusing. All you really need are the Open/Close button and the Play button. You can do the rest with the remote control.

5   Consider the features you want. Most players support these standard features: language choice for automatic selection of video scenes; audio tracks; subtitle tracks and menus (this feature must be supported with

### ✳ Tips

A film is stored on just one side of the disc, so there is no need to turn the disc over as with the earlier laser discs.

DVD offers scanning and scene selection, which VHS cannot.

A DVD can be loaded with a foreign-language track, subtitles and other additional material.

additional content on the disc); special-effects playback, including freeze, step, slow, fast and scan; parental lock for denying playback of discs or scenes with objectionable material (this feature only works on suitably equipped discs); programmability; playback of selected sections in a desired sequence; random play and repeat play; digital audio output; compatibility with CD and DVD-Audio formats.

6   Choose a DVD player that has an A/V receiver with at least a built-in Dolby digital decoder, enabling you to take full advantage of the digital sound. It will also allow you to upgrade your sound system to surround at a later time.

7   Select a DVD player that has good video outputs. All DVDs have both composite and S-video output jacks, and many higher-end models have the superior component video outputs.

8   Choose the best of a variety of audio outputs that are compatible with your TV. Lower-end models support stereo surround sound or Dolby Pro Logic surround sound. Higher-end players can be connected to a Dolby digital receiver to produce surround sound using six or more speakers.

---

## 128  Buy a Fax Machine

When looking for a fax machine, consider quality, price and special features. If you need to send faxes but not receive them, consider a computer-based fax modem as an alternative.

### ◎ Steps

1   Determine the type of machine you want. Choose a film-cartridge fax machine for adequate print quality; look for an ink-jet fax machine to achieve better print quality at a slightly higher price; if you can afford to pay more, buy a laser fax machine for the best print quality – if you receive a lot of faxes, the higher purchase price will quickly be offset by the low cost of use.

2   Look for machines with four choices for image quality.

3   Make sure the machine can print 64 shades of grey if you'll be receiving and copying both text and images. Colour-capable machines are also available, but they're expensive.

4   Consider how many – if any – speed-dial numbers you'll need.

5   Decide whether you need an integrated digital answering machine.

6   Compare each model's capacity for feeding multiple pages, storing received faxes when the machine is out of paper and "broadcast" faxing to a group of recipients.

7   Evaluate how easy the machine is to use.

8   Look for advanced business features, if necessary, such as delayed transmission, the ability to "poll" other fax machines, copy reduction and enlargement, and "shrink to fit" A4 pages.

9   Budget for everything you'll need, such as paper, extra cartridges, a mains surge suppressor and a service contract.

### ✳ Tips

You don't need to get a separate phone line (the fax or an attached answering machine may be able to tell incoming faxes from voice calls, or the sender can input a fax-activation code), but an extra line is convenient if you're doing a lot of faxing.

Be sure to budget for such consumable items as paper and cartridges or ink.

A typical film cartridge produces around 350 pages. To calculate out the cost per page, divide the price of the cartridge by the number of pages.

Toner cartridges for laser fax machines may produce up to several thousand pages, making them cheaper to run than ink-jet or film faxes; the basic cost of the unit may be considerably greater, though.

10  Consider the service contracts offered by the dealer. Do they include maintenance and cover normal wear?

11  Base your final decision on functionality and initial and ongoing costs.

## Choose a Mobile Phone                                                129

Can't bear to be out of contact with the rest of the world for a single second? Then get yourself a mobile phone.

### ⊙ Steps

1  Estimate how many calls per week you'll make on your mobile and how many minutes you'll spend talking.

2  Determine how much you're willing to pay for your mobile phone and for the monthly service.

3  Decide which features are important to you: size and weight, colour options, number storage, messaging, customised settings, fax, web capabilities, and caller identification to display the phone number (or name, if programmed) of an incoming call. Some of the new generation of mobile phones can even take photographs and send them to other suitably equipped phones, or download and play MP3 tunes.

4  Take accessories into account: You'll probably need an AC adaptor for charging the phone, and you might also want a car adaptor, a carrying case or fun goodies such as removable coloured faceplates ("fascias")

5  Consult consumer reports in magazines, newspapers, the web and other news media for opinions on different phones and providers.

6  Decide on a service provider in concert with your choice of phone (see the next eHow), since certain plans require the use of specific phones.

**✳ Tip**

Service providers sometimes offer deals including free phones or great discounts when you sign up for their plans. Look around for those.

**⚠ Warning**

Review the terms of the contract to ensure that there are no early-cancellation toos.

## Choose a Mobile Phone Service Provider                               130

Estimate your calling needs before you start investigating plans, and then find one that most closely matches how you think you'll use your mobile phone.

### ⊙ Steps

1  Estimate how much you're willing to pay, and whether to go for a pay-as-you-go plan or one that gives a set amount of "free" time for a monthly fee.

2  Decide what geographic coverage you need. Will you mostly be using your phone locally or will you also use it travelling overseas ("roaming")?

3  See what ALL of the mobile phone providers have to offer before taking the plunge. Since the UK has a very small number of players in this field, this kind of research can best be done in specialised mobile phone shops. Review the pricing plans, paying particular attention to charges for "roaming" (use outside the provider's area of coverage), texting, and making calls during peak hours.

**✳ Tip**

Subscribers who pay a higher fixed monthly fee for a greater amount of "free" talk time are rewarded with cheaper calls above their monthly limit.

**⚠ Warning**

Review the terms of the contract to ensure that there are no early-cancellation fees.

## 131 | Select a Pager Service

A wide assortment of pager services is available. Be careful not to pay for features you don't want.

### ◎Steps

1 Decide where and when you want your pager to work. Pager services now offer plans that can cover you nationwide or even worldwide.

2 Decide if you need to purchase a pager or just hire one temporarily – for an important business event, or the birth of a child, for example.

3 Determine whether you want the capability to send messages from your pager.

4 Decide if you want callers to be able to leave a voice message or just a phone number. Voice mail can prove convenient if you are out of range of the pager or you have turned the pager off when a call comes in.

5 Contact the major pager service providers – all of them should have dedicated websites.

6 Find out if the pager service offers customer service 24 hours a day, seven days a week.

7 Investigate whether it offers a live operator who can take messages.

8 Determine if each plan the service offers is flexible. Make certain that there is a means for you to get undelivered or stored messages when your pager is within the service area.

9 Find out if the pager service offers hardware – that is, a pager unit – that enables you to access all of the features in your chosen plan.

**❋ Tip**

Yearly plans are charged at a less expensive rate than month-to-month plans.

## 132 | Synchronise Your Palm Device With Your Computer

One of the greatest strengths of the palm computing platform is the ability to add information on either a computer or palm-held device, then synchronise the information between the two. (This eHow assumes that the Palm desktop has already been installed successfully on your computer.)

### ◎Steps

1 Be sure HotSync Manager is running.

2 On a Macintosh, launch HotSync Manager from the Instant Palm Desktop and make certain HotSync is enabled.

3 In Windows, check to see that the HotSync icon appears in the Windows task bar.

4 Place the palm device in the cradle. Then press the HotSync button on the cradle.

5 If nothing happens, tap the HotSync icon on the palm screen, then tap Local Sync.

**❋ Tips**

If you're having trouble performing a HotSync operation, try lowering the connection speed.

If you want to use a HotSync cable instead of a cradle, you must initiate the HotSync from the Palm device.

You can synchronize multiple Palm devices with one PC. You'll be prompted to select a user the first time you perform a HotSync.

6 Wait for the synchronisation to be complete, then launch Palm Desktop. You'll notice that items added to the palm device now appear on the Palm Desktop, and items added to the Palm Desktop now appear on the palm device.

## "Beam" a File to Another Palm Device · 133

One of the high cool factors in using a palm-held device is the capability to "beam" information wirelessly from one device to another. To beam and receive beams, you must be using at least a Palm III, or an earlier device upgraded to a Palm III.

### ⊙ Steps

#### Beam an Application Entry (Data)

1 Place the two palm devices facing each other, no more than a metre apart.

2 Select the file you want to beam.

3 Tap the menu icon, and then display the Record drop-down menu.

4 Choose Beam Memo if you are using the Memo Pad

5 Choose Beam Event if you are using the Date Book.

6 Choose Beam Address if you are using the Address List. You must have a specific address entry selected to beam an address.

7 Choose Beam Item if you are using the To Do List.

#### Beam an Application Program

1 Place the two palm devices facing each other, no more than a metre apart.

2 Tap the Applications icon (Palm III) or the House icon (above Palm III) to display the Applications list.

3 Tap the Menu icon, then choose Beam from the App drop-down menu.

4 Select an application from the Beam box, and then tap Beam.

5 Applications with a padlock symbol next to the size of the application are locked and cannot be beamed.

6 Tap Done to close the Beam box.

### ✱ Tips

It can be useful to beam an application entry – such as directions to a restaurant – from one device to another. It can also be fun to beam shareware games to all your friends.

You can beam entire categories of information from the Address Book, To Do list and Memo Pad.

If you are finding it difficult to beam, try placing both palm devices on a flat surface.

## 134 | Get Rich

It's easy to make a fortune: deal in stocks and shares, start your own internet company, win the lottery. Right? Wrong. To even be in with a chance of getting rich requires clear thinking.

### ⊙ Steps

1 Decide what "rich" means to you. Does it mean money for everything you need? Money for everything you want? Enough to retire where you live now? Enough to retire and live in the South of France?

2 Start saving. Most experts agree that investing 10 to 15 per cent of your gross monthly income will create a comfortable nest egg for later years.

3 Take advantage of compound interest – earning interest on your interest by letting investment returns accumulate and build on themselves.

4 Be conscious of cost. For example, if you buy a second-hand car instead of a new one, and invest the balance, you will have thousands of pounds more when you retire.

5 Take care of yourself. This will reduce medical costs later on in life, as well as extend the years you can work – and save.

6 A better education is more likely to result in high earnings. Some studies have shown that graduates are likely to earn an average salary of £15,000 more than those with no higher education. The gap is even higher for holders of a postgraduate degree.

7 Get married. Married people are generally healthier than single people. Plus, they can economise on expenses, and they have more to invest. And because married people live longer, they can work and save longer.

8 Enjoy yourself. Don't be so concerned with amassing a fortune that you neglect to enjoy life now. Strive for balance.

### ✱ Tips

Use a planning calculator (you'll find these on many personal finance web pages) to work out how much you need to save each year to achieve a specific goal.

Little expenses add up. Switch to regular coffee each morning, rather than a double-shot latte, put the pound you save in a fund, and you could have up to £50,000 more at retirement.

Work out how much you'll need to maintain your current lifestyle. Ask a financial adviser for help if you need it.

### ⚠ Warning

Don't waste the money you do have on "get-rich-quick" schemes, lotteries or gambling.

## 135 | Create an Investment Portfolio

A high-performing portfolio is every investor's goal. First, you'll need to develop your own objectives and strategies.

### ⊙ Steps

1 Determine what items or events you're saving for. These can be retirement, a new home, your children's education or anything else you choose.

2 Determine when you want to retire, purchase your home or send your children to college, to help you decide what percentage return you need to earn on your initial investment.

3 Decide how much money to invest. Invest what you can comfortably afford now, keeping in mind that you can change that amount later.

4 Determine how much risk you are willing to take. Some investments that generate high returns may be riskier than others.

### ✱ Tips

With less than £20,000 to invest, consider managed funds rather than individual shares to diversify and balance risk.

Tax-free government bonds usually generate lower returns, but they also pose less of a risk.

5  Once you decide the amount you are willing to invest, the returns you want to achieve, when you need the money and how much risk you are willing to accept, put together your investment portfolio.

6  Talk to a financial advisor or stockbroker. Tell them your objectives and ask them to suggest ways in which you can allocate your money. (Be aware that there is a fee for this kind of service, though.)

7  Re-evaluate your portfolio at least annually. Analyse each investment.

⚠ **Warning**

Allocate only a portion of your savings to stocks and shares, depending on your age and tolerance for risk. Invest the balance in other approaches, such as cash ISAs, pension plans or bonds.

## Make Good Investments | 136

Whether you are a first-time investor or an investment guru, mistakes happen. The key to avoiding mishaps is to keep on top of investment rules, tax codes and annual reports.

⊙ **Steps**

I  Study. Read financial news, personal-finance magazines, corporate annual and quarterly reports, registration statements and prospectuses for the financial products you're considering.

2  Develop goals and strategies to meet your goals. Use these to choose stocks and other investments. Ask for professional advice if you are uncomfortable investing on your own.

3  Diversify. Avoid putting large portions of your portfolio in a single stock or industry so that you're not so affected by its movements.

4  Take advantage of tax concessions by investing in ISAs or Stakeholder pensions.

5  Buy stocks that you plan to keep for three to five years. Remember that "good" stocks at unrealistically high prices are a bad buy. Aim to buy at a low price, sell at a high price (see 138 "Research Shares to Buy").

6  Invest in what you know, and avoid buying shares in unfamiliar industries and companies.

7  Shop for total value. That means learning to calculate key statistics, such as price-earnings ratios, so you can compare stocks.

8  Resist fads. If everyone is buying gold, variable annuities or some other investment, watch out. The herd soon will change direction – look what eventually happened to the internet company boom of the late 1990s.

9  Know when to fold. Your objective may be to hold particular shares or mutual fund for three to five years, but if its track record looks like terminal descent, bail out.

**Things You'll Need**

☐ financial newspapers and magazines

☐ corporate reports

☐ relevant prospectuses

## 137  Understand the Stock Market

Before you take the plunge, here are some key steps to consider towards building an understanding of the stock market.

### ⊙ Steps

1 Understand "equity securities". As an investor, when you buy stock you take an ownership stake in a company and assume a corresponding degree of risk – so you could end up losing all of your money.

2 Learn the language of the market, familiarising yourself with such financial terms as "price-earnings [PE] ratio", "margin", "option", "earnings per share" and "leverage".

3 Analyse the holdings of a number of successful fund companies, noting which stocks they have held – and those discarded – over the past three or four years.

4 Make a habit of reading the quarterly and annual reports filed by the biggest players on the FTSE 100 index.

5 Research companies of which you have personal knowledge – and a high degree of confidence. Evaluate their financial reporting, looking for trends that indicate growth and continuing profitability.

6 Get online. Dozens of companies offer financial news, advice and analysis online (see 138 "Research Shares to Buy").

7 Take advantage of all the information your stockbroker has to offer regarding individual shares. Always know what you are buying – and why – before you invest.

8 Invest on paper for a few weeks and carefully monitor the performance of your prospective portfolio before you actually apply to buy stocks and shares.

### ✱ Tips

Invest in reputable companies and stick with them for the long haul.

When paying for financial advice, make sure that you know the brokerage fees beforehand. These can vary to a surprising degree.

Set up an electronic portfolio of your stocks through an online service such as Yahoo! Finance. This will allow you to monitor your shares' performance throughout the day and to get the latest news about the companies you've invested in (see 140 "Monitor Shares").

If you don't have the time to do your own research, invest in a managed fund that has had good returns for at least three years.

### ⚠ Warning

Be prepared for a roller-coaster ride. The market can be volatile.

## 138  Research Shares to Buy

One of the most important parts of "playing the market" is researching companies.

### ⊙ Steps

1 Obtain quarterly and annual corporate financial statements. You can get such documents without charge from a number of sources, among them, Company Annual Reporting Online (www.carol.co.uk).

2 Analyse quarterly statements covering two or three years, noting trends in earnings per share and revenue.

3 Look for a trend of consistent growth in earnings per share.

4 Calculate the company's price-earnings (PE) ratio, a measure of a stock's value. (Divide the stock price by annual earnings per share.)

5 Compare the PE ratio with industry norms. The lower the ratio, the less expensive the stock is relative to earnings.

### ✱ Tips

Make sure the company doesn't ignore research and development – this may have implications for the future.

Calculate a sales-per-employee figure and compare the company with its competitors.

Assess the board. Use corporate reporting to discover where directors worked before they joined the company.

6   Beware of debt. Check out the company's balance sheet, looking for the extent of its long-term debt.

7   Check cashflow – the movement of cash through the company. You'll want the company to have positive cashflow.

## Buy Shares                                                                     139

Buying shares in a company is relatively easy once you've researched the companies you're interested in and have a broker or brokerage account to handle your purchase.

### ⊙ Steps

1   Educate yourself fully about shares before purchasing them. You can find information about shares and brokers on the internet.

2   Determine what you want in a broker or brokerage account. Do you want to meet with someone face-to-face? Will you want to be able to reach someone by phone? Do you require internet access? Is price your only consideration? Do you want to buy and sell only shares, or would you also like to buy and sell mutual funds, bonds or foreign stocks?

3   Choose a broker or brokerage firm to purchase the stocks on your behalf based on your needs. If you need a lot of advice, begin with a full-service brokerage: the less expensive brokers may not offer advice. If you are fairly confident and want low prices, go for an online broker.

4   Contact a broker or firm and request an application. Many firms offer online applications, although most require that you send a payment to actually open the account.

5   Deliver a cheque in person if possible to speed up the process.

6   Begin buying and selling shares once your account is open.

7   Review the statements you receive and re-evaluate your portfolio's performance. Are you moving towards your investment goals?

### ✱ Tips

Ask friends and colleagues for recommended stockbrokers. If you don't have a personal recommendation, read adverts in investment magazines, or such publications as the *Financial Times*.

An online broker is convenient and fast but can be susceptible to computer glitches. Ask if you will be able to make trades by telephone if ever necessary.

### ⚠ Warnings

Ask brokers to list all fees. Watch out for hidden costs (account transfer, electronic transfer or handling fees).

It can take a few days to open a brokerage account, so don't expect to be able to trade on the same day you decide to open an account.

## Monitor Shares                                                                 140

Monitoring the rising and falling prices of shares is an essential part of being a successful investor or shares trader.

### ⊙ Steps

1   Monitor the price of your shares on a daily basis, noting whether they are heading up, down or fluctuating. You can find your shares in the broadsheet newspapers or on the internet.

2   Track performance by reading monthly statements from your broker. Use the Internet for up-to-the-minute tracking when needed. (You can create a portfolio of shares on your personalised home page.)

### ✱ Tips

The stock market can be extremely volatile. It is advisable to keep a three-year horizon in mind. Day trading can be very profitable, but requires a high degree of knowledge as well as constant attention.

3   Closely monitor the shares you are interested in (not just those you own, but those you might buy). Monitoring can help you make an immediate decision on whether to buy, sell or hold.

4   Add to shares you like or those that are growing nicely when you have additional income to invest. Remember to diversify your investments.

5   Contact your broker by phone or the internet to buy or sell a shares.

6   Specify the action you want to take and at what price you want to take it. Your broker will do the rest and provide you with a confirmation of your transaction when your order is executed.

Read the *Financial Times* and read or watch any daily news that informs you about your stocks and events that affect the stock market.

A stock's performance should be compared with that of others in its group and evaluated over time – don't automatically sell your shares if you notice that it is declining in price.

---

## 141  Trade Online

Online trading depends on the same principles and skills as off-line trading, so use them to guide your thinking and actions.

### ⊙ Steps

1   Have a long, serious and brutally honest talk with yourself (and perhaps a trusted friend) about the kind of personality you have – you'll need to be disciplined and goal-orientated if you are to succeed.

2   Be sure you have at least £3,000 in easily available funds.

3   Set limits to your trading activity, such as number of transactions and/or commission paid, for an initial three-month period.

4   Research at least three online brokerage services and read all of the "terms and conditions" statements concerning trading accounts.

5   Open an account with the brokerage service you choose for the minimum amount necessary to trade.

6   Write down all of your trading (buys and sells) immediately after they have been executed: date, time, quantity and price per share of the actual purchase. Use these records for tax preparation and save them in case you are audited.

7   Evaluate your performance at the end of the three months. What were your gains and losses? Emotional reaction to the process? Did you stick to your goals?

 **Tip**

Free research online is available from many of the big investment firms. Avoid fee-for-service features of your account unless they will directly improve your ability to trade intelligently.

### ⚠ Warnings

All laws regarding securities trading apply to trading online.

Technical service calls and broker advice over the phone are rarely free – check first.

Never trade on advice from chat rooms, message boards or any other questionable sources.

Trade only with your savings until you are experienced. Only then consider borrowing to trade.

---

## 142  Invest for Your Child's Future

Using money you can put aside regularly, and your child's own contributions from allowance and birthday funds, you can create a tidy nest egg for your child's future.

### ⊙ Steps

1   Start early and let compound interest work in your favour.  If you can afford it, start paying into a stakeholder pension from birth. You can pay

 **Tips**

Ask relatives who regularly send cash gifts to consider putting that money into a savings account for your child.

in up to £2,808 per year and the government will top that up to £3,600. Even if you can only afford £10 per month, it will give your child a useful springboard from which they can eventually make their own regular contributions.

2 Be aware that any investment you make that involves stocks and shares could go down in value. As always, take a long-term view when investing in the stock market. Although performance has been poor in recent times, the overall picture has remained upwardly mobile for the past century.

4 When setting up a college fund, try to make the best estimate you can of the figures you wish to achieve by the time your child reaches student age. If the cost of a three-year degree course were presently around £20,000 (in living expenses and fees) it could be more than double that figure in 18 years' time.

5 Even if you invest a small monthly amount in a modest "safe" building society, the compound interest will accrue impressively over the years.

6 Monitor your funds carefully to ensure that they are on track to meet your needs. If, for example, your 13-year-old daughter announces that she wants to become a doctor you'll need to increase your contributions accordingly to cover the cost of training.

Teach the significance of finance from an early age. Try to give your children a say in how money is invested on their behalf. Let your children see the benefits of making their own contributions to their funds – how, say, contributing a proportion of their weekly allowance or part-time earnings could mean the difference between their having to work through college and having the time to devote to study and leisure.

---

## Determine the Type of Life Insurance You Need     143

The best life insurance to have is the kind that is in force when you die. But since most of us live a long time, some thought should go into the type of contract we choose.

### ◉ Steps

1 Determine how long you want your life insurance coverage to be in effect – for example, from now until your children finish college, your partner retires from work, or throughout your entire life.

2 Buy a term (fixed-length) contract with an increasing premium if that length of time is less than four years.

3 Buy a term contract with a level premium if you need coverage for a longer time (5, 10, 15 or 20 years).

4 Buy a permanent contract if you wish to provide a death benefit for your beneficiary no matter how long you live.

### ✱ Tips

Most types of permanent insurance (often called whole-life) have a cash value. You may be able to borrow against it at a low interest rate while keeping most of the death benefit in force.

If your employer offers term life insurance and that's what you need, buy all you can because group life is the least expensive term insurance available.

---

## Plan for Retirement     144

It may seem as if retirement is in the distant future, but it's never too early to start planning to enjoy it – and finance it.

### ◉ Steps

1 Start planning for retirement early. Think about how you want to live – and where. Calculate how much money you think you will need.

### ✱ Tips

Allocate retirement investment money to a mixture of stocks,

2   Plan for the possibility of living longer than you now expect. Include the possibility of being on a fixed income for as long as 20 or 30 years.

3   Create a financial plan either with a certified financial planner or by using computer software like Intuit's Quicken. (Remember to include your Social Security benefits.) This will help you figure out how much money you should invest for retirement on a regular basis.

4   Contribute funds weekly, monthly or annually to an ISA and/or pension plan (see 146 "Plan for Retirement").

5   Pay off your major debts – such as home mortgages, college loans and other significant cashflow drains – as quickly as you can.

6   As you approach your retirement, you may want to think about reducing your discretionary expenses and attempt to live on a fixed income – as you are likely to have to do when you retire. Adjust your asset allocation based on your spending patterns. If you are spending more than your assets are earning, you may have to lower spending and take more risks in the hope of increasing your returns. Ask for advice.

bonds and cash, according to your research and the thoughts of your financial advisors.

If you can't pay off your debt, try to put some towards the debt and some towards a savings plan. You may want to try reducing credit card and high-interest debt by taking out a low-interest loan or low-interest line of credit.

---

## 145 | Exploit Tax-Free Savings Opportunities

In most cases, interest you make from a savings account will be subject to tax – this will usually be deducted by the bank or building society. Here are some ways in which you can save without paying tax.

### ⊚ Steps

1   Anyone over the age of 16 is allowed to put cash into an Individual Savings Account (ISA). These are tax-protective "wrappers" for your money. Over the course of a tax year you can invest up to £3,000 into a cash mini ISA or you can put up to £3,000 into the cash component of a maxi ISA.

2   Besides being tax-free, many cash ISAs also pay excellent rates of interest compared with other savings products. (To make the best use of your cash ISA allowance, use it for money you don't expect to need in the near future – that way you don't lose the tax-free benefit.)

3   Monitor the rates paid by other cash ISAs – you are entitled to switch your ISA to another provider if they offer a more competitive rate of interest. A brief review of competing rates every few months should do the trick.

4   If you're a non-taxpayer then you shouldn't pay any tax on your savings. Banks and building societies are required to deduct tax from the interest they pay you unless you first fill out a form – officially known as an "R85" – confirming that you are a legitimate non-taxpayer. The interest on your savings is then paid to you in full.

### ✳ Tips

If you have a spouse who's a non-taxpayer, then open an account in their name and get them to fill in Form R85.

## ✓ 146 Plan for Retirement

Whether we like it or not, most of us don't expect to have to work beyond the standard retirement age: we expect *some* sort of mechanism to be in place to care for us – after all, we've spent all of our working lives contributing taxes for just this time, haven't we? Think again! With life expectancy in the UK ever on the increase it's going to be increasingly difficult to fund the traditional "old-age" pension. And the word from the experts is stark: the vast majority of us are not investing anything like sufficiently for that time. Although the pension route is the most common, it's only one of a number of approaches to saving for retirement.

### PENSION PLANS

A pension is an income that you receive when you retire. To build up a big enough pot to provide that income, there must first have been some serious saving going on. To encourage us to this end, the Government provides concessions, chipping in the tax that you have paid (or would pay) on that money you've saved. These contributions form a pension fund, which is invested over the years until your retirement. Pension plans take many different forms. Company schemes are usually good value for money since the employer also makes monthly contributions. "Final salary" schemes, in which the pension is based on your income at the time of retirement, are now increasingly hard to find: the occupational schemes in public services such as the police, fire, civil service and teaching professions are just about the best on offer anywhere. Supported by the government, the new "stakeholder" pensions are also worth considering for medium- or high-income earners – and for the self-employed, who have traditionally received a very poor deal from pension schemes.

FOR:

❏ Efficient way to save

❏ Stock market has traditionally provided the highest returns on investment

❏ Harder to succumb to temptation and spend the money before retirement

❏ Government contributes; employer contributes if in a company scheme

❏ Recent legislation makes it relatively easy to transfer between schemes

AGAINST:

❏ Charges higher and more complex than other investments

❏ Requires a degree of expertise (or at least an investment of time) to monitor progress

❏ Inflexible in respect to how you receive your pension money once you retire

❏ Not easy to estimate what your plan will be worth 10, 20, 30 or 40 years down the line

### ALTERNATIVES TO PENSIONS

Pensions have have some bad press in recent years. And not without due cause. It's not very helpful trotting out the great stock-market mantra, "think in the long term", when a market fluctuation has just wiped off 25 per cent of the value of your pension a week before you were due to retire. Unsurprisingly, some have chosen to look away from traditional pension plans. For the cautious, there are some very safe options, such as the National Savings and Investments' guaranteed income or equity bonds. These provide a risk-free way of playing the stock market – even if the returns on offer are not earth-shattering. In recent times, a popular – yet in many ways just as risky – alternative has been investment in property. Buying-to-let offers a regular income and, if you buy in the right area, a phenomenal growth on the value of your original investment. But that only holds true during a property boom. And they don't last for ever.

## 147 | Release Capital from Your Home

Many UK home owners are unaware that it may be possible to raise immediate cash based on the value of their property – or, in the case of mortgage-payers, on the equity they hold in that property.

### ⊙ Steps

1 Work out your equity: this is the current value of your home minus any money you still owe in loans or mortgages. If you own a home or you're a mortgage payer, the equity can be used to help you get a loan. If your home is worth £250,000, and your mortgage balance is £100,000, you have equity of £150,000 available to you.

2 The most straightforward way in which you can raise money against equity is to mortgage your property. This will only be possible if you own the property already. Most lenders will treat you in the same way as any other mortgage seeker, the amount they will lend you will depend on your personal circumstances (see 195 "Get a Mortgage").

3 If your mortgage is small relative to the market value of your home – a common occurrence in areas of the country that have seen property prices boom – you may be able to raise cash by taking out a secured loan. The lender will agree a loan value and fixed interest rate, and take your equity as security.

4 Consider a home reversion plan. Popular among the retired, this entails "selling" a percentage of your home to a finance company for a fixed sum or a monthly income: the proviso is that you retain the right to live there for the rest of your life. When your home is eventually sold on your death – or on your moving into care – the finance company takes the agreed percentage of the sale proceeds. If house prices have gone up, the company gets the benefit of the increase.

5 A home income plan (sometimes known as a mortgage annuity scheme) is a form of secured loan. In this case, with the cash you release you buy an annuity, which provides you with regular guaranteed income. This is not a good choice when interest rates are low.

### ✱ Tips

Although equity release schemes are most popular among the over-60s, an increasing number of younger people follow this route to pay for home improvements, a new car or their children's education.

### ⚠ Warnings

If you take out a secured loan you may put your home at risk. You will, however, benefit from a lower interest rate than would be offered with an unsecured loan.

Most equity release schemes involve legal and valuation fees – these could be as high as £1,000. (Some companies will reimburse these fees if you follow through with the loan.)

## 148 | Fill in Your Tax Return

If you are a self-assessed income tax payer you – or your accountant acting on your behalf – must fill in your annual income tax return. This provides the figures on which you pay your income tax.

### ⊙ Steps

1 Make sure that you have a copy of the Inland Revenue guide SA150, "How To Fill in Your Tax Return" (it should have been included with your blank tax return). This tells you how to complete every box in the form.

2 Begin by completing pages 2 and 3 of the form. This will tell you whether you need to acquire and supplementary pages. These can be ordered from the Inland Revenue web pages (www.inlandrevenue.gov.uk).

### ✱ Tips

You don't have to wait until the end of September/January deadlines to file your tax returns. Get them out of the way as soon as you can – it's one less thing to worry about.

3    If you send your completed tax return in by the end of September, the Inland Revenue will calculate the tax payable for you. Otherwise, forms (with calculations) must be returned by the end of the following January – failure will result in a £100 fine.

4    Gather together all of the financial information you need to fill in your tax return. This will include payslips and your P60 if you are an employee, or a copy of your accounts if you are self-employed or a partner. Don't send invoices and bank statements with your tax form – keep them safe in case they are required for inspection.

5    Taking a blue or black pen, work through the tax return filling in the boxes clearly when required. Unless otherwise requested, enter all figures numerically. Don't include pence – round the values down to the nearest pound.

6    Complete any supplementary pages that may be needed. Sign and date the form and return it to the Inland Revenue in the envelope provided. Don't send any documents or cheques with your tax return – requests for payment will be made soon enough!

You can also choose to fill in your tax return online. Look on the Inland Revenue's web pages: www.inlandrevenue.gov.uk.

## Claim Tax Credits                                149

Nine out of ten families with children are entitled to tax credits. But you don't need to have children to qualify. Here's how you can find out how to claim your entitlements.

### ◉ Steps

1    There are two different types of tax credit: Child Tax Credit and Working Tax Credit.

2    You can get tax credits if you are responsible for a child, or if you work but have a low income. By answering a few simple questions you can find out which tax credits you are entitled to and the amount you could get.

3    Look at the Inland Revenue's Tax Credits web pages. This has an online questionnaire which will automatically assess your entitlement and enable you to apply online (www.taxcredits.inlandrevenue.gov.uk).

4    To answer the entitlement questions you may need the following details: payslips or P60 and National Insurance number; if self-employed, your accounts and unique tax reference number (UTR); details of any Social Security benefits you and/or your partner received during the previous tax year; Child Benefit details; approved childcare provider's information; bank details; other income for the previous tax year, such as, income from savings or pensions.

### ❊ Tips

Families with combined incomes of up to £58,000 can claim child tax credits, while families earning up to £66,000 will receive some help during the first year of a child's life – it will be paid on top of the universal child benefit that all parents receive, regardless of their income.

The government says all families with one child and an income of under £13,000 a year will be guaranteed a total of £54.25 a week from April 2003.

## 150 | Change your Bank

Banks and building societies serve you, not the other way around: if you're unhappy with your service here is what to do.

### ⊙ Steps

1 Complain in writing to your bank. Many banking features – such as account charges – are at the discretion of the management. You may be able to get a better deal without changing accounts.

2 Almost all British banks and building societies produce packs that enable you to change accounts and automatically transfer standing orders and Direct Debits. This entails little more than filling out a form.

3 Don't close your existing bank account until the new one is up and running to your satisfaction.

4 Request an immediate overdraft facility.

5 Contact your employer's payroll department to have your salary paid into the new account.

6 Check that automated payments in and out have been made. If there have been no problems after three months, contact your previous bank to close your old account.

### ✳ Tip

Make sure that you have enough "float" to cover both accounts during the interim period when both are running concurrently.

## 151 | Pay Monthly Bills on Time

Paying your bills promptly will help you avoid penalty fees and interest charges. Follow these steps and keep your finances in good order.

### ⊙ Steps

1 Set aside a special place to put your bills when they arrive, such as a desk, a special section in a drawer or a bill inbox. As soon as you receive them, open your bills, then put them in this place.

2 Set aside two times each month – two weeks apart – to pay your bills. The middle and end of the month are good times.

3 If possible, phone the companies that send you bills and ask them to revise your payment due dates to correspond with one of the two times you plan to pay your bills each month.

4 Mark your calendar to remind you of bill-paying dates and to help you keep to your schedule.

5 Pay your bills with cheques or money orders, then note the cheque number, the date and the amount paid on the receipt portion of each bill.

6 Even if these are not business expenses, it's a good idea to file away and keep invoices for a few years. (In business you should keep them for seven years.)

7 Place the envelopes containing your payments next to your keys so that you will remember to take them with you and mail them immediately.

### ✳ Tips

Some credit card companies, mortgage lenders and finance companies change due dates. Check the due dates for such bills when they arrive.

Utility and phone companies are usually a little more flexible and will wait for a few days before they send you a reminder notice.

Some companies may give a discount for bills paid either by standing order or Direct Debit.

For added efficiency, consider getting a bank account that allows you to arrange for bills to be paid automatically from your current account. You can kick off the payment buy making a phone call or from the internet.

## Live Within Your Budget 152

Living within your budget can be challenging. A few simple practices can help ensure that you are successful.

### ◎ Steps

1   List all of your expenses, savings and income from the past year. Use your bank statement, credit card receipts and bills to do this. There are many computer-based financial programs that may help.

2   Determine, as accurately as possible, what expenses you expect to have over the next year. You can project expenses for a shorter period, such as the next three months, then multiply by four for yearly expenses.

3   Enter this information into a ledger or computer program (home finance software or as spreadsheet) to accurately track income and expenses.

4   Determine what you can reasonably afford to spend each month and then track how well you are doing by entering actual expenses into the ledger or computer program.

5   If you find that you are spending less than you had anticipated, you may want to put more money in your savings account to help out with unexpected expenses.

6   If you find that you are spending more than anticipated, try identifying the items you don't necessarily need (new clothes, CDs, eating out) and avoid purchasing them until you are back within your budget.

### ✱ Tips

Allocate a portion of your income for savings and retirement – for example, company, personal or stakeholder pension plans.

Consider setting aside up to 20 per cent of your take-home income for savings.

### ⚠ Warning

Avoid trying to forecast your expenses too far into the future. Doing so can result in inaccurate budgets and overspending.

## Calculate Your Net Worth 153

Calculating your net worth is easy if the necessary information is readily available. Doing this will help you when deciding whether to make major purchases.

### ◎ Steps

1   List all of your fixed assets, such as property and cars, at their current value.

2   List all of your liquid assets: cash, bank accounts, stocks and bonds.

3   List all jewellery, furniture and household items at their current value.

4   Add together all of the above. These are your total assets.

5   Subtract all of your debts, such as your mortgage, car loan and credit card balances, from your total assets. The result is your net worth.

6   Re-evaluate and update your net worth calculations on an annual basis.

### ✱ Tips

Be realistic when evaluating the current value of your assets. Such information can be useful in determining whether you are adequately insured. Share the information with your insurance company to help you decide.

Remember to use the net value (after-tax) of any stocks, shares and bonds when calculating their value.

## 154 | Calculate Your Credit Standing

Lenders use your debt-to-income ratio – or how much you owe on credit cards and loans compared with how much you earn – to help evaluate your credit standing.

### ⊙ Steps

1 Add up your total net monthly income. This includes your monthly wages and any overtime, commissions or bonuses that are guaranteed; plus any other payments received, such as interest or maintenance payment. If your income varies, calculate the monthly average for the past two years. Include any additional income.

2 Add up your monthly debt obligations. This includes all of your credit card bills, loan and mortgage payments. Make sure to include your monthly rent payments if applicable.

3 Divide your total monthly debt obligations by your total monthly income. This is your total debt-to-income ratio.

4 If your ratio is higher than 0.36 – which industry professionals would call a score of 36 – you need to take action. The lower the score, the better. A figure higher than 36 places you in danger of credit refusal, or may result in a higher interest rate.

**✱ Tip**

When you tally your total monthly debts, use the minimum payment on your statements.

**⚠ Warning**

Unreported earned income cannot be used in the calculation.

## 155 | Establish Credit

Credit isn't established overnight. Prepare yourself for financial emergencies by securing a good credit rating.

### ⊙ Steps

1 Get cheque and savings accounts in your own name.

2 Apply for a credit card or charge card in your own name from a retail store or financial institution. Make at least a minimum payment monthly to establish a record of managing debt.

3 Apply for a loan in your name to buy jewellery, furniture or another item that will be paid off in instalments for at least a year. Make all payments on time.

4 Secure a small loan from a finance company or bank and make sure that you pay installments on time.

5 Check your credit rating by calling your creditors or ordering a copy of your credit report.

6 If you experience trouble getting a loan, ask a friend or family member to guarantee it.

**✱ Tips**

Although not a credit indicator, a current or savings account shows how you manage money. Avoid bouncing cheques and add to your savings monthly.

The death of a spouse or a divorce could leave you without credit. Always establish credit in your own name.

Secure a job for several months before applying for credit.

## Obtain a Car Loan 156

Borrowing money to buy a car isn't hard if you have two things: sufficient income and a good credit rating.

### ⦿ Steps

1 Choose your new set of wheels and negotiate a price with the seller (see 923 "Buy a New Car").

2 Research interest rates. Compare the rates with those offered by your local bank, building society, finance company or car dealer.

3 Find out what your current car is worth as a trade-in using publications such as *What Car?*, *Parker's Guide* or *Used Car Price Guide*. Local newspapers will also give you some idea of going rates.

4 Determine how much of a deposit you can make. Talk with the car dealer that has the new car you want. Use your trade-in value and cash – or just cash – to come up with the deposit. (Deposit figures vary among finance companies.)

5 Apply where you find the best rates, and the length of the loan and monthly payment fit within your budget.

6 If you don't qualify, consider saving more for a deposit or choosing a less expensive car.

7 Build a better credit rating if that's what causes you to be turned down. Try again after six months of paying your bills on time.

**✳ Tip**

If you lack adequate income or a good credit history, lenders won't approve your loan until you prove you can repay it while meeting your other obligations.

## Obtain a Copy of Your Credit Report 157

Getting a copy of your credit report is fairly simple and allows you to keep track of your credit history and check for errors.

### ⦿ Steps

1 Credit ratings for millions of individuals in the UK are held by two main agencies: Equifax (www.equifax.co.uk) and Experian (www.experian.co.uk). The information they hold comprises your credit history, and will include details of unpaid bills, county court judgements (CCJs) and any previous applications for credit you have made. You can order credit reports from both companies for a cost of £2.

2 Decide whether you want to order a report online, by phone or by mail.

3 Have a credit or debit card handy if ordering online or by phone.

4 Include your personal details as requested by the agency. Sign your request and include your payment. You should receive a copy of your credit report within 15 business days.

5 Review the report closely for errors. If you do find errors, inform the agency in writing that you believe the information is in error. Include copies of any documentation to support your position.

**✳ Tip**

One reason why some people are turned down is that they are not on the electoral roll, which exists as proof of address. If you are not registered, you should arrange to do this as soon as you can so that the details show up on your file.

6 Note that these companies do not, themselves, make decisions about your credit rating – they merely hold information that finance companies may use to vet credit applications.

7 Consider using one of the services that reports information from all of the major agencies – they can sometimes report information differently.

## 158 | Repair a Bad Credit History

No matter how bad your credit may be, you can take steps to make it better.

### ⊙ Steps

1 Always pay all of your bills on time. Late payments – payments that are 30 days late or more – may have a negative effect on your credit rating.

2 Reduce the number of credit cards you carry. Write to your creditors to request that they close your accounts and report this status change to all three credit-reporting agencies.

3 Be aware that credit failures and County Court Judgements remain on the files of credit checking agencies for six years.

4 Ask a family member or friend to guarantee a small loan or credit card to help you re-establish credit. Make your payments on time.

6 Get a yearly copy of your credit report to catch any errors (see 157 "Obtain a Copy of Your Credit Report"). If you feel there are specific circumstances which might affect your ability to obtain credit – like the loss of your job through illness or redundancy – then you can ask for a Notice of Correction to be put on your credit file. Some lenders may take this into account.

### ⚠ Warning

Beware of credit repair agencies that claim to be able to have County Court Judgements (CCJs) removed from your credit file: CCJ's can only be removed under specific circumstances – and when this *can* take place, the procedures are quite simple and require no outside agency to be involved.

## 159 | Prevent Identity Theft

Some simple precautions, as well as the ability to spot trouble when it starts, may help you keep someone else from cashing in on your identity.

### ⊙ Steps

1 Be extremely protective of your PIN numbers, especially at cashpoint machines. Try to memorise your PIN numbers, but if you have to write them down, don't leave the note in your wallet or purse.

2 Change passwords often.

3 If you live in an apartment or shared house, remove letters from your mailbox promptly. If you suddenly stop receiving mail, call the post office immediately – criminals can forge signatures to have your mail forwarded elsewhere, then obtain information that will allow them to apply for credit in your name.

### ❋ Tips

If you find out that a forwarding order has been placed on your mail without your knowledge, go to the post office to check the signature and cancel the order.

To put a fraud alert on your credit file, contact the credit checking agencies Equifax or Experian.

4   Refuse to give your credit card number or other personal information to an unsolicited caller.

5   Tear up or shred credit card receipts, unused loan applications and any other items with personal information before throwing them away. Thieves often go through rubbish.

6   Obtain a copy of your credit report regularly to check for fraudulent accounts and other information. Report all errors.

7   Report stolen credit cards immediately.

8   Take the time to carefully review all of your bank and credit or cash card statements. Report any inconsistencies at once.

⚠ **Warning**

If a relative dies, do not throw out unused cheques or other personal documents – thieves have been known to steal steal the identities of dead people and clean out their bank accounts.

## Get Out of Debt                    160

Getting out of debt is challenging, but it can be accomplished with dedication and perseverance.

### ⊙ Steps

1   Cut up your credit cards except for one or two to use for emergencies. Throw away the pieces.

2   Contact lenders and request a lower interest rate on your debt.

3   Transfer as much debt as possible to the credit card that has the lowest interest rate, or get a debt-consolidation loan from a bank at a lower rate.

4   Use cash for all your purchases, and only buy what you can afford.

5   Commit to start paying off your debts one at a time and do it. Pay off the credit card and loans with the highest interest rate first.

6   Double your payments on the next debt by taking the payment you made on the first debt and adding it to the current debt.

7   Triple your payments on the next debt by combining payment amounts. Continue until all your credit cards and other debts are paid off.

✳ **Tips**

If you are a property owner, consider extending your mortgage to pay off other debts. (Do this only if your mortgage rate is lower than the interest rate you are paying elsewhere.)

Use consumer credit agencies to arrange repayment of debt. Many are free.

## Get Telemarketers to Stop Calling You        161

You can curtail or eliminate annoying calls from telemarketers. All it takes is a little effort and the following information.

### ⊙ Steps

1   Contact your phone company about caller ID services. With caller ID, choose not to answer numbers from callers who block identification.

2   Resist trying to reason with a telemarketer. Telemarketing companies have scripted responses for almost anything you say.

3   Prepare for those unwanted calls before they happen. Write the phrase, "Put my number on your don't-call list" on a memo by your phone.

✳ **Tips**

Don't set out to be offensive. Making these annoying calls is the telemarketers' job – they are not trying to personally assault you over the phone.

4  Stay on the line when a telemarketer calls. You actually have to speak to telemarketers in order to get them to stop calling you. Tell them that you wish to be placed on their "do-not-call" list.

5  Register your phone number with the Telephone Preference Service (TPS) – you can do this via their web pages (www.tpsonline.org.uk).

6  The Telecommunications (Data Protections and Privacy) Regulations 1999 makes it unlawful to place a direct marketing call to an individual who has objected, either directly to the company or through registration with the TPS.

## 162 | Get Your Name Off Mailing Lists

Most of us regularly receive unsolicited "junk" mail. Here are some steps you can take to prevent the daily deluge.

### ⊙ Steps

1  Register with the government-monitored Mail Preference Service (MPS). Write to: Mailing Preference Service, Freepost 22, London, W1E 7EZ. Or you can visit their web pages at: www.mpsonline.org.uk.

2  Junk mail should decrease within a few weeks of registering with the MPS. However, since postal advertising campaigns are prepared some months in advance, it can take up to six months for registration to take full effect. (If junk mail continues after this period, send the mail in question to: MPS Complaint Department, Mailing Preference Service, Haymarket House, 1 Oxendon Street, London, SW1Y 4EE.)

3  Call the customer service department of individual companies that send you junk mail. Ask to be removed from the company's mailing list. Have the mailing label with you when you call so you can relay exact names and codes from the label.

4  Tell mail-order companies with which you regularly do business not to give or sell your name to other companies. Do the same for any religious, political, professional and charitable organisations to which you may contribute, as well as for credit card companies, banks, schools and utility companies.

5  Watch out for tick boxes when filling out registrations forms, especially on the internet. Some will ask you explicitly to tick a box if you do NOT wish them to pass your details on to other companies.

6  Avoid sending in warranty registration cards. You'll still be covered by the warranty, but the company won't get the chance to use it to send you more information on its products.

7  Go ex-directory. Some mailing lists are formulated from names and addresses as they appear in telephone books.

### ✱ Tips

Registering with the MPS will stop most unsolicited mail. However, advertising leaflets from companies with which consumers have previously done business, or charities to which they have donated, will continue to be delivered.

The MPS cannot prevent the delivery of leaflets addressed to "The Occupier" or "The Householder".

Although stuffing business reply envelopes with nasty notes and sending them back at the company's expense might make you feel better, it probably won't help stop future mailings.

# ✓ 163 Choose a Business Structure

Going into business for yourself isn't just a matter of opening a bank account and getting some business cards and letterheads printed. When you set up on your own, you'll need to decide what type of business structure to establish for legal and tax purposes. The best structure for your business will depend on various factors, the most important of which are indicated in the table below. (Note, this is intended for initial guidance only. Before you start your business operation, it is essential you consult a solicitor and an accountant.)

| | OWNERSHIP RULES | LIABILITY OF OWNERS | CAPITAL | TAXES |
|---|---|---|---|---|
| Sole Trader | One owner. | Owner is personally liable for all of the business's obligations and debts. | Owner contributes majority of capital with balance from the bank if the business concept looks sound. | Business income, expenses and profit or loss are reported on the owner's annual tax return. |
| Partnership | Two or more owners working in partnership. | Each partner is liable for all of the business's obligations and debts. | Partners together contribute money or services for a portion of the profits and losses. Banks may provide funding if the project looks sound | The partnership submits a tax return but the tax is paid by the individual partners. |
| Limited Liability Partnership | One or more general partners and one or more limited partners | General partners are liable for all obligations and debts; limited partners have limited liability but do not take part in management. | Partners together contribute money or services for a portion of the profits and losses. Banks may provide funding if the project looks sound. | Similar to a traditional partnership |
| Limited Liability Company | Possible to have an unlimited number of shareholders. | Shareholders usually have no personal liability for any of the business's obligations and debts. Directors can be liable in certain situations. | Shareholders will contribute capital by purchasing shares. Banks and venture capitalists (VCs) may provide funding if the project looks sound. | The company is taxed on its earnings. Shareholders are taxed on any dividends they receive. Directors are taxed on their salaries. |

chart

## 164 | Decide Whether to Go Into Business for Yourself

If you want to satisfy your entrepreneurial urge, try owning a small business – but first consider whether your finances, personality and skills are up to the challenge.

### ◎ Steps

1 Think about whether you want to work for yourself. Do you enjoy being the boss? Or do you feel more comfortable working for someone else?

2 Determine how much of a risk taker you are. You must be willing to be patient and give the business enough time to get established and grow.

3 Consider how much time and effort goes into running a small business. Many entrepreneurs work harder for themselves than they ever have for a former employer.

4 Find the type of business that suits you. Assess your skills, interests and personal values and seek a business that is in line with these attributes.

5 Decide whether you want to start a business or buy an existing one. Launching a business may involve lower start-up costs, but the business will take time to get established. An existing business usually requires more money up front, but should be less risky.

6 Have enough money in the bank to get started. You'll need enough funds to pay for your everyday living expenses while sustaining the business until it turns a profit. Count on a minimum of three to six months, much more if you want to be a manufacturer.

### ✳ Tips

Talk to other entrepreneurs to get a perspective on what owning a small business entails.

Visit your local Business Advice Centre – or visit its web pages (www.businesslink.org) – to learn about any available help to get your business started.

There are many books on starting a business. Learn from others who have already been through the process.

## 165 | Become Self-Employed

Becoming self-employed – legally this is called "acting as a sole trader" – takes minimal effort. It's also the simplest type of business structure and the easiest to operate.

### ◎ Steps

1 You can start most businesses right away – with a few important exceptions there is no need for registration or licensing. (Contact your local Council or local Business Advice Centre to find out if you need a license or need to register your particular type of business.)

2 You can trade under your own name. If you want to use a business name you need to comply with the Business Names Act. Contact your local Business Advice Centre or see the Companies House web pages (www.companieshouse.gov.uk).

3 When you start trading, you must inform the Inland Revenue. If your turnover exceeds a certain threshold you will also need to register for Value Added Tax (VAT) with HM Customs and Excise.

4 Remember to keep receipts for everything you buy in relation to the business, and issue invoices ("bills") to your customers (unless you are a retailer). Keep a record of your business transactions in an accounts book or on a computer accounts program.

### ✳ Tips

Talk to your local Business Advice Centre (see Yellow Pages or www.businesslink.org) before you do anything and take advice from a solicitor and accountant.

Use a qualified accountant to help you do your tax returns.

### ⚠ Warning

Sole proprietors assume un-limited legal liability with no protection for personal assets if the business goes bankrupt.

5   You can employ staff, but if you do you must inform the Inland Revenue and take responsibility for the deduction of PAYE income tax and National Insurance. The law also requires you to have Employers Liability insurance.

6   Speak to your insurance broker as your domestic and car insurance may be invalidated by your business activities.

## Form a Partnership     166

If two or more people work together and no one is an employee then the law regards the arrangement as a "partnership".

### ◉ Steps

1   You can start most businesses right away – with a few important exceptions there is no need for registration or licensing. (Contact your local Council or local Business Advice Centre for more information.)

2   If you want to use a business name you need to comply with the Business Names Act. Contact your local Business Advice Centre or see the Companies House web pages (www.companieshouse.gov.uk).

3   When you start trading, you must inform the Inland Revenue. If your turnover exceeds a certain threshold you will also need to register for Value Added Tax (VAT) with HM Customs and Excise.

4   Keep receipts for everything you buy and sell. Keep a record of your transactions in an accounts book or on a computer accounts program.

5   You can employ staff, but if you do you must inform the Inland Revenue and take responsibility for the deduction of PAYE income tax and National Insurance. The law also requires you to have Employers Liability insurance.

### ✱ Tip

Although there is no legal requirement, it is recommended you have a Partnership Agreement, which tries to cover issues where disagreements are likely. This will require a solicitor.

### ⚠ Warning

Each partner has unlimited legal liability for all the partnership's obligations and debts, which means your personal assets are at risk if the business fails owing money.

## Set Up a Limited Company     167

A limited company is a legal entity in its own right. It must have at least one Director and a Company Secretary, who could be a second Director or another shareholder.

### ◉ Steps

1   A limited company has to be registered. Contact your solicitor or a company registration agent. Only buy from a reputable agent to ensure that what you are buying has no existing liabilities. (Companies House produces a series of booklets – these are free, or can be read online at www.companieshouse.gov.uk.)

2   Choose a company name that helps you to promote your business, but it must not be such that it can be confused with an existing company. The Business Names Act applies and in addition a company has to have its name on the outside of every place where it carries on business.

3   Contact your local Council or local business advice centre to find out if you need a license or need to register your particular type of business.

### ✱ Tips

Ensure your Articles and Memorandum of Association give you plenty of latitude in what the company can do.

Use a qualified accountant to help you do your tax returns.

### ⚠ Warning

Limited liability does not mean no liability. Directors can be held personally liable if the company trades fraudulently or they ignore their legal responsibilities.

Failure to obtain such permission may be a criminal offence. After you file, the office will let you know if the name has been taken.

4   When you start trading, you must inform the Inland Revenue. If your turnover exceeds a certain threshold you will also need to register for VAT with HM Customs and Excise.

5   Remember to keep receipts for everything you buy in relation to the business, and issue invoices ("bills") to your customers (unless you are a retailer). Keep a record of your business transactions in an accounts book or on a computer accounts program.

## 168  Research the Market for Your Product or Service

Before you start your business, test the market to make sure there will be demand for your product or service.

### ⊙ Steps

1   Learn about your market. Go to trade shows and network with other professionals in your line of business. Subscribe to trade publications.

2   Spend time with potential customers. Ask friends and acquaintances what they'd like in the type of product or service you want to sell.

3   Set up a focus group to gather opinions about your product or service. This could be a gathering of friends, or a more formal group assembled by a market research firm. Be sure to get reactions to your likely prices.

4   Send out a survey to potential customers. Make the form easy to fill out by asking multiple-choice questions. Ask the respondents if they would buy this product or service. Keep the survey short and enclose a stamped addressed envelope.

5   Analyse your findings to determine whether your idea is viable. How did people react to your product or service? What do people like or dislike about your product or service? Make adjustments, including the hardest one – letting go of your idea, if necessary, and finding another one.

### ✳ Tips

Make sure that the people you're surveying are indeed those who are potential customers.

Collect a large sample so that your findings will be accurate.

Create a well-designed survey. Ask very specific questions.

### ⚠ Warnings

Don't assume that what you like is what others will like. You must meet the needs of the greatest number of customers.

Be brutally honest with yourself – be prepared to accept that there may be insufficient demand for your idea.

## 169  Write a Business Plan

Every business should have a business plan. It is your road map to the future and is usually essential if you want to get finance.

### ⊙ Steps

1   Collect the information for your business plan. Include information on your business, product or service, customers, market, competition and potential risks.

2   Write a summary. This is the first section of the plan – a single-page description of all the elements covered in more detail later.

3   Describe your business. Spell out the purpose of your business plan. Talk about the skills you and your management team have.

### ✳ Tip

Gather all the information for your business plan before you start writing it. Limit the plan to about 10 to 20 pages (more for a major venture). Investors and lenders get business plans every day – most get a cursory look before they are either discarded or kept for further review.

4 Explain your product or service. Detail how you will make or provide it. Analyse the costs associated with this process. List your supply sources.

5 Talk about the market you're entering. Discuss general trends in the industry. Include details about the market segment you are pursuing, the niche you are targeting and your target customer; provide demographics on your potential customers and explain their buying habits. Analyse your competition. Be realistic.

6 Describe your marketing plan. Explain how you will generate sales through advertising, promotion and public relations. Estimate all costs conservatively.

7 Detail your yearly revenue projections and your expenses using a cash-flow forecast.

> ⚠ **Warning**
>
> A business plan is a never-ending process. As your business grows, update your business plan projections.

---

## Do a Cashflow Forecast                                      170

Plan, raise finance and manage your business successfully using a cash-flow forecast.

### ⊙ Steps

1 Use a spreadsheet program to help you create your cashflow forecast. Each horizontal row is for a specific category of "Cash In" or "Cash Out" which is listed in the first vertical column. Under "Cash In", there should be rows for "Sales", "Capital" and "Loans". Under "Cash Out" will be the categories of expenses relevant to your business.

2 Each subsequent column represents a month. Forecast for 12 months ahead, ending with a "Totals" column. Fill in the 12 months of figures – these are almost all estimates at this stage.

3 Ensure the figures are balanced – if you are selling a product where the typical mark-up is 100%, then your "Stock" line should run at about half that of your "Sales" line, otherwise you will be either run out of stock or find yourself overstocked.

4 Try different "what if" scenarios. In this way you can begin to see how much capital your business requires, sales targets you need to achieve, and where you are most vulnerable.

5 Update your cashflow forecast monthly to ensure you are running on track.

### ✳ Tips

Always be pessimistic about likely sales. Furthermore, allow time (at least six months for a service business – much more for a manufacturing business) before forecast sales reach a reasonable level.

Never underestimate your projected overheads.

> ⚠ **Warning**
>
> Never confuse cash inflow with profitability. Remember, the bottom line of a cashflow forecast does not represent either a "profit" or a "loss".

---

## Hire Employees                                              171

A business is only as good as the people it employs.

### ⊙ Steps

1 Determine what jobs you need done and what skills are needed.

2 Write precise job descriptions, including duties and skill requirements.

3 Conduct salary surveys among similar businesses in comparable locations to determine how much to budget for salaries.

### ✳ Tips

Create an annual employee budget to know how much you can afford.

4   Advertise in appropriate media. If you need general staff, advertise in local newspapers. If you need specialists, consider trade publications or other specialised media, including job fairs and the internet.

5   Interview carefully. Focus on the applicant's qualifications, track record, attitude and demeanour. Why did they leave their previous jobs?

6   Bring others into the interview process. Ask the applicant to meet others in your business so that you can get others' impressions.

7   Check references and employment history.

9   Put your offer in writing, spelling out the job description, hours, salary, benefits, holiday and other pertinent details. get your solicitor to check your offer letter.

Let current employees know about openings that might be of interest to them.

Make sure the job description is accurate, so people will know what they are applying for.

## ⚠ Warning

It is unlawful for an employer to discriminate on grounds of gender, race or disability.

---

## 172 | Write a Mission Statement

**Writing a mission statement will help you and your employees focus on a common goal and give everyone a benchmark to gauge performance.**

### ◎ Steps

1   Include everybody whose perception of your business matters. Collect as many ideas as you can.

2   Define your business. Think carefully about what role it plays in the industry and community.

3   State the things to which you're dedicated. Are you dedicated to quality, your customers, your success?

4   Assess the value of your product or service. Use written questionnaires to survey your customers, suppliers, partners and other external parties about the benefits of and ideals behind your business.

5   Set up a small committee to go through the ideas you have collected and incorporate them into your mission statement.

6   Give the mission statement high visibility; hang a copy in your work area. People will see it every day and be reminded of what their work means.

### ✱ Tip

Live your mission statement every day. In order to gain credibility with your employees, customers and suppliers, you must practise what you preach.

### ⚠ Warning

Be realistic. Set standards that are reasonable and attainable by you and your employees.

---

## 173 | Apply for a Business Loan

**Money to expand a business can come from a variety of sources. Most require you to provide a thorough financial profile.**

### ◎ Steps

1   Question yourself carefully about the loan: What is it for? How much do you need? When do you need it?

2   Decide on the type of loan you want and whether you want to obtain it from a bank or another lender.

### ✱ Tips

If two banks turn you down for a loan, your application may be unconvincing.

Apply for finance well before you actually need the money.

3   Update the balance sheet so that it reflects the current status of assets, liabilities and ownership.

4   Update the profit-and-loss statement with a summary covering business expenses, revenues and costs for a recent accounting period.

5   Develop cashflow projections for at least one year, showing how money will flow in and out of the business quarter by quarter.

6   Combine all of the above information into a business plan – this is the key document a lender will review (see 169 "Write a Business Plan").

7   Have your solicitor review any loan offer, documents or stipulations.

Owners with few business assets can expect to put up personal assets to secure a loan.

## ⚠ Warning

Be wary of lenders that want to secure your intellectual property or excessive assets as collateral for your loan.

---

## Secure Venture Capital Money 174

Venture capitalists (VCs) invest money in major start-ups in exchange for equity shareholding in the company. VCs receive hundreds of applications from entrepreneurs each year. Here's how to stand out.

### ⊙ Steps

1   Prepare a business plan. VCs will expect you to clearly define the purpose of your business, disclose pertinent financial information (including revenue streams and projections) and provide information on your executive management team.

2   Do internet research on venture funds and contact your local Business Advice Centre to find the appropriate fit for your company. Some VCs focus on retail and service companies, while others look specifically for technology start-ups.

3   Try to get a personal introduction to a VC rather than sending out your business plan. Introductions can be made by executives of companies already being funded by the VC or by lawyers and accountants who work with the firm. Try to contact four to five VCs.

4   Arrange a meeting with the VC. Consider bringing key members of the management team to the meeting.

5   Follow up your visit with a thank-you note and additional information.

6   Be persistent and polite.

### ✱ Tips

VCs want to see that you've done the basic groundwork and are ready to springboard to the next level. Spell out your next big step, and the resources you will need to get there. Investors want to see that you have a vision for your company and that you have plans to grow and expand.

Show off your top executive team. VCs want to see a solid management team which is knowledgeable, flexible, driven and committed.

### ⚠ Warnings

Acquiring funding is a demanding process – you'll need a thick skin, patience and determination.

VCs can be greedy – don't give too much equity away.

---

## Bring Your Business Online 175

Going online requires a strong business model and a sense of what you want to accomplish by having a website.

### ⊙ Steps

1   Decide whether your web pages is simply to provide information about your business or to transact online sales. Answering such questions can help determine the amount of effort required to build the site.

### ✱ Tips

When registering for a domain name, think of alternative names in case your first choice is taken.

2 Decide if you are going to develop your own web pages or have them designed by a professional. (Use a developer unless you are an expert.)

3 Gather information on web publishing via books, magazines and other current periodicals.

4 Browse other web pages for design and functionality ideas – good and bad.

5 Apply for a domain name.

6 Begin to develop the site. Install various checkpoints along the way to ensure that the project is progressing in the right direction.

7 Implement your marketing campaign before your site goes live, and step up your marketing efforts to bring traffic to your site after. (Be aware that it can take many months before search engines list your site.)

If you have a smaller business, consider selling your products through online classifieds and/or online auctions. These are simpler and less expensive ways of transacting commerce online.

## ⚠ Warnings

Begin planning as soon as you decide you want a site.

Don't automatically assume that your web pages will generate sufficient business to cover the costs of the site.

## 176 Apply for a Patent

A patent gives you the exclusive right (for a limited period) to make, use or sell a product or process that you have invented. The process of applying requires professional assistance and the costs can be considerable. If renewed annually a patent can last up to 20 years but is a territorial right – a UK patent is only effective within the UK. Applying for foreign patents involves further paperwork and expense

### ◎ Steps

1 Determine if your idea warrants patent protection. For more useful information, look at the Patent Office's web page (www.patent.gov.uk).

2 To be patentable, your invention must meet four key criteria:
(i) Be new – anywhere in the world.
(ii) Involve an inventive step which would not be obvious to an expert in the field.
(iii) Be capable of industrial application – i.e. be such that it can be made or used.
iv) Not be one of a number specifically excluded categories. (These include: discoveries, scientific theories; aesthetic creations; literary or artistic works; computer programs.)

3 If you think you have an invention that is patentable, you should not publicly disclose the invention before you apply for a patent. Any such disclosure – by word-of-mouth, demonstration, advertisement or article in a publication – could prevent the patent being granted.

4 In the UK, only a tiny minority of patents are by private individuals, the remainder are filed by companies, universities and government research agencies. Most private inventors find that their biggest challenge is getting their invention into production so they can earn something from their patent.

5 Once granted a patent can itself be bought or sold.

## ✱ Tip

The grant of a patent should not be taken as any indication that your invention has any commercial value. Most don't!

## ⚠ Warning

This information is by no means a substitute for professional advice. Refer to a qualified patent agent at a very early stage of your project and prior to any public disclosure.

## Decide if a Home-Based Business Is Right for You    177

Working from home sounds like the ideal way to work, but your personality, lifestyle and home life will dictate whether it is a viable alternative for you.

### ⊙ Steps

1   Ask yourself what you are trying to accomplish by starting a home-based business. Do you want more time to spend with your family? Do you want to have some flexibility in your work hours? Do you want to be your own boss? Do you want to make more money?

2   Consider your personality when making this decision. Are you the sort of person who enjoys the solitude of working alone?

3   Consider whether there are small children, pets or anything else that might distract you at home.

4   Decide what type of business you are interested in. Is it performing a service or creating a product? Is it best done at home, or will an office or additional workspace be required once you are successful?

5   Talk to other people who do the same or similar work from home. Ask what problems they run into.

6   Discover whether you can make enough money to meet your financial needs doing this sort of work.

7   Research what sort of resources will be required to get your business going – space, cash, equipment, marketing.

8   Can you do all the work yourself or will this business will require work from additional people? Can you use sub-contractors or will you have to hire employees? (The latter may be a problem in a home environment.)

9   Decide on a type of business that suits your personal needs and meets your financial commitments.

10   Get legal advice on any legal or planning constraints to using your home for business purposes.

### ✳ Tip

Ask yourself these key lifestyle/workstyle questions: Are you a self-starter? Can you meet deadlines without someone constantly reminding you? Do you need personal interaction throughout the day? Can you make decisions on your own? Do you enjoy having lunch with co-workers? Do you need a regimented workday? Do you prefer to leave your work behind when you leave the office? Do you prefer a flexible schedule that allows you to intersperse personal needs with work needs?

### ⚠ Warnings

Running a home-based business is not glamorous; it is hard work, requiring great time management and dedication.

Although working from home makes it easier to do things around the house, you might very well find yourself caught in a vice when family and work demands conflict.

## Set Up a Home Office    178

Once you're ready to set up shop in your home, it's time to turn that spare room or little corner into your office.

### ⊙ Steps

1   Establish a permanent space within your home for your office. If you have the space, a separate room is best.

2   Decide on an office arrangement. The best is a U-shaped arrangement, which lets you use three surfaces to keep everything within reach.

3   Choose an L-shaped arrangement that provides a secondary surface if space is limited. An alternative is a parallel arrangement which can provide two full-sized working surfaces if they are placed opposite one another.

### ✳ Tip

If you don't have a separate room available, use devices like screens, bookcases and directed lighting to create the necessary separation between home space and office space.

4   Consider a V-shaped arrangement, which consists of a small working area in front of you (generally used for a computer monitor) and two surfaces angled to your left and right if your office area is very small.

5   Establish two phone lines – one for voice and one for fax and/or internet – for your office. If you'll need to forward calls to other offices, ask your phone company about related services.

6   Buy office furniture that suits the arrangement you've chosen. Include desks and tables, chairs and desk lamps.

7   Buy a phone with a built-in answering machine and a hold button. If you'll be transferring calls from within your home office, make sure your phone has a transfer button.

8   Buy a computer system, including a printer and perhaps a scanner. Consider built-in fax software if you'll be sending and receiving files created on a PC. Buy a separate fax machine if necessary. To save money, buy a fax machine that also serves as a scanner and photocopier.

10  Stock your office with standard office supplies. If you're self-employed, budget the cost of these items in your monthly business expenses; otherwise, your employer may provide these supplies for you.

## Things You'll Need

- ❏ desk
- ❏ desk chair
- ❏ desk lamp
- ❏ phone lines
- ❏ telephone
- ❏ answering machine
- ❏ internet access
- ❏ computer
- ❏ printer
- ❏ fax modem or fax machine/copier
- ❏ office supplies

---

## 179 | Reduce Expenses in a Home-Based Business

Working from home is much less costly than renting office space. Once you've decided to forgo the hassle and expense of commuting, there are additional ways to reduce your costs.

### ⊙ Steps

1   Keep complete and accurate accounting records, and review your expenses every few months to determine where you could cut back.

2   Purchase multi-function office machines. For example, look for a fax machine that also copies and scans documents.

4   Take tax deductions for business use of your vehicle and home. Keep all your receipts

5   Earn supplier discounts. Sometimes a supplier may offer a small discount if an invoice is paid quickly.

6   Give free internet access services a try (see 91 "Evaluate Free Internet Service Providers").

7   Go over your insurance coverage with your insurance broker and look for ways to cut your premiums. Consider adding an incidental business option to your existing homeowner's insurance at a much lower cost than a standard business liability policy.

8   Check garage sales, classified ads or internet auctions for office cheap furniture. You can get great bargains, and sometimes you can even find like-new used or reconditioned fax machines and computers.

9   Shut off non-essential equipment at night.

**✳ Tip**

Consult an accountant before taking deductions for business use of your home and vehicle.

**⚠ Warning**

Don't get too budget-happy and stop buying items that are truly necessary to your operation, such as trade journals and training courses.

## Find a Flat     180

Finding the right flat – in the right price range, with the right amenities, in the right area of town – isn't hard if you know how to manage the process. Here's what to do.

### ⊙ Steps

1 Work out how much you can afford. Be sure to include utilities.

2 Think carefully about where you'd like to live. Consider commuting times to your workplace and the types of amenities you'd like your local neighbourhood to offer.

3 Write down what features are important to you, such as parking, security, proximity to public transportation, laundry facilities, acceptable pet policies, and number of bedrooms and bathrooms.

4 Scan the "flats to let" listings in the local newspaper where you want to live; ask friends and work colleagues to keep an eye out for vacancies; check online services, look for adverts in corner shops.

5 Keep a file of newspaper adverts, computer printouts and notes. Go through your file and call for appointments to see your choice. Make note of any additional information you get

6 Sign up with an agency service if you are new to the area, can't get around, don't have time to go through the classifieds or want fewer choices to consider.

7 Inspect flats carefully.

8 Agree terms with the landlord – most will require a deposit of one month's rent.

9 Establish a move-in date, sign a contract and arrange to pay the deposit and rent required.

### ✳ Tips

Drive by prospective buildings to get a feel for the neighbourhood.

The internet can provide useful information on prospective areas.

### ⚠ Warning

Flat-finding agencies often get commissions from landlords, so beware of any service that demands a hefty fee from prospective tenants.

## Determine How Much You Can Pay in Rent     181

It takes just a few simple calculations to determine how much you can afford to pay in rent.

### ⊙ Steps

1 Calculate your total monthly household net income after taxes, including your partner's income and any child-support or alimony payments (if applicable).

2 Multiply your total monthly net income by 0.3. This number will give you a general idea of the amount of rent you can afford to pay.

3 Add up all of your other monthly expenses, such as car and credit card payments. Include estimates for food, entertainment and transportation.

4 Add together the rent amount from step 2 and the amount from step 3. Make sure this total does not exceed your monthly income. If it does, adjust the amount of rent you can afford.

### ✳ Tip

Housing in some areas costs more than in others – set your target accordingly when you plan a move to another area.

## 182 | Assert your Rights as a Tenant

You may not be the owner of the property in which you are living, but the law affords you certain rights as a lease-holding rent payer.

### ⊙ Steps

1   If your landlord violates the lease, then he is in breach of contract.

2   If you are experiencing difficulties with your landlord it is important to get advice quickly. Greater problems can often arise if you don't take action at the right time. Keep copies of any letters you write and a note of any phone calls you make, including the time and date.

3   As a tenant, you have the exclusive rights to live in a property while your lease is valid – the landlord cannot move someone else in.

4   If you pay a deposit on the property before you move in, you should be given a receipt. You should get the full deposit back when you leave as long as there is no damage to the property under the agreement. If you pay weekly rent you must be issued with a rent book which shows your payments and is signed by the landlord.

5   Your landlord cannot enter the property without your permission or stop you having overnight guests. You should let in the landlord to do repairs but he or she should give you 24 hours' notice except in an emergency.

6   Get advice quickly if your landlord tries to change the locks, cut off gas, electricity or water, interfere with your post, or harass you. This is illegal. Contact your local Citizen's Advice Bureau (www.citizensadvice.org.uk) for help.

7   Landlords are responsible for most major repairs in rented property, such as roofing, garden fences, guttering, central heating and gas boilers. By law they must have the gas system checked every year by a registered CORGI (Council for Registered Gas Installers) engineer.

### ✳ Tips

The landlord is not necessarily the enemy. Do not jump to conclusions if your landlord is being unresponsive to your attempts at communication.

Here are some web pages that may be useful to renters:

Commission for Racial Equality (www.cre.gov.uk); Council for Registered Gas Installers (www.corgi-gas.com); Homeless Link (www.homeless.org.uk); Local Government Ombudsmen (www.lgo.org.uk/index.htm); The Housing Corporation (www.housing.org.uk); Tenant Participation Advisory Service (TPAS) (www.tpas.org.uk)

### ⚠ Warning

You cannot legally become a tenant in a property until you are 18 years old. If you are under 18 you may only be able to live in rented accommodation as a licensee.

## 183 | Negotiate a Lease on a Flat

Make sure you get all the details written out and agreed to before you sign on the dotted line. You'll have to abide by that agreement for the term of the lease.

### ⊙ Steps

1   Make a list of what is important to you and what details you want to include in the agreement.

2   Study the lease agreement as it is written and highlight any areas you want to change or negotiate.

3   Explain to the landlord your reasons for wanting or needing the change.

4   Be willing to give something up in order to get something else.

5   Act responsibly and respectfully. You'll have more success if you are pleasant to deal with.

### ✳ Tips

Remember that your ability to bargain depends on whether the landlord is anxious to have you as a tenant or there are plenty of other prospective tenants from whom to choose.

Negotiating the lease also involves such items as the rent payment date, move-in date and things to be repaired before the move-in date.

6   Provide documentation to support your worthiness as a tenant, such as a good credit report and a recommendation from another landlord or rental-management company.

7   Get everything in writing once you agree.

## Get a Landlord to Accept Pets                               184

If you can present your case in a persuasive manner, you may be able to get your landlord to accept your cats or dogs.

### ⊙ Steps

1   Provide your landlord with written statements from former landlords that commend your pet's behaviour and verify that your accommodation was well-maintained while you and your pet occupied the premises.

2   Invite your landlord to meet your pet and view the pet's behaviour.

3   Offer the landlord a "pet deposit".

4   Inform your landlord in writing that you will pay for damages caused by your pet during your lease.

## Get a Landlord to Respect Your Privacy                      185

Even though your landlord may own the property in which you live, the terms of your lease should spell out the circumstances in which he may be allowed to enter your home.

### ⊙ Steps

1   Never rent a property without signing a formal lease. This will contain clauses relating to your landlords' rights in respect of entering the property. If no such clause exists, insist that one be inserted.

2   Where no formal agreement exists, broach the subject with your landlord. It's not unreasonable to expect him to agree that he shouldn't be able to enter your home without a good reason or sufficient notice.

3   Write a letter to your landlord confirming the mutual understanding and thanking your landlord for agreeing to respect your privacy. Keep a copy for your own records.

4   If your privacy is consistently violated, follow up with a more serious letter that refers to your lease or rental agreement. Again, keep a copy for your records.

5   As a last resort, take legal action against your landlord.

### ⚠ Warnings

Make sure you fully understand your rights and responsibilities before threatening your landlord with legal action.

Never sign a lease that gives your landlord unrestricted access to your home. Other than emergencies – for example, water leaking from your flat into another while you are away on holiday – you should always expect to be given a reasonable period of notice.

## 186 Get a Landlord to Make Repairs

Landlords are required by law to maintain rented property in fit and habitable condition. But a landlord is typically responsible only for certain major repairs.

### ⊙ Steps

1 Make sure that your rental lease contains an unequivocal statement of your landlord's responsibilities.

2 Assess your situation. Repairs needed to keep the residence habitable would be considered major; minor repairs are matters of convenience. Examples of major repairs are a door that won't lock, a broken central heating boiler or a toilet that won't flush. Be aware that he may not share your view on what constitutes a major problem.

3 Make your request for a repair in writing, unless it's an emergency that requires immediate action. Detail the problem, how it affects you and what you expect to be done and when.

4 If your landlord fails to remedy the problem, start to build your case. Take pictures. Have a professional assess the problem and estimate repair costs. Gather forces and present your request as a group if other tenants suffer from the same problems.

5 Consider calling environmental health inspectors if repeated requests are ignored. Be prepared to provide documentation of the problem and your attempts to have it fixed.

6 Consider the repair-and-deduct option. Have the repair work done professionally and deduct its cost from your monthly rent. View your specific rental agreement in detail before taking this route.

7 Take extreme caution before you decide to withhold monthly rent payments as a tactic. However "moral" your case may be, it is certain to contravene your lease agreement. Such a course of action could lead to your eviction.

### ✳ Tips

Keep a careful record of all correspondence with your landlord. Write down the dates of any request that you might have made. You'll need comprehensive evidence of your dealings should the case enter a courtroom.

Provide as much detail as you can when you write to your landlord. Also, point out that the problem may worsen over time and become a much more expensive repair.

### ⚠ Warning

Before you withhold rent, sue or adopt any such drastic approach, make sure that such an approach is legal, that the necessary repair is major, that you have given your landlord adequate notice and time to act, and that you are willing to end your tenancy should the landlord or judge successfully evict you.

## 187 Tell Your Neighbour the Music's Too Loud

You don't want to rock the boat, but you do want to be able to sleep in on Saturdays. With a tactful approach, you can achieve your goal.

### ⊙ Steps

1 Start by smiling. Catch your neighbour's eye when he heads out in the morning or give him a friendly nod when he comes home.

2 Get to know this person if you don't already. What's his name? Where does he work? How long has he lived on your street?

3 Try to make pleasant conversation and find a common interest. What sorts of things does he like: sport? Gardening? Movies?

### ✳ Tips

Try to establish a friendly relationship with people in your neighbourhood at the outset – it's easier to make requests of them when the need arises.

In general, being friendly and direct will get you much better results than being hostile.

4   Mention, in an off-hand way, that you can hear his music from your house. Tell him it sometimes wakes you up. For many people, this will be enough to let them know that their behaviour needs to change.

5   Wait a week or two to see what happens.

6   Mention in a more direct way that you'd like the volume lower. Be clear and specific with your request – and don't forget to be friendly.

7   Find out if other neighbours are bothered, if no change happens, and ask them to mention it, too.

8   Consider soliciting the help of one of his friends on the block – he might be willing to heed the complaint from someone closer.

9   Wait a week or two to avoid creating a conflict that could become hostile.

10  If you have a repeated or frequent problem with a noisy neighbour, contact the Environmental Health department of your local council.

Be reasonable: we all like to party sometimes, so we should be tolerant of a neighbour who does the same.

⚠ Warning

This is your neighbour – a person you might see every day for a long time to come – so make sure you act tactfully and thoughtfully. You don't want to come home to a feud every day.

# Buy a House                                          188

You'll do a lot of house-hunting, deal with estate agents and building societies – and then hope the seller accepts your offer.

## ⊙ Steps

1   Work out how much you can afford to pay for your new house. Consider your deposit, stamp duty, estate agent's fee, mortgage, and buildings and contents insurance.

2   Decide where you want to live. Think about how long it will take to commute to work, local schools, and the re-sale value of the houses in the area.

3   Think about what kind of house you want. Do you want a newer house that requires little or no refurbishing? Would you prefer an older house with character that might require some repair work? One floor or two? Are you interested in a flat, terrace, semi-detached or townhouse?

4   Register with an estate agent. Have the details of properties that fall within your brief sent to you. Visit any properties that interest you: the more houses you look at, the better idea you will have of your likes and dislikes. This will help you filter out future choices.

5   You don't have to buy through an estate agent. Many people prefer to sell privately, advertising in newspapers or magazines.

6   Find a lender – usually an bank or a building society – and arrange to have pre-approved for a mortgage. A dedicated mortgage broker may be able to find a deal more suited to your needs – but you will be charged for the service.

7   Find your ideal house and make an offer.

8   Any mortgage lender will insist that you have the prospective property surveyed. (If you are paying the full quantity in cash you should still have the property surveyed.)

## ✳ Tips

Be patient. Finding a house that fits your family's needs can take some time.

House values fluctuate with the ups and downs of the economy.

Buying a house is likely to be the biggest single investment you'll ever make. Choose wisely.

9  Hire a solicitor specialising in buying and selling property. They will perform the necessary searches to prove that the property is registered in the name of the vendor. If you choose not to hire a solicitor you must do this for yourself – although possible, it is also time-consuming and arguably not worth the money you'll save.

10  Agree a date in which you can take possession of the property.

11  Once your solicitor has exchanged contracts with the vendor you can move in.

---

## 189 | Determine How Big a Mortgage You Can Afford

**Before you look for that dream house, you need to ask yourself what you can really afford to spend each month. And how much a mortgage lender is prepared to lend.**

### ◉ Steps

1  Before you begin house hunting, consult a building society, bank or mortgage broker to find out the maximum loan you are likely have at your disposal.

2  Be aware that the amount you are allowed to borrow will vary from lender to lender. This will depend on your personal circumstances, such as regular income or assets. A typical figure for the UK would be up to four times a single annual income (although multiples of six have been known in recent years) or 80 per cent the value of any owned property you intend to mortgage.

3  The maximum value of your loan will also depend on whether you are taking out a mortgage in your own name, or a joint-mortgage with a partner (or co-buyer). A typical multiple is two-and-a-half times the combined annual income.

4  To work out the maximum value of any property you can buy, take your mortgage ceiling and add the amount you have saved in cash to use as as a deposit (or the money you will have at your disposal following the sale of your current property).

5  To make a quick approximation of your monthly payments, see 196 "Estimate Your Mortgage Payment". (To do this you need to know the mortgage amount, the pay-back period, and the interest rate.)

6  Add to your monthly payments, the cost of mortgage insurance, any land rent or service charge associated with the property, Council Tax for the area (you'll need to know the Council Tax band for that property) and an estimate of the utility costs, such as gas, electricity and water.

7  Compare this figure with your monthly net income to work out whether the mortgage is affordable.

###  Tip

If you have regular monthly debt payments (for example, car loans or credit cards), take these into account when determining that bottom-line affordability figure.

### ⚠ Warnings

Lenders can only tell you what you might be able to afford based on your salary and debt level. You also have to feel comfortable with the reality of the monthly payment.

Don't assume that you can cut back your expenses and stretch yourself into a house payment. You can only live on beans on toast for so long.

If you take out a variable rate mortgage, be aware of the possible impact of a sudden increase in interests rate: When rates are around 5 per cent, a 25-year £200,000 repayment mortgage will require around £1,000 a month to be paid; if interest rates creep up to 7.5 per cent, your monthly payment will increase to around £1,500. Can your income sustain such an increase?

# ✓ 190 Evaluate a Neighbourhood

Property experts always say that the three most important things to consider when evaluating a property are location, location and location. That's because a home in a fashionable area with convenient shopping and good schools nearby will hold its value far better than an identical home in a less popular neighbourhood. Of course, it will also be much more pleasant to live in. Ask these questions to determine the quality of the neighbourhood you're considering, and to evaluate other local factors that go into making a house a good home – and a good investment.

❑ How well do residents keep up their properties?

❑ What is the ratio of renters to owners?

❑ How far away is the nearest shopping area? Is it easy to get to at the times you'll need to go?

❑ What is the quality of the local schools?

❑ Are local streets well-maintained?

❑ How much traffic is there? Is it safe for children?

❑ Is public transport nearby? Will it take you where you want to go?

❑ Is there a motorway or major road accessible from the area?

❑ How close are the nearest parks? Do they suit your family's needs?

❑ How close and accessible are cultural and entertainment facilities – theatres, museums and sports arenas?

❑ Visit the area after nightfall. Does it feel safe? How noisy is it?

❑ Check with the local police station. How much crime is there in the neighbourhood?

❑ Check with any local organisations. Is it a neighbourhood watch area?

❑ Check a map. How far is the nearest fire station or police station?

❑ Is there emergency medical service in the area?

❑ How far away is the nearest hospital? Is it close enough for your needs?

❑ Are you in the flight path of an airport? (Note that flight paths may change with weather conditions or at different times of day.)

❑ Is a fire station or train station so close as to cause noise pollution?

❑ If you are looking at a flat, check out any rules or regulations affecting the block. How do these fit in with your own style of decorating or living?

❑ Visit the council offices. Are any major new developments planned? What impact will these have on traffic, noise and school systems?

## 191 Use an Estate Agent to Buy a House

The easiest way to find the house of your dreams is to use the services of an estate agent.

### ◎ Steps

1  Look around areas that interest you. If you see a suitable property make a note of the address and the name and telephone number of the estate agent. Even if you fail to buy that property, the estate agent may have others on their books that are suitable.

2  Buy a local newspaper and take a note of all the estate agents in the area. Register with each one.

3  They will ask you for a detailed specification of the types of property and price range that interest you. Remember, the better you define your requirements, the more likely they will be to find you a match.

4  A good agent should know the local area well, and be able to show you examples of similar properties they've sold recently.

5  If you want to look at a property, contact the estate agent to arrange a viewing.

### ✱ Tips

You generally don't need to pay an agent who is helping you buy a house – the fee is paid by the vendor.

Get all agreements in writing.

## 192 Shop for a House Online

The internet offers myriad opportunities for house hunting, especially if you are looking to move into a new area.

### ◎ Steps

1  Decide on a location. Property web pages usually give you the choice of searching by county, town or postcode.

2  Decide on the property type and age of the house, or other features, such as number of rooms.

3  Surf the internet for sites that offer listings – such as Fish4.co.uk – or the web pages of estate agents operating in the area that interest you.

4  Contact the agent listed if you see a house that fits your criteria. Ask for further information, such as the property details or the schedule.

5  Set up an appointment to meet the agent if you are still interested.

### ✱ Tip

Request e-mail updates on available houses and additional information about the community you're considering.

## 193 Buy a Property at Auction

Buying at auction is one of the few ways of getting a bargain on the property market – if don't mind taking a few risks.

### ◎ Steps

1  Scour the internet for specialist property auction sites – all of the established auctioneers will have an online presence. (Enter something like "property auctions UK" into any web search engine.)

### ⚠ Warning

If a property you buy at auction turns out to be a dud, you have little come-back. This is a route for risk-takers!

2    Make sure you have the finance in place beforehand. You are unlikely to get an agreement for a mortgage on an auctioned property. (Although you could buy using a loan – with a substantially higher interest rate – and then get a mortgage to pay off the loan once you had purchased the property.

3    Order a catalogue for any upcoming auctions that interest you. (There is usually a substantial charge for these.)

4    Note the details of any property that interests you. It will be listed with its "reserve price" – the lowest price the vendor will allow the property to be sold.

5    Visit the property. If you intend to bid, have a professional survey done beforehand. This will reveal any major structural problems, and give you an estimate of its actual market value.

6    Before the auction, decide on the maximum figure you would be prepared to pay. Don't go above it – it's easy to get carried away in a bidding war.

7    At the auction, place bids by raising your hand. Some auction houses will allow bidding via the telephone or the internet.

8    When the gavel comes down, if your bid is the highest you are deemed to have made a legally binding contract.

9    Be aware of what is covered by homeowners' association insurance and what the association is responsible for, such as roots, common areas and landscaping.

## Make an Offer on a House                            194

So you've found your dream home, looked it over carefully, and are now ready to make your offer. Here are the steps you'll need to take.

### ☉ Steps

1    Consult a lender or mortgage broker to find out how much you can afford to spend on a house, or use a calculator on a financial website (see 189 "Determine How Big a Mortgage You Can Afford").

2    The amount you can borrow will vary from lender to lender, and will depend on whether you are taking out a mortgage on your own or a joint-mortgage with a partner (or co-buyer). A typical figure for the UK is three to four times one income, or two to three times a joint income.

3    Know how much money you have for a deposit. This will usually be at least 10 per cent (although in some cases first-time buyers may be able to secure a 100 per cent mortgage).

4    Decide what type of financing you want (see 195 "Get a Mortgage").

5    Know how much money you have for a down payment; typically 5 to 20 per cent of the purchase price is required, depending on the loan terms.

### ⚠ Warning

Consult a solicitor before you sign anything. What you agree to could severely limit the remedies available to you by law.

6   Make an offer to the vendor (or vendor's estate agent).

7   When approved, contact your solicitor to deal with contractual issues.

8   Now is the time to make a formal application for a mortgage.

## 195 | Get a Mortgage

For most of us, securing a home loan is the most important step in the home-buying process. Here are the basics for getting your finances in shape for the big purchase.

### ⊙ Steps

1   Find a mortgage lender. Traditionally, it was only building societies that arranged such loans, but now mortgages are widely available from banks and other financial institutions. First you should decide which type of mortgage you want.

2   A REPAYMENT mortgage is the most common type of loan. The buyer pays off a proportion of the loan each month and then pays interest on the remainder. All of the money goes to the lender. Some repayment mortgages are FLEXIBLE, allowing over- or underpayments to be made according to circumstances.

3   INTEREST ONLY and ENDOWMENT mortgages are more risky. The buyer pays only a monthly interest charge to the lender whilst at the same time paying into an independent scheme intended to pay off the full amount of the loan at the end of the period. The buyer must make up for any shortfall in value – which is likely with low interest rates and poor-performing money markets.

4   A CURRENT ACCOUNT mortgage puts your mortgage, saving and cheque accounts into one large loan, which can be paid into or drawn from at will. Most experts agree that this is the most economical way of running a mortgage, providing you are disciplined with your money.

5   Mortgages can have a fixed or variable interest rate. If you take out a fixed-rate mortgage you could lose out if interest rates fall; a variable-rate mortgage means that your monthly payments will depend on movements in interest rate.

6   Fill out a mortgage application form. Mortgages are signed in respect of a property, so whilst you may get an agreement in principle from a lender, the mortgage will only be formally approved when the lender has have approved the property you intend to buy.

7   Following approval, the mortgage lender will notify you in writing. This should take less than 14 days.

8   Once you have signed the mortgage agreement, the lender will make a payment to your solicitor – this will then be paid to the vendor's solicitor once the contracts have been exchanged (see 198 "Exchange Contracts on a Home You Are Buying").

### ✳ Tip

If you are a first-time home buyer, you may qualify for a lower deposit or interest rate. Check with banks, building societies and mortgage brokers to see what kind of deals are available.

### ⚠ Warning

Remember that if you default on your mortgage payments the lender may have the right to repossess your home. If this happens it will be auctioned and bring a considerably lower price than if you were to sell it on the open market.

# ✓ 196 Estimate Your Mortgage Payment

A home is the single largest purchase most of us are ever likely to make. This chart can help you get a handle on the daunting cost of a home by helping you estimate the monthly payment on a 25-year fixed-rate repayment mortgage. The figures in the left-hand column are annual interest rates. The headings across the top are loan amounts, – typically 80 or 90 per cent of the purchase price. So if you're putting down 20 per cent on a £250,000 home, look in the £200,000 column at your interest rate to find your monthly payment. (Be aware that these figures don't include other required payments, such as insurance. Nor do they include tax relief.)

Note: For loan amounts not listed, look in the £100,000 column at your interest rate and multiply by the appropriate factor – for example, for a £189,000 loan, multiply the mortgage payment by 1.89.

| RATE | £50,000 | £100,000 | £150,000 | £200,000 | £250,000 | £300,000 |
|---|---|---|---|---|---|---|
| 3% | £237.10 | £474.21 | 711.31 | £948.42 | £1,185.52 | £1,422.63 |
| 3.25% | £243.65 | £487.31 | £730.97 | £974.63 | £1,218.20 | £1,401.04 |
| 3.5% | £250.31 | £500.62 | £750.93 | £1,001.24 | £1,251.55 | £1,501.87 |
| 3.75% | £357.06 | £514.13 | £771.19 | £1,028.26 | £1,285.32 | £1,542.39 |
| 4% | £236.91 | £527.83 | £791.75 | £1,055.67 | £1,319.59 | £1,583.51 |
| 4.25% | £270.86 | £541.73 | £812.60 | £1,083.47 | £1,354.34 | £1,625.21 |
| 4.5% | £277.91 | £555.83 | £1833.74 | £1,111.66 | £1,389.58 | £1,667.49 |
| 4.75% | £285.05 | £570.11 | £855.17 | £1,140.23 | £1,425.29 | £1,710.35 |
| 5% | £292.29 | £584.59 | £876.88 | £1,169.18 | £1,461.47 | £1,753.77 |
| 5.25% | £299.62 | £599.24 | £898.87 | £1,198.49 | £1,498.11 | £1,753.77 |
| 5.5% | £307.04 | £614.08 | £921.13 | £1,228.17 | £1,535.21 | £1,842.26 |
| 5.75% | £315.55 | £629.10 | £943.65 | £1,258.21 | £1,572.76 | £1,887.31 |
| 6% | £322.15 | £644.3 | £966.45 | £1,288.6 | £1,610.75 | £1,932.90 |
| 6.25% | £329.83 | £659.66 | £989.50 | £1,319.33 | £1,649.17 | £1,979.00 |
| 6.5% | £337.60 | £675.20 | £1,012.81 | £1,350.41 | £1,688.01 | £2,025.62 |
| 6.75% | £345.45 | £690.91 | £1,036.36 | £1,381.82 | £1,727.27 | £2,072.73 |
| 7% | £353.38 | £706.77 | £1,060.16 | £1,413.55 | £1,766.94 | £2,120.33 |
| 7.25% | £361.40 | £722.8 | £1084.21 | £1,445.61 | £1,807.01 | £2,168.42 |
| 7.5% | £369.49 | £738.99 | £1,108.48 | £1,477.98 | £1,847.47 | £2,216.97 |
| 7.75% | £377.66 | £755.32 | £1,132.99 | £1,510.65 | £1,888.32 | £2,265.98 |
| 8% | £385.90 | £771.81 | £1,157.72 | £1,543.63 | £1,929.54 | £2,315.44 |
| 8.25% | £394.22 | £788.45 | £1,182.67 | £1,576.9 | £1,971.12 | £2,365.35 |
| 8.5% | £402.61 | £805.22 | £1,207.84 | £1,610.45 | £2,013.06 | £2,415.68 |
| 8.75% | £411.07 | £822.14 | £1,233.21 | £1,644.28 | £2,055.35 | £2,466.43 |

chart

## 197 | Change to a Better Mortgage Deal

Gone are the days when anyone wanting to buy their own home would be forced to beg from their bank manager. The mortgage world is now a competitive business with lenders doing all in their power to undercut one another.

### ☉ Steps

1 Check your current policy for any early payment penalty clause. If one exists (common among fixed rate repayment mortgages) the cost must be factored into any potential savings that might be made by moving.

2 If you have an endowment mortgage, seek advice in making any changes – with money markets volatile since the mid-1990s, most endowment policies will not pay for their loans without topping-up.

3 Look at the deals on offer from the banks and high-street building societies. Some may offer financial inducements or low interest rates to entice new customers.

4 Alternatively, contact a mortgage broker. He or she will know the best deals that apply to your circumstances. Be aware that there is usually a charge for this service (although some may obtain their fees from the mortgage lender).

**✱ Tip**

If you replace an endowment mortgage, it may be worth your continuing to pay into the endowment fund and view it as a savings plan.

## 198 | Close on the Sale of a House You Are Buying

When all the terms of the contract have been met, the solicitors of both parties will finally be able to transfer ownership of the property.

### ☉ Steps

1 Review all of your mortgage documents. Before you sign, make sure you are getting the mortgage you thought you were.

2 Make sure all inspections have been satisfactorily performed, all work completed, and clearances for completed work provided. Do this prior to signing any documents.

3 Do a walkthrough of the property prior to the signing of any documents. Make sure all agreed work has been completed to your satisfaction.

4 Agree on a date in which contracts can be exchanged and you can move in to the property.

5 Before you move in, contact the utility companies – telephone, water, gas and electricity – to ensure that you will have a service from that date.

6 Arrange to take possession of the keys once the transaction is recorded.

**✱ Tips**

Be sure to read all the paperwork you will be signing, and follow up to make sure that these steps have been taken.

Once the house is in your name, have the locks changed.

**⚠ Warning**

Do not sign loan documents until all necessary work has been completed.

## Obtain House Insurance

Insurance protects your home and your possessions. Most mortgage lenders will not fund a loan without building insurance.

### ⊙ Steps

1 As a home owner you can expect to pay two types of insurance. Building insurance covers your house, and contents insurance covers everything you own inside the building. Some insurers will give you discount if you take out a policy that covers both. (Some will go even further if you add car insurance to the deal.)

2 Call at least three different companies for rates. They should be able to give you a quote based on the replacement value of your home.

3 An insurance broker may find you the best deal on offer, but you may have to pay a fee for the service. (Be aware that some seemingly independent brokers have "favoured" insurers which often – by some strange coincidence – offer them the highest commission.)

4 Understand exactly what is covered in your policy. On "new for old" policies (where stolen or damaged goods are replaced) be sure to ask how the insurer defines replacement cost.

5 Ask about "valuables" – most insurers will require objects of above a certain value to be listed separately. There may be a value limit on any single item.

6 Some contents policies exchange lower premiums for an agreement that the holder pays for the first £50 or £100 of any claim.

### ✻ Tips

For items not covered by a standard policy, such as artworks or antiques, you should be able to buy add-on coverage.

If you work from home – or have a paying hobby – you may have to take out separate business insurance. Failure to do this may affect your other policies should you make a claim.

## Get Your House Ready to Sell

If your house makes a good impression on buyers, your chances of selling it faster and for more money are greater.

### ⊙ Steps

1 Make any required repairs and keep a copy of the list (along with receipts) to share with buyers.

2 Choose little fixes that make a big difference. Replace old grouting in the kitchens and bathrooms; retouch paintwork, and repaint if necessary; get carpets cleaned; get rid of clutter; use brighter lightbulbs and open curtains to make rooms look bigger; get rid of pet smells.

3 Decide on which upgrades to make – such as replacing old, worn carpet; or replacing old sink, taps and light fixtures.

4 Make the entrance grand. First impressions are important.

5 Make sure your garden is in top shape.

### ⚠ Warning

Don't spend too much money on changes that won't enhance your bottom line.

## 201 | Sell a House

If selling a house were easy, nobody would use an estate agent. But there are things you can do to make the process easier.

### ⊙ Steps

1 The most common starting point is to find an estate agent (see 202 "Use an Estate Agent to Sell a House").

2 Set the price for your house. Talk to an agent or study the sale prices of comparable houses in your neighbourhood to get an idea of what your house is worth.

3 Prepare your house to be shown. Clean it thoroughly, get rid of clutter and tidy up the garden (see 200 "Get Your House Ready to Sell").

4 Consider offers and evaluate contracts.

### ✱ Tip

Be prepared to answer these questions from buyers: How long has the property been on the market? Have there been any price reductions? Have there been any previous offers? How long have you owned the house? What improvements have you made?

## 202 | Use an Estate Agent to Sell a House

Contrary to popular opinion, estate agents are not (necessarily) the spawn of Satan. Unless you relish the challenges of selling a house on your own, you'll need a professional to assist.

### ⊙ Steps

1 Ask friends and families for a personal recommendation.

2 Make sure that any agent you consider belongs to a professional body, such as the National Association of Estate Agents. The NAEA sets certain standards for its members.

3 Look for estate agents who sell properties like yours – they will be more knowledgeable about that market and attract more suitable buyers. Look at the window displays of estate agents. Will your property get a clear photo with good details? Where do they advertise?

4 A good agent should know the local area well, and be able to show you examples of similar properties they've sold recently. Agents use comparisons to make their valuations, which can be difficult if your home is in some way unusual – all the more reason to use an agent who has recently sold a property like yours.

5 Interview at least three prospective estate agents before making a choice. Go with the agent you feel most confident with – not necessarily the one with the highest quote.

6 You don't have to use just one agent. However, if you give sole selling rights to one agent, the commission you pay will be lower.

7 Expect to pay between 1.5 per cent and 2.5 per cent of the selling price, depending on the area. Some may agree to a flat fee, which may be a good deal on an expensive property.

### ⚠ Warnings

Beware of agents who suggest they can get an unreasonably high sales price. An agent might use a high listing price to get your business, and then seek a lower price later.

Be aware that VAT is payable on estate agent's fees.

## Sell Your House Without an Agent

With a little savvy and a lot of tenacity, you can sell your house yourself – and save those commission costs.

### ⊙ Steps

1   Set a fair price for your house. Study the sale prices of comparable houses in your neighbourhood. (You can get this information from a local estate agent or newspaper.)

2   Use internet directory sites such as Fish4.co.uk to find out how actual sale prices compare to asking prices – use this as a guide to your "bottom line".

3   Clean your house thoroughly and get rid of all clutter (see 200 "Get Your House Ready to Sell").

4   Advertise in local or specialised newspapers.

5   Use a solicitor to handle the contractual side of the deal.

### ⚠ Warning

Take the time to thoroughly understand contracts and discuss anything you don't fully understand with a solicitor.

## Buy to Let

With mortgage rates enjoying a record low, why not consider buying a second property with the intention of renting it out. Buying to let gives you an asset that will (probably) increase in value as well as bringing in an additional monthly income.

### ⊙ Steps

1   Consider your finances. Even if you already have a mortgage, some building societies will give you a second mortgage for such projects. Common among couples is for each partner to carry a separate mortgage.

2   Choose your property carefully. Areas with a high student population are usually a good bet.

3   As a landlord you have a legal responsibility to provide accommodation that comes up to environmental health standards. You may have to spend money on a property to get it up to scratch.

4   Decide if you really want the hassle of maintaining another property. If you live far away from your new property, or you are short on free time, it may be worth paying a letting agent to deal with business on your behalf – but expect to pay up to 20 per cent of your potential rent in fees.

### ✳ Tip

If you have a son or daughter about to attend university, consider buying a house to let in that area. Not only will it provide "free" accommodation for your child – and allow them to choose and vet suitable house-mates – but you will also have someone living on hand to protect your investment and collect rent on your behalf.

## Buy a Holiday Home

Buying a holiday home is exciting, but, as with any other major purchase, it's important to think things through carefully.

### ⊙ Steps

1   Decide whether this is a place where you'd like to spend every holiday. If you're not sure, then it's probably not a wise to buy.

### ✳ Tips

You may get a better deal if you buy during the off-season.

2  Select the type of holiday home that best suits your needs.

3  Visit desired locations and tour properties for sale.

4  Determine whether the holiday property you are considering buying is priced fairly. Check local estate agents and newspapers to get a feel for the value of properties in the area. The process is then the same for buying any other property (see 188 "Buy a House").

5  Consider how you will maintain the holiday property throughout the year. Consider using a letting agent; a cheaper alternative is to find a reliable neighbour prepared to keep an eye on the place for you.

If you're seeking a time-share, look on the internet for people selling their weeks independently.

⚠ **Warning**

Most experts agree that you should buy a holiday home for pleasure rather than purely as an investment.

## 206 | Move Out of the City to the Country

Fed up with the pace of the big city? How about stepping back and taking in the country air?

### ⊙ Steps

1  Leaving the rat-race behind is one of *the* great romantic dreams, but don't get carried away with the moment – make sure that you act with a clear head.

2  Consider the practicalities. What about your career? Can you commute to your existing job? Can you work from home? If not, do you have the financial resources to support yourself while you seek alternative employment.

3  Think about your lifestyle. Most cities have a wealth of amenities – music venues, restaurants, theatres, cinemas, health clubs – that are lacking in more isolated areas. If you enjoy a busy social life, the peace and quiet may be appealing, but will you miss it in the long term?

4  How practical are you? Be aware that you may have to deal with many everyday household problems on your own – there might not be a handy local plumber to fix a burst pipe for you, for instance.

⚠ **Warning**

Be aware that the desire to "get away" may be symptomatic of a deeper underlying problem – if you're running from something the problem is likely to catch up with you eventually.

## 207 | Buy a Property Abroad

Once upon a time, buying a house abroad was only for the rich. But with house prices in much of mainland Europe substantially lower than in the UK, it has become possible for those of more modest means.

### ⊙ Steps

1  Overseas property seekers often are looking for sea and sun, so the coastline tends to be the most popular – and expensive.

2  Apply the same rules as if purchasing in the UK. Don't act on a whim. Do plenty of research. Start off by taking a holiday in the area you're considering. Are there enough facilities for what you require? Or do

✱ **Tip**

Seek out "ex-pat" clubs and societies to get first-hand experiences from those who have been there and done it before you.

tourist attractions out-number the local amenities? The best source of knowledge is those who have done it before: there is no shortage of "ex-pats" with stories from which you can learn.

3   Unless you're fluent in the local language, conduct your enquiries through a reputable third party. In London and the South East there are many reputable estate agents who are expert in dealing with overseas properties. Use established companies and beware of anyone who gives you the hard sell.

4   Make sure you have a good lawyer with an excellent command of English and the local language to deal with the endless stream of rules and regulations. (In Spain, for instance, you can inherit debts from a previous vendor.)

5   Make sure you have the finances in place before you put in an offer. You may find it difficult to get a mortgage in the UK to pay for a foreign home. Mortgaging and renting out a British home is a popular solution.

6   Start a direct debit from a local bank account to pay your regular utility bills. (Be aware that some foreign banks are considerably less lenient on late payers than the UK.)

7   Be aware that if you intend to remain resident in Britain, and wish to rent out your overseas property when it's empty, you could find yourself with income tax demands from both countries.

## ⚠ Warning

If acting independently, you must make sure that you understand your obligations under local legislation. Wherever you happen to be in the world, when dealing with the law, ignorance is never a defence.

---

## Decide Whether to Live Abroad                                    `208`

Many of us dream about leaving the country in search of a new way of life. In doesn't have to be very difficult to turn this dream into reality – as long as you are aware of the pitfalls.

### ⦿ Steps

1   Decide where you want to live, and try to imagine your day-to-day life in a new country.

2   Many people contemplate such a move after returning from their holidays. Be aware that a great time spent as a tourist is usually a rather different experience than being permanent resident.

3   Find out if it's possible to make such a move. Does the country in which you want to live have entry regulations? Australia, for instance, has a points system based on personal factors such as education or career. Others may take your wealth into consideration.

4   Scour the internet in search of people who have already made the move. Learn from their experiences.

5   Consider practical issues. Can you speak the native tongue? Will you be able to work? Is there are demand for your profession? Will your children be able to resume school without major disruption?

6   Contact the embassy for the country in question. Many of those that are actively seeking to recruit will produce useful information packs. At the very least they will be able to advise you of any unique pitfalls.

### ✳ Tip

Think carefully before committing yourself wholesale to a new way of life. Instead of selling up, why not rent out your home until you're satisfied that you want to make the permanent move?

## 209 | Repair a Tap

Modern taps usually feature a replaceable interior cartridge that houses the unit's moving parts. Drips and leaks can often be stopped by simply replacing this cartridge.

### ◉ Steps

1 Turn off the water at the water-supply valve. This is usually beneath the sink (or in the wall behind the shower assembly – often housed behind a removable panel). If there is no water-supply valve in the same room, turn off the water supply for the entire building.

2 Before taking the taps apart, turn them on full to drain the water from the pipes.

3 Remove the handle from the tap. Most handles are fixed with a screw, which is usually hidden under a decorative cap – depending on the make, this can be unscrewed or prised off with a small screwdriver. Remove the screw, then lift or jiggle the handle off. Put the handle in safe place after its removal.

4 Carefully pull the cartridge out of the fixture using a pair of pliers. (Some makes of tap may have a lock ring or lock nut that holds the cartridge in place. This must be removed with a screwdriver or pliers before the cartridge can be taken out.)

5 Take the cartridge to a hardware shop and purchase a replacement.

6 Install the new cartridge and reassemble the tap.

7 Turn the water supply back on, keeping an eye out for leaks.

### ⚠ Warning

When working with chrome or brass fixtures, be sure to protect the surfaces from tool damage using a piece of leather, heavy cloth or duct tape.

### Things You'll Need

- ☐ screwdriver
- ☐ pliers
- ☐ replacement water-valve cartridges

## 210 | Repair a Dripping Showerhead

A constantly dripping showerhead doesn't just waste water, it can also drive you crazy.

### ◉ Steps

1 Unscrew the showerhead from the water pipe. This can be done by hand but sometimes requires a monkey wrench or large pair of pliers. The head may be held on with a screw, which you'll have to remove.

2 Look at the screw thread inside the showerhead where it fixes into the pipe. You should find a small washer made of plastic or rubber. Replace it if it looks even a little damaged or brittle.

3 Wrap the showerhead stem with PTFE tape to seal the connection.

4 Remount the showerhead on the stem. Don't screw it on too tightly – hand-tightening should be sufficient.

5 Turn the water on and off. Wait several minutes and check for drips or leaks. If the showerhead is still leaking, you may have problems with the shower's water-control valve and need to call a plumber.

### ⚠ Warning

When working with chrome or brass fixtures, be sure to protect the surfaces from tool damage using a piece of leather, heavy cloth or duct tape.

### Things You'll Need

- ☐ monkey wrench or large pliers
- ☐ screwdriver
- ☐ replacement washers
- ☐ PTFE tape

# Fix a Running Toilet

If your toilet goes through more water than Niagara Falls, the problem is most likely to be the diaphragm of the ball cock or the water tank flap valve.

## ⊙ Steps

### Identifying the Source

1   Remove the lid of the cistern and place it out of the way on the floor.

2   Investigate the ball cock diaphragm. It's a valve attached to the float (which is either a metal or plastic ball on the end of a long rod or a plastic canister that slides up and down a vertical plastic pipe). If you can see water coming from this valve, it may need to be cleaned or replaced.

3   Reach down into the bottom of the tank and press down on the edges of the flap valve (a black or red rubber cone that fits into the tank's hole). If the sound of water running into the bowl stops, you know that the flap valve may be worn and needs to be replaced.

4   Get ready to work. Turn off the water supply to the toilet (this valve is most often found coming out of a wall near the toilet; turn the handle in a clockwise direction). Flush the toilet to drain some of the water and make your work easier.

5   If you need to replace the diaphragm or flap valve, take the old one with you to a hardware or plumbing supply shop to make sure you buy the correct replacement.

## Cleaning or Replacing the Ball Cock Diaphragm

1   Snap off the cover of the ball cock and put it out of the way.

2   Remove the screws holding down the top plate of the ball cock – the float-control arm is attached to this and may be spring-loaded. You'll see a rubber diaphragm.

3   Remove the diaphragm carefully, noting which side is up, and check its condition. Sometimes a piece of gravel or rust or a hard-water deposit can get lodged under the diaphragm and cause it to leak, or the diaphragm can simply become worn out with age.

4   Replace the diaphragm or clean it by rinsing it in the tank's water; flush the valve by turning on the water supply for the toilet just enough to get a flow of water for a couple of seconds.

5   Replace the top plate and secure it with its screws.

6   Turn the water supply back on, allowing the tank to fill, and replace the lid.

## Replacing the Flap Valve

1   Remove the flap valve. Some have a clamp-type assembly, while others hook to short posts that stick out from the overflow pipe; all attachments are fairly easy to remove by hand.

2   Install a new flap valve.

3   Turn on the water supply and replace the lid.

## ✱ Tip

If these strategies don't solve the problem, you may need to hire a plumber to disassemble the toilet to look for cracks or a worn connecting gasket.

## Things You'll Need

❏ screwdriver

❏ replacement diaphragm

❏ replacement flap valve

## 212 | Unblock a Toilet

A blocked toilet often can be cleared in a few simple steps.
Give these a try before you call in a professional cleaner.

### ⊙ Steps

1 Use the toilet as little as possible once you notice there's a problem.
This will help prevent overflow and water damage.

2 Insert a plunger into the toilet, making sure the rubber globe or cup has
fully sealed the drain opening.

3 Push down on the plunger handle with firm but careful strokes. Rough,
careless use can damage the toilet bowl. If the clog isn't too tight, these
bursts of increased water pressure should clear the obstruction.

4 Attack tougher problems with a plumber's snake (see 215 "Use a
Plumber's Snake").

5 Consider a chemical drain cleaner only as a last resort. Make sure that
any product used is specifically marked as safe for use with porcelain,
and follow the manufacturer's directions carefully. Never mix any of
these chemical agents, as dangerous reactions may occur.

6 Flush the toilet several times to remove the drain cleaner and to check
the flow.

### ✱ Tip

Buy the highest-quality plunger
you can.

### Things You'll Need

❑ plunger

❑ plumber's snake (optional)

❑ drain cleaner (optional)

## 213 | Retrieve a Valuable Dropped Down the Sink

Don't panic! Dropping something of value down the drain isn't
always the nightmare it seems. Try this method to get it back.

### ⊙ Steps

1 Turn off the water immediately to prevent the item being washed out of
reach.

2 Open the cabinet beneath the sink.

3 Find the trap – this is the U-shaped piece of pipe that connects the
vertical pipe running from the sink to the horizontal pipe that goes into
the wall.

4 Place a bucket under the trap.

5 Loosen the large threaded nuts that attach the trap to the other pipes.
Sometimes you can do this with your hands; otherwise, you may need
to use a large pair of pliers or even a plumber's pipe wrench.

6 Pull the trap away with a good yank, letting it fall into the bucket as
necessary. Beware, the trap will be full of dirty water.

7 Put on gloves. Empty the trap into your hand – over the bucket – and
look for your valuable.

8 Reassemble the trap, being careful not to overtighten the nuts.

### ✱ Tips

There may be another trap or
filter in the main plumbing
system, so if your valuable has
already passed the sink trap, it
may still be in the main trap.
Call a plumber.

If you're afraid of stripping or
marring the nuts holding the
plumbing together, place a thin
rag or tape around the nuts
before grabbing them with
the plumber's wrench.

### Things You'll Need

❑ bucket

❑ pliers or a plumber's wrench

❑ rubber gloves

**How to Do *(Just About)* Everything**

## Unblock a Sink

If your sink is blocked up, try these simple steps before calling in a plumber.

### ⊙ Steps

1  Remove the sink strainer or plug from the drain.

2  Fill the sink halfway with water, if it's not already full.

3  Place the plunger over the drain, making sure that the plunger's rubber globe or cup is full of water. Plunge five or six times using careful but forceful strokes.

4  Remove the plunger and give the sink a chance to drain.

5  After the sink is completely unblocked, run hot water down the drain for several minutes.

6  If that doesn't work, remove the trap (or U-bend) or use a plumber's snake (see 213 "Retrieve a Valuable Dropped Down the Sink" and 215 "Use a Plumber's Snake").

7  Consider a chemical drain cleaner only as a last resort and follow the manufacturer's directions carefully. Do not mix chemical agents, as dangerous reactions could occur.

8  Call in a plumber for problems you can't resolve on your own.

### Things You'll Need

- ☐ plunger
- ☐ plumber's snake (optional)
- ☐ drain cleaner (optional)

## Use a Plumber's Snake

A plumber's snake can be a helpful tool to have around the house. Use it with the proper care and you can avoid some major plumbing bills.

### ⊙ Steps

1  Put on a pair of gloves with a non-slip grip. The snake – essentially a long piece of wire – can get slippery and dirty.

2  Start with the smallest snake you can, graduating to a larger size if the first one doesn't work.

3  Insert the business end of the plumber's snake – the end opposite the handle – into the drain or toilet. Use care to avoid damaging sinks, toilet bowls and pipes.

4  Turn the handle slowly in a clockwise direction, gently pushing the snake. Let it find its own way through – this may take quite a few revolutions of the handle.

5  Fill the sink or toilet bowl about halfway with water to help lubricate and provide some pressure to wash the clog out once it begins to break up.

6  Pull out the snake when the snake crank becomes hard to turn, clean its end, and re-insert it into the drain.

7  Repeat this process until the drain is clear.

### ⚠ Warning

Some snakes are motorised. If you're using a motor-driven snake, don't spin it too quickly, and be careful when retrieving it from the drain – it may flail around and strike you as it comes out of the pipe.

### Things You'll Need

- ☐ pair of non-slip gloves
- ☐ plumber's snake

## 216 | Thaw a Frozen Pipe

Frozen pipes can be a huge inconvenience, and may cause water damage if they burst. Here are a few quick cures.

### ⊙ Steps

1  Turn on the tap nearest the pipe. Don't force it if it's too stiff.

2  Wrap the pipe in a towel and secure it with duct tape.

3  Pour boiling water over the towel. Repeat until the water has thawed and runs through the tap.

4  Alternatively, wrap the pipe in a heating pad or place a heat lamp next to it. If you don't have one of these, a handheld hair dryer or a small electric heater should do the trick.

### ⚠ Warning

Don't use electrical appliances if there is standing water.

### Things You'll Need

☐ duct tape

☐ heating pad, heat lamp, hair dryer or small electric heater

## 217 | Repair Leaky Pipes Quickly

You can stop – or at least slow down – a leak, thus preventing water damage until a plumber can do the full repair. These steps are for a temporary fix, not a long-term cure.

### ⊙ Steps

1  Tighten a threaded joint with a pipe wrench if the leak is there. If that doesn't stop the leak, it may at least slow it down until the joint can be replaced. (Note: Some older plumbing may require brazing – a kind of welding. If the pipe has no threads, or you see signs of welding, leave this job to the professionals.)

2  You may be able to plug a very small hole by inserting the tip of a sharp pencil. Break off the tip in the hole and cover with duct tape, wrapping it in several layers.

3  Alternatively, apply epoxy putty specially formulated for leaks caused by cracks or small holes.

4  Fix larger holes by clamping a piece of hose around the pipe. With a knife, cut a length of hose at least 5 cm (2 in) longer than the hole. (Rubber hose or even an old piece of garden hose will do.) You will also need three hose clamps. Slit the hose lengthwise and fit it around the pipe, then clamp the hose in place using a hose clamp at each end and one in the middle.

5  Catch the spillage with a bucket, or – better still – avoid using the leaky plumbing until proper repairs can be made.

### ⚠ Warning

Use caution – old joints and pipe can be fragile. Rough treatment may worsen the problem.

### Things You'll Need

☐ pipe wrench

☐ pencil

☐ duct tape

☐ epoxy putty

☐ hose

☐ knife

☐ hose clamps

## Assess Water Quality 218

The average person uses 275 l (60 1/2 gal) of water a day. But is that water safe? Water testing is expensive, so make sure you know what to test for and when to do it.

⊙ **Steps**

1 The quality of water in England and Wales is covered by the Drinking Water Inspectorate. Look on www.dwi.gov.uk for reports on each of the regional water companies. In Scotland, it is the responsibility of the Scottish Executive (www.scotland.gov.uk); in Northern Ireland, the Drinking Water Inspectorate for Northern Ireland (www.nio.gov.uk).

2 Run some tap water into a clear glass and look closely at it in good lighting. Is it clear or discoloured? Do you see sediment in the water? Smell the water – you should expect a faint smell of chlorine (like milder version of the smell you get in a swimming pool), but any other smell indicates a problem.

3 Check drains, fixtures and porcelain items such as toilets and tubs for red, green, blue or brown staining.

4 Water supply in the UK is in the hands of a number of different private or government-owned companies. These are legally obliged to provide you with safe, drinkable water. If you have concerns about the quality of your water, you should first contact your regional water company.

5 You could buy a home water test from a hardware store. While less accurate than a lab test, it's a less expensive alternative.

6 Be aware that the nature of drinking water differs depending on where you are in the UK.

7 Although every water company claims that their supply is safe to drink, an increasing number of people choose to buy bottled mineral waters. These are expensive but subject to the more stringent safety regulations associated with food and drink. And they certainly taste much more pleasant.

8 Note that water from a private well is not the responsibility of a water company, and should be tested independently before drinking.

✻ **Tips**

Sometimes tap water appears cloudy when first poured. This is usually simply caused by air bubbles, and should clear within a minute or two. It isn't anything to be concerned about.

If you use well water, be aware of agricultural activity in your area. This may affect the quality of your water. Test as you feel necessary after your first year on the property.

## Eliminate Hard Water 219

If your dishes have spots, your soap doesn't lather well and your white clothes look grey, you could have "hard" water – water with a high mineral-salt content. Here's what to do.

⊙ **Steps**

1 Water from some parts of the UK may be considerably harder than in others. This is less to do with the way in which water companies treat their supplies than geographical conditions. If you contact your water company (or look at their web pages) you should be able to discover the hardness of water in your region.

⚠ **Warning**

People monitoring their sodium intake may want to consult a doctor before installing an ion-exchange water softener – this will add salt to your water.

2  if necessary, call a water-conditioning specialist. They will be familiar with the quality of the water in your area and can recommend treatment.

3  If water is only moderately hard, buy water softener.

4  If you have a private water supply you may need a filtration system in addition to using a water softener. Remember that a water softener only removes hardness from your water, not the toxins.

### Things You'll Need

- ☐ water softener
- ☐ water conditioner
- ☐ filtration system

---

## 220 | Choose a Water-Filtration System

Filtration systems are designed to remove impurities from tap water. Although all drinking water provided by water companies in the UK is filtered before it reaches the taps, there are further steps you can take to improve the quality of your water.

### ⊙ Steps

1  The cheapest solution is a filter jug system. You fill a jug with tap water and it passes through a disposable filter leaving only "pure" water. Use filtered water for cold drinks, making ice cubes or in coffee machines. Filters must be changed regularly – once a month is normal – or else the process becomes worthless.

2  If you want to take things further, have your water tested so you know how much and what kind of filtration you need (see 218 "Assess Water Quality").

3  Decide whether you want a tap-mounted system, which is inexpensive and easy to install but requires frequent filter changes, or an in-line system, which mounts directly to your plumbing system. The latter is more costly but more comprehensive.

4  Use a carbon filter if your water contains chlorine, chloroform, pesticides or organic chemicals. Carbon filters are not effective against lead or other heavy metals, flouride or chloroform.

5  You may need an in-line reverse-osmosis filtering system if your water contains high quantities of sodium, ferrous iron, nitrates, lead, fluoride or organic contaminants.

### ✳ Tips

Install a sediment filter ahead of the carbon filter to remove solids that will clog the carbon.

Read product claims for removal and choose a system designed to treat your water conditions.

### ⚠ Warning

None of these filter types will solve hard-water problems.

## Replace a Light Switch                                      221

You can replace a broken light switch easily in a few minutes. But as with all electrical repairs, be sure to make safety your first concern.

⊙ **Steps**

1  Turn off the power switch at the main circuit breaker or fuse box. Test the power is off by flipping the light switch on and then off again. Make sure that everyone affected by the loss of power knows what you are doing. For extra security, put a notice near the circuit box so that no one mistakenly turns the power back on while you're working.

2  With a screwdriver, remove the two screws holding the cover plate and take the plate off – this is the piece of metal or plastic covering the switch unit.

3  Remove the two mounting screws holding the switch in place inside the electrical box.

4  Pull the switch out of the wall. The switch should come out far enough to expose the wires.

5  Remove the screws holding the two wires coming out of the wall to the switch. Make sure that you tag which wire came from which screw (they should be colour coded) with coloured pens or tape.

6  Take the switch to the hardware shop and get another one like it.

7  Take the switch home and hold it up against the wall, ensuring that it is right side up.

8  Attach the wires to the screws on the switch's back according to the tags you made earlier.

9  Secure the new switch in the box with mounting screws.

10 Replace the switch cover.

11 Turn the main power back on and test your work.

### ⚠ Warnings

Working with electrical systems is potentially dangerous. If you're unsure of your abilities or of any aspect of the project, call an electrician (see 259 "Hire an Electrician").

Whenever you turn the circuit breaker off or on, use only one hand and look away from the breaker to reduce the risk of injury should the breaker blow.

### Things You'll Need

☐ screwdriver

☐ replacement light switch

☐ coloured pens or tape

---

## Replace the Mains Cable on a Lamp            222

Replacing a lamp's electrical cable is often easier and safer than repairing it. Repaired cable is more likely to have loose connections or bad splices, which can cause fires or shocks.

⊙ **Steps**

1  Unplug the lamp. Remove the lamp shade and remove the lightbulb from the socket.

2  Unscrew or snap the socket from the lamp – you may need to use a screwdriver to gently prise the socket-shell base from the socket shell.

3  Unscrew the two wires from the socket's base.

4  Pull the wires off the screws, and then pull the cable out of the lamp from the bottom.

### ✳ Tip

When replacing a defective cable, also replace the plug (see 223 "Replace a Plug").

### ⚠ Warning

It is potentially dangerous to work with electricity. If you are unsure, call an electrician (see 259 "Hire an Electrician").

5  Push the new electrical cable into the lamp from the bottom up. Push slowly and evenly to avoid getting the wire stuck, particularly if the lamp is long.

6  Pull through a section of the new cable once it appears at the top of the lamp; it should be long enough to work with comfortably.

7  Separate the cable's two wires with a razor blade or craft knife, cutting 5 to 10 cm (2 to 4 inches) down the centre of the cable.

8  Strip about 2.5 cm (1 in) of insulation from the separated wire ends with a wire stripper. (Do not cut towards yourself, and take care not to pinch the palm of your hand.) Make sure there are no other nicks or cuts elsewhere on the cable.

9  Twist the ends of each exposed wire clockwise so they don't fray, then curl each into a small hook.

10  Place one hook over each screw in the socket, wrapping the wire in a clockwise direction (this will help ensure a snug fit under the screw).

11  Make sure the wires won't come into contact with each other, then tighten the screws.

12  Put the lamp back together: first screw in the socket; then replace the bulb and shade.

### Things You'll Need

- ☐ screwdriver
- ☐ replacement electrical cable
- ☐ razor blade or craft knife
- ☐ wire stripper

## 223 | Replace a Plug

**Instead of discarding lamps, appliances or extension cables with a damaged plug, follow these steps to replace the plug.**

### ⊙ Steps

1  Buy a replacement plug. These can be bought at any hardware shop or DIY store. If you have any doubts about the exact type of plug that you need, cut the old one off and take it and a short portion of the cable with you.

2  Select a heavy-duty plug; it may cost a little extra, but will last much longer.

3  Open up the outside cover of the replacement plug. It will have a screw or two holding it closed.

4  Cut off the old plug. Strip each wire in the cable using a wire stripper (if you don't have one, any sharp knife will do the business). Only 1 to 2 cm ($^1/_2$ to $^3/_4$ in) of bare wire is needed.

5  Look inside the opened plug and identify which of the three pins is Earth, which is Live and which is Neutral. This is always indicated in some clear way, typically by the letters E, L and N embossed on the inside of the plug alongside the appropriate pins.

5  Attach one wire under the screws at the end of each of the three plug pins. The green and yellow wire goes to the Earth pin, the brown wire to Live and the blue wire to Neutral.

6  Put the cover back on and snap or screw it into place. Your cable is ready to be plugged in.

### ⚠ Warning

Make sure that no bare wires make contact with anything other than the attachment they're supposed to be touching.

### Things You'll Need

- ☐ replacement plug
- ☐ screwdriver
- ☐ wire stripper

## Replace an Electrical Socket 224

You can fix a faulty electrical socket with a minimum of worry and cost. Just make sure that you put safety first.

### ⊙ Steps

1 Turn off the power switch at the main circuit breaker or fuse box. Make sure that everyone affected by the loss of power knows what you are doing. For extra security, put a notice near the circuit box so that no one mistakenly turns the power back on while you're working.

2 Test the socket with a circuit tester or an electrical appliance to make sure the power is off. Place the tester's probes inside the plug. If the tester's light goes on, check the mains until there's no power in the outlet.

3 Unscrew the cover plate and remove it.

4 Unscrew the socket and pull it away from the wall.

5 Using coloured pens or tape, mark where each wire was attached to the socket. The wires and screws should be different colours; note the places where they attach.

6 Loosen the screws holding the wires and remove the socket.

7 Take the existing socket with you to a DIY, hardware or electrical shop. A salesperson will be able to help you find the correct replacement. Keep the old socket as a guide to installing the new one.

8 Using the marks you made on the old socket as guides, attach the wires to the new socket. Wrap the wires around the terminals with needle-nose pliers or your fingers.

9 Tighten the screws around the wires.

10 Screw the socket back into the wall.

11 Screw the cover plate back on.

12 Reactivate the mains at the fuse box and test your work.

### ✳ Tip

Don't overtighten the cover plate, or you may cause it to crack.

### ⚠ Warnings

Working with electrical systems is potentially dangerous. If you're unsure of your abilities or about any aspect of the project, call an electrician (see 259 "Hire an Electrician")

Whenever you turn the circuit breaker off or on, use only one hand and look away from the breaker to reduce the risk of injury should the breaker blow.

### Things You'll Need

☐ circuit tester

☐ screwdriver

☐ coloured pens and tape

☐ replacement electrical socket

☐ needle-nose pliers

---

## Lubricate Door Hinges 225

If your door gives you a squeaky greeting each time you open or close it, apply a bit of oil to the hinge.

### ⊙ Steps

1 Buy some penetrating oil (WD40 is good for this). It will come in either a small can with a thin spout, or a spray can with a thin plastic tube that attaches to the nozzle for very accurate spraying.

2 Have a rag or paper towel handy to wipe off excess oil.

3 Apply oil to the round pin located between the flat plates of a hinge. (When the door is open, the pin is halfway between the door itself and the side post. The pin holds the plates together.) It's best to open the door and pull the pin halfway out of the hinge. Apply the oil into the exposed hole and onto the pin itself.

### ✳ Tip

Rusty hinges should be replaced.

### Things You'll Need

☐ penetrating oil

☐ rag or paper towel

4   Open and close the door until the hinge stops squeaking. Apply small amounts of oil at first, increasing the amount if squeaking persists.

5   Push the hinge pin back into its original position.

6   Wipe away any excess or dripped oil with your rag or paper towel.

## 226 | Maintain Windows

Maintaining the windows in your home is relatively painless and can save you money on heating, cooling and repair work later on.

### ⊙Steps

### Maintaining Wood-Frame Windows

1   Start with a visual inspection of the window-panes and the putty that holds the glass in place. Cracked panes and missing putty allow drafts. Replace broken panes or repair the putty (see 227 "Replace a Broken Window-Pane").

2   Look at the paintwork. If it is badly chipped, cracked or chalky to the touch, you will need to paint the exterior woodwork. A poor paint job allows moisture to penetrate the wood, causing rot and swelling – which in turn causes more paint damage.

3   Inspect where the window casing meets the wall. Use a high-quality paintable latex sealant to fill any gaps or cracks between the window frame and the siding or brick.

4   Make sure that the windows seal tightly when closed. If they are loose, you may need to add weather stripping around the window channels.

### Maintaining Metal- or Vinyl-Frame Windows

1   Start with a visual inspection of the window and frames. Rubber seals hold the glass in place. If the seals deteriorate over time, you'll have an air or water leak. The window sash will have to be removed from the unit and taken to a glass-repair shop to have the rubber replaced. You may need to call a professional to remove the window.

2   Check for cracked or broken glass, which should also be replaced by professionals at a glass shop.

3   Look for moisture between panes of glass if you have double-glazed windows. Moisture indicates that the seal between the panes has been penetrated. The space between the panes is usually filled with a gas to help provide insulation; if the seal is broken, the insulation value of the window is less effective.

4   Check around the window casing where it meets the wall; fill any gaps with a paintable latex sealant.

5   Make sure that any weather stripping is in good condition – you can find it seated in a groove in the window frame. Remove a short section of it from the window to take with you to the repair shop to find the right replacement. Remember to take measurements so that you get enough to do all the repairs needed.

### ✱ Tip

Window putty now comes in a tube that fits a sealant gun. The tip is designed to form beads of putty as you work.

### ⚠ Warnings

When working with broken glass, wear leather gloves and eye protection.

If your house is two or more stories tall, work carefully on ladders.

### Things You'll Need

☐ latex sealant and sealant gun

☐ weather stripping

## Replace a Broken Window-Pane  `227`

Do you have windows that are letting in more air than they should? With a little patience and care you can repair a broken window-pane – it's easier than you might think.

### ⊙ Steps

1  Remove the old glass carefully, wearing gloves and safety goggles. Using a chisel, chip out the old putty around the window and carefully remove the glazing brads (small metal tacks used to anchor the glass in place under the putty, also known as sprigs), so you can take out the glass. You may need to soften the putty with a heat gun or even a hair dryer on a high heat setting.

2  Measure the opening, then subtract 0.3 to 0.5 cm ( $1/8$ to $3/16$ inch) from the vertical and horizontal measurements. You don't want the glass to be jammed tightly in the opening.

3  Purchase new glass with the appropriate dimensions. Any glass shop and many DIY shops can cut glass to the size you need.

4  Set your new glass in place, and use at least two glazing brads on each side – more if the opening is larger than about 30 cm (12 in) square. Be careful that you don't press too hard against the glass, or you may break it.

5  Work the putty against the glass and the window frame. Smooth it down with a putty knife or a glazing knife, which looks like a putty knife with a bent end.

6  Let the window set for 24 hours before opening it.

7  Paint the putty to protect it, following the directions the putty came with. Some manufacturers suggest waiting for several days or even longer before painting.

### ✱ Tip

Large window-panes, or broken or cracked window-panes in metal or vinyl frames, should be left to the pros.

### ⚠ Warning

Be careful with broken glass, and dispose of it properly.

### Things You'll Need

- ☐ gloves
- ☐ safety goggles
- ☐ small chisel
- ☐ heat gun or hair dryer
- ☐ replacement glass
- ☐ glazing brads
- ☐ window putty
- ☐ putty knife or glazing knife
- ☐ paint

---

## Use a Sealant Gun  `228`

Using a sealant gun is the easiest way to seal against air and water. Use sealant to fill cracks between wood trim and your walls, inside the house and outside.

### ⊙ Steps

1  Clean the area to be sealed, removing dirt, loose paint and old sealant. Be sure the area is dry before you begin.

2  Load a tube of sealant into a sealant gun, making sure it's well seated at both ends.

3  Use a craft knife to cut the tip of the spout. Cut off as little as possible, taking into consideration the size of the "bead" of sealant you need. Some people like to cut the spout at an angle, while others cut it straight; it doesn't make much difference.

### ✱ Tips

There are many types of sealant available, including silicone, acrylic and latex. Silicone sealant is probably the longest-lasting, but does not take paint well.

Keep a bowl of water at hand. Dip your finger in the water before running it down the bead of sealant.

4 Hold the gun at a slight angle. If you're filling a crack, insert the spout if you can; otherwise, run it at the surface.

5 Pull away from the bead slightly as you squeeze out the sealant, rather than push into it, which can be very messy. Use just enough sealant to do the job. (Experiment in an unexposed area. You may find that you'll need less of a bead than you think.)

6 Use your finger to gently press the sealant into the corner or crack.

7 Use a damp towel or rag to clean off most of the excess sealant, then use a dry one to clean off the rest.

### Things You'll Need

- ❏ sealant and sealant gun
- ❏ craft knife
- ❏ nail or awl
- ❏ towels or rags

## 229 Re-Grout and Re-Seal Ceramic Tiles

**Is the grouting on your tiles badly stained or cracked? You can have it looking like new in no time.**

### ⊙ Steps

1 Buy a mildew-resistant grout – make sure it's the same colour as your existing grout. Some grouts are pre-mixed; for others, just follow the instructions on the box. You'll also need grout sealer.

2 Prise out old grout with a craft knife. Work carefully to avoid chipping or dislodging tiles. It's a good idea to wear safety goggles for this job.

3 Vacuum or brush dust and dirt from grout lines.

4 Work the grout into joints with a grout float. If you are only repairing a small area, use your finger. Wipe excess grout from the joint with a damp sponge, smoothing the grout to match existing joints. Clean any grout from the tops of the tiles with the sponge. Rinse your sponge often to speed the cleaning process.

5 Allow the grout to dry (this usually takes several hours at least, but overnight may be best).

6 Brush grout sealer onto the new dry grout. Sealing grout prevents it from absorbing water.

### ✱ Tip

If grout lines have cracked in wet areas, water may have seeped through to the plaster beneath. Allow this to dry thoroughly before re-grouting

### Things You'll Need

- ❏ grout
- ❏ grout sealer
- ❏ craft knife
- ❏ vacuum cleaner or dust brush
- ❏ grout float
- ❏ sponge
- ❏ brush

# ✓ 230 Do Preventive Home Maintenance

The best way to reduce home-repair costs and headaches is to perform preventative tasks on a regular basis. If you inspect your home regularly and keep everything in working condition, you'll cut down on repairs and nip emerging problems in the bud. Use this schedule to stay on top of home maintenance.

## Once a month

- Clear leaves and other debris from the path in front of your home.
- Scrub off any algae or moss from the path.
- Test the batteries in your smoke and carbon monoxide detectors.
- Pour a tablespoon full of baking soda down all drains, followed shortly afterward by a cup of vinegar. Let it stand overnight, then flush with hot water.
- Check fire extinguishers to see that they are still fully charged.

## Every three months

- Check for cracks in any masonry or stucco on the outside of your home. Seal cracks immediately.
- Check washing machine and dishwasher areas for leaks.
- Clean the filter in the cooker hood.
- Make sure attic vents are open to allow air to escape.
- Drain an electric water heater.

## Every six months

- Scrub off any mildew on the exterior of your home.
- Check for water and air leaks in the attic, basement and garage.
- Check the sealant in baths, showers and sinks, and replace it if necessary.
- Check for wood decay.
- Check that the TV aerial/satellite dish is secure.
- Look for any signs of rodent activity.
- Nail down any loose tiles or siding.
- Touch up the paint on the exterior of the house.

## Once a year

- Hire someone to inspect your chimney and clean it if necessary.
- Clean out gutters and drainpipes; clear any debris from the roof.
- Inspect the roof for damage.
- Check the seals on windows and doors, and weather-strip if needed.
- Have someone service your heating (and cooling) systems.
- Replace batteries in smoke and carbon monoxide detectors.
- Inspect flooring for wear; refinish or replace if needed.

calendar

## 231 | Choose the Right Adhesive for a Job

**Different glues are needed for different tasks; making the wrong choice may result in disaster.**

### ⊙ Steps

1   Read the labels. Make sure that the brand you choose is compatible with your purpose.

2   Consider the work surface. Is it porous or smooth? Wood, plaster, paper and cloth are porous; glass, metal, ceramic and plastic are not. Cyanoacrylate ("superglue") and white glue adhere to smooth, non-porous surfaces; hot glue and carpenter's (wood) glue are better for porous surfaces. Contact cement is suitable for both porous and non-porous work surfaces.

3   Decide how quickly you want the adhesive to dry. Superglue bonds instantly; hot glue is quick; water-based contact cement will stick immediately and should be dry within 30 minutes; white and carpenter's (wood) glues take a few hours; silicone sealant requires about 24 hours to cure; epoxies (heat-solidifying resins) vary.

4   Determine whether it needs to be water and/or heat resistant. Two-part epoxy, superglue, water-based contact cement and silicone sealant are resistant to both. Hot glue doesn't hold up well under extreme heat, but is waterproof. Carpenter's glue holds up under moisture and heat, whereas white glue doesn't fare well when exposed to either.

5   Think about cleaning. Silicone sealant, superglue and two-part epoxy can be cleaned up with acetone – which is flammable and toxic. Water-based contact cement, new water-based silicone sealers, carpenter's glues and white glues can be cleaned up with water.

### ✳ Tip

Latex-based products are nonflammable and far less toxic than solvent-based ones.

### ⚠ Warning

Always read all warning labels, and glue in well-ventilated areas.

## 232 | Patch a Vinyl Floor

**You can repair or replace vinyl sheet flooring and vinyl tiles with excellent results if you know the proper technique.**

### ⊙ Steps

1   Measure the damaged area.

2   Find a DIY store or floor-covering store that sells the pattern of vinyl flooring you need. Purchase enough sheeting or tile squares to repair the damaged area. (It's always a good idea to keep any scraps for future repairs.)

3   Use a sharp craft knife to cut a piece of new vinyl flooring that is larger than the damaged area if you're repairing sheet vinyl flooring. Use a straightedge to keep the blade vertical. Replace whole squares if you're using standard-sized tiles.

4   Line up the pattern of the new piece with the pattern along the edges of the damaged area.

5   Tape the replacement piece of vinyl over the damaged area with masking tape. (Make sure the new piece is secure and will not slip when cutting.)

### ✳ Tip

The cleaner the floor under the patch, the smoother the finished job will be. Raised areas will wear faster than the rest of the floor.

### ⚠ Warnings

Some adhesives can give off potentially harmful vapours, so always provide proper ventilation in your work area.

Always make sure to cut away from your body when cutting vinyl flooring.

6   Use a sharp craft knife to cut through both layers of vinyl. Cut an area just larger than the damaged spot. (This way the hole and replacement piece will be the same size.)

7   Remove both pieces of vinyl. Heat the old vinyl with a hair dryer to soften the adhesive before prying it up.

8   Clean debris and old adhesive from the floor with a putty knife. You can soften the old adhesive with a heat gun or hair dryer. Use a broom or vacuum cleaner for final cleaning.

9   Apply adhesive to the floor with a notched trowel or putty knife.

10  Press the new patch firmly in place starting at the centre and working towards the edges to get all the air bubbles out from under the patch.

11  Wipe excess glue from the edges with a damp sponge.

12  Roll the patch firmly with a rolling pin or hand roller. Wipe the edges again to remove any excess glue.

13  Let the adhesive dry well before allowing heavy traffic back in the repaired area.

### Things You'll Need

- ☐ measuring tape
- ☐ replacement vinyl flooring
- ☐ craft knife
- ☐ masking tape
- ☐ putty knife
- ☐ heat gun or hair dryer (optional)
- ☐ adhesive
- ☐ notched trowel (optional)
- ☐ sponge
- ☐ rolling pin or hand roller

## Replace Slate Roof Tiles                    233

You may not need a new roof, but replacing a few bad or missing tiles to avoid water damage can save you money later on.

### ⊙ Steps

1   Make sure the roof is dry before you climb on to it and that any ladder you use is sturdy and well-secured.

2   Check your roof at least twice a year and after bad storms, and look for loose, damaged or missing tiles.

3   Prise up a tile above one of the damaged ones, lifting it just enough to allow you to remove the damaged slate. Remove all the damaged slates in this way.

4   Cover the exposed area of roof with a piece of heavy plastic sheeting (a thick bin liner may do). Push the sheeting gently under the tiles above the damaged area and weight the other edges with bricks or stones.

5   Count the damaged tiles to tell how many you will need. Take one of the tiles with you to a builder's merchant to match colour and style.

6   Climb onto the roof. Test fit one of the new tiles in the space where an old one used to be.

7   Mark two nail holes on the replacement tile while it's in test position, as far under the upper tiles as you'll be able to reach when you come to hammer it into place.

8   Take the tile down to the ground with you and drill the nail holes.

9   Slide the new tile into place and nail it down with a hammer.

10  Slide a piece of felt under the upper tiles to cover the nail heads.

11  Repeat this process for all replacement tiles.

12  Make sure you remove any debris from the roof and gutters.

### ✳ Tip

Buy a few more slates than you strictly need, as you may suffer some wastage during the replacement process.

### ⚠ Warning

If you have a steep roof or a fear of heights, call in professionals. They have suitable equipment and experience to handle the toughest jobs.

### Things You'll Need

- ☐ ladder
- ☐ hammer
- ☐ tiles
- ☐ drill
- ☐ nails
- ☐ felt
- ☐ plastic sheeting

## 234 | Clean Gutters

Water trapped in gutters can cause major damage to your roof and walls. Maintaining clean gutters helps keep your home in good shape.

### ⊙ Steps

1. Gain access to the roof with a ladder. Don't lean the ladder against a drainpipe or gutter, which can easily bend or break.

2. Remove leaves and twigs from gutters by hand or with a large spoon, a gutter scoop or a small garden trowel.

3. Caked-on dirt can be difficult to remove without damaging the gutter. Dampen it and then remove with the gutter scoop or trowel.

4. Put debris in a bucket or plastic bin liner placed on the roof or ladder. If you use a bin liner, you can just drop it when it's full.

5. Check that the drainpipes aren't also clogged. Use water to unclog them by placing a garden hose in the opening. Be gentle at first; drainpipes aren't designed to withstand the same pressure as a house drain. If a plugged drainpipe can't be cleared with a hose, use a small plumber's snake or an unbent clothes hanger. Again, be gentle. Gutters are not as strong as house pipes.

6. Alternatively, use a leaf blower to clean the gutters; remember that you'll be high up – often in awkward postures – and carrying a piece of equipment that not only is awkward to use but also can blind you with dust.

7. Use the hose to flush the gutters with water after cleaning. (This is also the best time to find out if there are any leaks in the system.)

### ✱ Tip

Consider covering your gutters with wire or plastic mesh. This will cut down on debris.

### ⚠ Warnings

Never hold on to the gutter or drainpipe for support. They're not meant to support your weight.

Make sure the ladder is sturdy and well-secured.

### Things You'll Need

☐ ladder

☐ large spoon, gutter scoop or small garden trowel

☐ bucket or bin liner

☐ garden hose

☐ leaf blower (optional)

## 235 | Repair a Leaky Gutter

You can fix minor gutter leaks with roofing cement. Leaks in the drainpipe – often caused by leaky joints – require resealing.

### ⊙ Steps

#### Repairing Leaks in Gutter Railings

1. Clean the leaking area with a wire brush and water.

2. Dry the area and rub with coarse sandpaper.

3. Cover the hole with plastic roofing cement. Spread the cement at least 5 to 8 cm (2 to 3 in) around the hole.

4. Cover with a piece of flashing (sheet metal) if you're dealing with a large hole; press the flashing into the cement and feather the edges of the cement to hold the flashing in place.

#### Repairing Leaks in Drainpipes

1. Remove the leaking portion of the drainpipe.

### Things You'll Need

☐ wire brush

☐ coarse sandpaper

☐ plastic roofing cement

☐ flashing

☐ rubber gaskets

☐ silicone sealant

☐ gutter fasteners or connectors

**How to Do *(Just About)* Everything**

2   Clean old sealant or adhesive from the joint with a wire brush.

3   Replace rubber gaskets if you're dealing with vinyl or PVC gutters.

4   Apply a bead of silicone sealant on one joint and then put the gutter back together.

5   Re-attach the gutter with new fasteners or connectors if needed.

## Repair Wallpaper 236

Torn or damaged wallpaper can be repaired if you have extra wallpaper that matches the pattern. Here's how to make and apply a patch.

### ◉ Steps

1   With a craft knife, cut a piece of wallpaper a few inches larger than the damaged section.

2   Place it over the damaged section and hold it in place with "safety" masking tape, making sure that you match the pattern.

3   Use a sharp razor blade to trace the area to be removed, cutting right through both pieces of wallpaper at the same time. Try to make your cuts follow the pattern as best you can. (If possible, align your repairs along a seam.)

4   Carefully remove the top piece of paper and set it aside.

5   Use the razor to lightly score the wallpaper to be removed and apply water to loosen the adhesive (see 265 "Remove Wallpaper").

6   Use a putty knife to remove what you can't lift off with your fingers.

7   Clean or sand the area underneath the paper until it's smooth; use spackling compound to fill any dents. Apply primer (sizing) if you're down to a raw surface on the wall.

8   Apply wall-covering adhesive to the new wallpaper and place it on the wall.

9   Wipe away any adhesive on the surface with a damp sponge, then use a seam roller (see 266 "Hang Wallpaper") to press down the edges of the patch. Wipe the paper clean again.

### ✳ Tip

Repair a small tear by brushing on some wallpaper adhesive (or even white glue) and pressing the wallpaper back down. Repair a wrinkle or blister by slitting it with a razor and treating it as you would a tear.

### Things You'll Need

- ☐ craft knife
- ☐ replacement wallpaper
- ☐ "safety" masking tape
- ☐ sharp razor blade
- ☐ putty knife
- ☐ sandpaper
- ☐ spackling compound or primer
- ☐ wall-covering adhesive
- ☐ sponge
- ☐ seam roller

## Prepare a Room for Painting 237

It's all in the preparation. Take the time – probably more than you actual spend painting – to get the best results.

### ◉ Steps

1   Remove what furniture you can; move what's left into the centre of the room and cover with dust sheets. Use removable "safety" masking tape around mouldings, doors and windows, and dust sheets to protect floors and furnishings.

### ✳ Tip

Old blankets and duvet covers make excellent furniture covers when decorating.

2  Cover the smoke detector with a plastic bag and turn off heating while sanding or painting.

3  Sand or scrape loose and flaky paint with sandpaper and paint scrapers – down to bare surfaces if necessary.

4  Using a putty knife, fill all nail and screw holes using "plastic wood" or all-purpose filler; fill larger cracks with sealant. On woodwork, use epoxy filler (like that used on car bodies). Whatever you use, sand it down until it matches the area around it.

5  Wash all surfaces with sugar soap or a detergent solution to remove grease and dirt.

6  Rinse everything well with water to remove the sugar soap or detergent. Allow surfaces to dry thoroughly, and then dust and vacuum as needed.

7  Turn off the power to the room, then remove the cover plates from all electrical fixtures, outlets and switches. Place small pieces of masking tape over switch handles and sockets to protect them from paint. It's safest to leave the power off as you paint the room – if you decide to turn the power back on, work carefully around electrical areas.

8  Loosen or remove cover plates from all the light fixtures; cover what remains with plastic bags. Remember not to turn on the lights – melting plastic can smell terrible. Paint during the day to get maximum lighting in the room, or use an extension cable to bring in a light source from another room.

9  Remove heating vent covers.

## ⚠ Warning

If your home was built before 1980, it may contain lead paint. This is especially dangerous to children and pregnant women. Look on the Defra web pages for further information (www.defra. gov.uk/environment/chemicals/lead).

## Things You'll Need

- ☐ dust sheets
- ☐ "safety" masking tape
- ☐ plastic bags
- ☐ sandpaper
- ☐ paint scraper
- ☐ plastic wood/all-purpose filler
- ☐ putty knife
- ☐ sealant and sealant gun
- ☐ epoxy filler
- ☐ sugar soap or detergent

---

## 238 | Paint a Room

**To paint a room, start with the ceiling and then paint the walls. Finish with the trim.**

### ◎ Steps

1  Prepare the walls and ceiling (see 237 "Prepare a Room for Painting"). Use a stain-blocking primer to cover any dark mark you can't remove (stains, knots, ink, dark paint); otherwise, that area will bleed through. Never paint on wallpaper (see 265 "Remove Wallpaper").

2  Make sure there is adequate ventilation in the room.

3  Plan on three coats: one coat of primer and two coats of finish. Always use primer on patched and unpainted surfaces; raw surfaces suck up paint like a sponge – or even reject it altogether.

4  Paint into all the corners with a standard 5- or 8-cm (2- or 3-in) brush. Use the same brush to outline where the ceiling meets the wall (and vice versa), around doors and windows, above the baseboard and around any other trim or detailing – and wherever a roller won't fit.

5  Pour some paint into the roller pan and roll away on the ceiling and then the walls. Pour only a small amount of paint in your roller pan – this will keep the paint from drying out before you can use it.

### ✱ Tip

If you have mildew, consider adding a specially designed primer – or other additive – to your paint.

### ⚠ Warning

If you use anything other than water-based latex paint, never put paint-soaked or cleaner-soaked tools or rags in an enclosed area of any kind – even a metal dustbin with a lid. This is a recipe for spontaneous combustion.

6   Start rolling before the brushed-on paint has had time to dry, so that the rolled-on paint will blend in rather than become a second coat. Rolling out a "W", about 1 m (37 in) wide, and then filling it in, assures an even application of paint. Get as close into the corners as you can without making a messy paint line.

7   Paint from dry areas into wet. This will help reduce any paint ridges. Feather (thin out) all edges as you go, whether using a brush or a roller; this will also help reduce ridges.

8   Cover cans or buckets when you're not using them. Keep a rag and brush handy to deal with drips, spills and the general messiness of the process. If a drip becomes too dry to spread out, let it dry. Come back later, sand it and paint over it.

## Things You'll Need

- ❏ stain-blocking primer
- ❏ primer
- ❏ paint or finish
- ❏ 5- or 8 cm (2- or 3-in) brush
- ❏ paint roller
- ❏ roller pan
- ❏ rags
- ❏ sandpaper

---

# Paint Around Windows                                           239

As with all painting jobs, the more preparation you do now, the less work you'll have to do later. And of course the window will look nicer, too.

## ◉ Steps

1   Look for loose, flaky paint and remove it with a paint scraper and/or sander – all the way down to the wood if necessary. Sand down the areas you plan to paint.

2   If you're going to paint the outside of the window as well, check the putty between the glass and the frame. This seals the window and holds the glass in place – if it's cracked or crumbling, then you will need to replace it.

3   Check the outside for other areas where water could enter between the window frame and the house – or even within the window itself – and seal as necessary.

4   Remove or tape over all the hardware you can, such as locks, handles, latches or hinges.

5   Put masking tape on the glass next to the surface you're going to paint. It makes cleaning up easier.

6   Use primer if you've exposed any raw surfaces. Choose a primer which is appropriate to your surface – wood or metal require different paints.

7   Follow up with a coat of eggshell or gloss paint. It's durable and easy to clean.

8   Use an angled paintbrush and work from the top down. Paint the window frame first, then the trim on the wall around it. Make sure you don't paint windows shut (see Tips).

9   Scrape off any paint that has strayed onto the glass with a purpose-made razor blade – leave it until the paint has dried at least enough to be tacky. Gently run the blade, edge first, between the painted surface and the glass, then lay it flat (like a spatula) to scrape the rest of the paint off the glass.

## ✽ Tips

If you have sash windows (windows slide up and down behind each other), paint each window separately, allowing one to dry before painting the other, and leave them open a bit while drying so they don't stick to each other or the frames. Don't paint the vertical grooves on the side where the windows actually slide.

Vinyl-covered windows cannot be painted with anything at all.

## Things You'll Need

- ❏ paint scraper or sander
- ❏ putty
- ❏ sealant and sealant gun
- ❏ masking tape
- ❏ primer
- ❏ eggshell or gloss paint
- ❏ angled paintbrush
- ❏ razor blade

## 240 | Paint the Exterior of a House

This may be the most important painting (and preparation) you do. Paint and preparation vary with the type of surface: wood, stucco, metal, masonry. Check with your DIY store.

### ⊙ Steps

1  Consider the weather: You'll want to avoid extreme temperatures, wind and wet weather. Never paint right after it rains, as surfaces will be too wet. Always try to paint in the shade, as direct sunlight can cause the paint to blister. The temperate conditions of autumn and spring are usually best for painting outside.

2  Repair or replace any damaged surfaces, whether wood, stucco, masonry or metal.

3  Wash all surfaces with TSP (trisodium phosphate) and rinse thoroughly with water. Or use a pressure washer to reduce work (these can be hired easily enough). Make sure that surfaces dry thoroughly.

4  Use sandpaper or a paint scraper to remove any loose, cracked, chipping or blistered paint – down to raw surfaces if necessary. Use a small cloth to catch loose bits of paint and debris. If you decide the exterior needs to be sandblasted, hire a licensed professional.

5  Patch all nail or screw holes, gouges and cracks.

6  Seal such places as seams and corners, above door and window trim, and where trim meets siding – or where any material meets a different kind of material, such as trim over masonry. (Exception: Don't use sealant where siding or tiles overlap, or between tiles.) Always use high-grade exterior sealant. Better-quality sealants (such as silicone) actually bond to surfaces like glue and resist breaking down.

7  Use epoxy filler (the material used for car bodies) to repair more serious problems in woodwork.

8  Cover dark stains – for example, a wood knot, old paint, a wood stain – with a stain-blocking primer. The same goes for mildewed areas; you can find primers and additives made especially for mildew.

9  Sand all patched, raw and glossy surfaces; all paints need a slightly roughened surface to stick to. You can also use paint de-glosser on glossy surfaces. Remove sanding dust and debris.

10  Remove or cover all light fixtures, plumbing outlets, electrical covers and house numbers.

11  Remove all screens. You don't want to get paint on them; it's difficult (or impossible) to remove.

12  Place dust covers over everything you don't want to paint, such as plants, paths, cars and your neighbours' property.

13  Apply primer over all raw surfaces. Note that different surfaces – paint, metal, wood, stucco – require different types of primer.

14  Allow the primer to dry, then apply at least two coats of exterior paint. Let each coat dry between applications according to the manufacturer's instructions. Use a brush on all woodwork and a paint roller or spray machine for everything else.

### ❋ Tip

You can't paint vinyl or plastic. If there's a problem with any of these surfaces, you'll probably have to replace them.

### ⚠ Warnings

If your home was built before 1980, it may contain lead paint. This is especially dangerous to children and pregnant women. Look on the Defra web pages for further information (www.defra. gov.uk/environment/chemicals/ lead).

If you're using anything other than water-based latex, never put paint-soaked or cleaner-soaked tools or rags in an enclosed area of any kind – even a metal dustbin with a lid. This is a recipe for spontaneous combustion.

### Things You'll Need

- ☐ sandpaper
- ☐ paint scraper
- ☐ sealant and sealant gun
- ☐ epoxy filler
- ☐ stain-blocking primer
- ☐ paint de-glosser
- ☐ cloths
- ☐ dust covers
- ☐ primer
- ☐ paintbrushes
- ☐ exterior paint
- ☐ paint roller or sprayer

## Repair Concrete

Other than earth movement, moisture is the main cause of cracks in concrete. Here's how to deal with moisture damage.

### ⊙ Steps

1  Clean out cracks of any size as best you can, using a wire brush or even a strong spray of water.

2  Fill small cracks with sealant specially made for concrete. (Be sure cracks are dry before sealing.)

3  Fill larger cracks or small holes using patching products designed for use with concrete. These usually take the form of a powder that is mixed with water. They typically expand as they dry and become very hard.

4  Apply sealant or paint to the concrete.

### ✱ Tip

Patching compounds generally work better if the crack is damp or wet.

### Things You'll Need

☐ wire brush

☐ concrete sealant

☐ concrete patch product

☐ sealant

## Repair Masonry

Before you attempt to fix a serious crack in a brick, block or stone wall, determine the cause of the crack. This may be a job for a professional.

### ⊙ Steps

1  Look closely where you see cracks forming.

2  Suspect moisture as the culprit if the cracks appear in the mortar along the joints of the bricks, blocks or stonework.

3  See if you can find out where the moisture is coming from and look into ways to stop it. Remember that unless you treat the cause, the repair will only be temporary.

4  You should consult a professional builder or structural engineer if the bricks themselves are cracked – there could be foundation problems. If it's just one brick, it may be defective, and you can replace it.

5  Contact a professional builder or structural engineer if the crack is long and continuous. This type of crack indicates movement of the wall.

6  If the cracks appear along the joints of the bricks, re-pointing may be necessary. If the repair is fairly small, you may be able to do it yourself without having to call in a professional.

7  Use a cold chisel and mallet to knock out the mortar to a depth of about 1 to 2 cm ($\frac{1}{2}$ to $\frac{5}{8}$ in).

8  Wet the area thoroughly with a hose. The brick should be soaked so that it won't leach the water from the mortar and cause it to crumble.

9  Mix your mortar in a shallow bucket: one part cement, one part lime, six parts builders' sand. Alternatively, consider buying pre-mixed mortar if the repair is small.

### ✱ Tip

Be careful not to get mortar on the brick faces.

### Things You'll Need

☐ cold chisel

☐ mallet

☐ garden hose

☐ shallow bucket

☐ cement

☐ lime

☐ builders' sand

☐ pointing trowel

☐ mortarboard

10  Scoop a little bit of mortar with a pointing trowel and create a small cylindrical shape with it.

11  Press this cylinder into the area between the bricks. Hold a mortarboard or piece of cardboard under the area where you're working to catch falling mortar – it takes some practice to keep the mortar in the groove.

---

## 243 | Repair Stucco

Stucco can look great – unless it has a long, ugly crack running through it. Here's how to get it back into tip-top shape.

### ⊙ Steps

1  Note the direction of the crack. Vertical cracks from base to window or roof to door sometimes indicate a problem with the foundation. Before fixing the crack, call a foundation specialist to determine the condition of the foundation.

2  Fix very small cracks by filling them with a high-quality sealant – preferably one that can be painted over. Use your fingers to press it in well, and a damp cloth to clean up.

3  Use a cold chisel or an old screwdriver to clean out wider cracks.

4  Soak the area thoroughly with a hose so that the stucco won't absorb the water from the new mortar and cause it to crumble.

5  Mix your mortar in a shallow bucket: one part cement, four parts builders' sand and a little bit of water to make the mortar workable but not runny.

6  Cover the area to be patched with a polyvinyl acetate (PVA) bonding agent made for masonry.

7  When the bond is slightly tacky, fill the crack with the mortar mix.

8  Cover the patched area with a piece of bitumen-coated fibreglass. (Bitumen is a tar-like substance.)

9  Use a paint roller to press it into place, and apply a coat of bitumen over the patch.

10  Let the bitumen dry and then apply another coat, stippling it with a soft-bristled brush to match the rest of the wall.

11  Paint over the area with a primer made for stucco or bitumen patching. Allow the primer to dry.

12  Repaint the area – but be aware that you may have to repaint the entire wall so that the patch won't stand out.

### Things You'll Need

- ☐ sealant
- ☐ damp cloth
- ☐ cold chisel
- ☐ garden hose
- ☐ shallow bucket
- ☐ cement
- ☐ builders' sand
- ☐ PVA bonding agent
- ☐ fibreglass cloth
- ☐ bitumen
- ☐ paint roller
- ☐ soft-bristled brush
- ☐ primer
- ☐ paint

## Remove Corrosion From Aluminium                                    244

Aluminium patio furniture, window frames and other fixtures are not completely safe from corrosion. If a piece turns a dull grey and has globs of white crystals on it, it's corroded.

### Steps

1   Remove the crystals and grey discolouration using a fine wet/dry sandpaper dipped in white spirit. Don't try to polish the aluminium; simply rub it until it's bright again.

2   Wipe down the metal with a clean rag and some white spirit to remove grime and debris left from the sandpaper.

3   Allow the aluminium to dry.

4   Apply a chromate primer and allow it to dry completely.

5   Paint the aluminium or leave it with just the primer coating on it.

### Things You'll Need

☐ fine sandpaper

☐ white spirit

☐ rags

☐ chromate primer

☐ aluminum paint

## Help Keep a Cellar Dry                                              245

Most cellars can be kept free of flooding, and you can take many preventative actions yourself.

### Steps

1   Make sure the ground alongside the foundations is sloped away from the house. Your garden should be graded to direct water away to an appropriate drainage area.

2   Keep the gutters clean and free of obstructions so that water is directed away from the foundations (see 234 "Clean Gutters").

3   Seal any openings around cellar windows or doors.

4   Paint the basement walls with waterproof paint.

5   Install a sump pump that has an automatic switch.

6   Consult an established waterproofing or landscape contractor if there is a need for more serious work, such as installing underground drainage or re-grading your garden.

### Things You'll Need

☐ coalant and sealant gun

☐ waterproof paint

☐ paintbrushes

☐ sump pump

## 246 | Prepare Your Home for Winter

Some of these steps will require professional help – call early, as calendars fill up during the weeks leading up to winter.

### ⊙ Steps

1   Add a second layer of insulation to your loft. (If your house is relatively new, it is probably already suitably insulated.)

2   Seal around window and door glass and trim, and all exterior trim. Install or replace weather stripping on all doors and windows. Check for cracks around pipes entering or exiting the walls and electrical sockets.

3   Install secondary double-glazing if you have it. Consider purchasing secondary double-glazing if you have older windows that are not made from modern insulated or double-glazed glass.

4   Have your heating system checked by a licensed heating engineer. Most boiler manufacturers recommend at least annual inspections.

5   Check gutters and clean them if necessary. If there is substantial snowfall, clogged gutters can result in the basement flooding when the snow melts (see 234 "Clean Gutters").

6   Replace any roof tiles that are missing or damaged.

7   Have your chimneys inspected by a chimney service and, if necessary, cleaned (see 306 "Clean Out a Fireplace and Chimney").

8   Check the foundations for areas where water may puddle.

9   Trim trees away from the house. Have dead trees and branches removed by professional tree surgeons, or do it yourself.

10  Drain and shut off outdoor water taps.

11  Insulate any water pipes that are exposed to freezing cold.

12  Replace the batteries in smoke detectors, and check to make sure these are all in working order.

13  Check fire extinguishers and charge and replace as necessary.

14  Make sure you are stocked with salt, sand, and snow shovels if you live in an area where heavy snow is likely.

### Things You'll Need

- ☐ insulation
- ☐ sealant
- ☐ replacement weather stripping
- ☐ secondary double-glazing
- ☐ batteries
- ☐ salt
- ☐ sand
- ☐ snow shovels

## 247 | Burglarproof Your Home

Having your home burgled is a painful experience. Take these precautions to help prevent thieves getting into your house.

### ⊙ Steps

1   Keep windows closed and doors locked – don't take chances for even a few minutes. Bolt all exterior doors from the inside. Secure sliding glass doors by inserting a broomstick or dowel in the inside track.

2   Consider installing an alarm system or motion-detecting lights.

### ⚠ Warning

If you install an alarm system, learn how to use it properly to avoid false alarms.

3   Suggest that someone is at home by using electric timers to turn on the radio and house lights at certain hours. Vary the lights that you turn on.

4   Make sure that outside doors are made of metal or a sturdy wood.

5   Check to ensure that doors fit tightly in their frames. If they don't, install weather-stripping around them.

6   Etch valuables with your name and telephone number (or e-mail address) in visible places. If you don't want to ruin valuables by marking them, photograph them instead. Keep an inventory of your property.

7   Keep jewellery and other valuables in a safe.

8   Consider getting a dog – most will make enough noise to discourage burglars (see 619 "Select a Dog Breed").

9   Leave spare keys with a neighbour rather than hidden outside your house.

10  Keep shrubs and bushes trimmed so that they can't conceal prowlers.

## Replace a Lock                                    248

Replacing an existing lock – whether for security or mechanical reasons – is a relatively easy job. These instructions are for a deadlocking cylinder lock.

### ⊙ Steps

1   Take the old lock out of the door by using a screwdriver to remove the screws on the inside panel of the lock. Be sure to note how the lock comes apart.

2   Grasp the inside and outside pieces of the lock face.

3   Pull them away from the door.

4   Remove the screws from the lock-mechanism plate, which is on the edge of the door.

5   Measure the diameter of the hole in the door, or take the old lock to the hardware shop or lock shop to ensure that you purchase the proper-size replacement.

6   Place the new locking mechanism in the hole on the edge of the door.

7   Use the screws provided to attach the plate to the door edge.

8   Work the inside and outside halves of the lock cylinder into proper alignment. Secure them to the door with the screws provided.

9   Be sure that the bolt plate on the edge of the door is flush-mounted with the surface of the wood. Sometimes the hole for the plate will need to be enlarged slightly with a wood chisel.

10  Test the lock a few times from both the inside and the outside to ensure that it has been assembled properly.

### Things You'll Need

- ☐ screwdriver
- ☐ tape measure
- ☐ replacement lock
- ☐ wood chisel

## 249 | Choose a House Alarm System

Alarm systems for the home can be complex and expensive, so it's crucial to determine your security needs before you begin consulting with alarm companies.

### ⊙ Steps

#### Conducting Preliminary Research

1 Survey your home and determine how many windows and doors you want to be "switched" or integrated into the system.

2 Determine possible locations for the control panel and keypads. You might find it convenient to place a keypad close to the front door. You might also want a keypad close to the bedrooms. The control panel commands the system, and the keypads allow you to program the system and turn it, or its components, on and off.

3 Determine how far away windows and doors are from the control panel so that you know how far wires will be routed if you choose a wired alarm system or how far a wireless system needs to communicate with sensors. Keep in mind that it is difficult to install a hard-wired security system unless your house is still under construction.

4 Decide whether you want a security system that will be monitored 24 hours a day. The central monitoring station "watches" your home for a monthly fee. A less expensive alternative is a basic sensor system with a dialling accessory that connects the system to your phone lines and dials pre-selected numbers if the house's security is breached.

5 Consider your lifestyle. Does anyone in the family often get up in the middle of the night for a snack? Do you have a large pet that roams the house at night? Such circumstances will influence the type of motion sensor you select and how it is installed. It may also result in frequent trips to the keypad to prevent false alarms.

#### Choosing the System

1 Consult a reputable home security system advisor.

2 Choose a system with a control panel that can monitor all the zones you have in your home. Each window or door integrated into the system is considered a zone. A basic system is capable of controlling eight zones. However, many panels permit the addition of expansion modules that allow the system to watch up to 32 zones.

3 Determine if the routing of the wires for a hard-wired security system might be too long. With a wired system, you will have to drill holes in walls where wires will have to be routed. If the wire run appears too long to you, choose a wireless system.

4 Make certain that a wireless system can perform up to the distance of the farthest zone.

5 Be certain that the system you choose can accept fire-protection sensors, combustible-gas detectors, thermostatic switches (especially in cold climates) and water detectors. Make sure that panic buttons are or can be included.

### ✱ Tips

You may want to include some kind of alarm noisemaker. A blast of a siren or alarm bell not only alerts neighbours that an intruder is in your home, but also can scare the trespasser away.

A motion sensor outside the home can provide an early warning and, when used with a noisemaker, can discourage an intruder from entering your home.

6 Choose a system that is user-friendly. Make certain that inputting codes into the keypad is not a complicated process and is one that everyone in the family can learn quickly. You don't want to have to refer to the owner's manual as you input or try to interpret codes.

7 Work the keypad of the system you select to assure yourself that it is easy to use. Encourage all family members to work the keypad so that you will select one that everyone can use comfortably.

## Get your Loft Converted
`250`

With space at a premium in the more popular urban areas, more and more property-owners are effectively increasing the size of their homes by converting lofts into usable living space.

### ⊙ Steps

1 Loft conversion can be a complicated business. Consider what portion of the work you can realistically do yourself – doing the painting once the building work has been done, for example.

2 Loft conversions represent a significant investment, and can cost upwards of £20,000, but research shows that in the majority of cases they do add more value to the property than the initial outlay.

3 Ensure you have alternative space for items currently stored in your loft. It's easy to underestimate how much junk you've accumulated over the years when it's conveniently tucked away in the loft.

4 Building the shell of a loft conversion can take anything from four weeks to a few months to complete. If you're worried about the weather, try to get the work done in the summer.

5 There are two basic types of loft conversion: a Dormer conversion involves building an actual extension that protrudes from the roof; a Velux conversion involves putting in windows that are flush with the roof. The latter costs considerably less.

6 If the loft is intended for use as "habitable accommodation" – as an extra bedroom or home office, for example – your plans must comply with building regulations; for extensive structural alteration (most Dormer conversions) you will need planning permission from your local council.

7 For most conversion schemes, a decent building contractor will draw up the plans and carry out the work. More ambitious schemes may require the skills of an architect or structural engineer. Seek out contractors who specialise in loft conversions, and get at least three separate quotes.

8 Many people have difficulty in visualising what the end product will look like, so view previous examples of a builder's work. Before you engage a contractor, go through their quote carefully. Ensure you know exactly what you will get for your money

9 Try to have a good idea of what your finished room will look like before deciding where power sockets and light fittings will go. Mark them out on a plan and ensure your builder understands what you want.

10 Most conversions will require radiators, so check with a heating engineer whether your existing boiler will be able to cope with the extra strain on the system.

### ✳ Tips

For advice on getting planning permission take a look at www.planning.odpm.gov.uk/householders/index.htm.

### ⚠ Warning

Don't underestimate the costs involved – an average loft conversion costs about a third as much as moving to a more expensive house with an extra room. It will increase the value of your property, though.

## 251 | Build an Extension

With UK housing prices continuing to spiral ever upwards, the cost of moving up the property ladder has increased in recent years. Extending an existing property is a cost-effective way of gaining extra space without the expense of selling up and moving.

### ⊙ Steps

1   The design of your extension should be in keeping with the rest of the property. Try to match key features with those of the existing structure. Use similar materials and try to ensure doors and windows line up with existing fixtures. Avoid flat roofs if you can.

2   Your plans must comply with building regulations. You are also likely to need planning permission. If in doubt, contact the Planning Department of your local council – they will clarify exactly what you can and cannot do without their approval. (Be aware that if you go ahead without permission and are later found to have broken the law, you will certainly have to bear the cost of conforming to regulations and in extreme cases may even have to demolish your work.)

3   For most basic extensions, a good building contractor will draw up the plans and project manage the work. More ambitious schemes may require the skills of an architect.

4   Always get at least three separate quotes before choosing a contractor.

5   Building an extension is a big job. You will need to find the right experts to assist you. These will include bricklayers, carpenters, plumbers, electrician, roofers and plasterers. If in doubt, hire a contractor to project manage the work. In most cases they will recommend and find suitable tradesmen for the jobs.

6   Building work is messy, so be prepared to endure a period of dusty chaos and domestic upheaval. Ensure there is easy access for the builders to remove earth when the foundations are being dug. You should also be prepared for periods without water, gas and electricity. Keep pets and children away from the building work and use dust sheets to protect any access routes to the extension.

Think ahead. Consider such things as power points, telephone sockets and speaker cables, and plan their position *before* building begins.

### ✽ Tip

If you are looking for a local architect to plan and manage your work, take a look at www.archsearch.co.uk.

Personal recommendation is always the most reliable way of finding good skilled workmen. You can also find plenty of useful supplementary information on the official web pages of the Federation of Master Builders (www.fmb.org.uk).

### ⚠ Warnings

Be very wary if any of your chosen contractors asks for full payment up front. A deposit of 10 per cent is fair.

## 252 | Restore Original Features

Period properties are increasingly popular among home owners. And undoing years of dodgy DIY is one of the most effective ways of boosting the value of your home.

### ⊙ Steps

1   Find out as much as you can about the history of the property.

### ✽ Tip

Period design is now so popular that most of the major paint manufacturers – Dulux, Crown, Focus – produce their own "heritage" ranges.

2  Some of the original features may already be in place and simply in need of repair; others may have been lost for ever. Be prepared to tear down former owners' DIY – a cupboard or plasterboard wall may be hiding some fabulous design treasures.

2  Once you know the period and style in which your home was built, go to a university or art school library in search of research materials that might give clues to your property's original appearance. (If you live in or near London, visit the Geffrye Museum [www.geffrye-museum.org.uk] which has recreated typical English rooms from over the decades.)

3  Original Victorian and Edwardian fireplaces are widely available from architectural salvage yards. (But be prepared to pay what might seem like a lot for an item that may need further renovation.)

4  Delicate ceiling features from Georgian, Victorian and Edwardian homes will often have been lost – or blurred under decades of emulsion. Small repairs can be performed using plaster or filler, sanding or "carving" into shape when dry. However, creating the moulds for new plaster cornices and roses is a skilled art, requiring specialised labour.

5  To be as authentic as possible, study interior design fashions for the period in which your home was built. For example, Georgian homes favoured wooden wall panelling; many Victorian homes featured bold floral wall coverings and three-colour paint schemes; Edwardian styles were more restrained, with cream wall colourings the flavour of the day.

⚠ **Warnings**

Be aware that if you renovate period properties you may come into contact with old lead-based paints. These may be extremely hazardous, especially for kids and pregnant women.

## Install a New Kitchen                              253

There are many reasons for wanting new kitchen space. Not only will it make cooking more pleasurable but it will probably add to the overall value of your home.

### ⊙ Steps

1  Spend plenty of time thinking about the way you want to use your kitchen area. Is it just for cooking, or is it also for eating – or even a communal gathering space? Home interior design magazines can help you come up with ideas.

2  Consider practicalities such as gas or electrical appliances, cupboard and worktop space – even the number of power points you want in your kitchen.

3  Measure up your existing kitchen space, and draw it to scale on a piece of graph paper. Don't forget to mark important areas such as the doors, windows, mains electricity, gas, water and drain connections.

4  Visit a kitchen specialist or DIY store. Most have an in-house design facility: once you've found a range you like, a designer will lay it out using computer design software.

5  Plan the installation logically. Remember that you will first have to take out the existing kitchen, before you can do construction work on the floors, wall or ceilings.

 **Tip**

Be realistic about your own abilities – or the time you have to devote to the project. For between 10 and 15 per cent of your overall budget you could have the kitchen installed by professionals.

⚠ **Warnings**

Don't forget that while your kitchen is being installed you may not have access to your cooker or washing machine – you may even be without water.

6   Make sure that everything you need for your new kitchen has been delivered before you begin work. The last thing you want is to knock out your old kitchen only to discover that a supply problem means that a critical component can't be delivered for another month.

7   The true quality of a kitchen lies in the detailing. Some people go to the enormous effort of putting in a kitchen but leave out the final details, like poorly hanging cupboard doors or ill-fitting electrical units.

---

## 254 | Save Money on a Home-Improvement Project

With good planning and an honest assessment of your skills – and free time – you can probably save some money on your next big project.

### ⊙ Steps

1   Consider what portion of the work you can realistically do yourself. For example, if adding a room, maybe you can paint it when it's done.

2   Consider less expensive alternatives when designing an addition, such as a ready-built fireplace unit rather than traditional masonry.

3   Plan everything so you don't need to make changes once the contractor is working – changes often entail additional charges.

4   Get several prices for the work from recommended contractors. Price quotes may vary enormously in keeping with the contractor's schedule, the time of year and the distance from the job.

5   Try to schedule your project for an "off" time of year. For example, install central heating in early summer, not during the winter.

6   Shop for materials that are on sale. Building-supply stores often have various items (such as tile or wood flooring) on sale due to overstocking or other factors.

7   Make sure that your initial contract for the work is comprehensive and that the initial price covers all work to be done.

### ✱ Tip

Most people can handle light demolition, painting, landscaping and removal of debris, assuming that they have the time.

### ⚠ Warnings

If you have any doubts that the contract for the work is correct and complete, consult a solicitor before signing.

Be very wary if any of your chosen contractors asks for full payment up front. A deposit of 10 per cent is fair.

---

## 255 | Hire a Builder

Finding the right builder is essential to the success of your project.

### ⊙ Steps

1   Interview several builders. Ask an architect for recommendations. If an estate agent assisted you when you purchased your property, ask the agent for recommendations. Also consult friends and neighbours.

2   Review your completed plans with each builder, or ask the builders about designing plans for you.

3   Make sure that all the builders see the building site and are quoting to build the house on that site, including excavation and any other site-specific costs.

### ✱ Tips

Remember that you'll be working closely with the builder – be sure to select someone with whom you can establish a comfortable relationship.

Don't assume that the most expensive builder is the best, or the least expensive the worst. Price quotes vary based on a

---

4   Get price quotes from the builders and compare them, making sure that they each bid on the same items.

5   Ask for references – particularly previous customers – from each party. Check the references. Be sure to speak with them when the builder is not present. Look at some of the houses the builder has constructed.

6   If necessary, retain a solicitor with experience in construction cases to draft or review the contract. Be sure that the payment schedule for the builder is clear and understandable.

7   Make sure that the contract specifies the start and completion dates. Insist on some type of late fee or penalty if the completion is delayed beyond a certain grace period (notwithstanding circumstances beyond the builder's control, such as inclement weather).

8   Execute the approved contract.

9   Make any required deposit payment, and be sure to write your cheques according to the schedule (not earlier and not later).

builder's schedule, efficiency, overhead and distance from the job.

## ⚠ Warnings

Though recommendations from an estate agent can be a good way to find a builder, be advised that the agent may have a prior business relationship with the builder and that it may factor into the recommendation.

Be very wary if any of your chosen contractors asks for full payment up front. A deposit of 10 per cent is fair.

---

# Hire a Roofing Contractor                                     256

Roofing material ranges from cheap tiles to more expensive materials such as slate. It's important to hire a contractor who specialises in your type of roof.

## ⊙ Steps

1   Decide what type of roofing you want. Your decision will depend largely on the style of your home and your budget.

2   Contact several roofing contractors. Ask the builder, as well as friends and neighbours, for recommendations. If you're having difficulty locating contractors, try contacting the local builders association to see if it can suggest someone.

3   Have the contractors come out and quote prices on the project. Provide access to the property and make sure all the contractors are bidding on the same type of roofing.

4   Make sure the roofers are including the removal of old roofing in their bids. (Note that it's not always necessary to remove the existing roof when installing a new one.)

5   Find out if each roofer has experience with the type of roofing you're installing. Ask to see pictures of prior projects.

6   Ask for references and check them out. Are the previous customers happy with the work that was done for them?

7   Execute a contract for the work specifying cost, payment schedule, material to be used, start date and completion date. Try to minimise the deposit you pay to the contractor prior to the start of the work or delivery of materials.

## ✽ Tips

Roofing is outside work, so be aware that your project may be subject to weather-related delays. Roofing work is best carried out during the Spring and Summer.

## ⚠ Warnings

Be very wary if any of your chosen contractors asks for full payment up front. A deposit of 10 per cent is fair.

## 257 | Hire a Painter

Hiring a professional painter is much more costly than doing it yourself, but it's a quick and easy way to get the job done well. Here's how to hire a top-quality painter for the best results.

### ⊙ Steps

1   Determine which areas of your home need to be painted.

2   Consider any work you want to have done before painting. For example, do you want to replace or repair mouldings, patch damaged plaster or hang new doors?

3   Decide what colours and paints you want to use. You can get paint charts for all major brands at ant DIY store. The painter you hire may also have suggestions – take these seriously.

4   Contact several decorators. Ask friends, neighbours, builders and designers for recommendations. If you're having difficulty locating house painters, check the Yellow Pages.

5   Have the painting contractors inspect the site and quote a price for the job. Make sure the contractors are quoting on the same specifications – areas to be painted, number of coats and so forth.

6   Ask the painters for references and contact them. Were the customers happy with the job? Did the painter complete the project in a timely and professional manner?

7   Select a painter based on price, track record and your impressions.

8   Execute a contract specifying the work to be done, total cost, payment schedule, start date and estimated completion date.

9   Make sure the contract includes the paint brands and colours to be used in each location, as well as the number of coats.

10  Make sure the contract specifies that the painter is responsible for cleaning up and the removal of paint from all surfaces (windows, floors).

11  Remove all furniture and other movable items before the painter is scheduled to begin. Anything not removed should be piled together in the centre of the room and thoroughly covered with dust cloths.

### ❋ Tips

A good-quality paint job typically consists of one coat of primer and two finish coats of the colour.

If you intend to have customised painting done (such as sponging or other decorator techniques), first make sure that your painter has experience doing this type of work.

### ⚠ Warning

Be very wary if any of your chosen contractors asks for full payment up front. A deposit of 10 per cent is fair. Try to make your payment schedule match the pace of work and material deliveries.

## 258 | Hire a Hardwood-Floor Contractor

Hardwood is a popular flooring choice. Whether you're installing new hardwood floors or having older floors refinished, find a contractor who can do the best job.

### ⊙ Steps

1   Determine the areas where you want the hardwood flooring to be installed or refinished.

2   If you're having new floors installed, learn about differences in material costs for various flooring products, and decide which type of flooring you want to use. You can shop for flooring at a DIY store.

### ❋ Tips

Many types of wood-flooring products are available. The most common type is unfinished oak. These floors are sanded and coated with polyurethane after they have been laid.

3   Ask friends and relatives for recommendations to help find a contractor, or look in the Yellow Pages under "Floor".

4   Have contractors come to your home to measure and give estimates. Get several price quotes from competing contractors.

5   Discuss the finishing/coating options with the contractor. Do you have children or pets who make greater protection necessary?

6   Ask to see pictures of past jobs if you're looking for a contractor to do specialty work, such as elaborate parquet or inlays.

7   Learn whether each contractor is experienced in the specific work you want done. For example, a contractor may install very high-quality standard oak floors, but may not be sufficiently skilled to handle a more complex project with inlays or difficult cuts.

8   Ask the contractors for references and check them out. Are previous customers happy with the work that was done?

9   Select the contractor who provides the best combination of satisfied references and price.

10  Make arrangements with the contractor to cover damage to painted trim and other items that may be damaged when refinishing or adding a floor. (You may have to accept the fact that you'll have to repaint or touch up base mouldings in a room that's being worked on.)

11  Execute a contract specifying the work to be done, price, payment schedule, start date and estimated completion date. Try to pay the minimum possible deposit (no more than 10 per cent) and arrange a payment schedule that matches the completion of work and delivery of materials to the site.

New unfinished flooring has to arrive at the house a week or two before it is laid in order to adjust to the environment. For the same reason, it will have to remain unsanded for another week or two after installation.

## ⚠ Warning

The process for finishing wood floors requires several coats, laid down over two to three days (or more), during which you can't use the floors and may even have to vacate the house due to strong fumes.

---

## Hire an Electrician

Your home's electrical system is complex and can be hazardous with poorly handled renovations. Look for an experienced and reliable professional when hiring an electrician.

### ⊙ Steps

1   Evaluate what work needs to be done. Are you renovating or adding a room or rooms? Or do you need a repair to an existing system?

2   Consider your needs realistically – the number of electronic devices used in most homes means that additional sockets are often required. These are easy and inexpensive to add at the time of a renovation.

3   Ask friends and neighbours for recommendations, and then contact several electricians. If you are having difficulty locating an electrician, check the Yellow Pages or other trade directory.

4   Have the electricians inspect the site and bid on the job. Provide them with written specifications listing all aspects of the project.

5   Check to make sure that the electricians are properly qualified and have appropriate insurance coverage.

## ✳ Tip

Many electrical enhancements have been introduced in recent years. Discuss these with your electrician to determine if you want to add them to your project. Examples include mains surge protectors that can safeguard computers and other electronic devices. It is much cheaper and easier to install these items when conducting a renovation.

6   Inquire about the length of time each electrician has been in business.

7   Ask for past customers as references and contact them. Ask customers if they were satisfied with the work. Did the contractor come back promptly to address any problems?

8   Select an electrician, basing your choice on a combination of price, experience and your impressions.

9   Review your specifications with the electrician and discuss any necessary items you may have missed. For example, will you require an additional or upgraded power connection to support your renovation?

10  Execute a contract specifying the work to be done, cost, payment schedule, start date and estimated completion date.

## ⚠ Warnings

Make sure that the contractor provides you with a proper certificate of insurance before any payment is made or work commences.

Be very wary if any of your chosen contractors asks for full payment up front. A deposit of 10 per cent is fair. Try to make your payment schedule match the pace of work and material deliveries.

---

## 260 | Hire a Plumber When Building

When hiring a plumber for a big project, find someone who will do a quality job at a good price – and who will also be available for emergencies.

### ⊙ Steps

1   Evaluate what you need to have done.

2   Ask friends and family for recommendations and then contact several plumbers. For more possibilities, check the Yellow Pages.

3   Have all the plumbers give you price quotes on the project. Give the plumbers access to the site and provide them with written specifications (including detailed descriptions of materials – for example, "Kohler 'Vintage' sink in white").

4   Confirm that the plumbers are including the removal of existing fixtures (such as an old bath) as a part of their bids.

5   Make sure the plumbers are properly licensed and insured.

6   Ask how long each plumber has been in business. Look for one who has been in business for several years.

7   Ask for references and contact them. Were they satisfied with the work? Did the plumber return promptly to correct any problems?

8   Select a plumber based on price, experience and your impressions.

9   Execute a contract specifying the work to be done, cost, payment schedule, materials to be used for the project, start date and estimated completion date.

### ✳ Tips

When selecting a plumber, consider the firm's ability to provide someone on short notice for emergencies. Many plumbers have 24-hour emergency service available.

If your project is large, consider supplying the plumbing fixtures yourself (with the plumber supplying other material, such as pipe). Expensive baths and other fixtures are often marked up considerably by plumbers.

### ⚠ Warnings

Make sure your chosen plumber provides you with a certificate of insurance before you make any payments or work begins.

Be very wary if any of your chosen plumber asks for full payment up front. A deposit of 10 per cent is fair.

## Buy Replacement Windows

New windows can really improve the look of an older home while also improving energy efficiency.

### ⊙ Steps

1 Consider which windows you want to replace. Do you want to replace them all or just certain ones?

2 Consider the time of year. In all probability the project will take at least several days, during which time your home may be somewhat exposed to the elements.

3 Contact several window-installing companies.

4 Discuss the various window types the installers offer (wood, PVC, aluminium) and the merits and costs of each. PVC and aluminium windows do not require painting, so they are low-maintenance.

5 Discuss the energy-efficiency options (standard insulated glass, low-e glass and so forth) offered by the window company. Consider low-e and other high-tech energy-saving options in the context of the estimated savings on your heating and cooling bills. Do the expected savings justify the extra cost?

6 Ask the window company for references and check them: Were past customers happy with the work done? Was the work completed in a timely manner? Have they had any problems since the installation? Did the contractor leave the site in a clean and undamaged condition?

7 Select a window company based upon price, window type, references and your impressions.

8 Make sure that the window company offers guarantee(s). Sign a contract for the work. If ordering the windows separately from having them installed, make sure that the installer has signed off on the list to verify that the windows specified are correct.

9 Make sure that the window company is properly insured. Get a valid certificate of insurance from the contractor before you pay any money or before the work begins.

### ❋ Tips

The two most common types of windows are sash and casement. The former have bottom and top sashes that slide up and down to open or close the window; casement windows open like a door.

### ⚠ Warning

Your window installer will insist on a substantial deposit. Always try to negotiate the smallest possible up-front payment and a schedule that matches the pace of work and material deliveries.

## Decorate a Room So It Seems Bigger

Sleight-of-hand decorating can help to stretch the perceived dimensions of a room. Here are some ways to help a small room look large.

### ⊙ Steps

1 Open up the room by maximising views of the outdoors or of an adjoining, more spacious room.

2 Keep the walls light in colour, as light colours recede.

3 Provide good illumination, which will enhance the sense of space.

### ❋ Tip

Floor-to-ceiling mirrors definitely increase the sense of volume in a room. Keep in mind, however, that this is a look that comes and goes in popularity.

4   Paint mouldings, doors and the like in the same colour as the walls. Strongly contrasting elements chop up the space.

5   If there are too many small ornamental items, put some of them away – it will make the room seem cluttered.

6   Paint the ceiling white. Rooms have a greater sense of space with high ceilings, and white ceilings seem higher than darker ones.

7   Run linear flooring such as wood strips and ceramic tile on the diagonal. This creates the longest straight lines possible in the room, and the eye will follow them.

8   Use the same flooring material throughout the space to unify it and make it seem more expansive.

9   Select oversized ceramic tiles – even in small bathrooms.

10  Use furniture that is scaled appropriately to the room. For example, an oversize sofa will eat up too much space in a small room.

11  Decorate windows simply. Besides being the wrong scale for a small room, show-stopping treatments such as billowing curtains encroach into the space of the room.

---

## 263 | Select the Best Paint Colour for a Room

Choosing a paint colour can be a little tricky because it may be dramatically affected by lighting and shadows. Here are some tips for getting the colour just right.

### ⊙ Steps

1   Study colour schemes you admire in home-decorating magazines and tear out any particularly appealing examples. Take them with you when shopping for paint.

2   Remember that colour usually seems more intense on walls than it does on a sample card. When it doubt, go a shade or two lighter.

3   Keep in mind that yellow and rosey tones give a room a warm feeling. Greens, blues and greys are cooler colours.

4   Avoid snow-white except in ultra-modern, minimalist environments, because it will seem too harsh, giving a sterile, operating-room effect. It's better to go with a white that contains a hint of peach, beige or pink.

5   Save bold colour schemes for rooms where you don't spend long stretches of time, such as bathrooms and dining rooms. You may tire of these schemes if they're in the home office, kitchen, living room or other areas in which you stay for hours.

6   Take fabric with you if you're matching it. If you don't have a swatch, grab a sofa cushion, bedspread or curtain panel, for example.

7   Start small, buying just a litre or so of paint, and then cover a section of wall with a paintbrush or roller. Or test the colour on a large piece of plywood or wallboard scrap, or on a piece of cardboard; set it against the walls in the room as the light changes (including artificial light) and evaluate it for a few days.

✳ **Tip**

If you plan to sell your house soon, stick with mainstream colours. These are more likely to appeal to prospective buyers.

8 Test a two-tone colour scheme by painting two boards – or painting one board in both colours.

9 Repeat the test, tinkering with more pink, less peach or whatever seems appropriate, in small cans of paint until you're satisfied. Yes, the cost for sampling various paints can add up, but it can prevent the disaster of applying, say, three large tins of the wrong colour and being forced to repaint.

# Paint Woodwork                                                                 264

Excellent preparatory work and patience are the key secrets to successfully painting wood surfaces, such as skirting boards and door frames.

## ⊙ Steps

1 Clean the wood surface thoroughly with a specialised cleaner – one that doesn't leave a film that could interfere with the adhesion of the paint.

2 Let the wood dry.

3 Mask off the area around the woodwork carefully with professional masking tape, pressing down very firmly on the tape edges you intend to paint. Try pressing down the edges with a spoon.

4 Place dust sheets as needed.

5 Have one or more paintbrushes in widths appropriate to the wood you are painting. Purchase a high-quality brush or brushes with the type of bristles appropriate to the product you are using, either oil based or water based.

6 Apply a de-glossing product (liquid-sanding solvent) according to the directions, which will specify a waiting period before applying primer.

7 Apply primer; oil-based primer is best. Note that there's often a window of only 30 to 60 minutes in which primer can be applied successfully over de-glosser.

8 Sand rough areas after priming.

9 Let the primer dry; this may take a day or more.

10 Apply oil- or water-based paint, as desired.

11 Let the paint dry. Oil-based paint usually takes much longer to dry – a day or more – but experts generally feel it gives a more durable finish.

12 Apply the second coat of paint.

13 Let the second coat dry, and remove the masking tape. Oil-based paint should be thoroughly dry before you remove the tape, but some paint experts advise removing tape when water-based paint is still slightly tacky; do what your paint-can directions or paint store advises.

## ✳ Tips

High-quality paints and brushes will yield better results. Quality brushes provide a more even coat of paint and will last through many paint jobs.

Clean brushes thoroughly. Do not rest brushes with their weight on the bristles – it will deform the bristles and ruin the brushes.

Avoid painting on hot, humid days or immediately following rain to avoid getting bubbles in the paint.

## ⚠ Warning

When using solvent (oil-based) products, ventilate the work area thoroughly. Don't smoke or have any type of open flame (even a gas water heater) in the area.

## Things You'll Need

☐ wood cleaner and rags

☐ masking tape

☐ spoon

☐ dust sheets

☐ paintbrushes

☐ de-glossing product

☐ primer and paint

☐ sandpaper

## 265 | Remove Wallpaper

You won't know how difficult – or easy – removing old wallpaper will be until you try. Here are a few guidelines to help you tackle the job.

### ⊙ Steps

1 Move furniture away from the walls and cover the floor with dust sheets.

2 Pick a corner or an edge of the wallpaper and try to peel it off using your hands, a putty knife or a wallpaper scraper. Some papers are designed to simply peel off.

3 If the paper doesn't peel off, or if the pattern comes away leaving the backing in place, score the paper lightly using a blade or a wallpaper knife. Be careful not to cut into the plaster underneath.

4 Apply plain water, water mixed with a mild household soap, or a commercial wallpaper remover to the wall using a paint roller, squirt gun or large sponge. Saturate the wall several times if necessary; the paper will absorb the water until the glue begins to loosen.

5 Alternatively, rent or buy a wallpaper steamer. Take care – steamers get very hot.

6 Try again to pull the paper off with your hands. You might still have to use a scraper or putty knife, however.

7 Wash away as much of the glue as possible, until you are down to the original painted or primed wall. You might have to use a heavy-duty scouring pad. Wait until the wall is dry and use sandpaper to sand off what remains of the paper, backing or glue.

### ✳ Tip

If the wallpaper resists your efforts, sand it with very coarse sandpaper.

### ⚠ Warning

Wallpaper removers can be caustic, creating fumes that can irritate your lungs. Wear gloves, long trousers and sleeves, safety goggles, and a hat. Don't forget to ventilate the room well.

### Things You'll Need

- ☐ dust sheets
- ☐ putty knife or scraper
- ☐ razor blade or scoring tool
- ☐ wallpaper remover
- ☐ paint roller, squirt gun or sponge
- ☐ scouring pad
- ☐ sandpaper

## 266 | Hang Wallpaper

Hanging wallpaper can be an experience you'll never forget. These steps are for plaster walls that have been primed and painted but don't yet have wallpaper on them.

### ⊙ Steps

#### Preparing the Walls

1 Look for cracks, nail holes and loose paint or plaster on the walls. Fix them first.

2 Be sure that the walls are clean and dry and that every surface is either painted or primed. You don't want to apply paste to a surface that will just absorb it – the paper might not stick.

3 Remove light switch and socket covers after you've washed the walls.

4 Plan to start papering in a place that is inconspicuous, and remember

### ✳ Tips

Razor blades get blunt amazingly quickly, so replace them often. You'll be glad you did.

Avoid sliding the paper around. Even if you don't tear it, the paper might stretch.

### ⚠ Warnings

After removing electrical socket covers, you'll be wallpapering right over exposed electrical connections. Be sure to turn off the electricity to the room before cutting around these fixtures. Water, that your starting point will also be your ending point. (Corners and the areas behind opening doors are good places to start.)

5 Beginning at a doorway or corner, measure a distance that's slightly shorter than the width of your paper. Make a mark at this distance – be sure to make the mark as light as possible so that it won't show through the paper's background.

6 Using a spirit level and a pencil, draw a vertical line from the floor to the ceiling through this mark. If you start at a corner, be sure to use the level, not the corner, as your guide. You will align your paper to this line – again, be sure to make the mark as light as possible.

## Hanging the Paper

1 With a craft knife, cut a length of paper that's about 10 cm (4 in) longer than the wall, from ceiling to skirting board. (With a large repeating pattern, you might have to cut the strips longer to make sure the pattern matches up from piece to piece.)

2 Apply paste to the paper (see 267 "Apply Paste to Wallpaper"). Or, if using pre-pasted wallpaper, follow the manufacturer's instructions. (Most professional installers apply paste even to pre-pasted wallpapers, but be aware that this voids some manufacturers' warranties.)

3 Start at the ceiling, aligning the paper with the plumb line you drew on the wall. Allow roughly an extra 5 cm (2 in) to flop against the ceiling, and the same amount to flop below the top of the skirting board.

4 Smooth the paper using a smoothing brush or a plastic smoother (which looks like a wide spatula without the handle). Remove wrinkles by pulling a section of the paper away from the wall until you reach the wrinkle. Smooth out the paper as you lay it back against the wall.

5 Smooth from the middle out, applying enough pressure to push out the bubbles but not pressing so hard that you stretch or tear the paper. If you have an air bubble that just won't budge, poke it with a pin and press down on the paper before the adhesive dries.

6 Trim the paper. Using a wide putty knife, press the paper against the ceiling, skirting board, or corner and trim it with a sharp razor blade. (The putty knife provides a straight edge to guide the blade.)

7 Continue with the next piece, aligning it with the one you just laid down. If a pattern just won't line up between two strips, match it at the most obvious spot – eye level.

8 Roll each seam with a seam roller, but don't press so hard that you squeeze out all the adhesive. Go back 10 or 15 minutes later and roll each seam again.

9 When you reach the end – the place where you started – you'll want to create a clean final seam. Lap the final strip of paper over the first strip and trim both simultaneously.

10 Be sure to wipe any excess adhesive off the paper, ceiling, skirting boards and adjoining strips. Use a wet sponge, following with a dry rag.

electricity and metal are a dangerous combination.

Place pieces of tape over the sockets and switches to minimise their exposure to paste and water. But remember, the tape won't in any way protect you if the electricity is still on.

## Things You'll Need

☐ cleaning supplies

☐ tape measure

☐ spirit level

☐ pencil

☐ craft knife

☐ wallpaper

☐ wallpaper paste

☐ smoothing brush or plastic smoother

☐ pin

☐ wide putty knife

☐ seam roller

---

### 267 | Apply Paste to Wallpaper

Pasting wallpaper can be a messy job. Here's how to apply paste well and (relatively) neatly.

#### ⊙ Steps

1 Be sure that you have the correct adhesive paste for the job. Some papers, such as vinyl backed or lightweight, require a specific paste.

2 Mix wallpaper paste that comes as a powder in a separate bucket and then pour it into the paste bucket or roller tray you will use for the job. Stir well with a stirring stick to remove all the lumps, but not so well that you put a lot of air into the mix.

3 Pour liquid adhesive directly into a bucket or roller tray.

4 Lay a strip of wallpaper – already cut to size, pattern side down – on a long, flat, dry table (the table won't stay dry for long). Let one end of the paper flop over the edge of the table.

5 Use a paste brush or a paint roller to apply the paste to the half of the paper that remains flat on the table, being sure to cover every inch.

6 Fold the section you just pasted over onto itself, and slide the dry section of the paper onto the table. Apply the paste.

7 Fold the next section onto itself, then fold the two halves against each other, being very careful not to crease the paper. This process is called "booking". Booking keeps the paper moist, the paste from dribbling onto the floor and the pasted surface clean.

8 Set the paper aside in a clean spot for no more than 5 minutes before hanging it.

9 Keep your workspace clean: As soon as each strip of wallpaper is booked and set aside, use a clean, wet sponge to clean the table – but don't bother to dry the surface. Do this even if you're going to paste several pieces before you hang them; you'll want to get the adhesive off the table before it has dried.

#### ✳ Tips

You're going to get paste on the table, the pattern face of the paper and yourself. Don't be overly concerned – it's water-soluble.

Let the paper set after applying paste. This allows the paper to expand or shrink before you lay it on the wall. It also takes a few minutes for the paste to activate the dry adhesive on pre-pasted wallpapers.

#### Things You'll Need

☐ wallpaper paste

☐ buckets

☐ roller tray

☐ stirring stick

☐ paste brush or paint roller

☐ sponge

---

### 268 | Hang a Shelf on a Wall

Adding storage or display space in your home can be a simple matter. Here's how to mount a simple wooden shelf and two brackets to a wall.

#### ⊙ Steps

1 Buy a wooden shelf from a DIY store. Buy two shelf brackets – simple "L" shapes or something more decorative – making sure that the top leg of the bracket is no longer than the shelf is deep.

2 Buy screws if you don't have a supply at home or if they don't come with the brackets (see Tips).

3 Buy rawlplugs of a size corresponding to the screws.

#### ✳ Tip

Choose screws that will be able to go into the wall about 2.5 cm (1 in). Choose shorter screws for mounting the shelf on the bracket, so they won't penetrate the top of the shelf.

4   Determine where you want the bottom edge of the shelf to sit, then mark the position in pencil, using a spirit level as a guide.

5   Line up the top of each bracket with the pencil line and mark the attachment holes on the wall. Set the bracket aside.

6   Drill the holes to a depth appropriate to the screws. Check the depth of the screwholes by inserting the rawlplugs. They should nestle snugly in the holes.

7   Attach the brackets to the wall by screwing screws into the rawlplugs until they grip firmly. Lay your shelf on top, and screw the bracket into the shelf.

### Things You'll Need

☐ wooden shelf

☐ shelf brackets

☐ screws

☐ rawlplugs

☐ spirit level

☐ drill

---

## Measure Your Window for Curtains   269

Whether you make your own curtains, buy off the shelf or order custom made, knowing the correct measurements for your window is the key.

### ⊙ Steps

1   Decide what kind of curtains you want.

2   Decide where the curtain rod will go. You'll probably want it positioned about 15 cm (6 in) above the window frame, but you might want it higher or lower (or even – for a dramatic look on a tall, deep window – inside the frame).

3   Decide how much coverage you want. Curtains usually extend about 15 cm (6 in) above the window frame, 6 to 8 cm (2 to 3 in) on each side, and 6 to 8 cm (2 to 3 in) on the bottom. Consider how much light you want to block out – probably a lot if the window is east-facing and you like to sleep in of a morning – and how much privacy you want the curtains to provide.

4   Use a tape measure to measure from the curtain rod to the bottom point, and from side to side. Multiply the side-to-side measurement by two to allow for generously full curtains.

### ✻ Tip

Make sure the salesperson understands that these are desired finished dimensions of your curtains, and NOT the dimensions of your window. (It is of course helpful if you provide window dimensions as well.)

---

## Make Your Own Curtains   270

To have curtains made professionally can cost a fortune. Here are some simple steps you can take to make your own.

### ⊙ Steps

### Making the Curtains

1   First decide on the style of curtains you want to make. One common method for hanging curtains is to make a "sleeve" at the top of the curtain through which a curtain pole is threaded; the pole is then hung above the window. A popular alternative replaces the pole with a rail with mounted hooks which are attached to the curtain.

### ✻ Tips

If replacing old curtain hooks, make sure that anything you buy fits your existing curtain rails. These are usually specific to the manufacturer, so always take an old hook with you to the shop.

2 First measure the width of your window, and the length from the curtain rod to floor (or however far you want your curtains to hang).

3 Choose a good-quality, heavy material for your curtains, especially if they are intended to keep out drafts. Make sure that the material is appropriate to its use – kitchen and bathroom curtains should be made from a material that is easy to maintain.

4 Wash or dry-clean the material before you begin sewing.

5 Measure and cut your material to size. Since curtains are "gathered" at the top, double the width measurement. (If you want the curtains "lined" with the same pattern, double the length measurement and fold it back.) Add roughly an extra 50 cm (20 in) onto the length measurement – this extra amount allows roughly 25 cm (10 in) of material to use for the sleeve that the curtain rod passes through.

6 The size of the curtain rod will depend on the size of the sleeve that passes over it. If you have a standard size rod than you can take the cloth and fold it back to make the sleeve. Sew this down.

7 Place the panel on the curtain rod and decide on the curtain length. Pin up the bottom of the curtain, and then sew it to length.

8 When the curtains are finished, thread the curtain rod through and attach to mounting brackets on the wall.

9 If you are using a curtain rail, attach the hooks to the curtain. Make sure that you use the same number for each curtain. To ensure that they gather correctly when drawn, the hooks should be equal intervals apart.

## Cleaning the Curtains

1 The biggest maintenance problem is always going to be dust. Use the soft brush attachment on your vacuum cleaner, and always work from top to bottom.

2 If your curtains need more drastic attention, take them down from the rail or curtain pole, and place them in a dryer with a dryer sheet and a tennis ball. Turn it on for 20 minutes. This will dust and freshen them in one go.

3 When you take the curtains out of the dryer hang them up immediately. This should mean that they won't need ironing.

4 Small creases can be squirted with water spray - the weight of the water will smooth the fabric as it dries.

If you want your curtains to keep out the sun they will need to be lined with a sun-blocking fabric. This is best left to a professional (or experienced) curtain maker.

# Buy a New Carpet

Whatever your style or budget, you can find a carpet to fit your needs and tastes.

## ⦿ Steps

1 Decide which areas of your home you want to carpet.

2 Measure the rooms that you want to carpet.

3 Go to several carpet stores. Try both carpet-only showrooms and general DIY stores. Ask about installation costs – unless you plan to lay the carpet yourself.

4 Consider the various grades of carpeting available. Are you carpeting a high-traffic location or a less frequented area of your home?

5 Consider your long-term needs. Is it worth paying more for a carpet that will last ten years instead of five? Do you expect to move or re-decorate within that time?

6 Take samples of any carpet you are considering so you can view them with your walls and furniture.

7 Expect carpet prices to vary considerably according to quality and style. Typically sold by the square metre, carpeting can cost from under £10 per square metre for basic carpet and upwards of £50 per square metre for luxury carpeting. These figures may not include installation.

8 Make your selection after considering cost, style, colour and durability.

9 Decide what type of underlay you want beneath the carpeting. Often, a certain level of padding will be included in the installation price, and you will have the option to upgrade.

10 Ask the retailer to send someone to your home to measure the area to be carpeted.

11 Clean and empty the room before the installers arrive.

12 Check the carpet to make sure that it is clean and properly installed before accepting an invoice.

## ✱ Tip

Extra padding is an effective way to improve the feel of less expensive carpeting and is well worth the extra cost.

## ⚠ Warning

Be extremely careful cutting and measuring carpet if installing it yourself.

## 272 Buy a Sofa

A sofa is central to the appearance of most living rooms – and even more for its relaxation function. Here are some tips that will help you choose a sofa to meet your needs.

### ⊙ Steps

1   Determine potential size restrictions for your sofa. For example, if it will be moved up a flight of stairs or placed in a small room, determine the maximum measurements – depth and height as well as length.

2   Consider the colour carefully – a sofa will last many years, during which certain colours will drift in and out of fashion. A neutral sofa can be updated simply by swapping around the pillows.

3   Have an idea about upholstery before you shop. Tough leather may be ideal for a rough-and-tumble household with pets and toddlers; white cotton could be fine for careful adults who don't snack or drink red wine while sitting on the sofa.

4   Be aware that patterned, two-tone, tweedy and other multicolour fabrics will camouflage stains more effectively than solid colours.

5   Try out the sofa in the store. You and other family members should sit on it for several minutes, trying out both an outside cushion and a centre cushion to be sure they're comfortable.

6   Check the fabric for comfort. If it's scratchy or itchy, pass it by.

7   Examine whether the fabric's pattern is aligned where edges meet. If it's a stripe, plaid or big print, the pattern on the back of the sofa should align with the pattern on the cushion and then on down to the front of the seating base.

8   Look at the workmanship of the cushion cording. Does it snake around or is it straight?

9   Remove the sofa cushions and see what's under them. You shouldn't see any wood, just smooth, upholstered surfaces.

10  Ask the salesperson about interior construction. The frame should be wood with corner blocks and glue; don't buy a sofa with nailed, stapled or unbraced joints, as these will loosen and wobble.

### ✳ Tip

If the legs screw in (a mark of quality), this can be a help when moving the sofa. You'll be able to remove the legs to help the sofa turn a stairwell corner.

## Arrange Living Room Furniture

If you are bored with your present furniture arrangement maybe it's time for a reorganisation.

### ⊙ Steps

1   With a tape measure, calculate the dimensions of the room. Draw the outline to scale on graph paper.

2   Mark anything that would affect your arrangement: sockets for electricity and telephones; light switches; windows; doors that open into the room; space between windows; and sill height.

3   Make scale paper cutouts of your living room furniture and shift them on the room drawing as needed until a likely arrangement emerges.

4   Select a focal point for your room and subtly orient other furnishings and some of the lighting towards it. If there's a fireplace, that will nearly always be the focal point; other focal points might be bookcases or built-in shelving housing collectibles, or a sofa with a striking painting on the wall above.

5   Arrange the furniture in such a way that pieces viewed as a unit don't show dramatic variance in height and mass as the eye sweeps the room. When a high-backed chair is next to a low table, boost the visual height of the table by hanging a piece of art above it.

6   Set up cosy conversation areas so that when you entertain, people can be seated and chat rather than having to stand. Examples would include two chairs separated by a low table, or two love seats facing each other.

7   Pull furniture away from the walls for more flexibility in creating conversation areas. For example, use a sofa to divide space in a room.

8   Create a dramatic effect by positioning the sofa at a non-perpendicular angle to any walls. Perhaps put an area rug and coffee table parallel to the sofa.

9   Allow a bare minimum of 45 cm (18 in) for traffic lanes through the room. These will probably meander if you have two or three conversation areas in the room.

10  Freshen the room occasionally by shifting the furniture and accessories for a new look. Switch ornaments around, add fresh flowers, change potpourri or move pictures.

### ❋ Tip

If you're comfortable using a computer, you might find home design CAD (Computer Aided Design) software to be helpful.

### Things You'll Need

- ☐ tape measure
- ☐ graph paper
- ☐ pencil and eraser
- ☐ ruler
- ☐ scissors

## 274  Select a Mattress

Since the average mattress lasts about 10 years, buy the best you can afford. Here are guidelines.

### ⊙ Steps

1   Try out several mattresses before you make your decision.

2   Look at the warranty. Most premium mattresses come with at least a 10-year warranty. Note that many warranties are voided if the mattress has been stained or soiled in any way.

3   Wear loose, comfortable clothing when shopping for a mattress so you'll be comfortable lying down.

4   Think about whether you'll be sharing your mattress and how much room you need before you decide on a size.

5   Read labels to see what the ticking is made of. Quality ticking will be a cotton blend or damask, but ticking can also be a synthetic such as polyester or even vinyl.

6   Take off your shoes and rest on the mattress. This is the only way to tell if the padding is going to be comfortable.

7   Roll from the centre of the mattress to the edges to see if the support is the same at all points, and check to see if the mattress has further support around the edges where you would sit.

8   Buy a mattress with handles that are attached to the inner springs. They'll be less likely to break off.

9   Check the coil count. Coil construction and quality varies from company to company, but coils should start at 300 for a full, 375 for a double and 450 for a king. Ask about the diameter of the coils. The wider, the sturdier.

10  Purchase a mattress and box spring (the foundation for the mattress) in one set, as they work together as a unit. (Low-profile box springs are also available for those who prefer a lower bed placement. These are lower than traditional spring sets.)

### ✳ Tips

Beds in the UK come in four main sizes: single – 90 x 190 cm (36 x 75 in); double – 135 x 190 cm (54 x 75 in); king size – 150 x 200 cm (60 x 78 in) ; super king size – 180 x 200 cm (72 x 78 in).

Try to bargain for the best price. Shopping for a mattress is similar to buying a car in that there is often room for negotiation.

Cotton-foam and cotton-polyester are the best mattresses for everyday use because they weigh less and hold their shape well.

### ⚠ Warnings

Pillow tops add an extra layer of padding to the top of the mattress but tend to sag more quickly than thinner padding on mattresses.

Hard mattresses don't always offer the best support – it may add uncomfortable pressure to your hips and shoulders.

## 275  Select a Futon

Originating in Japan, futons are cotton or foam mattresses that can also double as couches. The style you buy will depend on whether it will be used as a couch, a bed or both.

### ⊙ Steps

1   Find out if the frame has at least a five-year warranty, especially if you're buying one that operates as both a bed and a couch.

2   Buy a futon with a mattress that's at least 15 cm (6 in) thick; anything thinner will probably be uncomfortable.

3   See what the futon is made from – usually either cotton, a cotton-foam combination, a cotton-polyester blend or a cotton-wool combination.

### ✳ Tips

Futon mattresses can last from 2 to 10 years, depending on their quality.

Check the wall clearance on a frame before buying it. Some futons need to be pulled away from the wall before they can be converted into a bed. Others simply rest against the wall and don't need to be pulled out.

4   Purchase the heaviest mattress available – either an all-cotton mattress or a cotton/foam/spring mattress – if you're not going to move or roll up the futon very often.

Buy a futon cover for your mattress to protect it from stains and dust.

5   Get a futon made of cotton and foam if you're looking for a mattress that weighs less. This combination also holds its shape and doesn't sag.

6   Try a cotton-polyester blend if you're looking for an even lighter futon. It's flexible and soft and holds its shape.

7   Think about buying a cotton-wool combination if you want a supersoft mattress. But keep in mind that cotton-wool is not very flexible.

8   Consider an innerspring mattress made of a spring unit that sits between layers of foam and cotton. It's flexible and gives the feel of a traditional mattress. However, it does weigh more than the cotton and combination futon mattresses.

9   Lie down on the futon and spread your weight out evenly to check for comfort and support. Make sure the futon isn't lumpy.

10  Choose between a three-way and two-way frame. the former is folded twice and uses the width of the mattress as the couch; the latter folds once and uses the length of the mattress as the couch, providing more seat room.

11  Southern yellow pine is ideal for futon frames because it's heavy and durable. Most other types of pine and wood are too brittle to withstand the daily wear and tear a futon endures, and they don't hold up as well.

## Arrange Bedroom Furniture                                      `276`

Bedrooms should be arranged for comfort and relaxation. Following are some tips to make your bedroom a cosy and welcoming retreat.

### ☉ Steps

1   Acknowledge that every room needs a focal point and that the focal point in a bedroom is nearly always the bed. Give it centre stage.

2   With a tape measure, measure the room. Draw the bedroom to scale on graph paper.

3   Be sure to measure short wall spaces – the distance between windows, the distance between the edge of a radiator to the corner and such – and include the measurement in the drawing. That way, you'll know whether your antique double wardrobe (or any other big, heavy piece of furniture) can squeeze into the space.

4   Mark all of the room's fixed features on the scale drawing. These can include heating ducts; windows (and the height of the sill from the floor); the curtains or blinds; radiators; electrical and phone sockets; light switches; doors (mark the swing width and direction); wall sconces; fire-places, and built-ins (bookcases, desks, dressing tables).

5   Measure your furnishings and make cutouts of their footprints according to your scale.

### ✻ Tips

Be bold in the planning stage – after all, there's no heavy lifting at this point. For instance, you could turn the bed diagonally into the corner – plan to put a tall plant, floor lamp or corner shelf behind the bed if the space looks empty.

Two heads are better than one. Enlist a friend or family member if you have doubts. And if the room is for a child, get his or her input for a happier result.

6 Arrange (and rearrange) the furniture cutouts on the room drawing until you have a layout that works for you. Allow a bare minimum of 45 cm (18 in) for traffic lanes, and set aside space for a bedside table (or pair of tables for a shared bed) as a perch for lighting, a glass of water, medicine, glasses, lotion, books or the TV remote control.

7 Place the bed so it doesn't impede the entry, closet or bathroom doors.

8 Decide on your final scheme and move the furnishings.

9 Tweak here and there as needed.

10 Position lamps and other accessories, including pictures on the walls. Note that most pictures should be visually anchored with a piece of furniture underneath.

### Things You'll Need

- ☐ metal tape measure
- ☐ graph paper
- ☐ pencil and eraser
- ☐ ruler
- ☐ scissors

## 277 | Strip Wood Furniture

Anyone who's ever found cherry or tiger oak underneath layers of old paint knows that while some pieces may not be worth the effort of stripping, others most certainly are.

### ⊙ Steps

1 Make sure there's no chance that your piece of furniture is an antique whose value could be destroyed by stripping the finish.

2 Set up your work area in a well-ventilated place with nothing around that could produce flames or sparks.

3 Remove drawer handles and other hardware and place the furniture on a layer of newspaper (or an old sheet). You may want to put some scrap wood or bricks udner it, especially if you're stripping the legs, to prevent it sticking.

4 Paint on a thick layer of stripper. Wear gloves and safety goggles.

5 Allow enough time for the stripper to work. (It usually takes 5 to 10 minutes).

6 Scrape the bubbled paint (or varnish) and stripper off in strips, using a paint and varnish scraper, an old spatula, or a putty knife; use an old toothbrush or cotton swabs for crevices. Take care not to scratch or mar softwood or gouge through thin veneers.

7 Repeat if necessary. Two applications are often required, especially if it's an old piece with several layers of stubborn paint or varnish.

8 Wipe down the piece of furniture with clean rags and white spirit, and allow to dry. Don't skimp on the white spirit – you want the piece to be as clean as possible.

### ✳ Tip

When you're finished, dispose of all brushes and remaining stripper as instructed by the paint stripper's manufacturer.

### ⚠ Warning

Even the new "safe" strippers are caustic. If any stripper gets on your skin, wash it off immediately with soap and warm water.

### Things You'll Need

- ☐ newspapers or old cloth
- ☐ stripper and brush
- ☐ gloves and safety goggles
- ☐ scraper
- ☐ toothbrush or cotton swabs
- ☐ clean rags and white spirit

## Paint Wood Furniture

Painting furniture involves sanding, priming and painting. Have the patience to apply that second coat of paint – you'll be rewarded with a better-looking, longer-lasting finish.

### ⊙ Steps

1 Make sure there's no chance that your piece of furniture is an antique whose value could be destroyed by changing the finish.

2 Set up your work area in a well-ventilated place with nothing around that could produce flames or sparks.

3 Remove drawer handles and other hardware. Place the furniture on a layer of newspaper or a disposable dust cloth.

4 Sand the piece of furniture until smooth using fine-grade sandpaper (or liquid sander). Wear gloves, safety goggles and a dust mask.

5 Remove any residual sawdust with a hand vacuum, brush or barely damp rag – you don't want to wet the wood.

6 Apply a coat of either white brush-on or grey spray-on water-based primer, depending on the size and area of the piece of furniture you intend to cover.

7 Allow the primer to become dry to the touch; this usually takes 1 to 2 hours. (Read the recommended drying time on your can of primer.)

8 If the primer coat looks spotty or thin, apply a second coat and allow it to dry.

9 Sand any rough areas.

10 Add a coat of water-based paint. Brush it on with even strokes, going in the direction of the wood grain. With spray paint, make slow passes with the can 20 to 30 cm (8 to 12 in) from the wood surface. Allow the first coat to dry.

11 Add a second coat and allow it to dry overnight.

### ✱ Tips

Wash paintbrushes immediately after use. Rinse them under fast-running water until the water runs clear from the bristles.

When using spray paint, cover a wide area with newspaper to protect adjacent surfaces.

### ⚠ Warning

Always work in a well-ventilated area.

### Things You'll Need

☐ newspaper or dust cloth

☐ fine-grade sandpaper or liquid sander

☐ gloves

☐ safety goggles

☐ dust mask

☐ hand vacuum, brush or rag

☐ paintbrushes or spray gun

☐ water-based primer

☐ water-based paint

---

## Apply Wood Stain

Stains are designed to enhance the natural colour of wood. The key is to put a stain on evenly and to keep your work area free of dust and other contaminants.

### ⊙ Steps

1 Set out a layer of newspapers to protect the work area.

2 Set the temperature in the room between 22 and 24°C (70 and 75°F). If it's too cold or too hot, the stain's drying time will be affected.

3 Sand the wood smooth and vacuum or brush off debris. Oil-based stains in particular will look patchy if the wood isn't smooth.

### ✱ Tip

Use the stain liberally. Don't pour it onto the wood's surface, but don't be stingy with it.

### ⚠ Warning

Be cautious with stains – they can be flammable. Use them in

4   Wet the wood slightly with a wide, clean paintbrush. This helps the stain spread more evenly.

5   Make sure that you have enough stain on hand for the job. If you have to buy more, it may come from a slightly different colour lot.

6   Apply the stain using a clean rag or paintbrush. Brushes are much more effective for staining ornate carvings, door frames, skirting boards and other irregularly shaped areas. Rags hold more stain and are easier to use on flat surfaces.

7   Use a spray gun to apply quick-drying alcohol-based stains (or dip the object in a stain bath for five minutes if a sprayer is too big or unable to reach fine details).

8   Wipe off excess stain with a paper towel.

9   Let the stain dry and then apply another coat if there are patchy areas.

10  Finish the project with varnish, shellac or wood polish to preserve the stain (see 280 "Apply Varnish").

11  Dispose of rags per instructions on the stain can.

well-ventilated areas, and wear gloves and a face mask when applying them.

## Things You'll Need

☐ newspapers

☐ sandpaper

☐ vacuum cleaner or brush

☐ wide paintbrush

☐ rags

☐ spray gun

☐ wood stain

☐ paper towels

☐ varnish, shellac or wood polish

---

## 280 | Apply Varnish

Varnishes protect wood from scratches and stains with a durable coating. These instructions apply specifically to oil-based varnishes, which are easiest to work with.

### ⊙ Steps

1   Set out a layer of newspapers to protect the work area. Make sure the area is well-ventilated.

2   A room temperature between 22 and 24°C (70 and 75°F) helps the varnish dry quicker without causing air bubbles and streaking.

3   Gather your disposable foam brushes, clean rags, steel wool pads and mineral spirits so that they are nearby when needed.

4   Strip any existing finish using a paint stripper. Wear gloves and a face mask while you work.

5   Clean the wood to be treated with a steel wool pad dipped in a mixture of five parts white spirit to one part linseed oil.

6   Use a clean rag to dry the wood.

7   Pour enough varnish into a separate container to do the first coat, and dilute it with 20 per cent white spirits (one part white spirit to four parts varnish). This coat seals the wood. (Read the label before use and follow the manufacturer's warnings and suggestions carefully.)

8   Use the foam brush to apply this diluted varnish into the wood. Work with the grain.

9   Let that coat dry at least 6 hours, but not more than 20.

### ✳ Tips

Keep things as clean as possible. A piece of lint or dust stuck in the varnish can ruin its smooth look. If you discover dust in the varnish, let it dry and then sand it with very fine sandpaper before applying the next coat.

Dragging the brush across the rim of the can will cause bubbles. Dab it instead. If you get too many bubbles, thin the varnish with a little bit of white spirit.

## Things You'll Need

☐ newspapers

☐ disposable foam brushes

☐ clean rags

☐ steel wool pads

☐ white spirit

☐ paint stripper

10  Apply the second coat (undiluted) with a new foam brush.

11  Put on up to five coats, depending on how much wear you anticipate the surface to receive. Use a new brush for each coat.

12  Dispose of rags, brushes and remaining stripper (as advised by the stripper's manufacturer).

☐ gloves and face mask

☐ linseed oil

☐ varnish

---

## Renovate Second-hand Furniture                                281

Second-hand furniture is often inexpensive and can easily be renovated. Here are some ways to update used furnishings.

### ⊙ Steps

1  Sand lightly, or use a liquid sanding product, and then paint wooden pieces (chairs, shelves, tables, sideboards) where the clear-coated finish has seen better days. Painted "antique" and faux finishes are popular; chequered and squiggle designs also are fun, or you may want to embellish that painted piece with decoupage (collage).

2  Disguise a bad tabletop by having a mirror cut to cover the entire table, edge to edge. This works for dining tables and side tables, too.

3  Or you can hide a bad tabletop with a layer of ceramic tile. Use moulding or sanded, varnished wood strips at the edges of the tile to fill to the perimeter of the table.

4  Re-upholster a dining-table chair with a pop-out seat. It's easy: you remove the old fabric and then cover with new one, using a staple gun to fasten it on the seat bottom. Make it taut but don't stretch it.

5  Cover up soiled or worn upholstery fabric on a dining chair by sewing a new chair pad that ties onto the back of the chair. A chair pad with a ruffle on the front and sides usually hides the old upholstery completely.

6  Camouflage the blemished upholstery on a sofa or easy chair with a throw. Tuck it down deeply behind the back of the cushions.

7  Cover up the soiled arms of an upholstered chair or sofa by draping a pretty table runner over each arm.

8  Apply decorative brass-nailhead trim to hide nicked edges on wood furnishings such as tabletop edges and shelving.

9  Renovate filing cabinets, bookcases or tables by covering them with textured wallpaper – the type that mimics plaster friezes or pressed-tin ceilings. You can then paint and glaze the piece. (Aged metallic finishes look spectacular on some types of furniture.)

10  Renew dull clear-coat finishes – varnishes, lacquer and the like – by cleaning with white spirit and possibly ultrafine steel wool; then apply a new coat of finish over the old (test first in an inconspicuous spot). This is a great way to save a picture frame or tabletop.

### ✳ Tip

Altering the finish on any piece of furniture that might be a fine antique could reduce its value tremendously. Have a qualified person examine and appraise the piece for you first.

### ⚠ Warning

Be especially cautious about upgrading old baby furniture. Crib slats on older furniture may be so far apart that they pose a strangulation hazard for the baby; old painted finishes may contain lead.

11 Revive an old trunk or cedar chest by scrubbing the exterior and lining the inside with wallpaper or by stapling in a tightly woven fabric, such as a new bed sheet. A flat braid can hide seams and corner imperfections.

12 Wrap a badly damaged table or nightstand with fabric. The fabric can be fitted, almost like a slipcover, in a box shape for a rectangular table or draped over a round table; have glass cut for the top so that a non-washable fabric won't be easily soiled.

13 Replace ugly, dated drawer pulls and knobs on a classically shaped chest of drawers, sideboard or similar piece.

14 Touch up small nicks and scratches on stained wooden pieces using special crayons (sold at paint and hardware stores) – or even with an eyebrow pencil or shoe polish.

## 282 | Apply Wax to Wood

**Wax can make an old finish look new again while protecting the wood underneath. Good waxes contain carnauba and beeswax, and some have a silicone element to add shine.**

### ⊙ Steps

1 Seal new wood with a coat of clear varnish before waxing.

2 Clean old wood along the grain with a mixture of one part linseed oil to three parts white spirit on a piece of fine steel wool. Go over the surface again with white spirit on a rag and let it dry. Make sure that you have adequate ventilation when working with white spirit.

3 Apply liquid wood wax with a soft cloth. Pour wax on the cloth, not directly onto the wood.

4 Use circular motions and cover the entire surface.

5 Wait an hour or so and buff the first coat of wax with a clean, soft cloth.

6 Apply another coat, working with the grain.

7 Buff it again after an hour, and then once more after six or more hours.

8 Dispose of rags soaked with white spirit according to the instructions on the manufacturer's label.

### ✳ Tip

Wax polish should be used only on indoor woodwork, as it lacks durability.

### Things You'll Need

- ☐ clear varnish
- ☐ linseed oil
- ☐ white spirit
- ☐ steel wool
- ☐ rags
- ☐ liquid wood wax
- ☐ soft cloth

## Clean Painted Walls 283

They may be vertical surfaces, but even your walls get dirty. When you get the notion, get your wall cleaning in motion.

### ⊙ Steps

1 Protect your floors with newspapers or towels.

2 Brush cobwebs and dust from the wall with a soft-bristled brush.

3 Remove any remaining dirt with a dry sponge. Rub it along the wall to lift away dirt.

4 Fill a bucket about three-quarters full with warm water.

5 Add a small amount of washing-up liquid – about as much as it takes to clean a sink full of dishes – to the bucket. This is the cleaning bucket.

6 Place a second, empty bucket near the cleaning bucket. (You'll use this when you wring out the cleaning sponge.)

7 Dip a small portion of the flat face of a sponge into the cleaning bucket until it is damp.

8 Spread the cleaning solution on the wall with the sponge, beginning at the top and working towards the bottom. Use a ladder to reach the high spots on the wall.

9 Squeeze – but do not wring out – the sponge over the empty bucket after wetting the entire surface of the wall.

10 Blot the surface of the wall you've just cleaned to lift any further dirt from its surface.

11 Repeat this process until you have covered the wall.

12 Dry the wall using a terry towel.

### ✱ Tip

Commercial products are widely available to remove oil-based or grease stains.

### Things You'll Need

☐ newspapers or towels

☐ soft-bristled brush

☐ dry sponge

☐ buckets

☐ washing-up liquid

☐ sponge

☐ ladder

☐ terry cloth towel

## Clean a Polyurethane-Coated Hardwood Floor 284

Polyurethane-finished hardwood floors are tough and will last for years with the proper care. Fortunately, caring for these floors is very straightforward.

### ⊙ Steps

1 Clear the room of rugs and as much furniture as possible. This helps to ensure that the entire floor gets equal treatment.

2 Sweep and/or vacuum the floor carefully. Dirt left on the floor during mopping can act as an abrasive.

3 Mix about 1 tsp of washing-up liquid into a large bucket full of warm water. The exact mixture isn't crucial; just keep the amount of detergent to a bare minimum.

### ⚠ Warnings

Be careful with water; you may need to spot-clean around any unsealed gaps between slats. Always buff the floor dry.

Never use cleaning oils or furniture polishes on polyurethane-coated floors – these can leave a residue that will cause refinishing problems later. Certain chemical-based strippers can damage the finish as well.

4   Start mopping in a corner along the wall farthest from the door, and mop the entire floor with firm strokes. Make sure the mop is well wrung out and not drippy. Both foam and string mop heads will work.

5   Use new solution when the water begins to grow cloudy or dirty.

6   Repeat the process with fresh water (not soapy) once the entire surface has been thoroughly mopped with the cleaning solution. This will pick up the soapy residue and leave your floor clean and shiny.

7   Buff dry with clean, dry towels.

**Things You'll Need**

- ❏ washing-up liquid
- ❏ bucket
- ❏ mop
- ❏ towels

## 285 | Deep-Clean Your Carpet

For heavily soiled carpets, shampooing is recommended, rather than spot-cleaning. Wet-cleaner machines spray and remove hot detergent solution while cleaning the carpet.

### ⊙ Steps

1   Purchase or rent a wet-cleaner machine, also known as a steamer, at a hardware or DIY store. When you rent a machine, the necessary cleaning products are usually included or can be purchased at the rental store.

2   Vacuum the floor thoroughly.

3   Spray heavily soiled areas with pre-spray or traffic-lane cleaner. For those really dirty areas, increase the amount of pre-spray used instead of increasing the amount of carpet shampoo.

4   Fill the machine's hose or reservoir with hot tap water.

5   Use the machine and carpet shampoo according to the steamer manufacturer's instructions.

6   Maximise the amount of water removed from the carpet by making a water-extraction pass with the water spray on, and then again with the spray off. Test the carpet with your hand. If your hand comes away with water droplets, extract again with the spray off; if your hand comes away damp and the carpet feels wrung out, you have extracted correctly.

7   Wait overnight for the carpet to dry before walking on it. To help it dry thoroughly, open windows and use fans.

**❋ Tips**

Special solutions are available to treat pet stains and odours.

To help your cleaning last longer, neutralise detergent residue left on the carpet by steaming with a rinse made up of a few drops of vinegar in a bowl of water.

**⚠ Warning**

Over-saturating the carpet can cause water to soak through and damage the floor underneath.

**Things You'll Need**

- ❏ wet-cleaner machine (steamer)
- ❏ pre-spray or traffic-lane cleaner
- ❏ carpet shampoo

## 286 | Clean Vinyl and Plastic Blinds

Don't go blindly into cleaning your window dressings. Follow these easy steps.

### ⊙ Steps

#### Cleaning Monthly

1   Lower the blinds and close the slats.

2   Wipe with a damp rag. Avoid applying too much pressure to the blinds when scrubbing, as most are prone to denting and bending.

**❋ Tips**

Cloth blinds should be vacuumed regularly and professionally cleaned every two years.

Most blinds can be professionally cleaned.

3   Close the slats in the opposite direction and wipe the other side.

## Cleaning Deeply

1   Remove the blinds from the window.

2   Release the blinds completely and lay them outside, on a drop cloth.

3   Spray the blinds with an all-purpose cleaner. Allow the cleaner to sit for a few minutes.

4   Scrub the blinds gently with a soft-bristled brush in a motion parallel to the slats.

5   Turn the blinds over and repeat this process.

6   Hang or hold up the blinds and rinse with a hose.

7   Shake as much moisture from the blinds as possible.

8   Hang the blinds outside and allow them to dry.

### Things You'll Need

- [ ] damp rag
- [ ] drop cloth
- [ ] all-purpose cleaner
- [ ] soft-bristled brush
- [ ] hose

# Clean Windows                                          287

Brighten up your outlook by stripping off those layers of grime. Here's how to get your windows squeaky clean and streak free.

## ◉ Steps

1   Prepare a cleaning solution of either a cap of ammonia or four to six drops of washing-up liquid in a bowl of water. Use as little as possible to avoid streaking.

2   Dip a sponge into the solution, allowing the sponge to absorb just enough water to cover the window without flooding it.

3   Wash the surface of the window with the sponge, paying attention to the sides and corners of the window frame, where dirt and grime tend to build up.

4   Dip a squeegee into a bucket of clean water.

5   Press the squeegee lightly into the surface of the window, starting at the top and pulling down vertically, stopping a few inches before the bottom of the window.

6   Wipe off the squeegee with a paper towel.

7   Press the squeegee down the area of the window directly beside the one you just cleaned, stopping at the same place.

8   Wipe off the squeegee with a paper towel.

9   Continue this process until the entire surface of the window except the final few inches at the bottom has been cleaned.

10  Pull the squeegee horizontally across the bottom section of the window and wipe the squeegee off with a paper towel.

11  Wipe off the water at the bottom of the window frame – where a great deal of moisture has by now collected – with a paper towel.

## ✳ Tip

For hard-to-reach windows, you can buy squeegee extension poles, specifically made for washing windows.

### Things You'll Need

- [ ] ammonia
- [ ] washing-up liquid
- [ ] sponge
- [ ] squeegee
- [ ] bucket
- [ ] paper towels

## 288 | Clean Wood Walls and Panelling

Some people hesitate to clean wood panelling for fear of damage. Here's how to clean those walls and panels safely.

### ⊙ Steps

1 Dust wood walls and panelling with a soft rag, or vacuum with a vacuum cleaner brush about every two weeks.

2 Use a soft cloth to apply oil soap to particularly dirty wood according to the oil soap manufacturer's directions.

3 For tough stains, clean the wood with white spirit as a last resort. To test for staining, use a soft cloth to apply the spirits to an inconspicuous area of the wall. If the spirits do not stain, moisten the cloth with mineral spirits and lightly dab the spot or stain. Allow to dry.

### ⚠ Warning

Don't use white spirit near heat or flame. Always allow proper ventilation.

### Things You'll Need

☐ soft rags or vacuum cleaner

☐ oil soap and soft cloth

☐ white spirit (optional)

## 289 | Clean and Care for Marble

Marble isn't as tough as you may think; it's a comparatively soft stone which is easily scratched and marred. Chances are you paid a lot for it, so keep it clean and take good care of it.

### ⊙ Steps

1 Wipe down marble surfaces with a damp rag and buff dry with a chamois for routine weekly cleaning.

2 Use a neutral, non-abrasive cleaner (such as acetone, hydrogen peroxide or clear ammonia) for tough stains.

3 Apply the cleaner with a cloth and buff dry.

4 After cleaning, polish marble surfaces using a marble polish containing tin oxide.

5 Protect marble floors with a stone sealer, and use standard non-abrasive floor cleaners to clean them.

6 Place coasters under glasses and put plastic under cosmetics on marble surfaces. Use rugs to cover marble floors.

7 Refer scratches of any depth to a professional.

### ⚠ Warnings

Powdered cleansers will scratch or damage marble.

Even weak acids – vinegar, wine, orange juice, cola – can damage marble, so make sure that you mop up spills immediately and rinse with water.

### Things You'll Need

☐ rags and chamois

☐ cleaner

☐ marble polish

☐ stone sealer

☐ floor cleaner

## 290 | Organise Your Kitchen

You've got three half-full bottles of vinegar in your cupboard and your utensil drawer is a minefield of knife tips and mangled wire whisks. Time to get organised!

### ⊙ Steps

1 Go through your kitchen and discard anything you don't use, along with any food, spices or medicines that are beyond their use-by dates.

2  Take everything out of your cupboards and drawers, and wash the insides with warm soapy water. Rinse, let dry and replace cupboard and drawer liners.

3  Store pots, pans and cooking utensils near the stove, nesting the pots and pans together to conserve space.

4  Store dishes and cutlery near your eating area and/or dishwasher. Use racks to maximise use of space.

5  Be sure that children are able to reach items they need to use. Put things they should not use – such as sharp tools, alcohol and cleaning chemicals – well out of their reach.

6  Store your spices in alphabetical order, and keep them near the stove on a spice rack or in a nearby cupboard on a revolving rack.

7  Remove large and seldom-used items from worktops and store them in a cupboard. For appliances that you use often, consider adding an American-style "appliance barn", which can store toasters, blenders, juicers and other pieces of equipment on the worktop without clutter.

8  Store food items that you use on a daily basis in accessible spots, and store all like food items together – for example, tea and sugar.

9  Put any food that may become infested with insects into sturdy plastic containers and seal them.

10  Use drawer dividers to organise utensils

## Things You'll Need

☐ racks and silverware holders

☐ spice rack

☐ appliance barn

☐ plastic containers

☐ drawer dividers

---

## Care for Silver 291

Extended exposure to air can tarnish your precious silver. Here's how to keep your silver flatware looking clean and new.

### ⊙ Steps

1  Handling helps keep silver free of tarnish, so use it regularly.

2  Avoid exposing silver for long periods of time to foods such as eggs, mustard and mayonnaise, all of which are high in sulphur, and can corrode silver.

3  Avoid leaving silver on rubber mats to dry – rubber also contains sulphur.

4  Wash and dry silver by hand.

5  Use a soft dish towel when drying silver.

6  Apply silver polish according to label instructions.

7  Rub the polish in thoroughly.

8  Buff the surface of polished silver with a fresh, dry polishing cloth until the silver has a bright sheen.

9  Thoroughly remove the polish from the silver before use; silver polish tastes terrible.

10  If silver is to be stored for a long time, pre-treat it with a tarnish-retardant polish before storing.

### ✳ Tip

Frequent polishing of silver-coated or -plated items may wear down their silver finish, leaving the base metal exposed. Rather than polishing such items, use them as often as possible and wash them by hand to prevent tarnishing.

### Things You'll Need

☐ silver polish

☐ soft dish towel

☐ soft polishing cloths

☐ tarnish-retardant polish

## 292 Polish Brass and Copper

Taking care of your brass objects and accessories is simple, and you may already have the necessary products.

### ⊙ Steps

1  Dust brass and copper regularly.

2  Wash in warm, soapy water; rinse and dry.

3  Use a commercial brass or copper cleaner as directed. A combination of toothpaste and Worcestershire sauce also works, although it is not as powerful as a commercial cleaner.

4  Apply with a soft cloth, wipe off, and buff with a clean, dry cloth.

5  Avoid using harsh chemicals, abrasive cleaners or scouring pads.

### ⚠ Warning

Do not polish lacquered brass or copper items.

### Things You'll Need

☐ brass or copper cleaner

☐ soft cloth

## 293 Clean a Coffeemaker

One way to make your coffee taste better is to keep your coffeemaker clean and free of hard-water deposits.

### ⊙ Steps

1  Put the filter basket in place.

2  Combine one part white vinegar with one part water in the pot; pour it into the coffeemaker and replace the pot. Turn the machine on.

3  Allow the solution to empty completely into the pot.

4  Turn the coffeemaker off and rinse the pot and filter basket with warm water.

5  Pour clean water into the coffeemaker and turn it on.

6  Allow the water to empty completely into the pot.

7  Rinse the pot.

8  Wipe the outside of the coffeemaker with a soapy sponge and polish it dry.

### ✱ Tips

Clean your coffeemaker weekly if you make a lot of coffee.

Consider purchasing a special coffeemaker cleaner. Follow the manufacturer's directions.

Rinse the pot and basket every day with warm water and once a week with mild soap and warm water.

### Things You'll Need

☐ white vinegar

☐ sponge

## 294 Clean a Fridge

Is there anything more unpleasant than opening a fridge door only to be greeted by some unexpected foul odour? It must be time to give your fridge a good going over.

### ⊙ Steps

1  Turn the temperature-control knob inside the fridge to "Off". If you have a fridge with a drip pan underneath, remove it to clean.

2  Take everything out of the fridge.

### ✱ Tip

Condenser coils should be vacuumed several times a year to prevent dust build-up.

3    Throw away any food that is mouldy, out of date or otherwise spoiled.

4    Take all removable parts out of the fridge, including shelves, wire racks and drawers.

5    Fill the sink with warm, soapy water (use a mild washing-up liquid).

6    Wipe any food matter out of the drawers.

7    Hand-wash the shelves, wire racks and drawers, then rinse them in warm water.

8    Let the shelves, wire racks and drawers drain in a dish rack, on paper towels or on newspapers.

9    Remove any food matter from the bottom of the fridge.

10   Wash the inside of the fridge using a sponge or dishcloth and the warm, soapy water. Remember the compartments and door racks.

11   Rinse the inside of the fridge with a sponge or dishcloth and clean warm water.

12   For odour control, use a solution of baking soda and warm water to wash the inside of the fridge (a solution of a few drops of vinegar in a bowl of warm water is also effective); apply and rinse. Leave a box of baking soda in the fridge to keep odours to a minimum.

13   Replace all shelves, wire racks and drawers.

14   Wash the outside of the fridge and the gasket – the rubber moulding around the door – with warm, soapy water; rinse and wipe dry.

15   Turn the temperature control knob inside the fridge back to the recommended setting.

16   Return the food to the fridge, first wiping off any bottles or jars that are sticky.

## ⚠ Warning

Never use harsh cleaners or scouring pads in or on the fridge.

## Things You'll Need

☐ mild washing-up liquid

☐ sponge or dishcloths

☐ baking soda or vinegar

---

## Clean a Toilet                                                          `295`

This will probably never be your favourite household chore, but it is one of the most important.

### ⊙ Steps

1    Open the bathroom windows and door, or turn on the fan. You need good ventilation when working with household cleaners.

2    Put on rubber gloves and lift the toilet seat. Flush the toilet to wet the sides of the bowl.

3    Apply a generous amount of powder or liquid toilet cleaner to the bowl, focusing on getting it along the sides, not just in the water. Be sure to follow the directions for your type of toilet bowl cleaner.

4    Let the cleaner stand for a minute.

5    Using the toilet brush, swab all around the interior of the bowl, paying special attention to the area immediately beneath the rim, and to the water line.

## ✱ Tip

High-pressure steam cleaners are very effective for cleaning toilets and bathrooms.

## ⚠ Warning

Never mix cleaners. The fumes could be deadly.

6   Flush the toilet to rinse. As the water in the bowl is replaced, thoroughly rinse the toilet brush in the incoming water.

7   Notice if the toilet bowl has developed a ring. If it has, scrub the stain with a wet pumice stone. Be sure the pumice remains wet throughout the process.

8   Spray the seat, the underside of the seat and the rim with disinfectant.

9   Wipe down the base, lid and tank top with disinfectant.

10  Allow the disinfectant to dry before using the toilet.

### Things You'll Need

- ☐ rubber gloves
- ☐ toilet cleaner
- ☐ toilet brush
- ☐ pumice stone
- ☐ disinfectant

## 296 | Clean a Bath

Scrub-a-dub-dub, there's soap scum in your tub; now how do you get it clean? With brushes and gloves you'll clean out that bath and give it a sparkling sheen.

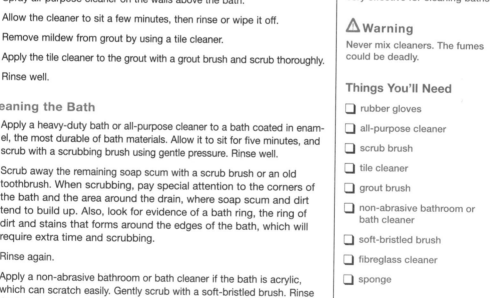

### ◉ Steps

#### Cleaning the Walls Above the Bath

1   Put on rubber gloves.

2   Spray all-purpose cleaner on the walls above the bath.

3   Allow the cleaner to sit a few minutes, then rinse or wipe it off.

4   Remove mildew from grout by using a tile cleaner.

5   Apply the tile cleaner to the grout with a grout brush and scrub thoroughly.

6   Rinse well.

#### Cleaning the Bath

1   Apply a heavy-duty bath or all-purpose cleaner to a bath coated in enamel, the most durable of bath materials. Allow it to sit for five minutes, and scrub with a scrubbing brush using gentle pressure. Rinse well.

2   Scrub away the remaining soap scum with a scrub brush or an old toothbrush. When scrubbing, pay special attention to the corners of the bath and the area around the drain, where soap scum and dirt tend to build up. Also, look for evidence of a bath ring, the ring of dirt and stains that forms around the edges of the bath, which will require extra time and scrubbing.

3   Rinse again.

4   Apply a non-abrasive bathroom or bath cleaner if the bath is acrylic, which can scratch easily. Gently scrub with a soft-bristled brush. Rinse the bath well.

5   Apply a specialised fibreglass cleaner or a non-abrasive bath cleaner to a fibreglass bath. Scrub gently with a sponge. Rinse well.

### ✳ Tip

Wipe down the bath with a washcloth or sponge after each use to avoid getting a bath ring.

High-pressure steam cleaners are very effective for cleaning baths.

### ⚠ Warning

Never mix cleaners. The fumes could be deadly.

### Things You'll Need

- ☐ rubber gloves
- ☐ all-purpose cleaner
- ☐ scrub brush
- ☐ tile cleaner
- ☐ grout brush
- ☐ non-abrasive bathroom or bath cleaner
- ☐ soft-bristled brush
- ☐ fibreglass cleaner
- ☐ sponge

# ✓ 297 Schedule Housekeeping Tasks

Keeping the house clean is an everyday chore, but you don't need to do it all every day. Some tasks you'll want to take care of daily; others you can put off for a week; still others you need to perform only once a year. To keep on top of the work, follow this schedule.

## Once a day

- Make beds.
- Pick up clutter.
- Throw dirty clothes in a laundry basket.
- Clean out bath and shower drains.
- Wipe off shower or bath.
- Wash dishes.
- Rinse kitchen sink.
- Empty kitchen rubbish.
- Wipe off kitchen counter.
- Wipe oven top and hobs.
- Sweep floor.

## Once a week

- Change bed linens.
- Vacuum carpets.
- Dust furniture.
- Clean shower or bath.
- Clean toilets.
- Throw out spoiled food in fridge.
- Empty all rubbish.
- Disinfect worktops.
- Flush sink disposal unit with cold water.
- Mop floor.

## Once a month

- Clean toothbrush and soap holders.
- Clean telephones.
- Clean the undersides of tables and chairs.
- Clean fridge shelves.
- Clean fridge exterior.
- Clean items on kitchen worktop.
- Disinfect rubbish bins.
- Clean oven, including range and backsplash.
- Check for cobwebs on ceilings, and vacuum.

## Every three months

- Wash or dry-clean quilts, duvets and bedspreads.
- Launder throw rugs and shower curtains.
- Wash blinds, shades, and curtains.
- Wash windows.
- Wash walls, mouldings and skirting boards.
- Wipe cabinets, wood-work and any smudges off walls.
- Clean fridge coils.
- Defrost freezer.
- Polish silver.

## Every six months

- Vacuum and turn mattresses.
- Empty bathroom cabinets and responsibly dispose of outdated medicines.
- Shampoo carpets.
- Wax or polish furniture.
- Empty kitchen cabinets and clean inside; throw away all outdated food.
- Clean tops of kitchen and bathroom cabinets.
- Vacuum behind large appliances.

## Once a year

- Empty dresser drawers and vacuum inside.
- Roll up area rugs and vacuum underneath.
- Clean ceiling fixtures.
- Re-seal wood floors.
- Go through all paperwork (bills, statements, notices) and recycle everything you don't need.
- Organise remaining papers in a filing system.

## 298 Clean Grout Without Scrubbing

Because sometimes it's OK to take the easy way out.

### ⊙ Steps

1   Put on rubber gloves.

2   Fill a spray bottle with a solution consisting of half liquid chlorine bleach and half warm water.

3   Turn the bottle nozzle to get a stream instead of a mist.

4   Spray the grout, saturating it with long, sweeping strokes.

5   Allow the saturated grout to sit for 10 to 15 minutes.

6   Repeat if needed.

7   Rinse or wipe off with a sponge.

### ✳ Tip

High-pressure steam cleaners are very effective for cleaning baths.

### Things You'll Need

☐ rubber gloves

☐ spray bottle

☐ chlorine bleach

☐ sponge

## 299 Remove Hard-Water Deposits From Showerheads

Hard water left on plastic surfaces causes lime and mineral deposits that can ruin your showerhead. Here's how to tackle these deposit problems on plastic showerheads.

### ⊙ Steps

1   Combine equal measures of white vinegar and hot water in a bowl.

2   Remove the showerhead from the pipe.

3   Submerge the showerhead in the vinegar-water solution for one hour.

4   Rinse and replace the showerhead.

### Things You'll Need

☐ white vinegar

☐ bowl

## 300 Make a Bed

These steps are for the traditional blanket and bedspread. If you use a quilt you can simply place it on top of the sheets without tucking it in. Pillows go on top.

### ⊙ Steps

1   Put the bottom sheet on the mattress. If it is a fitted sheet, it will have sewn-in corners and you can fit it snugly over the mattress. If it's a flat sheet, follow step 2 to make "hospital corners".

2   Lay the top sheet on the mattress so there's enough to tuck under the mattress on all four sides. Tuck the sheet snugly under the mattress at the foot of the bed and the head of the bed. Tuck the corners under the mattress on the long sides, making sure that the folds are flat. Tuck in the sides, pulling the sheet taut.

### ✳ Tip

A bed is a highly personal thing – choose bedding that will please the person sleeping there.

3   Place the top sheet over the fitted or bottom sheet, and again make hospital corners, but this time only at the foot of the bed.

4   Add blankets, repeating step 3.

5   Fold the top sheet back over the blankets at the head of the bed, pulling the sheet back about half a foot, and tuck under the side flaps.

6   Slip pillowcases over the pillows.

7   Place the pillows on top of the blanket and sheets at the head of the bed. Lay them flat, or prop them up against the headboard or wall.

8   Place the bedspread, quilt or comforter on the bed.

9   If you have a bedspread or thin quilt, fold the top of the spread down, lay the pillows on top, then fold the spread back over them, leaving part of the spread tucked under the pillows.

10  Place any remaining decorator pillows over the bed covering.

## Care for Down Pillows and Duvets                              301

Down pillows and duvets are luxurious on cold winter nights, but they require special care. The rule of thumb is: The less often you clean your duvet or pillow, the longer it will last.

### ◎ Steps

#### Caring for a Down Pillow

1   Cover your pillow with a pillow case at all times. This will keep your pillow free from dust, dirt and body oils.

2   Buy a pillow cover with a zip for an extra layer of protection under your pillow case. This will also help those who have allergies.

3   Clean the pillow cover and case regularly to keep your pillow fresh.

4   Launder or dry-clean your pillow yearly.

5   Spot-treat any stains before you wash your pillow if you're going to machine wash it.

6   Wash the pillow in cold water using a detergent that has a de-greaser so that oils are removed. Follow the pillow manufacturer's instructions for specific detergents to use.

7   Very gently squeeze out any excess water from the pillow after washing.

8   Dry the pillow with the dryer set on its lowest setting; put a tennis ball in with the pillow so that the fill moves as it dries.

9   Store your pillow in a dry and well-ventilated wardrobe or room when you are not using it, in order to avoid mildew.

#### Caring for a Down Duvet

1   Place a cover over your down duvet to protect it from dust, dirt and body oils.

2   Shake out your duvet weekly to prevent the down from bunching up.

**❋ Tip**

Thoroughly dry your pillow and comforter so that they will not mildew.

**⚠ Warning**

Do not use fabric softener when you wash – it will leave a coating on the down.

3   Air out your duvet occasionally to keep it fresh. Hang it on a clothesline or shake it out a window.

4   Take your duvet to a dry cleaner every three to five years if you decide not to launder it at home.

5   Use a Launderette with oversized washing machines if you have an oversized duvet, should you decide to machine-wash it.

6   Spot-treat any stains before you wash.

7   Wash your duvet in cold water using a detergent that has a de-greaser so that oils are removed.

8   Very gently squeeze out any excess water from the duvet.

9   Dry the duvet in the dryer on low heat setting with a tennis ball so that the fill moves as it dries.

10  Store the duvet in a dry and well-ventilated closet or room when you are not using it, in order to avoid mildew.

## 302 | Care for a Mattress

**Your mattress may be hidden under blankets and sheets, but it still needs special attention from time to time. If well cared for, it will last about 10 years.**

### ⊙ Steps

1   Cover your mattress with a cotton mattress pad, which will absorb perspiration and can be removed and washed to keep the mattress clean.

2   Rotate your mattress twice a year, or more often if instructed by the manufacturer. Flip it over completely after the first six months. Then, after another six months, flip it over and turn it so that the head is at the foot of the bed. Some new mattresses don't need turning over. Check with the manufacturer.

3   Use the handles on the sides of the mattress for positioning only – not for carrying. Lifting by the handles can damage your mattress.

4   Air out your mattress each morning by folding back the covers to the bottom of the bed for half an hour before you make it. This will also prevent moisture build-up.

5   Try not to sit on the edge of the bed in the same place every day, because this can lead to sagging.

### ✱ Tip

Leave the "do not remove" tag attached to the mattress. You will need this for filing warranty claims.

### ⚠ Warning

Avoid stain damage to your mattress. Many manufacturers void their warranties if there are stains.

# ✓ 303 Recycle Discards

Many local authorities have recycling schemes that pick up tins, bottles and newspapers. Some may also collect motor oil and other hazardous waste. But did you know that still other common materials can be safely recycled? Here's how to help find a few of these items a happy second home.

## Printer and photocopier cartridges

- Before you throw a cartridge away, be aware that printer cartridges can be recycled up to six times without any loss of quality.

- Read the manufacturer's instructions on the cartridge packing. It may tell you how to send back the cartridge free of charge so it can be refilled.

- You can find further information on dealing with used printer cartridges in the UK on the web pages of Eurosource (www.esel.co.uk) and the Cartridge Recycling Scheme (www.cartridge-recycling.org.uk) .

- Look at www.empty-inkjet-cartridges.com to find out how you can sell used printer cartridges.

## Packing "peanuts"

(These are the small "S-shaped" foam blocks used to protect items packed in boxes during transit.)

- Determine whether the peanuts are made from a vegetable derivative by running water on a few. If they disintegrate, they will decompose. Put them in a compost bin.

- Check with your local council to see if it will pick up large quantities of packing peanuts.

- Look under packaging or shipping in the Yellow Pages for a store that will accept the peanuts – some may let you drop them off.

## Computer Equipment

- Write down all the information about the old computer, such as its brand, type and model number, and which peripherals you wish to recycle.

- If you intend to continue using software currently loaded on an old machine, to avoid infringing copyright laws you should erase the contents of hard drives to be discarded. Obviously you should delete any personal files.

- Contact local schools or charities that might be able to make use of your equipment.

- Look at the web pages of Computer Aid (www.computer-aid.org) or UK Computer Recycling (www.uk-cr.org.uk) for more details on recycling computer technology in Great Britain.

## Batteries and Mobile Phones

- Take old car batteries to your local garage, or auto parts store.

- Many recycling centres will dispose of old car batteries.

- You can take unwanted mobile phones into any branch of Oxfam for recycling.

- Phone manufacturers such as Nokia will accept old phones. Look at their web pages (www.nokia.com).

- Look out for special trade-in offers where your mobile phone service provider may offer you a part-exchange deal on a new and better phone.

- FoneBak is a government-supported scheme for the recycling of mobile phones ( www.fonebak.co.uk).

reference

## 304 | Clean Out a Cupboard

Are the contents of your cupboards a mystery? Set aside a couple of hours to clean them out. All it takes is a little organisation to bring order to the chaos.

### ⊙ Steps

1 Start with a clean room, or you'll make an even bigger – not to mention more intimidating – mess as you clean out the cupboards.

2 Choose one area of the cupboard to focus on, such as a shelf, and begin there. It will make the overall task seem less daunting if you break it up into manageable parts.

3 Get three boxes and mark them "Rubbish", "Out of Place" and "Charity" (or "Car Boot Sale", if you're that way inclined).

4 Buy some stackable plastic bins with lids.

5 Evaluate each item you remove from the closet. Ask yourself if you have used the item in the past 12 months. If not, it's time to think seriously about getting rid of it.

6 Put things for charity shops in the "Charity" box.

7 Stash things that belong in other rooms in the "Out of Place box". (Give these things the 12-month test, too.)

8 Put as much as possible into the Rubbish box. You'll be surprised at how cathartic this can be!

9 Sort the items you want to keep into categories, such as "School Memorabilia", "Johnny's Artwork" or "Winter Accessories", and store them in the bins. Be sure to label the bins.

10 Label one bin "Odds & Ends". Here you can store "found" parts, orphaned gloves and other things that may eventually be reunited with their counterparts.

11 Stack the labelled bins neatly on the shelves and floor of the closet, making sure the ones you need to get into regularly are accessible.

### ✱ Tips

Give yourself a time limit. If you plan to devote 1½ hours to cleaning, don't do more than that. It will still be there later.

Some charities will come to your house to pick up unused items.

### ⚠ Warning

Get permission to throw away things that do not belong to you personally.

### Things You'll Need

☐ boxes

☐ plastic bins with lids

☐ labels

## 305 | Clean Brick Surfaces

Brick is an excellent and timeless building material for walls, home exteriors and other outdoor structures. However, it can get just as grimy as anything else. Here's how to clean it up.

### ⊙ Steps

1 Attack mould, mildew and lichens aggressively. They can change the colour of the masonry as well as affect its integrity. Prevent them from growing by keeping moisture to a minimum. Let as much air and sun reach the surface as possible.

2 Wear a dust mask and goggles when cleaning organic matter from brickwork. You'll create a lot of dust that you don't want to breathe.

### ⚠ Warning

Avoid using a wire brush, which will scratch brick surfaces.

3 Remove the crusties with a stiff scrubbing brush. To kill the spores, use a sponge to apply a solution of one part chlorine bleach to four parts water. Or use a commercial fungicide, available at garden centres.

4 Look for a white salt residue (efflorescence) on brickwork.

5 Remove it with the scrubbing brush. Don't use water - this will simply dissolve it, allowing it to soak into the brick.

6 Remove stains caused by mortar or cement by rubbing the area with a brick of the same colour.

### Things You'll Need

- ☐ dust mask and goggles
- ☐ stiff scrubbing brush
- ☐ sponge
- ☐ chlorine bleach

---

## Clean Out a Fireplace and Chimney | 306

A clean fireplace and chimney is your best defence against a dangerous chimney fire.

### ◎ Steps

1 Buy a set of chimney rods and brushes at the hardware shop.

2 Change into old clothes and don safety goggles and a dust mask. Lay out a clean dust sheet in front of the fireplace. Cover the fireplace opening with a plastic dust sheet held on with duct tape.

3 Open the fireplace's damper. This is the metal door up inside the fireplace, located just above the firebox; it prevents cold air from entering your home when you don't have a fire burning.

4 Carefully climb up on your roof, taking the rods and brushes with you.

5 Remove the chimney cap – sometimes called a spark arrestor – and check it for weather damage. The purpose of the chimney cap is to keep sparks from escaping your chimney. It also serves to keep out rain, small animals and debris.

6 Assemble the chimney rods and brushes according to the equipment manufacturer's directions.

7 Run the brush down the chimney, using a short up-and-down plunging motion. Some brushes are designed to twist as well.

8 Go back inside the house and use a short chimney brush to clean the flue, which is the pipe that runs between the fireplace and the chimney.

9 Use a vacuum cleaner or small broom and dustpan to remove the cold ashes and creosote from the fireplace and the damper.

10 Brush the floor and walls of the fireplace with a stiff scrubbing brush.

11 Use the brush to clean the creosote built up behind the damper.

12 Reach through the damper with a vacuum hose and vacuum the creosote out of the "smoke shelf", a cavity behind the fireplace.

13 Vacuum up all of the dust and debris.

### ✳ Tip

Depending on how often you use coal fires, consider hiring a professional to inspect your chimney and fireplace for any possible dangers, and to clean them out. This should cost less than £75.

### ⚠ Warning

Don't use water to clean the fire brick or cement blocks. It could affect heat retention.

### Things You'll Need

- ☐ chimney rods and brushes
- ☐ dust mask and goggles
- ☐ plastic dust sheets
- ☐ duct tape
- ☐ vacuum cleaner
- ☐ stiff scrubbing brush

## 307 | Clean a Barbecue Grill

To make your cleaning easier, try spraying the grill with a non-stick spray before you barbecue.

### ⊙ Steps

1   Put on rubber gloves.

2   Remove ash from the collector pan beneath the grill. (Make sure the charcoal is completely cool.)

3   Remove the grill's cooking and charcoal grates from inside the bowl.

4   Coat the bowl of the grill with spray-on oven cleaner.

5   Replace the grates and coat them with spray-on oven cleaner as well.

6   Wait as directed in the oven cleaner's directions.

7   Remove the grates again, and set them on newspaper. Scrub residue off the grates with a rag, steel wool or a wire brush, as needed. (If the grates have a non-stick coating, use a plastic scrubbing pad.)

8   Wipe out the bowl of the grill with wadded newspapers.

9   Use a high-pressure hose to rinse off the bowl and the grates.

10  Dry the grates and put a very light coating of cooking oil on each one.

11  Remove stains from the lid using warm, soapy water and a fine steel wool pad.

### ⚠ Warning

Avoid using harsh cleansers on any part of your barbecue grill.

### Things You'll Need

- ☐ rubber gloves
- ☐ oven cleaner
- ☐ newspaper
- ☐ rags, steel wool or wire brush
- ☐ plastic scrubbing pad
- ☐ hose
- ☐ cooking oil

## 308 | Clean a Crystal Chandelier

Your delicate chandelier will glow more brightly without all that dust and grime. Here's how to make it sparkle again.

### ⊙ Steps

1   Set up alternative lighting nearby (since you won't be able to use the chandelier for lighting while you're cleaning it).

2   Turn off the chandelier's power at the wall switch. Place a piece of tape over the wall switch so that no one can accidentally turn it on while you're working.

3   Cover any upward-pointing bulbs with sandwich bags. Secure the bags with rubber bands.

4   Place a dust cloth below the chandelier.

5   Mix a solution of one part isopropyl alcohol or ammonia in three parts distilled water. If you don't want to mix your own cleaner, you should be able to buy a special chandelier cleaner from many lighting retailers. Put some solution in a spray bottle.

6   Spray every part of the fixture with the cleanser, avoiding wires and other electrical components.

### Things You'll Need

- ☐ tape
- ☐ sandwich bags
- ☐ rubber bands
- ☐ drop cloth
- ☐ isopropyl alcohol or ammonia
- ☐ distilled water
- ☐ chandelier cleaner (optional)
- ☐ spray bottle

7　Allow the crystals to drip-dry. If your chandelier is too dirty for this drip-cleaning method, you'll have to hand-wash each individual crystal with the cleaning solution.

8　Remove the plastic bags from the lights once the crystals have dried, and wipe down light wells and other non-crystal parts with a soft cloth dipped in the cleanser.

9　Allow the entire fixture to dry overnight before turning its power back on.

---

## Remove Rust　309

Rust is tough, but you can get rid of it on most surfaces. Here's an overview of your options for treating and preventing rust on common objects.

### ⊙ Steps

1　Put on rubber gloves.

2　Treat the affected material (metal or otherwise) with a rust-removing agent that contains oxalic acid, taking care to follow instructions on the product label.

3　Treat the most severe rust stains (especially in toilet bowls) with a pumice scouring pad along with the rust-removing agent.

4　Prevent indoor metal items from rusting by keeping their surfaces dry, dusting regularly and wiping down occasionally with a damp cloth. Dry immediately after wiping down.

5　Keep outdoor wrought-iron structures rust-free by removing existing rust with a wire brush, some sandpaper or a sandblaster. Then go over bare spots with rust-inhibiting primer and paint the surface with rust-resistant metal paint.

### Things You'll Need

- ☐ rubber gloves
- ☐ rust remover
- ☐ pumice scouring pad
- ☐ wire brush, sandpaper or sand blaster
- ☐ rust-inhibiting primer
- ☐ rust-resistant metal paint

---

## Remove Stickers　310

Many common household items will help you remove stickers and adhesive-backed price tags from a variety of surfaces. You can also purchase products made especially for this purpose.

### ⊙ Steps

1　Remove stickers from glass, plastic or metal with alcohol-based products such as nail polish remover or 91 per cent rubbing alcohol. Oil-based products such as cooking oil, mineral oil and baby oil can also be used. Apply the liquid to a clean cloth and saturate the sticker; allow it to sit for a minute or so and peel the sticker from the surface.

2　Remove stickers from cardboard or paper with an alcohol-based product or with a commercial solvent. Apply the liquid to the sticker with a cotton swab until the sticker is saturated. Avoid getting too much liquid on the surrounding surface. Peel the sticker away.

### ✱ Tips

Remove as much of a laminated sticker as you can before you apply a liquid or solvent. Most products will not be able to penetrate the plastic coating.

Heat the sticker with a hair dryer before treating. (Do not use this method on plastics.)

3   Remove stickers from wood with furniture polish or any of the products
    listed in step 1. Again, saturate the sticker with the liquid and allow it to
    sit for 1 to 2 minutes. Peel the sticker away.

4   Saturate stickers that are on hard plastic surfaces (plastic tubs or food
    storage containers) with cooking oil. Allow the sticker to soften, then
    immerse it in water. Wipe the sticker away.

5   Repeat the sticker-removal process if any gummy residue remains after
    the first treatment. Scrape residue with a paint scraper or razor blade.

Avoid unnecessary stains. Test
the liquid or solvent on an inconspicuous area of the surface
before you proceed with the
sticker-removal process. Do not
use oil-based products on paper
or cardboard.

---

## 311 | Rid Your Home of Ants

**Ants enter homes looking for food, water and shelter.
Controlling them usually requires a combination of methods.**

### ⊙ Steps

1   Keep ants out. Seal all the cracks and crevices you find around your
    home's foundations; inside, pay special attention to areas where food is
    prepared.

2   Fix plumbing leaks. Remove food sources. Store food in clean, closed
    containers. Store rubbish outdoors in sealed containers.

3   Use poison to destroy nests. For an entire colony to be destroyed, ant
    poison must be slow-acting. Some of the chemicals that are effective in
    poisons are hydramethylnon, boric acid and fipronil. Poisons will work
    only if there is no other food source nearby.

4   If ants are inside, wash them away with warm, soapy water. This removes
    the chemical trail and is as effective as most of the insecticides.

5   Do not allow any wood – firewood, garden debris or foundations – to
    remain in contact with the soil. Damp wood provides a habitat for
    tree ants. Trim tree branches and shrubs away from buildings.

### ✳ Tip

For extreme ant infestations,
seek the help of a professional
exterminator.

### ⚠ Warning

Be sure to keep ant poisons
away from children and pets.

---

## 312 | Rid Your Home of Flies

**Flies spread disease, contaminate food and can place human
health at risk.**

### ⊙ Steps

1   Keep flies out with barriers, your first and best line of defence. Keep
    windows and doors closed. Seal all cracks and crevices.

2   Remove all outside organic-waste piles, which can be used as breeding
    sites: dog faeces, animal manure, piles of grass clippings. (Hot compost
    piles are inhospitable to breeding flies.) Keep rubbish in a container with
    a tightly fitting lid.

3   Put out traps – flypaper or sticky tape will catch a few flies. Use inverted
    cone traps to attract more flies with food poison.

### ✳ Tips

Egg-to-adult development in flies
can take place in as little as
seven days.

The best time to control the fly
populations is at their juvenile or
larval stage, by eliminating
breeding areas such as organic
rubbish and dog faeces.

Flies rapidly develop resistance
to insecticides, so use them only
as a last resort.

4   Remember that poison only works well if flies do not have access to other food sources. Place poisons well away from eating areas.

5   Cover and refrigerate food leftovers.

6   Use a fly swatter against the occasional fly that strays into the house.

⚠ **Warning**

Use non-residual pyrethrin sprays indoors, but carefully follow all directions.

## Rid Your Home of Clothing Moths                                  313

The worm-like larvae of clothing moths feed on fabrics, clothing, carpets, rugs, furs, blankets, wool products, upholstery, piano felts and brushes – any materials of animal origin.

### ⦿ Steps

1   Keep your house clean. Vacuum under furniture, along skirting boards, in corners, in closets and around heater vents and draperies. Get rid of full vacuum cleaner bags promptly, as they may contain eggs, larvae or adult insects.

2   Remove empty bird, rodent and insect nests from your home's perimeter, as they can also harbour moths.

3   Store out-of-season clothes properly. Dry-clean or wash them in hot water (above 49°C/120°F) for 20 to 30 minutes before storing. Brush out any pockets, along the seams and under collars. Store clothes in airtight containers.

4   Place mothballs, flakes or crystals in airtight containers, but include a layer of paper to keep clothing from making contact with the insecticides. (These products contain naphthalene or paradichlorobenzene, which can fuse plastic – including plastic buttons – into fabric.) Vapours from the insecticides will build up in the container and slowly kill the moths.

✱ **Tips**

Clothing moths are not attracted to light.

Clothing moths flutter close by the area of infestation.

⚠ **Warning**

The chemicals in mothballs can cause irritation to the skin, throat and eyes, and may be toxic if swallowed or inhaled. Follow the manufacturer's directions for use.

## Rid Your Home of Pantry Moths or Weevils                         314

Intruders in your flour and oatmeal? Suspect pantry moths or weevils. The first line of defence is good housekeeping.

### ⦿ Steps

1   Check for infestation. Examine all food packages for telltale signs of moth or weevil infestation: webbing in corners, grains clumped together with sticky secretions, or small holes in containers. Also look for small bugs in the food or little moths flying around the kitchen. If you find them, read on.

2   Clean infested areas. Vacuum cupboards, then thoroughly scrub all shelves with soapy water, paying close attention to cracks and corners. Dry the cleaned area thoroughly. Keep cupboard and food-storage areas dry.

3   Discard infested food.

4   Store food properly. Clean containers with hot, soapy water, then rinse and dry them thoroughly before refilling. Use tightly sealed metal, glass

✱ **Tips**

Pantry moth larvae eat a wide assortment of foods, ranging from flour to dried chillies and candy.

It takes six to eight weeks for the pantry moth to complete its life cycle.

⚠ **Warning**

Do not use pesticides in or around any area where food is prepared, or on food itself.

or hard plastic containers to store food; plastic bags are inadequate, as insects can get through them. Keep old and new food separate, and keep infrequently used items in the freezer.

5   Eliminate the pests' food sources (such as improperly stored food) and breeding grounds (such as rodent nests).

## 315  Rid Your Home of Cockroaches

Cockroaches can transmit bacterial diseases and hepatitis virus, and have been known to spread dysentery and typhoid fever. Many people are allergic to them.

### ⊙ Steps

1   Eliminate sources of food and water. Store food in sealed metal, glass or hard plastic containers. Remove rubbish from kitchens promptly, and place in containers with tight-fitting lids. Repair any plumbing leaks in or under your home. Place pet water bowls in a pan of soapy water at night.

2   Vacuum all corners to remove tiny food crumbs. If anyone in the house is allergic to roaches, be sure that your vacuum cleaner has a HEPA filter.

3   Prune plants away from vents near your home's foundation where roaches can creep in. Remove piles of debris.

4   Seal cracks and crevices wherever possible, both inside and outside.

5   Check furniture and appliances that have been in storage for egg cases.

6   Consider insecticide only if you must; cockroaches learn very quickly to avoid fast-acting insecticides such as insecticide spray. If you must use an insecticide indoors, dust a slow-acting one such as boric acid under cupboards and into cracks and corners. Remember that boric acid is permanently ineffective once it becomes damp.

7   Use poisons and sticky traps as effective alternatives to spraying indoors. Add insect-growth regulators to poisons to increase their effectiveness. Look for them where insecticides are sold.

**✳ Tip**

Tropical in origin, cockroaches require humidity and warmth as well as a food source. They prefer to live in cracks and tight crevices, and are nocturnal. Bathrooms and kitchens are favourite haunts.

**⚠ Warning**

Avoid the use of aerosol foggers. These can make things worse by dispersing the cockroaches over a wider area.

## 316  Rid Your Home of Spiders

Most spiders are beneficial, keeping many insect pests under control. Instead of killing spiders, take them outside and release them into your garden. Here's how to keep them outdoors.

### ⊙ Steps

1   Practise good sanitation for control. Vacuum and clear away all webs, being sure to remove any egg cases. Move and dust frequently behind furniture, stored boxes and appliances.

2   Eliminate the spiders' food sources – including flies, cockroaches and moths – and they will be less likely to return. Seal cracks by which spiders might enter the house.

**✳ Tip**

If you're determined to use a chemical control against spiders, keep in mind that these are only effective if the chemical lands directly on the spider. A fly swatter works as quickly.

3  Remove piles of wood, trash and debris from around the foundation of your home. Be sure to wear protective clothing: long-sleeved shirts, long pants, gloves and boots.

4  Hose off the outside of your home to destroy webs and egg cases.

5  Replace outdoor lights with yellow or sodium-vapour lightbulbs, which are less likely to attract insects and then spiders.

6  Shake out clothing that has been stored before putting it on.

# Rid Your Home of Mice                                            317

As with most pests, keeping mice out of your home in the first place is the best way to avoid infestation.

## ⊙ Steps

### Protecting Your Home

1  Keep your lawn mowed. Mice do not like to travel through short grass.

2  Remove wood piles, rubbish and debris from your home's perimeter. Elevate wood piles 46 cm (18 in) above ground level. To protect yourself when cleaning out wood piles, rubbish or debris, be sure to wear protective clothing: long-sleeved shirts, long trousers, gloves and boots.

3  Check all vents.

4  Check where pipes enter the building. In wooden walls, place sheet-metal collars around those entrances. In stucco, stone or brick walls, use cement fill.

5  Fill cracks and crevices around the foundation and eaves with sealant or foam. Steel wool can be used, although it rusts.

6  Remove food sources by placing all food items, including pet food and bird seed, in tightly sealed containers. Clean up fallen bird seed. Keep rubbish in containers with tight-fitting lids.

7  Avoid vacuuming or sweeping mouse droppings, due to the dangers of hantavirus, a deadly virus spread to humans through contact with rodents and rodent urine and droppings. Droppings should be misted with a strong household disinfectant (chlorine bleach) and wiped up with paper towels.

### Trapping and Poisoning

1  Place traps or poison pellets near holes and in places where you've seen mice. The trigger should be as near to the hole as possible.

2  Use fruit, sweets or peanut butter if your traps require bait.

3  Check traps daily.

4  Put on thick gloves and remove the carcass from the trap once a mouse has been caught.

5  Seal the carcass in old newspaper or a plastic bag and place it in an outdoor rubbish bin.

## ❋ Tip

Mice are prolific breeders and can have as many as 13 litters per year. They can squeeze through a hole as small as a pencil rubber and are excellent climbers.

## ⚠ Warning

Be aware that mice can carry diseases. Some of them – such as hantavirus – are potentially fatal.

## 318 | Design a Small Urban Garden

Whether you are starting from scratch or taking on a mature garden, it is worth making a design at the start. Even if you can't do all the work at once, you'll know what you are aiming for.

### ⊙ Steps

1 Think about what you want to use your garden for. Is it a family play area, a quiet haven for a drink at the end of the day, a wildlife paradise or simply somewhere pretty to look at out of the window?

2 Decide, too, how much time you can spare to maintain the garden. Are you willing to be out there daily at some times of the year, watering and checking the plants, or do you want somewhere that will look good with the minimum of upkeep?

3 Look at what you have already. Draw a plan of the garden to scale on squared paper and sketch in anything that is already there – borders, a shed, a large tree and so on. Test the soil acidity using a kit.

4 Watch and plot on your plan where the shadows fall at certain times of day. Are some areas in sun all day and some constantly in shade?

5 Set a budget. Be realistic – plants and materials are not cheap when you add them all up, so do not go beyond what you can afford

6 Start to create your design, using the information you have collected. Decide whether you want to move a shed, or cut down a tree (an established tree lends height and maturity to a garden, but may also create too much shade). Plot on tracing paper over the plan the main features you want to include, positioning them in the best place – so a patio could go a sunny part of the garden, or a compost heap in a far corner, or a greenhouse in a spot with a mix of sun and shade. If plants are your priority, choose the best sites for the sorts of plants you wish to grow.

7 Consider how you will move through the garden. Do you need to add some paths? Can you include an arch or screen an area to create extra interest? While straight lines can suit a formal, modern design, simple curves can provide a more fluid, softer look.

8 Plan your boundaries. In a small garden it's vital to use every bit of space, and planting climbers up the walls and fences, or fastening a planter to a dull wall can make a huge difference.

9 Plan the planting. Look at surrounding gardens to see what thrives in your area. Visit gardens open to the public to get ideas on which plants look good together and their mature sizes. Match the plants to your soil type and plan to improve the soil if necessary. Think too plants for different seasons (see also 339 "Design and Prepare a Flower Bed").

10 Work up your plan in three dimensions. This is essential for planning heights, planting distances and quantities of plants in the border as well as the scale of walls, patios and paths. You can obtain simple computer programs that help with designs, and show you how plants will look over time. Keep experimenting.

11 Make a schedule for the work. Some planting is best done in spring or autumn, while the hard structures can be built at any time. Allow yourself plenty of time to obtain the plants and materials.

### ✳ Tips

Take plenty of time before you start working on the garden to think about what you need and like as well as what is there already. Time spent thinking and watching the garden is never wasted.

Lawns are not essential in a small garden. They often have to be small and so may be overused, and in a city thay may be shaded so the grass will never thrive.

For instant colour while other plants are maturing, use annuals (see 342 "Growing Annuals").

### ⚠ Warning

Don't try to include everything in a small garden or the design will end up looking bitty. It's best to aim for a simple and strong design for maximum impact rather than anything too fussy.

# Plan a Large Garden

A large garden offers great opportunities. There is space to include different areas within the garden and a variety of features. It all takes careful planning to make sure it hangs together.

## ⊙ Steps

1   Use the same design principles as for a small garden (see 318 "Design a Small Urban Garden"): think about what you want to use the garden for, how much time and money you can spend on it and what's there already.

2   Look at what surrounds your garden. Are you overlooked or would you like to "borrow" the surrounding landscape, making it part of your garden? Do you want privacy or openness?

3   Assess the style of your house. Is it built of local stone or does it include architectural features that you would like to continue in the garden? Or is it fairly plain, offering you the chance to create a garden that makes a statement in its own right?

4   What is the prevailing wind direction? Do you need to make or maintain tall boundaries to shelter the garden? If you are by the sea, there will be salt borne on the winds    this will affect the plants you choose.

5   Test the soil's acidity and texture in several places. This will also affect your planting – you could plan a damp garden for the moist foot of a hill, for instance – and you may need to plan to improve the soil.

6   Make a scale plan of the plot and house, including level changes, soil type and existing large features such as trees and hedges. Is the whole garden visible in one sweep from the house? If not, indicate areas that cannot be seen. Use these for functional aspects of the garden or perhaps for creating a "secret" garden within a garden.

7   Start making rough plans on tracing paper over your scale drawing. Try as many as you want. A large garden is often more interesting if it is divided up into areas. The divisions can be subtle, like a change of planting, or more obvious like hedges and gates. Position vegetable beds, water features, greenhouse – all the large elements. If you can't get an area of the plan to work, look at the whole again.

8   Include seating areas, from patios to benches. These will enable you to enjoy your garden from several angles and will provide focal points.

9   Choose the materials for any hard features like patios and paths, ensuring they complement the materials used in the house.

10  Decide on your framework plants. Will you have some trees to give scale, or hedges, or an arbour for climbing roses? These large plants will be a feature in their own right and set the tone for the rest of the planting.

11  Plan the planting in detail (see 339 "Design and Prepare a Flower Bed"). In a large garden, swathes of the same plants look most striking in borders. Choose plants that suit the style of garden you want. For a formal look select plants with a strong shape. In an informal, cottage garden plants can be more easy-going in habit.

12  Make a three-dimensional plan (see 318 "Design a Small Urban Garden") and keep adjusting it. Create a schedule for the work.

## ✳ Tip

Keep an open mind and allow the plan to evolve over time. Look at where the good spots are to spend time in the garden at different times of day and year and use this knowledge to improve your plan.

## ⚠ Warning

It will take several years for the garden to mature. Do not be tempted to plant too closely as the plants will not thrive, and you will waste time and money. If you can afford to buy them, a couple of larger trees or shrubs will add an established air to the garden – but they need very careful watering and care for the first year or two to help them settle in.

## 320 | Select Basic Gardening Tools

You don't need to spend a lot to start a garden, but you do need some basic tools. You can get started for under £100 – less if you can find tools at jumble sales or second-hand shops.

### ⊙ Steps

1 Select a garden fork as your first tool. Before you plant anything, you will need to open and improve the soil. A fork is used to dig down into hard soil and break up the ground. A smaller version, known as a border fork is a lightweight alternative, but will not manage heavy jobs.

2 Next, choose a hoe. A hoe is useful for weeding and cultivating the surface of the soil to allow for penetration of nutrients and water.

3 Choose a watering can. Long nozzles allow the water to come out at a very gentle flow rate and are useful for reaching across long distances. Select a watering can that has a detachable spray head – this type of watering can is perfect for watering young seedlings.

4 Select a spade for larger digging projects, such as planting shrubs and trees. A border spade is smaller and good for light work in small spaces.

5 Buy a good garden rake, with the rake head made from one piece of steel for strength. It's used for levelling the soil after it has been turned and prior to planting, or for removing large clods of earth or rocks from the soil. You can also turn the rake over and use the flat side to smooth soil in preparation for planting.

6 Select a pair of secateurs that fits comfortably in your hand. Secateurs, sometimes called clippers, are used for pruning, shaping and removing foliage or branches. Don't buy the most expensive secateurs until you decide you like gardening.

**✳ Tip**

These are the basic garden tools. Others might come in handy but are not essential.

**⚠ Warning**

Don't buy the most expensive tools when you are just starting out. You may find that you don't really like gardening – and if that is the case, you will not have lost a large investment.

**Things You'll Need**

❑ garden fork

❑ hoe

❑ watering can

❑ spade

❑ garden rake

❑ secateurs

## 321 | Begin a Compost Heap

Make the greatest organic matter you can ever add to your soil – start a compost heap. Recycle your garden and kitchen waste and watch nature's most basic process unfold in your garden.

### ⊙ Steps

1 Start a very basic compost simply by piling up leaves and grass clippings. If you do nothing else, you can dig out compost after about six months of warm weather.

2 For something a little more thought-out, start by finding a good place for your heap – somewhere that is handy for the garden and kitchen, yet not prominently in view.

3 Enclose that compost with a simple frame – loosely roll 2 m (6 ft) of chicken wire to make a ring. Leave three cut ends of wire exposed to secure the ring to itself and stand it up.

**✳ Tips**

Healthy compost smells pleasantly earthy – turn it more often and add more dry brown matter if yours smells bad.

Water your compost heap only during extended dry weather, and then only enough to moisten it, not drench the contents.

Many excellent compost bins of varying sizes are available ready-made at different prices.

4  Build a more permanent compost bin from slatted wood or recycled pallets. Leave it open on one side for access – adding, turning and digging out compost from the bottom – and do not cover the top.

5  Understand the two basic elements that make compost: green (grass clippings, old annuals) and brown (dry leaves, soil) garden debris. Try for a balance of one part green to one to two parts brown, until the mix is damp but not wet.

6  Put a layer of leaves 10 cm (4 in) thick in the bottom of your heap, then 2.5 cm (1 in) of your good garden soil. Next add 5cm (2 in) of grass clippings or old plants, then more brown and green in alternate layers.

7  Turn with a fork one week after building your heap. Begin burying coffee grounds, eggshells and green kitchen waste into the heap and turn it weekly. You'll have compost in about two months.

8  Make another ring or bin and turn the compost from one into the other to neatly mix it up and aerate the heap for fastest results. (Start another heap after yours has grown to 1 cubic m/1 cubic yd.)

9  Begin digging out compost from the bottom of the heap when you turn it over and cannot recognise the component parts any longer. Dig out shovelfuls of crumbly brown compost to use in your garden, and use the partially composted matter for mulch or to start another heap.

## ⚠ Warning

Do not compost animal waste, meats, oils, diseased plants or plants treated with weed killers.

## Things You'll Need

❑ garden and kitchen waste

❑ chicken wire or wood

❑ garden fork

---

## Maintain a Container Garden

### 322

Plants in containers offer a great opportunity to brighten up a patio, terrace or balcony. Provided that you water, feed and care for them well, they will flourish.

### ◉ Steps

1  Choose the right compost for your plants and avoid using garden soil, which becomes stale and may harbour pests. Composts can be loam-based or loam free. They contain different nutrient levels; a low-nutrient compost is ideal for short-lived annuals, while a high-nutrient one is good for shrubs and trees. Use a lime-free compost for lime-haters such as azaleas.

2  Water carefully and regularly, up to several times daily in hot, dry summers. Hanging baskets in particular dry out very quickly. Try mixing water-retaining granules with the compost to hold water for longer. Use crocks in the base of containers to keep drainage holes clear.

3  Feed containers regularly in the growing season with a liquid fertiliser. Feed fast-growing annuals more often than more permanent plants.

4  Keep plants healthy and tidy. Deadhead regularly and pinch out or prune plants that are straggly or uneven (see 351 "Deadhead Flowers" and 353 "Shape and Revive a Plant"). Clear fallen leaves from in and around pots.

5  Repot at the end of the season. For long-term plants, repot if the roots are starting to emerge from the base of the container, choosing a larger container and adding fresh compost. Replace tired-looking annuals with new plants or bulbs.

### ❋ Tip

For thriving plants, choose those that like the conditions you have. If you have a sunny spot, choose sun-lovers, or for a shady corner choose shade-lovers.

### ⚠ Warnings

If you are using windowboxes, make sure they are securely fixed to the sill.

Take care when lifting heavy plants. Lift with a straight back and bent legs, or ask for help.

### Things You'll Need

❑ compost

❑ watering can

❑ fertiliser

❑ clean pots

# ✓ 323 Care for Your Garden, Season by Season

Your garden follows an annual cycle of growth and dormancy. And you, the gardener, must keep up with this cycle. Use this guide to help remind you of the tasks that need to be completed every spring, summer, autumn and winter. Keep in mind that this is a general guide; adjust the tasks to your local conditions.

## Spring

- Sow annuals in containers indoors.
- Transplant seedlings into the garden when any chance of frost damage is past.
- Feed shrubs, trees, climbers and ground cover plants.
- Stake climbing and tall plants if needed.
- Deadhead spring-flowering annuals and perennials.
- Prune shrubs that flower on new growth.
- Prune shrubs that have finished flowering.
- Prune climbers to shape them.
- Lay turf or sow seeds for a lawn.

## Summer

- Transplant annuals for summer and autumn flowering.
- Feed fruit-bearing plants.
- Continue to deadhead flowering plants.
- Remove dead branches from evergreens.
- Prune climbers that flower on old wood after flowering.
- Mulch to save water and control weeds.
- Dig up, divide and store spring-flowering bulbs.
- Feed roses after each flush of blooms.
- Prepare soil in areas where you plan to plant in the autumn.
- Keep summer flowers and vegetables constantly moist.

## Autumn

- Plant spring-flowering bulbs.
- Plant lettuce and other cool-season vegetables.
- Lay turf or seed for a lawn.
- Plant hardy perennials.
- Net ponds to stop leaves falling in.
- Rake and dispose of fallen leaves and other debris.
- Divide perennials.
- Remove dead and diseased wood from shrubs in late autumn
- Move frost-intolerant container plants to a protected spot.

## Winter

- Plant bare-root trees, roses and other shrubs before spring growth starts.
- Protect plants from severe cold with plastic sheeting, hessian or other material.
- Prune dormant fruit trees and soft fruit bushes before spring growth starts.
- Mulch young fruit trees and bushes.
- Sharpen lawn mower blades and shears.
- Prune roses in winter to early spring, depending on climate.
- Start seeds of flowers and vegetables indoors.

calendar

# Create a Lawn 324

Create a healthy lawn as a key part of your garden and reap more rewards than beauty alone. It can also be a functional part of the garden, for relaxing or for children to play.

## ⊙ Steps

1 Choose the right type of grass for your needs. Decide whether you will start with grass seed or turf.

2 Sow grass seed in spring or autumn (or summer if there is a good watering system). Lay turf at any time of year, but not in very dry weather.

3 Test your soil – the simplest way is to test it yourself with a home kit, but you may be able simply to check with neighbours or a nursery that knows local conditions. Find out what nutrients you have and lack, what the pH is, and whether or not you need lime or sulphur. Check also how free-draining the soil is.

4 Improve the soil by spreading 5–8 cm (2–3 in) of organic matter, such as compost or ground bark, over the planting area. Also spread a starter fertiliser, which is usually high in potassium and phosphorous, if it's called for after a soil test.

5 Dig over the soil to incorporate the organic matter to a depth of 15–20 cm (6–8 in). Firm the soil thoroughly to create a level surface.

6 In dry areas or for large high-quality lawns, consider an irrigation system to simplify watering. Place enough sprinklers or hoses and pipes around to irrigate, or have an underground system installed.

7 Smooth the planting area with a the back of a rake.

8 Sow seed or lay turf over the planting area.

9 Keep the area moist until the grass is firmly established (six to eight weeks on average).

## ✳ Tips

Much of the equipment needed to plant a lawn can be borrowed or rented from your local nursery.

To make raking easier, water the area thoroughly three or four days before planting.

## ⚠ Warnings

Keep kids and dogs off the grass until it's at least 4 cm (1½ in) tall and ready for mowing.

Avoid letting your newly planted lawn dry out. You may need to water more than once a day for at least a week after planting.

## Things You'll Need

❑ grass seed or turf

❑ soil testing kit

❑ organic matter

❑ fertiliser

❑ fork

❑ rake

# Plant a Lawn From Seed 325

Planting grass from seed is an inexpensive way to grow a beautiful new lawn, but you need to prepare the soil carefully and watch over the sprouting seeds. Here are the basics.

## ⊙ Steps

1 Select the right type of grass seed. The most common mix for a hard-wearing surface is perennial ryegrass with red fescue, smooth-stalked meadow grass and browntop or highland bent. Other mixtures are available for high-quality lawns or shady areas.

2 Measure the area of your new lawn to determine how much seed you'll need. Purchase the seed at a local nursery or garden centre. Information on the packet will tell you how much to buy.

3 Prepare and level the soil, as described in 324 "Create a Lawn".

## ✳ Tips

Once you have thoroughly watered the seedbed after planting, you only need to water enough to keep the top 2.5 cm (1 in) moist. Germination will take 5 to 14 days, depending on weather and grass type.

When the grass is 2.5–5 cm (1–2 in) high, you can begin to water less often; avoid letting the planting area go completely dry.

4   Set your seed spreader at the appropriate setting and fill it with half the seeds.

5   Walking at a steady pace, sow the seed over the planting area, moving back and forth in opposite directions. Repeat the process using the rest of the seeds, walking at a 90-degree angle to your original paths. This will ensure that the seed is sown evenly.

6   Rake over the area lightly. This will help keep the seeds from drying out.

7   Push a roller over the entire area to make sure the seeds and soil are in good contact.

8   Water the seedbed thoroughly so the soil is moist to a depth of 15–20 cm (6–8 in). Apply the water slowly so that the seeds do not wash away.

9   Keep the seedbed moist (but not soggy) until the seed germinates and the new grass is a few centimetres high. In hot weather you may have to water more than once a day.

⚠ **Warning**

Heavy watering may wash away the seeds, and watering too frequently may rot the seedlings.

**Things You'll Need**

☐ grass seed

☐ seed spreader

☐ rake

☐ roller

☐ watering equipment

---

## 326  Plant a Lawn From Turf

Planting turf (living green grass) turns a patch of dirt into a beautiful lawn instantly. Here are the basic steps.

### ◎ Steps

1   Select the right type of grass for your area (see 325 "Plant a Lawn from Seed").

2   Measure the area of your new lawn to determine how much turf you'll need. Purchase fresh turf at a local nursery or garden centre, or have it delivered from a local turf farm.

3   Prepare and level the soil, as described in 324 "Create a Lawn." The final level should be 2.5–5 cm (1–2 in) lower than the final lawn height to accommodate the thickness of the turf.

4   Pick up the turf or arrange to have it delivered on the day you are ready to lay it. Inspect the turf carefully to make sure it hasn't dried out. Reject it if it has dried, curled or cracked edges, or yellowing grass.

5   Start laying the turf along a straight edge, such as a drive or path. To create a straight edge, stretch a string across the centre of the lawn.

6   Position the turf pieces so the ends butt up tightly against an edge or previously laid piece. Unroll the turf. Place edges as close as possible, but don't overlap them.

7   Stagger pieces as you move from row to row (as if you were laying bricks) so the ends don't all line up.

8   Use an old kitchen knife to cut turf to fit in odd-shaped areas.

9   Fill in any large spaces between pieces of turf with soil.

10  Push a roller over the entire area to make sure that turf and soil are in good contact and to help level the area, or firm with the back of a rake.

11  Water thoroughly so the soil is moist to a depth of 15–20 cm (6–8 in).

### ❊ Tips

Lay the turf on dry soil to avoid a muddy mess.

When laying turf, kneel on a plank of wood so you don't disturb soil or damage turf, and use kneepads to keep your knees from getting sore.

Laying turf is hard work. Enlist help, and use a wheelbarrow to cart pieces around.

Keep pets and kids off your new lawn by enclosing it with stakes and string.

⚠ **Warning**

Avoid letting turf dry out. Occasionally sprinkle it with water from a handheld hose, and store pallets of turf in the shade.

**Things You'll Need**

☐ turf

☐ string

☐ old kitchen knife

☐ roller or rake

12  Keep the planting bed moist (but not soggy) until the turf roots knit with the soil below. In hot weather, you may have to water more than once a day to prevent turves drying out and shrinking.

## Mow, Edge and Trim a Lawn 327

Conscientious mowing, followed by edging and trimming, reduces weeds, thickens turf and improves the lawn's appearance and vitality.

### ⊙ Steps

#### Mowing

1  Choose the proper mower for your type of lawn. Cylinder mowers provide a fine finish on a high-quality lawn, while rotary mowers are good for mowing large areas. Hover mowers are ideal for small or awkward areas.

2  Set mower blades to the proper height according to grass type and time of year. Set the blade height by placing the mower on a flat, paved surface. Use a ruler to measure between blades and pavement. Adjust according to the manufacturer's instructions.

3  Mow the lawn when the grass is about a third higher than the recommended mowing height.

4  Leave grass clippings on the lawn, unless the grass has grown very tall between mowings. They will contribute organic matter and nutrients as they break down.

#### Edging and Trimming

1  Use grass shears around trees, under hedges or in places that are hard to reach.

2  Use a nylon-line trimmer (strimmer) to trim and edge large lawns or to cut grass too tall to mow.

3  Create a neat edge to your lawn by using a half-moon edger (a small semicircular blade) between beds and lawn. Push the blade in with your foot so that it slices off a thin piece of turf, leaving a clean, straight edge of soil between lawn and bed. You can also use this to cut edges on worn pieces of turf, or to cut out and remove turves.

4  If you use a half-moon edger, return slices of soil to the garden beds to break down; chop slightly and bury them under the mulch for a neat, nourishing edge.

5  Use edging shears to trim grass that is overhanging the edge of the lawn.

### ✳ Tips

Mow more frequently in summer when the grass is growing quickly. When mowing for the first time at the end of winter, give a high cut initially, then lower the blades slightly with each cut. An average guide for the height of cut to aim for is 1–2.5 cm ($\frac{1}{2}$–1 in).

Mow at the upper end of the height range during hot weather or periods of drought. Taller grasses have deeper roots and survive heat and drought better than shorter grasses.

### ⚠ Warning

Wear protective footwear and eye protection and follow manufacturers' safety instructions. Remove young children and pets from the area being mown.

### Things You'll Need

☐ lawn mower

☐ grass shears

☐ nylon-line trimmer

☐ half-moon edger

☐ edging shears

## 328 | Remove Weeds From a Lawn

Annual weeds can quickly invade lawns, and once perennial weeds are established they are hard to remove. Ensure you get rid of any weeds before they set seed.

### ⊙ Steps

1 Prevent weds from becoming established by fertilising to keep your lawn healthy and lush. Healthy turf grass will crowd out weed seeds before they can germinate and grow.

2 Water your lawn thoroughly on a less frequent basis to encourage the grass roots to grow deep into the soil; this makes the grass stronger.

3 Dig or pull out weeds as soon as they appear, in the early spring. Use a daisy grubber or trowel to pull out all of the roots of perennial weeds such as dandelions.

4 Use chemical controls only if the weeds have become a pest. Use a herbicide to spot-treat weedy patches in the lawn. For larger areas, dilute soluble lawn weedkiller and water it on according to the manufacturer's instructions. If herbicide leaves large bare patches, see 329 "Reseed Bare Patches in a Lawn".

### ⚠ Warning

If using chemical sprays, wear protective clothing as recommended by the manufacturer, including long sleeves and long trousers and boots. And avoid spraying on a windy day.

### Things You'll Need

❑ lawn fertiliser

❑ daisy grubber or trowel

❑ lawn weedkiller

## 329 | Reseed Bare Patches in a Lawn

Whether they're caused by pests, weeds, dog urine or a bad golf swing, those little bare spots in your lawn are easy to repair. The trick is to keep on top of them.

### ⊙ Steps

1 Rake and remove the dead grass and debris from the bare patch.

2 Use a fork or hoe to loosen the soil in the bare area.

3 Incorporate 5–8 cm (2–3 in) of compost into the prepared area.

4 Smooth the area with the back of a rake until the new soil is level with the surrounding area.

5 Seed thickly and evenly (taking care not to overcrowd the seeds or jumble them on top of each other). Incorporate the seeds into the soil gently, using the back of the rake.

6 Cover the seeded area with a thin layer of fine compost or other organic matter to act as a protective mulch.

7 Water gently so you don't wash the seeds away.

8 Protect the area from birds if they are a problem. Insert 30 cm (12 in) long wooden stakes into the ground surrounding the perimeter of the patch, keeping the stakes 25–30 cm (10–12 in) apart. Tie humming tape or aluminium foil strips to the stakes. This will frighten birds away.

9 Keep the repaired area moist until the seed germinates. Once the new grass is established, resume regular watering.

### ✱ Tip

If the bare patch is due to a petrol spill or dog urine, flood the area with water to dilute the problem fluid. Other measures may be needed in order to control lawn disease or insects.

### Things You'll Need

❑ rake

❑ fork or hoe

❑ compost

❑ grass seeds

❑ wooden stakes

❑ humming tape or aluminium foil

**How to Do** *(Just About)* **Everything**

## Shop for Flowering Bulbs                                330

Local nurseries and garden centres are convenient places to buy standard flowering bulbs like tulips and daffodils. Generally, though, you'll find a wider selection in catalogues and online.

### ⊙ Steps

1   Select bulb varieties and types based on colour, flowering time, height, ability to grow in sun or shade and hardiness. Much of this information will be on the packaging or in catalogue descriptions.

2   Choose healthy, firm bulbs, free of blemishes, bruises or soft spots. Usually bigger is better.

3   Choose the highest grade of bulb (if the bulbs are graded) unless cost is a major factor, as when purchasing large quantities. Higher-quality bulbs generally produce more flowers.

4   Make sure to note how closely the bulbs can be planted (the descriptions may say, but you might have to double check in a book on bulbs or ask the nursery salesperson). Spacing helps determine the quantity of bulbs needed for each planting area.

5   Select hardy spring-flowering bulbs, such as daffodils, tulips, crocuses and hyacinths, for autumn planting.

6   Choose tender summer-flowering bulbs, such as begonias and gladioli for spring planting.

**✳ Tip**

Try to buy your bulbs from a reputable source. Check before buying that your bulbs are from cultivation rather than gathered from the wild. It is illegal to collect wild bulbs.

**⚠ Warning**

Bargain bulbs are not always as good a deal as they may seem. They're often smaller or lower-quality bulbs that don't bloom as well as more expensive choices.

## Plant Bulbs in Autumn                                  331

Spring-flowering bulbs such as daffodils, tulips and hyacinths are generally planted in autumn. Here's how to do it right and ensure a wonderfully colourful spring.

### ⊙ Steps

1   Select bulb types as described in 330 "Shop for Flowering Bulbs".

2   Arrange for delivery, or make your purchase, so you can plant in autumn. If you are not going to plant them for a while, store them in a cool, dry place.

3   Improve the soil, if necessary, by incorporating ample organic matter. Soil preparation is not always necessary as long as drainage is good.

4   With a spade or trowel, dig holes the appropriate depth for your bulb type. Consult packaging, catalogues or a book on bulbs for planting depth. A depth of two to three times the length of the bulb is a good rule of thumb.

5   Add bone meal to the bottom of the hole and roughly mix it into the soil.

6   Place the bulb in the hole. Make sure you have the right side up (usually point up, roots down). The bottom of the bulb should rest firmly on the bottom of the hole.

7   Refill the planting hole, tamping the soil lightly and water thoroughly.

**✳ Tips**

Many spring-flowering bulbs can be planted under deciduous trees. They will bloom before the tree comes into leaf and shades the planting area.

There are many tools to help you when planting a lot of bulbs. Some make perfect holes by removing small cylinders of soil.

Alternatively, dig a long trench instead of individual holes.

**Things You'll Need**

❑ spring-flowering bulbs

❑ spade or trowel

❑ bone meal

## 332 | Do Basic Winter Pruning

Deciduous trees and shrubs shed their leaves and go dormant over the winter. This is the perfect time to prune them without fear of interrupting their growth.

### ⊙ Steps

1 Remove any growth that comes from below the graft (where the top of the plant was originally joined to rootstock). Cut the growth as close to the main body of the plant as possible.

2 Look for and remove any dead, diseased or injured wood. Branches that are different in colour from the main body of the plant are suspect. Injuries may look like splits or blisters. Diseases may show up as black patches along the branch.

3 Cut into the tip of a suspect branch to make sure that it is dead. If it is green on the inside, it is still alive. If the branch is brown on the inside, it is probably dead. Keep cutting back from the tip until you reach green wood.

4 Remove any branches that cross through the centre of the plant; this will improve air circulation and discourage fungal disease.

5 Cut out any competing leaders – the upright growing limbs that will eventually turn into the main trunk. Most trees should have only one main branch heading vertically; multiple leaders and then trunks sap the energy from a tree and weaken it over time.

6 Prune for shape and size. In the case of fruit trees, keep the branches low so that you can reach the fruit. Most maples look best with a rounded crown, and most roses should be pruned in a low goblet shape. Know the basic shape of the plant you are working on.

7 Remove any water shoots from fruit trees. These are non-productive and light in colour and grow straight up, whereas fruiting wood is crooked and dark.

8 Rake up and remove all prunings and fallen leaves. Insects overwinter in fallen plant debris.

✳ **Tip**

Sharpen and oil your pruning tools before you start cutting.

⚠ **Warning**

Once the plants begin to grow leaves, sap is flowing through the branches. If you prune then, you take the chance of causing excessive bleeding.

**Things You'll Need**

❑ secateurs

❑ loppers

❑ long-handled loppers

❑ rake

---

## 333 | Plant a Bare-Root Tree or Shrub

Many kinds of shrubs and trees are sold while leafless and dormant, with roots bare of soil. A bare-root plant may look pathetic, but if you start it off properly and care for it well, it will thrive.

### ⊙ Steps

1 Plant bare-root trees and shrubs in late autumn, winter or early spring (from mid-November to April in most parts of the country) when the plants are dormant and the ground isn't frozen solid. They'll have a chance to put out new roots before they have to cope with hot sun, drying winds and the added stress of producing leaves.

2 Remove any packing material carefully, and rinse off or gently pull off any clumps of earth clinging to the roots; trim off any dead or damaged roots.

✳ **Tips**

Unless you're planting a small shrub or a tree in a confined space, avoid improving the soil in the planting hole. The "good" soil will encourage the roots to confine themselves within that small area rather than spread out as they need to.

3   Immerse the roots in a bucket of water to soak for at least one to four hours, but no longer than overnight. Supplying enough moisture is key to the success of bare-root planting.

4   Dig a hole that's at least 60 cm (24 in) wider than the root system and about as deep as the point where the roots flare from the trunk (or stems in the case of a shrub). Using your spade, loosen the soil on the sides of the hole so it doesn't solidify around the plant's roots.

5   Mound soil in the bottom of the hole so that the peak reaches just about ground level.

6   Place stakes in the hole if you're planting a tree that will need support.

7   Set the tree or shrub on top of the mound so the roots cascade down over the sides. Spread them gently with your hands if you need to, and add or remove soil so that the crown of the root system is just at the surface of the ground. Use the soil mark on the plant as a guide to the correct planting depth.

8   Fill the hole about halfway with soil and tamp it lightly with your foot to remove large air pockets.

9   Make sure the tree or shrub is standing straight up, then water slowly to saturate the soil and remove any remaining air pockets.

10   Finish filling the hole with soil and water again.

11   Keep the soil moist for the first year after planting. Mulch to retain moisture, but keep at least 15 cm (6 in) bare around the trunk. Check frequently; if you see yellow leaves or the soil feels dry, water immediately.

Deep, thorough watering is the key to healthy shrubs and trees. Give new trees at least 2.5 cm (1 in) of water a week all around the root zone. (The roots of a woody plant extend about the same distance as its branches.)

## ⚠ Warning

Use the bare-root method only for deciduous trees and shrubs of the standard size sold in nurseries. Larger deciduous plants and all evergreens will suffer too much stress without an extra cushion of soil around their roots.

## Things You'll Need

❑ secateurs

❑ bucket

❑ spade

❑ stakes (optional)

❑ mulch

---

## Plant a Root-Balled Tree or Shrub      334

A root-balled tree or shrub comes with a hessian- or netting-wrapped clump of soil around its roots. Many evergreens are traditionally sold this way.

### ◉ Steps

1   Buy root-balled trees or shrubs for planting in autumn or spring. Plants can also be set out during mild spells in winter if soil conditions allow.

2   Keep your tree or shrub in a cool, shady place until planting, cover the rootball with mulch, and keep the roots moist.

3   Calculate your hole dimensions carefully: A root-balled plant is heavy, but the roots are easily damaged. The less you have to move it, the better. You'll want to set the plant into the hole so that the bottom of the trunk (or trunks) is just above the soil surface.

4   Measure the rootball, then dig a hole about 15 cm (6 in) wider all around and roughly as deep. Lay a cane across the hole, measure the distance from the cane to the bottom of the hole and adjust the depth as needed.

5   Loosen the sides of the hole with your spade, and if your plant is too large to lift and lower without strain, cut down one side of the hole so that it forms a slope. You'll be able to simply slide the plant down the ramp and into the hole. Place stakes in the hole if you're planting a tree that will need support.

### ✳ Tips

Unless you're planting a small shrub or tree in a confined space, avoid improving the soil in the planting hole. The "good" soil will encourage the roots to confine themselves within that small area rather than spread out as they need to.

Deep, thorough watering is the key to healthy shrubs and trees. Give new trees at least 2.5 cm (1 in) of water a week all around the root zone. (The roots of a woody plant extend about the same distance as its branches.)

6  Move the plant to the hole very carefully. Ease the plant onto a plastic sheet and drag it to the site; don't roll it. If your plant is large, or if you have several, it pays to rent a special plant-moving trolley from a nursery or hire shop.

7  Lower the rootball into the hole, covering and all. Remove any synthetic wrappings or fastenings. Leave natural hessian and twine in place (they'll rot quickly), but cut away any hessian around the trunk; if it sticks out above ground it will wick moisture away from the roots.

8  Fill the hole about half way with soil and tamp it lightly with your foot to remove large air pockets. Make sure the tree or shrub is standing straight then water slowly to saturate the soil and remove any remaining air pockets.

9  Finish filling the hole with soil. Use any extra to build a temporary ridge at the drip line (the place on the ground directly below the outer edges of the foliage) and water again.

10  Keep the soil moist for the first year after planting. Mulch to retain moisture, but keep at least 15 cm (6 in) bare around the trunk. Check frequently; if you see yellow leaves or the soil feels dry, water immediately.

## ⚠ Warning

Even small root-balled shrubs are heavy. Unless you're dealing with tiny specimens, don't risk your back or the plant's roots and limbs – get help at planting time.

## Things You'll Need

❏ spade

❏ bamboo cane

❏ plastic sheet

❏ mulch

---

## 335 | Plant a Tree or Shrub From a Container

Many common nursery plants are sold in containers of various sizes and materials. Unlike bare-root and root-balled, container-grown plants can be planted even while growing vigorously.

### ⊙ Steps

1  Plant a container-grown tree or shrub in spring or autumn for the best results, especially if it's an evergreen. If that timing is not possible, though, any time except midsummer will work, as long as the soil is not bone-dry, saturated or frozen.

2  Dig a hole at least 15 cm (6 in) wider than the container and about the same depth. Then roughen up the sides of the hole with your spade.

3  Remove the plant from its container even if the label says you don't need to; the roots will spread out more quickly. With a small tree or shrub, it's easy to do this job before you lower the plant into its hole; with a larger plant, it's easier to handle if you place it into the hole first and then cut away the container.

4  Knock a plant out of a rigid plastic container. Simply tilt the pot onto its side, tap it lightly, and gently slide out the rootball. If the container is made of a soft material such as peat, cut the pot away using a knife or scissors.

5  Gently tease out any roots that are encircling the rootball with your fingers so that they are free, taking care not to break up the ball of soil. Then trim off any damaged roots.

6  Place a stake in the hole if you're planting a tree that will need support.

7  Set the plant into the hole at the same depth it was growing in the pot, and begin filling the hole, checking as you go to make sure the plant is

### ✱ Tips

Unless you're planting a small shrub or tree in a confined space, avoid improving the soil in the planting hole. The "good" soil will encourage the roots to confine themselves within that small area rather than spread out as they need to.

Deep, thorough watering is the key to healthy shrubs and trees. Give new trees at least 2.5 cm (1 in) of water a week all around the root zone. (The roots of a woody plant extend about the same distance as its branches.)

When purchasing a tree or shrub in a container, make sure no roots are growing through the holes at the bottom of the container. The appearance of roots indicates that the plant is root-bound and may be under stress.

standing up straight. Add about 10 cm (4 in) of soil and gently firm it with your foot or a hoe to remove any air pockets. Repeat the process until the hole is filled.

8 Water slowly to saturate the soil and remove any remaining air pockets.

9 Use any extra soil to build a temporary ridge at the drip line (the place on the ground directly below the outer edges of the foliage) and water again; the ridge will prevent the water from running off the soil.

10 Keep the soil moist for the first year after planting. Mulch to retain moisture, but keep at least 15 cm (6 in) bare around the trunk. Check frequently; if you see yellow leaves or the soil feels dry, water immediately.

**Things You'll Need**

❑ spade

❑ mulch

❑ knife or scissors

❑ secateurs

❑ stake (optional)

❑ hoe

## Sow Seeds Indoors

**336**

Starting plants from seed indoors is a great way to get a head-start on spring. Although it takes a bit of a knack, it's not hard – especially when you know a few tricks of the trade.

### ⊙ Steps

1 Consider your timing. Some plants need to be planted as much as 12 weeks before your region's last average frost date, while others do best when started just two weeks before.

2 Choose your seed-sowing container. Nearly any container with drainage will do, but good candidates include milk carton bottoms, egg cartons, plastic produce boxes, peat pots, special seed-starting trays and modules divided into individual sections. (Punch drainage holes into containers that need them.)

3 Plant seeds in sterile seed compost. It has no soil to cause disease problems and is lightweight – perfect for baby plants to get off to a good start. Sprinkle vermiculite over seeds that require covering. Its lighter colour helps you see just what you've covered.

4 Follow seed packet directions about the depth of planting. As a rough rule, the larger the seed, the deeper it's planted. Some very small seeds are just scattered directly on the soil and not covered up at all.

5 Water gently. Either set the container in 2.5–5 cm (1–2 in) of warm water and allow the water to wick up to the soil surface, water gently from above with a fine-rose watering can, or dribble water from your hand.

6 Slip the container into a clear plastic bag to minimise draughts and conserve moisture. Twist the end shut.

7 Put the seeds in a spot at the correct temperature. (Check the seed packet.) Keep the seeds out of direct sunlight or risk fatally overheating them. Seeds usually need either cool temperatures of 10–18°C (50–65°F) or warm temperatures of 21–30°C (70–85°F). Find the right spot by checking with a thermometer in different locations in your house.

8 Check the seeds daily. If water drops form inside the bag, open the end to air it. Once the seeds germinate, remove the plastic and put the seedlings in the brightest indoor spot possible.

9 Put the new seedlings in a sunny, unobstructed south-facing window.

### ✱ Tips

If you've planted the seedlings more than a couple of weeks before the last frost date, it's a good idea to prick them out, transplanting them into individual pots so that they have plenty of room to grow. To do this, lift the seedlings out gently with a kitchen knife and plant them in regular potting soil.

### Things You'll Need

❑ seeds

❑ containers

❑ seed compost

❑ vermiculite

❑ clear plastic bag

## 337 | Sow Seeds Outdoors

Whether you're planting flowers, vegetables or herbs, sowing seeds outdoors is simple. All it takes is good garden soil and a little follow-up care to get loads of great plants.

### ⊙ Steps

1  Read seed-packet directions carefully. Many annuals and perennials can be sown directly in the ground, but some should be started in containers, then transplanted.

2  Consider your timing. Some plants like to be planted outdoors in early spring, while temperatures are cold. Others must wait until after your area's average last frost date. Again, consult the packet.

3  Prepare the soil. Most seeds demand optimum conditions. Work in plenty of compost with a spade or fork to a depth of at least 30 cm (12 in). The soil should be loose and crumbly and moist before planting. Rake smooth.

4  Sow the seed. Follow packet directions on sowing depth. As a rough rule, the larger the seed, the deeper it must be planted. Some very small seeds are just scattered directly on the soil and not covered up at all.

5  Water gently. It's easy for seeds to be washed away by heavy watering. Mist the soil gently with a water sprayer or use a watering can that has a gentle sprinkle. Be sure to keep soil moist until seedlings emerge.

6  Thin out seedlings by gently pulling them out, if the seed packet directs, once they are 2.5 cm (1 in) or so high. This will ensure that those you want to survive have adequate room to grow big and healthy.

7  Pinch out most seedlings when they've made three sets of true leaves. Just take the top part of the tiny plant off with your fingernails to encourage bushy growth and more roots. Check the packet first to determine whether pinching is recommended.

8  Look after your seedlings. Make sure they continue to have all the sun they need. Also keep the seedlings watered and weeded. Add up to 5 cm (2 in) of organic mulch as soon as seedlings are up and growing.

### ✳ Tips

Some plants are easier than others to start from seed: marigolds, zinnias and nasturtiums are easy-to-start examples.

It's better to trim crowded seedlings off at soil level than to disturb the ones you want to keep by pulling the crowding ones out by the roots.

### Things You'll Need

❑ seeds

❑ spade or fork

❑ rake

❑ watering can or water sprayer

❑ mulch

## 338 | Transplant Seedlings

Whether you grow your fledgling plants from seed or buy them at the nursery, extra care at planting time will get them off to a good start in your garden.

### ⊙ Steps

1  Double-check the planting date on the seed packet, in a comprehensive garden book or on the plastic tag stuck into the soil (for plants you bought at a nursery). You must hold off planting most flowers and vegetables until all danger of frost has passed. Some cold-tolerant varieties such as cauliflower can go into the ground a bit earlier; heat lovers such as tomatoes should wait until the ground has thoroughly warmed up.

### ✳ Tip

If the plant has been growing in a peat pot, break away a few pieces from the bottom or sides so the roots won't be confined, and loosen the soil a little with your fingers.

2  Prepare the planting bed. Use a spade or fork to work the soil to a depth of 25–30 cm (10–12 in); incorporate organic matter as needed.

3  "Harden off" your seedlings by leaving them outdoors for longer and longer periods. Start by sheltering the young plants under a porch or bench by day, then bringing them back in by night or during inclement weather. After two or three days, you can safely keep them in the sun for half a day. By the end of a week, they'll be tough enough to soak up the rays all day.

4  If you can, transplant the seedlings to the garden on an overcast day to ease the shock of transition from pot to ground. If a light drizzle is falling, so much the better. Water both the ground outside and the plants before you move them into the garden.

5  Remove each plant from its pot by turning it upside down and tapping lightly on the bottom; it will slide out easily. Gently run your fingers through the roots to loosen them a little.

6  Use a trowel to dig a hole about twice the size of the rootball and set the plant into the hole so the rootball will be covered by about 5mm of soil. Press the soil firmly around the roots to ensure good soil-to-root contact.

7  Space the plants according to the directions on the packet.

8  Water well immediately after transplanting and again every day until the plants are well established and growing – usually within a week. If some plants show signs of wilting, shield them with a piece of lattice until they perk up, which shouldn't take more than a few days.

## ⚠ Warning

If you live where late frosts can hit unexpectedly, be prepared to protect your tender seedlings. When the weather forecast predicts low temperatures, cover them with Styrofoam cups, plastic bottles cut in half or one of several commercial products made for the purpose. Or invest in some cloches. Traditional beautiful, bell-shaped glass covers have been used for centuries to shield tender plants from sudden cold, or simply to prolong the growing season.

## Things You'll Need

❑ seedlings

❑ spade or fork

❑ organic matter

❑ garden trowel

❑ watering can or garden hose

---

# Design and Prepare a Flower Bed          | 339

A well-prepared flower bed not only looks good but promotes good drainage, has plenty of nutrients, makes watering and weeding easy, and discourages disease and pests.

## ◉ Steps

1  Choose a spot for the bed and walk around it. Visualise plants of different shapes and sizes. Consider their needs for sun and shade. Make rough sketches.

2  Sketch a plan of the bed you want to plant. Tall plants should go at the back of a bed that's adjacent to a wall or fence and in the middle of a bed that will be viewed from all sides. Plants that need frequent attention, such as pruning, deadheading or spraying, should go where they can be reached without your crushing other plants.

3  Sprinkle flour or sand to trace the outline of your prospective flower bed. If you don't like the way it looks, brush it away and start again.

4  Use a trowel or small spade and cut along the lines you've just marked out, then remove the grass from the surface.

5  Have your soil tested, or test it yourself with a home kit, and improve it as necessary. A local nursery can recommend the best products to use.

6  To eliminate weeds, dig over the area. Then leave it for at least a week to allow annual weed seeds in the soil to germinate. Hoe or dig it a second

## ✳ Tips

There's no need to limit your bed to a rectangular shape. Flower beds can be any size or shape you wish.

Unless you've got a budget big enough to buy full-grown perennials, the plants you put in the ground now will look very different in a year or two. Leave room for them to grow. You can fill in bare spots with annuals.

## ⚠ Warning

This method for creating a new flower bed works only if the soil is reasonably good. In areas with very sandy or very heavy clay soil, raised beds are your best bet. Or if you don't mind the work, dig out and dispose of the time to remove the weeds. Alternatively, spray the area with a non-selective herbicide, following directions carefully, especially regarding how long to wait until planting.

7   Spread 8–10 cm (3–4 in) of compost and any other fertilisers over the top of the area you intend for the bed.

8   Till or dig up the soil to a depth of at least 20–25 cm (8–10 in), up to 60 cm (24 in) if you're planting perennials.

9   Toss out any large stones that appear on the surface.

10  Rake the surface smooth, and you are ready to plant.

11  Add edging, if desired. Edging isn't a must but does help keep out grass and some other weeds while creating a neat appearance.

problem soil, and replace it with a mixture of compost and high-quality topsoil.

## Things You'll Need

❏ flour or sand

❏ trowel

❏ compost

❏ hoe or spade

❏ rake

---

## 340 | Plant a Garden Bed

After you've prepared the soil and raked it smooth, the next step is to add the plants. Here's what to do.

### ⊙ Steps

1   Remove seedlings from their containers, and loosen the roots gently if they're root-bound. Place the unpotted plants back into the nursery tray, lying on their sides with the foliage all facing the same direction. Work quickly so the roots don't dry out.

2   Begin planting at the back of the garden bed. This way you won't be stepping all over the plants you've just put into the ground. Keep the tray of plants where you can easily reach it.

3   Use a trowel to make a hole for each plant. Stab the trowel into the soil, trying to gauge the depth so that the hole is only as deep as the rootball. The crown (the area where the foliage meets the rootball) of the plant should be at the surface of the soil.

4   Pick up the rootball of a plant with your free hand.

5   Lower the plant into the prepared hole.

6   Adjust the depth if necessary. With your trowel, shovel in a little soil to fill the hole around the plant, or scoop out a little more soil to make room for the plant. You want the top of the rootball to be at the surface of the soil.

7   Push the soil into place around the roots with your trowel.

8   Continue working backwards, planting as you work toward the front of the bed.

9   Cover your footsteps by roughing up the soil with your trowel. Tender young roots push through soft, uncompacted soil much faster than through compacted soil.

10  Water the newly planted garden immediately after you've finished planting the entire bed. Use a hose at low volume or a watering can. Try not to get water on the foliage; apply it near the roots to settle the soil.

### ✻ Tips

Plant in the early morning or late afternoon to prevent roots from drying out.

Avoid using fertiliser until you begin to see new growth.

Stand up and stretch your back every 15 minutes while planting.

### Things You'll Need

❏ seedlings

❏ garden trowel

❏ garden hose or watering can

## Mulch Flowers

A mulch is a layer of material applied to the soil's surface. It cuts down on weeds and conserves moisture so you water less.

### ⊙ Steps

1 Choose your mulching materials. Grass clippings, wood chips, shredded bark, pine needles, cocoa bean husks and many other materials all make excellent mulch materials, but vary in cost and have subtle advantages and disadvantages. Check with your local garden centre for advice on the best mulch to use in your area.

2 Apply the mulch to your flower bed in late spring after the last frost. If you apply it earlier, you'll prevent the soil from warming up – and you need adequately warmed soil for good plant growth.

3 Spread the mulch 2.5–8 cm (1–3 in) thick, depending on the size and sturdiness of the flowers. Large, mature perennials can handle 8 cm (3 in) of mulch, while small, newly planted annuals might get lost.

4 Spread the mulch right up to the plant but don't push it against the base.

5 Plan on replacing a mulch annually; it breaks down into the soil.

### ✳ Tip

It's easy to confuse mulching that you do in the spring and mulching you do in the autumn (to protect plants over the winter). Mulch applied in the autumn is usually very airy and lightweight (straw, shredded autumn leaves) so the plant doesn't suffocate.

### Things You'll Need

❑ mulch

❑ spade

## Grow Annuals

Plant annuals (plants that live one season only) in the ground at the right time of year and they'll provide long-lasting colour that few perennials can match.

### ✳ Tips

Annuals are usually divided into two groups, hardy annuals and half-hardy annuals. Hardy annuals withstand some frost and can be started early in the season. Half-hardy annuals are damaged or killed by cold. If planted too early in spring, they'll languish in cold soil or be nipped by frost.

Never let annuals wilt. Instead, feel the soil to see if it's dry or water whenever the glossy leaves lose their sheen.

### ⊙ Steps

#### Choosing Annuals

1 Determine if you want to start your annuals from seed or from established plants. Established plants are fastest and easiest but cost much more and are available in a limited variety. Starting from seed takes a bit of skill and more time, but you can have hundreds of flowers for what you'd spend on just one tray of established annuals.

2 Browse the catalogues or display racks carefully when buying seeds. Beginners should choose annuals that are recommended as being especially easy or that perform especially well. Also look for fast germination times. A plant that germinates in 4 or 5 days is easier to grow than a plant that germinates in 20.

3 Look for short, stocky (not leggy) established plants that don't have flowers on them and don't have roots coming out of the drainage holes at the bottom of the pot. Blooms indicate that the plant is putting too much energy into flowering when you want it first to put energy into root development at planting time; roots coming out of the bottom of the pot are a sign that the plant has been in the pot too long.

4 Read the label or packet carefully and note the plants' needs for sun, soil, water and other conditions. Make sure you're able to provide those conditions.

### ⚠ Warning

Never buy a plant that is showing signs of disease or wilting. It's likely to go downhill once you take it home and may spread disease to other plants in your garden.

## Planting Annuals

1 Prepare the planting area well, as described in 339 "Design and Prepare a Flower Bed". Also work a little slow-release granular fertiliser into the planting area if desired. Fertiliser can help fast-growing annuals reach their maximum height and bloom. Follow the packet directions exactly.

2 Pinch off any flowers or buds on the plant. (There will be some in most cases.) This will help the plant get established and produce more flowers in the long run.

3 Plant annuals about 25 per cent closer than recommended on the label. Those distances are recommended for maximum plant health, not for the best visual effect. Plant in groups. Most annuals look far better when grouped in plantings of 12 or more.

## Caring for Annuals

1 Mulch most annuals (see 341 "Mulch Flowers"). Use a mulch such as grass clippings or wood chips. Mulch suppresses weeds, conserves moisture and prevents some soil-borne diseases. Apply a layer 2.5–8 cm (1–3 in) thick over the area.

2 Keep annuals appropriately watered (see 345 "Water Flowers"). Most annuals are fairly thirsty – they'll need about 2.5 cm (1 in) of water per week, either as rainfall or watering. It's better to water them deeply and occasionally rather than giving them just a little water here and there.

3 Deadhead most annuals regularly (see 351 "Deadhead Flowers"). This means trimming or pinching off spent blooms every few days. This not only keeps the plant looking tidy, but it encourages more flowers.

4 On well-prepared soil, annuals do not usually need feeding. If necessary, fertilise during the growing season, using food formulated for flower production. Follow the instructions on the packet.

5 Dig out annuals when they're spent. They stop flowering and the foliage starts to die back in autumn. Dispose of healthy annuals in a compost heap. If disease has been a problem, put them in a separate area or throw them out with the rubbish.

### Things You'll Need

❏ annual seeds or seedlings

❏ spade or fork

❏ rake

❏ compost

❏ fertiliser

❏ mulch

❏ scissors

---

## 343 | Grow Perennials

Perennials flower for several seasons. Most die back into the ground partially or fully over the winter, but many stay evergreen in mild years.

**✱ Tip**

Check individual plant requirements, because not all perennials need the same treatment.

### ◉ Steps

#### Choosing Perennials

1 Look for perennials at nurseries year-round. Spring and autumn are good times for planting, but summer is a good time for seeing the top-growth of what you are buying.

2 Select perennials that grow well in your conditions.

3 Choose healthy-looking plants that have signs of new growth in leaf and flower bud in spring and summer.

## Planting Perennials

1   Choose a spot for perennials that is well-suited to their needs – "sun" means 6 hours of sunshine a day; "light shade" or "dappled shade" comes from tall trees; "dark shade" comes from something solid like a house; and "part shade" means 3 hours of sunshine a day.

2   Prepare the planting area as described in 339 "Design and Prepare a Flower Bed".

3   Add a light application of organic fertiliser to the planting hole.

4   Place the plants no deeper than they were growing in their containers.

5   Set the plants an appropriate distance apart, depending on how wide they grow.

6   Mulch the plants with 2.5–8 cm (1–3 in) of organic compost to help retain water and keep down weeds while the plants are establishing.

7   Water new plants well, until the soil is completely moist. Do this weekly during their first summer.

## Caring for Perennials

1   Apply an organic fertiliser to the soil in early spring – except for perennials that do not need annual fertilising.

2   Mulch around but not on top of the plants with 8 cm (3 in) of organic compost in early spring (see 341 "Mulch Flowers").

3   Cut old flower stems off spring-blooming plants to a place on the stem just above where you see new leaves growing. This will encourage the plant to bloom again.

4   Water most perennials well until the soil is completely moist; do this weekly in summers with little rainfall.

5   Cut back old stems and flowers in late autumn (for spring flowering perennials) or early spring (for perennials that bloom in summer and autumn).

## Things You'll Need

- ❑ perennial plants in containers
- ❑ spade or fork
- ❑ rake
- ❑ trowel
- ❑ organic fertiliser
- ❑ mulch
- ❑ secateurs

---

# Care for Roses                                    344

Roses have an undeserved reputation for being fussy, hard-to-care-for plants. Some roses do require more maintenance than others, but growing roses is something even a beginner can do.

## ◉ Steps

1   Prune roses in winter or early spring once the rose starts to show signs of new growth, usually in the form of tiny red buds swelling. These buds will become new branches.

2   Cut out any obviously dead or damaged branches first. Then cut out all but four or five healthy main stems.

3   Cut the stems back by a third to a half, depending on how tall you want the bush to be. Make these cuts right above an outward-facing bud – that is, a red bud that's on the outside of the rose bush. This directs the

## ✹ Tips

Use sharp secateurs for most pruning. To cut branches over 1 cm (½ in) thick, use loppers.

Many shrub roses do not require the typical pruning described in the steps. Instead, simply cut them back by a third

bud to grow up and out, leaving the centre of the rose bush open for a prettier shape and better air circulation.

4 Start feeding roses regularly at the start of the growing season. Roses are hungry plants, demanding lots of nutrients for best growth and flowering. Fertilise roses with a liquid fertiliser watered on to the soil every three to four weeks during the growing season or according to packet directions. Using a liquid feed directly on the leaves (foliar feeding) is not usually necessary.

5 Water diligently. Roses need a steady source of water during the growing season, about 2.5 cm (1 in) a week from rain or watering. In dry areas or for a large planting of roses, consider installing a drip irrigation system. It is better to water less often and more thoroughly to encourage the rose to root more deeply.

6 Mulch. Roses need less frequent weeding and watering and suffer from fewer diseases if you lay down a 2.5–5 cm (1–2 in) layer of organic mulch, such as bark chips, grass clippings, horse manure or other biodegradable materials.

7 Deadhead. This simply means trimming off spent roses to encourage the bush to produce more. While some roses bloom only in one big flush in June, others are bred to keep producing off and on all season long. All benefit from prompt deadheading. Use secateurs to cut old flowerheads off to a shoot further down the stem.

8 Deal with pests and diseases. Try simply trimming off the affected portion of the plant or giving a plant covered in aphids a good strong blast from a hose. If you cannot identify the problem from a specialist reference book, take the affected part that you have trimmed off to a reliable garden centre, where the staff can prescribe the correct treatment. As an alternative, you may want to deal with problems by spraying.

9 Pull off suckers (shoots emerging from below ground level) as soon as you see them. Avoid using secateurs on these.

10 Stop fertilising roses in early autumn, at least one month before the first frost. Fertilising too long into autumn encourages roses to produce tender new growth that will get scorched by cold.

If your rose is a climber or rambler, prune with caution. Some will bloom only on old wood from the previous year.

Each rose grower has his or her own favorite feeding method. One of the easiest is to buy a slow-release granular rose food and work it into the soil so it can feed the plant all season long.

## ⚠ Warnings

Read pesticide and fungicide labels carefully. Even organic products can be hazardous if used incorrectly, so follow packet directions to the letter.

## Things You'll Need

❑ secateurs

❑ loppers

❑ fertiliser

❑ mulch

---

## 345 | Water Flowers

Water your annual and perennial flowers badly and you'll waste time – and have sickly plants. Water them well and you'll save yourself time and be rewarded with healthy, beautiful blooms.

### ⊙ Steps

1 Water early in the day. Watering in the cool of morning (even before dawn) minimises evaporation if you're using a sprinkler. It also allows foliage to dry off quickly, preventing fungal diseases.

2 Avoid wetting the blooms. Some blooms close up if wet or are damaged in a hard spray.

3 Water occasionally and deeply rather than often and lightly. You want water to soak in as deeply as possible, encouraging the plant to send

### ✳ Tips

In optimum (loamy) soil conditions, most plants need 2.5–5 cm (1–2 in) of water per week.

As you design and plant your garden, try to cluster plants according to watering needs.

down deep roots. The soil should be moist to the bottom of the plant's roots when you insert your finger into the soil.

4    Learn to look for signs of dryness before flowers wilt, including a loss of sheen on leaves and hard soil surrounding the plant. Never let flowers wilt. This weakens them and makes them more prone to a host of diseases.

5    Check plants in containers once or even twice a day, since they can need watering that often in hot, sunny or windy weather.

6    Let technology help you. If you have difficulty keeping up with watering needs, check out your local garden centre's supplies of soaker hoses, drip hoses (including some for containers), and timers to connect to your outdoor tap. Or try adding water-absorbing crystals to your containers – the crystals can cut watering needs significantly.

7    Mulch (see 341 "Mulch Flowers"). Not only does this suppress weeds, but it keeps the soil around your flowers cool and moist, minimising the need for water.

## ⚠ Warning

Avoid planting flowers whose watering needs will be difficult to keep up with. If you live in a dry area, for example, it's silly to fight nature by planting lots of moisture-loving plants.

---

## Water Vegetables                                      346

Most vegetables need about 20 l of water per sq m (0 gal per 10 sq ft) every 7 to 10 days to survive. In most years, in most places, rain alone won't supply enough.

### ◎ Steps

1    Pull back any mulch, dig down about 10 cm (4 in), scoop up a handful of soil and squeeze it. If the soil holds together, it's moist enough; if it crumbles in your hand, you need to water. Very sandy soil never forms a ball. If it feels gritty and sticks to your fingers, it's moist; if the particles flow through your fingers, the soil is too dry.

2    Cultivate before you water to loosen the soil; otherwise, the water will cause a crust to form on the soil's surface, preventing both water and air from reaching the roots.

3    Water in the morning. Avoid watering during the heat of the day, when a lot of water will be lost to evaporation, or in the late afternoon or evening; water that remains on stems or foliage overnight encourages fungus disease.

4    Apply water slowly and uniformly to a depth of about 15 cm (6 in); you'll encourage deep roots that can seek out water at different levels in the soil. Adapt your technique to the particular needs of vegetables – flood the furrows if you grow in rows; sink a reservoir made of a perforated pipe next to melons and squash; and locate sprinklers close to the ground for less evaporation around large leaves.

5    Install a drip irrigation system for maximum watering efficiency and ease. This will deliver water to individual plants, not to your driveway or the weeds growing in the garden path. A large nursery can supply and install the system for you. It's not cheap, but it can cut your water costs by half.

6    Accomplish similar results at a lower cost with a drip soaker: a hose with holes punched in it or a porous hose that oozes water along its length. You simply lay the hose so that it reaches the base of each plant.

### ✳ Tips

Enrich your soil with organic matter to improve the way it handles water.

Use mulch to conserve moisture.

### ⚠ Warnings

Some vegetables need more water than others. Heavy drinkers include celery, artichokes and asparagus. Beets and tomatoes are modest imbibers. Many herbs, including marjoram, oregano, thyme and garlic, need very little liquid sustenance. In fact, they'll taste best if you hold off watering until they look ready to wilt.

Too much water will cause as much damage as too little: it will drown plant roots and wash away nutrients.

# ✓ 347 Grow Popular Vegetables

Home-grown produce almost always tastes better than shop-bought. Look for seeds and seedlings in nurseries and catalogues and on websites, and choose with an awareness of what will grow best in your region and climate.

| | SOIL AND SUN | PLANTING | SPECIAL CARE | WATERING | HARVESTING |
|---|---|---|---|---|---|
| Carrots | Choose a site in full sun. Dig at least 30cm (12 in) deep, and remove all rocks and debris. Add plenty of organic matter. | Sow directly in the ground from about two to three weeks before the last expected frost. | Thin seedlings before tops entwine. Pinch out the leaves to thin – pulling the carrots whole attracts carrot fly. Mulch with compost. | Water in dry spells and when plants are young, but do not overwater; cut back on watering as they near maturity. | Begin harvesting when roots have turned bright orange. |
| Courgettes | Choose a site with full sun. Courgettes need soil that's rich, moisture-retentive and well-draining. Dig in plenty of compost and well-rotted manure. | Sow seed indoors in mid- to late spring or outdoors in early summer. Plant out home-grown or bought plants in early summer when frosts are over. | Feed if plants appear to be growing slowly. Train trailing courgettes over wires. | Water regularly, especially during flowering. | Harvest when the flowers fall off or when the courgettes are about 10 cm (4 in) long If left longer, flavour deteriorates. |
| Lettuce | Plant in full sun or in light shade in midsummer. Dig the soil thoroughly, breaking up clumps and removing stones and debris. Work in plenty of compost and well-rotted manure. | Sow seeds outdoors as soon as the soil can be worked in spring. Keep sowing through the season for continuous crops. Plant bought lettuce plants 15–25 cm (6–10 in) apart. | Feed occasionally with liquid fertiliser if growth seems slow. | Keep the soil moist, especially in dry weather, but avoid watering in the evening; foliage that stays wet overnight is prone to disease. | Begin cutting leaf lettuces as soon as they're big enough to use. Harvest heading types when heads are firm and fully formed. |
| Peas | Choose a site with full sun and well-draining soil. Dig in plenty of compost. Avoid any high-nitrogen soil additives. | Sow directly outdoors as soon as soil can be worked. Plant 2.5 cm (1 in) deep, 8–10 cm (3–4 in) apart, in rows 90 cm (3 ft) apart. Install supports. | Help ensure heavy yields by using liquid fertiliser twice during growing season. Guide climbing types upwards as soon as they're long enough to climb. | Give young plants about 1 cm (½ in) of water a week (twice that in very sandy soil). When plants begin to flower, give them 2.5 cm (1 in) per week. | Expect peas to be ready for picking about three weeks after the plants begin to flower. |
| Potatoes | Choose an open, sunny site. Work in plenty of well-rotted manure the autumn before planting and add a fetiliser. | Prepare tubers by "chitting" them: put them in trays in a cool, light place until they produce short green shoots. Plant the potatoes in holes or trenches 30–38 cm (12–15 in) deep. | Earth up potatoes as they grow, piling soil around the stems to ensure the potatoes do not come to the soil surface. | Water well to keep the plants and tubers moist but not waterlogged. | Harvest early potatoes when the plant flowers. Leave maincrop potatoes longer to increase in size. |
| Tomatoes | Tomatoes need full sun and plenty of warmth. Improve the soil with compost. | Move seedlings to the garden when they have their first flower buds and all danger of frost is past. Dig a hole the size of a football for each plant. Mix in a spade of compost. Set plants 38–45 cm (15–18 in) apart. | Mulch soil and install any supports the plants will need as they grow. Feed with low-nitrogen fertiliser: after the first flowers appear, when fruits are as big as golf balls, and when you spot the first ripe tomato. | Keep plants continually moist, especially during dry spells. Erratic watering results in poor fruits. | Pick tomatoes when their colour is glossy and even, and their texture is midway between soft and firm. Pick green tomatoes at the end of the season and leave in a warm place to ripen. |

## Prevent Weeds

Fighting weeds is a constant battle during the growing season. The key is to get them under control and then prevent them from returning.

### ⊙ Steps

1  Dig, chop, hoe or remove any weeds that have invaded your garden. You need to start with a clean slate in the war against weeds.

2  Place a thick layer of mulch over the clean soil. Mulch can be anything that covers the surface of the soil, including shredded bark, newspaper, leaves or even old carpet. It prevents weeds from germinating by shading the soil and keeping it cool. An 8–10 cm (3–4 in) thick layer will prevent all but the most noxious weeds from growing.

3  Encourage shrubs to grow to full size by fertilising during the growing season. Shrubs will shade the surface of the soil and choke weeds before they become established.

4  Use fast-growing ground cover such as periwinkle or rose of Sharon to choke weeds out of existence. Once the surface of the soil is covered with foliage, the weeds won't have anywhere to grow.

5  Pull stray weeds as they appear, and never allow them to go to seed in your garden.

**✴ Tip**

Use a thick layer of mulch around new plantings until shrubs and ground cover become well-established.

**⚠ Warnings**

Always start out with the least toxic method of weed control.

If you do use chemicals for weed control, wear protective clothing, including a long-sleeved shirt and trousers and gloves. Follow the manufacturer's instructions carefully.

Never spray chemicals on a windy day or they may affect plants other than the weeds.

## Deal with Foxes

Foxes are increasingly becoming a nuisance in urban areas where they come to scavenge for food and breed. They are virtually impossible to eliminate but can be deterred.

### ⊙ Steps

1  Avoid leaving food to tempt foxes into the garden. Clear up any scraps that fall from bird tables each evening. Use dustbins with a secure lid so that foxes cannot get to the contents.

2  Do not use bonemeal or dried blood to fertilise plants; the foxes smell it and come in search of food.

3  Use secure hutches for rabbits, chickens and other small animals to keep them safe. If the hutches or enclosures have a soil base, bury chicken wire underground around the edges to prevent foxes burrowing underneath.

4  Buy a proprietary deterrent. Strong-smelling ones are made to deter foxes and milder ones are for cats and dogs but can also work up to a point. The downside is the unpleasant smell, especially in a small space.

5  Discourage foxes by the above means, but if a fox makes its home or "earth" in your garden, it is hard to remove it. Try to erect a barrier or gradually fill in the hole. Do this in September to December outside the breeding season or there may be fox cubs inside.

**✴ Tip**

If you are happy to live with foxes but don't want them damaging a particular area such as a vegetable bed, use wire around it to prevent foxes burrowing.

**⚠ Warnings**

Poisoning is illegal and poses a danger to other pets and animals in the area.

Humane trapping is legal, but foxes are territorial and once one is removed another is likely to move in.

## 350 | Protect Your Garden From Slugs and Snails

There's no sure way to get rid of slugs and snails in your garden. All you can do is be vigilant and try to discourage them. Here are some ways to keep slugs and snails off your plants.

### ⊙ Steps

1 Be aware of what slugs and snails like best – seedlings, small annuals, climbers, herbaceous perennials and vegetables. Try planting seedlings out at a later stage when their leaves are less appealing to slugs, or grow particularly precious plants in pots, where they are less likely to suffer.

2 Dig over the soil regularly to expose slug and snail eggs so that birds will eat them.

3 Clear away fallen leaves and other debris under which slugs and snails hide during the day.

4 Water on some nematodes; these are minute parasites that attack and kill slugs. You can buy them by mail order and they should be applied between March and October when the temperature is 5–20°C (41–68°F). Each set of nematodes is effective for up to six weeks.

5 Spread grit or broken shells or eggshells as a mulch around plants prone to attack. Slugs and snails dislike the rough surface.

6 Set traps. Put out halves of grapefruit or melon peel in the evening, open side down – the slugs and snails will crawl in attracted by the smell and you can collect them and dispose of them in the morning. Alternatively, sink a container half-filled with beer or milk into the soil, leaving 2–3 cm (1 in) of rim above ground. The slugs and snails will crawl in and drown, while beneficial ground beetles will stay out.

7 Make a ring of copper tape around precious plants or pots. The copper strips emit an electrical charge when in contact with slug and snail slime.

8 Go out at night with a torch and collect the slugs and snails by hand.

9 Apply slug pellets and liquids. Aluminium sulphate-based products are least harmful to other wildlife.

### ✱ Tip

A nighttime patrol is even more effective after rain, when slugs and snails particularly like to feed.

### ⚠ Warning

Slug pellets can harm cats, dogs and birds that eat the poisoned slugs. Use them as a last resort, and if there are pets in the garden, put the pellets in a tube beside vulnerable plants so that the dead slugs and snails are less visible and so less likely to be eaten.

## 351 | Deadhead Flowers

A flowering plant's goal is to set seed. If you repeatedly deadhead – trim off the spent flowers – the plant goes into overdrive, putting out more and more flowers in an effort to reproduce.

### ⊙ Steps

1 Deadhead when a flower starts to brown, wither, shatter or otherwise deteriorate.

2 Deadhead tall flowers that sit on long, slender stems by cutting the stem at the base of the plant.

### ✱ Tip

Plants respond differently to deadheading, depending on climate, variety, rainfall and other variables. Experiment. Take comfort in the fact that in most cases, the worst you can do is give them a bad haircut. It's almost impossible to kill a plant by deadheading.

3  Trim bushy plants with many small flowers with handheld shears or small hedge clippers. Trim the whole plant at once – even if there are still some nice flowers left – rather than trying to tediously trim one flower at a time.

4  Deadhead other plants by simply snapping or pinching off the flowers with your hand or cut them off with shears, a knife or scissors.

5  Treat annuals and perennials that have dying or ragged foliage by cutting back (shortening) the foliage by one-third to two-thirds. Do this either when the plant has stopped blooming or when it starts to get that overall tatty look. It will usually send out a new flush of healthy, fresh foliage with flowers.

### Things You'll Need

❑ secateurs, shears or small hedge clippers

---

## Train a Climber                                              352

Climbers are quick-change artists that can hide garden eye-sores. There are four basic types of climber, each growing in a different way.

### ⊙ Steps

1  Plant climbers such as ivy or climbing hydrangea at the base of any wall or fence you want to cover. Stand back and watch them scramble upwards. They will send out rootlets that will cling to any support they encounter.

2  Plant climbers with tendrils such as grapes and sweet peas where they can hang on to their supports. Their tendrils grow out from their stems and can wrap themselves around thin supports such as string, wire or the stems of other plants. Match the support to the size and weight of the mature plant; a grapevine needs a sturdy support with strong wires, while sweet peas need only a simple wire or nylon mesh trellis.

3  Plant twining climbers such as clematis and morning glory near any trellis, arbour or openwork fence. As the plants grow, they'll twine themselves around both vertical and horizontal supports. Guide the first shoots up the fence and fasten them loosely; once they start weaving their way through the openings, they will need no more help.

4  Fasten climbers with no means of self-support, such as jasmine, directly to a fence or trellis. Secure the shoots loosely using plastic-coated wire or nylon twine tied in a figure-of-eight. To cover a wall or solid fence, drive in galvanised nails at 45–60 cm (18–24 in) intervals, and as the shoots grow, tie them to the nails.

### ✳ Tips

Look to the future if you plant a perennial climber. Wisteria, for instance, will live 50 years or more, and a mature plant is heavy. It needs a sturdy, well-designed structure that will both show off its beauty and bear its weight.

Arrange the shoots of tendril climbers in the direction you want them to grow, and fasten them loosely with twine or coated twist ties for a day or so until the tendrils begin to grip.

### Things You'll Need

❑ twine or other ties

❑ trellis

❑ galvanised nails

## 353 | Shape and Revive a Plant

Many plants benefit from occasional barbering, whether the purpose is to promote more flowers or simply to produce a more pleasing shape. The method to use depends on the plant.

**Things You'll Need**

❏ secateurs

### ◎ Steps

1 Deadhead (trim or pinch off regularly) the spent flowers of all annuals and the many perennials that bloom over a period of time instead of all at once (see 351 "Deadhead Flowers"). There are dozens of long-blooming perennials, including yarrow, salvia and peony.

2 Pinch back annual flowers, vegetables, herbs and late-blooming perennials such as chrysanthemums and asters. You'll help the plants produce more flowers and make them fuller and denser.

3 Shape perennials that bloom in a single flush, such as lavender, to produce a form that blends well with other plants in your garden. Use secateurs to cut foliage back by about a third, creating a shape that blends in with later-maturing plants in your garden.

4 Cut plants prone to legginess all the way back to the ground after they bloom. Hardy geraniums, Japanese anemone and black-eyed Susan all lend themselves well to this treatment.

## 354 | Trim Hedges

Plant a hedge to mark a boundary, form a barrier, create a background or define a planting bed. All hedges will look best if kept trimmed and in good health.

**✳ Tip**

The ideal hedge plant has scaffolding branches that start at the ground. Box, holly, juniper and privet are all excellent choices for hedging.

**⚠ Warning**

Evergreen hedges such as juniper and Leyland cypress should never be trimmed below the foliage or they won't grow back. Clip only a few centimetres from the previous year's growth.

### ◎ Steps

1 Begin trimming hedges when they're first planted. Young plants respond well to shaping and training.

2 Cut a few centimetres off the top of a hedge plant as soon as it has been planted. This will help form bushy plants.

3 Use a string guide to keep your hedges even when trimming. Place a bamboo stake at either end of the hedgerow. String a line between the two stakes at the desired height of the finished hedge. Use shears or hedge trimmers and follow the string line.

4 Shape the hedge so that it's wider at the bottom. Sunlight will reach all the leaves if the hedge is pruned this way. Taper the plants in as you near the top.

5 Trim during the active growing season. You may have to trim more than once, but you'll avoid making mistakes that can't be rectified.

6 Trim lightly at the end of the growing season to keep hedges looking good throughout the winter months.

**Things You'll Need**

❏ shears or hedge trimmers

❏ string

❏ bamboo stakes

## Divide Perennials

Are your perennials blooming less prolifically or getting too crowded? Then it's time to divide them. The method depends on your plants' growth habit.

### ⊙ Steps

#### Dividing Clump-Forming Perennials

1 Dig up the entire root system using a spade or fork – including all the soil from about 15–20 cm (6–8 in) around the roots.

2 Separate the root clumps with your hands by shaking off excess soil and pulling the roots apart into divisions.

3 Separate tightly growing clumps with two forks. Stick them between clumps with their backs together, then push the handles apart.

4 Replant the new divisions in the ground, or plant them in containers filled with potting compost.

5 Water new plantings well until the soil is completely moist.

6 Discard the oldest section at the centre of the clump if it looks woody and has little new growth.

#### Dividing Single-Stemmed Perennials

1 Use the following method for perennials that have runners (underground stems) and those that spread by sending roots through the soil and producing more stems above ground.

2 Plunge a shovel or spade straight down into the soil between groups of upright stems that are above ground. This separates the whole plant into sections.

3 Dig up a clump of soil that has roots and three or four stems growing out; dig about 10–15 cm (4–6 in) down. These are your new plants.

4 Replant or pot the extra divisions.

5 Refill the original hole with compost.

6 Water the remaining plant and the new divisions well, until the soil is completely moist.

### ✱ Tips

Most perennials can be divided in late autumn or early spring.

Dividing perennials means you get more and more plants every year – plants you can use in your own garden or share with friends.

### Things You'll Need

❏ spade

❏ two forks

❏ compost

---

## Prepare Your Garden for Winter

Readying your garden for winter is essential in cold-winter regions, where freezing, drying conditions can tax even hardy plants. Even in warmer climates there's plenty to do.

### ⊙ Steps

1 Plant spring-blooming bulbs such as tulips and daffodils. Plant them any time from September – as long as the ground can be easily worked.

2 Rake up leaves and dispose of them, preferably in a compost heap. Failing to rake up leaves can result in a dying or diseased lawn.

### ✱ Tip

Save your favourite plants before frost hits. Small annuals and herbs are wonderful for digging up and planting in pots to spend the winter in a sunny window inside.

3   Pull up any annual flowers or vegetables blackened by frost. Dispose of these in the compost heap; if you suspect disease, throw them away.

4   Cut back almost to the ground any perennials whose foliage has become unsightly. The seedheads and dried foliage of some perennials add interest during the winter months, while others just look messy.

5   Weed. Autumn action prevents weeds from getting a head start next spring, saving you work in the long run.

6   Dig up tender bulbs. Cannas, tuberous begonias, dahlias and most other summer-blooming bulbs don't survive cold winters. Store bulbs in vermiculite in a paper bag in a frost-free, dry spot.

7   Apply a winter mulch to perennials in cold areas. Simply lay a lightweight organic mulch, such as shredded autumn leaves or straw, over beds to protect plants from winter's extremes. Avoid more compact mulches and whole leaves (which can mat), since they can suffocate plants.

8   Water evergreens and small trees and shrubs if the autumn weather is especially dry. Their foliage and stems need to be nice and plump to prevent damage from drying winds now through early spring.

9   Check plants in containers. Bring in any tender plants to a cool, light spot to overwinter. For large plants that are hard to move, wrap the container in hessian and straw or bubble wrap to stop the rootball freezing.

10  Protect tender plants on a wall with straw packed between the branches held in place with netting.

## ⚠ Warning

Don't fertilise or prune plants at the end of their seasons. Either could promote tender new growth that will get nipped by cold. The exception is trimming out dead or damaged branches or foliage.

## Things You'll Need

❑ leaf rake

❑ secateurs

❑ mulch

❑ straw, hessian and netting

---

## 357 | Water Houseplants

More houseplants die from too much water than from not enough. Here's how to determine when your plants need water.

### ⊙ Steps

1   Poke your finger right into the soil, 2–3 cm (1 in) below the surface or up to your first knuckle. If the soil feels dry to the touch below the surface, it's time to water. If it feels damp, wait a day or two and test again.

2   Use an inexpensive moisture meter to check the moisture level in the soil as an alternative to the fingertip test.

3   Provide extra water for plants that require moist soil, such as ferns and philodendrons. The soil should feel like a wrung-out sponge.

4   Use self-watering pots if you don't have the time to check your plants daily. These handy pots allow the plants to help themselves to a drink. You will need to check the pots' water reservoirs every two weeks.

5   Use tepid or warm water for tropical plants. Allow the water to sit in the watering can overnight to warm to room temperature. For lime-hating plants use tap water or distilled water.

6   Mist plants frequently. They do take in moisture through their leaves, and the humidity mimics their tropical environment.

7   Avoid watering too much in winter when plants are dormant. Water more often once they start into active growth in spring.

### ✱ Tips

Plants in bright light will use more water than those in low-light areas.

Make a humidity tray by placing gravel in the saucer. When you water, moisture will evaporate from the gravel up through the foliage.

### ⚠ Warning

Never allow plants to sit in standing water. Drain saucers a half-hour after watering.

## Feed Houseplants **358**

You need to feed houseplants during their growing season, which is spring and summer.

### ⊙ Steps

1. Select a liquid fertiliser formulated for houseplants, and use it as directed during the growing season (spring and summer).

2. Add the concentrated fertiliser directly to the watering can.

3. Remove a plant from its saucer and place it in an area where water can run freely through the soil, such as in a sink or bath.

4. Pour the fertiliser solution onto the surface of the soil. Make sure it flows from the pot's drainage hole.

5. Allow the water to drain through the pot thoroughly before replacing the plant on its saucer.

6. Consider another method: use a slow-release fertiliser in the form of granules or spikes. Apply the product according to label directions.

### ⚠ Warnings

Don't feed more than is recommended, or you may burn your plants or get a salt build-up on the terracotta pot.

Try not to get any fertiliser on the foliage; it may burn the leaves and cause spots.

### Things You'll Need

- ❑ liquid fertiliser
- ❑ watering can
- ❑ slow-release fertiliser

---

## Propagate Houseplants From Cuttings **359**

Propagating from stem cuttings is an economical way to add to your houseplant collection.

### ⊙ Steps

1. Cut the tips (including the end leaf and the second and third leaves in from the end) off trailing or branching houseplants such as Swiss cheese plant, wandering Jew or weeping fig.

2. Remove the bottom two leaves. Roots will form at the nodes where the leaves were removed, not from the leaves themselves. If left on the cutting, the leaves may rot and contaminate the water.

3. Dip the cut end of the cutting into a rooting hormone. Rooting hormones encourage new root growth.

4. Place the prepared cutting into a small pot filled with damp sharp sand. You may also use damp perlite or vermiculite.

5. Set the cuttings in a bright, warm location, away from direct sunlight. To increase humidity while roots are forming, place the cuttings (in their containers) in a clear plastic bag. To prevent the bag from collapsing onto the young plants, place two or three chopsticks or wire hoops into the sand to support the bag. Tie the plastic bag loosely at the top with twist ties or rubber bands.

6. After roots form, transplant each cutting into a small pot filled with damp potting soil. Tug gently on a leaf to check for root development. If the plant pulls out of the sand easily, It's not ready. If there's some resistance, roots have formed and the cutting is ready to transplant.

7. Treat your new plant as you would any other houseplant. Be extra careful about proper moisture and light until the plant has fully established itself.

### ✱ Tips

Cuttings from foliage plants should not be longer than 8–10 cm (3–4 in), unless the plant is very large. Take several cuttings to ensure success in propagation.

African violets can be grown from a single leaf. Remove the leaf from the plant, dip the cut end into rooting hormone, place the cutting in damp sand, then transplant when roots form.

### Things You'll Need

- ❑ clean secateurs
- ❑ rooting hormone
- ❑ small pots
- ❑ sharp sand
- ❑ clear plastic bag
- ❑ chopsticks or wire hoops
- ❑ twist ties
- ❑ potting soil

## 360 | Select a Basic Set of Kitchen Equipment

You'll be able to prepare most recipes with just a few basic pots, pans and utensils.

### ⊙ Steps

1 Assess your needs. Basic equipment is adequate for those who mostly cook for themselves and don't go gourmet too often.

2 Look for basic equipment at larger markets and kitchen stores. Quality yet affordable equipment is available at kitchen shops and department stores. Supermarket equipment will work but often is of lesser quality.

3 Choose a 23 or 25 cm (9 or 10 in) frying or sauté pan with a lid, a 3.5 l (6 pt) saucepan and a baking or roasting tin to start with. You can cook most recipes with these three items.

4 Add to your basic set with an extra sauté pan, a 1 or 2 l (2–3½ pt) saucepan, and an 8 or 10 l (14–16 pt) stock pot.

5 Avoid plastic handles if possible – they can't withstand high oven temperatures – and choose cookware with riveted or welded handles. (There's nothing worse than a handle coming off in your hands as you attempt to remove a pot from the stove.)

6 Choose stainless steel or thick aluminium equipment if possible.

7 Start out with a spatula, tongs, a vegetable peeler and a few wooden spoons as your basic cooking utensils.

8 Be sure to get at least one high-quality, sharp knife; a good choice is the all-purpose, medium-size kind often labelled "cook's knife".

### ✳ Tip

Non-stick surfaces such as Teflon work well but are usually necessary only in frying or sauté pans. Use only wooden or coated utensils for non-stick surfaces.

### Things You'll Need

❑ 23 or 25 cm (9 or 10 in) frying or sauté pan

❑ 3.5 l (6 pt) saucepan

❑ baking or roasting tin

❑ 1 or 2 l (2–3½ pt) saucepan

❑ 8 or 10 l (14–16 pt) stock pot

❑ spatula

❑ tongs

❑ vegetable peeler

❑ wooden spoons

❑ cook's knife

## 361 | Season a Cast-Iron Saucepan

Seasoning a cast-iron pan with oil gives it a protective coating that keeps food from sticking and the pan from rusting. Do this when the pan is new or food is starting to stick to it.

### ⊙ Steps

1 Scrub a new pan with steel wool or a plastic scrubbing pad and mild, soapy water to get it very clean. (If re-seasoning an old pan, just scrub with hot water and a brush.) Rinse well and dry thoroughly.

2 Use a paper towel to coat the pan lightly with solid white vegetable fat (don't use butter).

3 Heat the saucepan, uncovered, in an oven for 1 hour at 180°C (350°F/Gas mark 4).

4 Let it cool before use and store uncovered.

### ✳ Tips

Once you've seasoned a pan, avoid washing it with soap. Clean instead by wiping with a damp cloth after each use – use a little salt as a mild abrasive to remove bits of stuck food, then coat with solid white vegetable fat.

If you must wash it, clean with mild soap, rinse and wipe dry. Then grease lightly with solid white vegetable fat.

## Sharpen Kitchen Knives 362

A sharpening steel, a whetstone and a commercial knife sharpener all can help keep an edge on your good chef's knives. Here are the basics on all three.

### ◎ Steps

#### Sharpening Steel

1 To maintain the edge, use a sharpening steel – a metal rod with a handle and a crosspiece to keep the knife from hitting your hand – every time you use the knife.

2 Hold the steel in one hand and the knife in the other. Place the heel of the knife blade near the tip of the steel.

3 Move the knife blade down the steel in the direction of the cutting edge and along the edge from heel to knife tip, at about a 10- to 20-degree angle. Repeat on the blade's other side.

#### Whetstone

1 Use a whetstone to give a knife back its edge. Choose wet or dry – experts differ on which is best. Choose one with a coarse side and a smooth side.

2 Place the whetstone on a stable surface, coarse side up. Position the knife blade at about a 20-degree angle to the stone.

3 Draw the knife across the stone several times in the direction of the cutting edge and along the edge from heel to knife tip. Repeat the process on the other side of the blade, about 10 times per side.

4 Repeat the same process a few more times on the fine side of the stone.

#### Commercial Sharpener

1 Use a commercial sharpener to sharpen and maintain blades. First, find out about the variety available: electric and manual, with a variety of sharpening surfaces, including ceramic and diamond. The best automatically position the knife blade at the correct angle.

2 Search online for "knife sharpeners" to find suppliers and information about the different products. Expect to pay anywhere from £10 to £25 for a sharpener.

### ✱ Tips

Make sure yours is a good knife that can be sharpened. Most high-quality chef's knives today are made of high-carbon steel.

Store good knives in a knife block or on a magnetic rack – not tossed randomly into a drawer – and cut only on cutting boards.

A professional sharpening service can do a great job on your knives if you're willing to be without them for a little while. Check online directories or the Yellow Pages for ones near you. Cutlery and cookware shops, as well as butchers, also sometimes offer this service.

### ⚠ Warning

Using a whetstone correctly takes practice and can be frustrating – consider having a cooking teacher or chef show you how to do it.

## Chop an Onion 363

Chopping an onion may very well be the most common kitchen task other than washing dishes. Still, it can be daunting.

### ◎ Steps

1 Make sure you have a firm, clean cutting board and a sharp knife.

2 Use a knife that's at least twice as long as the onion. You'll need the length to slice through the vegetable.

### ✱ Tips

To avoid tears, make sure your kitchen is well-ventilated so the sulphuric compounds released from the onion are dispersed.

3 Place the onion on the board so you can see both the root and the stem.

4 Hold the onion carefully and position the knife's blade along the onion so that it will cut it in half vertically, through both the root and stem ends.

5 Start the cut and then stop to make sure the blade is lined up properly.

6 Take your hand off the onion and place it on top of the knife, so that if the knife slips it won't cut you.

7 Finish cutting the onion in half.

8 Place each half on the cutting board, cut side down.

9 Cut off about 1 cm (½ in) from the root and stem ends, and either discard them or save them for stock. Remove the peel from the two halves.

10 Hold one half of the onion against the cutting board with the fingers of one hand at the very top, the fingertips curled under to keep them away from the knife blade.

11 Hold the knife in the other hand with the flat of the blade parallel to the cutting board. Cut the onion into a stack of horizontal slices, still connected at the root end – that is, don't cut all the way through it.

12 Turn the knife so the tip is pointing toward the root end and the blade is perpendicular to the board. Cut the horizontal slices into sticks, still not cutting through the root end.

13 Point the knife tip away from yourself and cut the sticks crosswise to make dice. Repeat with the other half of the onion.

A really sharp knife makes this process a breeze.

All onions, including shallots, are basically the same and can be cut the same way. If using leeks, discard the dark green part and wash the remaining white part well between each layer. Leeks don't need to be peeled.

Do not cut onions in half horizontally, so the stem is on one half and the root end on the other. Onions are difficult to work with and to keep together when cut this way.

Chop the onion more finely (if desired) using the "hinge" method: hold the knife with one hand and place the fingers of your other hand on top of the knife, down by the tip, to keep the tip lightly pressed to the cutting board. Use a rocking motion, with the tip of the knife acting as a hinge, to chop the onion into smaller pieces.

## 364 | Chop Fresh Herbs

**Fresh herbs are an important part of many recipes, and chopping them to the right size helps blend in their flavours.**

### ⊙ Steps

1 Rinse your herbs in cold water and carefully dry them with paper towels.

2 If using herbs with a woody or thick stem, like rosemary, basil or older thyme, strip the leaves off the stems with your fingers.

3 Remove the lower, leafless stems from herbs like parsley or coriander.

4 Pile the herbs on a clean cutting board.

5 Chop the herb pile roughly first, drawing the herbs back into a pile as you rechop them.

6 Finely chop the herbs using the "hinge" method: hold the knife with one hand, and place the fingers of your other hand on top of the knife down by the tip, to keep the tip lightly pressed to the cutting board. Raise the knife handle up and down rapidly, using a rocking motion, with the tip of the knife acting as a hinge.

7 Use the knife to draw the herbs back into a neat pile after every few strokes to make sure they are chopped evenly.

8 Use the herbs in your recipe as soon as you've finished chopping them.

### ✱ Tip

The best knife for chopping herbs is a sharp one with a wide blade, such as a chef's knife or a Chinese cleaver, that lets you chop without hitting your fingers on the cutting board. Don't use a serrated-edge knife because it won't cut cleanly.

# ✓ 365 Choose Produce

Follow the pointers in this chart to select the best tasting, ripest fruits and vegetables. If you have any doubts or questions, ask the greengrocer or store department manager. Note that imported produce may be available in seasons other than those listed.

| | WHAT TO LOOK FOR | PEAK SEASON |
|---|---|---|
| **Apples** | Bright colour, firm texture; no bruising or wrinkling | September to November (but available year-round) |
| **Asparagus** | Straight stalks with closed (not open or mushy) tips | February to June (hothouse asparagus may be available year-round) |
| **Avocados** | Heavy weight for size; no bruises or cuts; ready to use if they give to gentle pressure; ripen further if still firm | Hass avocados – summer; Fuerte – autumn and winter |
| **Bananas** | Bright yellow with green tips need further ripening; perfectly ripe when speckled with brown spots | Available year-round |
| **Broccoli** | Florets closed, dark green or purplish; not soft and mushy; fresh smell | October to April (but available year-round) |
| **Cherries** | Attached stems; firm but not hard; not soft or bruised | May to August |
| **Citrus fruit** | Heavy for their size; faint, sweet fragrance appropriate to variety | Available year-round (lemons peak in the summer) |
| **Grapes** | Silver-white bloom on skin; no brown spots; firmly attached to moist, flexible stems | Available year-round |
| **Mangoes** | Red blush over yellow skin when ripe; choose larger rather than smaller ones | May to September |
| **Melons** | Slightly sweet fragrance; slight softness at blossom end for musk melons; dull, not shiny, rind for watermelons; sound hollow when thumped; avoid bruised melons | Musk melons (such as cantaloupe and honeydew) – late summer to early autumn; watermelons – May to September, but peak from mid-June to late August |
| **Mushrooms, button** | Light colour; closed caps; pleasant, earthy smell; dry-looking, not slimy | Available year-round, but peak in autumn and winter |
| **Peaches and nectarines** | Intense fragrance; yellow, pink or white (not green) background colour; give slightly to pressure | Peaches – May to October; nectarines – May to late September, with a peak during July and August |
| **Pears** | Firm texture (avoid pears with soft spots); blemish-free skin; fresh fragrance | Mid to late summer to early November (and later if pears are from storage) |
| **Pineapples** | Fresh looking, leafy green crown; no visible bruises; sweet pineapple smell at stem end | Available year-round, but peak from March to July |
| **Plums** | Silver-white bloom on some types; very slightly soft; no bruises or wrinkles in skin | Peak in midsummer to autumn |
| **Potatoes** | Red, white, brown or purple skin free of discolouration; no decay, blemishes, green or sunken spots | Year-round (one variety or another) |
| **Raspberries** | Vivid colour, plump and slightly firm; not green; avoid soft berries | Midsummer and autumn |
| **Strawberries** | Bright colour, plump and glossy with green caps still attached; avoid mouldy, soft berries | April to midsummer |
| **Squash** | Blemish-free skin with no mushy spots; summer squash firm, heavy and smooth-skinned; winter squash firm, hard and heavy | Summer squash – early to late summer; winter squash – early autumn to the winter |
| **Sweetcorn** | Golden-brown silk; bright green, snug husk; rows of tightly packed, plump kernels extending to the tip | May to September |
| **Tomatoes** | Heavy for size; firm and well-shaped; give slightly to pressure; rich colour characteristic of variety | Available year-round, but peak from June to September |

chart

## 366 | Dice Vegetables

A diced vegetable is cut into small cubes. It's easy to dice quickly and evenly – just think "slices, sticks and cubes".

### ⊙Steps

1 Clean your cutting board and knife.

2 Peel the skin from the vegetable, if necessary, and discard it.

3 For round vegetables like carrots and potatoes, cut in half lengthwise and place them cut side down on the board. This will keep the vegetable from rolling.

4 Cut the vegetable lengthwise into even slices, then stack the slices and cut them into long sticks. (Long, relatively thin vegetables like celery and leeks need only be sliced into sticks.)

5 Gather the sticks and cut them crosswise into cubes. Make sure to cut the cubes as evenly as you can.

### Dicing Tomatoes

1 To dice a tomato, cut it in quarters vertically, through the stem. It is not necessary to cut out the stem just yet.

2 Cut away the inner pulpy part of each tomato quarter, removing the stem with it.

3 Slice the remaining outer flesh into thin strips, then cut the strips crosswise into dice.

### Dicing Cucumbers

1 To dice a cucumber, peel the skin with a vegetable peeler and cut the cucumber in half lengthwise.

2 Using a teaspoon, scrape the seeds and pulpy interior from each half.

3 Slice the cucumber into thin strips and then cut crosswise to dice.

### ✱Tips

A small dice is generally considered to be a 5 mm (¼ in) cube, a medium dice is about 1 cm (½ in), and a large dice is 2–2.5 cm (¾–1 in).

This technique will vary for specific vegetables, but you will almost always be aiming to get the vegetable into strips, which you can then easily cut into cubes. Vegetables made up of flowers, such as broccoli and cauliflower, are not typically diced, but broken into "florets."

To julienne vegetables (a type of cut that makes long, thin strips), follow steps 1 to 4 to slice the vegetables into even strips 5 mm (¼ in) thick and about 5 cm (2 in) long.

## 367 | Peel and Mince Garlic

Garlic is one of the most common ingredients in cooking. Using fresh garlic that you peel yourself gives the best results.

### ⊙Steps

1 Select a whole bulb of fresh garlic whose cloves are held tightly together and are not discoloured.

2 Separate the cloves by placing the garlic bulb, root side down, on a cutting board and pressing down on it firmly with the heel of your hand.

3 To peel the cloves, arrange them on the cutting board and whack or press them firmly with a heavy object, like the flat side of a chef's knife, a kitchen mallet or a small pan.

### ✱Tips

Wetting your fingers with water from time to time will prevent them from getting sticky from the garlic.

If salt is called for in your recipe, try adding a little to the garlic as you're mincing it. The salt will make the garlic less slippery and make mincing easier.

4   Cut away the end of the garlic clove where it was attached to the bulb.

5   Discard the skins and clean the cutting board before mincing.

6   First chop the garlic coarsely. Use the same technique as with an onion: Make a series of horizontal cuts on the clove (separating it into thin slices), then a series of vertical cuts (separating it into thin sticks). Then cut the sticks crosswise to make tiny dice.

7   Mince the diced garlic by chopping it with a rocking motion: Keep the tip of the knife on the cutting board and move the handle up and down.

8   Stop every few strokes and use the knife blade to draw the garlic pieces back into a neat pile before continuing. Scrape off the garlic that has stuck to the side of the blade.

## Peel and Seed Tomatoes                           368

So often, recipes call for peeling and seeding tomatoes. But how do you do it? Here you go.

### ⊙ Steps

1   Place a saucepan three-quarters full of water over a high heat and bring to the boil.

2   Immerse tomatoes in the boiling water for 1 minute.

3   Remove tomatoes with tongs or a slotted spoon and set aside to cool enough so that you can handle them.

4   Barely pierce a tomato's skin with the tip of a sharp knife. Loosen the skin with the knife and peel away.

5   Cut the peeled tomatoes in half horizontally – that is, not cutting through the stem end.

6   Hold a tomato half in your hand over a small bowl.

7   Gently squeeze the tomato half so that the seeds and the clear pulp surrounding them drip into the bowl. Discard.

8   Use tomatoes as the recipe requires.

### ✱ Tips

Some people cut a small X in the base of the tomato before dipping it in the boiling water. The skin splits slightly around the X; peel back the corners of the X to remove the skin.

If the tomatoes don't peel well, dip them in the boiling water for another 30 seconds.

## Bone a Fish                                      369

You can bone fish either before or after cooking. The bones separate quite easily after cooking, but it's often more pleasant to eat fish when the bones have been removed beforehand.

### ⊙ Steps

1   Place the gutted and rinsed fish on a cutting surface. The following steps give you fillets.

2   Hold the fish by the head (if the head is still attached) and slice into the fish behind the gill until you feel the knife touch the backbone.

### ✱ Tips

The sharper the knife, the better. Fish flesh is usually very delicate, especially trout and smaller fish, and requires a very sharp knife to cut cleanly. Serrated knives and electric knives are not recommended – they will make a mess.

3   Turn the knife so it's flat against the backbone, touching the ribs. The cutting edge should face the tail.

4   Cut along the backbone from head to tail, under the fillet.

5   Turn the fish over and repeat this cut. At this point two sets of bones will remain in the fillet.

6   Cut away the rib cage bones, which will be visible, by sliding the edge of the knife between the rib bones and the meat of the fillet.

7   Pull out the smaller set of bones, called pin bones, that run through the centre of the fillet. Use your finger to press gently and feel for the pin-bone tips sticking out of the fillet. Use tweezers to grab the tips and pull them out.

Raw fish should be gutted and rinsed in clean water.

## 370 | Take the Skin Off Chicken

Chicken skin contains most of the bird's fat, and by removing skin you can lower the amount of fat in your diet. Many recipes call for skinless chicken meat.

**⊙ Steps**

1   Place a whole raw chicken on a clean cutting board with the breast facing down.

2   Slice through the skin along the backbone.

3   Cut off the wings at the first joint.

4   Cut around the end of each drumstick to loosen the skin from the legs.

5   Carefully peel the skin away from the chicken, starting with the cut you made at the backbone.

6   Cut or pull the skin from the breastbone.

7   Skin a single piece of raw chicken by grasping one end of the skin firmly and pulling it.

8   To skin a whole cooked chicken or a cooked chicken piece, wait until it is cool enough to handle, then pull the skin away.

**✳ Tip**

Leave the skin on during cooking and peel it away afterwards – meat won't absorb a significant amount of fat from the skin during cooking. Skin will also protect the meat from drying out during cooking and will add a little extra flavour.

## 371 | Bone a Chicken Breast

The more work done to prepare chicken before sale, the more it costs per pound: skinless, boneless breasts are much more expensive than the bone-in variety.

**⊙ Steps**

1   If the recipe allows, cook the chicken breast with bones intact. They protect the meat as it cooks, which helps keep it juicy, and they help the breast retain its shape.

**✳ Tips**

When you're finished cutting raw chicken, be sure to thoroughly clean everything the chicken touched.

2   If you want to cook with a boneless breast, place the raw chicken breast, skin side down, on a clean cutting board. The bones will face up.

3   Look for the rib bones. Breasts sold with the bones attached still retain the ribs and part of the breastbone.

4   Hold the breast by the rib bones, and use the tip of the knife to make a thin incision between the ribs and the breast meat.

5   Use the knife tip to make small cuts across the rib cage, between the ribs and the meat, so you gradually separate the meat along the entire length of the rib cage.

6   Follow the contours of the rib cage with the tip of the knife, holding the breast by the ribs.

7   Continue making small cuts until the meat has completely separated from the bone.

8   The meat is now ready for your recipes.

9   Save the bones for stock or discard them.

A sharp boning knife is best for cutting chicken. Boning knives have thin, flexible blades about 15 cm (6 in) long that can manoeuvre around the bird's small bones.

## Shuck Oysters 372

Opening oysters requires practice to do just right and preserve most of the oysters' liquid. It's a good idea to use a specialised sturdy oyster knife to make the job easier and safer.

### ⊙ Steps

1   Make sure the oysters are still alive by checking that their shells are tightly closed.

2   Scrub the oysters with a stiff brush under running water.

3   Hold an oyster in the palm of your hand with a towel so that you don't cut yourself. Or wear leather oyster gloves to protect your hands.

4   Work over a bowl so that you can catch the oysters' juices.

5   Position the oyster in your hand with the cup side down – so that its curved shell faces down and its flatter side faces up.

6   Insert a strong paring or oyster knife between the shells, near the hinge.

7   Twist the knife so that the oyster's muscles are detached.

8   Remove the top shell.

9   Scrape the meat from the top shell into the bottom shell.

10  Use the knife to cut the oyster free from the bottom shell.

### ✱ Tip

Always try to determine that shellfish originated in a body of water untainted by pollution or other hazards. The best way to do this is to become the regular customer of a reputable fishmonger. Try calling a restaurant chef or your local newspaper food section for recommendations.

### Things You'll Need

❏ stiff brush

❏ leather gloves

❏ oyster knife

## 373 | Devein Unshelled Shrimp

The "vein" is actually the shrimp's digestive tract. You don't have to take it out, but many people prefer to remove it for appearance's sake.

### ⊙ Steps

1   Cut down the back of the shell with a knife or kitchen scissors to make it easier to access the vein.

2   Use your fingers and a shrimp pick, a skewer or the tip of a small, sharp knife to remove as much of the vein as you can. Keep pulling out pieces until all of the vein has been removed.

3   Rinse in cold water.

### ✳ Tip

You can devein the shrimp and leave the shell on; the shell adds flavour to the dish and can protect the meat if you're grilling the shrimp.

## 374 | Clean and Crack Cooked Crab in its Shell

With its pincers and hard shell, a live crab can be intimidating to handle – and a cooked one only a little less so. But the reward of sweet crabmeat is worth it.

### ⊙ Steps

1   Place a cooked crab on a work surface, belly side up.

2   Pull off the triangular-shaped belly flap, or "apron".

3   Turn the crab over and remove the top shell by inserting your thumb between the body and shell at the rear end of the crab and pulling up on the shell.

4   Pull off the spongy gills and small paddles at the front of the crab's body and discard them.

5   Use a spoon to scoop out crab meat and roe ("crab butter") from inside the body. Keep the roe if you like.

6   Twist off the claws and legs. (Note: Some people like to leave the smaller legs on as handles to hold while they pick out the meat.)

7   Use a knife to cut the crab's body in half lengthwise and then into quarters, if desired, or simply snap the body in half. Pick out meat.

8   Use a nutcracker or small hammer to crack open the leg shells. Tap the shells sharply to break them into pieces that you can then remove.

9   Pick out meat from the legs and body of the crab with a lobster pick, fork or tip of a crab claw.

### ⚠ Warning

Watch out for live crabs' pincers. They are strong enough to cause injury.

## Boil an Egg

**375**

Just in case your mother never explained this to you, here are the simple steps involved in boiling an egg.

### ⊙Steps

1  Fill a small saucepan with water.

2  Bring the water to a simmer.

3  Place the egg in the water and turn the heat to medium.

4  When the water begins to boil, reduce the heat to low.

5  Continue simmering for 3 to 5 minutes for soft-boiled eggs or 10 to 15 minutes for hard-boiled eggs.

6  Remove the egg with a spoon or ladle and let it cool slowly, or run cold water over it to cool it more quickly.

**✳ Tip**

Cooking times given are for room-temperature eggs. Allow a couple of minutes more for eggs straight out of the fridge.

## Separate Egg Whites From Yolks

**376**

Working slowly is the secret, as is getting a good first crack.

### ⊙Steps

1  Lightly crack an egg on the edge of a bowl.

2  Turn the egg upright and carefully open the shell into two halves, keeping the egg in the lower half.

3  Over the bowl, pour the egg from one half of the broken shell into the other, letting the egg white fall into the bowl but keeping the yolk intact in the shell halves as you pour.

4  Repeat until all of the white has fallen into the bowl and only the yolk remains in the shell.

**✳ Tip**

If you plan to whip the egg whites, take care not to get any yolk in them, separating each egg over a small bowl before transferring the yolk and white to separate larger bowls. Whites that have yolk or any fat at all in them will not whip properly. It's usually not a problem to have a little white left in the yolk.

## Shell a Hard-Boiled Egg

**377**

Don't crack the egg too sharply or you'll sacrifice some of the egg along with the shell.

### ⊙Steps

1  Hold a boiled egg in one hand and a spoon in the other.

2  Lightly strike the egg in the middle of its side with the edge of the spoon.

3  Rotate the egg 90 degrees and repeat.

4  Continue until the egg is cracked all the way around.

5  Hit the side of the egg above the crack.

6  Slightly squeeze the egg in the middle.

**✳ Tips**

Squeeze the egg just a little or you will crush it.

The fresher an egg, the harder it is to peel when cooked. If you can't get the shell off, put the egg in the freezer for a few minutes and try again.

7   With a slight twisting motion, lift off the shell's top.

8   Hit the side of the egg below the crack.

9   With the same twisting motion, lift off the shell's bottom.

## ⚠ Warning

Even though they are thoroughly cooked, hard-boiled eggs need to be refrigerated to store them.

---

## 378  Stew Anything

Stewing is a good way to prepare foods that don't do too well with other cooking methods. A great use of leftovers, stews are easy to make, freeze and reheat.

### ⊙ Steps

1   Start the stew by cutting the ingredients into pieces roughly the same size so that they cook evenly. Stews are usually made up of smaller pieces of meat and vegetables so that they can be bite size and their flavours can mingle.

2   Heat a large saucepan or stock pot over medium heat and add a few tablespoons of oil – enough so that the ingredients won't stick.

3   Season the meat with salt and pepper and add it to the pan. The pan should be hot enough for the meat to sizzle. Brown the meat thoroughly, but don't cook it all the way through.

4   Remove the meat when it is browned and add sturdy vegetables (but not potatoes just yet). Most stews use a mixture of onions, celery and carrots. Cook these for a few minutes, stirring them around, and then add a generous sprinkle of flour. This will thicken the stew as it cooks. Add about 1 tbsp flour for each 600 ml (1 pt) of cooking liquid you will use in step 7.

5   Stir the flour into the vegetables and cook for a few minutes before returning the meat to the pot.

6   Add herbs, such as bay leaf or thyme, if desired.

7   Cover the stew with liquid. Most stewing liquid is water, stock, wine or a combination. Homemade stock is best, of course, but stock from a cube or powder will do. Any dry wine will work; different wines will give your stew different tastes – just don't use a sweet wine.

8   Bring the mixture to the boil, lower the heat to simmer, cover and cook until the meat is done (see Tips for approximate cooking times). Add any potatoes, cut in quarters or large cubes, about 40 minutes before the end of the cooking time. Check if it is done by removing a piece of meat and tasting it; it should be tender but not mushy.

9   Sprinkle on freshly chopped parsley or another herb and serve.

### ✳ Tips

Stew made with vegetables only takes 20 to 35 minutes to cook. Check such a stew constantly because, unlike meat stew, vegetable stew is easy to overcook.

Poultry stews take about an hour to cook, lamb and veal stews about 90 minutes, and beef stews up to 3 hours.

Tougher cuts make the best stew meat, because the slow cooking tenderises the meat, while long stewing will actually make tender cuts tougher. Look for "stewing meat" for sale. It's usually the least expensive. .

Potatoes are indispensable in many stews. The trick is to add them after the stew has simmered for a while so that they don't overcook and disintegrate.

## Marinate Meat 379

Marinating meat is one of the best ways to give it more flavour and tenderise it at the same time. It's foolproof if you follow a few simple guidelines.

### ⊙ Steps

1 Trim the meat so that it's ready for cooking. You shouldn't have to cut or trim the meat after it's been marinated.

2 Mix the marinade according to its recipe (see 380 "Make a Basic Marinade" or 381 "Make a Red Wine Marinade").

3 Notice whether the marinade contains any of these three key ingredients: an acidic ingredient (such as wine, lemon juice or vinegar), salt and alcohol. Each one reduces the amount of time the meat should marinate.

4 Combine the meat and marinade in a sealed, non-metal container. Make especially sure not to use aluminium or cast iron, as these react with acids, and try to avoid metal altogether, if possible.

5 Marinate in a sealable plastic bag if you can. You can turn the bag over often, ensuring that all surfaces get coated.

6 Immediately place the container in the refrigerator. Never marinate meat at room temperature.

7 See Tips for marinating times.

8 When the marinated meat is ready to cook, be sure to treat it with the same care you would treat any raw meat.

9 Discard the marinade after use.

### ✱ Tips

Any marinade that contains acidic ingredients, alcohol or salt should not be used for very long, because it will chemically "cook" or denature the food in it. In general, marinate food for less than 4 hours; however, marinades that contain no salt, acidic ingredients or alcohol can be used to marinate overnight or, in some cases, longer. Marinades that contain citrus juices, especially lemon or lime juice, should be used for 2 hours or less.

Although marinades inhibit bacterial growth, remember that the food in them is still raw and must be treated as such.

### ⚠ Warning

Do not reuse a marinade or baste with it less than 5 minutes before food has finished cooking.

## Make a Basic Marinade 380

This easy marinade will add great flavour to chicken, fish and prawns. You can use many different combinations of fresh herbs. This makes enough for up to 900 g (2 lb) of food.

### ⊙ Steps

1 Mince the garlic and place it in a mixing bowl.

2 Rinse the herbs in cold water and dry them carefully with clean paper towels. Parsley, thyme, oregano and marjoram are good in this marinade, in virtually any combination. Coriander and basil lose their flavour quickly and are best avoided for marinades. Use them fresh, instead, on the finished dish.

3 Chop the herbs into small pieces and place them in the bowl with the remaining ingredients. If using rosemary, remove the leaves for use and discard the woody stems before chopping.

4 Mix the ingredients well.

5 Carefully place the food to be marinated in a sealable plastic bag or a clean container.

### ⚠ Warning

Once raw food has been stored in this marinade, discard the marinade immediately after use and do not use it again.

### Ingredients

❑ 6 to 8 cloves garlic

❑ a good handful of chopped fresh herbs (parsley, thyme, oregano or marjoram)

❑ 300 ml (1/2 pt) olive oil

❑ 1 tbsp freshly ground black pepper

6   Pour the marinade over the food and mix everything together well.

7   Marinate food in the refrigerator for several hours or up to two days. Because this marinade contains no salt or acid, food can be left in it for longer periods of time.

8   Use the marinade on fish, shellfish (such as shrimp) and poultry, especially white meat from chicken and turkey.

9   Take the food out of the marinade and cook it on an outdoor grill for the best flavour. You can also roast or sauté marinated foods.

10  Make this marinade in advance for more convenience. Store it in a covered container in the refrigerator for several weeks.

## 381 | Make a Red Wine Marinade

Here is the quintessential marinade for beef, especially tougher cuts such as pot roasts and ribs. This recipe makes about 700 ml (1¼ pt), enough for one pot roast or 1–1.5 kg (2–3 lb) of ribs.

### ⊙ Steps

1   Place all ingredients in a non-reactive saucepan and bring to the boil over a high heat. Boil briskly for 5 to 6 minutes.

2   Remove the saucepan from the heat and allow the marinade to cool.

3   Use the marinade as a cooking liquid in a stewed or braised dish. Once it cooks for a while with beef, it makes a fantastic sauce.

### Ingredients

❏ 1 (750ml) bottle red wine

❏ 1 carrot, chopped

❏ 1 medium onion, chopped

❏ 5 or 6 sprigs fresh thyme

❏ 5 or 6 sprigs fresh parsley

❏ 1 bay leaf

❏ 1 tsp black peppercorns

## 382 | Sauté Anything

Sautéing is the same as pan-frying – cooking quickly in a little fat. It comes from the French word meaning "to jump", because the food in the pan is sometimes quickly stirred or tossed.

### ⊙ Steps

1   Sautéing is a quick cooking method, so have everything ready to go and near the stove before you begin.

2   Set a ring to a medium heat or higher.

3   Place the frying pan on the ring and allow it to heat. This is an important step; the pan should never be cold when you add the cooking oil or the food. Cookware with a non-stick coating shouldn't be heated dry for more than 30 seconds. Add the cooking fat before this, because the non-stick coating will degrade if heated dry for too long.

4   When the pan is hot, add enough oil or other cooking fat to thinly coat the bottom. Sautéing properly depends on the cooking fat's forming a

### ✳ Tips

The high heat is necessary to brown the outside and cook foods quickly enough so that the inside doesn't dry out. This is especially true of meat, in which the fibres contract as they cook, squeezing out moisture as they do so.

Almost anything can be sautéed, as long as it's reasonably thin and isn't too wet. Use paper towels to dry damp items, because sautéing depends on enough heat to vapourise the water in the layer between the food and the pan, so make sure you use enough. Too little oil will cause food to cook unevenly and probably stick. Yet if you use enough and heat the pan properly, the food won't absorb a lot of fat.

5   Don't overheat the oil; it should never start smoking. One common test to see whether the pan is hot enough is to drop a minute pinch of flour into it; if the flour bubbles and sizzles rapidly, the pan is hot.

6   When the oil is hot, add the food you're going to sauté. Place it in the pan carefully, because the pan should be hot enough now for it to sizzle rapidly. The sound should tell you whether the pan is hot enough. No sizzle means it's too cold, and if it splatters and pops, the pan is too hot.

7   Foods that have been cut up, perhaps for a stir-fry, will need to be stirred regularly so that each piece has the same amount of contact with the bottom of the pan. Larger pieces, such as chicken breasts and fish fillets, are best left undisturbed and flipped only once, so that each side gets the same amount of contact with the pan.

outer layer of foods, which leads to browning. Too much water will cause the food to steam instead.

Vegetable, sunflower or olive oil will work in virtually all recipes, but if you use the latter, make sure your dish will benefit from its taste – also be aware that extra-virgin olive oil has a low smoking point. Butter can't be heated as much (the dairy solids in it burn), so it's best used for eggs, vegetables and other foods that cook fast and at lower temperatures. Animal fats such as lard and bacon fat work very well, but add distinctive flavour.

## Stir-Fry Anything                                                   383

Stir frying is an Oriental technique for cooking meat and vegetables quickly. It typically involves a quick sauté over high heat, occasionally followed by brief steaming in a flavoured sauce.

### ⊙ Steps

1   Invest in a non-stick or carbon-steel wok. While you can stir-fry in any old pan, the wok's depth and sloping sides (it's cooler there, so you can move ingredients up and away from the hot bottom) are ideal.

2   Cut all your vegetables and meats and prepare your sauce before you begin to stir-fry. Stir frying is fast; you won't have time to chop the broccoli while the onion is cooking.

3   Make sure that your vegetables and meats are all cut approximately the same size – bite size, as a matter of fact. Stir-frying uses high heat, so pieces must be small enough to cook through without burning.

4   Learn the different cooking times of meats and vegetables, so that you can add ingredients according to how long they take to cook. (For example, you'd add onions first and stir-fry for about 2 minutes, then add broccoli florets and stir-fry for 3 to 4 minutes, then add red bell pepper and stir-fry for 2 more minutes.) If you've got a wok-full, stir-fry the meat completely first and remove it, then add it back in at the end.

5   Follow this order when stir-frying: heat the pan first, then add oil. When the oil is hot, add aromatics, such as ginger and garlic, and stir-fry for a few seconds, or until you smell them. Then start adding your other ingredients, according to their approximate cooking times. When the food is about two-thirds done, add your sauce. If the food will take more than a few additional minutes to cook, cover and steam until done. If it will take a short time, continue to stir-fry.

6   Practise the basic technique of lifting the food in the wok with a spatula or other flat utensil and moving it to the side.

### ✳ Tip

For a basic stir-fry sauce, combine 2 tbsp soy sauce, 2 tbsp water or broth, 1 tbsp plain or rice vinegar, 1 tbsp Chinese rice cooking wine or dry sherry, a pinch of sugar, and 1 to 2 tsp of Oriental chilli garlic sauce (or a few dashes of hot pepper sauce). Whisk 1 tsp cornflour into the cold mixture as a thickener.

## 384 | Keep Food From Sticking to Pans

From saucepans to baking tins, follow these tips to keep food from sticking.

### ⊙ Steps

#### Saucepans and Frying Pans

1  Buy high-quality, heavy pots and pans. Thin pots and pans can develop "hot spots", which cause food to burn and stick. Heavy non-stick pans are great for cutting down on sticking, but some cooks believe that food doesn't brown as well in them, and even the highest quality non-stick coating degrades over time.

2  Make sure your pots and pans are completely clean before you use them. Old food build-up can burn and make food stick. Black spots indicate food build-up. Scrub it off with a non-abrasive cleanser.

3  Try to have your food at room temperature before adding it to the pan.

4  Heat the pan, then add a small amount of cooking oil or other fat. When the oil is also hot, add the food. (Non-stick pans are an exception: heating them without oil for more than 30 seconds will damage the coating.)

5  If food does burn, wait for the pan to cool, then soak it in hot water.

#### Baking Tins

1  Buy well-made tins, and keep them free of food build-up.

2  Follow your recipe carefully. Most recipes will indicate if a pan should be greased, greased and floured, or left ungreased.

3  If in doubt, grease. Use non-stick cooking spray or wipe on butter or oil with a paper towel. Coat thinly and evenly.

4  To grease and flour a pan (usually for baking a cake), coat the pan with cooking spray or butter from a pastry brush, then add a tablespoon of flour to the pan. Knock the pan from side to side until the pan is dusted evenly with flour. Throw out the excess.

### ✳ Tips

If you overcook food, it is more likely to stick to the pan.

If you use non-stick pans, don't use metal utensils, as these can scratch the coating.

Season cast-iron pans and carbon-steel woks before you use them, to prevent sticking (see 361 "Season a Cast-Iron Saucepan").

Non-stick cooking sprays can leave a gummy build-up on pans, causing food to stick later. If you do use a non-stick spray, apply it to a cold pan, then put the pan on the heat. If your pan feels sticky or gummy after you've washed it, remove the build-up with a non-abrasive cleanser.

Avoid using metal scrubbers to clean pots, as these can leave tiny scratches in the finish where food can build up and stick.

## 385 | Braise Anything

Braising is a cooking method usually used for tougher cuts of meat, and sometimes for vegetables. The food cooks in liquid, similar to stewing, and the result is meltingly tender.

### ⊙ Steps

1  Make sure that all your ingredients are roughly the same size so they will cook evenly.

2  Heat the pan, then add a little oil and heat that, too.

3  Season the meat or vegetables on both sides with salt and pepper, or whatever seasonings your recipe requires.

### ✳ Tips

Pot roasts, chuck roasts, ribs and poultry legs and thighs are best for braising.

If you want to use the braising liquid as a sauce, leave the pan uncovered so that moisture can evaporate, thus concentrating

4   When the pan is hot, add the meat or vegetables and sauté at high heat to quickly brown the outside. This adds colour and flavour.

5   When they're nicely browned, add enough liquid to the pan to come about halfway up the sides of the meat or vegetables. Liquid used for braising is usually water, stock, wine or a combination.

6   Lower the heat and simmer the ingredients slowly until everything is tender, or place the whole dish (provided the pan is ovenproof) in the oven and bake it. What's important is that the meat or vegetables cook slowly in the liquid and that the liquid never evaporates. (See Tips to decide whether to cover the dish.)

7   Check whether it is ready according to what you're cooking. Be aware that braising is a slow-cooking method. Most braised dishes take from 30 minutes (or less, for vegetables) to 6 hours (for tough ribs).

the flavours. Only do this with cuts that take less than 90 minutes or so to cook. Add other ingredients, such as vegetables or herbs and spices, to flavour the liquid. Make sure the liquid level doesn't get too low, or you'll be baking and not braising.

Vegetables that braise well include onions, fennel and root vegetables; you can even braise fruit such as pineapples and apples. In each case, it's easiest to cut the vegetable or fruit in half and brown it on the flat cut side.

# Steam Vegetables                    386

Steaming is one of the best ways to cook vegetables. It leaves more of the vegetable's natural taste, texture and colour intact than any other method, and it requires no added fat

## ⊙ Steps

1   Bring a few centimetres of water to the boil over a high heat in a large pot. Always use a high heat to steam vegetables. Since steam is hotter than boiling water, vegetables will cook faster and will absorb less water.

2   If you're using a steaming-rack or a bamboo steamer (works great!), make sure it's clean and have it ready.

3   Trim and cut your vegetables when the water is boiling. It's best to do this as close to cooking as possible so they won't dehydrate or oxidise. Cut all the vegetables the same size so they'll cook evenly.

4   Place the vegetables in the steamer or steamer rack and cover.

5   Steam them only until they're done; most cut vegetables only need to steam for a minute or two. Thicker pieces might steam for 2 to 3 minutes. Potatoes take 15 to 30 minutes.

6   Serve immediately, because the longer the vegetables sit, the mushier they'll get.

**✱ Tips**

A bamboo steamer is preferred to all other containers because the wood inhibits condensation. Choose bamboo steamers that are 100 per cent bamboo. Some contain metal linings or metal racks, and these will allow condensation, which can lead to soggy vegetables. Bamboo steamers are best used in a wok.

The most important tip is not to overcook steamed vegetables.

# Blanch Vegetables                    387

By boiling vegetables briefly, chilling them in ice-cold water, then reheating them slowly, you can preserve texture, colour and flavour. The boiling and chilling technique is known as blanching.

**✱ Tips**

Blanching is best for vegetables like asparagus, broccoli, cauliflower, green beans and spinach. If you were to serve these

## ⊙ Steps

1   Bring a large pot of water to a rapid boil over a high heat. Add enough salt so that the water tastes faintly salty.

2   While the water heats, fill a medium bowl about three-quarters full with ice, then add enough cold water to come just to the top of the ice.

3   When the water is boiling and the ice bath is ready, trim the vegetables to the size you need. It's best to trim them just prior to cooking so they won't oxidise or dehydrate.

4   Add the vegetables to the boiling water in batches small enough to ensure that the water doesn't lose its boil.

5   Boil the vegetables only until they're barely cooked through but still tender. To test, remove one piece with a slotted spoon, dip it into the ice bath to cool, and eat it.

6   As soon as the vegetables are done, remove them as fast as you can and submerge them in the ice bath.

7   Remove them from the ice bath as soon as they are no longer warm.

8   To reheat the vegetables, you can use any cooking method you wish, such as sautéing, grilling or boiling; just make sure to barely heat them up and not to cook them again.

vegetables right out of the boiling water, they would continue to cook and might become too mushy. These vegetables, blanched, are also great for crudités (vegetable platters). Serve with aioli (garlic mayonnaise) or another dip.

You can also boil and chill pasta this way, for cold pasta dishes or for pasta you plan to reheat later.

## 388  Make Mashed Potatoes

In some families, making mashed potatoes is an art form. Here's a recipe that will be a hit. Makes six servings.

### ⊙ Steps

1   Peel, cut into large chunks and boil four to six medium-size potatoes for 20 to 25 minutes or until tender when pierced with the tip of a knife.

2   Drain the potatoes, return them to the pot they were boiled in and shake over a medium heat until the potato pieces are dry and mealy.

3   Purée the potatoes by passing them through a food mill or potato ricer, by whipping them with an electric mixer, or by mashing them with a potato masher or heavy fork. Work out lumps as best as you can.

4   Whisk in 2 to 4 tbsp melted butter, a pinch of salt, pepper to taste and 200–300 ml (1/3–1/2 pt) warmed milk. Whisk potatoes until smooth.

5   Serve immediately.

### ✳ Tip

Never use a food processor to make mashed potatoes. They will become gooey.

### Ingredients

❑ 4 to 6 potatoes

❑ 2 to 4 tbsp butter

❑ salt and pepper to taste

❑ 200–300 ml (1/3–1/2 pt) milk, warmed

## 389  Toast Nuts

There are two ways to toast nuts – in the oven or in a tin. Both use high heat and short cooking times to bring out the nuts' best flavour.

### ⊙ Steps

1   Make sure the nuts are shelled and of uniform size.

2   For toasting in the oven, spread nuts in a single layer in a baking tin (one with sides is best). Cook at 200°C (400°F/Gas mark 6) for 7 to 10 minutes or until the nuts turn golden. Shake the pan halfway through toasting.

### ✳ Tips

Toasted nuts have a deeper, more concentrated flavour than raw nuts.

Nuts have high concentrations of natural oil, so it is not necessary to add oil when toasting them.

3   For toasting in a pan, place nuts in a single layer. With the pan over a medium-high heat, stir or shake the nuts continuously.

4   Cook the nuts only until they start to turn golden and parts of them still appear raw, about 5 to 7 minutes; they should smell toasty, though. Don't let them get any darker than light brown or they won't taste good. Remove them from the cooking pan as soon as they're done. Let them cool before using.

## Choose a Steak 390

To pick the best steak for your money (and it can be a lot of money), pay attention to the type of cut and the grade – as well as to a few things that are not so obvious.

### ⊙ Steps

1   Get to know the cuts, which are sold under many different names. Fillet steak is boneless and is the most expensive; sirloin (or contre filet) is a large cut, sold with or without bone and includes the fillet and the very thin minute steak; T-bone and porterhouse steaks are also part of the sirloin, and include a large bone; rump steak is a lean and tender cut.

2   Determine how tender you like your steak. The most tender cuts come from the part of the animal that gets the least exercise. Fillet is a very tender cut, but often less full of flavour than rump.

3   Get to know a good butcher whom you trust. The quality of beef depends on the age, breed and sex of the animal and how it was reared (organic is often excellent meat). The best beef has the most marbling, or fat within the meat, which helps to keep the meat moist and tender as it cooks. Avoid meat with much gristle.

4   Check with your butcher to find out if the meat has been hung, which tenderises and mellows the flavour.

5   Allow at least 125 g (4 oz) of steak per serving – double or triple that for hungry eaters, or if the steak contains a bone.

### ✳ Tips

The more marbling, or streaks or flecks of fat, the more flavourful the steak. Be sure that the marbling is evenly distributed.

Look for meat with a smooth, tight grain.

A general rule of toughness: the closer the meat is to a hoof or horn, the tougher it will be.

## Grill Meat 391

Grilled meat is cooked very close to the heating element. Because it takes such high, direct heat, grilled food gains a pleasantly brown exterior, and it usually cooks quickly.

### ⊙ Steps

1   Choose tender steaks and chops that can be cooked quickly – or sliced ham, bacon, fish or baby beef liver. Preheat the grill for at least 5 to 7 minutes. It needs to be very hot.

2   Season the meat and place it on a grill pan, or on a rack in a shallow baking tray.

### ✳ Tip

Grilling works best on quick-cooking cuts – less than 2.5 cm (1 in) thick. Thicker cuts can be browned in the grill and finished in a 190°C (325°F/Gas mark 5) oven.

3   Put the grill pan in the oven about 13 cm (5 in) from the heat source. Place thicker foods farther from the heat, thinner foods closer. Cuts that are too thick must be cooked another way.

4   Grill until the side closest to the heat turns a pleasant, deep golden brown. Take care that the meat doesn't burn. Depending on the cut, start checking after about 5 minutes.

5   Turn the food over and cook the other side until it is done. Test to see if it is ready with an instant-read cooking thermometer (the most accurate way), or cut steaks or chops in the thickest part to see how well they are cooked. Most red meat is rare at an internal temperature of about 55°C (130°F), medium rare at 63°C (145°F) and medium at 66°C (150°F). Pork and poultry should be completely cooked through – at least 71°C (160°F) for pork, 77°C (170°F) for poultry breast meat and 82°C (180°F) for poultry thigh meat. Fish should flake easily.

6   Learn to test by pressing with a finger; meat firms as it cooks. Be careful not to burn yourself.

⚠ **Warning**

If something catches fire, do not pour water on it, because this can splash flaming grease. Shut the oven door and immediately turn off the grill. Most grill-pan fires will suffocate themselves. If the fire persists, use a fire extinguisher.

---

## 392 | Roast Meat

Roasting is used for large, tender cuts. Beef rib cuts, pork loins, legs of lamb and whole poultry all roast well.

### ◉ Steps

1   Preheat the oven to 230°C (450°F/Gas mark 8).

2   Assess the size of the roast. If it's small enough for you to quickly brown the outside in a very hot pan or a barbecue grill, season the roast with salt and pepper, oil it lightly and brown it.

3   Put the meat in a roasting pan, fat side up.

4   If the meat is already browned, lower the heat to 170°C (325°F/Gas mark 3) and cook it until done.

5   If the meat is too large to brown before roasting, cook it at 230°C (450°F/Gas mark 8) for about 20 minutes, then lower the heat to 170°C (325°F/Gas mark 3) and cook it until done.

6   Test to see if it is ready with an instant-read kitchen thermometer. Beef, lamb and veal are generally rare at about 55°C (130°F), medium-rare at about 63°C (145°F), and medium at 66°C (150°F). Pork and poultry should be completely cooked through – at least 71°C (160°F) for pork, 77°C (170°F) for poultry breast meat and 82°C (180°F) for poultry thigh meat.

7   Place foil over the meat and wait 10 to 20 minutes to carve it. (Waiting helps to ensure that juices settle back into the meat, rather than spilling all over the cutting board.)

### ✱ Tips

If you don't have a meat thermometer, refer to a meat chart in an all-purpose cookbook to determine cooking time by weight.

In general, don't cover a roast; you don't want it to steam in its own juices. If, however, you're cooking a large roast or turkey and it browns too quickly, cover only the browned parts with foil.

## Use a Meat Thermometer

The best way to tell if meat is done is to use a meat thermometer. These directions are for the type of thermometer you leave in during cooking.

### Steps

1   Push the thermometer into the thickest section of the meat you are cooking before you place the meat in the oven.

2   Make sure the thermometer is not touching bone but is embedded deeply in the meat itself.

3   Put the meat in the oven at the recommended temperature.

4   Leave the thermometer in the meat throughout the cooking process.

5   Check the thermometer close to when the recommended cooking time for the cut of meat you are preparing is almost finished. The reading on the thermometer – check the levels for the kind of meat you are cooking – will indicate when the meat is cooked throughout.

### ✳ Tips

Meat thermometers come in a variety of styles, including instant-read, dial types, probes and stand-up types. Some probe thermometers allow you to connect the thermometer to a worktop unit that gives you the temperature reading without having to open the oven.

Instant-read thermometers are not left in the meat while it cooks. They register temperatures within a few seconds of insertion.

## Make Beef Stock

Beef stock, or beef broth, is widely available in cubes or ready-made. But you'll feel like a real pro making your own – and it does taste better. Makes about 2 l (3 1/2 pt).

### Steps

1   Preheat the oven to 230°C (450°F/Gas mark 8).

2   Put the soup bones in a large, shallow roasting tin.

3   Bake the bones for about 30 minutes, or until they're well browned, turning at the 15-minute point.

4   Put the soup bones in a large pot. Pour 120 ml (1/4 pt) water into the roasting tin and stir with a wooden spoon to scrape up and dissolve any crusty browned bits. Add the water mixture to the pot.

5   Add carrots, onions, celery, parsley, peppercorns, basil, bay leaves, garlic and salt to the pot.

6   Add 3 l (5 pt) water to the pot and bring to the boil. Reduce the heat, cover and simmer for 3 1/2 hours. Remove the soup bones.

7   Line a colander with two layers of muslin. Set it over a heatproof bowl and pour the broth into the colander to strain.

8   Discard the vegetables and seasoning.

9   Chill the broth, then lift off the solidified fat.

10  Store the broth in a covered container in the refrigerator for up to three days, or freeze for up to three months.

### Ingredients

- 1.8 kg (4 lb) meaty soup bones (short ribs or beef-shank crosscuts)
- 3 l (5 pt) water
- 3 carrots, chopped
- 2 medium onions, chopped
- 2 celery stalks with leaves, chopped
- 8 sprigs fresh parsley
- 10 black peppercorns
- 1 tbsp dried, crushed basil
- 4 bay leaves
- 2 halved garlic cloves
- 1 1/2 tsp salt

## 395 | Make Chicken Stock

Homemade stock is the best! It's so easy, and it also fills your kitchen with great aromas. Makes about 2 l (3½ pt).

### ◎ Steps

1   Warm the vegetable oil in a stock pot or large saucepan over a high heat.

2   Brown the vegetables for a few minutes, until they are golden in places.

3   Add the wine, water, chicken, salt, peppercorns, bay leaves, parsley and dill and bring to a simmer. Skim any foam from the surface.

4   Reduce the heat to low, cover partially and simmer for 2 hours.

5   Remove the chicken.

6   Strain the stock into a bowl, reserve the meat for later use and discard the remaining solids. Taste the stock. If it seems too bland, bring it to the boil and reduce it (let it boil and evaporate) until it tastes rich enough.

7   Chill the broth, then lift off the fat.

8   Store the broth in a covered container in the fridge for up to three days or freeze for up to three months.

### Ingredients

☐ 1 tbsp vegetable oil

☐ 2 large yellow onions, chopped

☐ 3 celery stalks with leaves, coarsely chopped

☐ 3 carrots, coarsely chopped

☐ 250 ml (9 fl oz) dry white wine

☐ about 2.5 l (4½ pt) water

☐ 1 (1.5–1.8 kg/3½–4 lb) chicken, in quarters to fit stock pot

☐ 1½ tsp salt

☐ 6 peppercorns

☐ 2 bay leaves

☐ 10 sprigs fresh parsley

☐ 5 sprigs fresh dill

## 396 | Make Vegetable Stock

A savoury vegetable stock is a staple of vegetarian cooking. It doesn't get better than this. Makes 3½–4 l (6–7 pt).

### ◎ Steps

1   Preheat the oven to 230°C (450°F/Gas mark 8).

2   In a roasting tray, roast the carrots, leeks, celery, white and red onions and garlic, uncovered, for 1 hour (cut vegetables to fit in the tray).

3   Transfer the vegetables to a large stock pot.

4   Add the thyme, bay leaf, peppercorns and water. Turn the heat to high.

5   Bring to the boil, reduce heat and simmer, covered, for 1 hour.

6   Remove from the heat. Strain through a fine-mesh sieve.

7   Chill the stock. Store in a covered container in the fridge for up to three days or freeze for up to three months.

### Ingredients

☐ 5 carrots

☐ 3 leeks

☐ 3 celery stalks

☐ 2 white onions

☐ 1 red onion

☐ 1 head garlic

☐ 2 thyme sprigs

☐ 1 bay leaf

☐ 5 peppercorns

☐ 4 l (7 pt) water

## Make and Use a Roux 397

A roux is a cooked mixture of flour and a cooking fat, such as vegetable oil, that is used to thicken sauces and gravies.

### ⊙ Steps

1 Pour about 4 tbsp of oil into a small, sturdy pan and place the pan over a medium-low heat.

2 When the oil is warm but not too hot, start stirring in flour with a wooden spoon until the mixture is thick – about the texture of wet concrete or plaster of Paris. Add more oil or flour until the consistency is right. Roux is usually equal parts by weight of flour and fat, but most chefs make it by simply adding flour to hot oil and looking for the proper thick texture.

3 Stir continuously with the wooden spoon over the heat so the roux cooks. The flour will gradually begin to brown. The roux can be used when the flour is light golden in colour. The darker you cook the roux, the more flavour it will add to the sauce. Don't cook it past a mahogany colour, though.

4 Transfer the roux to another container to cool.

5 Store the roux in the fridge for a week, or freeze in tablespoon-size waters for later use.

6 To thicken a sauce with roux, let it cool so it won't splatter, and whisk it into your boiling sauce base, such as broth or pan drippings. One tbsp of roux will thicken 300–425 ml (½–¾ pt) of liquid.

7 Lower the heat to a simmer and continue to whisk until all the roux has been absorbed.

8 Simmer the sauce for at least 20 minutes until it has thickened and the texture is smooth.

### ✳ Tips

Any cooking fat can be used to make a roux, including bacon fat or chicken fat.

Butter should be used only for very light-coloured roux. The milk solids in the butter will burn easily if it's cooked too long.

For best results, reserve some roux and some liquid when making your sauce so you can adjust the thickness later.

Roux-thickened sauces will thicken further as they cool.

### Ingredients

☐ about 4 tbsp vegetable oil

☐ about 4 tbsp plain flour

## Thicken a Sauce 398

There are hundreds of ways to thicken sauces, but only a handful are commonly used, and here are four of them. In each case, you'll need to start with some sort of base liquid.

### ⊙ Steps

1 Thicken most broths for gravies with roux, a cooked mixture of flour and a cooking fat such as vegetable oil (see 397 "Make and Use a Roux"). Roux needs to be cooked first, but gravies made with it are virtually lump-free. Many cream soups are also thickened this way.

2 Use cornflour to thicken fruit and vegetable juices. Dissolve 1 tbsp of cornflour in 2 tbsp of ice-cold water, then whisk the mix into 300 ml (½ pt) of boiling liquid. Simmer the sauce for at least 15 minutes to allow the starch to work. Cornflour is also commonly used to thicken stir-fries and many other Oriental dishes.

3 Use a cooked-vegetable purée to make a rustic sauce. For example, sautéed onions braised with a pot roast can be strained out, puréed

### ✳ Tips

Most sauces benefit from some simmering before you thicken them. This allows them to reduce, which means that excess moisture will evaporate and what's left will be more concentrated.

Reducing sauces can be tricky, because the amount of salt and other seasonings will also concentrate, so make sure to underseason everything and correct it only at the end.

and whisked back into the liquid to create a flavourful sauce with no added fat.

4 Use butter to thicken powerfully flavoured liquids such as wine and concentrated pan juices. Butter softens the flavours and smooths the texture. Whisk in partially softened cubes of butter over very low heat, tasting as you go, and serve these sauces in tiny amounts. Don't heat them, or they'll separate.

### Ingredients

- ❑ vegetable oil
- ❑ plain flour
- ❑ cornflour
- ❑ butter

---

## 399 | Make Hollandaise Sauce

Essential to many dishes, including eggs Benedict, hollandaise sauce is about as rich and luxurious as a sauce gets. It's excellent with fish. Makes about 600 ml (1 pt).

### ◉ Steps

1 Place the white wine, white wine vinegar, shallots and peppercorns in a saucepan and bring to a simmer.

2 Simmer until the liquid has reduced by three-quarters, and then strain the liquid into another container. Discard the seasonings.

3 Bring a little water to a simmer in the bottom of a saucepan.

4 Melt the butter completely in another small saucepan over low heat.

5 Skim off and discard the white foam that rises to the top. Ladle off and reserve the clear yellow liquid in the middle (this is clarified butter) and discard the milky liquid at the bottom.

6 Place the egg yolks in a medium metal bowl and whisk them together.

7 While whisking the egg yolks continuously, place the bowl over but not touching the simmering water in your saucepan for about 20 or 30 seconds, and then remove it and whisk for a few more seconds. Repeat.

8 Heat the yolks slowly so that they don't form scrambled curds. If they scramble, you'll need to start again.

9 Keep whisking until the yolks thicken. Look for the ribbon stage, when they're firm enough that when you lift the whisk out of the yolks and drizzle some back onto the surface, it forms a ribbon-like pattern that lasts for a few moments before sinking back into the yolks.

10 Slowly drizzle some of the melted clarified butter over the beaten yolks, whisking constantly. When a ladle or two of butter has been blended in, begin alternating between the melted butter and the vinegar mixture.

11 Notice when the mixture has thickened and begins resembling a sauce, then season with salt and begin tasting. If it's too tart, whisk in more melted butter – if it's not tart enough, squeeze in some lemon juice.

12 Keep the sauce in a warm place until you're ready to use it. It will thicken as it sits.

### ✳ Tips

An overly thick sauce can be thinned by whisking in a little hot water. The same remedy will help a sauce that begins to separate.

This sauce can't be reheated and will separate if you try to do so.

### Ingredients

- ❑ 300 ml (½ pt) white wine
- ❑ 300 ml (½ pt) white wine vinegar
- ❑ 2 shallots, chopped
- ❑ 1 tsp black peppercorns
- ❑ 450 g (1 lb) unsalted butter
- ❑ 3 egg yolks
- ❑ juice of 1 lemon
- ❑ salt

## Make Turkey Gravy | 400

This recipe assumes that you have just roasted a turkey and are set to make gravy from its dripping. Makes 1.2 l (2 pt).

### ⊙ Steps

1   Set the turkey aside after it has finished cooking. Pour all the dripping from the turkey's roasting tin into a glass measuring jug that can accommodate 1.2 l (2 pt) of liquid. Leave any browned bits on the bottom of the pan. (These are actually quite tasty and help give the gravy its flavour.)

2   Let the dripping stand until the fat rises to the top of the measuring jug. Spoon off the fat and reserve.

3   Add stock so that there are 1.2 l (2 pt) of liquid in the measuring jug.

4   Set the roasting tin over a medium-low heat. (You may need to use two rings at once.)

5   Spoon out 6 tbsp of the reserved fat and put it back in the roasting tin. Discard the remaining fat.

6   Sprinkle the flour over the fat and whisk. Whisk the flour and fat for 1 to 2 minutes until the flour turns golden brown.

7   Pour the dripping and stock mixture into the tin and, with a wooden spoon, scrape off the encrusted bits on the bottom of the tin.

8   Simmer the mixture for 2 to 3 minutes, whisking every so often.

9   Adjust the thickness of the gravy. If it is too thin, simmer it, whisking often until the gravy is as thick as you want it. If it is too thick, whisk in a little more stock.

10  Season the gravy with salt and pepper to taste.

11  Strain the gravy if you want to get rid of any remaining bits you loosened earlier. Pour the gravy into a gravy boat and serve.

### ✳ Tip

You can substitute ready-made chicken stock for the turkey or chicken stock.

### Ingredients

☐ turkey drippings

☐ 6 tbsp plain flour

☐ turkey or chicken stock

## Store Leftovers | 401

Handling your leftover lunch or dinner safely helps prevent food poisoning.

### ⊙ Steps

1   Wash your hands well with soap and warm water before and after handling leftovers, each time.

2   Refrigerate leftovers within 2 hours of the time they were prepared.

3   Cool food in the fridge instead of on the worktop. Small portions of leftovers cool down faster. Stir or turn larger quantities frequently so they cool evenly and completely. Don't put piping-hot foods in the fridge, though, for they can raise the temperature of chilled foods inside.

4   If you have large amounts of leftovers, divide them among several clean, shallow storage containers.

### ✳ Tips

Use a fridge thermometer to make sure your fridge stays between 2 and 5°C (35 and 40°F).

Bacteria grows most easily between 5 and 60°C (40 and 140°F), so keep hot food hot and cold food cold.

5   Make sure that storage-container lids seal tightly, or cover them with aluminium foil or clingfilm.

6   Place storage containers at least 5 cm (2 in) apart in the fridge – this allows cold air to circulate.

7   Use leftovers containing meat within three days; use other foods within five days.

## 402 | Make a Basic Vinaigrette

A vinaigrette is a basic sauce, usually used as a salad dressing, that can be made from a few simple ingredients in about 3 minutes. Makes about 300 ml (1/2 pt).

### ⊙ Steps

1   Whisk the mustard and vinegar together in a medium bowl.

2   Season lightly with salt and pepper.

3   Continue whisking the mustard/vinegar mixture and drizzle in the oil in a thin, steady stream.

4   Start tasting the mixture when about half of the oil has been incorporated. You may need to add some more salt and pepper. The basic ratio for vinaigrette is one part vinegar to three or four parts oil. Use whatever ratio tastes right to you, though; some people like significantly more vinegar, some less.

5   Keep whisking in the oil until the vinaigrette tastes smooth and slightly tart. If it's too sour, keep whisking in oil.

### ✳ Tips

You can substitute any acidic liquid for the balsamic vinegar, such as lemon or other citrus juice, other vinegars, or champagne.

Add fresh herbs, such as basil, parsley, thyme or marjoram.

### Ingredients

❏ 1 tbsp Dijon mustard

❏ 4 tbsp balsamic vinegar

❏ salt and pepper

❏ 200–300 ml (1/3–1/2 pt) olive oil

## 403 | Fry Chicken

Here is a simple but classic method for making fried chicken. This recipe uses a flour coating rather than batter. Makes four servings.

### ⊙ Steps

1   Put flour, salt, pepper, paprika and cayenne pepper in a plastic bag. Shake to mix.

2   Add chicken pieces, with or without bones, to the bag. (Smaller pieces cook more quickly, so consider cutting each breast half in two.) Shake to coat the chicken with the seasoned flour.

3   Heat 2 cm (3/4 in) oil in a heavy frying pan (preferably cast-iron) over a medium-high heat, until it reaches 180°C (350°F). Use a 5 cm (2 in ) deep pan if possible to reduce spatters.

4   When the oil is hot, shake any excess flour off the chicken and add the pieces to the pan a few at a time. Don't allow the pieces to touch in the pan. Fry the chicken in batches if your pan won't hold them all with space to spare.

### ✳ Tip

Frying chicken is a messy business. Spread newspapers on the floor in front of the cooker to keep the floor clean. Consider moving anything on the hob out of the way so it won't acquire a coating of grease.

### ⚠ Warning

Be very careful when working with hot oil. It can splatter and cause bad burns. Add chicken carefully to the pan, handling it with long metal tongs if possible.

5   Cook the chicken pieces for about 10 minutes per side. Regulate the heat as the chicken cooks, keeping the oil temperature below 190°C (375°F) – use a deep-frying thermometer to check the temperature.

6   Check the chicken to see if it is done. The meat should no longer be pink, and the juices should run clear when the meat is pierced.

7   Drain the chicken on paper towels.

**Ingredients**

- ☐ 125 g (4 oz) plain flour
- ☐ 1 tbsp salt
- ☐ 1 tsp pepper
- ☐ ½ tsp paprika
- ☐ ½ tsp cayenne pepper
- ☐ 1 1.4–1.8 kg (3–4 lb) chicken, cut into at least six pieces
- ☐ 1 l (1¾ pt) cooking oil

---

# Bake Chicken    404

Chicken can be baked whole or in pieces. Leave the skin on during cooking, even if you discard it later, to protect the meat from drying out. Makes four to six servings.

## ◉ Steps

1   Preheat the oven to 180°C (350°F/Gas mark 4).

2   Season the chicken with salt and pepper.

3   Coat the chicken with a marinade, glaze or breadcrumbs if desired.

4   Place a whole chicken in a roasting tin or large ovenproof dish, or place pieces skin up on a lightly greased baking tray.

5   Cook a whole chicken for 1 to 1½ hours, uncovered. Cook pieces for 35 to 40 minutes.

6   Use a meat thermometer to check the chicken during cooking. When the internal temperature reaches 77°C (170°F) for breast meat, 83°C (180°F) for thighs (measured in the thickest part not touching the bone), the chicken is done.

7   Test without a thermometer by cutting into the thickest part of the thigh. If the meat is no longer pink and the juices run clear, the chicken is done.

**✽ Tips**

Try rubbing the raw chicken with different dry seasonings.

Squeeze a lemon over the chicken (and inside the cavity of a whole chicken) before you cook it.

To avoid contamination, be sure to carefully clean everything the raw chicken touched.

**Ingredients**

- ☐ 1 1.1–2.25 kg (2½–5 lb) chicken
- ☐ salt and pepper
- ☐ marinade, glaze or breadcrumbs (optional)

---

# Roast a Chicken    405

Roasting a chicken is far easier than the browned and succulent result would make it seem. Your guests don't need to know. Makes four to six servings.

## ◉ Steps

1   Preheat the oven to 200°C (400°F/Gas mark 6).

2   Remove the chicken from its plastic bag, if it is in one.

**✽ Tips**

Try rubbing the bird with 1 tbsp Dijon mustard mixed with 1 tbsp olive oil. Put fresh herbs in the cavity of the bird, or squeeze a lemon inside it and leave the lemon halves inside.

3  Remove the bag of giblets from the cavity of the bird.

4  Remove any large deposits of fat from the cavity.

5  Trim any loose skin with a sharp knife.

6  Remove the tail, if you want, or leave it on. Rinse the chicken inside and out with cold water. Pat dry with a paper towel.

7  Place a roasting rack in a baking tray with sides at least 2.5 cm (1 in) high.

8  Place the bird on the rack with its breast side up.

9  Grind fresh pepper onto the bird, and sprinkle with a little salt. Salt and pepper the cavity as well. Rub the bird all over with olive oil and stuff it with fresh herbs and a quartered lemon if desired.

10  Place the baking tray on a shelf in the oven's lower-middle part.

11  Roast for 45 to 70 minutes or until the juices run clear when a sharp knife is inserted between the body and the thigh, or until a meat thermometer registers 77°C (170°F) for breast meat, 83°C (180°F) for thighs.

12  Remove the chicken from the oven, cover it loosely with foil and let it rest for 10 minutes before carving.

If the chicken seems to be browning too much, cover it loosely with foil.

Make sure your kitchen is well ventilated. In small spaces, the roasting process has been known to set off smoke alarms.

### Ingredients

☐ 1 1.1–2.25 kg (2½–5 lb) chicken

☐ black pepper

☐ salt

☐ olive oil

☐ fresh herbs (optional)

☐ lemon (optional)

☐ Dijon mustard (optional)

---

## 406 | Roast a Turkey

The turkey in this recipe is not stuffed, so you might want to prepare a stuffing on the side. Makes six servings. For a turkey this size, allow 0.34 to 0.45 kg (¾ to 1 lb) per serving.

### ⊙ Steps

1  Preheat the oven to 170°C (325°F/Gas mark 3).

2  Remove the turkey from its wrapping and remove the neck and giblets from inside the cavity. Set them aside to make gravy later.

3  Rinse the turkey inside and out with cold water. Dry with paper towels.

4  Put the oven shelf on the lowest level.

5  Place the turkey on a roasting rack, breast side up, in a roasting tin.

6  Rub the outside of the turkey with olive oil.

7  Salt and pepper the turkey's body and cavity.

8  Roast the turkey for about 3 hours for a 5.5–6.4 kg (12–14 lb) bird, or until a meat thermometer inserted in the thickest part of the thigh registers 80–83°C (175–180°F).

### ✳ Tips

A turkey should be roasted for 20 to 25 minutes per kilo (10 to 12 minutes per pound) if it is not stuffed and 25 to 30 minutes per kilo (12 to 15 minutes per pound) if it is stuffed.

In general, you shouldn't cover a roasting turkey; you want the skin to get a deep brown all over, and you don't want it to steam. However, you can loosely cover parts that are browning too quickly with aluminium foil.

### Ingredients

☐ 1 5.5–6.4 kg (12–14 lb) turkey

☐ olive oil

☐ salt and pepper

## Carve a Turkey      **407**

After hours of preparation and anticipation, be sure to carve the turkey in a way that preserves its flavour and texture.

### ⦿ Steps

1   Choose a sharp, thin-bladed knife. Running your knife along the bottom of the turkey, find the places where the thighbones meet the body.

2   Slip your knife into the joint to separate thigh from body on each side.

3   Separate the drumstick from the thigh using the same technique (cut through the joint, not the bone, wiggling the drumstick to locate the joint).

4   Running your knife along the bone, separate the meat from the thigh and drumstick – try to get as much as possible in one piece.

5   Cut thigh and leg meat into thin slices.

6   Use your knife to find where the wings and body connect.

7   Slip your knife into the joint to separate wings from body on each side.

8   Carve thin slices off one side of the breast, cutting parallel to the breast.

9   Repeat with the other side of the breast.

### ✳ Tips

If you are carving soon after roasting, cover the turkey with foil and let it stand for 15 minutes first.

Cut dark meat before light meat, as it will stay moist longer.

## Make Toad-in-the-Hole      **408**

This traditional dish is easy to prepare and is the ultimate in comfort food. Makes enough for four people.

### ⦿ Steps

1   Heat the oven to 220°C (425°F/Gas mark 7).

2   Pour the vegetable oil into a small roasting tin and put in the sausages, rolling them around to coat them in oil. Place them in the oven until they are lightly brown all over.

3   Sift the flour and salt into a medium mixing bowl and make a hollow in the centre.

4   Break the egg into the hollow and add half of the milk and water mix.

5   Mix together into a smooth paste, making sure that all the flour is incorporated from around the edges of the bowl.

6   Add the rest of the milk and water and beat the mixture until it forms a smooth batter.

7   Pour the batter into the roasting tin on top of the sausages.

8   Bake in the oven for about 40 minutes.

### Ingredients

- ❏ 450 g (1 lb) sausages
- ❏ 2 tbsp vegetable oil
- ❏ 125 g (4 oz) plain flour
- ❏ 1/4 tsp salt
- ❏ 1 egg
- ❏ 300 ml (1/2 pt) mixed milk and water

## 409 | Grill Hamburgers and Hot Dogs

**Grilled hot dogs and hamburgers are a hit with kids of all ages.**

### ⊙ Steps

1  Season the minced beef as desired by adding salt, chopped onions, dry onion-soup mix, Worcestershire sauce; salt and pepper.

2  Form the mince into patties using hands or a mould: grab a tennis ball-size piece of beef and flatten it into a patty. Be sure the patty is the same thickness on the edges as it is in the middle. Each patty should be about 2 cm (¾ in) thick.

3  Stack the beef patties on a plate, separating them with pieces of greaseproof paper. Refrigerate the patties until it is time to cook them.

4  Prepare a fire on a barbecue or turn a grill to high.

5  Place hamburgers and hot dogs on the grill.

6  Hot dogs should be turned often until slightly blistered on all sides, 5 to 6 minutes.

7  Cook hamburgers on one side until brown (approximately 10 minutes).

8  Using a spatula, flip hamburgers over and cook the other side.

9  When hamburger juices are no longer pink, use a small knife to cut into one hamburger and check if it is done. If one is done, the rest will be too. If making cheeseburgers, let cheese melt on top of the burgers for about 1 minute before removing the burgers from the grill.

10 Place grilled hamburgers and hot dogs on a clean plate.

11 Serve as desired – plain or on buns – with such accompaniments as cheese, lettuce, tomatoes and onions.

### Ingredients

☐ minced beef (about 175 g/6 oz per serving)

☐ salt

☐ chopped onions

☐ dry onion-soup mix

☐ Worcestershire sauce

☐ salt and pepper

☐ hot dogs

☐ buns

☐ mustard and ketchup

☐ cheese, lettuce, tomatoes and onions

## 410 | Grill Vegetables

**Grilled vegetables can be an easy accompaniment to other grilled foods or the centrepiece of a vegetarian meal.**

### ⊙ Steps

1  Choose vegetables that take well to grilling, such as peppers, aubergines, tomatoes, corn on the cob, mushrooms and courgettes.

2  Clean and trim the vegetables. Cut large ones into smaller pieces.

3  Boost flavour by marinating vegetables for 15 minutes before grilling (see Tips). Or just brush them lightly with oil so they don't stick to the grill – unless you will use a foil pouch.

4  Prepare a medium-hot fire in a barbecue or turn a grill to medium.

5  Put the vegetables directly on the grill, on skewers or inside a foil pouch. Start vegetables first that take the longest to cook. The time for cooking vegetables varies greatly. Tomatoes may take 3 minutes per side, while whole peppers can take up to 20 minutes in total.

### ✳ Tips

Marinades can be made the day before and stored, covered, in the refrigerator.

Try this basic marinade: Combine 2 parts olive oil and 1 part lemon juice with 1 peeled and crushed garlic clove.

### Ingredients

☐ vegetables

☐ marinade, oil or butter

6   Turn the vegetables often, brushing on more marinade as needed.

7   Remove the vegetables when they can be easily pierced with a fork.

---

# Grill Fish `411`

Grilling on your barbecue is a superb way to cook fish. Most fish take well to quick cooking over direct heat. Use fish fillets no more than a couple of centimetres thick.

## ⊙ Steps

1   Get a hot fire going on your barbecue or turn on an automatic barbecue to its highest heat setting. Let it heat up for at least 20 minutes or so.

2   Season the fish well with salt and pepper or your desired dry seasoning.

3   Make sure that you have all your tools next to the grill, along with a clean plate or dish to hold the cooked fish.

4   Oil the grill grate lightly, then repeat. This coat of oil will prevent the fish from sticking and will promote the formation of grill marks.

5   Lay the fish in the centre of the grill directly above the heat source. It should sizzle audibly. Avoid cooler sections and indirect heat.

6   Wait about 2 minutes, then slide the prongs of a fork between the bars of the grill grate and under the fish. Gently lift up a section of fish to check the cooking and look for grill marks.

7   When grill marks have formed, use the fork to lift up a corner of the fillet, and slide a spatula under the fish.

8   Turn the fish over and cook the other side.

9   Use the fork to flake open a section of one fillet to check if it is done. If the interior is no longer translucent, the fish is cooked.

10  Remove the fillets as soon as they're done.

## ✳ Tips

Almost every species of commercially available fish can be grilled. Salmon and halibut grill especially well, whereas more delicate fish, such as smaller flatfish and trout, will require extra care.

High heat is important to sear the fish instantly and keep it firm. Lower temperatures and slower cooking will dry out the fish and make handling it more difficult.

The ideal size for a piece of grilled fish is the size of your spatula, for easy flipping.

## Ingredients

❑ 1 175–225 g (6–8 oz) fish fillet per serving

❑ salt and pepper

❑ vegetable oil

---

# Prepare and Cook Mussels `412`

Mussels are tasty, succulent and easy to prepare once you know how.

## ⊙ Steps

1   Place the mussels in a large colander and rinse them thoroughly under cold running water. Use a sharp knife to scrape off debris and remove their "beards". Continue until no sand runs out of the colander.

2   Dispose of any mussels that do not close when the shell is tapped.

3   Set a frying pan on a high heat and immediately add the mussels, cooking them for about 5 minutes or until the shells open. If there are any that remain closed, throw them away.

## ✳ Tip

Never buy mussels with cracked shells or shells that do not close when tapped. These mussels may be dead and so could cause food poisoning if eaten.

4   An alternative is to put the mussels in a pan of water or wine with herbs and onions and simmer for a few minutes until they open, again discarding any that do not open.

5   Serve them at once, with melted butter and lemons, adding garlic and herbs if you wish.

**Ingredients**

❑ melted butter

❑ fresh lemons

❑ fresh garlic and herbs (optional)

## 413 | Boil Lobster

Boiling is an easy way of preparing lobster. You can eat the lobster by itself – it's simple and elegant with some melted butter – or use the meat in recipes such as crêpes, salads or risotto.

### ⊙ Steps

1   Fill a large saucepan with enough water to cover the lobsters, and bring to the boil over a high heat.

2   Salt the water and add lemon juice.

3   Put live lobsters headfirst into the boiling water. If you choose to kill them quickly before boiling, do this now (see Tips).

4   Allow the water to boil again, and then turn the heat down to medium.

5   Cover the pot and cook 12 minutes for the first 450 g (1 lb) of a lobster's weight and an additional 5 minutes for each additional 450 g (1 lb). Like all shellfish, lobsters overcook almost instantly, so remove them from the water as soon as they're done.

6   Remove the lobsters from the water and drain them on paper towels.

7   To prepare the lobsters for the table, twist off each large claw, leaving the claw joints intact (there's a lot of meat in the joints). Crack the claw shell with a nutcracker or mallet.

8   Hold the body of a cooked lobster with a clean kitchen towel (the lobster should still be hot) and twist off the tail with your hands. Remove the tail meat by separating and removing the tail shell with your fingers.

**✱ Tips**

To kill the lobsters quickly just before boiling them, place the tip of a sharp knife on top of a lobster's head where the lines in the shell form a T. Push the knife down with a quick cutting motion.

At the fishmonger's, select the liveliest lobster. Make sure the tail curls under, the shell is not damaged and the claws are secured with bands.

**Ingredients**

❑ lobsters

❑ salt

❑ fresh lemon juice

## 414 | Eat Lobster

The shell is a small obstacle to that rich, tender lobster meat. Here's how to get at your dinner.

### ⊙ Steps

1   Allow the lobster to cool after cooking.

2   Remove the large claws from the body by twisting them off at the joints.

3   Crack the claws. A nutcracker works well for this.

4   Bend the body back from the tail – it will crack, and then you can remove the tail. Break off the small flippers on the tail.

**✱ Tip**

You can mash the liver, add a little stock or cream, and use it as a sauce.

5  Push the tail meat out of the tail. It should come out in one piece. Remove the black vein in the tail and discard it.

6  Dip the lobster meat in melted butter and enjoy. Repeat as you unshell more of the meat.

7  Find the liver (it's green) and eat or discard it.

8  Note that the coral-coloured roe in a female lobster is also edible.

9  Crack the body apart to find the meat in the four cavities where the small legs join the body.

10 Look for meat in the small walking legs, too, if you have a lobster weighing over 0.9 kg (2 lb). Push a skewer into the legs to get the meat out.

⚠ **Warning**

Pregnant women and breast-feeding mothers are advised not to eat the liver in lobster due to high dioxin levels. Others are advised to limit consumption to one meal per month.

## Boil Pasta                                                      415

Boil some pasta, make a quick sauce or open a jar, and you have the quintessential quick, easy meal.

### ⊙ Steps

1  Fill a large pot three-quarters full with cold water.

2  Place the pot on the stove and turn the ring to high.

3  When the water begins to boil, add 1 to 2 tsp salt, depending on how much pasta you're making.

4  Add the desired amount of pasta and stir.

5  Return the water to the boil.

6  Cook for as long as the packet instructs. Stir occasionally so the pasta doesn't stick to itself.

7  To test when the pasta is done, taste it at the earliest time indicated on the packet. It should be tender but still firm to the bite ("al dente", which means "to the tooth" in Italian). If you can still see a little uncooked core in the pasta, it needs another minute or so. But keep in mind that it will continue to cook a little after you remove it from the stove.

8  When the pasta is done, remove the pot from the ring immediately and carefully pour the contents into a colander in the sink.

9  Shake out any excess water over the sink.

10 If you want, use a couple of drops of olive oil to prevent the pasta from sticking; but if you're saucing the pasta, you really don't need to.

11 Serve immediately.

**Ingredients**

☐ salt

☐ pasta

☐ olive oil

## 416 Make 10-Minute Tomato Sauce

This recipe uses tinned whole tomatoes and tastes fresher than any bottled sauce. It can be used on its own or as the base for other sauces. Makes enough for a 450 g (1 lb) pasta.

### ⊙ Steps

1  Heat the oil in a saucepan and sauté the garlic for 30 seconds.

2  Open the tin of tomatoes and add it to the pan.

3  Bring the liquid to a fast simmer and cook for about 5 minutes.

4  Blend or chop the tomato. You can use a hand blender to coarsely purée the tomatoes or use a large spoon to mash them right in the pot; or transfer the mixture to a blender or food processor.

5  Season to taste with salt and pepper and continue mashing or puréeing until the sauce is evenly coarse.

6  Add the basil and serve.

### ❋ Tip

Don't worry too much about precise measurements. Season to taste.

### Ingredients

- ❑ 1 tbsp olive oil
- ❑ 2 tsp minced or chopped garlic
- ❑ 2 400 g (14 oz) tins whole tomatoes
- ❑ salt and pepper
- ❑ a handful of fresh chopped basil

## 417 Make Lasagne

Here is a recipe for lasagne at its simplest. Modify it to your own taste by adding any extra ingredients you like to the sauce. Makes six to eight servings.

### ⊙ Steps

1  Break or tear the basil leaves with your fingers. Set aside.

2  Warm the olive oil in a saucepan over a medium-low heat, and add the garlic. Allow the garlic to sizzle for 3 to 4 minutes without letting it get too brown. Remove the garlic.

3  Add the passata to the hot oil and stir. Add the basil.

4  Turn the heat to very low, cover the pan and allow the sauce to simmer for 30 minutes, stirring occasionally.

5  As the sauce simmers, fill a large pasta pot with water and a large pinch of salt. Bring to the boil.

6  Carefully place the lasagne in the boiling water and stir occasionally to ensure that the sheets do not stick together. Cook until al dente, or tender but still chewy.

7  Drain the lasagne but don't rinse the sheets.

8  Generously grease the bottom of a baking dish.

9  Cover the bottom of the dish with a layer of lasagne.

10  Spread the sauce over the lasagne with a spoon and top the layer with a little of each cheese.

11  Repeat until the dish is full, saving most of the cheese for the top.

### ❋ Tip

This recipe assumes that the lasagne pasta needs pre-cooking. Many packets of lasagne can simply be added dry to the dish and will cook in the oven, with no boiling required beforehand. Cooking time may be longer in the oven – check the packet

### Ingredients

- ❑ 1 large sprig of fresh basil
- ❑ 5–8 tbsp extra-virgin olive oil
- ❑ 1 garlic clove, cut in half
- ❑ 1 400 g (14 oz) jar of passata (or tomato sauce, see 416)
- ❑ salt
- ❑ 1 box dried lasagne
- ❑ 225 g (8 oz) grated Parmesan
- ❑ 225–350 g (8–12 oz) ricotta
- ❑ 225 g (8 oz) grated mozzarella

12  Top with remaining sauce and cheese.

13  Cover and bake at 180°C (350°F/Gas mark 4) for 20 minutes. (You may
    need to cover the lasagne for the first 10 minutes to melt the cheese,
    then uncover it for the last 10 minutes to brown it.)

14  Let the lasagne stand for 10 minutes before serving.

## Make Basic Cheese Enchiladas                                    418

**The zesty sauce in this recipe can be used for most types
of enchiladas. Makes four to six servings.**

### ⊙ Steps

#### Making the Sauce

1  Bring the chillies and water to the boil in a large saucepan. Remove from
   the heat and let cool.

2  Remove the chillies from the water. Save the water for puréeing.

3  Purée the chillies and garlic in a food processor. Add enough water to
   the food processor to give the puree a gravy-like consistency.

4  Heat 2 tbsp of vegetable oil in a saucepan over a medium-high heat and
   add the flour while constantly stirring. Add the chilli purée, garlic powder
   and salt.

5  Simmer for 15 minutes, stirring occasionally. If the sauce gets too thick,
   stir in a little more chilli water.

#### Making the Enchiladas

1  Preheat the oven to 180°C (350°F/Gas mark 4).

2  Heat the remaining lard or vegetable oil in a small sauté pan over a
   medium-high heat. Using tongs, dip a tortilla quickly in the oil and place
   it in a baking dish that will hold 12 rolled enchiladas in a single layer.

3  Sprinkle a little of the cheddar cheese in a line across the middle of the
   tortilla. Starting at an edge of the tortilla that is directly across from the
   line of cheese, roll the tortilla until it just folds over itself.

4  Place the rolled enchilada in the baking dish, flap side down. Repeat this
   process until all tortillas and cheese are used.

5  Pour enough chilli sauce over the tortillas to just moisten the entire surface. Bake for 20 minutes uncovered.

6  Remove the enchiladas from the oven and sprinkle with the parmesan.

7  If desired, garnish the enchiladas with shredded iceberg lettuce,
   chopped plum tomatoes and chopped onions.

### ✱ Tip

For a quicker version, canned red
enchilada sauce makes a good
substitute.

### Ingredients

❑ 12 stemmed and seeded
  chillies

❑ 1 l (2 pt) water

❑ 1 garlic clove, peeled

❑ 6 tbsp vegetable oil

❑ 2 tbsp flour

❑ ¾ tsp garlic powder

❑ ½ tsp salt

❑ 12 corn tortillas

❑ 450 g (1 lb) grated cheddar
  cheese

❑ 125 g (4 oz) Parmesan cheese

❑ shredded iceberg lettuce
  (optional)

❑ chopped plum tomatoes
  (optional)

❑ chopped onions (optional)

## 419 | Make a Curry

You don't need jars of curry sauce – it's simple to make your own curry and you can adjust the spiciness to your taste. This recipe is for a basic, creamy lamb korma. Serves two.

### ⊙ Steps

1   In a large saucepan, heat the butter and slowly fry the onion, garlic and ginger until they are tender and translucent.

2   Crush the coriander, cardamom pods and peppercorns in a pestle and mortar.

3   Add them to the saucepan and stir in well.

4   Turn up the ring and add the pieces of lamb to the pan gradually, stirring the mixture all the time. Repeat until all the lamb is evenly coated in the spice mixture.

5   Add the turmeric, lemon juice and ground almonds, and stir again to mix thoroughly.

6   Cover and simmer gently until the lamb is tender and cooked through. This may take up to 1 hour.

7   When you are almost ready to serve the dish, stir in the double cream gradually, allowing it to heat through.

8   Sprinkle the lemon zest on as a garnish (or chives if you wish) and serve with rice or naan bread.

### Ingredients

- ❑ 50 g (2 oz) butter
- ❑ onion, chopped
- ❑ minced garlic
- ❑ finely chopped root ginger
- ❑ 1 tsp coriander seeds
- ❑ 3 cardamom pods
- ❑ ½ tsp black peppercorns
- ❑ 450 g (1 lb) lamb, diced
- ❑ 1 tsp turmeric
- ❑ lemon zest and juice
- ❑ 25 g (1 oz) ground almonds
- ❑ 100 ml (3½ fl oz) double cream
- ❑ chives (optional)

## 420 | Make Fried Rice

Fried rice is an easy and filling dish – you just have to remember to have cooked rice on hand. Makes two or three servings.

### ⊙ Steps

1   Heat a wok or large pan over a high heat.

2   Add a little oil and wait a few moments for it to heat up. You only need a tablespoon or so to keep the rice from sticking.

3   Break the eggs into the wok and stir quickly to scramble.

4   When the egg is well set, remove it and chop it into bite-sized pieces.

5   Wipe out the wok and add a little more oil. Wait for it to heat.

6   If the rice is clumpy, break it up with your hands to separate the grains.

7   Add the cold rice to the wok. Move the rice quickly around the hot pan by sliding your spoon or spatula under the rice and turning it over. (This is the basic stir-frying technique.)

8   After a minute or so, add the carrot and stir-fry it with the rice.

9   After 3 minutes, add the peas and stir-fry.

10  After 2 minutes, add the scallions, egg and meat, if using.

### ⚠ Warning

Don't use hot rice; you'll have a sloppy mess. Cooling the rice makes the grains separate.

### Ingredients

- ❑ oil
- ❑ 2 eggs
- ❑ 175 g (6 oz) cooked rice, cold
- ❑ 1 carrot, finely diced
- ❑ 50 g (2 oz) frozen peas
- ❑ 4 minced scallions
- ❑ 50 g (2 oz) leftover meat, chopped (optional)
- ❑ salt or soy sauce

11 Once the ingredients are well mixed, season the rice with salt or soy sauce. Cook another minute or until everything is heated through.

12 Remove from heat and serve.

## Make Chow Mein 421

This recipe calls for chicken, but you can substitute beef, pork, seafood or vegetables. Makes four to six servings.

### ⊙ Steps

1 Look for fresh Chinese egg noodles in the supermarket refrigerator section. These are best to use. Pick them apart (they will be stuck together in a clump) before you cook them.

2 Toast sesame seeds by tossing them in a dry, hot pan for a minute or until golden.

3 Cook the noodles according to packet directions and drain. Toss with a small amount of the peanut oil to prevent sticking.

4 Heat a wok or pan over medium-high heat. Add the remaining oil and garlic and cook, stirring, until the garlic is golden but not brown.

5 Add the chicken and stir continuously until it is no longer pink. Add the bamboo shoots, mushrooms and celery, and cook for 3 minutes.

6 Add 600 ml (1 pt) of the broth to the pan and bring to the boil. Cover, reduce the heat to medium and cook for 7 minutes.

7 Add the onion and cook for another 2 minutes. Add the bean sprouts and stir until most of the liquid has evaporated.

8 Mix the cornflour with the remaining broth and soy sauce; stir into the pan. Stir until the sauce thickens, then add the noodles.

9 Toss to heat through and taste. Add more soy sauce if preferred.

10 Serve in a large bowl, garnished with the sesame seeds and coriander.

### Ingredients

- ❏ 450 g (1 lb) Chinese egg noodles
- ❏ 2 tbsp white sesame seeds
- ❏ 3 tbsp peanut oil
- ❏ 3 garlic cloves, minced
- ❏ 675 g (1½ lbs) chicken breast or thigh, cut into thin slices
- ❏ 2 small cans bamboo shoots, drained
- ❏ 350 g (12 oz) button mushrooms, thinly sliced
- ❏ 2 celery stalks, rinsed and sliced thinly crosswise
- ❏ 850 ml (1½ pt) chicken broth
- ❏ 3 small onions, peeled and sliced thinly
- ❏ 350 g (12 oz) bean sprouts
- ❏ 3 tbsp each cornflour and soy sauce
- ❏ 2 tbsp freshly chopped coriander

## Use Chopsticks 422

Practice makes perfect when it comes to using chopsticks. The key is that the bottom chopstick remains still while the upper chopstick moves to grasp the food.

### ⊙ Steps

1 Position one chopstick so that it lies at the base of your thumb (on the joint) and at the lower joint of the middle finger. This chopstick shouldn't touch your forefinger.

2 Place the other chopstick between your thumb and forefinger so you can move it up and down.

### ✱ Tip

If you have trouble manoeuvring the chopsticks, try supporting the second chopstick against your ring finger as well.

3   Keeping the tips of the chopsticks parallel and the first chopstick stationary, practise moving the second chopstick toward the first.

4   Use this technique to position the chopsticks around a piece of food.

5   Hold the food firmly as you lift it towards your mouth.

⚠ **Warning**

Though you may be tempted to spear food with your chopsticks as an act of desperation, it is considered impolite.

## 423 | Make Muesli

Make a large batch of this muesli to last several days. It makes a quick and healthy breakfast, and you can experiment with quantities and different sorts of dried fruits and nuts until you get it just how you like it.

### ⊙ Steps

1   Roughly chop the dried apricots.

2   Cut the hazelnuts in half and toast them lightly in the oven or in a frying pan (see 389 "Toast Nuts").

3   Place the oats, raisins or sultanas, apricots and almonds in a large bowl and stir them until they are evenly distributed.

4   Add the apple juice and mix in well.

5   Leave the mixture for about quarter of an hour so that the fruit, nuts and oats soak up the juice.

6   Serve with yoghurt and honey or fresh fruit such as banana, chopped apples and pears.

7   Pour the remaining muesli into an airtight container and store it in the refrigerator.

### Ingredients

❑ 125 g (4 oz) dried apricots

❑ 125 g (4 oz) hazelnuts

❑ 175 g (6 oz) oats

❑ 175 g (6 oz) sultanas or raisins

❑ 300 ml (1/2 pt) apple juice

❑ plain yoghurt

❑ honey

## 424 | Scramble Eggs

Scrambled eggs are easy, but to make your eggs creamy, you need to cook them slowly over low heat. Makes one serving.

### ⊙ Steps

1   Crack one to three eggs into a bowl.

2   Add a splash of milk.

3   Add a dash of salt and pepper.

4   Beat with a fork or whisk until well combined.

5   Heat a pan over a medium-low heat.

6   Melt the butter in the pan.

7   Pour the beaten eggs into the pan.

8   Let the eggs cook undisturbed until they begin to set, then push them gently from the bottom of the pan.

✳ **Tip**

Eggs cooked for a shorter period of time are "scrambled soft". If cooked longer, they are "scrambled hard". The "ideal" scrambled eggs are soft and creamy.

### Ingredients

❑ 1 to 3 large eggs

❑ milk

❑ salt and pepper

❑ 1½ tsp butter

9   Continue cooking until the eggs are the consistency you like.

10  Stir cheese or any other additions into the eggs 1 or 2 minutes before
    you're going to serve them.

---

## Make Porridge                                          425

A traditional Scottish dish, porridge makes a warming and
hearty start to the day and is popular with adults and children
alike.

### ⊙ Steps

1   Put the oats, water, milk and salt into a saucepan. Experiment until you
    find the proportion of milk to water that you like best. Purists use salt;
    some use sugar instead.

2   Bring to the boil over a medium heat.

3   Once it is boiling, turn it down and simmer it gently for about 10
    minutes, stirring so that it does not stick or become lumpy. The
    porridge will gradually thicken.

4   Once it has thickened add the cream and stir it in.

5   Remove the porridge from the heat.

6   Pour into bowls at once.

7   Use the topping of your choice: sugar, honey, treacle or even chocolate
    are good if you have a sweet tooth; fresh or stewed fruit makes a
    healthier breakfast.

### ✳ Tip

The size of cups does not matter
when measuring porridge; the
important thing is to have twice
as much fluid as oats.

### Ingredients

❏ 1 cup porridge oats

❏ 2 cups water or milk or water
    and milk mixed

❏ pinch of salt

❏ 1 tbsp cream

---

## Make Chocolate Chip Cookies                            426

We eat more chocolate chip cookies than any other type, and
for good reason. They're the most familiar and most satisfying.
Makes about 20 cookies.

### ⊙ Steps

1   Stir together the flour and salt. Do not sift.

2   Beat the butter until creamy, then add the sugars and vanilla and stir
    them in until combined.

3   Add the beaten egg, mixing well.

4   Stir in the flour mixture. Stop the instant it's all been incorporated.

5   Stir in the chocolate chips until they are distributed evenly.

6   Form the dough into a log, wrap it and chill for at least 30 minutes.
    Chilling the dough is an important step. It allows the flour to relax, the
    sugars to partially dissolve and the flavours to begin to come together.

### Ingredients

❏ 175 g (6 oz) self-raising flour

❏ ½ tsp salt

❏ 75 g (3 oz) softened unsalted
    butter

❏ 75 g (3 oz) brown sugar

❏ 75 g (3 oz) caster sugar

❏ 1 tbsp vanilla essence

❏ 1 egg

❏ 125 g (4 oz) chocolate chips

7   Heat the oven to 180°C (350°F/Gas mark 4) and grease baking sheets.

8   Cut the dough into thin rounds, place on baking sheets and bake for 10 minutes or until the edges begin to turn golden.

## 427 | Make Peanut Butter Cookies

These all-time favourites taste great and are easy to make. Try using "natural" peanut butter (the kind that separates – stir it together first) or crunchy. Makes about two dozen cookies.

### ⊙ Steps

1   Use a wooden spoon or electric mixer to beat the butter and peanut butter until combined, about 30 seconds.

2   Add the sugars and beat until combined.

3   Add the vanilla and the egg, and beat until combined.

4   Stir in the flour until it's incorporated. The dough will become thick and difficult to work at this point; you may want to chill it for an hour or so until it's easier to work with.

5   Heat the oven to 170°C (325°F/Gas mark 3).

6   Roll the dough into 2.5 cm (1 in) balls and place them well apart in rows on baking sheets.

7   Butter the prongs of a large fork and use it to press the cookies flat. Make a design of perpendicular lines with the fork. Re-butter the fork as necessary. You can also dip the buttered fork into granulated sugar before pressing; some of the sugar will then stick to the cookies.

8   Bake for 15 to 18 minutes or until the cookies start to brown around the edges.

9   Remove the cookies from the cookie sheet to cool.

### Ingredients

❑ 50 g (2 oz) unsalted butter

❑ 50 g (2 oz) peanut butter

❑ 50 g (2 oz) caster sugar

❑ 3 tbsp light brown soft sugar

❑ 1 tsp vanilla essence

❑ 1 egg

❑ 2 tbsp self-raising flour

## 428 | Make Chocolate Brownies

For pure decadence, try icing these brownies when cool with a chocolate fudge icing. Makes 24 small brownies.

### ⊙ Steps

1   Preheat the oven to 180°C (350°F/Gas mark 4).

2   Grease the baking tray. Set aside.

3   Melt the butter and chocolate in a bowl over a medium-size saucepan of boiling water over a low heat (take care not to burn the chocolate). Remove from the heat.

4   Stir in the sugar. Add the eggs and vanilla. Beat lightly with a wooden spoon until just combined.

5   Stir in the flour and nuts.

### Ingredients

❑ 65 g (2½ oz) unsalted butter

❑ 50 g (2 oz) plain chocolate

❑ 175 g (6 oz) caster sugar

❑ 1 tsp vanilla essence

❑ 2 eggs

❑ 65 g (2½ oz) self-raising flour

❑ 50 g (2 oz) chopped walnuts

6 Spread the mix in the baking tray. Bake for 30 minutes. Don't overbake.

7 Cool the brownies in the tray on a wire rack. Cut into bars.

## Make a Victoria Sponge 429

This is the classic sandwich cake, perfect for traditional teas and party cakes. It's quick to make and uses simple ingredients, so also makes a good standby.

### ⊙Steps

1 Bring out the butter or margarine so it is at room temperature.

2 Grease and line two 18 cm (7 in) sandwich tins.

3 Preheat the oven to 190°C (375°F/Gas mark 5).

4 Beat the butter or margarine and sugar together in a large mixing bowl until the mixture is light, pale and creamy. Use a wooden spoon or an electric mixer.

5 Add the eggs a little at a time and beat well so that they are fully incorporated. Again, use a wooden spoon or electric mixer.

6 Add the vanilla and beat again.

7 Add the flour in two batches, folding it into the mixture with a metal spoon. Use as few strokes as possible so the mixture stays light.

8 Pour the mixture into the prepared cake tins. Bake for about 20 minutes, until the sponges have risen and spring back when touched, and are turning golden.

10 Invert the tins to remove the cakes and cool them on a wire rack. Once cooled, sandwich them together with a layer of jam, choosing the most even half to go on the top

11 Top with your preferred icing (see 431 "Ice a Cake").

**Ingredients**

- ❏ 175 g (6 oz) butter or margarine
- ❏ 175 g (6 oz) caster sugar
- ❏ 3 eggs, beaten
- ❏ vanilla essence
- ❏ 175 g (6 oz) self-raising flour
- ❏ jam
- ❏ icing or caster sugar to top

## Make a Rich Fruit Cake 430

This is perfect for Christmas or for special occasions. The quantities are for a 20 cm (8 in) round or a 18 cm (7 in) square tin.

### ⊙Steps

1 A day before you intend to bake the cake, put the dried fruit, glacé cherries and mixed peel in a large bowl, add the brandy, mix well, cover it up and leave it to stand and absorb the brandy.

2 The next day, prepare the cake tin by greasing it and lining it with two thicknesses of greaseproof paper. Tie brown paper around the outside.

3 Preheat the oven to 140°C (275°F/Gas mark 1).

4 Put the butter and sugar in a large mixing bowl and whisk them together.

**Ingredients**

- ❏ 1 lb (450 g) currants
- ❏ 200 g (7 oz) raisins
- ❏ 200 g (7 oz) sultanas
- ❏ 50 g (2 oz) glacé cherries
- ❏ 50 g (2 oz) mixed peel ➤

www.ehow.com

5   Add the eggs to the butter and sugar, beating the whole time until they are fully incorporated.

6   Sift the flour, spices and salt into another bowl and then fold them into the sugar, butter and egg mixture using a metal spoon.

7   Finally, add the brandy-soaked fruits and peel, the flaked almonds and the lemon zest and fold them in so they are well mixed.

8   Spoon the mixture into the tin and gently smooth the top with the back of the spoon to eliminate air pockets. Make a slight hollow in the middle.

9   Bake for up to 4½ hours, covering the top with greaseproof paper after an hour. It is ready when a skewer inserted in the middle comes out clean.

10  Leave to cool in the tin, then take it out and place it on a wire rack.

❑ 2–3 tbsp brandy

❑ 225 g (8 oz) butter

❑ 225 g (8 oz) brown soft sugar

❑ 4 eggs, beaten

❑ 225 g (8 oz) plain flour

❑ ½ tsp mixed spice

❑ ½ tsp nutmeg

❑ ½ tsp salt

❑ 50 g (2 oz) flaked almonds

❑ zest of 1 lemon

## 431 | Ice a Cake

**Icing helps seal the moisture in a cake – not to mention adding extra flavour. Make sure the layers are cool and free of crumbs before you apply the icing.**

### ◎ Steps

1   Cool the cake halves or layers in trays on the wire rack for 5 minutes.

2   Cover another rack with a tea-towel; place the rack, towel side down, on top of the cake and invert as a unit. Remove the pan.

3   Place the original rack on the bottom of the cake; turn over both racks (as a unit) so the cake is right side up. Remove the top rack and towel.

4   Repeat with the other half. Allow the halves to cool completely.

5   Before icing the cake, brush loose crumbs from the sides and edges of the cooled halves. Support the cake firmly with one hand and brush crumbs with the other.

6   Place one half, rounded side down, on the cake plate and spread filling (such as jam or butter icing) to within 5 mm (¼ in) of the edge.

7   Place the second half, rounded side up, on top. Coat the side with a very thin layer of icing to seal in crumbs.

8   Swirl more icing on the side, forming a 5 mm (¼ in) ridge above the top of the cake.

9   Spread the remaining icing over the top, just meeting the built-up ridge around the side. Make swirls or leave the top smooth for decorations.

### ✱ Tips

If you don't let the cake cool, the icing will melt on it and run off.

If your cake is bumpy or has a hump in the middle of it, slice off the bumps to make the layer level. If the cake falls apart or part of it sticks to the baking tray, try sticking it together with the icing.

Scatter hundreds and thousands in spirals or strips or around the edge as a border.

Decorate with candles, sweets, coconut or chopped nuts.

Dip the spatula in hot water as you ice to give the icing a smooth look.

## Make Basic Shortcrust Pastry     432

The secret of tender, flaky pastry is not to overwork it. Makes enough for one pie in a 23 cm (9 in) tin.

### ◎ Steps

#### Making the Dough

1 Sift the flour and salt together into a bowl; cut in the chilled solid butter and lard with a fork or two knives then rub it with your hands until the mixture resembles breadcrumbs.

2 Add water a tablespoon at a time, sprinkling it evenly and stirring it in until the mixture comes into large lumps.

3 Gather the dough into two balls and chill for at least 20 minutes.

#### Rolling it Out

1 Flour a board lightly. Also flour the rolling pin.

2 Roll the dough into a 28–30 cm (11–12 in) circle, about 3 mm (1/8 in) thick, using fairly firm pressure. Roll from the middle of the dough out to the edges, not back and forth. Press the dough together to mend any cracks.

3 To transfer the dough to the baking tin, loosely roll it around the rolling pin, and then unroll it in the tin. You can also try folding the dough into quarters, and then unfolding it in the tin.

4 Trim the crust edges so that there's a 2.5 cm (1 in) overhang around the rim.

5 Unless your recipe calls for the pastry to be pre-baked, add the filling.

6 For a one-crust pie, make a decorative edge by pressing the prongs of a fork into the dough, or pinching it into scallops.

7 For two-crust pies, place the top crust on the filling, using either the rolling pin or folding method.

8 Trim the dough to a 2.5 cm (1 in) overhang.

9 Fold the top crust under the bottom crust and pinch the edges together, and then pinch as for a one-crust pie.

10 For a two-crust pie, score the top with a knife to let steam escape.

### ✻ Tips

Use just butter or margarine instead of the lard.

If your recipe calls for pre-baking the pastry case (or "baking blind"), cover the pastry in the tin with foil or greaseproof paper and add dried beans to cover the base.

Don't stretch the dough into the baking tin. It will shrink when baked.

Flakiness is enhanced by handling the dough as little as possible. Make every attempt not to re-roll the dough.

Brush beaten egg white over the pastry case before baking to yield a beautiful, glossy finish.

### Ingredients

❑ 225 g (8 oz) plain flour

❑ 1/4 tsp salt

❑ 50 g (2 oz) butter

❑ 50 g (2 oz) lard or white vegetable fat

❑ cold water

## Make Apple Pie     433

Use tart apples for your pies – Granny Smiths and bramleys are good choices. Makes one 20 cm (8 in) pie.

### ◎ Steps

1 Make pastry (see 432 "Make Basic Shortcrust Pastry" for instructions) or use frozen pastry.

2 Preheat the oven to 190°C (375°F/Gas mark 5).

### Ingredients

❑ basic shortcrust pastry

❑ 900g (2 lb) cooking apples

❑ 2 tbsp plain flour

3　Peel and core the apples, then cut them into 1 cm (½ in) thick slices.

4　Toss the apples lightly with the flour, sugar, lemon juice, spices and salt.

5　Roll out the pastry for the bottom crust and place it in the pie dish. Trim the edge to a 2.5 cm (1 in) overhang.

6　Drain the apples and add to the dish. Top with the pieces of butter.

7　Roll out the pastry for the top crust. Place it over the pie and trim the edge, leaving a 2.5 cm (1 in) overhang.

8　Fold the top edge of the upper crust over the lower crust and squeeze them together.

9　Seal the edges by pinching small sections of dough with your fingers.

10　Use a sharp knife to cut five 2.5 cm (1 in) steam vents in the top.

11　Sprinkle the upper crust with sugar for sparkle.

12　Bake for 40 to 50 minutes, until the crust is golden.

- ❏ sugar to taste
- ❏ 1½ tbsp fresh lemon juice
- ❏ ½ tsp cinnamon
- ❏ ¼ tsp ginger
- ❏ ½ tsp allspice
- ❏ ¼ tsp grated nutmeg
- ❏ ¼ tsp salt
- ❏ 1½ tbsp butter, cut into pieces

## 434 | Make Treacle Tart

**This is a traditional teatime treat or dessert that is simple to make and a favourite with young and old.**

◎ **Steps**

1　Make shortcrust pastry (see 432 "Make Basic Shortcrust Pastry"), roll it out and line the tin, then put it in the refrigerator for at least 30 minutes. Chill the leftover pastry.

2　Preheat the oven to 190°C (375°F/Gas mark 5).

3　Pour the golden syrup into a saucepan, add the lemon zest and juice, and heat very gently.

4　Sprinkle the breadcrumbs over the base of the pastry case.

5　Pour in the syrup and lemon slowly to maintain the even covering of breadcrumbs.

6　For a traditional finish, roll out the remaining pastry and cut it into long strips about 1 cm (½ in) wide and lay these over the tart to form a lattice pattern. Brush over the lattice with the beaten egg.

7　Bake in the oven for 20–25 minutes, or until the filling is just set.

### Ingredients

- ❏ shortcrust pastry
- ❏ 225 g (8 oz) golden syrup
- ❏ zest and juice of 1 lemon
- ❏ 75 g (3 oz) fresh breadcrumbs
- ❏ 1 egg, beaten

## Make Cheesecake     435

This lemon cheesecake is simple to make and needs no baking. You need to make it the day before and keep it in the refrigerator. Makes one 20 cm (8 in) cheesecake, about 12 servings.

### ⊙ Steps

1 Have all the ingredients, especially the cream cheese, at room temperature.

2 Place the digestive biscuits in a plastic bag, tie the top, and then crush the biscuits with a rolling pin or large spoon until they are fine crumbs, all roughly the same size.

3 Put the butter into a small pan, and melt it slowly.

4 Add the sugar and the digestive crumbs and mix them all together.

5 Tip the mixture into a 20 cm (8 in) loose-bottomed tin and press it down flat with a spoon or the base of a glass.

6 Beat the cream cheese with a mixer until it is smooth and workable, then add the condensed mild and lemon zest and juice, beating until they are fully mixed together.

7 Whip the double cream in another bowl until soft peaks form.

8 Gently fold the whipped cream into the cheese and lemon mix.

9 Pour the cheesecake mix into the cake tin to cover the base and smooth the top with a knife. Cover it and put it in the refrigerator overnight.

10 Remove the cheesecake from the tin and slide it off its metal base.

11 Spread soured cream over the topping.

12 Decorate with fruit just before serving.

### ✱ Tip

Use any fruit you wish to decorate the top of the cake; seasonal fruit will be particularly tasty.

### Ingredients

❑ 175 g (6 oz) digestive biscuits

❑ 50 g (2 oz) butter

❑ 25 g (1 oz) demerara sugar

❑ 350 g (12 oz) cream cheese

❑ 1 400 g (14 oz) tin of condensed milk

❑ finely grated zest and juice of 3 lemons

❑ 150 ml (¼ pt) double cream

❑ 150 ml (¼ pt) soured cream

❑ fruit to decorate

## Make Pancakes     436

Forget that mix. Pancakes are easy to make from scratch. Makes about eight pancakes.

### ⊙ Steps

1 Sift the salt and flour into a large mixing bowl.

2 Make a well in the centre and break the egg into it. Beat the egg and flour together to form a paste.

3 Beat in the milk gradually, making sure to mix in all the paste from the sides of the bowl. Aim for a smooth batter mix.

4 Pour a little oil into a heavy-based frying pan and heat it up. Pour away any surplus oil – you need a minimal amount.

5 Pour or ladle in enough batter to just cover the base of the pan.

6 Cook until golden, turning or tossing the pancake so both sides are even.

### ✱ Tip

It's normal for the batter to be lumpy after you stir it.

### Ingredients

❑ ½ tsp salt

❑ 125 g (4 oz) plain flour

❑ 1 egg

❑ 300 ml (½ pt) milk

❑ vegetable oil for frying

7 Slide the pancake onto a plate.

8 Repeat with the rest of the batter, oiling the pan again only if it is necessary. As the pancakes are cooked, place them on top of each other with a layer of greaseproof paper in between.

9 Serve with sugar and lemon juice or a topping of your choice.

## 437 | Make Bread and Butter Pudding

A traditional nursery favourite, this uses simple ingredients to make a sweet and gooey dessert. Makes enough for four.

### ⊙ Steps

1 An hour or so before you start making the pudding, take the butter out of the refrigerator so it is at room temperature.

2 Preheat the oven to 170°C (325°F/Gas mark 3).

3 Cut the crusts off the bread, then spread the slices with butter on both sides. Cut them into squares.

4 Use half of the squares to line a 1 l (1³/₄ pt) ovenproof dish.

5 Sprinkle the fruit and half of the sugar over the bread in the dish.

6 Place the rest of the bread over the top and sprinkle over the rest of the sugar.

7 Add the eggs to the milk and beat well, then pour over the bread in the dish. Leave it to stand for about half an hour.

8 Bake for about 45 minutes until it is set and golden on top.

### Ingredients

- ❑ 6 slices of bread
- ❑ 50 g (2 oz) butter
- ❑ 50 g (2 oz) currants or sultanas
- ❑ 40 g (1¹/₂ oz) caster sugar
- ❑ 2 eggs
- ❑ 600 ml (1 pt) milk

## 438 | Make Christmas Pudding

Make your pudding at least a couple of weeks before Christmas to allow all the flavours to blend well together. This pudding is a large one that serves eight people.

### ⊙ Steps

1 Prepare a large pudding basin – about 1.5 l (2³/₄ pt) – by greasing it thoroughly.

2 Half fill a large saucepan or steamer with water and put it on to boil.

3 Sieve together the flour and all the the spices and salt.

4 Put all of the ingredients into a large mixing bowl.

5 Stir the mixture well until all the ingredients are evenly distributed. It's traditional at this stage for all the family to have a go at stirring the rich, sloppy mixture.

6 Pour the pudding mixture into the greased pudding basin.

### Ingredients

- ❑ 100 g (4 oz) plain flour
- ❑ ¹/₄ tsp nutmeg
- ❑ ¹/₄ tsp cinnamon
- ❑ ¹/₂ tsp mixed spice
- ❑ pinch of salt
- ❑ 275 g (10 oz) currants
- ❑ 175 g (6 oz) raisins
- ❑ 175 g (6 oz) sultanas
- ❑ 75 g (3 oz) fresh breadcrumbs

**How to Do (Just About) Everything**

7 Cover the bowl with two sheets of greaseproof paper and some foil. Tie some string firmly around the top of the bowl to ensure the foil stays in place and the top is sealed.

8 Place the basin in the saucepan or steamer and steam for about 8 hours.

9 Check the water level regularly and top it up with boiling water so that it does not boil dry.

10 Once the pudding has been steamed, allow it to cool in its basin with the foil lid in place.

11 When it is cool, unwrap it carefully then rewrap it in clean foil and store it in a cool place.

12 To reheat it ready to serve, place it in a steamer for about $2^3/4$ hours.

❏ 100 g (4 oz) shredded vegetable suet

❏ 100 g (4 oz) dark brown soft sugar

❏ 25 g (1 oz) almonds

❏ zest of half a lemon

❏ 150 ml (¼ pt) stout

❏ 2 eggs

## Make Hot Chocolate                                                439

Chocolate was actually first enjoyed as a drink by the Aztecs. You can use skimmed milk, but whole milk gives the best consistency. Makes about 10 servings.

### ◉ Steps

1 Chop the chocolate into small pieces and place in a mixing bowl.

2 Heat the milk in a saucepan over a medium-low heat until it steams and is very hot.

3 Add the sugar and vanilla and stir the mixture until the sugar has dissolved. Remove from the heat.

4 Ladle out about 300 ml (½ pt) of the milk and pour it over the chocolate.

5 Let the chocolate melt slowly. Stir it with a whisk to blend all the chocolate into the milk.

6 Continue adding the remaining milk and stir until all the milk has been incorporated. Serve hot.

### Ingredients

❏ 175 g (6 oz) high-quality plain chocolate

❏ 2.25 l (4 pt) whole milk

❏ 225 g (8 oz) sugar

❏ 1 tsp vanilla essence

## 440 | Brew a Pot of Coffee

Filter coffee can be made in a coffee percolator or simply by placing a filter holder over a pot or cup.

### ⊙ Steps

**Using a Coffee Percolator**

1 Fill the percolator's jug with fresh, cold water.

2 Place a filter in the percolator's filter cone.

3 Add 2 tbsp coffee to the cone for every 175 ml (6 fl oz) of water. (Sometimes the cups marked are more than 175 ml (6 fl oz), so check the instructions.)

4 Pour the water into the reservoir and replace the jug.

5 Turn on the percolator.

**Using a Filter Holder (Manual Method)**

1 Boil water, then let it rest briefly to achieve the optimum brewing temperature of 90–96 °C (195–205 °F).

2 Place a filter holder over a coffeepot or cup.

3 Place a filter in the holder.

4 Add about 2 level tbsp ground coffee to the filter holder per 175 ml (6 fl oz) of water, or adjust if you like it weaker or stronger.

5 Pour about 3 tbsp of water over the grounds to wet them.

6 Wait a few seconds for the grounds to expand.

7 Pour the rest of the water over the grounds. Let it drip through the grounds, but be sure to remove the grounds before the last of the water has drained into the pot or cup. Coffee grounds can overextract and get a bitter taste.

### ✱ Tip

Keep coffee warm on a ring or hot plate for no more than 20 minutes. After 20 minutes, coffee takes on a "stewed", bitter taste. Reheating coffee increases its bitterness and is not recommended.

## 441 | Brew a Pot of Tea

When you're feeling parched, there's nothing more refreshing than a cup of tea that has been properly brewed in the traditional way in a teapot.

### ⊙ Steps

1 Fill a kettle with fresh, cold water, adding enough to make the desired amount of tea, plus some extra to allow for evaporation and to pre-warm the teapot.

2 Wait until the water is near boiling, then pour a little into the teapot and swirl it around. This warms the pot so that it is at an optimum temperature for holding the tea. Empty the pot.

3 For each cup of tea, place 1 rounded teaspoon of leaves into the warmed pot. (If your pot has a strainer basket, use that.)

### ✱ Tips

If you do not want to use a strainer, place the tea leaves in a tea infuser, filter or mesh tea ball instead. You can also purchase tea pots with removable infusion baskets. You can use tea bags in a teapot, but the quality of tea in bags is never as good as that of loose tea.

4   Allow the water to come to the boil.

5   Pour the water from the kettle over the leaves in the teapot.

6   Let the tea steep for 3 to 5 minutes, depending on the size of the leaves. Allow a longer steeping time for larger leaves.

7   Stir just before serving, then pour the tea through a strainer into the cups. You might add sugar, milk, honey or lemon (or a combination, but don't use lemon and milk together).

8   Keep the pot covered with a tea cosy to keep the tea warm, and enjoy.

Transfer steeped tea into another heated teapot to avoid the bitter taste that can result from its sitting on the leaves for a long period of time.

## Make Lemonade                                      442

Lemonade, that classic summer quencher, is easily made from scratch. The best version combines a simple sugar syrup and freshly squeezed lemon juice. Makes two servings.

⊙Steps

1   Make sugar syrup: combine the sugar and 300 ml (½ pt) water in a saucepan and heat to boiling. Remove from the heat, stir to dissolve the sugar completely and allow to cool. (You'll only use a couple of tablespoons per serving – but this is a good item to make ahead and store in the refrigerator, covered. It keeps for weeks.)

2   For each serving, combine the juice of half a lemon, 2 tbsp of the sugar syrup and 225–300 ml (8–10 oz) cold water in a tall glass.

3   Add ice and sprigs of mint. Serve immediately.

### Ingredients

❏ 225 g (8 oz) sugar

❏ 300 ml (½ pt) water

❏ 1 large lemon

❏ 450–600 ml (16–20 fl oz) cold water

❏ mint sprigs

## Make a Dry Martini                                 443

The classic, elegant martini has undergone quite a resurgence lately. Makes one martini.

⊙Steps

1   Pour gin and vermouth over ice in a cocktail shaker.   .

2   Shake or stir well.

3   Strain into a chilled martini glass.

4   Serve straight up with an olive. (To make this drink a Gibson, serve with a pickled onion.)

### Ingredients

❏ gin

❏ dash of extra-dry vermouth

❏ 3 or 4 ice cubes

❏ cocktail olive

## 444 Make a Cosmopolitan

A Cosmopolitan is a fruity, refreshing drink of fairly recent origin that has become a classic. Makes one serving.

### ⊙ Steps

1  Wet the rim of a chilled martini glass with cranberry juice in a saucer and dip in sugar in another saucer.

2  Put ice in a cocktail shaker.

3  Add the vodka, cranberry juice, lime juice and Cointreau to the ice.

4  Shake twice.

5  Strain into the cocktail glass.

6  Add a lemon twist.

### Ingredients

❑ 30 ml (1 fl oz) cranberry juice plus extra for dipping glasses

❑ granulated sugar

❑ 3 or 4 ice cubes

❑ 50 ml (2 fl oz) vodka

❑ 30 ml (1 fl oz) lime juice

❑ dash of Cointreau

❑ lemon twist

## 445 Mix a Frozen Margarita

Break out the tortilla chips and salsa: you're making frozen margaritas! Just serve them as soon as they're made, for best results. Makes one serving.

### ⊙ Steps

1  Rub a cut lime around the rim of a margarita glass and then dip the glass into a plate of coarse salt if desired.

2  Put the tequila, fresh lime juice and triple sec or Cointreau in a blender with the crushed ice.

3  Blend at medium speed for 5 to 10 seconds and pour immediately.

4  Garnish with a lime wedge.

### Ingredients

❑ cut lime

❑ coarse salt

❑ 50 ml (2 fl oz) tequila

❑ 25 ml (¾ fl oz) fresh lime juice

❑ 30 ml (1 fl oz) triple sec or Cointreau

❑ crushed ice

❑ lime wedge

## Choose Wine for a Special Occasion

Whether the occasion is a birthday or a christening, a discreet lovers' tryst or a formal dinner party, a quality wine is often what is required. But which wine should you choose?

⊙ **Steps**

### General Points

1 Consider the price that you are prepared to pay. Decent wines can be bought for £5 and upwards, and some quite excellent ones for between £10 and £20. But if you really want to impress, there are wines available at luxury prices in the hundreds of pounds.

2 Decide whether you intend to buy a wine to be drunk on its own or with food. Remember that if you are buying a wine to go with a meal being cooked by someone else, your choice may not match the food.

3 Decide on the general characteristics of the wine that you want to buy. Do you want a white wine that is sweet or one that is dry? Are you looking for a red that is light and fruity or heavy and oaky? Learn to read wine labels carefully, since they will inform you on these characteristics

4 Remember that you are not buying the wine for your own satisfaction but for another or others. Give primacy to their tastes. If you don't know what their tastes are, ask them. There is no point in buying a good bottle of white wine to share with a person who only ever drinks red.

5 Know that a shot in the dark – buying a wine by the attractions of its label, name or price – will often lead to disappointment. Discuss your choice with an experienced and honest vintner if you possibly can. Alternatively, take advice from friends.

### Specifics

1 Choose a sparkling white wine as the universally acknowledged drink for celebrations of all kinds. Buy a sparkling wine that is bone dry and ensure that it is thoroughly chilled. Select French Champagne if you can afford it – it is still unrivalled in its prestige.

2 Buy a white wine for drinking as an aperitif before food or with nibbles. Select a New Zealand Sauvignon Blanc, rather than a similar wine from France. Choose a Chardonnay from Australia or California, where the extra sunshine brings a flavour rich in fruit.

3 For an intimate evening with love in the air, try a sweet desert wine such as a Muscat or Beaumes de Venise. Consume with some light and tasty sweet food, such as Italian cantucci or a good quality ice cream.

4 Choose a hefty vintage red wine to impress as your contribution to a dinner party. Ensure that, if you hand the bottle over to your host on arrival, he or she is aware that the wine requires to be uncorked immediately – it will need to "breathe" before it is consumed.

✳ **Tips**

Educate yourself about wines before you confront this situation. Read about the different regions and grape varieties – there is information available in books, magazines and on the Internet. Above all, experiment with a range of wines and build up a personal taste.

If possible buy a wine that you already know and like, even if it's not especially fancy. One advantage is that you aren't likely to be disappointed. Also, you'll be able to proffer the wine with a personal recommendation, which usually creates a good impression.

## 447 | Open a Wine Bottle

It's actually pretty simple to open a bottle of wine. These steps are for a double-action, or wing, corkscrew, which has two arms (or wings) that help lever the cork out of the bottle.

### ⊙ Steps

1  Remove the top of the foil by cutting around the rim of the bottle with the sharp point of the corkscrew. The arms of the corkscrew will have to be raised for this step. You can also make a slit in the foil and remove the whole thing before beginning.

2  Stand the bottle on a flat, hard surface at mid-chest level or lower. Lower the arms of the corkscrew. Holding the corkscrew as vertically and straight as possible, place the sharp end directly into the middle of the cork.

3  Securely grasp the top of the bottle and the lower end of the corkscrew with one hand.

4  With the other hand, begin turning the handle of the corkscrew clockwise, applying an even, constant downward pressure into the cork. As the corkscrew goes into the cork, its arms will begin to rise.

5  Apply more pressure if the corkscrew will not penetrate the cork.

6  Keep turning the handle until the arms of the corkscrew are completely raised and the screw is well into the cork.

7  With one hand on each arm of the corkscrew, press the arms down. This will lift the cork out of the bottle.

8  Wrap your hand around the base of the corkscrew and lift straight up.

9  Remove the foil, if necessary.

10  Twist the cork off the corkscrew.

11  Wipe the rim of the bottle with a clean, damp towel before serving, to remove any stray pieces of cork.

### ✳ Tips

Avoid corkscrews that penetrate the cork with a solid, ridged metal screw, which won't grip a cork well and can tear it apart. Instead, use a corkscrew with a metal spiral resembling a cartoon pig's tail.

If for some reason you just can't get the cork out on the first try, twist the corkscrew into a different part of the cork until the arms are raised, and repeat the process. But if you keep turning the corkscrew handle until the arms are completely raised, you shouldn't need to do this.

### Things You'll Need

❑ double-action (wing) corkscrew

## ✓ 448 Pair Wine and Food

Choosing the right wine for a meal can strike fear into the heart of a host. There are no hard-and-fast rules – you're best advised to serve the wine that you personally feel will complement the dish. If you're still unsure, check below for some guidelines.

### Seafood

- Pair a delicate-flavoured fish such as sole or plaice with delicate wines: a Muscadet or Vouvray from France, or a Sauvignon Blanc from New Zealand.

- For fuller-flavoured fish such as trout or sea bass, consider a full-bodied Chardonnay or one of the lighter red wines.

- For rich seafood such as salmon, consider a Chablis, a full-bodied Chardonnay or an elegant pinot noir.

- For shellfish such as oysters, crisp Muscadet, Chablis and sparkling wine are classic. For richer shellfish, such as lobster, try a Chardonnay or a Chablis.

- For spicy seafood dishes, try a spicy wine such as a Gewürztraminer from Alsace, a New Zealand Riesling, or alternatively a dry sparkling wine.

### Poultry

- Pair delicately flavoured chicken dishes with crisp, delicate white wines such as Vouvray, Muscadet or Sauvignon Blanc.

- For any grilled poultry, try a medium-bodied red Burgundy or Pinot Noir, a South American Cabernet or a fruity Californian Zinfandel.

- For heavily spiced chicken or turkey, try a spicy white wine, such as a Gewürztraminer from Alsace.

- For rich duck dishes, consider a rich, gamey red from Burgundy, Hermitage or Châteauneuf-du-Pape, or a wine high on acidity such as Italian Sangiovese or a white Burgundy.

- Pair game birds with earthy reds: a Rioja or Châteauneuf-du-Pape – or even a mature Cabernet-based wine.

### Meat

- For grilled meats, choose intense, smoky reds: Italian Barolo or Barbaresco, a big Napa Valley Cabernet Sauvignon or an Australian Shiraz.

- Pair full-flavoured dishes such as pepper steak with spicy reds such as Grenache from California, Australia or Gigondas in France. Also good: Côtes-du-Rhône or a peppery Californian Zinfandel.

- For hearty, spicy stews, pick spicy Syrah-based Rhône wines from Hermitage and Côte-Rôtie or California's Central Coast. Zinfandel is another option.

- Lighter meats can sometimes go well with big or off-dry whites. Try an oaky Chardonnay with veal, for example, or a Riesling or Gewürztraminer with baked ham.

### Vegetarian

- Pair strongly flavoured dishes, such as those made with garlic, with robust reds: Syrah or Cabernet Sauvignon. Try a Sangiovese for tomato-based dishes.

- For more subtle dishes, try a crisp white: a Sauvignon Blanc from New Zealand or a Vouvray from France.

- For strong, mushroomy dishes, select Pinot Noir for its delicate, earthy aromas.

- For Mexican dishes with sweetcorn or green chillies, try a crisp Chablis or a slightly grassy New Zealand Sauvignon Blanc – as long as the dish isn't too spicy.

- For spicy dishes, such as curry, try a slightly sweet German Riesling, a Gewürztraminer or a French rosé.

reference

## 449 | Choose Champagne

Sparkling wine – called Champagne if it comes from the Champagne region of France – is made from Chardonnay, Pinot Noir, Muscat and other grape varieties.

### ⊙ Steps

1 Learn to look for the words "méthode champenoise" on the label. True Champagnes and the best sparkling wines from other regions are made by this process of double-fermentation – once in barrels or vats and a second time in bottles.

2 Learn the different types of sparkling wines, from extra-brut (the driest) to extra-sec (very dry), sec (dry), demi-sec and doux (sweet). The great vintage Champagnes are found in the brut category.

3 Taste various types of sparkling wine and Champagne to get an idea of what kinds appeal most to you. One way to do this is to check the wine seller's events calendars and attend Champagne tastings.

4 Ask friends whose taste you respect for advice and recommendations, and talk to wine sellers, too.

5 Learn the histories and winemaking styles of various sparkling wine houses in France, California and elsewhere. Remember that Germany, Spain and Italy also make sparkling wines.

### ✳ Tips

Sparkling wine terms can be confusing. "Brut," for example, is drier than "extra dry."

Only sparkling wines from the Champagne region of France are correctly called Champagnes – but the term is still casually used for all sparkling wines, especially in the United States. Some California sparkling wines will even say "Champagne" on the label.

Less expensive sparkling wines are usually made by the charmat bulk process, in which all the fermentation takes place in vats.

## 450 | Open a Champagne Bottle

It takes some skill to open a bottle of Champagne so that the bubbly ends up in the flutes and not all over your guests.

### ⊙ Steps

1 Remove the foil from the cork.

2 Angle the bottle away from everyone so that if the cork pops out, it won't injure anyone.

3 Untwist the wire restraint securing the cork.

4 Wrap the bottle's neck and cork in a clean napkin.

5 Take hold of the cork with the napkin and gently untwist.

6 Continue untwisting, or hold the cork in place and twist the bottle itself.

7 Slowly ease the cork out of the bottle's neck. Wait for a soft pop. Pour.

### ✳ Tips

Keep glasses nearby and ready to catch the foam.

To preserve and best appreciate the effervescence of any sparkling wine, use the tall, narrow glasses known as flutes. Old-fashioned wide Champagne glasses allegedly cause bubbles to dissipate quickly.

## Make Mulled Wine 451

This comforting hot drink is easy to prepare and is a great warmer on a cold winter's night or for a festive pre-Christmas drink, especially if served with heated mince pies.

### ⊙ Steps

1 Pour the wine into a large saucepan and add the spices and sugar.

2 Lightly pound the orange and lemon zest to release the aromatic oils, and place it in the wine.

3 Heat slowly so that all the flavours infuse, but do not allow it to boil.

4 Pour the wine into a bowl and ladle it out, hot, into glasses.

5 Add a lemon or orange slice to each glass to decorate.

6 Lace with brandy if desired.

### Ingredients

- ❏ 1 l (1¾ pt) red wine (usually claret or burgundy)
- ❏ 2 tbsp soft brown sugar
- ❏ 6 cloves
- ❏ 1 cinnamon stick
- ❏ nutmeg
- ❏ zest of 1 orange and 1 lemon
- ❏ orange or lemon slices
- ❏ brandy (optional)

## Make Egg Nog 452

"Nog" derives from an old English term for strong ale or liquor. However, this version can be made plain or spiked. Makes eight small servings.

### ⊙ Steps

1 Heat the milk, cloves and peppercorns over low heat in a non-reactive saucepan until the mixture steams and is very hot.

2 Meanwhile, place the egg yolks, nutmeg, sugar and vanilla in a bowl and beat thoroughly.

3 When the milk mixture is hot, turn off the heat and strain out the cloves and peppercorns.

4 Start whisking the egg yolk mixture vigorously, and slowly ladle about 4 tablespoons of milk into it.

5 Switch the whisk to the saucepan and whisk the hot milk while slowly pouring the egg/milk mixture into the saucepan.

6 Return the saucepan to a low heat and stir continuously with a wooden spoon or heatproof flexible spatula. Make sure to stir the mixture off the bottom so the portion in contact with the pan doesn't overcook. The mixture will thicken as it cooks.

7 Test to see if it is ready by dipping the spoon or spatula in the mixture and dragging your finger across the back of it; the eggnog is done when your finger leaves a path through the thickened milk and the milk doesn't run. (This might take as long as 20 minutes. Keep the heat low and don't rush it, or you might curdle the eggs.)

8 Pour the mixture into a mixing bowl. Stir in the remaining extracts and, if you wish, single cream to taste.

9 Chill thoroughly before serving.

### ❋ Tips

If rum essence is not available, substitute ½ tsp orange essence.

To spike this egg nog recipe, add a dash of rum, brandy or whisky per serving.

### Ingredients

- ❏ 600 ml (1 pt) whole milk
- ❏ 5 or 6 cloves
- ❏ 10 white peppercorns
- ❏ 6 egg yolks
- ❏ ½ tsp nutmeg
- ❏ 175 g (6 oz) sugar
- ❏ 1 tsp. vanilla essence
- ❏ 1 tsp rum essence
- ❏ ½ tsp almond essence
- ❏ single cream (optional)

## 453 | Set the Table

Whether your dinner is very formal or not so formal, there are a few basic guidelines to setting a table.

### ◎ Steps

1   Consider how many guests will be attending. If several children will be in attendance, consider having a children's table. If you would like to include the children at the main table, consider booster seats if the children are small.

2   Determine where everyone should sit. For convenience, the cook may want to sit near the kitchen door. Parents should sit next to their children. If there is a male guest, he is traditionally seated on the hostess's right. A female guest is traditionally seated on the host's right. For large parties, determine who would interact best with each other. Some hosts like to alternate men and women, but this isn't necessary. You may want to use place cards to avoid everyone's rushing for a seat at the last minute.

3   Decide if you will use a tablecloth. If the tablecloth is damask, you will need a pad under it to prevent it from slipping. Also, the middle crease should be arranged so that it runs in a straight and unwavering line down the centre of the table from head to foot. The tablecloth should hang down about 45 cm (18 in) for a seated dinner. For a buffet table, it should hang down to the floor.

4   Once you've put the tablecloth, if you're using one, on the table, you can set it. Begin by folding napkins and placing them in the centre of each diner's place.

5   Place the large dinner fork to the left of the napkin and the smaller salad fork to the left of the dinner fork.

6   Place a salad plate to the left of the forks. The dinner plate should not be on the table when guests sit down.

7   Place a knife to the right of the napkin. For poultry or meat, you might want to use steak knives.

8   If serving soup or dessert, you will need one spoon for each. A small dessert spoon (or fork) may be placed horizontally across the top of the setting. Place the soup spoon to the right of the knife. (You can also wait and bring the dessert spoons or forks out just before dessert.)

9   Place a bread plate with a butter knife (if you have them) about 5 cm (2 in) above the forks, with the knife across the top of the plate.

10  Place a water glass about 5 cm (2 in) above the knife. Place wine glasses to the right of the water glass and slightly closer to the dinner guest.

11  If you will be serving coffee, the cup and saucer should go to the right of the glasses; or bring out the coffee cups when serving the coffee.

### Things You'll Need

- ❑ tablecloth
- ❑ napkins
- ❑ silverware
- ❑ china
- ❑ glasses for water
- ❑ wine glasses
- ❑ coffee cups and saucers

## Eat at a Formal Dinner

The silverware is placed on the table in the order in which it will be used, starting with the outside pieces. Let this be your guide as you work your way through a meal.

### ⊙ Steps

1. Put your napkin on your lap. Unfold it, but don't spread it.

2. Use the outside fork for the first course, unless soup is served – then use the outside spoon.

3. When you are finished with the course, place your fork at the right end of your plate, on a slight diagonal. This signifies that you are finished. For a soup course or another course that uses a wide bowl, place the spoon on the plate below the bowl. If a shallow bowl is used, place the spoon on the bowl in the same manner as a fork on a plate.

4. Continue by using the new outside fork. If the course requires a knife, use the knife farthest to the right.

5. Use the fork closest to your plate to eat your main course. The spoon or fork at your plate's head is for dessert.

6. Drink water from the largest glass at your setting.

7. Drink red wine from the rounder glass; drink white wine from the narrower glass.

8. If a little bowl of water is on the table at your place, or appears with the dessert, it is a fingerbowl. Wash the tips of your fingers in it. Dry them with your napkin.

9. Place your napkin on your chair if you leave the table temporarily. Place it next to your plate (don't fold it) when you leave the table.

### ❋ Tips

It is proper etiquette for the guests to wait for the host or hostess to unfold the napkin and begin eating before they do the same.

If you're uncertain about how or when to use a certain utensil, watch others and do what the majority of them do.

When eating bread, tear off pieces with your fingers – don't cut it or take bites from larger pieces. Also, butter the piece you've just torn just before you eat it; don't butter the whole piece first.

To eat soup, dip the spoon into the soup, then remove it in a motion away from your body, not towards it. Quietly sip the soup off the side of the spoon, rather than placing the whole spoon in your mouth.

## 455 | Get on TV

You thought that being on TV was just for superstars? Maybe it's about time you stepped out in front of the cameras – even if it is standing behind a court reporter outside the Old Bailey.

### ⊙ Steps

1   Are you really good at anything? So good that it would simply be a crime if you failed to share your talents with the world? That's still probably (just about) the best way to get on TV. If not, perhaps it's *Big Brother* for you.

2   Do you have any major problems? If so, researchers on such talk shows as *Kilroy* (www.bbc.co.uk) or *Trisha* (www.angliatv.com/trisha) are just waiting to hear from you. And remember: the weirder – and more sordid – the better your chances of appearing.

3   Ever wondered who all those "nobodies" are that routinely wander in the background scenes of your favourite shows? If you fancy being spotted wandering through Albert Square or down Coronation Street then you'll need to register with an "extras" agency – do a search on the internet, or try www.tv-filmextras.co.uk or www.extras.tv/information.htm.

4   Are you unusual to look at, or even – to be blunt – downright ugly? There are a number of modelling agencies that specialise in finding "character" faces for TV shows or commercials – try Ugly (www.ugly.org).

### ✱ Warnings

Being on TV, especially as the star of a reality show, may sound like a good idea at the time, but it can seriously backfire.

Remember, the "stars" of these programmes are often only noted for one thing and it's generally not for being Brain of Britain.

## 456 | Be in the Audience for a TV Show

A night out at the theatre or comedy club can cost an arm and a leg these days, especially if it's a big name you want to see. But how would you fancy a night out that doesn't cost you a penny? Interested?

### ⊙ Steps

1   Look at the BBC's ticketing web pages (www.bbc.co.uk/whatson/tickets). Here you can find a list of all the TV and radio shows that are being recorded over the coming months. You can make your choices and order the tickets online. For shows broadcast on Channel 4, you can order tickets from www.channel4.com/tickets.html.

2   Some shows are produced independently. At the end of a programme's credits, make a note of the production company. You should be able to find a contact either by doing a web search or looking it up in one of the many broadcasting industry directories – you'll find them in most public libraries.

### ✱ Tip

As the shows are free it's not uncommon for people to order their tickets and not turn up. Consequently, many more tickets are usually sent out than can be accommodated in the theatre. Make sure that you arrive early since seating will be on a first come first served basis.

## Be a Contestant on a Game Show 457

It doesn't matter whether it's *Who Wants To Be A Millionaire?* or *Family Fortunes*, for a TV game show to work it must have one vital ingredient – a contestant. It has to be someone, so why not you?

⚠ **Warning**

Be prepared for disappointment: contestants are not always chosen for their capabilities but for other characteristics, such as photogenic appearance or particular type of personality.

### ◉ Steps

1 Identify the quiz show in which you want to take part. Have a pen and paper ready – often you will hear details of how to apply at the end of the show. If it's produced by an independent TV company, note the name – you may need to contact them later.

2 If the quiz show was broadcast on the BBC you should be able find details on the BBC web pages (www.bbc.co.uk); similarly with pro-grammes made on Channel 4 (www.channel4.com), ITV (www.itv.com) and Channel 5 (www.channel5.co.uk).

3 Contact independent producers directly.

## Spot Celebrities 458

Although it may sometimes seem as though they inhabit another world altogether, getting a good "star spot" may be easier than you think – you just need to look in the right places.

⚠ **Warnings**

There can be a fine line between spotting celebrities and turning into a stalker.

Not all stars like to be accosted by strangers, and so may not be as friendly as they seem on your favourite shows. Be aware that the experience could be a very disappointing one for you – for every Dustin Hoffman who'll happily talk to your Mum on your mobile phone, there'll be a Jay Kay ready to bloody your nose.

### ◉ Steps

1 Think about where the stars are based. You'll clearly have a better chance of spotting a TV celebrity wandering around London's Soho than in a shopping centre in Swindon.

2 Find out about film premieres and award ceremonies. That's where you'll find your favourite celebs looking their most glamourous.

3 Subscribe to the biggest celebrity magazines, such as *OK!* and *Heat.* Gossip columns will often talk about bars, hotels and restaurants where the rich and famous hang out. (If you can get a table at The Ivy in London, you're guaranteed a star spot: if you can't get a table – or can't afford one – hang around outside for a few hours.)

4 In recent years, it's become fashionable for some of Hollywood's biggest names to tread the boards on London's West End. So, if you know the theatre and are prepared to hang around by the stage door, you might just get a glimpse of such A-list stars as Kevin Spacey or Nicole Kidman.

5 Shop with the stars! Take a trip to some of London's coolest fashion houses. Every celeb's favourite department store? Forget Harrods – that's for the tourists – instead, head for Harvey Nichols. Indeed, any of the big designer names in Sloane Street have the potential to come up with the goods.

## 459 | Whistle

If singing is not your biggest strength, try whistling your favourite tunes. Follow these steps and practise until you can whistle with comfort and ease.

### ◎ Steps

1   Purse your lips into a tiny O shape, leaving a small opening for air.

2   Place the tip of your tongue behind your bottom teeth or against your inside bottom gums.

3   Gently expel air through your mouth.

4   Adjust your tongue position and the small opening formed by your lips until you hear a note.

5   Once you can sound one note, experiment with your tongue position and the strength of your breath to produce different notes.

6   Practise!

### ✳ Tips

Try not to blow too hard at first; it's much easier to whistle with a small amount of air.

You may find it easier to produce a strong, pure note if you wet your lips first.

## 460 | Waltz

The waltz, which evolved from a German folk dance, is danced to a triple beat. It is popular throughout Europe and the United States, especially at formal social events.

### ◎ Steps

1   Get into position by facing your partner. If you are the leader, place your right hand on your partner's waist slightly around the back and extend your left hand to your side with your elbow bent and your palm raised, facing her. With that hand, grasp your partner's right hand in a loose grip, and make sure your partner has her left hand on your right shoulder, with her elbow bent. She should mirror your movements.

2   On the first beat, step forwards gracefully with your left foot. Your partner should follow your lead by doing the opposite of what you do on each beat – in this case, stepping back with her right foot.

3   On the second beat, step forwards and to the right with your right foot. Trace an upside-down letter L in the air with your foot as you do this.

4   Shift your weight to your right foot. Keep your left foot stationary.

5   On the third beat, slide your left foot over to your right and stand with your feet together.

6   On the fourth beat, step back with your right foot.

7   On the fifth beat, step back and to the left with your left foot, this time tracing a backward L. Shift your weight to your left foot.

8   On the final beat, slide your right foot towards your left until your feet are together. Now you're ready to start again with your left foot.

9   Repeat steps 2 to 8, turning your and your partner's orientation slowly to the left by slightly varying the placement of your feet.

### ✳ Tips

It helps to count as you go – "one, two, three; one, two, three" – placing the emphasis on the "one" as you count.

Practise to a slow waltz until you become comfortable with the moves.

# Tango                                                461

Born in the brothels of Argentina, the tango is synonymous with passion. Although the dance is relatively free-form, you can do a lot with two basic moves: the walking step and the rock step.

## ⊙ Steps

1   Face your partner and stand closer together than you would in most other ballroom dances – close enough for your torsos to touch.

2   If you're the leader, place your right hand on the middle of your partner's lower back. Extend your left hand out to your side with your arm bent and grasp your partner's right hand in a loose grip. Your partner should place her left hand on your right shoulder and place her right hand lightly in your palm with her right elbow bent.

3   On the first beat, walk forwards slowly with your left foot, placing down your heel first and then your toes. Your partner will mirror each of your movements on every beat throughout the dance – in this case, moving her right foot backwards, landing her toes and then her heel.

4   On the second beat, step forwards slowly with your right foot so that it moves past your left. You should feel as if you are slinking forwards.

5   On the third beat, step forwards quickly with your left foot, then immediately slide your right foot quickly to the right side and shift your weight to that foot.

6   On the fourth beat, bring your left foot slowly to your right, leaving your left leg slightly bent as your feet come together. Your weight should still be on your right foot.

7   Now, shift your weight to your left foot and do a right forwards rock step: While making a half-turn clockwise, step forwards quickly on your right foot, and then quickly shift your weight back to your left foot. With your right foot, slowly step forwards to complete the half turn.

8   Bring your feet together, bring your left foot up next to your right and repeat steps 3 to 7.

**❋ Tips**

Bear in mind that your feet barely leave the floor as you dance.

This isn't a subtle way to meet people.

# Salsa                                                462

Listen to the rhythm of the music as you learn this popular Latin dance. You can learn the basic salsa steps in less than an hour, and sashay all over the dance floor before you know it.

## ⊙ Steps

1   Get in position by facing your partner. If you are the leader, place your right hand on your partner's waist, slightly around the back. Extend your left arm diagonally to chest height with your elbow bent at a right angle and your palm raised. Grasp your partner's right hand in a loose grip; your partner's left hand should be on your right shoulder.

2   On the first beat, step forwards with your left foot. Your partner will mirror each of your movements throughout the dance; for example, on the first beat she will step backwards with her right foot.

**❋ Tips**

You can add more complicated moves once you've grasped the basic salsa step.

Don't use exaggerated hip movement. That sexy swing will come naturally as you let yourself feel the rhythm.

3   Step in place with your right foot on the second beat.

4   Step back with your left foot on the third beat so that you are back in the starting position, and hold in place for the fourth beat.

5   Step back with your right foot on the fifth beat.

6   Step in place with your left foot on the sixth beat.

7   Step forwards with your right foot on the seventh beat so that you are back in the starting position, and hold for the eighth beat.

8   Repeat, starting at step 2.

Some salsa clubs offer free or inexpensive introductory classes or specials on certain nights of the week.

## 463   Jive

Modern jive is a dance style that evolved in the 1990s. It can be danced to many kinds of music, from rock'n'roll and swing to much of contemporary pop. There are hundreds of possible variations, but here is a basic move to get started.

### ⊙ Steps

1   Get in position by facing your partner. If you are the leader (usually the man), turn your hands palm upwards in front of you at waist level. Your partner lays her hands lightly over yours.

2   Initiate the dance with a step backwards by both partners. Bend your fingers to create a grip and stretch your arms so that you can feel the tension of your two bodies pulling away from one another. Keep the handhold light – neither of you should grip with your thumbs.

3   Step together on the next beat, at the same time turning anti-clockwise through 90 degrees, so that you are side by side.

4   Both twist 180 degrees clockwise on the next beat so that you are again side by side but facing in the opposite direction.

5   Both twist 90 degrees anti-clockwise to face one another. If you are the leader, raise your left hand to shoulder height. The partner mirrors this by raising her right hand. Ensure the hands are palm to palm, touching but not holding.

6   If you are the leader, push downwards to propel the partner into a spin. The partner spins through 360 degrees and returns to face the leader.

7   Resume the light grip with both hands and both step back, once more creating tension in the arms as you pull apart. You are ready to repeat the move or try another variant.

### ✻ Tips

Keep your arms at waist level most of the time. When pulling apart, don't extend your arms out fully straight – if you do, the effect is jerky and definitely uncool.

Some jive clubs offer inexpensive introductory classes on certain nights of the week. You will need lessons to pick up enough moves to make jiving worthwhile.

**How to Do** *(Just About)* **Everything**

## Write a Sonnet

The sonnet, a 14-line poem, has two main types: English (or Shakespearean) and Italian (or Petrarchan). Here, we present the format for writing a Shakespearean sonnet.

### ⊙ Steps

1 Select the subject matter for your sonnet. Themes have often focused on love or philosophy, but modern sonnets can cover almost any topic.

2 Divide the theme of your sonnet into two sections. In the first section you will present the situation or thought to the reader; in the second section you can present some sort of conclusion or climax.

3 Compose your first section as three quatrains – that is, three stanzas of four lines each. Write the three quatrains with an *a-b-a-b, c-d-c-d, e-f-e-f* rhyme scheme, where each letter stands for a line of the sonnet and the last words of all lines with the same letter rhyme with each other. Most sonnets employ the metre of iambic pentametre (see Tips), as seen in these three quatrains from Shakespeare's "Sonnet 30":

*When to the sessions of sweet silent thought* (a)
*I summon up remembrance of things past,* (b)
*I sigh the lack of many a thing I sought,* (a)
*And with old woes new wail my dear time's waste·* (b)
*Then can I drown an eye, unus'd to flow,* (c)
*For precious friends hid in death's dateless night,* (d)
*And weep afresh love's long since cancell'd woe,* (c)
*And moan th'expense of many a vanish'd sight:* (d)
*Then can I grieve at grievances foregone,* (e)
*And heavily from woe to woe tell o'er* (f)
*The sad account of fore-bemoanéd moan,* (e)
*Which I new pay as if not paid before.* (f)

4 Compose the last section as a couplet—two rhyming lines of poetry. This time, use a *g-g* rhyme scheme, where the last words of the two lines rhyme with each other. We refer once more to "Sonnet 30":

*But if the while I think on thee, dear friend,* (g)
*All losses are restored and sorrows end.* (g)

### ✱ Tips

An iamb is a type of metrical "foot" used in a poem. It is composed of two syllables, with the accent on the second syllable. Examples: "to*day*" or "en*rage*". Pentameter means that there are five metrical feet per line. Iambic pentameter means that each line of the poem consists of five iambic feet, or 10 total syllables. An example from Shakespeare: "Good pilgrim you do wrong your hand too much."

In the Italian sonnet, use an *a-b-b-a-a b-b-a* rhyme scheme for the first section (called the "octave"), and a rhyme scheme of *a-d c-d-e or c-d-c-d-c-d* in the second section (called the "sestet").

## Write a Short Story

The model described here is the pyramid plot. The upward slope establishes setting and characters and builds tension; the tip is the climax; and the downward slope is the resolution.

### ⊙ Steps

1 Choose a narrative point of view. You can write your story as if you were one of the characters (first person), as a detached narrator who presents just one character's thoughts and observations (third-person limited), or

### ✱ Tips

There are many possible variations of this model, all of which allow for perfectly good short stories.

as a detached narrator who presents the thoughts and observations of several characters (third-person omniscient). A first-person point of view will refer to the central character as "I" instead of "he" or "she".

2   Create a protagonist, or main character. This should be the most developed and usually the most sympathetic character in your story.

3   Create a problem, or conflict, for your protagonist. The conflict of your story should take one of five basic forms: person vs. person, person vs. himself or herself, person vs. nature, person vs. society, or person vs. God or fate. If you choose a person vs. person conflict, create an antagonist to serve as the person your protagonist must contend with.

4   Establish believable characters and settings, with vivid descriptions and dialogue, to create a story that your readers will care about.

5   Build the story's tension by having the protagonist make several failed attempts to solve or overcome the problem. (You may want to miss out this step for shorter stories.)

6   Create a crisis that serves as the last chance for the protagonist to solve his or her problem.

7   Resolve the tension by having the protagonist succeed through his or her own intelligence, creativity, courage or other positive attributes. This is usually referred to as the story's climax.

8   Extend this resolution phase, if you like, by reflecting on the action of the story and its significance to the characters or society.

Keep your language concise, specific and active. For example, write "Steve ate the apple" instead of "The fruit was eaten by someone".

---

## 466  Write a Limerick

There once was a fellow called Larry,
Who sought to write lim'ricks for Carrie.
   With the help of eHow
   He wrote one, and now
Young Larry is married to Carrie.

### ⊙ Steps

1   Prepare to write five lines of verse. If you're stumped, try starting off your limerick with the traditional "There once was a ...".

2   Create the following stress pattern in lines one, two and five: da-*da* da-da-*da* da-da-*da*-da. For example, "There *once* was a *fel*-low called *Lar*-ry....". You can omit the last, unstressed syllable if you prefer.

3   Create the following stress pattern in lines three and four: da-*da* da-da-*da*. For example, "He *wrote* one, and *now*". You have the option of adding an extra unstressed syllable before the first stress and one or two syllables after the last stress.

4   Make sure your limerick's rhyme scheme is *a-a-b-b-a*. In other words, the first, second and fifth lines all rhyme with one another; the third and fourth lines rhyme with each other.

5   Exploit puns and wordplay.

### ✱ Tips

The racier, the better. Limericks are notoriously bawdy and obnoxious.

The last line should deliver a punch, whether surprising, funny or naughty.

You can be flexible about rhythm as long as you make sure there are three strong beats in lines 1, 2 and 5, and two in lines 3 and 4.

## Paint a Landscape With Watercolours 467

Painting outdoors is a peaceful way to enjoy a beautiful day. Keep a backpack full of painting supplies and you can be ready to go whenever the inspiration strikes.

### ⊙ Steps

1  Tape a piece of watercolour paper to a heavy piece of cardboard using masking tape. Run the tape along the entire edges of all four sides of the paper.

2  Use a soft lead pencil to begin your painting with a simple sketch.

3  Locate and draw the horizon line, which is the line formed where the sky and the land meet.

4  Sketch in the background objects: hills, mountains, distant trees. Background objects are typically smaller and have less detail than objects in the foreground.

5  Sketch the objects in the foreground. These objects will be larger and more detailed.

6  Use clear water and a flat brush to dampen the sky area of your picture.

7  If you're painting on a sunny day, use a medium round brush to paint a blue sky over the sky area while the paper is damp. This is applying what is called a "wash".

8  Create clouds by blotting the sky with a crumpled tissue while the paint is still wet.

9  Use the same wash technique to paint in large areas of background colour such as hills, mountains, water and grass.

10  Wait until the watercolour paper is dry or almost dry to paint details; your paintbrush should also be nearly dry. This technique, which gives you more control over the paint flow, is called "dry brush".

11  Paint in details using a small round brush. Mix paint with more water to create softer, lighter hues. Use less water to create darker, more vivid colours and harder edges.

12  Allow your finished painting to dry completely, then carefully peel away the masking tape from the edges of the paper. This will leave a nice white border around the edge of your painting.

### ✱ Tip

Consider buying a watercolour block, which is a pad of watercolour paper that is glued on all four sides. A watercolour block is rigid, which makes it easy to take anywhere so you can do without a drawing board.

### Things You'll Need

❑ cardboard
❑ masking tape
❑ watercolour paper
❑ pencils and rubbers
❑ watercolour paints
❑ water and container
❑ watercolour brushes
❑ paper tissue

## Finger Paint 468

Finger painting is an easy way to show off your artistic talents. It's great for both the beginner and the advanced artist, and it has always been very popular with children.

### ✱ Tips

To reduce the paint's chipping or cracking, avoid leaving thick concentrations of paint on your paper.

### ⊙ Steps

1  Gather your supplies together: rough, thick paper or card, and tempera paint, which is most commonly used. However, almost any nontoxic water-based paint will work.

2　Select your work area. A large, smooth, flat surface that is easy to clean is best. Cover it with newspaper or plastic, and wear old clothes or an apron that you don't mind getting dirty.

3　Lay out your paper. Using a brush, sponge or even your hand, dampen the surface of your paper with water. This smooths out the paper and makes it easier to spread paint.

4　Pour the paint into baking tins or bowls.

5　Use your fingers, a spoon or a brush to scoop a generous amount of paint onto the paper.

6　Smear the globs of paint around with your fingers to create your painting. Don't be timid when finger painting; lots of bright colours and bold strokes are the keys to good results. Use your fingers, hands and even feet for effect.

7　If your paint begins to dry before you're finished, add water to keep the paint fluid and easy to work with.

8　Sign your masterpiece when you've finished and let it dry on a flat surface. It's better not to hang your picture for drying, as the paint may run.

9　Clean up with soap and water.

You can also use oil paint with your fingers, though it's more difficult to clean up and not good for beginners or children. Wear latex gloves when finger painting with oil paint, since it is toxic.

Sprinkle glitter on your painting before it dries.

## ⚠ Warning

Use nontoxic paints when painting with children.

## Things You'll Need

❏ finger-painting paper

❏ tempera or other water-based paint

---

## 469　Start a Collection

**An informed collector is a happy collector. Know what you're buying and the best price before you buy the item.**

### ◎ Steps

1　Work out what kind of items you are interested in collecting, or determine if you already have three or more of a certain object. You may have begun a collection without knowing it.

2　Subscribe to collecting magazines or newsletters that are devoted to your object(s) of interest.

3　Purchase books and do the research required to become an expert in your subject of interest. It will save you money in the long run because you'll recognise bargains and rip-offs when you see them.

4　Allocate a space in which to store the collection. It's best if this space is easily viewed so that you can enjoy the fruits of your obsession. Purchase display cases or shelves if necessary.

5　Set a budget so you don't spend too much money on the collection.

6　Use the internet or newsletters to form a loose network with other collectors and sellers.

7　Thoroughly research each item before you purchase it.

8　Keep a ledger listing your contacts, the items in your collection and the date and cost of purchase.

### ✳ Tips

Monitor online auction sites, such as eBay, to find out general price ranges and typical rates.

Let family and friends know that you are starting a collection. It will help them come up with gift ideas for you.

Many collections can be assembled or started without making special purchases with items such as matchboxes, bottle caps, seashells or pine cones.

## Find the Books You Loved as a Child 470

New books get published every year, but the ones you loved as a child are like comfort food. It's natural to want the children you love to have the books that were your childhood favourites.

### ⊙ Steps

1 Remember as much about the books as you can. Titles and authors' names are, of course, exceedingly useful, but any tidbit, including the setting (Scotland? San Francisco?), the main character's name (Betsy? Harriet? Tom?) or the theme (a magic garden? a swan that can play the trumpet?) can come in handy. Make notes as you mull it over.

2 Ask the librarian at your public library for help, especially with books you don't remember well. Many librarians have not only a deep passion for children's literature, but also an encyclopedic memory for plots and characters.

3 Frequent car-boot saloo. As people are having fewer children and having them later, parents with grown up children are quite likely to be selling off the books that they bought for their kids, rather than waiting for the distant day when they might become grandparents and be able to pass them down another generation.

4 Find out if there's someone in your local second-hand bookshop who knows about children's books. It's a common passion, and these people tend to be knowledgeable. Some will even keep wish lists and notify you when they find the book you're looking for.

5 Keep an eye out for library book sales. Many collectors look askance at books that were once in a library because they're less than pristine. Still, they're often in surprisingly good condition – well loved, but not destroyed.

6 Make use of online services. Most of the larger online shops (such as www.amazon.co.uk) offer book-search services, while sites that specialise in used and out-of-print books (for example, www.alibris.com) link networks of small independent book dealers.

### ✳ Tips

Memory can play tricks on you, and even reference books can contain typographical errors. Whether you're searching in reference books or online, check a few different spellings if you can't find what you're looking for.

Make this a family project. Ask your family and friends of your own age to help you jog your memory.

## Make Decorative Paper 471

Give scrap paper a new life by blending it with water to make decorative paper. You will need a fine mesh and a tub larger than the screen to do this project.

### ⊙ Steps

1 Gather a pile of scrap paper and tear it into small bits.

2 Boil water, remove it from heat, and soak the paper bits in the hot water for 2 to 3 minutes. The ratio should be two parts water to one part paper.

3 Blend the water and paper bits in a blender. Run the blender for a few seconds at a time until the mixture is a very fine pulp.

4 Pour the mixture into a large plastic bowl (a baby bath works well) or a large baking pan.

### ✳ Tips

If the mixture is too thick, add more water to thin it out. If your mixture is too thin, add more paper bits. Then blend again.

In place of glitter you can add sequins, slivers of aluminium foil, flower petals or waterproof ink to the pulp. Add these items to the pulp mixture in the tub before you dip in the screen.

5   Use a large spoon or your hands to stir the mixture until the pulp is evenly distributed in the bowl or pan.

6   Repeat with more scrap paper until the mixture in the bowl is deep enough to dip the mesh into.

7   Add some glitter to the bowl and stir again until the glitter is evenly distributed throughout the mixture.

8   Submerge the mesh in the mixture, dipping it below the mixture at a shallow angle and then holding it in a horizontal position.

9   Use your hands to distribute the pulp on the mesh evenly and then slowly lift the mesh up and out of the bowl, keeping it horizontal.

10  Hold the mesh over the bowl until water stops dripping from the bottom (this should take less than a minute). Gently turn it from side to side to make sure all excess water drains out.

11  Quickly flip the mesh over and lay it pulp-side down on a short stack of absorbent towels.

12  Gently lift the mesh off the layer of pulp so that the pulp remains on the towels in one piece.

13  Place another stack of towels on top of the pulp layer to blot the pulp.

14  Press firmly on the stack with your hands or use a rolling pin to squeeze out the water.

15  Carefully transfer the pulp to a new, dry stack of towels if the original stack becomes soaked. Continue blotting until hardly any water comes out when the stack is pressed.

16  Gently remove the sheet of paper and place it on a flat, dry surface to air-dry overnight.

17  Once the paper has dried, use scissors to trim the edges as desired. Some people prefer to leave the edges naturally rough.

You can use stacks of newspapers to blot the paper instead of stacks of towels; however, the ink in the newspapers may run into the pulp.

## Things You'll Need

❑ fine mesh

❑ plastic bowl or baking pan

❑ scrap paper

❑ blender

❑ glitter

❑ towels

❑ rolling pin

❑ scissors

---

## 472 | Play Charades

Charades, believed to have originated in 18th-century France, is a classic party game that's fun for all ages. You'll need at least six people to play.

### ⊙ Steps

#### The Game

1   Divide the group into two teams of at least three people each. Decide on a time limit – between 3 and 5 minutes – for each round.

2   Ask each team to write titles of books, TV shows or movies, or other phrases (see Tips), on individual scraps of paper, then fold them to hide the writing. Each team then places its scraps in a separate bowl.

3   When it's your turn, close your eyes and pick a piece of paper from the other team's bowl. Read its contents to yourself.

4   Without speaking, help your team try to guess the title by giving signals using appropriate gestures (see the following section).

### ✳ Tips

In addition to book, film and TV titles, popular charades topics include well-known quotations, song titles and names of famous people, rock bands and places.

Arrange other signals with your partners before the game, if you wish, but remember that it's against the rules to arrange an "alphabet code" to act out the spelling of a word.

It is improper to point to people or objects in the room for hints.

5   Stop when your team guesses the title or time runs out.

6   Sit down and watch the other team draw a title and act it out.

7   When it's your team's turn again, watch as one of your teammates draws a new title out of the bowl; now it's your turn to try to guess what your team mate is acting out.

8   Record how many clues it takes each team to guess correct titles (or add up the number of correct guesses per team) to determine the winner.

## The Clues

1   To indicate a book title, put your hands together as if you are praying, then unfold them flat.

2   To indicate a film title, form an O with one hand to pantomime a lens while cranking the other hand as if you are operating an old-fashioned movie camera.

3   Indicate a television show by making a box with your fingers.

4   Make quotation marks in the air with your fingers to indicate a quote.

5   Pose like Napoleon (with a hand on your chest and the tips of your fingers tucked partway into your shirt) to indicate a famous person.

6   Pull on your ear to indicate that the word being guessed sounds like another word.

7   Hold up fingers to indicate the number of words in the title, quotation or name; hold up a number of fingers again to indicate which word you want your teammates to guess.

8   Hold fingers against your arm to indicate the number of syllables in a particular word.

9   Pinch your thumb and forefinger or open them up to indicate a short or long word.

10  Confirm that your partners have guessed a word correctly by tapping your index finger on your nose and pointing to the person or persons who made the correct guess.

11  Wipe your hand across your forehead to let your team mates know that they are getting warm.

12  Cross your arms and shiver to let them know that they are getting cold.

## Play Twenty Questions                                                    473

This is a terrific way to occupy children on a rainy day or during a long car ride. One player thinks of an object and the other players ask questions to determine what that object is.

### ◉ Steps

1   Choose one person to start. This person must think of an object. To make the game easier, he or she can classify the object as animal, vegetable or mineral.

### ✳ Tips

If the players use up their 20 questions without guessing the object, the player with the object in mind reveals it and thinks of a new one.

2   Have another player ask a question about the object that can be answered yes or no.

3   The person who has the object in mind should answer the question with a simple yes or no.

4   After hearing the answer, the questioner is allowed to guess the object. The players are allowed to ask a total of 20 questions.

5   If the guess is correct, the winning questioner now thinks of a new object. If the answer is incorrect, another player is allowed to ask a yes or no question.

This game works best with four or fewer players.

## 474 | Play Draughts

**Draughts has been around for centuries and is played in most parts of the world. Try it – you'll find it's not just for kids!**

### ⦿ Steps

1   Flip a coin to decide who will play white and who will play black. Whoever wins the toss chooses. The white player will make the opening move.

2   On the white player's side, place one white draught on each black square in the first three rows of squares.

3   On the black player's side, place one black draught on each black square in the first three rows of squares.

4   Make sure there are 12 staggered draughts on each side of the board with two empty rows in the middle.

5   The white player begins by moving one red draught forwards diagonally on to an adjacent free black square.

6   Take turns moving one draught, one square forwards diagonally, at a time.

7   "Jump" your opponent's draught if it is in a square directly diagonal and adjacent to your own draight and there is a free square on the other side. To do this, move your draught over your opponent's draught and place it on the opposite square. Take possession of your opponent's jumped draught by removing it from the board.

8   If you jump a draught and land in a position to jump another of the other player's draughts, jump that draught as well during the same turn.

9   "King" one of your draughts when it reaches the furthest row from your starting side (your opponent's back row). Signify a kinged draught by having your opponent stack one of your jumped draughts on top of the kinged draught. Kinged draughts can move both forwards and back-wards, but still can only move diagonally to adjacent black squares, one square at a time.

10  The first player to remove all of the opponent's draughts from the board by jumping them wins the game.

### ✳ Tips

If one of your draughts is in a position to jump, you must jump; the alternative is to forfeit the game. If more than one of your draughts is in a jumping position, you are allowed to choose which one will jump.

White and black are the most common colours for draughts. Another popular colour pair is red and white (white goes first).

These rules are for standard draughts. Other variations exist.

## Do a Cryptic Crossword Puzzle
### 475

Cryptic crosswords, such as the one that appears daily in *The Times*, are a source of lifelong pleasure for some people, but a complete mystery to others. Here are some clues to get started.

### ⊙ Steps

1  Know that each clue normally consists of two parts, one that gives you a devious, riddling way to work out the solution, and the other that gives the literal meaning of the solution. For example, "Endless hate for headgear" would have the solution "hat". (Cryptically, the word "hate" without its end, or final letter, and also literally, "headgear".)

2  Try to work out which part of the clue gives the literal meaning, but remember that the most obvious answer is unlikely to be the right one!

3  Look out for anagrams – letters to unscramble – as these are often among the easier types of clue to solve. Anagrams are usually indicated by words such as "confused" or "changing" (clue: "Changing places? It is requiring particular skill"; solution: "specialist" – an anagram of "places it is", meaning "someone with a particular skill").

4  Look out for "hidden word" clues, where the solution is to be found in consecutive letters embedded in the clue. For example, clue: "Holdall found in cab again"; solution: "bag" (a holdall is a bag, and the word "bag" is found in "caB AGain".

4  Learn key words that are regularly used in clues with a special purpose. For example, "sailor" is often used to indicate the syllables "tar" or "ab" (nickname for a sailor and initials for "able-bodied seaman"); "flower" is very likely to mean "river" (get it?); "saint" or "holy man" may indicate the letters "st"; and so on.

5  Look at each clue as many ways as you can. Mental flexibility is the key to solving cryptic crosswords.

6  If you're stumped, put the puzzle down for a while and try again later.

7  Go through the correct solutions in the following day's newspaper. Compare the solutions with the clues and see if you can understand how the clues worked.

### ✱ Tips

Filling inspired guesses into the crossword square is often a useful way forwards for beginners. Use a pencil so that you can rub out mistakes easily.

A question mark at the end of a clue means that it is somehow especially devious. Such clues may not have the classic two-part structure of a cryptic clue. An example from *The Times*: "Great banana summit?"; solution "It must be an anagram" (which is an anagram of "great banana summit"!)

The puzzles in newspapers such as *The Times*, *Guardian* and *Telegraph* are easiest on Monday and get progressively harder throughout the week.

## Play Darts
### 476

If you're competitive, think about improving your darts play at home so you can impress at the local watering hole. Here's how to get started if you need to set up from scratch.

### ⊙ Steps

1  Hang the dartboard so that the centre is 1.73 m (5 ft 8 in) from the floor.

2  Mark the throwing line, or "oche" (rhymes with "hockey"), with nonskid tape. The line should be 2.37 m (7 ft 9¼ in) from the face of the dartboard (not the wall), according to the World Darts Federation.

### ✱ Tip

For an alternative game of darts, throw five sets of three darts for each player and tot up the total scored. The highest scorer wins.

3   Make sure the tape mark lies so that the front edge is the actual line. In other words, a player may step on the tape, but not past it.

4   Give each player or team three darts, and determine who throws first by having each player or team representative throw one dart. The player or team whose dart is closest to the bull's-eye gets to go first.

5   Warm up, as competitive darts players do, by alternating throws until each person has thrown nine darts.

6   Once the game begins, take your turn by throwing your three darts.

7   Start from 301 and count downwards, subtracting each score from the total. The first player or team to reach exactly zero wins.

### ⚠ Warning

Resist the temptation to hang your dartboard on the back of a door, unless the door is kept permanently locked.

---

## 477 | Play Marbles

Although most of us think of marbles as an old-fashioned pastime, the game is still fun for children of all ages and is played around the globe.

### ◉ Steps

1   Draw a circle about 1 m (3 ft) wide. Use chalk on asphalt or concrete, a stick on earth, or a string on carpet or tile.

2   Select your shooter and place any marbles you wish to play with as targets inside the circle; the other players do the same. Shooters are designated marbles used to knock targets out of the ring. Your shooter should be larger than the other marbles so it's powerful enough to do its job. It should also look different from other marbles so you can distinguish it from them easily.

3   Take your turn when the time comes by shooting your marble from outside the ring at any marble or marbles inside the ring. Shoot by kneeling on the ground and flicking your marble out of your fist with your thumb.

4   Gather any marbles you've knocked out of the ring.

5   Shoot again if you knocked any marbles out of the ring. Let the next player shoot if you haven't knocked any marbles out and/or your shooter remains in the ring.

6   Continue shooting in turn until the ring is empty.

7   Count your marbles at the end of the game. The winner is the player with the most marbles.

8   Return the marbles to their original owners unless you're playing "keepsies". In that case, each player keeps the marbles he or she won during the game.

### ✳ Tips

These are the rules for a version of "ring taw" marbles, an older, more common variant. There are many other ways to play.

One way to decide playing order is called "lagging". The players line up opposite a line 3 m (10 ft) away (the "lag line") and shoot their marbles at it. The player whose marble ends up closest to the line goes first, the next closest goes second, and so on.

# ✓ 478 Choose Gifts for Kids of All Ages

Are birthdays or holidays approaching? Use this chart to help you find the right gift for everyone on your list – but don't follow it too rigidly. Children develop at different rates, and any of the gifts may interest either gender, so check both columns and adjacent ages. Be careful buying toys for children under 3, as they tend to put everything into their mouths.

| AGE | FEMALE | MALE |
|---|---|---|
| One | Board books shape sorters, clothes, blocks, push toys, hammer and pegs, stuffed animals | Board books, shape sorters, clothes, blocks, noise makers, sit and ride toy, hammer and pegs |
| Two | Sponges and toys for the bath, a bucket and spade for the beach, toy buggy, play cooking set, doll, tricycle, jigsaws, modelling clay, picture books | Tricycle, play cooking set, picture books, wooden cars, sand box, jigsaws, sponges and toys for the bath, modelling clay, building bricks |
| Three | Simple memory games, doctor's kit, picture books, clothes for dressing-up, bicycle with stabilisers, modelling clay, play cooker, shop or till | Train set, toy earth mover for a sand box, toy car to ride in, clothes for dressing-up, picture books, play cooker, shop or shop, simple memory games |
| Four | Board game, tea party set, alphabet puzzles, an outing to the park or zoo, picture books, puppets, garden slide, climbing frame, chalks and crayons | Glow-in-the-dark stars; action figures; pyjamas with a favourite animal; alphabet puzzles; blocks or magnets; trucks or trains; picture books |
| Five | Painting set, dollshouse, gift certificate for clothes, lunch box, marbles, insect-collecting kit, sticker set, puzzles, books, CD-Roms, puppets, music | CD-Roms, books, music, sports equipment, simple board games, activity kits, school supplies, puzzles, paints, puppets, marbles, play castle |
| Six | Childproof camera, small basketball, concentration game, swimming or gymnastics lessons, books, board games, educational games, crafts set | Kite, soccer or swimming lessons, electric trainset, school supplies, books, crafts set, board games, educational games |
| Seven | Books, garden basketball hoop, make-up kit, computer game, trip to the cinema or theme park, card game, board game, watch | Rocket or car model kit, board game, outing to a sporting event or theme park, books, card game, garden basketball hoop, computer game, watch |
| Eight | Kids' magnetic poetry kit, electronic memory game, board game, watch, personal radio, posters for room, mystery novels | Remote-controlled aeroplane, computer game, sporting equipment, adventure and suspense books, watch, board game, posters for room |
| Nine | Three-dimensional puzzle, bath gel, make-your-own-jewellery kit, book on horses, inflatable furniture, kite, CDs, clothes, diary | Construction kit, radio-controlled helicopter, mini-planetarium, book about astronomy, adult-level puzzles, diary |
| Ten | Diary, chess set, manicure set, "young adult" book, trendy clothes, tape recorder, teen music, school supplies, computer game, kids' cookbook | Word game, kids' cookbook, aquarium, whale- or bird-watching trip, ship-model kit, radio-controlled plane, clothes, school supplies, computer game |
| Fifteen | Magazine subscription; day-planner; address book; software; camera; portable CD player; record tokens which cover CDs; tickets to a theme park, cinema or sporting event; perfume; sunglasses; watch; hair accessories; cosmetics; earrings; cash | Magazine subscription; day-planner; address book; software; camera; portable CD player; record token; tickets to a theme park, a cinema or a sporting event; battery-operated games; cologne; penknife; tools; cash |
| Twenty-five | Clothes; record tokens which cover CDs; gym membership; luggage; gift certificate for a massage, facial, manicure or pedicure; tennis lessons; TV; VCR; aromatherapy candles; perfume; cosmetics; jewellery; bottle of wine, personal stereo | Personal stereo, record tokens which cover CDs or dinner at a favourite restaurant, concert tickets, tickets for a sporting event, clothes, TV, VCR, beer-of-the-month club membership, something for his car or computer, gym membership |
| Sixty-five | Gift certificate for hair styling, manicure or pedicure; gift basket of "splurge" foods; jewellery; magazine subscription; family portrait; home-made gifts from her grandchildren; membership of an organisation such as the National Trust | Gift certificate to a local restaurant or cinema, round of golf or a fishing trip, a year's pass to a museum or art gallery, magazine subscription, book, prepaid tickets to the local car wash, family portrait, point-and-shoot camera |

chart

## 479 | Juggle

Juggling is a matter of learning to catch and throw at the same time. Work up from one ball to two balls to three balls.

### ⊙ Steps

1 Hold a ball in your right hand.

2 Be aware that as you juggle, you'll be moving your hands in two independent circles – your right hand clockwise and your left hand anti-clockwise. The left hand lags about half a rotation.

3 Throw the ball with your right hand so that the apex – the highest point – of its path is about head-high.

4 Catch the ball as it drops into your left hand, then throw it up again, catching it with your right hand. Practise this manoeuvre until you go blind with boredom.

5 Proceed with a ball in each hand and continue as you did with one ball, throwing the second ball just as the first reaches its apex, and catching each ball with the other hand.

6 Practise with two balls until you feel confident. Try starting with the left hand once you've mastered starting with the right.

7 Add a third ball by starting with two balls in your right hand and one ball in your left hand.

8 Begin as you did with two balls, by throwing one of the balls from your right hand and then throwing the ball from your left hand when the first ball reaches its apex.

9 Catch the first ball with your left hand.

10 Throw the third ball (from your right hand) when the second ball reaches its apex.

11 Catch the second ball in your right hand.

12 Throw the first ball from your left hand as the third ball reaches its apex.

13 Catch the third ball in your left hand.

14 Keep throwing each ball just as the ball thrown from the opposite hand reaches its apex. You will always have at least one ball in the air, and you will never have more than one ball in either hand.

### ✳ Tips

Juggle facing a wall to keep the balls from running away from you. Also, try juggling things that don't bounce – such as bean bags – so you don't have to chase after them.

Stand over your bed or sofa while juggling so you don't have to bend down as far to retrieve dropped balls.

If you're having trouble reacting quickly enough, try throwing the balls higher to give yourself more time to catch them.

## 480 | Walk on Stilts

Stilt-walking is an ancient art that only requires a pair of stilts, optional protective padding and lots of practice. Soon you'll be able to view the world from a whole new perspective.

### ⊙ Steps

1 Begin with a low pair of stilts that places your feet about 30 cm (1 ft) off the ground. If you're concerned about injuring yourself in a fall, you might also want to wear a helmet and protective padding on your knees, elbows and wrists.

### ✳ Tips

Learn how to fall correctly. You want to curve yourself inwards a little and try to land on a wide part of your body, such as your shoulders, which can better absorb the impact.

**How to Do (Just About) Everything**

2   Select a firm, even surface on which to walk – the stilts could sink into softer ground, making them difficult to manoeuvre. Also, try to position yourself next to a wall that you can use as support, or between two low surfaces that you can use to prop yourself up, the way a gymnast uses parallel bars.

3   Make sure you have someone to "spot" (or catch) you who can handle your entire weight. Alternatively, string a rope tightly across your training area at the level where your hands will be when you're on stilts. Use this for support and balance.

4   Grasp one stilt in each hand, set one foot on the little ledge sticking out from one stilt, and straighten your leg. Have your spotter prop you up if need be.

5   Once the first stilt feels secure, raise your other foot on to the second stilt and straighten this leg.

6   Practise stepping in place to get a feel for lifting your legs with the stilts properly. Begin walking only after you feel comfortable taking steps.

7   Take your first step forwards and then keep moving – it's easier to keep your balance that way.

8   Pretend you're marching – picking up each stilt high as you walk – so you don't trip on bumps on the ground.

9   Practise until you feel comfortable.

10  Progress to taller stilts as you feel ready.

Take slow, small steps in the beginning to avoid "the splits".

---

# View a Lunar Eclipse                                          481

A lunar eclipse occurs when the sun, earth and moon are aligned so that the earth partially or totally blocks the sun's rays from reaching the moon, casting it in shadow.

## ⊙ Steps

1   Consult an astronomy field guide, telephone hotline or website, or check with local weather forecasts for the date and time of an upcoming lunar eclipse. On average, lunar eclipses occur at least twice a year, but the majority are not total eclipses, nor are they visible everywhere.

2   Go to the darkest place possible on the appointed night, as far away from streetlights and city lights as possible. Although the moon is widely visible, you'll enhance your view by eliminating any extra light.

3   Place a blanket on the ground.

4   Lie on your back and look up at the moon; binoculars will magnify your view but are not essential.

5   Observe the umbra, or darker part of the earth's shadow, as it slowly starts to cover an edge of the moon.

6   Watch the shadow gradually cover more and more of the moon.

7   Expect the disk of the moon to be dark and reddish when the eclipse is complete. For the next hour or two, gradually less and less of the moon will be in shadow.

## ✳ Tips

An entire lunar eclipse usually takes at least a few hours. Most people are content to watch just the beginning of the eclipse plus the moment of totality if it's a total eclipse.

Remember to bundle up or even take a sleeping bag if the weather is going to be chilly. You'll lose body heat very quickly lying quietly on the ground.

## Things You'll Need

❏ blanket or sleeping bag

❏ binoculars (optional)

## 482 | View a Partial Solar Eclipse

In a solar eclipse, the moon moves between the sun and the earth. Here's how to view solar eclipses with an indirect viewing system – never look directly at the sun.

### ⊙ Steps

1   Pick a viewing area that's not too crowded and has a good view of the sky. Visit the site beforehand to make sure no trees or buildings will block your view of the eclipse.

2   Punch a small hole into the centre of a white piece of cardboard with a sharp pencil or a pin. The hole should be about the size of a pencil point. Thick paper will also work if cardboard is unavailable, but make sure it is opaque.

3   Turn your back to the sun during the eclipse, and hold the punched cardboard about 45 cm (1½ ft) above a second sheet of cardboard. The sun should be shining through the hole in the cardboard.

4   Adjust the distance between the sheets to get a clear, sharp image of the eclipse. Moving the sheets closer to each other will give you a smaller, sharper image.

5   View the eclipse as it occurs by looking at the image projected on to the second piece of cardboard. As the moon moves across the sun, a similarly shaped shadow will move across the bright disc of the sun's image on the cardboard.

### ✷ Tip

Most solar eclipses are partial, occurring when the moon crosses the sun only part way. Total solar eclipses occur when the moon passes directly in front of the sun; they last only a few minutes. In annular solar eclipses, the moon passes in front of the sun but is too far from earth to cover the sun's disc. This creates a dark circle in the middle of the sun, surrounded by a bright ring.

### ⚠ Warning

Never look directly at the sun during a solar eclipse.

### Things You'll Need

❑ 2 pieces of white cardboard

❑ sharp pencil or pin

## 483 | Bird-Watch

Bird-watching is one of the fastest-growing hobbies in Britain. If you're looking for a new pastime, join the ranks of amateur ornithologists, or "twitchers".

### ⊙ Steps

1   Choose a beginner's field guide that covers the birds of Britain.

2   Study the book and learn the characteristics of different bird families.

3   Use the book's range maps and identify the birds of your region.

4   Invest in a pair of binoculars to help you see birds more closely.

5   Begin to identify the larger birds that you see in your garden with the naked eye.

6   Try to identify smaller birds, such as blue tits and robins.

7   Start a journal listing the birds you have seen and positively identified. List the bird type, location and date.

8   Expand your bird-watching explorations from your garden to local parks, coastal locations such as cliffs and marshes, and other habitats such as moors or woodland. Continue to keep lists and notes on birds seen.

9   Join a bird-watching club to further expand your horizons.

10  Plan bird-watching trips to other countries.

### ✷ Tip

Find out if there are daytime or evening classes in bird-watching available in your area. Also check for local expert-led bird-watching excursions.

### Things You'll Need

❑ bird field guide

❑ binoculars

❑ notebook and pen

## Make a Simple Bird Feeder      484

You don't need to spend a lot of money on a fancy bird feeder to attract feathered visitors to your garden. Try this easy make-it-yourself model.

### ◉ Steps

1 Wash an empty 4-pint plastic milk bottle thoroughly, removing any milk residue from it.

2 Put the cap on.

3 Stand the milk bottle right side up on your work surface.

4 Cut large holes – about 8 to 10 cm (3 to 4 in) in diameter – in two adjacent sides of the bottle opposite the handle. Cut the holes in the middle of the side and high enough that the seed won't spill out of the container when you put it in.

5 Use a large nail to punch a smaller hole below each of the large holes, and insert a dowel, which the birds will use for perching, through diagonally. The perch should be long enough to stick out about 5 cm (2 in) on both sides to provide perching spots for your birds.

0 With the large nail, punch two holes in the neck of the milk jug, about 2.5 cm (1 in) below the cap.

7 Run a 60 cm (2 ft) piece of wire through these two holes, twisting the wire tightly above the cap with several turns.

8 Fill the feeder with birdseed and use the wire ends to hang it from a strong branch or other support.

### ✳ Tip

Clean your bird feeder every time you change the seed or whenever the seed gets wet.

### ⚠ Warnings

Adults should supervise children using scissors, nails and wire.

Make sure that the feeder is located in an area safe from the local cats. Try to place it so it's inaccessible to squirrels.

### Things You'll Need

❏ 4-pint plastic milk bottle

❏ scissors

❏ large nail

❏ dowel or smooth stick

❏ thin but sturdy wire

❏ birdseed

## Make a Snowman      485

Building a snowman provides an entertaining, creative way to enjoy classic winter weather. You'll need a reasonable fall of snow on the ground; wear gloves or mittens.

### ◉ Steps

1 Test to see if you have "packing snow", which clumps together easily and isn't too wet. The snow must pack to make a snowman.

2 Shape a handful of snow into a ball. Continue adding more snow and packing the ball until it's too large to hold.

3 Place the ball on the snow in front of you and slowly roll it away from you. As more snow accumulates on the outside of your ball, pack the snow by pressing on it with your gloved hands.

4 Roll and pack the ball over and over until it is the size you want for the bottom of the snowman's body.

5 Repeat for the midsection and head. The bottom should be the biggest ball, and the top should be the smallest.

### ✳ Tips

If you're having a hard time rolling and packing the snow into sections, try using buckets. Find three that are of descending size and pack them with snow, then upend them, dumping the snow from one bucket on top of the other.

Your snowman's days are numbered, so take plenty of pictures.

6   Pack some extra snow between the layers to make them stick together. Place sticks down the centre where the sections meet if your snowman is having trouble standing erect.

7   Give the snowman a face. Use coal, stones, buttons or anything dark and round for the eyes. A horizontal stick or twig will make a good mouth, and a carrot is fine for the pointy nose. If you don't have a carrot, a banana will do the job.

8   Cover the top of his head with an unwanted plant for hair, or give him a knitted hat to wear. Top hats will blow away unless secured.

9   Add arms, legs and other accessories. Push sticks into the sides of the middle section and hang old mittens on the ends, then place boots at the bottom for legs. Also consider adding items such as a shirt, a scarf or a pair of sunglasses.

## Things You'll Need

❑ gloves or mittens

❑ coal, stones or buttons

❑ stick or twig

❑ carrot

❑ hat

❑ other accessories

---

## 486  Build a Sandcastle

Indulge your artistic side and create medieval fantasies by building your very own sandcastle.

### ⊙ Steps

1   Draw a rough sketch of the castle you'd like to build.

2   Choose a spot near the water, but not so close that waves will destroy your castle as the tide comes up. Make sure you have enough room for your castle plans.

3   Dig a hole down to the water table, where the sand is dark and moist, or bring up large buckets of water from the sea.

4   Scoop wet sand on to the centre of the area in which you'll be working. Work fast so the sand stays wet.

5   Build towers by forming and stacking sand patties about the size and shape of thick pancakes. Place larger patties on the bottom, and gently shake the patties from side to side as you pile them so that the sand settles. Seal your towers by gently pouring water over them.

6   Build walls to connect the towers of your castle by jiggling – gently shaking from side to side – wet sand into brick shapes and laying them on top of each other.

7   Carve the towers and the walls into shapes using tools such as a small trowel, a putty knife or plastic utensils.

8   Dig a moat around the castle to protect it from invaders.

### ✴ Tips

Extremely wet sand is easiest to work with. Use a spray bottle to wet down the sand if your castle begins to dry and crumble during construction.

Be sure to jiggle the sand while building, as pounding, beating or pushing the sand might destroy your castle. Another popular method is the drip method, where you squeeze a fistful of extremely wet sand and let it drip out of your hand into piles.

### Things You'll Need

❑ paper and pencil

❑ shovel or trowel

❑ buckets

❑ putty knife or plastic utensils

❑ spray bottle

## Skip Stones 487

Nothing accompanies deep thought better than skipping stones across a body of water.

### ⊙ Steps

1 Select a stone that's round, flat and smooth.

2 Stand at the edge of a large, placid body of water.

3 Hold the stone horizontally – flat side down – with your index finger curling around one edge.

4 Aim the stone, ensuring there is no one near your line of fire.

5 Throw the stone low and parallel to the water's surface. Throw sidearm so that your hand travels past your waist and the stone travels horizontally across the water.

6 Release the stone with a snap of the wrist to give it a horizontal spin. Your elbow will be next to your hip as the stone leaves your hand.

7 Count the number of times the stone skips.

### ✳ Tips

The harder you throw the stone, the higher it may ricochet after the first skip. Three or more skips is very good. Eight is extraordinary. More than 12 is mythical.

You want the flat part of the rock to skip along the water's smooth surface.

## Find Fossils 488

Fossil collecting is an excellent pastime for adults and children alike. You aren't likely to find a dinosaur, but with the right approach you will find fossils that are as old as the dinosaurs – or even older.

### ⊙ Steps

1 Start by doing some research, to find out where fossils are to be found in your area or the area where you're holidaying. Get hold of geological maps or books on the geology of the area, either from a bookshop or your local library. Or visit websites such as www.discoveringfossils.co.uk that give information on fossil-rich sites around Britain.

2 Choose the location for your fossil hunt. Note the characteristics of the site and consider how it affects the clothing and equipment you need – if the fossils are embedded in mud you will need wellington boots and a trowel, while for fossils found in cliff faces and quarries you will need a hammer and chisel, goggles to guard your eyes from rock chips, and possibly a hard hat to protect against falling rocks.

3 Pack a strong bag with a notepad and pen, a camera, a magnifying hand lens, your trowel and/or hammer and chisel, a map of the area, a selection of plastic bags, some newspaper or kitchen paper, and protective clothing if necessary.

4 If the site is on the coast, check the times of high and low tide; it is best to search for fossils when the tide is going out.

5 Look around the site on arrival and try to locate the likeliest places for finding fossils. At seaside locations, examine the surface of flat rocks extending from the bottom of cliffs across the beach, or scour the high-tide line where fossils washed from the cliff tend to accumulate.

### ⚠ Warnings

Searching for fossils at the foot of cliff or quarry faces is a hazardous activity that should not be undertaken without the wearing of a hard hat.

Be sparing in the removal of fossils. They are generally best left where they are.

Do not use a hammer and chisel unless absolutely necessary, and if you do, wear goggles to guard your eyes against rock chips.

### Things You'll Need

❑ stout bag

❑ notepad and pen

❑ map

❑ magnifying lens

❑ hammer and chisel (optional)

❑ hard hat (optional)

❑ trowel

6   When you find some fossils, examine them with your lens, photograph them in position and make a note of your find in your notebook.

7   If you decide to collect a fossil, remove it from its surroundings with great care. Always leave a generous margin of rock or sedimentary material around the fossil when you lift it out.

8   Wrap the fossil in newspaper or other protective wrapping and then place it in a plastic bag.

❑ newspaper for wrapping

❑ plastic bags

---

## 489  Make Papier-Mâché Paste

Making a figurine, dinosaur or bowl is fun, easy and economical with papier-mâché. The first step is mixing up the paste, which helps to hold all the newspaper strips together.

### ◉ Steps

1   Gather all your materials and spread a plastic cover over your work area, including the floor.

2   Pour equal parts of flour and water into a plastic bucket or bowl and blend with a mixing spoon. The amount you make depends on the size of the project. Two cups each of flour and water is good for a smaller project; you can always make more if you run out.

3   Add flour to thicken the mixture or water to thin it until you reach the desired consistency – a smooth liquid with no lumps. The paste should stick smoothly to paper strips without dripping off.

4   Add salt to the paste to keep it from getting mouldy; add white glue for extra stickiness.

**Things You'll Need**

❑ all-purpose flour

❑ water

❑ mixing spoon

❑ plastic bucket or bowl

❑ salt

❑ white glue

---

## 490  Make a Papier-Mâché Bowl

Use a bowl of almost any shape or size as a mould for this papier-mâché creation, as long as it's completely concave.

### ◉ Steps

1   Choose a bowl for your mould, and spread a thin, even coat of petroleum jelly on the inside of it. This will prevent the paper from adhering to the inside of the bowl.

2   Tear newspaper into strips 5 to 7.5 cm (2 to 3 in) wide. Each strip should be long enough to cover the interior of the bowl from rim to rim and extend about 5 cm (2 in) past the rim at each end.

3   Make papier-mâché paste (see 489 "Make Papier-Mâché Paste").

4   Coat one newspaper strip at a time with the paste. Dip it into the bowl of paste and then run the strip through your fingers to ensure an even coating and get rid of excess paste.

**✳ Tips**

Have a rag handy to keep your hands clean while you work. It will be difficult to run the strips through your fingers if you allow paste to build up on them.

You can use a variety of concave or cylindrical household containers to create other papier-mâché vessels.

5  Cover the interior of the bowl with the strips, placing each strip in the bowl as soon as it's dipped. Start at the centre of the bowl and work outwards, placing the strips all the way across the bowl; each strip should overlap the previous strip by about 2.5 cm (1 in).

6  Repeat the previous step six or seven times, making crisscrossed layers. After you lay down one layer, turn the bowl 90 degrees and lay down another layer. The number of layers you need depends on how large a bowl you're making – a larger bowl requires more layers. Allow the paper to dry at room temperature for 36 to 48 hours.

7  Remove the paper bowl from the mould; use a butter knife to gently loosen it from the mould, if necessary. Place it upside down to continue drying on a baking rack, and let it dry at room temperature for another 12 hours or so.

8  Use scissors to trim the bowl's rim evenly to the desired width.

9  Lightly smooth the interior and exterior of the bowl with sandpaper.

10  Paint the bowl with two coats of a solid-colour tempera or other water-based paint – white makes a good primer. When that's dry, paint your designs on the bowl and lightly apply a protective varnish, if desired.

## Things You'll Need

- ❏ bowl
- ❏ vaseline
- ❏ newspapers
- ❏ papier-mâché paste
- ❏ scissors
- ❏ sandpaper
- ❏ tempera or other water-based paint
- ❏ varnish (optional)

---

## Make Beanbags 491

Small, easy-to-make beanbags can help kids learn how to play catch. Plus, they put your scrap fabric to good use. Follow these steps to make 10 small beanbags.

### ◉ Steps

1  Start with your own fabric scraps, or search through the remnant bins at fabric stores to find suitable material. Any sort of closely woven fabric will do. To make 10 beanbags 10.2 cm (4 in) square, you'll need approximately 45 cm (½ yd) of 1.1-m (45-in) wide fabric.

2  Purchase enough filling material for the desired number of bags. Use fibrefill or plastic pellets sold especially for beanbags. These items can be found at most fabric and craft stores.

3  Use a yardstick or ruler to draw an 11.4-cm (4½-in) square on heavy paper or cardboard (the extra margin on each side is for stitching together the edges). Cut out this square to use as your template.

4  Iron your fabric, if necessary, and lay it down on a flat surface, wrong side up.

5  Place your template on the fabric and use a fabric-marking pen or chalk to trace 20 squares. Use scissors to cut out the squares.

6  Pin two pieces of fabric together to make one beanbag, right sides together (inside out).

7  Use a sewing machine to stitch a 60 mm (¼ in) seam – that is, 60 mm (¼ in) from the edge – around the edges of the fabric square, starting 2.5 cm (1 in) from any corner. When you reach a corner, keep the needle inserted in the fabric, lift the presser foot of your sewing machine and swivel the fabric 90 degrees. Then release the presser foot and sew the

### ✱ Tips

Make your bags from a variety of fabrics. The total quantity needed does not have to come from just one piece of fabric.

Make your beanbags any size you desire. Just be sure to make your template slightly larger all around – for the seam allowance.

Avoid using beans, rice or birdseed for bag filling. These items can work very well as filling but they have a tendency to attract insects.

## Things You'll Need

- ❏ fabric
- ❏ fibrefill or plastic pellets
- ❏ heavy paper or cardboard
- ❏ fabric-marking pens or chalk
- ❏ scissors
- ❏ dressmaker's pins
- ❏ sewing machine or needle and thread

next side. Stop sewing 5 cm (2 in) short of where you began, to allow an opening that will let you turn the bag right side out.

8  Turn your bag right side out at the 5 cm (2 in) seam opening, and fill your bag with the fibrefill or pellets.

9  Use a needle and thread or a sewing machine to stitch up the opening.

10  Repeat steps 6 to 9 to make the remaining beanbags.

## 492 | Make a Beaded Necklace

You only need a few items to complete this necklace. Once you're done, you'll have the basic skills necessary to tackle more complex beading and jewellery projects.

### ◉ Steps

1  Choose a length for your necklace and purchase that much beading thread, plus a few extra centimetres.

2  Make sure you have enough beads, including spacer beads (the small beads that go between the larger beads). You will also need a clasp and two bead tips, which are used to secure the ends of your necklace so that the clasp can be attached.

3  Lay your beads out on a flat surface, on top of a towel to keep them from rolling away. Determine the design of your necklace and in what order the beads will be strung.

4  Knot a thread end and use scissors to trim off the excess thread. The knot should be at the very end of the thread, but not so close that it runs the risk of unknotting.

5  Push the unknotted end of your thread through one open end of the bead tip and thread it through the hole. Pull the thread all the way through so that the knot you made rests firmly against the hole.

6  Place a small amount of craft glue on the knot to keep it from coming undone, and allow it to dry.

7  String your beads and then thread on the other bead tip so that the open end of the tip faces away from the strung beads.

8  Tie a loose knot in the thread end and use a long, straight pin to push the knot down into the open end of the bead tip. The knot should rest securely against the hole. Trim the excess thread and use pliers to close the bead tip.

9  Affix one clasp piece on to one bead tip hook so that the loops at the end of each are joined. Use the pliers to close one ring over the other. Repeat with the remaining clasp piece at the other end of the necklace.

### ✱ Tips

Look for bead tips under the name "clam shells" or "oyster shells", so named because of their shape.

Use a double strand of beading thread for extra strength.

Place glue along 2.5 to 5 cm (1 to 2 in) at the end of your thread before stringing the beads and allow it to dry. This will stiffen the thread end and make the beads a lot easier to string.

### Things You'll Need

❑ beading thread

❑ beads

❑ jewellery clasp

❑ 2 bead tips

❑ towel

❑ scissors

❑ craft glue

❑ straight pin

❑ pliers

## Make Salt Dough Badges     `493`

Salt dough is easy to make and use. Roll it out like pastry and then cut out whatever shapes you fancy. Once you've baked the dough shapes, paint them in bright colours, fix badge findings to the backs and decorate your jumper or coat.

### ⊙ Steps

1. In a mixing bowl stir together 100 g (3½ oz) salt with 340 g (12 oz) of sieved plain flour.

2. Gradually add 225 to 350 ml (4 to 6 pt) of lukewarm water, stirring all the time.

3. When you have a soft dough, knead it for 5 minutes until smooth and then place in a plastic bag for half an hour to settle before using.

4. Draw the shapes you want for your badges on a piece of card. These might include fish, birds, wild animals, cats and dogs, flowers, musical instruments, trains, cars and buses, the moon, faces, hearts. Cut out your chosen shapes to make templates.

5. With a rolling pin, roll out a sheet of salt dough to about 1 cm (2½ in) thick. Place your templates on top of the dough.

6. Cut around the templates with a knife. Mark any details within the shape, such as wheels, windows, or facial features with the knife.

7. Put the dough shapes on a baking tray and bake them for ½ hour to 1½ hours at 170°C (360°F) or Gas Mark 2. Tap them to check if they're ready: if they sound hollow, they're done.

8. Leave the shapes to cool. Then paint the fronts. First give them a coat of white emulsion to provide a smooth, white surface on which to paint your design. Then, using acrylic, emulsion or poster paints and the appropriate sized round paintbrushes, paint your design carefully.

9. Let the last paint application dry. Then, coat with polyurethane varnish to create a glossy finish and prevent the paint from chipping off.

10. Finally, using a strong craft glue, stick a badge pin-clip to the back of each shape. Once that's dry, they're ready to wear.

### ✳ Tips

Clean your brushes in plenty of water before applying each coat of different-coloured paint, or you'll create a muddy effect.

### ⚠ Warning

Before varnishing your badges, make sure the room is well ventilated. Varnish can be dangerous if you breathe in too much of it. Open a window if in doubt.

### Things You'll Need

- ❏ 100 g (3½ oz) salt
- ❏ 340 g (12 oz) plain flour
- ❏ 225–350 g (4–6 pt) water
- ❏ sheet of card
- ❏ mixing bowl, wooden spoon and knife
- ❏ range of paintbrushes
- ❏ acrylic, poster or emulsion paints
- ❏ polyurethane varnish
- ❏ craft glue
- ❏ badge pin-clips

## Make Bubble Mix     `494`

Reuse bubble jars and blowers again and again by making your own bubble mix. For just a few pence, you can make enough mix to fill an entire afternoon with bubbly fun.

### ⊙ Steps

1. Combine 125 ml (4 fl oz) washing up liquid, 2 tsp. sugar and 300 ml (10 fl oz) water in a mixing bowl.

2. Mix gently. This recipe yields 425 ml (14 fl oz) of bubble mix.

3. Use immediately or store in a plastic container.

### ✳ Tips

This mixture is very sticky – it's best used outside.

Use baby shampoo in place of soap, if desired.

## 495 | Make a Giant Bubble Wand

A giant bubble wand is a big hit with kids and works on the same principle as the smaller, shop-bought versions. This wand is simple and quick to make.

### ◎Steps

1 Bend a wire clothes hanger into a circle; for large bubbles, the more perfect the circle, the better it works.

2 Twist the hook opposite the circle to form a handle.

3 Wrap the handle with insulating tape, taking special care to cover the wire's two sharp ends with tape.

4 Wrap the circle with cotton twine to absorb more soap mixture so you can make bigger bubbles.

### ✳ Tip

Use floral wire to make smaller wands with interesting shapes.

### Things You'll Need

☐ wire clothes hanger

☐ insulating tape

☐ cotton twine

## 496 | Make a Paper Aeroplane

You don't need to be a pilot to get an old-fashioned introduction to aviation. Grab a piece of paper and start flying jets in your own back garden.

### ◎Steps

1 Find a rectangular-shaped piece of paper. A sheet of computer printing paper or school notebook paper is a good size and weight.

2 Lay the paper on a table with one of the long edges closest to you.

3 Fold the paper in half lengthwise. When the two edges match up, use your thumbs to make a sharp crease along the fold.

4 Take the upper left corner of the top layer of paper and fold it diagonally down towards the first crease you made. When the edges match up, use your thumbs to make a sharp crease along the new fold, which should create a small triangular flap.

5 Turn the paper over.

6 Take the upper right corner of the top layer of paper and fold it diagonally towards you, until the edge lines up with the first crease you made. When the edges match, make a sharp crease along the new fold. (This is a mirror of what you did in step 4.)

7 Take the newly formed diagonal edge on the right side of the paper, and fold it straight down towards the first crease you made. When the edges match, make another sharp crease.

8 Turn the paper over, and again fold the diagonal edge down towards the first crease you made; make another sharp crease. The paper should now look like a triangle with a 90-degree angle.

9 Form the wings by flipping the airplane over and repeating steps 7 and 8.

10 Hold the paper in one hand along the first crease you made. Let the wings of the plane flare out.

### ✳ Tips

Experiment with the size and weight of the paper.

Experiment with the location of the tab.

Make sharp creases to ensure a good flight.

**How to Do (Just About) Everything**

11  At a point about 20 cm (4 in) from the nose of the plane, make a 1.3 cm (½ in) rip in the bottom part of the plane; make another rip 1.3 cm (½ in) behind it. Fold this tab up.

12  Hold the aeroplane near the tab and toss the plane with an overhand, horizontal forward motion.

## Fly a Kite                                                                   497

A windy day in the park might keep you from flying a paper aeroplane outdoors, but it could be the perfect day to practise launching a kite.

### ⊙ Steps

1  Check your local weather report to see if conditions are favourable for kite flying. Look for light to moderate winds if you're a beginner at kite flying, or gustier winds if you are more experienced. A wind speed of 8-24 kph (5-15 mph) is best for kite flying.

2  Find a large and windy open area free of trees and power lines – two things that are notoriously dangerous for kites and their owners.

3  Hold the kite in both hands and toss it lightly into the wind until the wind catches it. This works well when the wind is moderately strong.

4  Alternatively, let out a small length of kite string and, holding the string in your hand, run with the kite behind you until the wind lifts it.

5  Begin letting out string until the kite reaches a height with which you are comfortable. Good heights range from 15 to 30 m (50 to 100 ft).

6  Keep an eye on your kite, as it may come crashing down because of sudden changes in wind. If it dips, run or pull in the string a bit to give it some lift.

7  Bring the kite down by slowly winding the kite string around a kite spool.

8  Reach out and grab the kite before it hits the ground to avoid damaging it.

### ✱ Tips

Tighten the string around a spool and secure the spool to the ground if you want to tend to other activities.

Tie additional ribbon or strips of cloth to the tail to increase the stability of diamond kites in gusty winds.

### ⚠ Warning

Stay away from electricity power lines! If a kite becomes entangled, leave it there. And never fly your kite during a thunderstorm.

## Dry Flowers                                                                  498

Dried flowers are wonderful for year-round floral arrangements. You can dry flowers by hanging them or by placing them in a box of desiccant, which preserves the blossoms better.

### ⊙ Steps

#### Air-Dry Method

1  Pick flowers when their blossoms are half-open, and leave the flowers on their stems.

2  Strip the lower leaves from the stems; don't remove the leaves closest to the flower on the stem.

3  Gather 8 to 10 stems together, and tie them with string or secure them with rubber bands.

### ✱ Tips

Make floral arrangements out of dried flowers or use them in craft projects.

Rapid drying in a warm, dry and brightly lit place (near a sunny window, for example) will provide bright blossoms; slower drying in a more humid spot (for instance, near a water heater) will produce more muted colours.

4 Hang the bundle upside down in a well-ventilated area. After 10 days (in warm weather), the flowers should be dry. When drying multiple bundles of flowers, leave space between them to ensure thorough drying.

## Box Method

1 Line a box with fine, dry sand, borax or silica gel.

2 Place the whole heads of the flowers face down in the box. Dahlias, roses and zinnias dry well using this method.

3 Sift more sand or borax on to the flowerheads until they are covered.

4 Place the box in a warm, dry area for two weeks.

You can find borax in the laundry section of the grocery store.

### Things You'll Need

❑ flowers

❑ string or rubber bands

❑ box

❑ dry sand or borax

---

## 499 | Arrange Fresh Flowers

You don't have to have specialist equipment to arrange fresh flowers. Trust to your instinct and give your creativity free rein.

### ◉ Steps

1 Decide on the type of arrangement you want to create. Consider the impact of position on the size and shape of the arrangement. Do you intend to place it on a table, the floor or on a shelf? Will it be seen from all sides or just one? What colours will surround the arrangement?

2 Choose a container that coordinates with the surroundings in its colour and style, and choose flowers that complement the container.

3 Fill three quarters of the container with water and add a little bleach and sugar to it to help preserve the flowers.

4 Remove the lower leaves from the stems, where they will sit below the waterline, to prevent them from rotting. Cut the stems at the base at an angle and scrape away 5 cm (2 in) of each stem for quick water uptake.

5 Select just one or two types of flower or a variety of colours of the same type of flower. Set these off with some textural foliage, such as fennel.

6 Set the tallest stems at the centre of the arrangement and step down the lengths of the stems either side and to the front to create a flat-backed or all-round "fan shape".

### ✳ Tips

Do not be over-ambitious to start with. A simple display of red and pink roses in a china vase can look stunning on the windowsill.

Try to keep the arrangement in proportion. As a guideline, the tallest stem should be twice the height of the container.

---

## 500 | Hollow Out an Egg

Lots of egg-decorating projects call for hollow eggshells. After you empty the egg, save the white and yolk to make scrambled eggs, quiche or an omelette.

### ◉ Steps

1 Wash and dry a raw egg.

2 Insert a long needle into the large end of the egg to make a small hole. Twist the needle as you push it into the eggshell as far as you can while still grasping it.

### ✳ Tip

Save empty egg cartons for storing the hollow eggs before and after you decorate them.

3  Use the needle to make a slightly larger hole in the small end.

4  Push the needle into the center of the egg and move it around to break the yolk.

5  Hold the egg over a bowl with the small end down.

6  Place your lips over the hole at the large end of the egg and blow firmly until all the egg comes out of the hole at the small end.

7  Rinse out the egg by running a thin stream of water into the larger hole.

8  Blow out the water in the same way that you blew out the egg.

9  To dry the eggshell, prop it up in a dish drainer with the large end facing down.

⚠ **Warning**

Do not swallow any of the raw egg. Raw eggs can carry the salmonella bacteria, which can cause serious illness.

## Dye Polka Dot Eggs                                501

Save your used birthday candles to make these eye-catching polka dot eggs.

### ⊙ Steps

1  Hard-boil or hollow out several white eggs to decorate (see 500 "Hollow Out an Egg").

2  Lay out newspaper on your work area to protect it from dripping wax.

3  Choose your dye colours – you'll want a lighter base colour for the polka dots and a darker colour for the rest of the egg surface. Prepare the dye according to the directions on the package.

4  Dye the egg your base colour. It should be a light colour, such as yellow or pale pink.

5  Place the egg on a paper egg holder (see Tips) and let it dry thoroughly.

6  Light a candle. For this project, you will need the small candles that are sold as birthday candles.

7  Hold an egg in one hand and the lighted candle in the other.

8  Allow the melted candle wax to drip onto the egg, forming small circles of wax on the shell. Take care not to burn your fingers.

9  Turn the egg slowly so that the wax cools as you go and drips of wax cover the top half of the egg evenly, spacing the circles evenly apart to create a polka dot effect. It's difficult to control exactly where the drops of melted wax will fall on the egg. However, the spontaneity of the drops adds to the beauty of the finished egg.

10  Set the egg on a paper egg holder to allow the wax to cool and harden. You won't be able to wax the whole egg without burning your fingers, so do one end, let it dry, then repeat steps 7 to 9 to do the other.

11  Dye the egg with the darker colour to tint the surface that does not have wax on it.

12  Allow the egg to dry.

### ✳ Tips

You can make a simple egg holder by rolling up a strip of thick paper into a small cylinder about 5 to 7.5 cm (2 to 3 in) high and about 2.5 cm (1 in) in diameter and then securing it with tape. A section of a toilet paper roll could also work.

You can dye the egg more than two colours. Follow steps 1 to 12. Then scrape off some of the wax dots and dye the egg in the darkest colour before scraping away the remaining wax dots. A good dye sequence would be yellow, orange, red or yellow, green, blue.

### ⚠ Warnings

Handle burning candles with extreme caution. Both the flame and the hot wax can cause serious burns.

Never allow children to handle burning candles or matches.

13  Remove the wax by scraping it off with your fingernail if the egg is hard-boiled. Or, if you're using a hollowed-out egg, wrap the egg in foil and place it in the oven at 90°C (200°F) for 5 minutes, or until the wax softens. Then wipe off the wax with a paper towel.

**Things You'll Need**

❏ eggs

❏ egg-dye kit

❏ birthday candles

❏ matches

---

## 502 | Carve a Pumpkin

In recent years British parents have become used to their children demanding a carved pumpkin head at Halloween. This activity requires more tenacity than skill.

### ⊙ Steps

1  Select a fresh pumpkin in a shape that pleases you. Some people prefer their pumpkins low and round, while others like them tall and oval-shaped.

2  Draw a circle or hexagon on top of the pumpkin in preparation for making an opening large enough for your hand to reach through.

3  Cut through the stem end of the pumpkin along your outline with a sharp knife. Use a back-and-forth slicing motion to cut through the thick, tough skin.

4  Remove the stem end, which will act as a cap, making sure you scrape off any seeds or pulp.

5  Use a large spoon to scoop out the seeds and pulp from inside the pumpkin. Hold the spoon by its bowl to get a better grip while scooping.

6  Draw a pattern for the face on the clean pumpkin with a felt-tip pen, or scratch the lines into the skin using a pencil. Be sure to make the eyes, nose and mouth large enough; you'll have a hard time cutting out tiny features when you're using a big knife blade to saw through tough skin.

7  Follow your pattern as you cut all the way through the pumpkin.

8  Push out the cut-out features gently from the inside of the pumpkin and discard the pieces.

9  Place a candle inside the pumpkin to create an eerie glow.

**↑ ↑ ↑**

### ✱ Tips

Coat the cut edges with cooking oil to keep your jack-o'-lantern fresh longer.

During the Halloween season, some supermarkets sell sturdy plastic pumpkin-carving tools.

### ⚠ Warnings

Candles should be used with care, especially around children.

Always cut away from your body.

### Things You'll Need

❏ pumpkin

❏ sturdy, sharp knife

❏ large spoon

❏ felt-tip pen or pencil

❏ candle

---

## 503 | Carve a Fancy Pumpkin

With this technique, you remove the tough orange skin from some areas, and carve out other sections completely to let the light from a candle or small torch shine through.

### ⊙ Steps

1  Select a pumpkin with a smooth surface.

2  Draw a pattern on a separate piece of paper. Some suggestions are bats, skulls, spiders and ghosts.

**↑ ↑ ↑ ↑**

### ✱ Tips

A slip of the knife can sometimes be mended by pinning the skin back in place with a toothpick.

3   Cut away the top section of the pumpkin surrounding the stem, and remove any seeds and pulp from inside.

4   Follow the pattern and draw the design on the pumpkin, thinking about which areas you'll cut out completely, and where you'll remove just the orange skin. Areas where the orange skin is left in place will appear darker than those where the skin is removed. In the case of a ghost, for example, you would completely carve out the eye holes and perhaps a mouth, but remove only the pumpkin's skin in the area of the ghost body.

5   Cut an outline around your design using a sharp knife.

6   Remove the areas that are to be completely cut.

7   Cut around any raised areas, such as folds of fabric or spider legs.

8   Slowly and carefully remove the orange skin from the desired areas with a vegetable peeler or a specialised pumpkin-carving tool. Take your time, as this is the hard part. Variations in depth will create a more interesting design.

9   Place a candle or battery-powered light inside the pumpkin to create an eerie glow.

Try cutting off the bottom of the pumpkin and removing the insides from this end, especially if the pumpkin is lopsided or the stem is very small.

## ⚠ Warnings

Be extremely careful. Carving tools are sharp.

Be especially careful with candles near small children.

## Things You'll Need

❑ pumpkin

❑ sturdy, sharp knife

❑ vegetable peeler or special pumpkin-carving tool

❑ candle or small battery-powered light

---

# Make a Haunted House                                504

Create the spookiest entertainment in your street, and terrify children and adults alike on Halloween night.

## ◎ Steps

1   Find a safe place large enough to accommodate all the things you plan to do. You can use your house, basement, shed or garden.

2   Draw up a plan. Using a diagram of the space available, work out what you want to have in your haunted house and where it might go. Plan an entrance and an exit.

3   Do the hard stuff first. Order or construct props, including such items as fake headstones, guillotines and coffins.

4   Put the haunted house together. Make it dark using black plastic rubbish bags or blankets over windows, then add eerie lighting. Include lots of unexpected scary sounds and sensory experiences to startle visitors. Bear in mind the need for adequate ventilation.

5   Use peeled grapes as eyeballs, placing them where people will touch them in the dark. Use Styrofoam heads from a beauty supply house and turn them into monsters.

6   Spray visitors' faces with cold water in the dark, or have visitors walk through spider webs made of stretched cotton or wet string (be careful young children don't get entangled).

7   Create a bubbling-cauldron effect with the aid of dry ice. Fill a rubber glove with water coloured with food colouring and freeze it, then remove the glove and float the "frozen hand" in the cauldron.

## ✳ Tips

Start planning early in the year and gather or make the necessary items in time for Halloween.

Check out your local fancy-dress or novelty shop, or browse online to find items for your haunted house. If your local library has an audio section, you may find scary music there.

Mix citrus soda and blue punch for a bright green beverage.

## ⚠ Warnings

Small children may be terrified of the goings-on in a haunted house. Set an age range, or put up a sign warning children of the level of scariness within.

Do not allow dry ice to touch anyone's skin.

8   Invite several adults to participate with you. They can dress in costume and be part of the haunted house, but can also keep an eye on things and help supervise participants.

9   Advertise. Whether the haunted house is simply for trick-or-treaters in your street or a community affair, put up a sign telling kids where to find some haunted fun on Halloween.

Keep anything wet safely clear of electrical effects or outlets. Do not use any candles or other live flames.

Always remember: safety first.

---

## 505 | Create a Unique Halloween Costume

Forget the passé ghosts and goblins this year. Instead, fire up your imagination and create a costume that will be the talk of the town.

### ⊙ Steps

1   Toss out any clichés immediately. Forget anything related to traditional Halloween costumes, such as witches, werewolves and monsters.

2   Play off common words, titles or phrases in unexpected ways. For example, a surfer costume covered with fake spider webbing could be a "web surfer".

3   Make a list of themes that are unique to you. Play off your name, a nick-name, a personal legend or an unusual physical attribute.

4   Shop at charity shops. These treasure troves are home to some of the most unusual and useful clothes and accessories.

5   Use common household items to transform your look. Burn a piece of cork and rub it on your face for a 5 o'clock shadow, or use spirit gum to attach fake fur to your face for a beard.

### ✳ Tips

Consider dyeing old clothes or accessories to fit your costume. You'll save money and cut down on shopping time.

Surf the web, watch cartoons or check out your local bookshop for ideas to spark creativity.

---

## 506 | Make Scary Spiders

Spiders are easy to make using cardboard egg cartons. This project is easy for young children, although they'll need supervision when cutting or painting. One carton makes six spiders.

### ⊙ Steps

1   Spread several layers of newspaper on your work surface.

2   Cut or tear the top off an empty cardboard egg carton.

3   Paint the entire bottom of the egg carton, inside and out, using black tempera paint.

4   Let the paint dry for a few minutes, then cut the egg carton cells apart. Touch up the edges with black paint.

5   Turn the cells so the open side is down, and insert eight black pipe cleaners into each cell, four on each side. Bend the pipe cleaners to look like legs.

### ✳ Tip

Make several spiders and hang them together for a spooky effect, especially in low light.

### Things You'll Need

❑ cardboard egg carton

❑ black tempera or other water-based paint

❑ paintbrush

---

6   Glue on googly eyes from a craft shop, or make eyes for the spiders out of thick paper or card.

7   Hang each spider using a needle and piece of thread. Thread the needle and tie a knot at one end; then pierce it through the egg carton cell from the bottom. Use a light-coloured thread to make it less noticeable.

❑ black pipe cleaners

❑ glue

❑ googly eyes

❑ needle

❑ thread

---

# Make an Evergreen Wreath      507

Alongside the Christmas tree, wreaths are a traditional Christmas decoration. Wreaths are easy to make from common greenery found just outside your home.

## ◎ Steps

1   Gather a large shopping bag full of 15-cm (6-in) garden trimmings. Some suggested trimmings are cedar, pine, fir, magnolia and oak. Remember to include holly or other red berries in your collection. The tip ends of the branches work best.

2   Use a wire wreath frame or make your own from a wire coat hanger. (Simply unbend it from the familiar shape into a circle; you can use the hook to hang your finished wreath.)

3   Attach florist's wire anywhere along the wire wreath frame. Tie it to the frame at that point and keep unspooling it and wrapping as you go around the frame with the bundles of greenery.

4   Select several of the garden trimmings and place them together in a bunch with the stems at one end.

5   Place this bundle on top of the frame where the florist's wire is attached.

6   Hold the bundle in place and wrap the florist's wire around the bundle and frame. You will need two hands for this: one to hold the bundle in place against the frame and one to wrap the wire.

7   Wrap the florist's wire around the bundle a second time and then pull it tight. Make sure to leave the wire attached to the frame – you still have a long way to go.

8   Gather another bundle of foliage and place it so that the leaves overlap the first bunch and cover the stems. Make sure that the stems on both bunches face the same direction.

9   Continue overlapping the bunches of foliage and wiring them to the frame until you complete the circle.

10   Add pine cones by twisting a new piece of florist's wire around the base of the cone, leaving a tail of 20 to 25 cm (8 to 10 in). Tie the wired cone's tail to the wreath.

11   Lift the first bundle that you wired on to the frame and tuck the last bundle under it.

12   Twist the wire tightly around the last bundle. Knot the wire on to the frame, leaving enough wire to hang the finished wreath.

13   Trim the wire with scissors or pruning shears when you're finished.

## ✱ Tips

Thick bundles make fat wreaths. The more plant material you add, the fuller your wreath will appear.

Make a bright red bow and attach it with wire to the top of your wreath.

A wreath makes a striking gift for your hostess during the Christmas party season.

## ⚠ Warning

Once your family and friends see your wreath, they will all want one. Buy or make plenty of wreath frames to supply the overwhelming demand.

## Things You'll Need

❑ scissors or pruning shears

❑ garden trimmings

❑ wire wreath frame or wire coat hanger

❑ florist's wire

❑ pine cones

## 508 | Decorate a Christmas Tree

Decorating a Christmas tree can be huge fun – and all the family can join in. Decide together on the theme you would most like, then get collecting and making.

### ⊙ Steps

1   Decide on your colour theme. Do you want a traditional, vibrant red and green Christmas tree, a more sophisticated silver and green tree, or a flamboyant tree decorated with all the colours of the rainbow?

2   Decide on your decorative theme. Do you want to have an edible theme or a dried flower theme? Perhaps you would like to reflect a particular culture – Chinese or African, for example – and cover your tree with shop-bought and home-made decorations inspired by these cultures.

3   Select your Christmas tree lights to reflect your colour theme – tiny pin-pricks of silver light or more dominant red candle lights. Drape these over the tree, starting at the top and winding evenly down to the bottom.

4   Collect any shop-bought globes, chains and swags that appeal to you and that accord with your colour scheme or decorative theme.

5   Make paper chains out of gold or silver paper, tissue paper or crêpe paper, according to preference. Drape them on the tree.

6   Make a star template and cut out thick coloured card in star shapes. Paint these with designs of your choosing and fix loops to the top to hang them onto the tree.

7   Cut strips of ribbon and tie into bows. Wire these onto the branches of the tree.

8   Fix florist's wire to pine cones for hanging. Spray the cones with silver paint and dip them in glitter. When dry hang on the tree.

9   For an edible theme, make gingerbread men and biscuits, and decorate them with coloured icing. Thread cord through a hole at the top of each.

### ✱ Tips

Once you've decided on your colour scheme or decorative theme, stick to it.

### Things You'll Need

❑ Christmas tree lights

❑ paper, card and ribbon

❑ florist's wire

❑ spray paint and glitter

❑ gingerbread or biscuit ingredients

❑ thin cord

## 509 | Make a Snowman Pop-Up Card

Let your children send their own 3-D Christmas greetings with this easy pop-up card.

### ⊙ Steps

1   Use a blank greeting card or a piece of card stock that has been cut to the desired size and folded in half. A folded card measuring 15 cm by 20 cm (6 in by 8 in) works well for this project.

2   Draw or trace a snowman shape on to a separate piece of heavy white paper. Card stock or cardboard is best. The snowman should be one-half to three-quarters of the length of your greeting card and three-quarters of the width of the open greeting card.

3   Outline the snowman shape with a black felt-tip pen or permanent marker. Use crayons, acrylic paint or markers to decorate the snowman.

### ✱ Tips

Use a snowman-shaped biscuit cutter as a template. You can also make other shapes, such as a star, angel or heart to create pop-up cards.

Make sure that the tabs are the same colour as the interior of the greeting card. You may have to draw your snowman on a white piece of paper and then glue it on to paper that matches the greeting card.

4　Use a ruler and pencil to draw one vertical line along each side of the snowman. Place each line 5 cm (2 in) from the snowman's widest point.

5　Use scissors to cut along the outside of the snowman outline so that the black marks made in step 3 remain. Leave uncut the 5-cm (2-in) long tab of paper on the centre of each side of the snowman. Make sure both tabs are centred and even with each other. Note that if your card is smaller than 15 by 20 cm (6 by 8 in), make the tabs 2.5 cm (1 in) instead.

6　Fold the snowman in half vertically, blank sides together. Make a sharp crease and unfold. Fold the tabs on the sides of the snowman under by about 1 cm (1/2 in). Make a sharp crease.

7　Position the snowman over the open greeting card so that the snowman's centrefold lines up with the centre of the card; keep in mind that the snowman fold should oppose the card fold. Decide where to place the tabs depending on how far you want the snowman to pop up. Mark the two spots for the tabs with a pencil, making sure that they are equidistant from the edges.

8　Glue the folded-back portion of the tabs to the surface of the greeting card so that the pop up shape remains in the position decided in step 7. Allow the glue to dry.

### Things You'll Need

❏ card stock paper

❏ black felt-tip pen or permanent marker

❏ crayons, acrylic paints or markers

❏ ruler

❏ pencil

❏ scissors

❏ glue

---

# Make Pomanders　510

Pomanders – fruits studded with cloves – have been used for centuries for their fragrance. They will add a wonderful Christmas scent to your home.

### ⊙ Steps

1　Choose a variety of fruits for your pomanders. Apples, lemons, tangerines and oranges work best.

2　Use a toothpick or a wooden or metal skewer to pierce the skin of the fruit. Insert cloves into the fruit so that cloves form close, vertical rows. Make patterns with the cloves, if you desire. The goal is to cover the fruit with cloves as completely as possible.

3　Combine the powdered orrisroot, ground cinnamon, ground allspice and ground nutmeg in a large zip-up bag. (This mixture will cover approximately two pieces of fruit.)

4　Place the fruit in the bag, and roll the fruit around in the spice mixture. Cover the entire fruit with spices.

5　Remove the fruit from the bag and shake off excess spice powder.

6　Wrap the fruit in tissue paper and store in a cool, dry place for three to four weeks.

7　Unwrap the pomander and display as desired.

### ✱ Tips

Hang pomanders in doorways, on mantles or even on a Christmas tree.

Display four or five pomanders in a bowl filled with potpourri.

### Things You'll Need

❏ apples, lemons, tangerines or oranges

❏ toothpick or skewer

❏ cloves

❏ 1 tbsp powdered orrisroot

❏ 1 tbsp ground cinnamon

❏ 1 tbsp ground allspice

❏ 1 1/2 tsp ground nutmeg

❏ large zip-up bag

❏ tissue paper

## 511 Make Pot-Pourri

A fragrant mix of flower petals, herbs, spices and essential oils, pot-pourri is a decorative way of perfuming a room. The most simple method of making pot-pourri is to combine all the ingredients in a jar and leave to cure for 6 to 8 weeks.

### ⊙ Steps

1  Select and dry your preferred scented flowers or leaves. Perfumed roses and lavender are the most popular flowers to use as a basis for a pot-pourri mix but any fragrant flower or herb that appeals to you can be used, for example, lily-of-the valley, peonies, or rosemary.

2  Place the dried flower petals in a mixing bowl.

3  Add the fixative. Ground orris root, with its violet scent, and ground cinnamon are suggested here but you could use frankincense. Fixatives are in themselves aromatic and add to the overall bouquet of the pot-pourri but their main function is to hold the perfume of the flower petals.

4  Add the essential oil: lavender oil is used in this recipe but you could use any essential oil with a perfume you liked.

5  Transfer the mixture to a large storage jar. Seal the jar and store it in a dry place at room temperature for about 6 to 8 weeks. Shake the mixture daily to ensure the ingredients are well combined.

6  Place the mixture in a container of your choice and place in the room.

### ✳ Tips
Any fragrant petals are suitable for pot-pourri: experiment with different combinations of scents and colours.

### Things You'll Need
- ❑ 500 ml (1 pt) dried rose petals
- ❑ 500 ml (1 pt) dried lavender
- ❑ 1 tabsp ground cinnamon
- ❑ 1 tbsp ground orris root
- ❑ 8 drops lavender oil
- ❑ mixing bowl
- ❑ storage jar with lid
- ❑ container for display

## 512 Make Scented Sachets

Scented sachets, or sweet bags, have been used for centuries to perfume clothes in drawers and wardrobes. They not only infuse clothes with subtle scent but also help keep moths away.

### ⊙ Steps

1  Make a pot-pourri according to your preferred scent (see 511 "Make Pot-Pourri).

2  Choose a fabric for your sachets – cotton or linen are most popular. Select a fabric design that suits your taste.

3  Cut out two identical circles of the fabric, 10 cm (4 in) in diameter.

4  Place the two circles right sides together and stitch together neatly around the edges, leaving a small gap of 5 cm (2 in).

5  Turn the pouch the right way out and spoon in some pot-pourri mixture, being careful not to overfill the sachet.

6  Sew up the gap carefully and conceal with a hanging ribbon loop and bow. Use the loop to hang the sachet in a wardrobe.

7  Repeat until you have made all the scented sachets you require.

### ✳ Tips
To make these sachets even prettier, try edging them with lace.

### Things You'll Need
- ❑ length of cotton or linen fabric
- ❑ cotton and needle for sewing
- ❑ ribbon for decorating
- ❑ pot-pourri mix (see 511 "Make Pot-Pourri")

## Wrap a Gift                                    513

These instructions are for a rectangular gift box, but they can be applied to any size or shape of box.

### ⊙ Steps

1   Gather your materials and lay them out on a flat work surface. Remember to remove the price tag from the gift before wrapping it.

2   Place the box along the length of wrapping paper and unroll enough paper to wrap it around the box, leaving at least a 5 cm (2 in) overlap. Make sure there is enough wrapping paper at each end of the box to cover the ends completely when folded over them.

3   Use a pencil to mark where this overlap ends and cut the wrapping paper in a straight line at this point. Fold the paper or use a ruler to guide you in cutting a straight line.

4   Eyeball the wrapping paper at the ends of the box. Trim away any extra paper so that the remaining flaps are long enough to cover the box but short enough to fold over smoothly into flaps.

5   Open the paper you've just cut and lay the box in the centre of the unprinted side, top down.

6   Bring one lengthwise edge of the wrapping paper to the centre of the box and secure it with tape. Turn the opposite edge of the paper under approximately 2.5 cm (1 in) and bring this to the centre of the box as well so that it overlaps the first edge, and tape it down.

7   Position the box so that one short end is facing you. Grasp the left and right edges of the wrapping paper and push the sides in so that top and bottom flaps are formed. Make sure the edges are pushed in as far as they will go without ripping the paper. Tape the edges to the box.

8   Bring the upper flap down against the side of the box, making sure the flap is sharply creased at its folds. Tape the flap to the box.

9   Bring the lower flap up against the side of the box. Crease and secure it as you did the upper flap.

10  Repeat for the opposite end of the box.

11  Position the package so the seamless side is facing down.

12  Wrap a long piece of ribbon around the box lengthwise, then twist the ribbon at the lengthwise seam to wrap it around the box widthwise.

13  Turn the box over so that the seamless side is facing up and tie the ribbon into a bow on top of the present where the ribbons cross.

14  If you have a card, slide it under the ribbon and secure it with tape on the underside. If you have a gift tag, use the loose ends of the ribbon to secure the gift tag (if it has a hole in it), or stick it directly to the gift (if it has adhesive on it.)

### ❋ Tips

If your gift is not rectangular, find a box you can put it in to make it easier to wrap.

Check the label on any package of gift-wrapping paper to make sure there is enough paper to wrap your gift box.

Choose gift-wrapping paper that comes on a tube instead of precut sheets of paper that come folded into squares. The latter have deep creases, which can give your package a crumpled, untidy appearance.

Transparent cellophane tape, especially the nonglossy kind ("magic tape"), will give your package a tidier appearance than can be achieved with other types of tape.

### Things You'll Need

❑ wrapping paper

❑ pencil

❑ scissors

❑ transparent cellophane tape ("magic tape")

❑ ribbon

❑ card or gift tag

## 514 | Be Happy

Happiness has different meanings for everyone; we each have to define and seek it for ourselves.

### ⊙ Steps

1   Decide what is important to you in life. For example: Do you value a certain kind of job; material things; a relationship; time alone or with others; time to relax or to be creative; time to read, listen to music or have fun? These are just a few of the possibilities.

2   Think about times when you have felt happy, good, or content. Where were you? Whom were you with? What were you doing, thinking or experiencing that made you feel happy?

3   Decide to make more time in your life to do more of what is important to you and makes you feel happier. To be happy, you have to make happiness a priority in your life.

4   Start with little things and work up to bigger ones. Little things might include reading an engrossing book for 15 minutes; taking a walk; telephoning a friend; or buying scented soap, shampoo, candles or tea that you will enjoy every time you use them.

5   Focus on what is positive about yourself, others and life in general instead of dwelling on the negative. Write down as many positive things as you can think of in a journal. Keep it handy to read over and continue adding to it.

6   Appreciate what is working in your life at the moment. In the major areas of your life, such as your health, job, love life, friends, family, money and living situation, what is going well?

### ✱ Tips

Ask other people, "What makes you happy?" or "What is something that makes you feel good?"

It's OK to ask for professional help. Talk to someone, such as a psychotherapist, career counsellor or spiritual adviser (minister or teacher) to help you sort out what would make you happy.

Read books on the subject of happiness. Wise people have been writing about it for hundreds of years. In the bookshop, look under psychology, spirituality, or philosophy.

## 515 | Overcome Shyness

Everyone feels shy sometimes, but being too shy can hamper many aspects of your life.

### ⊙ Steps

1   Determine why you're shy in the first place. For example, are you afraid of what someone might say about your physical appearance? Remember, there's an underlying reason for how you react in situations.

2   Act as if you're not shy. In private, behave as if you're oozing confidence. Hold your chin up, stand up straight and tall, stride confidently and speak firmly. It may seem ridiculous, but you will see results when you're out in public.

3   Practise making eye contact and smiling when you have interactions with others. Strike up casual conversations with strangers about the weather or current events.

4   Look your best. One way to reduce self-consciousness is to always look good and limit opportunities for being self-critical.

### ✱ Tip

See 843 "Overcome a Phobia" for progressive relaxation techniques. These same steps can be applied to situations that cause you to feel shy.

5   Decrease your fear of rejection by imagining the worst possible out-come. If you approach someone, he or she may say no to your overture or may just walk away. Everybody has been rejected at some point, but no one has to dwell on it.

6   Look and learn. Watching friends or even strangers who aren't shy is a good way to learn some tips first-hand.

7   Develop a positive feeling about yourself, don't get frustrated, and have fun. Keep in mind that the real goal is to meet people who will like you for who you are.

## Find the Best Places to Meet People                    516

Still looking for the man or woman of your dreams? If you're wasting hours on end hanging out at the corner bar or the local gym, you might want to change your strategy.

### ⊙ Steps

1   Choose a place that interests you. This increases your chances of meet-ing people who are interested in similar things.

2   Be creative about where you go. Parties and other social gatherings are the most obvious places to make new acquaintances, but don't leave out other options, such as club meetings and classes.

3   Go academic: college and university are great places to meet people. Why not sign up for a summer school or evening classes.

4   Mingle: parties, dances and cinema queues are fun places to meet people who make an effort to go out.

5   Don't overlook opportunities in public places: supermarkets, laun-derettes, bookshops, cafés and restaurants are all casual spots to meet new people.

6   Ask around – friends and relatives are good sources for helping you meet other people.

7   Look around locally. Proximity plays a big part in friendships as well as romantic relationships, and you may find that the special someone you seek is right around the corner.

8   Look in your community. Familiar places like your church, synagogue or mosque are good venues for seeing who's out there.

9   Use the newspaper. Place a personal ad or respond to one.

10  Try meeting people online. There are numerous websites that feature chat rooms, personal ads and individual photos.

### ⚠ Warnings

If you meet a potential romantic partner at work, think carefully before proceeding – is it worth the possible complications?

Try not to seem desperate – people may find this unattractive.

## 517 | Flirt

**Not a natural flirt? Don't worry – anyone can learn the basic social skills that will attract others.**

### ⊙ Steps

1   Be confident – it's the magical charm that makes others want to get to know you.

2   Smile, smile, smile.

3   Think playful thoughts when gearing up to flirt. Flirts are fun and engaging, and they love to play with others.

4   Compliment a stranger or acquaintance on his or her clothes, eyes, smile or sense of humour, for starters.

5   Keep your body language open and inviting: make eye contact, lightly touch the person's hand or arm when telling a story, toss your head back when you laugh.

6   Initiate stimulating conversation. At a loss for words? Ask open-ended questions about the flirtee's job, home town, family, recent films seen or thoughts about a painting on the wall.

7   Open up about yourself, giving someone even more reason to like you. But don't go on and on – the goal is to engage and intrigue, not bore.

8   Gauge the person's interest carefully. If you sense a red light – or worse, smug ridicule – make your exit graciously and immediately. You've got nicer people to meet.

9   Progress in your flirtation, paying attention to cues from the object of your interest. If you perceive a sensual or sexual connection, make a bold move – ask for a date.

### ✳ Tips

Avoid negative body language, such as crossing your arms, scowling, appearing overly stressed, looking downwards or walking in a hurry when you don't really need to.

Give yourself time to learn the types of conversation starters that work for you. Practise flirting wherever you can – at the local shop or launderette, or with your friends.

### ⚠ Warning

Sexually suggestive remarks or touching is inappropriate among colleagues. Keep any office flirting innocent at all times.

## 518 | Survive the Bar Scene

**You agreed to go out with your friends to a bar or club. Instead of dwelling on how you allowed such a thing to happen, have fun by following these simple tips.**

### ⊙ Steps

1   Enjoy yourself, first and foremost. Would you rather be at home washing the dishes? If the answer is yes, keep thinking of mundane chores until you find one you would not want to be doing at the moment.

2   You see someone you think you'd like to know better. He or she ignores you. So? Pat yourself on the back for knowing that your soul mate is not necessarily hanging out in a meat market. Let it go and find someone else with better manners.

3   Be someone you're not – try on a new hat. Play the part of the spoiled rich girl, the alpha-wolf guy, the dumb blonde.

### ✳ Tips

Be sure you know how you're getting home before you go out.

Interestingly enough, 71 per cent of men report success when they use the pickup line "Hi".

### ⚠ Warning

Don't put yourself into a dangerous situation, such as being alone in a dark alley with a strange man – or woman.

4   Be careful not to drink too much, in case you are approached by some-
    one with a bad pick-up line. "May I end this sentence with a proposi-
    tion?" might work on you if you have had a few too many.

5   Remember, though, that as lame as pick-up lines might be, the person is
    making an effort to show an interest in you. If you are even remotely
    interested, laugh, say hello and begin a normal conversation.

6   Be polite if someone wants to talk to you and you aren't interested. If the
    person won't leave you alone, say that you have a boyfriend or girlfriend.

7   Save your flirting for when you really want to use it.

---

# Make Small Talk                                                          519

Small talk can be a big challenge, but preparation and
confidence are all you really need.

## ☉ Steps

1   Practise. Converse with everyone you encounter: cashiers, waiters, peo-
    ple you're in a queue with, neighbours, co-workers, and kids. Chat with
    people unlike yourself, from the elderly to teenagers to tourists.

2   Read everything: cookbooks, newspapers, magazines, reviews, product
    inserts, maps, signs and catalogues. Everything is a source of informa-
    tion that can be turned into interesting conversations.

3   Force yourself to get into small-talk situations, such as doctors' waiting
    rooms, cocktail parties, and meetings at the office. Accept invitations or
    host your own gathering.

4   Immerse yourself in culture, both high and low. Television, music, sports,
    fashion, art and poetry are great sources of chat. If you can't stand
    Shakespeare, your dislike of the bard is also a good topic for discussion.

5   Keep a diary. Write down funny stories you hear, beautiful things you
    see, quotes, observations, shopping lists, and phone calls you made.
    That story about the time when the long-distance operator misunder-
    stood you could become an opening line.

6   Talk to yourself in the mirror. Make a random list of topics and see
    what you have to say on the subjects. Tennis, Russia, butter, hip-hop,
    shoes – the more varied your list, the better.

7   Expand your horizons. Go home a new way. Try sushi. Play pinball. Go
    online. Paint a watercolour. Bake a pie. Try something new every day.

8   Be a better listener. Did your boss say that she suffers from migraines?
    Has your doctor just had twins? These are opportunities for making
    small talk.

9   Work on building up your confidence, overcoming shyness and banish-
    ing any feelings of stage fright. Remember, the more you know, the more
    you know you can talk about.

## ✳ Tips

Be yourself. Confidence and
uniqueness are superb substitutes for comedic genius.

Keep a few exit lines in mind. For
example, "Thanks for the wonderful conversation, but now I
have to give the impression I'm
interested in everybody else."

## ⚠ Warning

Keep your fellow chatterers in
mind; naughty stories and loose
language will be frowned upon in
many circles. Similarly, your
French quips and scientific dis-
courses will be wasted on some.

## 520 | Know if Someone Is Lying

There are often cues and signs that a person may be lying. But there may also be understandable reasons for the lie.

### ⊙ Steps

1 Look for body language that might indicate someone is lying, such as not looking you in the eye when speaking to you, being fidgety, or seeming nervous or uncomfortable.

2 Listen for inconsistencies in what the person tells you, such as different stories on different days, different time frames, mistakes in remembering details or mixing up details.

3 Notice if the person steadfastly resists answering any of your questions. Extreme defensiveness could mean that he or she is hiding something.

4 Notice if the person accuses you of lying or being deceitful when you haven't been. This could reflect the accuser's own underlying behaviour, which he or she is projecting onto you rather than owning up to.

5 Listen to your gut reaction, or intuition. You may just know someone is lying. If you are not sure, don't jump to conclusions. Try to get some evidence to back up your hunch.

6 Consider asking directly if the person has lied to you. Many people feel guilty if they are caught lying and find it a relief to finally be honest.

7 Try to be understanding and listen to the person's reasons for lying. Was he trying not to hurt you? Was she afraid you would be angry or upset?

8 Look at your possible role in the situation. Are you someone who gets so upset hearing the truth that others feel they can't be honest with you?

### ⚠ Warning

Try not to assume that someone is lying unless your evidence is solid. Body language and intuition can provide clues but not proof.

## 521 | Compliment a Man Who Catches Your Eye

A cute guy has just entered the café. What do you do? A straightforward compliment can lead to a beautiful friendship – or at least brighten his day.

### ⊙ Steps

1 Be sincere and friendly; compliment him in the same way you would want to be complimented.

2 Smile at him as he walks by. Giving special attention and obvious appreciation might be all you need to do.

3 Mention that he has a nice smile – but don't be lecherous. Simply say, "You've got a nice smile."

4 Note an attractive part of his outfit: "Like your shades!" "Cool sweater!"

5 Don't ogle.

6 Keep your appreciation of his Adonis-like features or body to yourself – anything you say about his physique will probably sound cheesy.

### ✳ Tip

Try not to be too extravagant, for example, saying you love something of his. Simple, straightforward compliments are best and leave little room for misinterpretation.

### ⚠ Warning

Use compliments sparingly lest you appear insincere.

7   Give him credit for his pluck and originality if he sports a magenta, green or blue hairdo.

8   Compliment him in the context of the situation at hand. For example, tell him you admire his taste in reading material.

## Compliment a Woman Who Catches Your Eye                522

You spot an intriguing woman and must establish contact or live with regret for the rest of the day. How do you compliment her without appearing too aggressive? Or, worse, tasteless?

### ⊙ Steps

1   Think about commenting on actions over looks: "Great moves!" for the groover on the dance floor, or "Healthy diet!" for the good-looking woman buying greens at the supermarket.

2   Commend a woman for her wit or intelligence ("Funny joke!" "Great idea!") rather than her beautiful breasts.

3   Compliment a woman's appearance – hair, clothes, jewellery – only if you can do so with a sincere smile, or she'll think you're giving her a line and you might get a frosty response.

4   Consider compliments that may lead to conversation: "Love your bike – where do you like to ride?"

5   Consider asking her first if she likes receiving compliments. If she smiles encouragingly, tell her she's got a great smile; if she gives you a dirty look, just look the other way.

6   Get creative. If a woman has unbelievable violet eyes or an extraordinary and exotic name, she's probably used to getting compliments about these unusual features. Compliment her on something less obvious – she'll appreciate that you noticed what others usually don't.

### ✳ Tip

Watch out for half-compliments that could do more damage than good: "You're going to look so beautiful when you finally get your braces taken off."

### ⚠ Warning

Avoid sarcasm and smirking when you give compliments, especially if those behavioural no-nos tend to occur when you're nervous.

## Know if Someone Likes You Romantically              523

Sometimes the direct approach is best – just ask. But if that seems too bold, look for some of these telling signs.

### ⊙ Steps

#### Behaviour

1   Pay attention to your conversations with the person in question. Does this person show a special interest in talking with you and, once it's started, make an effort to keep that conversation going?

2   Does this person "accidentally" run into you in places where he knows you will be, such as at your desk? At the launderette on Tuesdays? At your brother's birthday party?

3   Notice whether this person mentions future plans to spend time with you: "That band is coming here soon. We should really get tickets."

### ✳ Tips

Trust in your intuition and listen to your feelings.

Feel flattered if a friend or co-worker likes you romantically, but don't view it as a personal crisis if you can't return the affections. Your admirer will probably move on once you make it clear that you don't feel the same way.

4   Notice if the person is making an effort to spend time alone together. Cancelling other plans in order to be with you longer, or finding excuses not to leave, could be a sign of romantic interest.

5   Has the person been calling for seemingly random reasons, such as, "I was wondering if you knew what that pizza place down the street is called", followed by, "Are you hungry?"

6   Has the person taken a sudden interest in your life and hobbies? This is a sure sign that she is interested in something – and it's probably not your stamp collection.

7   Observe how the person acts around your friends – he might be extra friendly to your closest pals for a reason.

## Body Language

1   Sometimes seeing someone you have a crush on results in telltale physiological signs. Does the person in question blush when you look at her? Her sympathetic nervous system is probably going into overdrive. Does she jumble her words when talking to you?

2   See if the person mirrors your movements: when you lean back, he leans back; when you put your elbows on the table, he does the same.

3   Notice whether this person sits or stands in the open position – that is, facing you with arms uncrossed, or crossing her legs in your direction if the person is a woman.

4   Does he move closer to you and/or touch you subtly, such as patting your hand or touching your cheek?

5   Look for other elements of body language, such as frequent eye contact, holding your gaze and looking down before looking away, energetic speech coupled with open hands, or flashing palms.

6   Does the person you're wondering about smile at you a lot?

---

## 524 | Ask for a Phone Number

Say you're at the supermarket and out of nowhere comes your dream mate. Don't just stand there speechless in aisle 9 – ask for a phone number!

### ○ Steps

1   Approach the person. Remember that eye contact and a gentle smile are crucial in appearing friendly.

2   Enter the conversation with a compliment, then introduce yourself. Try not to be too cute with your delivery; sincerity usually goes down better than an elaborate pick-up line.

3   Talk. You'll get a strong sense of whether the person would be willing to give you a phone number. If no eye contact or smile is coming your way, and you're making a solid effort, then maybe you should give up.

4   Ask for the number if you're getting positive signals. Try not to be pushy, and show respect for the person's private information. Avoid "How about

###  Tips

Opt for a person's work number if he or she appears uncomfortable with giving you a home number.

If you get a phone number, wait two days before calling so as not to appear desperate. Avoid waiting too long, though; he or she may forget about you.

giving me your number?" Instead, use: "It would be great to get to know you better. Is there a number where I can reach you?"

5 Offer your own phone number after getting the other person's, if you feel comfortable doing so. Some women are not comfortable giving out their number, so if a woman declines to give you hers, you may still want to offer your own.

## Ask Someone on a Date                                                      525

You'll never know whether the other person is interested unless you ask. So gather up all your courage and follow these steps.

### ⊙ Steps

1 Introduce yourself to that person you've been admiring from afar.

2 Ask for the person's telephone number, or tell a common friend that you would like the number.

3 Call at a time that's not intrusive. Make the call when you feel comfortable, regardless of what your friends might say about romantic protocol.

4 Reintroduce yourself once you're on the phone by saying something like, "Hi, it's Emma. We met at the art gallery."

5 Using as little pretence as possible (ideally none), ask the person if he or she would like to meet for a cup of coffee or do something similarly informal. If you are politely refused, take the hint and get off the phone.

6 Arrange to get together casually for a brief time – half an hour or so. If that goes well, suggest a more formal date, such as lunch.

### ✳ Tips

Some of the best ideas for a date are the things you love to do the most, such as going to an art museum or getting muddy on a mountain bike ride.

If your invitation is rejected, congratulate yourself for trying and move on.

### ⚠ Warning

Going to see a film may not be ideal for a first date; it shows a lack of creativity and does not allow the two of you to spend much time talking.

## Plan a Date on a Budget                                                    526

You don't need to blow your bank account or rack up debt on your credit card to plan a fantastic date. All you need is a little imagination and the following pointers.

### ⊙ Steps

1 Determine how much you can spend and the types of things you and your date might enjoy doing together.

2 Opt for the less expensive meet-at-a-café date or the drink-after-work date for a blind date, or if you don't yet know your mutual interests.

3 Consider an afternoon bike ride or walk through the park, or simply sitting by the river watching the boats go by.

4 Plan an evening picnic in the park, weather permitting. Coordinate with a free outdoor musical or play, and pack a bottle of wine, together with bread and cheese.

### ✳ Tip

Ask the person to lunch and a matinee at the weekend – the inexpensive version of a Saturday-night dinner-and-a-film date.

### ⚠ Warning

Avoid pretending you have money when you don't. But don't draw attention to the fact that you have little to spend – financial distress is never a turn-on.

5   Consider inviting your date to a party; make any necessary introductions to your friends, have fun, then leave together after a relatively short time and go for a drink.

6   Try cooking dinner and renting a film. (This may or may not be an appropriate first date.)

---

## 527 | Refuse a Date to Ensure No More Requests

Unless you want to be asked out again by this person, be direct and leave no room for misinterpretation.

### ⊙ Steps

1   Be clear, consistent and gracious in your refusal. Be politely neutral rather than emphatic.

2   Don't hesitate, procrastinate or ask to think about it.

3   Express regret, if you'd like, but never say anything you don't mean, such as, "Maybe another time."

4   Devise an impersonal, generic explanation if you prefer, such as, "I never date colleagues" or "I'm involved with someone else." Otherwise, simply refuse the invitation with a polite "Thank you for thinking of me. I'm sorry, I'll have to say no."

### ✱ Tip

If a person persists in asking you out, just persist in being firm and clear. Sooner or later, you'll get the message across.

---

## 528 | Refuse a Date to Ensure Another Request

Sometimes circumstances are beyond your control. Here's how to refuse a date when you truly wish you could accept.

### ⊙ Steps

1   Smile and make eye contact if the invitation is made in person.

2   Communicate your complete attention if the request is made by phone. Consider saying something like "Excuse me while I close the door" or "I was hoping you'd call."

3   Express your thanks in whatever style is genuine and comfortable for you – a joke, a simple thanks, a great big "Wow!"

4   Communicate your regret at having to refuse, and explain why you need to decline the invitation.

5   Suggest another specific day, or express your general wish to find another time that works for both of you. A straightforward "I can't this time because I have to go to Glasgow, but I would love to make it another time. How about next Friday?" has candour to recommend it.

### ✱ Tips

People look for acceptance, so be open and enthusiastic.

If you simply say that you can't make it, the person may interpret that as a brush-off. Always provide an explanation.

Be clear, candid and gracious.

### ⚠ Warning

Asking someone out can be difficult, so make it as easy as possible for the other person.

## Cancel a Date at the Last Minute 529

You've changed your mind about the date – or life has simply got in the way. How do you cancel at the last minute?

### ⊙ Steps

### If You Want to Be Asked Out Again

1  Call as soon as possible. It's not likely you'll be forgiven easily if you let your date show up and wait for you, just to have you cancel.

2  Blame it on outside circumstances: an unexpected meeting, deadline or assignment. You really, really want to go, but ...

3  Tell the truth: you're tired, you don't feel well, you've had a rotten day. You'd rather stay in and rest than go out and not be very much fun.

4  Create an excuse: you forgot that you were meeting your friends for dinner, you need to go to your grandmother's to move her furniture, you lost your keys and can't leave until you find them.

5  Leave the conversation open for another invitation.

6  Suggest an alternative date.

7  Offer to make it up to him or her   and then do it. Send a card or a bouquet of flowers.

8  If your date calls later to check up on you, be where you said you'd be and thank him or her for being thoughtful.

### If You Don't Want to Be Asked Out Again

1  Call as soon as you realise you want to cancel. Keep in mind how much easier cancelling is on the phone than in person.

2  Blame it on outside circumstances. Believable: you are really busy at work and don't have time for dating. Unbelievable: your power has been shut off so you haven't had a shower in four days.

3  Tell the truth: you're not interested; you've had a revelation that he or she is not The One.

4  Tell a white lie: you're seeing someone else, or you've decided that you don't want to date anyone just now.

5  Stay on the phone only long enough to deliver your message; be careful not to give the impression that you are interested.

### ✳ Tip

If you don't want another date, keep the conversation short. Don't apologise for not wanting to go out with this person. Ever.

## 530 | Create a Romantic Atmosphere

When planning an intimate dinner or other event, use your imagination and ingenuity to arouse the senses with beautiful sights, sounds, flavours and aromas.

### ⊙ Steps

#### Indoors

1 Set the mood by playing some soft, romantic music. Classical music is usually a safe bet, as are jazz and soul.

2 Fill the room with a dramatic array of flowers to add visual interest as well as inexpensive elegance.

3 Light the room with either bright, slow-burning candles or, if possible, the glow from a fireplace to add a warm, intimate tone to the evening.

4 Plan and prepare a simple yet elegant meal. Try to find out beforehand which foods your date particularly enjoys and serve them.

5 Include classic romantic fare, such as champagne and strawberries.

6 Use your best china, and select table linens and napkins in soft and sumptuous fabrics. If chosen well, these items can be purchased for little money but appear stylish and sophisticated, giving your date the impression that you've gone all out for the occasion.

#### Outdoors

1 Coordinate your plans with seasonal or natural events, such as a sunset, a full moon or the turning of the leaves during the autumn.

2 Plan and prepare a simple yet elegant meal. If possible, include your date's favourite foods. Don't forget the wine or champagne.

3 Pack the meal and the necessary utensils in a picnic basket. Again, use the best china you have.

4 Bring along a picnic blanket as well as a big, soft blanket for warmth, should the night turn cold.

5 Bring along some candles or torches to provide light and warmth. Citronella candles are especially handy for warding off insects.

### ✱ Tips

Flowers are a staple of romance – use them liberally.

When planning an outdoor event, be sure to check the weather forecast and have an alternative plan in mind, just in case.

### Things You'll Need

❑ music

❑ flowers

❑ candles

❑ romantic food and drink

❑ china

❑ table linen and napkins

## 531 | Keep a Dozen Red Roses Fresh

To make that special and romantic gift last as long as possible, follow these guidelines.

### ⊙ Steps

1 Store the roses in a cool place – ideally a refrigerator – if you can't get them into water immediately. A cool environment will help to slow the deterioration process.

### ✱ Tips

There are many other factors that go into the duration of a cut rose, including rose type, gardening methods and climate; however,

How to Do *(Just About)* Everything

2   Fill a vase with warm or tepid water. Make sure it's no cooler than room temperature. Warm water will be absorbed more quickly.

3   Add floral preservatives to the water if you have some available. Follow the package instructions.

4   Cut off any foliage that will lie below the waterline (it will rot), as well as any torn leaves.

5   Cut off about 2.5 cm (1 in) of the stems, either straight across or at a slant, using a knife rather than scissors. Do this while the stem is sub-merged in a basin of warm or tepid water.

6   Place the roses in water immediately after cutting them.

7   Change the water and recut the stems daily, taking extra care to remove any leaves that may have wilted or dipped into the water. This will help prevent bacteria build-up. If you're using preservatives, add more solution every other day.

8   Keep the flowers in a cool, dry place, away from direct sunlight, heaters, air conditioners and draughts. At night, move your roses to the coolest part of the house. This will help them last longer.

following these steps will allow you to keep your roses fresh for as long as possible.

You can make your own floral preservative using a citrus-based soft drink. Add one part soft drink for every three parts water.

## Make a Great First Impression on a Date    532

Want to make sure your date will be eager to go out with you a second time? No problem.

### ⊙ Steps

1   Dress attractively but comfortably. Don't wear clothes that make you feel stiff or self-conscious.

2   Be aware of your posture – it speaks volumes about you. You want to appear alert and confident by sitting up straight.

3   Compliment your date. Don't just say "I like your shirt." Be sincere and notice something that he or she took time with.

4   Learn to flirt (see 517 "Flirt") and try it out. Don't overdo it, though.

5   Realise that you don't have to tell people how great you are. It's better to show them instead.

6   Be interested and interesting. Listen actively to what your date says. Ask questions and don't interrupt.

7   Enjoy yourself, no matter what. If you're easygoing and fun to be around, and if you can go with whatever comes your way, you can't help but make a great impression.

8   Thank the other person for the date – always, without exception. Good manners will get you far.

### ✱ Tips

Don't talk about anything nega-tive or complain on a first date.

Be cautious about drinking – it will give you a false sense of confidence and your inhibitions will be lowered. You may say or do things you'll regret later.

## 533 Read Your Date's Body Language

Your date claims to be having fun, yet you catch him or her yawning uncontrollably. Body language says a lot about what your date is really thinking.

### ◎ Steps

### Positive Body Language

1 Notice if your date's posture is good yet relaxed. A slouched date probably isn't having a good time. A date who's sitting up is paying attention.

2 Observe whether your date makes good eye contact. If he keeps looking into your eyes, you've got it made.

3 Is your date leaning forward? Then you aren't a stranger any more.

4 Be aware of any physical contact. Holding hands is a great sign.

5 Notice if your date has her palms up, which indicates a friendly warmth.

6 Know that your date is listening to you if he nods at appropriate times during the conversation; this indicates that your words are being heard.

7 Pay attention to whether your date is in sync with you and constantly reflecting your behaviour. Does she shift in her seat when you do? Does he pick up your speed and tone when he's speaking? This occurs unconsciously and indicates a good rhythm between you – it's not just a copycat game.

### Negative Body Language

1 Take note if your date's arms are crossed. This suggests there's a wall between the two of you.

2 Beware if your date is yawning. This is a bad sign – unless it's because she was up all night thinking about you.

3 Notice if your date is nodding at inappropriate times or seems to be nodding constantly during your conversation. Your date may be thinking about something else.

4 Is your date looking at everything but you? Be worried.

5 Notice if your date is keeping some distance between you. Personal space is one thing, but if your date is not standing next to you when you're waiting in a cinema queue together, that's a bad sign.

### ✳ Tip

Interpreting body language isn't cut-and-dried; allow for the fact that your interpretation may be wrong.

### ⚠ Warning

Avoid pointing out your date's body language to him or her – this may put your date on the defensive.

## 534 Kiss on a Date

The date's gone well, and now it's almost over. Here are some tips on the how and when of kissing.

### ◎ Steps

1 Look for positive body language, such as eye contact, uncrossed arms and head tilted towards you.

2 Do it. Waiting just makes the moment awkward.

### ✳ Tip

Keep the kissing simple for now. Use a soft touch that will calm your date, especially if this kiss is the first one.

 How to Do *(Just About)* Everything

3    Maintain eye contact as you close in. Try not to close your eyes until after making lip contact.

4    Tilt your head slightly to one side to avoid bumping noses.

5    Press your lips gently against your date's. Try not to suck his or her breath away just yet.

6    Release. Look into your date's eyes. If he or she isn't looking back at you the same way, then you probably shouldn't continue.

7    Kiss your date again. There's more flexibility to this kiss.

8    Explore – softly kiss your date's neck, ears and eyelashes. By this time, you'll have a better feel for how and where to kiss your date.

## Decide Whether to Go on a Third Date                535

You made it past the first and second dates. Now it's time to decide: is this worth pursuing?

### ⊙ Steps

1    Assess the relationship. Who is making the plans? Is it both of you or just one of you? Are the decisions truly mutual?

2    How interested are you? You probably don't know each other very well yet, but are you beginning to feel comfortable with this person? Can you talk about some of your thoughts and feelings?

3    Does he or she seem interested in you?

4    Think about your shared interests. Do you have any of the same hobbies? Do you enjoy the same kinds of weekend activities?

5    Take note of your differences. Some can be a problem, while others may add interest. Do you have fun listening to his fishing stories, even though you'd never go yourself? That's a good sign. Are you put off by her vocal political opinions? Better forgo the third date.

6    Do your conversations keep getting more interesting? Or are you already running out of things to talk about?

7    Do you talk on the phone apart from setting up dates?

8    Have you seen any signs of psychological gamesmanship? If so, don't continue this unless you really enjoy the abuse.

9    Were you thanked on the first two dates? Regardless of who paid, it's nice to know that someone appreciated spending time with you.

10   How comfortable would you be meeting his or her parents? That may tell you a lot about how well you're clicking.

### ✱ Tips

If you decide to go on a third date, make sure to take it slow. Even though all the signs are looking positive, you need time to get to know each other better before getting serious.

If you decide against a third date, be firm and respectful in letting the other person know. Treat him or her the way you would like to be treated in this situation.

## 536 | Know When It's Over

**Is it time to call it quits?**

### ⊙ Steps

1  Be realistic. If you're being abused, hurt, cheated on or lied to, it's time to cut your losses and get out.

2  Think about the future you're creating. If your partner is jealous, obsessive, possessive or overly emotional, consider the extra burden you are carrying in dealing with those behaviours.

3  Is he a shameless flirt? Is she bossy? demanding? insecure? These are more signs of a rocky road ahead.

4  Do you truly enjoy each other's company, or do you find yourself relieved whenever you part company? If the latter, it doesn't bode well.

5  Evaluate your role in maintaining the relationship. If it feels as though you're doing all the work, it's time to talk or walk.

6  Does he promise to call and then forget? Is she terminally late? Be honest with yourself. Is this what you want?

7  Do you feel accepted and appreciated? If not, move on.

**✳ Tip**

Make sure you want to end the relationship because the person is wrong for you and not because you fear commitment. You don't want to send Prince Charming packing just because you have commitment jitters.

## 537 | Break Up Peacefully

**If you're ready to end a relationship, consider how you can break up without conflict.**

### ⊙ Steps

1  Acknowledge that the relationship is really over. Come to terms with your own feelings and make a firm decision to end the relationship.

2  Don't delay the inevitable. Once you decide to break up with your partner, immediately think about how, when and where you will take action.

3  Make sure you're the one who personally delivers the news. Don't give a third party the opportunity to tell your partner that you want to break up before you have the chance to discuss the matter alone.

4  Select a private place to meet your partner to end the relationship.

5  Find or schedule an appropriate time. Approach the topic when both of you are calm and rational. Don't announce your intention to break up during a heated argument or a moment of anger.

6  Show your resolve by being firm, decisive and honest. Help your partner understand why you want to end the relationship. Be tactful, not brutal.

7  Remind your partner that you'll never forget the positive qualities in your relationship, but emphasise that you're ready to move on with your life.

8  Give your partner the closure that he or she needs to accept the break-up; answer questions and talk it over instead of leaving loose ends.

9  Stay positive as you both make plans to go your separate ways.

**✳ Tip**

Let go of old grievances during a break-up. The end of a relationship isn't the appropriate time to bring up old grudges.

**⚠ Warning**

If your partner does not agree to the break-up, don't allow him or her to manipulate you into staying in the relationship.

## Handle a Break-Up

Whether you're the one doing the dumping or the one getting dumped, breaking up is always hard to do. Although you might feel as if you'll never get over this, you will.

### ⊙ Steps

1 Call all your friends – even those you may have ignored during your recent relationship – and make plans immediately. Now is not a good time to be alone.

2 Vent when the need arises. Good friends will let you take out the photo album (again) and cry (again) and rant (again) – and they'll still love you.

3 Allow yourself time to grieve. If you don't let yourself wallow in self-pity for a while and mourn the good times lost, your heart may harden to future relationships and love.

4 Realise that this sadness will pass.

5 Distract yourself with fun once you're tired of mourning. Films, group sports, classes or a favourite CD can help take your mind off your loss.

6 Indulge yourself when you're feeling lonely. Try a massage, a weekend trip away with a best friend, a great new outfit – whatever helps you feel good about yourself.

7 Begin dating again when you're ready. Let friends set you up, and go to all those parties you might otherwise skip.

8 Analyse what went wrong in the relationship only after you have rebuilt your self-esteem. If you attempt to do this too soon, you're headed for another downward spiral.

9 Remember the good aspects of the relationship (there must have been some), and then get excited about the new direction your life is suddenly taking. Change can be great!

**✻ Tip**

Keep in mind that clean breaks are generally better than those mini-breaks or sort-of break-ups that are a bit easier to deal with at the time. Upon breaking up, attempt to resolve lingering issues, then take some time away from each other, even if you intend to remain friends.

**⚠ Warnings**

Never sleep with an ex unless you like to torture yourself.

While you're upset, don't do anything you'll regret later. The transition back into single life is a highly vulnerable time. Get support from your friends.

## Know if You're in Love

Determining if you're in love involves serious soul-searching.

### ⊙ Steps

1 Clarify what love is for you. Write down all your thoughts and feelings about what a loving relationship would be like for you. Ask other people how they define love or know if they love someone.

2 Distinguish between love (as you've defined it) and lust or infatuation. Lust is an intense sexual desire. Infatuation refers to the initial stage of a relationship, when you are "mad" about your new love interest; this feeling usually fades over time.

3 Write down how you do feel about the person. For example: you enjoy his or her company, have similar interests, feel safe, trust the person, think he or she is attractive, and so on.

**✻ Tips**

Infatuation, when you may think you are in love and have found the perfect person, lasts about six months. But it often takes more time to tell if you are truly compatible and if you can love the whole person in the longer term.

4   Think about how well the two of you relate to each other. For example, how well do you communicate with each other? How do you deal with conflict? Do you bring out good or bad parts of each other? Can you show different sides of yourself?

5   Ask yourself if you see and accept your love interest as a whole person. True love isn't just about loving the parts of someone that are easy to appreciate, but choosing to love that person overall.

Read books on the subject of love. Wise people have been writing about it for hundreds of years.

---

## 540 | Say "I Love You"

Ready to take the plunge and introduce that most romantic phrase into your relationship's dialogue?

### ⊙ Steps

1   Decide if you do, indeed, love your mate. Most partners can see through a halfhearted "love ya" – which won't do your relationship any good.

2   Consider the possibility that your partner might not respond with the hoped-for "I love you, too." If you can handle that and still want to express your love, go for it. If you can't, then consider holding off until either you're certain your partner will respond as hoped or you're OK with it if he or she doesn't.

3   Think about how you'd like to let your partner know the way you feel, keeping in mind that uttering those words may give birth to a lifelong memory. If spontaneity works for you, wait for the perfect moment. If you're more methodical, consider writing a love letter first, then telling your mate in person the next time you get together.

4   If you decide in advance when to reveal your love, plan a special evening around it. Such relationship milestones warrant celebration.

5   When you tell your partner you love him or her, do so while making total eye contact, and while you are holding each other. This gives the moment the intimacy it deserves.

### ✱ Tip

Avoid saying the "L" word for the first time in the heat of passion – your partner may doubt the sincerity of your proclamation.

---

## 541 | Write a Love Letter

Here is how to profess everlasting love for your one and only in a proper love letter.

### ⊙ Steps

1   Select stationery appropriate to your personality and sentiment. Decide whether you prefer torn-out notebook paper, perfumed sheets covered with flowers, or elegant note cards.

2   Determine the letter's purpose. Are you writing to tell your longtime love that you miss him or her, or initiating contact with someone you don't know very well?

3   Date your letter for posterity's sake.

### ✱ Tips

Handwrite the letter. Laser printing isn't very romantic.

Write a draft, set it aside briefly, then read it again. Tone the letter down if necessary.

---

4  Begin with Dear, Dearest, Beloved, My Precious, or whatever endearment or salutation feels appropriate for the depth of your relationship.

5  Be sure to thank your lover if you're responding to a letter, and mention the number of times you've reread it. Flatter your lover by repeating a couple of choice phrases he or she used.

6  Describe how your loved one makes you feel. Try to be original, but put sincerity ahead of creativity. The purpose of the letter is to express your feelings, not to stun your partner with a brilliant metaphor.

7  Mention his or her adorable traits. Bring up specific qualities or idiosyncrasies you appreciate. Be sparing with references to eyes and smiles, which can seem forced or clichéd, and try not to get melodramatic.

8  Recall your past times together and describe your hopes for the future.

9  Close with an exhortation to write back quickly, a mention of the next time you expect to see each other, or another appropriate comment.

10  Affix a proper valediction – such as "Yours", "Love" or "Feverishly Awaiting Your Letter" – depending on how you feel.

11  Read your letter aloud to check for awkward or stilted phrasing.

12  Finish your letter or envelope with a wax seal. Consider affixing a flower to it or enclosing a poem.

Consider other creative means of expressing your devotion: scrawl confessions on a mirror, fan or piece of cloth. Fire off a quick succession of postcards.

---

## Make a Long-Distance Relationship Last　542

Whoever first said that absence makes the heart grow fonder never contended with the weekend airport rush. Here are some ways to hold on to your long-distance lover – and your sanity.

### ⊙ Steps

1  Keep in touch daily. If large phone bills are a concern, send e-mail, letters, cards and even faxes.

2  Plan reunions to keep both of you pleased about the relationship. If your partner needs closeness, set up plans to meet often. Having a date to look forward to can help you through the rough times.

3  Reaffirm your love and commitment to one another. Try not to assume that the relationship is thriving. Listen to your partner's concerns and communicate your own before they become bigger problems.

4  Keep your partner informed about your life. You may live separately, but sharing information about your activities and friends is still important.

5  Trust one another. Suspicion will only break the relationship down.

6  Keep the relationship a high priority. Avoid cancelling reunions or putting off a phone call.

7  Focus on the future. Make plans to live in the same city eventually.

### ✳ Tips

Plan a reunion in a city other than the ones you live in. Having a weekend getaway or holiday together can help recharge the relationship and reinforce your commitment.

Find ways to reduce the costs of travel and phone calls so you can meet and talk more often.

Surprise your loved one with an unexpected visit or a bouquet of flowers to keep the passion alive.

Be patient – it may take time for long-term plans to work out.

## 543 | Ask for Forgiveness

Saying you're sorry can seem awfully tough, but it gets easier with practice and delivers bountiful rewards.

### ⊙ Steps

1 Think about what happened and what it is you are sorry for doing.

2 Write down your apology; this will help you organise your thoughts and calm your nerves.

3 Practise what you plan to say until you feel comfortable with it.

4 State clearly what it is you are sorry for doing.

5 Acknowledge your actions without making excuses.

6 Share your feelings about what happened – avoid blaming, exaggerating or saying empty words.

7 Listen to the other person's response without getting defensive.

8 Offer to make amends if appropriate.

9 Move on. Once you've apologised, let it go.

### ✳ Tips

Think of an apology as a commitment to the relationship rather than an act of weakness.

Be honest. Only apologise for things you truly feel responsible for; don't apologise just to make an unpleasant situation go away.

Say it in writing if a personal confrontation is just too scary.

Give the other person some time to sort out his or her feelings – don't be discouraged if you aren't completely forgiven the moment you apologise.

## 544 | Forgive

Forgive and forget, let go and lighten your load. A grudge can be a heavy weight to bear.

### ⊙ Steps

1 Think about what happened.

2 Acknowledge all your feelings. There is often anger lurking behind any hurt or sadness you might feel.

3 Express your feelings – write them out, talk to a friend or simply allow yourself to feel what you feel.

4 Accept responsibility for your own emotions. Although you were wronged and your emotions may be justified, it is still up to you to decide when you're ready to stop feeling angry or upset.

5 Talk to the other person about the behaviour that upset you and how it made you feel. The odds are that you won't feel truly ready to forgive until you know this person has heard and understood your perspective.

6 Try to understand the other person's perspective, even if you don't really agree with it.

7 Rebuild trust in the relationship. Make agreements about acceptable future behaviour whenever appropriate.

8 Make the decision to forgive and communicate your forgiveness to the other person. Once you've done this, make every effort to move on and let it go completely.

### ✳ Tips

You can forgive someone without condoning his or her behaviour; forgiveness isn't the same thing as approval.

Avoid a defensive reaction by first venting your emotions outside the presence of the wrongdoer – this will help the interaction to be more productive.

Wait until you are truly ready to forgive. Respect your feelings and take all the time you need.

## Know if You Will Marry Your Significant Other

**545**

Is the object of your affections the right one for you? Keep your eyes open for signs that this is the person you want to marry.

### ⊙ Steps

1 Examine your conversations. Does your partner include you in her plans when she talks about the future?

2 Consider the compatibility of your activities and values. Are you interested in your loved one's work and hobbies? Does your partner seem to be interested in your job and pastimes, even if she doesn't share your passion for them?

3 Consider whether you're both travelling along the same pathway in life. Do you want the same things, such as kids, stability, money, career?

4 Evaluate how your partner treats you in private and in public. Does he brag about you? Does he seem proud to be with you, or does he avoid being seen with you in public? Does he stick around when you're having a bad day, or does he disappear when you need him the most?

5 Evaluate how your significant other treats your friends and family. Is she willing to be nice to them, even if she doesn't like them?

6 Assess your partner's honesty and trustworthiness. Does he do what he says he's going to do? Do you feel you can trust him?

7 Think about all the reasons why you really like this person. Remember that infatuation fades, but genuine compatibility endures.

8 Communicate with your partner and discuss these issues to figure out if you're meant for each other.

### ✱ Tip

If the person seems secretive or ashamed to be seen with you in public, reevaluate your relationship. He or she may be trying to hide something or someone from you.

## Get Him to Propose

**546**

You've found the man of your dreams, and you know you're meant for each other, but he needs a little nudge. Here's how to point him in the right direction.

### ⊙ Steps

1 Make him aware of your interest in a lifetime commitment. Drop subtle hints from time to time, such as, "We'd make a great team" or "I can't imagine my future without you", rather than incessantly bombarding him with demands about marriage.

2 Point out your shared interests, values and common goals. Open his eyes so he'll realise that you're the one for him.

3 Remember that actions speak louder than words. Show him what a great lifetime partner you could be through thoughtful actions, sincerity, kindness and other appealing traits.

4 Create opportunities for him to pop the question. Plan a candlelight dinner, arrange a romantic evening out or have a weekend away together.

### ✱ Tip

Make sure not to fixate on this issue, as it may have a detrimental effect on the relationship. Give him the time he needs to sort things out.

5   Remind him of several happily married couples who are mutual friends of yours, pointing out how much you have in common with them and how successful their marriages are.

6   Express your happiness, love and devotion to him. Show him by your actions and words that you've found the man of your dreams – and you're ready to marry him!

## 547 | Propose Marriage to a Man

You're not the type of girl to wait around for Prince Charming. You know what you want, so why not ask for it? Here are some thoughts on how to propose to the man in your life.

### ◉ Steps

1   Know your beloved well and anticipate his response. Will he be swept away by this romantic gesture? Or could he feel threatened by a woman's proposing marriage? (If so, you may want to reconsider.)

2   Set the stage. Pick his favourite place – whether you consider it romantic or not – to pop the question. This might be a secluded camp site, a fancy restaurant, a golf course at sunset ... or a bar. Let your lover's taste be your guide.

3   Keep your plans flexible. You may have an evening of French cuisine and fine wine in mind; he may be in the mood for burgers and beer. Unless your plans involve other people or events, go with the flow.

4   Make a splash if your beloved appreciates the theatrical. Put your question up in lights at a dance, or bring in a soloist to croon over pasta.

5   Keep the occasion subtle if your partner tends to like things more subdued. Pop the question over dessert, or during a private game of pool.

6   Bring or plan an engagement gift. Of course, you could get him a ring, but a puppy with a note tied around its neck might be a better choice. Or a motorcycle. Something that will last for a long time.

7   Give him some time to be surprised and tongue-tied. Remember, even though he loves you for the unconventional woman you are, he probably won't see this one coming.

### ⚠ Warning

If you've already been dropping hints and he hasn't been receptive, don't use a proposal to force the issue. Your attempt at romance may backfire.

## 548 | Propose Marriage to a Woman

This is a moment that will be recounted over and over to friends, family and even your children. Make it memorable.

### ◉ Steps

1   Try to keep your plans to yourself.

2   Consult your intended's father before asking, if you are a traditional kind of guy.

### ❋ Tip

It may be best to pop the question first and buy the ring together later, especially if you're not sure of her taste.

3   Make sure the proposal reflects your personal style. Get on one knee and propose at the top of a mountain, during a romantic weekend or while you're on a tropical holiday.

4   Have champagne and flowers waiting.

5   If your partner says yes, call the people that matter to let them know.

6   Be prepared to start talking about wedding plans immediately.

7   Don't be offended if your new fiancée is not taken with the ring you selected. She can choose another setting later if she desires.

## Buy an Engagement Ring                            549

Bucking tradition might be necessary when it comes to selecting an engagement ring that she'll wear for the rest of her life. It's always best to get input from the bride-to-be.

### ☉ Steps

1   Discuss styles, stones and budget with your bride-to-be if you're going to be shopping together.

2   Expect to pay about £2,500 to £3,500 per half carat for a quality diamond. This is a rough estimate that will depend on several factors, including the diamond's size – larger diamonds are rarer, and therefore more valuable (see 705 "Buy a Diamond").

3   Go shopping with your intended after your proposal, or shop alone so that you can surprise her.

4   If you shop alone and aren't sure what style she wants, buy just the stone, make an appointment with a jeweller to return later for a setting, and pop the question using a fun imitation ring. After she's accepted, go back and pick out a setting together.

5   Have the ring made or buy one ready-made, once you've discussed styles with your sweetheart.

### ✳ Tips

Despite the old adage that the ring should be worth two months' salary, if you can't spend that much money, go for a simple design that can be dressed up with the wedding band.

Use the stone from a family heirloom to make a unique and less expensive ring she'll treasure.

If you buy the ring without the bride's input, don't fret if she doesn't like your choice. Get a basic setting with an understanding from the jeweller that you can come back and trade up.

## Decide on a Form of Wedding Ceremony             550

Have you always had your heart set on a church wedding? Or does a quiet registry office ceremony sound ideal? Perhaps you like the idea of a civil wedding but fancy an unusual location or one that is special to you. The choice is yours.

### ☉ Steps

1   If you want a church wedding, make an appointment to see the vicar or priest of your local church to discuss the ceremony.

2   If you want to get married in a register office, make an appointment to attend the register office in the district where you live. You can discuss with them the personalisation of your ceremony with special readings and/or music, available dates and the fees involved.

### ✳ Tips

Look into all the options thoroughly with your intended. You may discover that you have very different ideas about the style of wedding you prefer!

Consider the various costs involved before making the final decision.

3 Consider getting married at one of more than 3,000 approved premises in England and Wales. These include stately homes and museums, boats, castles and more unusual venues, such as the British Airways London Eye in London and Epsom Racecourse.

Log onto www.confetti.co.uk for a list of current approved venues for marriage in the UK and abroad.

4 Once you have chosen your venue, contact the register office in the same district and ask about the availability of the registrar to come out to the venue and the fee involved.

5 Decide whether you would like to get married outside or in your own home. At the moment, the only possibility within the UK is Scotland, where you can marry half-way up a mountain if you choose. Alternatively, you could marry in a register office and arrange your own private ceremony in your garden or an outdoor space special to you to follow immediately afterwards.

6 Consider getting married on a beach in the Seychelles or on a Carribbean island. There are several tour operatours that offer wedding packages in holiday destinations all over the world. Look at a few of them and decide if this is the right option for you.

## 551 | Plan a Wedding

Now that you've recovered from the delightful shock of your engagement, take a deep breath, grab a notebook and your address book, and then let the countdown to the big day begin!

### ⊙ Steps

1 Imagine your wedding from beginning to end. Where and when have you dreamed the wedding would take place? How formal would you like the event to be? What will the wedding party wear? What kind of food would you like to serve?

2 Pick a date.

3 Set a budget – one that is functional and provides for some flexibility. Here is where you must combine fantasy with practicality.

4 Ask friends and family to recommend a reputable jeweller. Order your engagement and/or wedding rings.

5 Book the wedding and reception sites.

6 Meet with the officiant of your wedding. Now is the time to be clear about rules and restrictions regarding the ceremony and ceremony site.

7 Select your wedding attendants – your wedding party can be as big or small as you like.

8 Choose a dress and wedding attire for the rest of the wedding party.

9 Make a guest list. You may have to compromise on the number of guests if your budget is limited.

10 Plan your pre-wedding parties, ceremony, reception and honeymoon. Consider menus, decorations, favours and music.

11 Interview and hire suppliers: wedding coordinator, photographer, video recordist, caterer, florist and entertainment.

### ✱ Tips

Ask your parents early on in the planning stage for their input.

Be kind to yourself and your betrothed—this can be an extremely stressful time.

Keep a notebook to fill with things like swatches of fabric, notes and supplier contracts.

Be sure to take time away with your partner and give attention to your relationship.

12  Check state requirements for obtaining a marriage licence, and find out how long the licence will remain valid.

13  Take care of the rest of the paperwork, from ordering invitations to setting up a wedding list.

## Register for Marriage  552

There are just a few things you absolutely have to do before the big day. One of them is to register with the district in which you plan to marry. Here's how to go about it.

⊙ **Steps**

1  Contact the register office in the district where you intend your wedding to take place.

2  Check with this office a minimum of three months before your wedding date.

3  Make a list of any documents the office tells you to bring with you when applying for a marriage licence.

4  Be prepared to provide the bride's and groom's legal names, addresses, ages and previous marital histories, if any. If either of you has been married before, you will have to show records of annulment or divorce, or the previous spouse's death certificate.

5  Ask about fees. Cash and credit cards are usually accepted.

6  Be prepared for a waiting period, although this varies across the country.

7  Bear in mind that special rules may apply if your prospective spouse does not have British nationality. Be sure to ask about this.

8  Remember to ask what you must do once the ceremony is completed, in case there are any follow-up forms that need to be filled in.

**✱ Tips**

It's usually best if you have all the paperwork out of the way before the big day.

You may need a birth certificate or a positive identification, such as a driver's licence or passport.

## Set up a Wedding Gift List  553

Make it easy for yourself and your guests – be organised and offer them a wide selection in both price and types of gifts they can buy you.

⊙ **Steps**

1  Discuss what you truly want as a couple, and draw up a wish list.

2  Explore your options. You can go the traditional route – home accessories, formal place settings, silverware and fancy linens – or you can break the mould and sign up for tools, contributions towards a trip or a special purchase such as a home, or donations to a selected charity.

3  Scout around – visit a number of department stores until you find one that suits your personal taste and satisfies your needs.

**✱ Tips**

Check the cut-off date by which time guests must purchase their gifts from the list. Many department stores close the books 6 weeks before the wedding date.

Keep track of who sent what as soon as gifts arrive. This will help you later on when you are writing thank-you notes.

4    Consider registering at two or three specialist shops, a good option if you and your betrothed want to cover unusual ground or you simply can't agree on a single gift list theme.

5    Set up a list soon after your engagement, but not more than nine months prior to the wedding day.

6    Give as much detail as possible when filling out the list at your chosen department store or specialist shops. Make the buying experience easier for guests by providing information about brand, pattern or model, size and colour. This will be easy if the store has a computerised system, in which case the details will simply be scanned into the database as you choose each item.

7    Find out whether the shop or chain has a computer database for tracking; whether it takes phone, fax or online orders; whether it offers direct shipping; and what kind of refund and exchange policy it has.

8    Ask the store for a complete list of what you've registered for, so you can verify that your list and your mailing address have been entered accurately in the shop's database.

9    Jot down the name of a contact person at the shop so you'll know who to contact should complications arise.

⚠ **Warning**

Double-check the shop's return deadlines and policies.

---

## 554 | Write a Wedding Invitation

**Send out invitations at least six weeks before the ceremony to give your guests plenty of time to make travel arrangements.**

### ⊙ Steps

1    Decide who is announcing the wedding – the couple's parents or the bride and groom themselves.

2    Determine if your invitation will be formal or informal. You can say "Mr and Mrs Marcus Melendy request the honour of your presence" or use a more casual phrase like "please join us".

3    In general, use the term "the honour of your presence" if the ceremony will be held in a place of worship. Otherwise use "the pleasure of your company" or another less formal phrase.

4    For a traditional invitation, list the bride's name – usually first and middle – after her parents' names. For example, "Mr and Mrs Barry Harrison request the honour of your presence at the marriage of their daughter, Penny Jane."

5    Follow the bride's name with the full name of the groom: "to John Jacob Williams". You may choose to name the groom's parents: "son of Mr and Mrs Robert Williams".

6    Write out the date: "Saturday, the seventh of June, two thousand and three".

7    Mention the time of the ceremony: "at ten o'clock".

8    List the location and full address.

9    Enclose a separate map and a stamped, self-addressed reply card.

### ✳ Tips

Invitations to a small or informal wedding are usually handwritten, not engraved. In designing them, feel free to use your imagination.

Include all the guests' names on the envelope. Avoid impersonal terms such as "and family".

If you want to depart from the traditional wording, consult your stationer for ideas – or look at wedding invitations you've received, and decide which ones you like best.

## Handle Family Tension at Your Wedding                                    555

Tensions between relatives can dampen the joy of your wedding day, but with the right attitude and a positive approach, you can practically eliminate family friction.

### ⊙ Steps

1  Present a united front with your spouse-to-be. Talk about your apprehensions and decide how you'll face them as a couple.

2  Open a current account expressly for wedding expenses, and have all contributors (parents, in-laws) each submit a predetermined amount. This will prevent unnecessary comparisons and the "I paid for this" superiority complex.

3  Sit down with everyone involved (individually, if the situation is awkward) and air your concerns. Explain that your wedding day should be one of your happiest and that family members can help by putting aside their differences for one day.

4  Split up wedding duties – if you want to ask the bride's biological father to give her away, consider granting her stepfather the first dance with her at the reception.

5  Separate hostile parties. At the ceremony, seat your mother and her spouse in the front row and your father and his spouse in the third row; at the reception, avoid forcing them to sit at the same table.

6  Talk to your officiant if things seem too hard to handle. This person can talk you through your concerns and can be a positive source of support.

**✱ Tip**

Show affection and respect when communicating with family members – let them know you value their opinions and beliefs.

## Be a Best Man                                                            556

Being chosen as best man is an honour and a responsibility. Here's how to fill the role.

### ⊙ Steps

1  Arrive on time or early to every event connected with the wedding.

2  Plan a stag party that suits the groom's personality.

3  Oversee the ushers' morning suit rentals and fittings – make sure the morning suits are picked up and ready the day before the event, as well as returned on time after the wedding.

4  Hold the ring (or rings) until needed, unless a ring bearer is present.

5  Be sure the groom has the marriage licence. You are an official witness and may sign it.

6  Remind the groom to be ready with his suitcases for the honeymoon, tickets and anything else he may forget.

7  Help the groom get dressed before the wedding.

8  Get the groom to the wedding with plenty of time to spare.

**✱ Tip**

Remember that the other ushers as well as the groom will be affected by your attitude, so be enthusiastic and have fun.

9  Make the first toast to the bride and groom at both the rehearsal dinner and the wedding reception.

10  Read out any congratulatory cards, e-mails or telegrams from absent friends or relatives at the reception.

11  Dance with the bride and attendants during the reception.

12  Unless the couple plan to drive away on their own, arrange for a car, or drive them from the ceremony to their hotel or the airport.

## 557 | Be a Maid of Honour

As one of the bride's closest friends or relatives, you'll have a major part in the wedding festivities.

### ⊙ Steps

1  Ask the mother of the bride if you can help in any way aside from performing your ceremonial duties.

2  Consider offering accommodation to out-of-town guests if you live near the place where the wedding is being held.

3  Offer your support as the bride plans (and perhaps obsesses over) every wedding detail – from floral arrangements to dinner menus.

4  Organise a hen night.

5  Help the bride get dressed before the wedding.

6  Attend to the flower girl and ring bearer if there is no one else available to direct them.

7  Serve as one of the official witnesses to the wedding, if asked.

8  Hold the bride's bouquet and the groom's ring during the ceremony. Help the bride with her veil or train if necessary.

9  Act as a liaison between the bride and the bridesmaids during the reception.

10  Give a toast at both the rehearsal dinner and the reception – usually after the best man.

11  Dance with the best man at the reception.

12  Help the bride prepare for her departure after the reception. Alert the bride's and groom's parents when the newlywed couple is ready to leave the reception.

### ❋ Tip

Keep any negative opinions of the bridesmaids' dresses or any other wedding details to yourself.

## Be a Bridesmaid

Whether the bride is an old schoolmate, a favourite new friend, a trusted sister or your brother's fiancée, be honoured that she has asked you to share in this joyous – and hectic – special time in her life.

### ◎ Steps

1 Let the bride know you feel privileged to be chosen as a bridesmaid. She will appreciate your enthusiasm.

2 Offer to help the bride and maid of honour with any tasks they'll be facing prior to the big day. This could include housing out-of-town guests.

3 Organise a hen night – or assist the maid of honour in doing so.

4 Keep in mind that your bridesmaid dress is part of the big picture – if you are not crazy about the material or design, keep it to yourself. It is your responsibility to pay for the dress, shoes and lingerie.

5 Attend as many prenuptial events as you can – and give the bride one less thing to worry about by being punctual.

6 Contribute to the bridesmaids' gift to the bride, in addition to your own.

7 Pack an emergency kit for the bride for the wedding day: hairpins, safety pins, hair spray, hair dryer – anything she may forget to bring and can't live without.

8 Be ready to fill in doing odd jobs, such as serving as an impromptu seamstress if the need should arise.

9 Jump-start the party – dance with the best man and ushers and bring other guests onto the floor.

10 Mingle and help everyone feel comfortable.

11 Toast the newlyweds at the reception, alone or with another bridesmaid.

### ✳ Tips

Be sensitive to the bride's wishes, if and when you throw a hen night. Remember, it is your friend's wedding and you'll want to respect her desires.

Budget your expenses for the months to come. The costs for parties, meals and clothes may add up to more than you expect.

## Change Your Name After Marriage

Whether the wife takes the husband's name as tradition dictates, he takes hers, or both make the decision to hyphenate, follow the necessary steps to make it official.

### ◎ Steps

1 If you are a woman changing your name to your husband's after marriage, simply order extra certified copies of your marriage certificate and send them to all the numerous government departments, companies and organisations that you deal with so they can amend your records.

2 If you're a man changing your name at marriage, either to your wife's or to a combination of both your surnames, then you will need a deed poll or statutory declaration to get new documents.

3 Advise the Inland Revenue and Department of Social Security of your

### ✳ Tip

Because a woman traditionally takes her husband's name when she is married, a certified copy of her marriage certificate is sufficient documentation for a woman's name change, even if it doesn't contain a space for her new name. A man will need to change his name by deed poll or by a statutory declaration drafted and sworn before a solicitor.

change of name. Send them your marriage certificate or deed poll.

4   Advise the DVLA of your change of name, sending in the marriage certificate or deed poll along with your driving licence.

5   Obtain and complete a Passport Amendment Application. Send this along with appropriate fees, your current passport(s), and your marriage certificate or deed poll to the nearest passport agency. You can do this two months before your marriage, so that you have a new passport to use if going abroad for your honeymoon.

6   Order replacements for cheques, business cards, credit cards and other documents that contain your old name.

7   Call your employer or college (if you are a student) to let them know your new name, and ask them to change it in their records.

8   Change your name on your car registration, and with your insurance and mortgage companies. Contact the post office, utility companies and registrar of voters.

9   Make the announcement to friends and family (ideally to your in-laws first), using stationery or thank-you cards with your new name printed on them, or order name-change cards designed for such an occasion.

---

## 560 | Write a Wedding Thank-You Note

Send personalised thank-you notes to all of your gift-bearing wedding guests. This is your chance to let them know how much you appreciate their thoughtful presents.

### ◎ Steps

1   Consider ordering formal note cards with your married name or monogram on them. These cost about £150 or more for 50 cards, depending on the quality of paper and number of details you include. Order these notes at the same time that you order your invitations.

2   You can also opt for preprinted thank-you notes from a card or stationery store. These are much less expensive, and there are lots of styles to choose from. Expect to pay £5 to £10 for eight cards.

3   Be sure to purchase plenty of extra cards. You may receive more gifts than you expected.

4   Handwrite each note.

5   Mention each gift and tell the giver how you will use the item, if possible.

6   Refer to any special effort the person went to for you, such as travelling a long distance to attend the wedding or giving a special toast.

7   Consider adding a line telling invited guests who were unable to attend the wedding how sorry you were that they couldn't be there with you.

8   Send separate notes for wedding gifts.

9   Be timely. A thank-you note should be written within two to three weeks of receiving a gift – six to eight weeks at the very most.

### ✳ Tips

Use collectors' stamps from the post office for creative flair.

If possible, include a photograph of you taken with the person who gave the gift, at your wedding. People will enjoy this gesture.

Send thank-you notes to all your wedding suppliers to show how much you appreciated their efforts. Also send notes to your wedding party to thank them for taking part in your big day.

### ⚠ Warning

Even if you thanked guests in person, you are still expected to send out a formal note.

## ✓ 561 Select a Wedding Anniversary Gift

Whether you're celebrating your own anniversary or buying a present for another couple, these traditional and modern themes can give you some ideas. Feel free to interpret these suggestions either literally or creatively – for example, a coral anniversary could mean coral jewellery, or it might mean an exotic holiday that includes a visit to a coral reef.

| | TRADITIONAL | MODERN |
|---|---|---|
| 1st | Paper (stationery, book, scrapbook) | Clock (watch, grandfather clock) |
| 2nd | Cotton (clothing, linens, towels) | China (teacups, garden art) |
| 3rd | Leather (luggage, jacket, armchair) | Glass or crystal (champagne flutes, vase, lamp) |
| 4th | Fruit, flowers, linens (gift basket, bouquet, flowering plant) | Electrical appliance (cappuccino maker, ice cream maker, blender) |
| 5th | Wood (picture frame, firewood, cello) | Silverware (cake server, silver chopsticks) |
| 6th | Sweets, iron (candy dish, cast-iron pot) | Wood (jewellery box, salad bowl, tree) |
| 7th | Copper, wool (pots and pans, sweaters) | Desk set |
| 8th | Bronze, rubber (sculpture, rubber stamps) | Linens, lace (napkins, lacy curtains) |
| 9th | Pottery, willow (vase with willow vines) | Leather (boots, gloves, book, diary) |
| 10th | Tin and aluminum (antique tin toy, aluminum lamp or picture frame) | Diamond jewellery (tiny studs for her, diamond cufflinks or tie pin for him) |
| 15th | Crystal (glassware, chandelier) | Watch or clock (stopwatch, kitchen timer) |
| 20th | China (cake plate, gravy boat, figurine) | Platinum (watch, cake server, brooch) |
| 25th | Silver (earrings, cufflinks, vase) | Silver (desk accessories, picture frame) |
| 30th | Pearl (suit studs, strand of pearls) | Diamond jewellery (earrings, cufflinks) |
| 35th | Coral (earrings, necklace, ring) | Jade (jewellery, sculpture, paperweight) |
| 40th | Ruby (necklace, ring, earrings) | Ruby (decorative box, picture frame) |
| 45th | Sapphire (earrings, bracelet, tie tack) | Sapphire (blue glass, sapphire-cut steel) |
| 50th | Gold (ring, bracelet, cufflinks) | Gold (hair accessories, picture frame) |
| 55th | Emerald (necklace, tie tack, ring) | Emerald (stick pin, vase) |
| 60th and 75th | Diamond (necklace, cufflinks, bracelet, earrings, ring) | Diamond (watch, photo in diamond-shaped frame) |

chart

## 562 | Create a Successful Marriage

As with most good things, a long and satisfying marriage takes time and effort – on the part of both spouses. Your reward is happiness of the highest order.

### ⊙ Steps

1 Cherish compatibility. Seek out the things that interest, please and delight both of you.

2 Respect and treasure your differences. Learn from one another. Appreciate and understand your spouse's distinctive style, approach and personality – especially when it diverges from yours. Differences can often turn into delight.

3 Cultivate patience. Give your spouse enough time to reach a comfortable middle ground in his or her own way.

4 Learn how to be understanding, and develop the ability to see through your spouse's eyes.

5 Share your feelings in regular talk sessions. A nice atmosphere in a good restaurant helps open the doors to intimacy and sharing. Really listen to your partner. Be sure to look directly into the eyes of your loved one.

6 Strive for a high ratio of positive to negative in comments and actions.

7 Allow time to pass when you're surprised by a disappointment. Solutions will become evident when there is patience. A good night's sleep will help additional insights to surface.

8 Resolve the inevitable differences in a way that strengthens and deepens your love. Strive to communicate your feelings without being aggressive or defensive. Listen to each other with an open mind and seek resolutions that you both can be happy with.

9 Learn to express thankfulness for the smallest things. This gratitude can be brief and must be genuine.

**✳ Tip**

Especially after children arrive, schedule time to be alone together, and make it fun. Enjoy each other's company and laugh together.

## 563 | Impress Your In-Laws

In-law jokes have been part of world cultures for centuries. It can sometimes be tricky to forge a positive relationship with your spouse's parents, but it's a good idea to try.

### ⊙ Steps

1 Treat your spouse well. Nothing pleases parents more than knowing that their son or daughter is being well-loved and cared for.

2 Present a united front. Never squabble with your spouse in front of his or her parents. If you think hot issues may come up, discuss how you will deal with them ahead of time.

3 Contact them without waiting for them to contact you, and invite them to visit before they invite themselves. This allows you to get your home ready and to prepare yourself emotionally for a visit on your own terms.

**✳ Tip**

Begin making your own cherished family holiday traditions at home, especially if family holidays become a tug-of-war about whose family to visit and it isn't possible to visit both. Or go away and enjoy the holidays in an entirely different way.

4 Ask their advice, regardless of whether or not you plan to take it. Your spouse's parents will be glad to feel that they still have some influence in their child's life.

5 Be creative. If it bothers you that your mother-in-law always tries to wash up after dinner at your house, offer her another task, such as serving coffee or playing with the baby.

6 If you and your in-laws are completely incompatible, just handle it as gracefully as possible, avoid contact whenever you can, and remember that even if you will never love your in-laws, they did something wonderful when they created your spouse.

⚠ **Warnings**

Avoid confrontations with your in-laws. Try to let criticism or differences of opinion wash over you.

Try to get along well with your in-laws, but don't let them take over. This can be especially important when children arrive. Set reasonable ground rules for everyone in the family.

## Resolve Conflict in a Marriage 564

Of course, there will be disagreements in any marriage. The key is how you resolve them. Do it right and your marriage will grow stronger and deeper by the day.

✳ **Tip**

Practise conflict resolution with small matters, such as picking out silverware, before moving to complex, possibly disharmonious decisions, such as choosing pets and naming children.

◉ **Steps**

1 Separate complaints, which can be destructive, from constructive criticism, which you can learn from and build upon.

2 Understand your spouse's emotional needs. Listen to what your spouse is saying, but also try to understand why he or she is saying it.

3 Learn to communicate non-defensively and non-aggressively. Presenting facts or feelings in a neutral manner helps avoid escalation.

4 Stay calm and be direct. Be truthful with your spouse and with yourself. What are you really feeling?

5 Keep studying those first four steps. Practice makes perfect. And perfecting your marriage is worth all the practice you can put into it.

## Be a Better Listener 565

As you've probably heard, good communication is the most important part of a successful marriage. And careful listening may be the most important part of good communication.

✳ **Tips**

Your questions and comments reflect how closely you have been listening. Good listeners might incorporate bits of what the speaker has said, sometimes much earlier in the discussion, into their questions.

Keep an open mind and avoid jumping to conclusions.

◉ **Steps**

1 Position yourself so that you can be engaged with your spouse and the conversation: Face your spouse and make eye contact. If you are doing something else (for example, typing or reading the paper), stop.

2 Close the door to minimise interruptions and let your partner know you're willing to listen.

3 Pay attention to your spouse's words. Stop daydreaming and letting your mind wander elsewhere.

4 Pay attention to non-verbal cues: notice pitch, tone and inflection. Observe facial expressions and posture. Is your partner slouching,

turned away from you, or sitting with his arms crossed? These postures may indicate that he is upset – try to find out why.

5   Be conscious of your spouse's personality – and your history together – when you're evaluating his words.

6   Try to determine what your spouse wants from you, even if it's not explicitly stated. Sympathy? Advice?

7   Try to rid yourself of biases or preconceptions that can distort what you hear or your understanding of it.

8   Avoid interrupting the speaker before he has finished talking. You might be thought rude, but more important, you might misinterpret what your partner is saying if you don't let him finish.

9   Respond appropriately. Encourage your partner with an understanding nod or say "I see" or "That makes sense".

10  Ask questions to clarify what you don't understand and to demonstrate your interest. Open-ended questions (such as "How did that make you feel?") promote further discussion.

## ⚠ Warnings

Avoid turning the focus of the conversation onto you. For example, if your spouse is trying to confide a personal problem, avoid saying "That's just like the time I ..." and digressing into unhelpful stories about yourself or your own problems.

Avoid trying to plan your next comment while the other person is talking – this can detract from listening and hearing.

Don't let your emotions cloud what the other person is saying.

## 566 | Get a Divorce

**In Britain more than two out of every five marriages end in divorce. The process boils down to controlling what you can – and normally, what you won't be able to control is your spouse.**

### ◉ Steps

1   Make every effort towards keeping your relations amicable. The angrier your spouse is, the uglier your divorce will be.

2   Consult a solicitor or two – most will meet for an initial consultation just to explain the process and your immediate options. Be aware that divorce laws in England and Wales differ from those in Scotland and Northern Ireland.

3   If the divorce is uncontested and there are adequate grounds for divorce, consider a "quickie" DIY divorce. This is not usually appropriate if there are issues to be resolved relating to children or finances.

4   Gather your financial documents, including tax returns for the last five years, all retirement accounts and all financial accounts.

5   Close or freeze joint accounts. You and your spouse may want to divide equally all funds accumulated during your marriage.

6   Keep track of all debts incurred or paid (credit cards, repairs to the family home and so forth) once you separate from your spouse.

7   Determine whether maintenance or child support is warranted. If you are the spouse in need of support, make sure to initiate court proceedings as soon as possible, because you won't receive support until you file. Consult a solicitor or other resource.

8   Keep track of any money you give your spouse as maintenance or child support, and write cheques rather than give cash.

### ✻ Tip

It's best to consult with a lawyer who specialises in family law, even if you plan to represent yourself throughout the process.

### ⚠ Warnings

Expect the divorce process to be long and potentially costly.

Remove your emotions from the legal process by seeking therapy to deal with them. Don't use your lawyer or the system to retaliate against your spouse; it will just cost you more money.

9   Realise that there will be at least a six-week waiting period between the time you file for divorce and the time your divorce is final.

10  Research your spouse's pension plans, retirement accounts and other savings accounts. You may not be aware of all the plans to which your spouse contributes, or to which an employer contributes on behalf of your spouse.

11  Negotiate a custody plan if children are involved; you will have to.

## Date as a Single Parent 567

As a single parent, you may feel reluctant to date again. Take it slowly, listen to your instincts and try to have fun.

### ⊙ Steps

1   Date when you feel you're ready, not when others tell you that you should (see 525 "Ask Someone on a Date").

2   Ignore guilt. You're a human being and you need adult companionship. You deserve an occasional night out.

3   Take it slowly. Don't fill your calendar with dates all at once. It will take time for you and your children to adjust to the idea of your dating.

4   Make sure your children are cared for by someone you trust while you're on a date.

5   Talk to your children. Explain that you're going to spend some time with a person you like. Do not talk about remarriage or new daddies or mummies, but be honest about its being a date. Answer any questions your children have, but keep personal details to yourself.

6   Decide whether you want the person you're dating to meet your children. On a first date it is probably not advisable. When you do introduce them, keep it light, easy and quick. Don't plan any "family" outings yet.

7   Try not to talk about your children too much during dates, but don't feel you need to hide their existence, either.

8   Introduce the new person to your children gradually if you feel that your relationship is becoming more serious.

9   Avoid letting your children see you in bed with anyone.

10  Consider how much affection you're comfortable expressing in front of your children. Follow your instincts. You can always kiss after the kids are in bed.

11  Be prepared for your children to be angry, resentful, hostile, sad, shy or nervous about the situation. Help them through it as best you can.

12  Be patient. It may take time to become comfortable on dates after being out of practice for so long.

13  Keep your ex-spouse out of it. He or she is bound to find out about your dating and may try to discuss it with you or become involved. Remember that you are divorced and it is your life to live as you please, so long as your children are not harmed.

 **Tip**

If you or any of your children are having a very difficult time coping with the situation, consult a counsellor or therapist.

## 568 | Prepare Siblings for a New Baby

**Whether baby makes four, five or six, the change in your family will undoubtedly both excite and confuse your children.**

### ⊙ Steps

1 Wait until Mum is showing before breaking the news; this will make the wait seem shorter for siblings-to-be.

2 Involve your children by letting them listen to Mum's belly and feel for hiccups and kicks.

3 Allow young ones to ask questions about the baby's impact on their lives.

4 Give your children a doll to introduce them to the concept of a new baby. Teach them how to change nappies and bathe the doll.

5 Show your children the ultrasound photo of the new baby, then bring out their own ultrasound photos and discuss similarities and differences.

6 Read books together about children who have brothers and sisters.

7 Bring a present to the hospital for each of the siblings so they can receive it as soon as their new brother or sister is born. Explain that the present is from the baby.

8 Give the baby a small present from each brother and sister, and let the siblings find a good place for the gifts in the baby's room.

### ✱ Tip

Children may have serious concerns about where the baby will sleep, whether the baby will play with their toys, and how much he or she will divert Mum and Dad's attention from them. Respond to all questions thoughtfully and with reassurances.

### ⚠ Warning

Although your goal is to encourage a bond between siblings and new babies, caution your older children specifically about any actions that could harm the baby – for example, accidentally smothering the baby with a blanket, hitting the baby or trying to feed the baby solid food.

## 569 | Decide Where to Have Your Baby

**It is important to feel as comfortable as possible when giving birth – minimising stress can ease the process. For some women hospital will be the best place, others will choose a home birth.**

### ⊙ Steps

1 Ask your midwife and doctor what is available in your area. Take a tour of the maternity units in hospitals local to you. Large hospitals have midwives and a full team of doctors and consultants on hand. Smaller cottage hospitals or midwife-led units may be able to deal with uncomplicated births but need to transfer mothers to larger maternity units should problems arise.

2 Consider the "Domino" scheme. Domino stands for "DOMiciliary IN and Out" – a midwife comes to your home when labour starts and takes you into hospital to deliver your baby, attended by hospital staff and a GP only if needed. If all goes well you go home within a few hours. This may depend on the availability of midwives in your area.

3 Look at birth at home. Medical staff in some areas are very supportive of home births. Often, however, first births at home are discouraged as are home births where there may be complications (such as twins, breach births or if there have been problems in pregnancy).

4 Give yourself time to assess your options. You can change your mind during your pregnancy. Go with what feels right to you and your partner.

### ✱ Tips

Involve fathers in choosing where to give birth.

If you are going for a hospital birth, investigate their rates of caesarians and other interventions, which can vary widely. If you want a birth with minimal interventions, you may need to choose your hospital carefully. Likewise, many hospitals are reluctant to provide elective caesarians unless there is a good medical reason for doing so.

Independent midwives and doulas (experienced mothers providing emotional support) are available to mothers before, during and after birth. If you are interested in such support, arrange to meet them early on in the pregnancy.

✓ **570 Choose a Traditional Name for Your Child**

If you want your child to grow up honouring his or her heritage, a name may be a good way to start. If family names don't suit you, you can try the chart below. It lists some traditional names, along with their meanings, from a variety of ethnic groups and languages.

| | BOY | GIRL |
|---|---|---|
| **Arabic** | Adil, righteous; Akbar, greatest; Alam, universe; Cemal, attractive; Fadil, generous; Haidar, lion; Nailah, success; Nazeer, friend; Nizam, leader; Roni, joy is mine | Aisha, life; Najma and Najmah, star; Nureen, light; Rashieka, descended from royalty; Sadiya, lucky; Shula, bright; Razi, my secret |
| **Chinese** | Ho, good; Hu, tiger; Lei, thunder; Li, strong; Liang, excellent; Lok, happy; Kong, sky; Yong, courageous; Yu and Yue, universe | Lian, graceful willow; Ling, delicate; Mei, pretty; Meiying, beautiful flower; Xiaoli, small and beautiful; Xiu Mei, beautiful plum; Yang, sun; Yen, yearning |
| **French** | Antoine, praiseworthy; Bernard, brave as a bear; Guillaume, determined guardian; Henri, leader; Jean, Marc, Luc and Jacques, love | Aimée and Cheri, love; Annette, gracious; Chantal, song; Charlotte, little and womanly; Juliette, youthful; Nicole and Nicolette, victorious people |
| **German** | Baldric, brave ruler; Dardolf, bright wolf; Dieter, army of the people; Len, brave as a lion; Medwin, faithful friend; Ottokar, happy warrior; Otto, rich | Annchen, gracious; Delana, noble protector; Gretchen, Greta and Gretel, pearl; Hedy, delightful and sweet; Katrina, pure; Mina, love; Raina, mighty |
| **Greek** | Alexander, defender of humankind; Constantinos, firm or constant; Nicos and Nicholas, victorious people; Platon, broad-shouldered | Alexandra, defender of humankind; Athena, wise; Callista, most beautiful; Helena, bright one; Kay, rejoicer; Katina, pure; Philana, love |
| **Hebrew** | Ethan, strong and firm; Gibor, powerful; Levi, joined in harmony; Joel, God is willing; Joshua, God is my salvation; Josiah, fire of the Lord; Jonah, dove | Ahava and Haviva, beloved; Aliza, joyful; Evelyn, life or life-giving; Ariel, lioness of God; Danielle, God is my judge; Dara, compassion; Liora and Meira, light |
| **Indian (Sanscrit, Hindi)** | Hari, sun; Jitendra, conqueror; Rajiv, lotus flower; Ranjit, victory; Sanjay, triumphant; Suresh, sun. | Anisha, without a master; Chandra, moon; Lakshmi, wife of Vishnu; Pooja/Poojan, worship; Sharada, autumn; Sunita, righteous |
| **Irish** | Aron, strength; Conn, Conan and Quinn, intelligence; Eoin and Owen, gift from God; Jack, John and Sean, grace; Kacey, brave; Kevin and Keeley, beautiful | Aingeal, angel; Caronwyn, Cavan and Keeley, beautiful; Dara and Ida, intelligence; Grace, Hannah and Jane, grace; Shauna and Siobhan, gift from God |
| **Italian** | Angelo and Angelino, angel or messenger; Davide and Amadeo, love; Giovanni, has favour with God; Nicolo and Nicolas, victorious people | Angela and Angelina, angel or messenger; Beatrice, blessed; Isabella, dedicated to God; Lucia, light; Natalia, Christmas; Pia, devout; Sofia, wisdom |
| **Polish** | Andrzej, manly; Czeslaw, rocky fortress; Dawid, beloved; Eryk, peaceful ruler; Jan, God is gracious; Krzysztof, Christbearer; Leon, lion; Pawel, small | Agnieszka, pure; Ala, truthful; Elka, Elzbieta and Izabella, consecrated to God; Filomena, loved one; Janina, God is gracious |
| **Russian** | Aleksandr, Aleksey and Sasha, defender of humankind; Danila, God is my judge; Leonid, brave as a lion; Misha, like God; Nikolai and Koyla, victorious people; Vitya, conqueror; | Anya, gracious; Dodya, love; Katya and Ekaterina, pure; Nika, belonging to God; Nikita, victorious people; Sonya, wisdom; Tania, fairy queen |
| **Scottish** | Angus, unique; Duncan, brown warrior; Gregor, watchful shepherd; Mungo, beloved; Ninian, an early British saint; Rory, red king | Catriona, pure; Eilidh, bright; Janet, the Lord is gracious; Kirstie, Christian; Morag, tall; Rowan, red-headed |
| **Spanish** | Alfonso, noble and eager; Alejandro, defender of humankind; Carlos, strong and manly; Fernando, daring and adventurous; Jose, God will increase; Pablo, small; Pedro, small rock | Alicia, truthful; Carmencita, song; Clarita, bright and clear; Juana, God is gracious; Monica, adviser; Paloma, dove; Rosa, rose; Susana, lily; Teresita, reaper |
| **Welsh** | Aled, a river in Wales; Dafydd/Dewi, beloved; Dylan, tide or sea; Hefin, summer; Huw, heart or soul; Meredydd, great leader | Bethan, oath of God; Era, snow; Gwen, holy and blessed; Haf, summer; Heulwen, sunsine; Rhiannon, maiden or queen; Siriol, cheerful |

chart

## 571 | Name a Baby

Whether you decide to go with a traditional name or with a more unusual one, make sure the name will fit your baby throughout life.

### ⊙ Steps

1 Decide whether you lean towards unusual names or more traditional ones (see 570 "Choose a Traditional Name for Your Child").

2 Collect names from both partners' family trees. Look for names of people who have played a meaningful role in either of your lives or who have names you both like.

3 Write down your favourite artists and writers; favourite characters from novels, films or plays; and figures from history or mythology.

4 Think about cities and countries significant to you and your partner – geographically inspired names have become popular in recent years.

5 Think about your heritage. Do you want to recognise a particular nationality or ethnic background in your baby's name? Could you use other elements in your family's history, such as place names?

6 Buy a book of baby names and highlight the ones you both like.

7 When you've compiled a list, think about how your favourites sound with the baby's last name. You'll probably want to avoid rhymes, long first names combined with long last names, or combinations that add up to a celebrity's name or a pun, or that have any unflattering nicknames.

8 Using all of the above information, narrow your list down to two girls' names and/or two boys' names (depending on whether you know the sex of the baby).

9 After the baby is born, either bestow a name immediately or, if you prefer, observe your baby for a day or two and decide which of your choices seems most appropriate.

### ✳ Tip

Try not to divulge your top choice. It's a fun surprise when the day finally comes. Plus, you don't want someone else who's also expecting to poach your favourite name.

## 572 | Be a Good Parent

A big part of good parenting is establishing respect between parents and children. Your child needs to know what you expect of her, and you in turn must learn to listen and wait.

### ⊙ Steps

1 Slow down. Babies and children live in a different time frame from adults' – usually a much slower one. Keep this in mind as you talk to your child, care for her and go about your day together.

2 Observe your child. You'll be amazed at how well you'll get to know your child by sitting back and watching. This focused awareness will help you better understand moods, abilities and temperament. Listening is important, too.

### ✳ Tips

Build more time into your day so you can slow down with your child and enjoy your time together. Continuous hurried behaviour creates stress for both you and your child.

3   Stay optimistic. Optimism is contagious; so is negativity. Show your child through your behaviour how to overcome minor setbacks. Children emulate their parents' attitudes and habits, so it will help if you have a positive outlook.

4   Accept and acknowledge your child's feelings and desires. Let her know it's OK to feel sad, scared or angry. You can say, "It looks as if you're sad because your friend has gone home" or "It seems that you're cross because I put the ball away".

5   Tell your child your expectations. Children won't always comply right away, but they need to understand clearly what a parent expects: "I want you to put on your sweater. We're going outside", or "I want your feet to stay off the couch".

6   Set appropriate limits. Even when you acknowledge a feeling or desire, you must make a child aware of appropriate behaviour and rules: "I can see you're angry at your friend because he took the toy from you, but I won't let you hit him. Hitting is not something we do in our family. What else can you do?"

7   Wait. Let your child do as much as she can on her own – learn to walk, put on socks, resolve conflicts with friends. Anxiety or the desire to help often tempts parents to rush in and solve the problem for the child. A better response would be to wait and see what your child can manage on her own. One might surprise you.

8   Behave genuinely. Just as you accept your child's moods, though not always her behaviour, it's OK to have a sad or angry thought yourself and express it appropriately: "I'm really tired right now but I'm listening to you". A parent's genuineness prepares a child for life.

9   Look after yourself and your marriage. Make arrangements to have some guilt-free time to take care of your own needs. Plan a date with your partner and forget the kids for a while. You'll be a happier person and a better parent.

Start a babysitting group with local parents so you can have a few hours to yourself or a night out with your partner. Ask friends, grandparents or a responsible teenage niece to babysit. Get out of the house and have some adult fun.

⚠ **Warning**

Monitor your child if he or she is having a dispute with a friend. Feelings can quickly escalate, and a parent may need to intervene. Safety should always be your number one consideration.

---

## Breast-Feed Your Baby Successfully                    573

Breast-feeding is nature's way to feed an infant – but that doesn't mean it comes naturally. Here's how to get started.

◉ **Steps**

1   Make sure your hands are clean.

2   Choose a breast-feeding position: on your lap, baby at your side or lying on your side (reclining position). Use pillows to support your back and arms as necessary.

3   Hold your baby very close, with head, shoulders and hips facing you. While his mouth is close to your breast, tickle his mouth with your nipple. When he opens his mouth (the "rooting" reflex), bring him in the rest of the way. If he is latched on correctly, his lips will be flared out and he will take a good portion of your areola into his mouth.

4   Expect to feel a pulling of the nipple, or even some pain initially. If pain lasts beyond a few seconds, the baby is probably sucking on just the tip of the nipple; remove him from the breast and try latching him on again.

✱ **Tips**

Eat a balanced diet and drink plenty of fluid. You may want to have water or juice nearby as you feed.

Delay bottle feedings for at least three to four weeks to avoid nipple confusion. If a delay is not possible, ask a feeding specialist or health visitor about alternative feeding methods.

5   Let your baby feed on the first breast as long as he wants, to ensure that he gets enough to eat and that your milk supply will keep pace with his needs.

6   To remove your baby from the breast, insert a clean finger into his mouth to release the suction, and then pull him away.

7   Burp your baby after he finishes the first side, then offer the other breast. If he doesn't take the other breast, offer that breast at the next feeding.

8   Breast-feed initially at least 10 to 12 times a day, or whenever your baby seems hungry. Signs of hunger include increased alertness or activity, mouthing and rooting. Crying is a late indicator of hunger.

You will know that breast-feeding is going well if your baby gains weight gradually. He or she will lose some weight in the first week, but should be up to birth weight by two weeks and start to gain steadily after that.

⚠ **Warning**

If breast-feeding isn't going well, get support. Some hospitals employ breast-feeding specialists. La Leche League is an excellent support group for nursing mothers; visit www.laleche.org.uk or phone 020 7242 1278.

---

## 574 | Store Breast Milk

**Whether you are expressing breast milk daily so you can return to work or you're just doing it before a night out, storing it properly is essential.**

### ⊙ Steps

1   Express your breast milk using a breast pump.

2   Pour the milk into either clean, plastic or glass bottles or plastic bottle-liner bags.

3   Store the breast milk in 60–120 ml (2–4 oz) portions. These cool down more quickly than larger portions.

4   Cap the bottles tightly. Tape the bags shut or use ones with built-in twist ties.

5   Label each bottle or bag with the date.

6   Refrigerate or freeze breast milk as soon as possible after collecting it.

7   Store breast milk in the refrigerator for up to 72 hours; if you need to store it longer, use the freezer. A freezer compartment inside a single-door refrigerator can keep breast milk safely frozen for up to two weeks; the freezer section of a double-door refrigerator can store milk for three months.

✳ **Tips**

Wash bottles well with hot, soapy water and a brush. Sterilise them before adding milk.

Use the oldest milk first when thawing it.

⚠ **Warning**

Throw out any breast milk that has been at room temperature for more than 6 hours.

## Heat a Baby's Bottle

**575**

Whether they take breast milk or formula, some babies prefer having their bottles warmed up. It takes off the chill and generally helps infants accept the bottle.

### ⊙ Steps

1   Look at alternatives to clear plastic bottles and consider replacing them with opaque ones, since some studies have indicated that chemicals may leach from plastic bottles made out of polycarbonate.

2   Defrost breast milk if necessary, either by thawing it in the refrigerator overnight or putting it in a bowl of warm water for half an hour.

3   Warm a bottle of either formula or defrosted breast milk by submerging it in a bowl or pan of warm (not boiling) water, by running the bottle under warm tap water, or by using a commercial bottle warmer, available at baby shops.

4   Test the temperature of the milk or formula in the bottle by shaking a few drops onto your inner wrist. It should feel tepid, not hot.

5   Continue warming the milk or formula until it's the desired temperature.

6   Some babies also like to have the teat of the bottle warmed; run it under warm tap water or submerge it in a pan of warm water for just a few seconds. Test it on your inner arm to make sure it's just warm, not hot.

### ✱ Tip

To make life more convenient when you are out and about, you may want to start introducing a bottle closer to room temperature – so your baby does not grow accustomed to always having a nice, toasty bottle.

### ⚠ Warnings

Avoid microwaving formula or breast milk; it distributes heat unevenly in the bottle.

For your baby's safety, never reuse formula or breast milk once you've heated it. Bacteria may have formed in the liquid.

## Get Dad Involved With Baby Care

**576**

It's important for new fathers to help care for their babies – it promotes family bonding, gives new mothers much-needed support, and is emotionally rewarding for dads and babies alike.

### ⊙ Steps

1   Make sure Dad is there at the baby's birth. For many fathers, the bonding experience begins when they help cut the baby's umbilical cord. If you have to deal with any birth complications or a caesarean section, he can spend time with the baby while you're recovering.

2   Give Dad a special, unique task of his own. In many families, fathers take care of bath time, nappy-changing or winding.

3   Trust him to work things out for himself (as long as everyone stays safe). He may not perform all baby-care tasks exactly as you do, but the difference may not matter. So what if the baby's outfit isn't colour-coordinated?

4   Let him share in the nighttime parenting. Dancing, cuddling and rocking are wonderful ways for a father to nurture his baby. Even a middle-of-the-night nappy change can offer a tranquil moment of bonding between father and child.

5   Encourage him to play with his baby. Even very tiny infants benefit from Daddy time.

### ✱ Tips

If you're looking for a sling that Dad can wear, too, get one with adjustable straps. Some slings even come in larger sizes to accommodate tall men.

Take photographs and videos of Dad and baby together. It will give you a record of the special moments they share and encourage Dad to stay involved as your baby grows.

### ⚠ Warning

If you're breast-feeding exclusively, resist the urge to let Dad give an occasional bottle, at least in the early stages; using artificial nipples in the first three to four weeks of life can cause nipple confusion and may lead to breast-feeding difficulties.

6   Let him carry his baby in a sling or other infant carrier. When the baby gets older, Dad can carry his toddler in a backpack.

7   Give Dad reading material, such as the many books on fatherhood that can help him deal with his new role.

## 577 | Reduce the Risk of Cot Death

Most parents worry about cot death (sudden infant death syndrome or SIDS), but the chances of an average baby dying from cot death are less than 2 in 1,000. Try to reduce the risk.

### ◎ Steps

1   Place your baby on her back to sleep, not on her tummy.

2   Give your baby a firm mattress.

3   Keep your baby away from smoke.

4   Never put your baby to sleep on a water bed or beanbag chair.

5   Don't use plastic top sheets or allow plastic bags or film near the cot.

6   Make sure your baby doesn't get overheated – avoid multiple layers of clothing and hot blankets.

7   Keep stuffed toys, pillows and heavy blankets out of the cot along with anything else that might smother the baby.

8   If your baby suffers from sleep apnea (cessation of breathing), which can be life-threatening, consider purchasing a monitor that signals you if your baby suddenly stops breathing.

### ✱ Tips

Babies who have survived a life-threatening incident in which they turned blue, stopped breathing and required significant intervention or resuscitation are at a higher risk for cot death. Premature and low-birth weight babies may also be more susceptible.

Most deaths occur between the second and fourth months, at home, in the cot, in cold weather and between midnight and 8 am. Consult your doctor or health visitor for more information about cot death.

## 578 | Change a Baby's Nappy

Not much has really changed since the days of nappy pins – whether you choose to go the route of cloth or disposable nappies, you'll follow more or less the same procedure.

### ◎ Steps

1   Lay a fresh nappy on a changing table, or on a towel or mat on the floor.

2   Place your baby, tummy side up, on top of the clean nappy.

3   Unfasten the nappy tabs on the soiled nappy.

4   Hold your baby's feet together and very gently lift them up, raising the baby's bottom. Use the clean part of the nappy to wipe away any excess stools, then fold over the soiled section of the nappy and set the old nappy aside.

5   Wipe your baby's buttocks and genitals gently from front to back with baby wipes. Don't forget the lower back and the skin folds of the thighs. (A baby girl might get stools around her labia and vagina, so clean that area gently with baby wipes.)

### ✱ Tip

Wash your hands before and after all nappy changes, and remember that frequent changes help prevent nappy rash.

### ⚠ Warning

Never leave your baby unattended on a changing table.

6   Lower your baby's bottom onto the clean nappy.

7   Pat the area dry with a towel.

8   Apply nappy-rash cream to the area if necessary.

9   Make sure to pull up the back of the clean nappy high enough to prevent leaks. Position the front of the nappy just under the baby's abdomen.

10  Bring the tabs around from the back of the nappy and fasten them to the front.

11  Turn changing into a game of peek-a-boo to distract your baby.

## Things You'll Need

❏ changing table

❏ nappies

❏ baby wipes (or wet washcloth or cotton wool balls)

❏ towel

❏ nappy-rash cream

## Wind a Baby                                                            579

Winding a baby can reduce sickness and relieve bloating caused by swallowed air. Here are some tried-and-trusted methods.

### ⊙ Steps

1   Put a clean towel, cloth nappy or muslin cloth over your shoulder or wherever your baby's head will rest

2   Position the baby over one shoulder with his stomach against your chest and with his head resting on your shoulder.

3   Gently pat your baby on the back and rub it in a circular motion until he burps.

4   Alternatively, place one hand across the baby's chest, supporting his chin with your thumb and index finger. Lean your baby across that support hand and gently pat or rub his back with your free hand.

5   Opt for a "lap burp". Position yourself so that you can comfortably place the baby's head on one thigh and his stomach on the other. Using an upwards and circular motion, gently pat the baby's back until he burps.

6   Try getting exercise while you walk and burp your baby. Stand up and place your arm under the baby's rib cage, with the baby's back to your chest. Walk around slowly, leaning the baby over your arm until he burps. And be patient: sometimes burping takes several minutes.

### ❋ Tips

Never try to burp a baby while he or she is vomiting.

Don't worry if your baby is sick occasionally – what looks like a lot of liquid is probably no more than a teaspoon. Very frequent sickness or projectile vomiting could signal a problem; contact your doctor.

Breast-fed babies tend to swallow less air than bottle-fed babies, so don't worry if your breast-fed baby rarely burps, as long as he or she seems comfortable.

If breast-feeding, wind the baby when you switch sides or finish feeding. If bottle-feeding, wind every so often or whenever he or she seems uncomfortable.

## 580 | Get a Baby to Sleep

You've just put her down for a nap, and now she's awake and crying again. You could let her cry it out, or try these ideas to get her back to sleep.

### Steps

1 Rock your baby. Most babies enjoy rocking and cuddling as part of their bedtime routine.

2 Nurse your baby. Babies love to fall asleep while breast-feeding; in fact, sometimes it's hard to keep them awake long enough to finish a meal. But don't let this become such a habit that your baby will never sleep without nursing first.

3 Swing your baby. Mechanical swings or rocking cradles can calm fretful babies and help them drift off to sleep.

4 Swaddle your infant. Many newborns enjoy the feeling of being snugly wrapped – though others don't enjoy being swaddled.

5 Dance with your baby. A good lullaby or smooth jazz CD, a dark room and a slow dance often send a baby to sleep.

6 Bath your baby. A warm bath about an hour before going to bed is a great way to relax your baby and help her sleep.

7 Go for a drive or walk. Many babies who resist falling asleep in a cot or bed will happily drift off in a car seat in a moving vehicle, in a sling or frontpack, or in a pushchair.

8 Read, talk and sing to your baby. Even if she's too young to understand the words, the gentle rhythms of your voice may help her get to sleep.

9 Turn on a fan or other source of white noise. The steady buzz of a fan, or even the static from a baby monitor with the transmitter turned off, can help a baby tune out other sounds.

10 Do the washing. The gentle vibration and white noise of a washing machine often help a baby get to sleep. Some desperate parents even put the baby in her car seat on top of the dryer.

11 Develop a routine. Mealtime, bath time, cuddle time and story time will naturally lead to bedtime once your baby gets used to the pattern.

### ✳ Tips

Some babies are night owls by nature. If your baby is like this, don't worry about enforcing a 6 pm bedtime. If she falls asleep at 9 or 10 pm, she may sleep later in the mornings, giving you time to yourself at the start of the day.

Get black-out blinds for the room where your baby will sleep. This will help keep the room dark for naps and ensure that your baby doesn't always get up with the sun.

### ⚠ Warning

Avoid leaving your baby in a swing for too long; extended periods of sitting upright can hinder spinal development in young babies.

## 581 | Calm a Colicky Baby

About one in five babies has colic – a set of symptoms that include inconsolable screaming, clenched fists, increased bowel activity and wind. The cause is unknown.

### Steps

1 Rock your baby in your arms, a pram, a swing or a cradle (but not until your baby is at least six weeks old). Experiment with a variety of rocking positions, since all babies are different.

### ✳ Tips

Always consult your doctor about colic. A doctor can make a proper diagnosis, eliminating possible causes such as an intestinal problem or an allergy to formula.

2  Sing a lullaby to your baby.

3  Walk around with your baby in a sling or backpack.

4  Wrap your newborn snugly in a soft blanket, as some infants are soothed by being swaddled.

5  Gently massage your baby's back, tummy and thighs.

6  Give your baby a warm bath if he likes it.

7  Place your baby across your lap, tummy down, and stroke his back.

8  Walk around to relieve pressure, placing your forearm under your baby's rib cage with the baby facing outwards .

9  Soothe your baby with sound: some babies enjoy rhythmic noises, such as music, a vacuum cleaner or a dishwasher. They may also find being driven in a car very soothing.

He or she may recommend medication for wind relief, or a different baby formula.

Most babies outgrow colic by the end of their fourth month.

## ⚠ Warning

Never rock or shake your baby vigorously.

# Wash a Baby

582

As soon as the umbilical cord has healed, your baby is ready for a bath. Bathing your baby is not only easy, it can be fun for you both.

## ◎ Steps

1  Place an baby bath in the kitchen sink.

2  Fill it with lukewarm water. Test the water on the sensitive skin inside your wrist or elbow to make sure it's lukewarm, not hot.

3  Add a few squirts of baby wash.

4  Carefully place your baby in the bath, being careful to support his head and neck.

5  Wash the infant with a baby washcloth, patting and rubbing gently.

6  Gently dab your baby's face with the washcloth.

7  Pour warm water onto your baby's hair from a small plastic cup, shielding his eyes.

8  Apply a pea-size dollop of baby shampoo and wash the baby's head and scalp.

9  Shield the baby's eyes and rinse his head with lukewarm water, again using the cup and being careful to avoid the eyes.

10  Lift your baby out of the bath.

11  Wrap him in a soft, warm towel.

## ⚠ Warning

Never leave a baby unattended in the bath, even for a few seconds. Babies and toddlers can drown in very shallow water.

## Things You'll Need

❑ baby bath

❑ baby wash

❑ baby washcloth

❑ small plastic cup

❑ towel

## 583 | Clean a Baby's Eyes, Nose and Ears

A daily sponging is all that's really required to keep your baby's eyes, nose and ears fresh and clean.

### ⊙ Steps

1 Dip a clean, soft baby facecloth or cotton wool ball into warm water and squeeze it to remove any excess water. (As baby skin is very sensitive, avoid using soap on the face.)

2 Sing or talk softly to your baby to distract her as you clean.

3 Use the cloth or cotton wool ball to clean the corners of your baby's eyes, wiping gently from the inside corner to the outside edge of each eye.

4 Use a soft, damp facecloth or baby wipe to remove mucus around your baby's nose, wiping gently around each nostril.

5 Use a facecloth to wipe the outer part of your baby's ears, but not inside. Check behind each ear, and wipe away any dirt or debris.

### ✳ Tip

Earwax keeps ears clean and naturally moves outwards. But if wax buildup seems excessive or doesn't move outwards, talk to your doctor.

### ⚠ Warning

Never put anything inside your baby's eyes, nose or ears. Cotton buds or fingers could rupture the eardrums or make the walls of your baby's ears bleed.

## 584 | Wean Your Baby Off the Bottle

When you decide to wean your baby from a bottle to a cup, a variety of techniques can make the transition easier on you both.

### ⊙ Steps

1 Offer your baby a cup instead of a bottle, and follow his cues. He may seem interested and may drink from it properly; if he has trouble or just refuses, try again in a few days.

2 Make a family policy that your baby can't walk around with his drink or play with his bottle. This will make it clear that he needs to eat at regular meal and snack times, rather than always holding on to the bottle. Follow similar rules yourself so you don't send mixed messages.

3 Substitute other things that will comfort your baby if he seems to be using his bottle as a dummy. These should include extra attention and affection, as well as special games, toys and books.

4 If your baby gets thirsty at night, keep a spillproof cup of water nearby and offer it to him in lieu of a bottle when he wakes. The nighttime bottle is often the most difficult to lose, but doing so is important. Using formula milk or juice at night harms your baby's dental health, as the liquid will pool in the mouth, coat the teeth and lead to severe decay. Bottles also pose a choking hazard.

### ✳ Tips

If your baby does not seem fond of cow's milk, don't despair. There are many other excellent sources of calcium and protein, such as tofu and yogurt.

Remember that your baby still needs good nutrition; a 1-year-old should drink about 600 ml (1 pt) of milk daily, depending on how much solid food he takes in.

Many babies become addicted to juice during weaning; try to make it an occasional treat rather than a regular part of your baby's diet.

Try using a cup that features your child's favourite book, TV or film characters; this may help him get excited about using it.

## Wean Your Baby Off the Breast 585

Weaning can be a difficult time for both mother and baby, but doing it gradually with lots of love can ease the transition.

### ⊙ Steps

1 Proceed slowly. Your baby may find abrupt weaning traumatic, and it can lead to uncomfortable engorgement and mastitis in your breasts. Mastitis is an infection that can cause fever and flu-like symptoms, as well as pain, hardness, redness, or heat in your breast – usually just one breast, not both.

2 Eliminate one daily feeding session at a time over a period of weeks or even months, starting with the feeding session that seems the least important to your baby emotionally.

3 Offer your baby a substitute for the breast. If she is less than one year old, you may need to substitute formula in a bottle to make sure she gets the nutrition she needs. If she is past her first birthday, eating a variety of foods and drinking from a cup, you may be able to offer her food or distract her with a fun game or activity.

4 Give extra affection. Weaning can make babies feel vulnerable for a while, and your baby may need added reassurance that you still love her.

5 Keep your baby occupied by going to the park, taking a walk or playing in the garden.

6 If your baby clearly wants to feed, and if your attempts to distract her with other snacks or activities aren't working, it's OK to feed. This way, you can avoid a battle of wills.

7 Continue to feed for comfort if necessary. Often, a more or less weaned baby will want to feed after a fright or a fall. This is OK. It will take her a while to get used to the other forms of comfort you offer.

8 Contact your doctor, a health visitor or your local La Leche League or NCT if you experience pain or engorgement while waiting for your milk to dry up. They can offer some solutions for a safe and pain-free transition.

9 If you wean your baby from breast to bottle, avoid putting her to bed with a bottle. It poses a choking hazard and promotes tooth decay. If she gets thirsty at night, keep a spillproof cup of water nearby and offer it to her when she wakes.

### ✱ Tips

According to UNICEF, optimal breast-feeding practices include exclusive breast-feeding (breast milk with no other foods or liquids) for the first six months of life, and continued breast-feeding for up to at least two years old.

After the first year, weaning often becomes easier, as you can offer your baby a wider variety of foods.

Avoid feeling that you have to wean your child; many mothers breast-feed beyond the first year, and some feed their babies well into toddlerhood. Eventually, all children lose interest in breast-feeding, so follow your heart and do what feels right.

When substituting other liquids for breast milk, avoid offering your baby large quantities of juice or sugary drinks; they will fill your baby up without providing adequate nutritional value, and can cause tooth decay.

## Take a Baby or Toddler to a Restaurant 586

Don't let your family outing turn into a food fight or the quickest meal on record. These strategies can make eating out together fun for everyone.

### ⊙ Steps

1 Plan to go to a restaurant during your child's normal mealtime.

2 Make a reservation if you have a large party. Often restaurants take reservations for parties of more than six people. If not, ask about the wait. Hungry tummies and long waits do not mix.

### ✱ Tips

Ask other families about restaurants geared to kids. Some restaurants have generous children's menus, pass out balloons or crayons, or sing silly songs for birthdays.

3   Enquire about the availability of high chairs and booster seats. Take a hint if the restaurant doesn't have high chairs or booster seats on hand: this may not be the best place for young kids.

4   Keep a portable booster seat in your car in case the restaurant has already given out all its high chairs.

5   Change your baby's nappy before entering a restaurant.

6   Try to sit near other families. Other parents tolerate squeals and tantrums much better. Plus, with other kids around, any noise and commotion that occurs at your table may just blend in rather than drawing unwanted attention.

7   Consider sitting outside or near a window to provide distractions for your child, and to keep any noise away from the central dining area.

8   Assess the table arrangement. Move out of reach all sharp utensils, breakable plates, glassware and any other objects not safe for young children to handle or hurl.

9   Bring food or a bottle for your child or baby and offer it early in the meal. If ordering food for your child, flag down the waiter soon after sitting down to get food to the table as soon as possible.

10  Provide age-appropriate books and toys for your child to play with while you are eating.

11  For very young babies investigate how to place your child in a car seat safely on a chair. Ensure there is no chance it can fall. Booths work well.

12  Leave a good tip if you have caused the staff extra work, such as cleaning up after your baby.

Save four-star restaurants for nights out with your partner.

### ⚠ Warning

Avoid placing the car seat on the ground when your baby is sleeping, in case of spilled beverages.

---

## 587   Deal With Stranger Anxiety in Babies

Stranger anxiety, which starts as early as three months, is a normal, self-protective process. The anxiety should lessen after the first birthday as your child learns to handle new faces.

### ⊙ Steps

1   Greet a friend or relative who's new to your baby with a handshake, a kiss or whatever seems appropriate. This will give your baby a hint that Mum or Dad accepts this stranger.

2   Stay in view of your baby when you're at the market, the doctor's surgery or anywhere where strangers are present. Hold or comfort your baby if she's anxious.

3   Don't force a child to be held or kissed by anyone who seems to cause anxiety, even if that person is a friend or relative. Babies go through phases when even Grandma or a neighbour can provoke anxiety.

4   Ask grandparents, friends or anyone to whom your baby has become sensitive to approach her slowly so that she has time to warm up to them.

### ✱ Tips

Talk to your baby. You can say, "This is Aunty Carol. We went to her house last week. Remember?"

Avoid telling your baby there's nothing to be scared of. The fear that babies and children experience is real to them.

## ✓ 588 Developmental Milestones and Immunisations

### Developmental Milestones

Set out below is a guide to the main stages of a child's development during the first three years. Bear in mind that the range of what is normal is wide, and while a child may be quick to talk, he will not necessarily also be an early walker.

#### 0–3 months
- First smile
- Follows you with his eyes
- Recognises you and other familiar faces and objects
- Makes first non-crying noises, such as cooing and gurgling

#### 3–6 months
- Rolls over
- Moves more purposefully; for example, reaching for toys, kicking mobiles
- Grasps objects, passing them from hand to hand
- Begins babbling, making "ga" and "goo" sounds

#### 6–12 months
- Sits up on his own
- Pulls himself up to stand
- Crawls or shuffles on his bottom
- Plays "peekabo" games and claps his hands
- Follows simple instructions, such as "Kiss bear"

#### 12–18 months
- Starts to walk alone
- Uses thumb and forefinger to pick up tiny objects
- Manages a spoon well
- Builds with a few bricks
- Speaks first intelligible words
- Points to parts of the body

#### 18 months – 2 years
- Walks confidently; able to stop, start, sit down, stand up, squat and climb
- Uses hammer-and-peg toys, threads large beads, does simple jigsaws
- Has a vocabulary of up to 70 words; can make two-word sentences

#### 2–3 years
- Climbs stairs; throws and kicks a ball; pedals a trike
- Probably has daytime control over bowel and bladder
- Draws and paints shapes; models with dough
- Has vocabulary of up to 400 words; uses short sentences and phrases

### Immunisations

Vaccinations will prevent your child from contracting potentially deadly diseases. The following recommendations come from the Department of Health. Consult a doctor or health visitor for the most up-to-date information.

#### At 2, 3 and 4 months
- Polio
- Diphtheria, tetanus and pertussis, and Hib (DTP-Hib)
- Meningitis C (MenC)

#### Around 13 months
- Measles, mumps and rubella (MMR)

#### At 3–5 years (booster)
- Measles, mumps and rubella (MMR)
- Diphtheria, tetanus and acellular pertussis (DTaP)
- Polio

#### At 10–14 years
- BCG (against tuberculosis)
- Rubella (girls only)

#### At 13–18 years
- Tetanus and low-dose diphtheria

calendar

## 589 | Choose Childcare When Returning to Work

Choosing childcare can be one of the hardest decisions a new mother (and father) have to make. There is an increasing range available, so it is vital to make time to look at all the options.

### ⊙ Steps

1 If you think you'd like to return to work after having your child, start to plan childcare while you are pregnant. In some areas you need to book a place for your child well in advance. Also, it can take considerable time to look at all the childcare in your area and assess your feelings about it.

2 Put your child first. You need to balance their needs with your family circumstances and your own needs as a mother or father (economic and emotional). Think laterally to try to find the best solution for all of you.

3 Investigate local childminders, daycare nurseries, nannies and au pairs. If you have a relative who is willing to look after your child, this can be a great option, but it needs to be assessed alongside others.

4 Childminders look after children in their own home. They are registered and inspected by Ofsted and strict rules govern how many children of different ages they can look after. Childminders offer flexible childcare in a home environment and can become an extension of the family for many years as children grow up. Find out about them from your local authority.

5 Nurseries offer a range of options and hours. They give a sociable environment with other children and are reliably available. There are state, voluntary and private nurseries, which charge a variety of fees, all inspected by Ofsted. Find out about them from your local authority.

6 Nannies usually look after children in the child's home. They can often fit around the parents' working hours. You are responsible for their wage or salary as well as income tax and National Insurance. Find out about nannies from a nanny agency. Au pairs and mother's helps are also available.

7 Whatever childcare you look at, ask as many questions as you can think of, including: "How long have you been working with children? What is your training and qualifications? Where will my child rest? What kind of food and drink is available? What will my child do all day?"

8 When visiting childcare, look to see if the children are calm, safe and happy. Do they play together? Do the staff listen to children and answer them carefully? Do they join in with what the children are doing? Is the premises clean, safe and well-kept? Is there access outside for play?

### ✳ Tips

Listen to your feelings. If you are not 100 per cent happy with the childcare, don't go for it.

Talk to local parents about their experiences but remember that the final decision is yours.

Once your child is in childcare, keep an open mind and listen to him or her. Children and their needs change, childminders and nannies leave or alter their arrangements and you may have to rearrange childcare several times between babyhood and school age.

Always take up references.

### ⚠ Warnings

Unless a relative or highly trusted friend is looking after your child, always choose a registered childminder.

Nannies who work for no more than two families at once are not registered and inspected. Unless you know a nanny personally or one is recommended by another family whom you know and trust, go through an agency when employing a nanny.

Au pairs are not usually trained to look after young children and should never be given sole responsibility for a child under three years old.

## Help Your Child Adapt to Your Returning to Work 590

Not having you around all day every day is a big change for a little one. Do all you can to ease the transition.

### ⊙ Steps

1 Give your child time to adapt. He will almost certainly protest if he is suddenly left with someone new. Spend time with your child and their new carer before leaving your child alone with the carer. Then leave the child and carer together for progressively longer. If the childcare is in a new place – the carer's home or a nursery – your child may take longer to get used to it.

2 Be calm, confident and positive at all times. These attitudes communicate themselves to your child and may help to calm him.

3 Take important toys or blankets along to the carer to ensure some continuity. Explain your child's routines, sleep times and mealtimes carefully so that the carer can keep to them as much as possible.

4 Avoid obviously temporary arrangements. If your child is happy with an arrangement, think twice about changing it. If you do need to change childcare, go through the whole process again – do not assume that your child will automatically adapt to new surroundings and people.

### ✳ Tips

Give yourself time to adapt, too. Initial separation from your child can be hard to deal with; ensure the carer is happy to provide progress reports and will phone you if there are any problems.

Put your child first. If he seems happy and thriving with the carer, that's the main thing. Even if a nanny or au pair doesn't do all you would wish in the way of housework stick with him or her if your child is happy.

## Cope with an Au Pair 591

An au pair comes from another country and stays with your family while learning English. He or she can help for up to five hours a day. If ground rules are set from the start, and au pair can be a valuable and fun addition to the family.

### ⊙ Steps

1 Au pairs are there to live as part of your family. They are not full-time carers – they have no training as such and it is not part of the arrangement. If there is respect on both sides, neither is likely to take advantage of the other.

2 Draw up a contract with your au pair and stick to it. Include all the duties you'd like the au pair to undertake and include aspects such as smoking and privacy.

3 Avoid giving all the "horrible" jobs to the au pair. If you don't like doing it, chances are they won't either. Arrange for them to do a mixture of chores and fun activities, like taking the children swimming.

4 Although it's important to set out guidelines at the start, try not to be too prescriptive. Allow the au pair some leeway to contribute to your family in his or her own way.

5 Air any grievances or issues that arise in a polite and friendly manner. There is nothing worse than a strained atmosphere at home. Your au pair may feel confident enough to raise problems with you, but since you are their host, it may be up to you to start the discussion.

6 Stick to your side of the bargain, though ensure you don't make promises you can't keep.

### ✳ Tip

For more information on au pairs, telephone the Home Office on 08706 067766.

### ⚠ Warning

Because au pairs are not usually trained to work with young children they are often not suitable for looking after them when parents are out. They can be ideal for providing after-school care, though.

## 592 | Feed a Finicky Toddler

Some toddlers are so reluctant to eat that they seem to live on air. Even a fussy eater can still get adequate nutrition fairly easily, though.

### ⊙ Steps

1 Don't worry if your child's weight gain slows or even stops. Many children stop gaining weight for a short period around the time they hit toddlerhood; that's because their intense activity level causes them to burn off lots of extra calories.

2 Maintain a positive and matter-of-fact attitude about food. Don't turn it into an emotional issue. Often, a child may resist eating even more if he figures out that it gain him more attention.

3 Don't take food too seriously. Playing with food is a natural part of a toddler's development and is not likely to become a behaviour problem.

4 Make sure you are offering your child foods from all the necessary food groups every day; this will help him maintain a balance of nutrients as he grows.

5 Offer your child choices, but don't overwhelm him with them. Two or three options are easier to deal with than five or six.

6 Try to reduce or remove distractions at mealtimes. This will teach your child that mealtimes are for focusing on food and family, not on TV, toys or other activities.

7 Consider presenting food in imaginative ways. For example, you could use biscuit cutters to turn toast, a sandwich or French toast into fun shapes. This may encourage your toddler to eat more.

8 Follow your child's cues as much as possible while still providing a balanced mix of healthy foods. If he shows a preference for mashed foods, for example, you may get him to eat more than just bananas and potatoes by mashing other foods you offer him.

9 Offer small servings – about 1 tablespoon of each food for each year of your child's age.

10 Keep track of your child's weekly nutritional intake rather than worrying about it every day. Some kids may eat a lot on some days, then next to nothing on others. This almost always balances out over the course of a few days. As long as you are offering a range of healthy food choices, you will probably find that your toddler is eating fairly well overall.

### ✷ Tip

Many children prefer to eat small, frequent meals and snacks, rather than three large meals each day.

### ⚠ Warning

If your child begins to lose weight rapidly, refuses to eat altogether for more than a few hours, or shows any other signs of malnutrition (including bleeding gums, brittle hair and nails, or loose, wrinkled skin), contact your doctor immediately.

## Discourage Temper Tantrums

A tantrum is a natural way for a young child to experiment with feelings. But you can take some steps to help her work through frustration and bring emotions like anger under control.

### ⊙ Steps

1  Set a good example. If you act aggressively when you are frustrated or angry, it is only natural for your child to react in the same way when faced with the same emotions. Try to remain calm and neutral in voice and posture when dealing with tantrums or other frustrating situations.

2  Talk openly about your emotions. Say things like, "Mummy gets angry when you throw your food on the floor. I get frustrated when you throw your toys around the room. It looks messy and is more work for me. I feel sad and angry when you yell at me and call me names." Teach your child how to express feelings verbally by expressing yours.

3  Observe your child. If you see a tantrum coming on, go and sit near your child. Ask whether something is bothering her and whether you can help in some way. Helping your child learn to work through a problem is a valuable lesson.

4  Once a tantrum gets started, try to ignore it. If your child is not a threat to herself or others, let her work through the anger or frustration. By ignoring the tantrum, you are telling your child that you are not interested in the behaviour.

5  Resist the urge to reason with your child. Your child is very preoccupied with emotions and can't listen to or comprehend reason.

6  Remind your child, in a friendly, uncritical voice, of the appropriate response. Say things like, "I know you are angry. Let's try again. Why don't you take your toy to your room to be alone? You can be angry and cry, but you cannot hit people."

7  Try not to give in. If your child is throwing a tantrum because you took something or said no, giving in to your child's demands will encourage more tantrums in the future.

8  Remove your child from the room if necessary. Especially if you are in a public place, sometimes your child needs a quiet or empty room to work through frustration or anger.

9  If ignoring the tantrum isn't working or isn't an option, try distracting your child with another toy or activity. Because young children have naturally short attention spans, redirection can be an effective way to draw attention away from a frustrating activity and channel energy into a more constructive activity.

### ✳ Tips

Praise your child often for good behaviour.

Keep behaviour charts for older children. Teach your child to monitor and control behaviour by marking charts and setting behaviour goals.

Keep track of your child's tantrums, and try to eliminate or reduce the occurrence of situations that bring on a tantrum.

### ⚠ Warning

It is natural at times for a parent to feel frustrated or angry when a child has a tantrum. If you experience extreme frustration or anger when trying to discipline your child, however, consult your family doctor or another health care professional.

## 594 | Toilet Train Your Toddler

There are many ways to toilet train your child, and various experts consider many of them controversial. Remember that your child will give you signs to indicate readiness for the big step.

### ⊙ Steps

1  Assess your toddler's readiness for toilet training. Ask yourself these questions: Does your toddler follow simple instructions? Dislike having a soiled nappy? Know words for passing a motion and urine? Sit for 5 minutes or more attending to a project? Understand the physical signals indicating the presence of urine or a motion? Have dry periods for 2 hours or longer? Wake up dry from naps? These are all good indications that you can start introducing your toddler to the potty.

2  Buy a potty or toilet seat. Choose one that will suit the needs and preferences of both you and your toddler. Do you want one you can take with you anywhere? Do you want one that will rest safely on public toilets? Don't be surprised if your child doesn't agree with the one you think is right.

3  If you feel comfortable, have your child sit on his potty with clothes on while you, your spouse, or another person of the same sex as your child goes to the bathroom. Don't try to restrain your child or force him or her to sit down. If your toddler shows extreme fear or disdain for the potty, put it away and try again, or let your child explore the toilet seat independently.

4  Sit your child on the toilet seat without a nappy when he or she shows no signs of fear. Explain to your child what is supposed to happen on the potty. Don't be surprised if nothing happens for a long time. After two-plus years of passing urine and faeces in a nappy, change will come slowly.

5  Create a toilet routine. Following a routine will set up your child for success. Place your toddler on the toilet at specific times of day – first thing in the morning, right before or after a nap, and right before bed.

6  Be patient. Some children become "clean" before becoming "dry". Other children wet the bed up to age 7 or 8. All children develop and accept change differently.

### ✱ Tips

Reward your child for making it to the potty.

If your child has an accident on the floor or in training pants, use gentle, encouraging words. Let your child know that he or she is learning something new and that accidents are OK.

Read toilet-training books for kids together to show your toddler that other children learn this skill, too.

## 595 | Throw a Children's Birthday Party

With a little planning and imagination, you can help your child have the best birthday celebration ever.

### ⊙ Steps

1  Decide on the number of guests to invite. In some schools with small classes, if you invite more than half a class it's a good idea to invite the remainder of the class to avoid making anyone feel left out. This can prevent hurt feelings.

2  Get your child's input. Let him or her decide on a theme, such as a cartoon character, a film, or a favourite sport or other activity.

### ✱ Tips

For younger guests, plan the party for around mid-afternoon, after their naps. Plan on the party lasting no more than 2 hours, and allot time accordingly for eating and playing games.

3   Select party room and table decorations, snacks and games to illustrate this theme.

4   Pick a location for the party, whether it's at home, in a park, or at an indoor play area or restaurant. Make sure the environment is appropriate for the kids' age and energy level.

5   Choose entertainment for the guests, such as arts and crafts or old-fashioned games like musical chairs, musical statues and pin the tail on the donkey. If your child is older, consider throwing a pool or sleepover party.

6   Keep foods simple – pizza, ice cream, crisps, biscuits, fruit and juice are perennial favourites.

7   Decide, based on the age of the guests, whether you want to include a time for opening presents or wait to open them later. Keep in mind that younger guests may get confused as to whom the presents are for.

8   Send invitations directly to the guests, or send them via their parents or guardians, and ask for an RSVP. When the parents call to confirm, you can discuss party logistics, such as food and dress.

9   Request that an adult accompany children under 5. Provide for the needs of the adults at the party as well. For older kids who are being dropped off, be sure to let the parents know when they can expect to pick their children up.

When entertaining guests under 6 years of age, avoid choosing competitive games, which may upset them.

If you're giving out goody bags (a popular practice at kids' birthday parties), keep in mind that a modest, well-thought-out bag can be just as much fun as a more expensive one. Try linking the goody bags to the party's theme.

### Things You'll Need

☐ invitations

☐ party decorations

☐ snacks and drinks

☐ games

---

## Discourage Thumb Sucking

**596**

Children who suck their thumbs after around the age of 6 may become the target of teasing and criticism; they may also end up with dental and speech problems.

### ⊙ Steps

1   Wait for the problem to go away. Most children, but not all, outgrow the habit by the time their permanent teeth come through (at about 6). After this age, thumb sucking can cause dental and speech problems, but before then, many children still have a fairly strong impulse and need to suck.

2   Start to work on kicking the habit a little while before you expect your child's permanent teeth to come through. That way you can deal with it before it becomes a real problem.

3   Try to keep your child talking, which will make it hard for her to keep her thumb in her mouth.

4   Offer her activities to keep her hands busy: crayons or pencils and paper, squishy dough or toys to fiddle with, or models and puzzles to work on.

5   Consider working out a reward or praise system, using stickers and a chart or calendar.

6   Encourage your child with positive reminders that she is a big girl, and that big girls don't need to suck their thumbs.

 **Tips**

Encourage your child to wash her hands frequently to avoid constant transfer of germs from her hands to her mouth.

Take a look at your child's thumb. If it is callused or sore from sucking, she is almost certainly sucking it too much.

Look for hidden stress in your child's life if she suddenly develops a thumb-sucking habit. Dealing with the source of the stress may eliminate the problem.

7   Explain to your child in simple terms why it is important for this habit to go away, and ask her to suggest a few possible solutions. Many children will come up with some creative possibilities.

8   Try putting a brightly coloured adhesive plaster on your child's thumb as a reminder not to suck.

9   If your child sucks her thumb at night, consider having her wear a glove or sock on her hand while she sleeps.

10  Talk to your dentist, who may have helpful suggestions and who can also explain the dental consequences and options for treatment if thumb-sucking continues when the permanent teeth come through. Ask your dentist to have a talk with your child, if you think it will help.

11  Be patient with your child. Although thumb sucking is an unattractive habit, many children can't help themselves. Take the time your child needs to eliminate the habit gently and gradually, rather than criticising or punishing.

## 597 | Teach Your Child Manners

**It's never too early – or too late – to teach your child about proper etiquette.**

### ⊙ Steps

1   Set a good example. It's unfair to expect politeness of a child if his parents are not polite themselves.

2   Teach your child manners in stages, as his comprehension and skills develop. It probably won't do any good to ask a 2-year-old to stop chewing with his mouth open; he probably lacks the understanding and physical coordination to comply. But by 4 or 5 years of age, your child should have the ability to grasp the reasoning behind such a rule.

3   Start using words and phrases like "please", "thank you", "excuse me", "I'm sorry", and "may I?" as early as possible around your child. Encourage your child to do the same.

4   Take care what language you use around children; they mimic the way adults speak.

5   Ask your child to address adults with a certain degree of formality – that is, Ms Lee, Mrs Jones, Mr Smith – unless the adult tells them to do otherwise.

6   Review the other basics of etiquette with your child whenever necessary. He should learn how to shake hands, show respect for older people, behave quietly in public places, and avoid interrupting other people in conversation. He should also learn not to play with other people's belongings unless given permission to do so.

7   Avoid ignoring bad behaviour or waiting to talk about it. Address a rule as soon as your child breaks it.

8   Bring up the behaviour again in private so you can discuss it more thoroughly and make sure your child understands how to behave in the future.

9   Praise your child for good behaviour.

### ✱ Tip

When teaching or correcting manners, try never to embarrass your child in public.

## Encourage Young Siblings to Share

Refereeing in the neverending game of which toy belongs to whom can lead to premature grey hair. These steps can help you spend more time playing and less time blowing the whistle.

### ☉ Steps

1 Set aside a specific time when you will interact and play with your children. Young children learn and remember best when a parent works with them directly for consistent periods of time.

2 Suggest some toys to play with, and help your children get them out. Bring the toys to an open area so you all have room to play.

3 Establish a positive and constructive play activity while letting your children remain in control of their play. If you want your children to play with blocks instead of climbing on the furniture, start building a tower.

4 Monitor your children and their play. Watch for an older sibling teasing a younger one. Keep mental notes of how long a turn one child takes with a toy other siblings want to play with.

5 If one child takes a toy from another, give the upset child a toy the other child likes. If she also tries to take away that toy, tell her she must give one of the two toys to the upset child. Explain that sharing is fair.

6 If a child refuses to share toys, place her in a time-out area – a predesignated spot, separate from the play area, where she can be alone, calm down, and get ready to return in a more cooperative mood. She must give the upset child a toy and apologise before returning to play.

7 Praise your child for sharing or helping independently. Say things like, "What a good sharer you are. Nice manners!"

8 Follow these steps during playtime and use them during the course of the day to reinforce the skill of sharing.

### ✳ Tips

Maintain a calm, neutral tone when explaining how sharing works: "It is nice manners to share. Look how Tommy gets upset when you take away a toy. Please be nice and share with your brother."

Try to use positive terms by telling your children what you want them to do instead of telling them what you *don't* want them to do. For example, say "Please give Tommy a truck to play with" instead of "Don't take that away!"

## Teach Your Child Financial Responsibility

From piggy banks to credit cards, there's plenty you can teach your child about money matters at any age.

### ☉ Steps

1 Start talking about money with your child as early as age 3. Take her to the shops and explain that you earn money so that you can buy things you need.

2 Give your child a small amount of money and let her buy something on her own.

3 Begin giving your child a small amount of pocket money weekly when she is 6 or 7 years old, and set guidelines about how she can use it.

4 Pick a date, such as a birthday, on which to give your child an annual rise. Increase her responsibilities as you increase her pocket money.

### ✳ Tips

When deciding on an amount for pocket money, consider the child's age, her needs and your family's financial situation. Talk to other parents if you'd like to get an idea of typical allowances in your area, or do an online search to find various national polls on the topic.

Encourage your older child to work and save by offering to match each deposit she makes to a savings account.

5 Avoid withholding pocket money if your child doesn't fulfil a responsibili-ty; choose another form of discipline instead. It's hard for a child to learn budgeting skills if she doesn't know how much money will be coming in each week.

6 Start talking about long-term goals, such as saving for college or a car, when your child is between 11 and 14. Encourage her to earn extra money by mowing the neighbour's lawn or babysitting.

7 Consider opening a bank account in your child's name as an aid to saving and spending her earnings.

8 Consider encouraging your child to find a part-time job when she is 16 to 18 years old.

9 Consider giving her a credit card when she enters college, and discuss how to use it responsibly. Determine together what expenses you will pay for and what she must pay for. If the card is to be used only in emergencies, make that clear.

10 Teach your child about social responsibility as you teach her about money – for example, you could both donate money to a charity or volunteer your time.

## ⚠ Warning

Keep your college-age child's credit card use under careful supervision, providing guidelines as well as clearly stating the con-sequences of misuse.

---

## 600 | Talk to Your Daughter About Menstruation

A young girl may find the onset of menstruation both an excit-ing and an anxiety-provoking time, and it's important that she enter this phase of her life with the information she needs.

### ⊙ Steps

1 Make sure you talk to your daughter early so she won't be surprised when she gets her first period. Some girls can begin menstruating as early as age 9 or 10, so age 8 can be a good time to discuss it. If your daughter is beginning to develop breasts and pubic hair, menstruation is probably coming soon.

2 Approach the subject tactfully. Girls just entering puberty are often sen-sitive and easily embarrassed.

3 Make sure she knows you are proud of her. Make it clear to your daugh-ter that entering womanhood is a wonderful event, and that there is no reason to feel uncomfortable or ashamed of the changes in her body.

4 Be realistic. While menarche (the onset of menstruation) is an important rite of passage, menstruation is also a physical event your daughter will go through every month throughout her childbearing years. Let her know what to expect physically and emotionally. Tell her in as straightforward a way as possible, without either overstating or sugarcoating the facts.

5 Discuss her options. Present the pros and cons of pads and tampons, and discuss how to deal with any premenstrual symptoms or cramps. See if she wants to chart her cycle on a calendar or in a diary.

6 Reassure her. On a practical level, menstruation won't change her life all that much. Women of earlier generations may have avoided certain activi-ties during menstruation, but it is now common knowledge that women can swim, exercise and go on with life as normal during their periods.

## ✱ Tip

Prepare yourself in advance with any books and materials you may need to help you explain the more technical aspects of men-struation to your daughter.

7 Talk about the implications of menstruation. Once your daughter begins menstruating, she has the ability to bear children. This may be the time for you to begin seriously discussing the issues of sexuality, reproduction and contraception with her.

## Talk to Your Child About Sex 601

More than 25 per cent of 15-year-olds have had sexual intercourse – many start as early as age 12 or 13 – so it's wise to broach the subject of sexual responsibility early.

### ⊙ Steps

1 Prepare for this important conversation beforehand by thinking through what questions your child may have, and gathering any information you may need to answer them clearly.

2 Ask what your child knows about sex so you'll have a starting point. Depending on your child's age and knowledge level, you might begin by explaining the physical aspects of sex, or answering questions about this – even older kids may be unclear on some points. Be direct and use the exact words for sex organs so there's no room for misinterpretation.

3 If your child is mature enough, discuss the emotional side of sexual intimacy. Acknowledge that sex can be pleasurable, but point out that emotions surrounding it can at times be complicated, confusing or even painful, and that these issues may be more difficult to deal with if a teenager becomes sexually active early. Remind your child that it's up to him or her to decide when he or she is ready for sex, and to stick to that resolution, even if it means resisting peer pressure or pressure from a girlfriend or boyfriend.

4 Remind your teenager that there is never any excuse for pressuring someone into sex. Make it clear that if your child is coerced into sex, he or she is not to blame – and should not continue in that relationship.

5 Address the topic of pregnancy. Adolescents are often incapable of thinking far into the future. Familiarise your child with the possible consequences of living for the moment. Discuss contraceptive options, and remind your adolescent that none of these are foolproof.

6 Explain the risks of contracting a sexually transmitted disease. Teenagers account for many of the new cases of sexually transmitted diseases annually. Stress that abstinence is a viable option and that contraceptives are always available. Even if you emphasise abstinence, make sure your teenager understands how to protect himself or herself when he or she does decide to become sexually active.

7 Anticipate questions your child might have, whether those involve facts or advice about decision making, and be prepared to provide concrete answers and support. If you don't have answers to every question, consult your family doctor, a therapist, or a medical book or website that specialises in this area.

8 Strive to maintain open lines of communication. Make sure your teenager knows that you are always available for advice or assistance, whether that means sorting out relationship issues or finding a reliable form of contraception.

### ✱ Tips

Your primary goal as a responsible parent should be to provide your teenager with enough information to make intelligent choices.

Clarifying your own thoughts and values beforehand will help you decide on the exact message to convey. This, in turn, will help you avoid delivering an ambiguous message that could be challenged or, worse, ignored.

### ⚠ Warning

Avoiding this topic could have strong negative effects, such as your child becoming pregnant or contracting a sexually transmitted disease.

## 602  Plan a Teenage Sleepover

**Some planning – and some rules – will help everyone sleep a little easier.**

### ⊙Steps

1  Sit down with your teenager and decide how many kids to invite. Consider the size of your living room (or whichever room they will sleep in), how light a sleeper you are, and any other specifics of your house that affect how many teenagers can fit in your house.

2  Send out invitations a week ahead of time, or pass the word by phone. Ask guests to RSVP. Make it clear that the party will be supervised, with an adult present for all of the activities.

3  Ask everyone to bring a sleeping bag and pillow.

4  Have at least three or four age-appropriate videos for the kids to watch, and make the sleepover spot convenient for the TV and video if possible.

5  Be prepared in case the kids want to listen to music, go swimming or play games.

6  Stock up on snacks and beverages. If you have concerns about spills on your carpet or furniture, limit eating to the kitchen.

7  Don't forget to lay in supplies for breakfast. Cereals and orange juice are fine, or you can get more elaborate items.

8  When the kids arrive, spell out the rules from the start. Discuss what rooms the kids can use and when they can make noise, and set limits on phone and kitchen use. If you don't want them to leave the house for any reason, tell them up front. If you're not sure your child will be comfortable laying out the ground rules, take the responsibility yourself.

### ✳ Tip

If you don't want the kids going off on their own in the middle of the night, or if you don't want any members of the opposite sex showing up during the night, make those rules very clear at the beginning.

### Things You'll Need

❑ invitations

❑ videos

❑ games

❑ snacks and drinks

## 603  Teach a Teenager to Drive

**Patience and calm are your best friends when teaching a teen-ager to drive. If you can't handle it, have your spouse, a trusted friend or relative, or a driving teacher take on the job.**

### ⊙Steps

1  Make sure your teenager has a provisional licence or any other require-ment necessary before beginning to teach them to drive.

2  Go over the rules of the road at home or while you are driving before you let your child get behind the wheel.

3  Drive to an empty car park, industrial estate or driving course.

4  Explain the basic workings of the entire car, inside and out, before letting your child start the engine. Go over each part and process in detail, including everything under the bonnet, the dashboard controls, the petrol tank, the tyres and the emergency equipment. Repeat until you're sure your teenager understands.

### ✳ Tip

For your child's safety as well as your peace of mind, teach him or her how to change a flat tyre before driving alone (see 945 "Change a Flat Tyre").

### ⚠ Warning

Discuss the dangers of and laws against drinking and driving or using drugs and driving. Also dis-cuss the hazards of driving when tired or when distracted by rowdy passengers, blaring music or difficult weather conditions.

5 Demonstrate how everything works: the lights, seat belts, windscreen wipers, indicators, horn, emergency lights, gear transmission, seat adjustment, steering wheel, mirrors and heated windows.

6 Sit in the passenger seat and ask your child to start the engine.

7 Point out how acceleration, braking and smooth gear changes feel.

8 Give corrections, warnings and tips as you make your way around the course, and discuss overall points when you've finished.

9 Sprinkle your lesson with what-if scenarios. Cover such possibilities as a child running across the road, traffic signals failing, emergency vehicles pulling up behind, a tyre going flat, and so forth.

10 Remind your teenager that it's important to always have the car's registration and insurance information accessible in the car, and to carry a driving licence.

11 Note skill improvements and make the course progressively more difficult, finally going out into traffic when you think your child is ready.

12 Practise again and again.

## Set Rules for Using the Car 604

**Make the rules clear and fair so you won't have to renegotiate every time your teenager wants to use the car.**

### ⊙ Steps

1 Decide who will pay for the teenager's insurance coverage, which can be a big expense, especially for young male drivers. You can add your child to your existing policy, which will drive up the rate, or obtain a new one. Either way, you can pay for it yourself, require your teenager to pay for it, or split the cost in any way you think is appropriate.

2 Discuss petrol usage and who will pay to fill the tank.

3 Write out the times when the teenager can have access to the car.

4 Clarify permissible destinations, such as within a 25-mile radius of the house, to school, to work or to a friend's.

5 Set down any other conditions for use of the car. For example, you could say that the teenager can use the car only after completing homework or cleaning up their bedroom.

6 Make rules concerning who is allowed in the car when the teenager is driving. Letting a carload of friends accompany a new driver is not a good idea.

7 Explain your policy regarding lending the car to friends or letting friends drive it.

8 Tell your teenager what you expect when he or she is using the car. Issues may include removal of litter, adjusting radio stations, locking the car in the driveway after use, or washing the car.

 **Tip**

Make certain your teenage driver understands what to do in case of an accident.

## 605 | Encourage Responsible Dating

This parenting hurdle takes particular patience and understanding. You'll find a sense of humour a valuable asset.

### ⊙ Steps

1 Broach the subject of dating early on, perhaps during your child's first years at secondary school, or even sooner.

2 Set down some basic rules, including what you consider a proper dating age for both your teenager and their dates. Also discuss expectations about group or single dating, curfews, and appropriate destinations. For example, you might feel that only going out in groups is appropriate until the age of 16, or that teenagers should not leave your town on their dates.

3 Put all of your rules and expectations in an informal written document that you share with your teenager. As they mature, bring it out and make changes if appropriate.

4 Talk with your teenager about issues of sex and morality. In addition to discussing your moral views, talk about AIDS, sexually transmitted diseases, pregnancy and emotional issues related to sex – critical issues for teenagers. If you have trouble communicating about these issues with your teenager, or if you feel that your child is experiencing problems that are too large for you to handle, get help from a counsellor, clergy member or medical professional.

5 Explain that if your teenager winds up in a difficult situation, you are willing and available to pick him or her up – whenever or wherever that might be, no questions asked.

6 Tell your teenager where in the house to find some extra cash in case he or she is going out and doesn't have money available. They should always carry enough cash to take a cab home in case of emergency.

7 Insist that your teenager's date come into the house upon arrival for an introduction. Small talk and friendly questions are fine – this is not the best time for interviews, warnings or giving the third degree.

8 Make yourself available after the date to talk if your child wants to. Show your interest, but avoid prying. If you decide not to wait up that night, be sure to let your child know beforehand that you'll be available to chat in the morning.

9 Keep your ears, eyes and mind as open as possible. A parent's intuition will often spot the first signs of trouble, whether that means alcohol, drugs, an abusive relationship, a significant age difference, or anything else that worries you.

### ✱ Tip

If your teenager doesn't have a mobile phone, give him or her change for a pay phone in case of emergency. Make sure they have a phone number for reaching you or a trusted friend.

### ⚠ Warning

Consider counselling if you feel a dating situation has got out of hand and you can't effectively communicate with your son or daughter about it.

## Help a Teenager Find a Job 606

Networking, answering ads and creative thinking are the keys to a successful teenage job search.

### ⊙ Steps

1 Sit down together and assess skills, expectations and requirements, just as you would do for yourself.

2 Discuss options, taking into account your teenager's time availability and transport needs.

3 Think creatively: if your daughter wants to be a tennis star, maybe she can work at the local tennis club. Or your wannabe reporter can call local newspapers and radio stations for a trainee position.

4 Help your teenager create a CV, even if this is her first working experience. A CV can include academic and extra-curricular information and can mention achievements, prizes and relevant skills and interests.

5 Role-play with your teenager. Listen to her ask for the job and describe her strengths, and coach her on what she should say in response to questions the interviewer may pose.

6 Make a list of possible contacts, both yours and your child's. Get phone numbers and encourage the teenager to call for job possibilities.

7 Check local newspapers for lawn-care, babysitting, removals or painting jobs around town.

8 Once your teenager has applied for a job, encourage her to make a follow-up call if the management doesn't respond within a week.

### ✳ Tips

Usually, a teenager must be 16 to legally get a traditional job, although there are exceptions.

Make sure your son or daughter knows about good grooming and the importance of articulate, respectful and punctual behaviour.

## Plan a Family Reunion 607

Organise a memorable family reunion to renew lost contacts, introduce new ones and celebrate your heritage.

### ⊙ Steps

1 Make a list of family members, including spouses, partners and children. Get contact information for all the people on your list.

2 Choose a date when most people can attend. Summer months are often ideal, since children are off from school.

3 Decide how long you want the reunion to last and where to have it. Hold it near most family members, if you're clustered in one area; or if you're scattered, pick a central location.

4 Develop a budget and decide how much each family will need to contribute. Avoid making costs prohibitively high.

5 Visit reunion sites – such as hotels, inns and country clubs – and reserve one early.

6 Determine the menu – perhaps one that celebrates your family's heritage. Find a caterer or restaurant that can supply food for the event.

### ✳ Tips

Try making family reunions a consistent event – every one, two or five years – at the same time of year.

If your reunion is large, consider organising a reunion committee, with a secretary for communications, a treasurer and a social-events planner.

Have attendees send cheques several weeks before the reunion so you can shop for food, prizes or whatever else you'll need.

7   Appoint a family historian to take photographs or videos during the event.

8   Plan social activities for the reunion – icebreaker games, sports, contests and talent shows. Include activities that will appeal to all ages. Buy prizes for your games or for distinctions such as oldest family member or longest distance travelled to attend.

9   Send an initial mailing to gauge interest and preferences, and to ask for help with planning. Send invitations later, with relevant information, directions and a map. Ask for a cheque from each family for its part of the reunion expenses.

## 608 | Make a Family Time Capsule

A time capsule can be a great family project to commemorate a special occasion. Fill it with photographs and mementos, and put it away for as long as you like.

### ⊙ Steps

1   Determine how long you want to put your time capsule away. Is it something you want to look at in 5 years? 10? 20? Will you take it out for a special occasion, such as an anniversary or a 21st birthday? Or do you want to hide it away for the next generation to find?

2   Decide where to put it. Keep in mind that you may move before the appointed time, so think about putting it where you can easily find it.

3   Decide what container to use. You can buy containers designed for time capsules, or use any waterproof, airtight and preferably fireproof vessel.

4   Ask everyone in the family to contribute an item – cuttings, photographs, letters, arts and crafts, toys or just about anything else that fits into the capsule.

5   Protect the contents from decay. Put them into individual, airtight plastic bags and store them in a cool, dry location. For extra protection, consider copying them onto acid-free paper first.

6   Store photographs correctly – ask at a photography shop if you aren't sure how to treat your photos.

7   Leave out any substance that could decay and damage the other contents of the box. This includes rubber, wool, wood, PVC, and any perishable or edible item. If you must include any of these, put them in an airtight plastic bag.

8   Mark everything clearly so you or others will know where each item came from and who included it when the time comes to open the capsule. Don't assume you will remember all the details. You may also want to include a detailed inventory of all the items.

9   Fill the capsule and seal it, then put it out of sight and out of mind. Make sure you store your capsule in a place where your kids won't get impatient having to look at it every day.

10  Leave yourself a reminder about the time capsule in a place where you are likely to find it if you move or if your home suffers any damage.

### ✳ Tips

Black-and-white photos last longer than colour photos and will not fade as much – use them whenever possible.

Have each family member include a letter to the older version of himself or herself, or to future generations, if the capsule will be stored that long. Mention favourite foods, music, books, films and hobbies.

If you plan to seal the time capsule away for more than a generation, include instructions for using any equipment or recordings you include. Your compact discs and videotapes may very well be obsolete 100 years from now.

### Things You'll Need

❏ container

❏ memorabilia

❏ plastic bags

❏ acid-free paper

## Plan a Funeral

Planning a funeral is a difficult task, in which you must consider the wishes of the deceased as well as the survivors.

### ⊙ Steps

1 Meet the other principal mourners to discuss their wishes and preferences. Find out if the deceased left any instructions for the funeral. Discuss religious preferences and how much money the family is willing to spend.

2 Consult a religious leader or a funeral home if you would like help with any of the details, including location of a burial site or site for the ashes, coffin or cremation container selection, transport, legal issues, flowers and music.

3 Choose the site where the funeral will take place. This is most often a church or crematorium. (You may also decide on a more informal memorial service.)

4 Select someone to conduct the service. This could be a religious leader or a friend of the family.

5 Appoint pallbearers if you are having a formal funeral. Pallbearers can include special friends or business associates of the deceased, though the funeral directors can usually provide them.

6 Assign someone to give the eulogy. Typically, the family will choose a family member, religious leader or close friend. Contact the person who will give the eulogy as soon as possible to give him or her time to talk with the family and organise notes for the service.

7 Consider including music in the service. Choose a piece with special meaning for the family, perhaps having a family friend sing or play an instrument.

8 Choose flowers for the service. What is appropriate depends on the family's wishes and the amount of money it wishes to spend.

9 Place an obituary in the local newspaper announcing the date, time and place of the funeral.

10 Consult the funeral directors about having printed programmes for the funeral service. Get input from the family regarding their design.

11 Buy a guest book for guests to sign as they arrive, if one is not provided.

12 Coordinate all of the above with the funeral directors, which will arrange to transport the coffin to the funeral, remove the coffin to the burial site, or take care of other details as requested.

### ✳ Tip

You are not obliged to purchase any goods or services from the funeral directors, and doing some things yourself can save a great deal of money. Ask the funeral directors for a general list of all the services it offers – with prices – and choose only what you want to pay for or can't do yourself.

## 610 | Give a Eulogy

A eulogy is a speech in praise of a person who has died. One of the most important elements of a funeral, it can be given by a family member, friend of the departed or religious leader.

### ⊙ Steps

1 Talk to the family of the deceased. Write down details of the person's life, major awards or recognition he or she received, names of family members, and special memories that family members share. Ask if the family would like you to say anything specific during the eulogy.

2 Take your notes home. Try to find a theme or ethic that defined the person's life and build the eulogy around it. For example, was family most important to the deceased? Did he or she have a great sense of humour?

3 Begin at the beginning. Most eulogies begin with the departed person's birth and give a brief outline of his or her life. Include anecdotes, memories and details that capture the person's spirit.

4 Try to quote a memorable statement made by the person or relay specific incidents that bring him or her to life for family and friends. Anything that paints a portrait of the individual is perfect.

5 Use your personal memories of the individual, if you have any. For example, if you knew the deceased in your youth, recall those times.

6 Infuse your eulogy with a little humour, especially if the deceased was a joker or had a good sense of humour. Keep all humourous references appropriate to the occasion.

7 Be as brief as you can while still doing justice to the life of the deceased. Brevity is the key to a well-received eulogy.

### ✱ Tips

Try to avoid high-flown, moralistic speeches, and don't portray the deceased as a saint unless he or she truly was.

If you're not sure how much time you should take to deliver the eulogy, ask the person conducting the funeral or the family what they expect.

You may want to rehearse the eulogy a few times so you'll feel more comfortable delivering it. You don't need to memorise it, though; using typed sheets or note cards is perfectly acceptable.

If you find yourself becoming too emotional to continue, stop for a moment and try to collect yourself. If you feel you are are unable to resume, you can ask the clergy member who has been officiating to read the eulogy for you.

## 611 | Comfort a Grieving Person

Comforting a grieving person entails offering support and allowing the person to go through whatever he or she is feeling.

### ⊙ Steps

1 Allow the person to talk about his grief and express his feelings. Listen without offering advice or interrupting.

2 Be patient with the grieving person's changeable moods. It's normal for someone who is grieving to alternate between anger, sadness, numbness and acceptance.

3 Give the person as much time as he needs to grieve. Telling him to "get over it" or "let it go" won't help him grieve any faster.

4 Ask the bereaved what you can do to help. Try not to get frustrated if he doesn't know what he needs.

5 Offer suggestions of what you could do to help. For example, does the grieving person need more space? Does he want you to be around more? Are there tasks or errands he needs done?

### ✱ Tips

There is no "correct" amount of time to mourn a loss. The grieving period varies with the individual.

Be sensitive to significant dates such as birthdays, holidays and the anniversary of the death or loss; the grieving person may find these especially difficult times.

6   Show affection such as hugs or hand-holding if the bereaved seems receptive. If he seems uninterested in affection, try not to get irritated – this will pass with time.

7   Encourage the grieving person to join a grief support group or get bereavement counselling. He can call his doctor for a referral.

8   Urge the grieving person to get professional help if he's so depressed that he's unable to function day to day. Assist him in setting up an appointment with a doctor to discuss counselling or possible medication.

## Find Vital Records     **612**

You can obtain official birth, death and marriage certificates for England and Wales from the General Register Office. Follow these directions to get a copy.

### ⊙ Steps

1   Visit the website of the General Register Office, which is part of the Office for National Statistics (www.statistics.gov.uk). Alternatively telephone them on 0870 243 7788.

2   The General Register Office holds a register of births, marriages and deaths from 1837 onwards, apart from those in the previous 12 months. For certificates issued in the past year contact the Register Office where the birth, death or marriage took place.

3   Apply to the General Register Office by downloading an application form from the internet or by telephone. You can also apply by post or fax.

4   Give as much information as possible when requesting a certificate, including the full names of the person whose certificate you wish to trace, as exact a date as possible and the place where the event took place.

5   Enclose the appropriate fee. You can also request a priority service if you need the certificate urgently.

 **Tip**

Scotland and Northern Ireland each have their own General Register Office. Contact these for details of how to obtain certificates relating to records there.

## 613 | Deliver Puppies

Your dog's whelping (delivering) puppies can be an exciting and educational experience for your family. In all likelihood you will only have to observe and be available in case of emergencies.

### ⦿ Steps

1   Contact your vet to arrange a pre-whelping examination and consultation. Your vet can offer last-minute advice and will be familiar with your dog should she need assistance during delivery.

2   Provide a whelping box of sturdy material that the puppies can't chew through and that's big enough for the mother dog to lie in and stretch out with her puppies. The sides of the box should be at least 15 cm (6 in) high – high enough to prevent 4- to 6-week-old pups from escaping, but low enough to allow the mother to get in and out easily.

3   Present the whelping box to your dog one to two weeks before delivery and place it in semi-private, familiar surroundings. Put soft, clean towels in the box.

4   Check the temperature of the mother-to-be daily after day 50 of pregnancy. When her temperature drops to 37°C (99°F), labour will begin in 10 to 24 hours.

5   Look for signs that the dog is ready to give birth, such as her licking the genital area, or the appearance of an amber fluid or a bulge (the amniotic sac) protruding from the birth canal. This indicates that a puppy should be delivered within a few minutes.

6   During labour, avoid upsetting the dog. Remain calm when she is restless, nervous, anorectic (not eating), vomiting, pacing, shivering or panting. This can be normal behaviour for dogs in labour.

7   If the mother has not removed the amniotic membrane from her pup within 1 minute after delivery, intervene. Gently grasp the puppy in a clean towel and pull away the slimy material. Make sure that the nose and mouth are free from fluid and tissue.

8   Don't panic if the mother delivers a puppy without expelling the placenta. Sometimes the placenta of the previous birth will be expelled with the following birth.

9   Cut the umbilical cord about 5 cm (2 in) from the puppy's body, using sharp, sterilised scissors. (Use isopropyl alcohol to sterilise the scissors.)

10  Consult a vet if your dog is in active labour for more than 30 minutes but has not yet delivered a puppy. If you notice that a puppy seems to be stuck, gently grasp it and pull it from the birth canal, twisting slightly if necessary.

11  Make sure all puppies are safe and warm and are not getting stepped on as the mother is delivering the other puppies. Multiple births followed by resting is common, but a delay of more than 1 hour between births warrants a call to the vet.

12  Make sure each puppy nurses soon after delivery. It's essential that puppies nurse within the first 24 hours to acquire vital antibodies supplied by their mother's milk.

### ✳ Tips

Labour lasts 6 to 12 hours. Stage one of labour begins with uterine contractions and ends with the full dilation of the cervix. This is not externally visible. Stage two of labour begins with full dilation of the cervix and ends with full delivery of the first puppy. Stage three begins after delivery of the first puppy and ends with the expulsion of the placenta. The length of the second and third stages is variable – anywhere from 10 to 30 minutes.

If you suspect a puppy is not breathing, rub it with a towel along the shoulders and back to stimulate breathing. A healthy cry or whimper indicates an unobstructed airway.

### ⚠ Warning

Prepare yourself and your children for the possibility of a stillbirth. Should this happen, bury the puppy yourself or take it to the vet.

### Things You'll Need

☐ cardboard box

☐ clean towels

☐ sterilised scissors

☐ commercially prepared milk substitute for puppies

13 Be prepared to give the puppies commercially prepared milk substitute in case the mother doesn't have enough milk or some other emergency arises. This is available wherever pet supplies are sold.

14 Take the mother and her puppies – in the whelping box, with a blanket for warmth – to the vet for an examination. Do this within 24 hours after the last puppy is born.

## Deliver Kittens                                                    614

Mother Nature can usually guide the birth of kittens, but if you do get involved, follow these steps to ensure your cat's safe and comfortable delivery of her kittens.

### ◉ Steps

1 Contact your vet if you think your cat is pregnant to ensure that you will have professional help if needed.

2 Choose a quiet, warm location to place a basket or box lined with clean towels large enough for the mother cat to lie in and stretch out with her kittens. The sides should be at least 10 to 15 cm (4 to 6 in) high – high enough to keep 4- to 6-week-old kittens from escaping, but low enough so that the mother can get in and out easily.

3 Avoid disturbing the mother during delivery, but observe her closely every few minutes to see how she is getting on. Delivery should begin within 20 minutes of the first strong contraction; birth of the first kitten may take up to 60 minutes, but you should call your vet if a kitten has not been delivered within 30 minutes since it may take a while to track down some help. Signs of labour include licking of the genital area, and straining in general.

4 Watch for amber fluid or a bulge (the amniotic sac) protruding from the mother's birth canal – this indicates that a kitten should be delivered within a few minutes.

5 If the mother has not removed the amniotic membrane within 1 minute after delivery, intervene and gently grasp the kitten in a clean towel and pull away the slimy material. Be certain the nose and mouth are free from fluid and tissue.

6 Rub the kitten with a towel along the shoulders and back to stimulate breathing. A healthy miaow indicates an unobstructed airway.

7 If the mother has not chewed through the umbilical cord, sever it about 5 cm (2 in) from the kitten's body, using sharp, sterilised scissors (sterilise with isopropyl alcohol). Gently pull the afterbirth from the birth canal.

8 Expect kittens to be delivered 15 to 45 minutes apart, but call your vet if strong labour continues for 30 minutes without producing a kitten. Average litters contain three to six kittens.

9 Make sure that nursing begins in a few minutes. It is essential for the kittens to feed from the mother to provide protection against disease. Supplement with commercially prepared milk substitute, available wherever pet supplies are sold, following your vet's advice.

### ✱ Tip

Make sure the basket or box is readily accessible so you can closely observe the mother during her delivery.

### ⚠ Warnings

Watch closely when the mother is cleaning the newborn kitten. She may attempt to eat the afterbirth (placenta), and may inadvertently injure a kitten if it is wrapped tightly in the tissue.

Once in a while a kitten will be born dead – prepare yourself and your children ahead of time. Should this happen, bury the body or take it to the vet.

### Things You'll Need

☐ basket or box

☐ clean towels

☐ sterilised scissors

☐ commercially prepared milk substitute for kittens

10 Take the mother and her kittens to the vet for an examination in a covered container or box. Do this within 24 hours after the last kitten is delivered.

## 615 | Get Your Pet Spayed or Neutered

Having your pet spayed (an ovario-hysterectomy, for females) or neutered (castration, for males) will help stop pet overpopulation and contribute to your pet's well-being.

### ⊙ Steps

1 Contact your vet about recommendations concerning age, vaccination requirements and other health-care issues as soon as you adopt your pet.

2 Understand that spaying or neutering information will vary depending on the type, age and sex of the pet you have chosen. Surgery at an early age – 6 to 12 weeks – is now widely accepted for dogs and cats.

3 Ask the local animal shelter or your vet about special programmes available to have your pet spayed or neutered at a reduced cost.

4 Ask the staff what is involved in the surgery and about pre- and post-operative care. This helps you make an educated choice about where to have the procedure done and how much you should pay.

5 Realise that post-operative pain management is a standard part of any acceptable surgical protocol; the vet of your choice should recommend pain medication.

6 Make an appointment for surgery, and follow the veterinary hospital or clinic staff's instructions about pre-surgical care.

7 Take your pet to the veterinary hospital or clinic.

8 Pick up your pet as soon as allowed after the surgery, and administer post-surgical care as directed. Some vets will discharge your pet on the day of surgery, while others prefer to keep pets hospitalised overnight for observation.

9 Watch for signs of swelling, discharge or complications such as not eating or vomiting. You should have an after-hours contact number to call if you suspect anything is wrong.

10 Call the clinic the day after surgery, and let the staff know how your pet is. They should be interested in your pet's recovery.

11 Make sure that you stop your pet from licking at the incision or chewing out any sutures – your vet may provide a special coilar to help prevent this.

12 Make an appointment for a follow-up examination and suture removal.

### ⚠ Warnings

Spaying or neutering your pet is a major surgical procedure that should be performed by a qualified veterinary surgeon, under a general anaesthetic, in a sterile surgical environment. Exercise care and good judgement when selecting someone to do this once-in-a-lifetime procedure on your pet.

General anaesthesia and surgery do involve risk, but the benefits to pet and pet owner greatly exceed the risk involved.

## Obtain a Passport for Your Pet 616

Under the Pet Travel Scheme (PETS for short), you can take your dog or cat abroad without facing the nightmare of lengthy quarantine for your pet on your return to the UK.

### ⊙ Steps

1   Check that your travel destination is included in the scheme. You can find an up-to-date listing on the Department for Environment, Food and Rural Affairs website, www.defra.gov.uk, or by phoning the PETS Helpline, 0870 241 1710.

2   Contact a vet and have your pet fitted with a microchip that conforms to official standards.

3   Have your pet vaccinated against rabies.

4   Thirty days or more after the vaccination, take the pet to a vet again for a blood test, to prove that the vaccine has taken effect. The vet will than issue a PETS certificate – the "pet's passport".

5   Remember to take all documentation with you when you travel.

### ✳ Tip

Start early – remember that it is going to take at least seven months to make your pet eligible for foreign travel.

### ⚠ Warning

Your pet also has to be treated for tapeworm and ticks between 24 and 48 hours before you check in for your homeward journey. Without a certificate to show that this has been done, your pet will face quarantine.

## Choose the Right Dog for Your Family 617

By evaluating the dog's breed and background as well as your home and lifestyle, you can assure your family of a fun and loving companion.

### ⊙ Steps

1   Consult a vet, who can provide useful advice on a breed's behaviour and temperament as well as potential medical problems. A vet's opinion is apt to be less biased than that of a breeder, who is trying to sell a particular breed.

2   Consider your daily routine. Are you or someone else at home often enough to care for a dog? If not, consider adopting a more independent pet, such as a cat.

3   Think about your family. Do you have young children in the house? If you do, be sure to choose a breed that generally gets along well with children.

4   Evaluate your living environment. Is it rural or urban, a flat or a house? A Chihuahua or Yorkshire terrier may love your one-bedroom flat, but larger breeds need more room to roam.

5   Supplement the information you receive from a vet with further study about different breeds. For an overview of breed characteristics, see 619 "Select a Dog Breed" or check the pet section of your local library. Talking to dog owners can provide additional advice.

6   Decide whether you want a pedigree or a mixed-breed dog. If you plan to show or breed your dog, then choose a pedigree. If not, keep in mind that mixed-breed dogs can be just as loyal and lovable.

### ✳ Tips

Be aware that the average life span of a dog is 12 to 15 years, depending on the breed.

Adopting an adult can save you from the surprise of not knowing what the size, appearance and disposition of the dog will be as it gets older.

### ⚠ Warning

It's not fair to the animal to adopt it and then "return" it if you decide things aren't working out. Do your research and soul-searching beforehand, and once you've made a decision, try your best to honour the commitment.

7   Decide whether you want a puppy or an adult dog. Many wonderful puppies and adult dogs have been abandoned or given up to animal shelters or breed rescue groups, and adopting a pet from one of these sources may mean saving a life.

8   Ask the seller to tell you about particular habits or personality traits the dog exhibits.

9   Ask the seller about the parents of the puppies when visiting a pedigree litter. Be sure that each parent belongs to an entirely different family and has been screened for common genetic or inheritable diseases.

## 618 | Introduce Your New Dog to Your Home

Prepare yourself and your home so that your new dog can quickly become comfortable in his new abode.

### ⊙ Steps

1   Collect supplies for your new puppy or dog: a comfortable bed or crate, dog food and treats, food and water dishes, toys, a collar, a lead and an identification tag.

2   Dog-proof your home. Check and repair any damaged fencing, gates, doors or windows. Place poisons out of reach, remembering to check behind the fridge for small objects or forgotten rat or mouse poison (see 654 "Protect Dogs and Cats From Household Dangers").

3   Pick up your puppy or dog at a time when you or someone else will be around the house for a couple of days.

4   Introduce the newcomer to other pets and family members, and then let him explore the house.

5   Supply a nice, plush bed or a cosy box. Consider placing the bed or box in an area where your new pet can keep an eye on you when he beds down.

6   Take your puppy outside to relieve himself after meals, after playtime, upon waking and, if necessary, every 15 minutes. Adult dogs can wait 2 hours or longer.

7   Listen for your puppy's cues that he needs to relieve himself in the middle of the night. It may take a while before he can sleep through the night without a potty break. Remember, it was your choice to get this puppy (see 642 "House-Train Your Puppy").

8   Play with your pet on and off throughout the day.

9   Take your pet to a vet for a check-up and vaccinations as soon as possible.

### ⚠ Warning

Dogs will eat or drink anything – that's how they explore and learn – so be thorough in removing items that pose a risk to your dog.

# ✓ 619 Select a Dog Breed

No matter where you live or what your lifestyle, there's likely to be a dog breed that will suit you. Here are brief descriptions of popular breeds recognised by the Kennel Club; for details visit the website at www.the-kennel-club.org.uk.

| BREED | APPEARANCE | CHARACTERISTICS | CARE |
|---|---|---|---|
| Airedale terrier | Large; tan and black | Gentle, protective | Exercise twice daily |
| Akita | Large; erect ears | Intelligent; loyal; good watchdog | Sheds heavily; prone to bloating |
| Alaskan malamute | Large; muscular; thick coat | Affectionate, obedient | Sensitive to heat and humidity |
| Australian shepherd | Medium-sized; medium-length coat | Energetic; good watchdog | Exercise daily |
| Basset hound | Medium-sized; large ears | Friendly, loyal, calm | Exercise to keep weight down |
| Beagle | Small; short, dense coat | Friendly with people and pets | Exercise daily |
| Boston terrier | Small; brindle, seal or black and white | Friendly, intelligent | Good indoor dog |
| Boxer | Large, muscular | Friendly, protective | Needs a garden |
| Bulldog | Medium-sized, stubby | Friendly; loyal; gentle with children | Clean face to avoid skin problems |
| Chihuahua | Small; large eyes and ears | Attentive; suspicious of visitors | Sensitive to cold |
| Cocker spaniel | Medium-sized, silky coat | Obedient; gets along well with people and animals | Coat needs regular trimming and grooming |
| Collie | Large; long or short hair | Loves people, good with children | Sensitive to heat |
| Dachshund | Small; low body | Bold, curious, adventurous | Walk or exercise daily |
| Dalmatian | Large; white with spots | Energetic, playful | Daily jog or walk; prone to deafness |
| Doberman pinscher | Large, powerful, regal | Loyal; intelligent; good watchdog | Likes warmth; not an outdoor dog |
| German shepherd | Large; strong; agile | Intelligent; loyal; excellent watchdog | Sheds heavily |
| Golden retriever | Large, powerful; golden coat | Playful; energetic; friendly; reliable | Sheds heavily; lots of exercise |
| Great Dane | Large, powerful, glossy coat | Gentle; friendly; eager to please | Twice as much food as other dogs |
| Jack Russell terrier | Small; smooth coat | Energetic; affectionate; athletic | Space and exercise; loves to dig |
| Labrador retriever | Medium-sized and strong; short, dense coat | Gentle; outgoing; eager to please | Very active, lots of exercise |
| Miniature schnauzer | Small; hard, wiry coat | Playful; spirited; obedient | Groom once or twice a week |
| Pekingese | Miniature; long, full coat | Dignified; stubborn | Groom weekly; sensitive to heat |
| Pug | Small; stocky; smooth coat | Even-tempered, playful, charming | Excessive shedding; indoor dog |
| Rottweiler | Medium-large and robust; black with rust markings | Headstrong; confident; excellent watchdog | Lots of exercise, training, companionship |
| Saint Bernard | Large, powerful, imposing | Loyal; friendly; calm | Lots of exercise and food; drools; sensitive to heat |
| Scottish terrier | Small; wiry coat | Bold; stubborn, feisty | Groom two or three times a week |
| Shar-pei | Medium-sized; wrinkled head | Loyal; excellent watchdog | Sensitive to heat |
| Shih tzu | Miniature; long, full coat | Outgoing; happy, affectionate | Groom and exercise daily |
| Siberian husky | Medium-sized; well-furred | Energetic; independent; impish | Fenced-in garden; may try to escape |
| Standard poodle | Large and elegant | Intelligent; obedient | Groom a few times a week |
| Weimaraner | Medium-sized; sleek; grey | Active; headstrong; friendly | Exercise; fenced-in garden, training |
| Yorkshire terrier | Miniature; long steel-blue and tan coat | Spirited; independent | Groom daily; must live indoors |

reference

## 620 | Tame a Feral Cat or Kitten

With a little patience and time, most feral (wild) cats can be tamed into loving pets.

### ⊙ Steps

1 Enclose the cat or kitten in a small space at first – a bathroom or bedroom works best.

2 Turn out the light if the cat is terrified; this often has a calming effect.

3 Put a bed, a litter box, food and water in the room. If the cat is very young (6 to 12 weeks), put her in a large carrier with a grated door and small windows.

4 Spend at least 2 to 3 hours a day with the animal. Just sitting quietly in the same room will allow the cat to learn that you are not a threat.

5 Gently compel the cat to let you touch her. Carefully wrap a blanket around her if you have to, hold her on your lap and pet her. Stroke her coat and touch her ears, face and neck as you talk to her in soothing tones. Even if the animal doesn't seem to be enjoying the attention, she is. Hold the cat by the scruff of the neck if she attempts to leave. (The mother cat will do this to carry or train a kitten – it doesn't hurt, and it actually relaxes the animal.)

6 Present special treats such as chicken or tuna, and leave them if the cat will not eat from your hand.

7 Gradually allow the cat to roam about in more rooms.

8 If the cat tries to run away from you repeatedly, enclose her in a smaller space and start again.

### ✳ Tips

Don't get discouraged early on; young feral cats can become very affectionate pets.

Younger cats are more apt to adjust quickly: 6- to 8-week-old kittens typically take two to three weeks to adjust to a domestic environment. An older cat that has been wild for a long time is difficult and sometimes impossible to tame, and may be better left outside. If you catch one, have the animal spayed or neutered and vaccinated, and then turn the cat loose where caught, or contact a professional.

### ⚠ Warning

Handle feral cats with extreme caution. Use gloves and protective clothing as required. Cat bites and scratches can result in serious health problems.

## 621 | Move to a New Home With Your Cat or Dog

Don't let your four-legged friend get lost in the shuffle of a move. Relocating your pet to a new home can be a smooth transition for everyone involved if you follow these simple steps.

### ⊙ Steps

1 Obtain a copy of your pet's medical records to give to a vet in the new area. Make sure all vaccinations are current.

2 Get a health certificate and proof of rabies vaccination if you're moving abroad, and ask your vet about any other requirements to move animals out of the country.

3 If moving abroad, call the local animal-control agency or animal welfare organisation. Ask about any licensing requirements.

4 Arrange for your pet to travel with you. Buy a crate if he'll be travelling with you by air.

5 Feed your pet 5 to 6 hours before travelling. Give him water 2 hours before travelling. Give your pet medication to calm him, with your vet's advice, if he becomes over-excited or anxious while travelling.

### ✳ Tips

Get your pet used to the crate a few weeks before the move so he will feel comfortable and secure while riding in it.

As soon as you know your new address and phone number, order a pet-ID tag with this information in case your pet gets lost in the new neighbourhood.

If your cat is missing, check open vents and crawl spaces. Cats have been known to crawl between walls and other small spaces in an effort to hide and feel secure in a new place.

6   Bring food and water along. If you're travelling by car, make frequent stops to let your pet stretch, relieve himself and drink water.

7   Keep your pet confined when you get to the new home. He can easily escape during the moving process. Release him once all doors and windows are closed, and allow him to become familiar with the house.

8   Use familiar bowls, bedding and toys. Put them in locations similar to where they were in the old house.

9   Accompany your pet outside until he's familiar with the area. It's best to keep cats indoors for about two weeks after the move until they are accustomed to their new home. Disorientated cats sometimes run away in an attempt to get back to their old homes.

10  Try to stick to a regular schedule in the first days after the move.

11  Locate a vet in your area. Make an appointment for your pet, and take your pet's records along.

### ⚠ Warning

Check your new home closely for dangers such as discarded poisons or chemicals inadvertently left by others.

---

## Introduce Dogs and Cats                   622

The best time to introduce dogs and cats is when they are young. If possible, start when puppies are less than 12 weeks old and kittens are less than 7 weeks old.

### ◉ Steps

1   Realise that kittens usually attach themselves to adult dogs, who in general aren't threatened by kittens.

2   Understand that dogs instinctively chase animals that run or move suddenly, even if they're used to being around other cats.

3   Introduce the kitten while the dog is either closely monitored by someone else or is on a lead. Do this several times over a period of several weeks, to allow time for each animal to become comfortable.

4   Make introductions a positive experience for the dog, and reward her with plenty of praise and treats when she shows appropriate behaviour.

5   Give an immediate and sharp "No!" if the dog is unfriendly towards the kitten, but avoid shouting if the dog behaves inappropriately.

6   Realise that an adult cat may perceive the dog as a threat to his status and may protest by marking his territory. This is normal behaviour for a cat under stress.

7   Avoid allowing a puppy or dog to roam the house freely during the first few weeks of her introduction to an adult cat.

8   Provide a special area for the cat that's inaccessible to the dog. Be sure to place food, water and a litter box in the area.

9   Be aware that both the dog and the cat need space and special attention; bathing and grooming should take place in private.

10  Place the cat on a table and pet him for reassurance, while letting the dog sit on the floor nearby.

### ✳ Tips

Don't fret if your dog and adult cat never bond. Most adult cats don't do well with change and are independent and solitary by nature.

Trim your cat's nails prior to introductions (see 641 "Trim Your Cat's Nails").

If after two weeks there are no improvements in relations, you may have to relocate one of the pets. Contact a pet behaviourist.

### ⚠ Warning

A dog can injure or kill a cat with a single bite, so proceed with caution. Avoid leaving the two together for even a brief period without supervision.

11  Alternatively, place the puppy or dog in a cage, and let the cat approach.

12  Allow the cat to swat at the dog (within reason) when they finally meet nose to nose. This is a cat's way of establishing space boundaries.

---

## 623 | Introduce Your New Baby to Your Dog

Introducing your new baby to your dog is almost like bringing a baby home to a sibling – if handled incorrectly, it can cause rivalry and hurt feelings. Take a few simple precautions.

### ⊙ Steps

1  If you need to change house rules, change them before the baby arrives. Otherwise, your dog may associate the baby's arrival with her sudden banishment from the couch.

2  Consider a series of obedience classes before the baby arrives, especially if your dog doesn't know the basic commands: sit, come, stay.

3  Have your dog thoroughly checked out by a vet before your baby comes home. This will give you time to deal with parasites or other problems that could pose a family health risk.

4  Let your dog get used to the sights, smells and sounds of a baby in advance. Let her sniff baby blankets and lotions, and get her used to the sounds of rattles and other baby toys.

5  Before bringing your baby home from the hospital, send home a blanket or gown that the baby has been wrapped in. This will get your dog used to the baby's scent.

6  Let Dad or someone else carry the baby inside at the first homecoming, so that Mum is free to greet the dog with open arms. That way the dog will be less jealous of her attentions to the baby.

7  Praise your dog when you're near the baby so she will think of the child as a positive influence on her life – she gets praised more when the baby is around.

8  Reassure your dog, each time your baby cries, that this is a normal sound, and train her not to bark when she hears it. Use positive reinforcement as much as possible – a treat or a hug for doing the right thing.

9  Spend one-on-one time with your dog while the baby is napping, or during walk time (your baby can ride along in a sling).

10  Be patient – it may take some time before your dog is really comfortable around your baby.

### ✳ Tips

Teach your dog to heed a "Quiet!" or "Hush!" command if she tends to bark when someone comes to the door. This will mean she can still do her job of guarding the house, but you can quieten her quickly if your baby is sleeping.

Keep your dog's nails trimmed (see 640 "Trim Your Dog's Nails"). Train her not to jump on people if this has been a problem.

### ⚠ Warning

Never leave your dog alone with your baby, no matter how well trained and friendly the dog may be. Even the best-behaved dog can become frustrated with a baby's cries, and will act instinctively rather than rationally in some situations.

## ✓ 624 Select a Cat Breed

When you're buying a pedigree cat, you have the choice of a "pet-quality," "breeder-quality" or "show-quality" animal, each showing greater conformance with breed standards at a correspondingly higher price. When you're selecting any kitten, inspect her to make sure she's healthy. Get a written health guarantee from the breeder, and bring your kitten to a vet for a check-up as soon as possible. For more information about breeds, visit the website of one of the many ailurophile organisations, such as the Cat Fanciers' Association (www.cfainc.org).

| BREED | APPEARANCE | CHARACTERISTICS | HEALTH AND CARE |
|---|---|---|---|
| Abyssinian | Solid brown, fawn, blue or red, with large ears and almond-shaped eyes | Active, playful, affectionate | Susceptible to kidney disease. Brush teeth weekly to help prevent gingivitis. |
| American curl | Unusual curled ears, a genetic mutation | Loving; adapts well to other animals | Don't force the ears to uncurl, or you could break the cartilage |
| British shorthair | Stocky and sturdy; dense and firm, short hair | Reserved yet affectionate; loves children | Prone to haemophilia B (hereditary bleeding disorder) |
| Burmese | Sleek and silky, with round gold eyes. Sable is the most popular colour; other colours are blue, champagne and platinum. | Playful, affectionate, intelligent; a great lap cat | Hardy and long-lived if kept indoors |
| Korat | Silver-blue fur, luminous green or amber eyes | Extremely loyal, with a gentle disposition; highly acute hearing | Prone to corneal dermoids, treatable surgically |
| Manx | Tail length varies from non-existent to normal | Mellow and affectionate, but may attack intruders; likes high places | Prone to severe spinal defects |
| Maine coon | Shaggy tail, tufts on paws and ears, longer fur on belly | Gets along well with other cats, even dogs; can be trained to walk on a lead | Tends to inherit hip dysplasia and hypertrophic cardiomyopathy |
| Persian | "Smooshed-in" face and long, flowing fur | Serene, quiet, dignified | Sometimes has respiratory problems such as wheezing and eye drainage |
| Siamese | Blue eyes and either triangular or apple-shaped face; darker shadings on feet, ears and tail | Affectionate, good with children; vocal and demanding | Sometimes cross-eyed; occasionally has a kinked tail. May inherit heart defects. |
| Somali | Available in silver, blue, fawn, red (sorrel) and ruddy colours | Personable and active; likes to snooze on laps, but also needs to run and play | Needs a special "PCV" blood test. May be prone to autoimmune hemolytic anemia (AIHA) and renal amyloidosis. |
| Sphynx | Appears to be hairless, but colour and pattern are visible in a downy coat and on underlying skin | Gregarious, active, affectionate; gets along well with other animals | Needs a warm indoor environment to maintain its hairlessness. Prone to sunburn, even through a sunny window. Must be bathed often to combat oily skin; ears are prone to wax buildup. |

reference

## 625 | Introduce Your New Baby to Your Cat

When you bring your new baby home, your cat may not be favourably impressed – but there's a lot you can do to help the two of them become good friends.

### ⊙ Steps

1   If you need to change house rules, change them before the baby arrives. Otherwise, your cat may associate the baby's arrival with his sudden banishment from the foot of your bed.

2   Set up a cot or Moses basket for your baby ahead of time and train your cat not to sleep in it. Cats and infants should not sleep together, because it poses a risk of suffocation or allergic reaction for the baby.

3   Have your cat thoroughly checked out by a vet before your baby comes home. This will give you time to deal with parasites or other problems that could pose a family health risk.

4   Before bringing your baby home from the hospital, send home a blanket or gown that the baby has been wrapped in. This will get your cat used to the baby's scent.

5   Let Dad or someone else carry the baby inside at the first homecoming, so that Mum is free to greet the cat with open arms.

6   When introducing your baby to your cat, don't hold or restrain the cat; let him approach and explore the baby at his own pace.

7   Spend time with the cat while your baby is sleeping. Cuddle him, brush him and play with him as much as possible to reassure him that you still love him.

### ✳ Tips

As your baby grows and becomes mobile, teach her as early as possible how to pet your cat gently, and make sure she doesn't grab at your cat's tail or ears. This will help your child and your pet to become friends rather than adversaries.

Be sure to keep your cat's nails trimmed (see 641 "Trim Your Cat's Nails"). Don't declaw him, though – especially if he spends any time outdoors. Just train him to be gentle around your baby.

### ⚠ Warning

If your baby will be sleeping in a nursery, consider making it a cat-free zone. Your cat probably won't hurt your baby deliberately, but it is dangerous to leave them together unsupervised.

## 626 | Find a Pet Sitter

Use a pet sitter as an alternative to a kennel when you travel. Here's how to find a loving pet nanny.

### ⊙ Steps

1   Ask your vet or pet groomer if they can recommend any pet sitters in your area.

2   Check the Yellow Pages under Pet Services for companies that offer pet-sitting services.

3   Have the potential sitter come to your home for an interview. Introduce your pet, to gauge both parties' reactions. If your pet is a dog, have them go for a walk to see how the sitter handles your dog on a lead.

4   Determine how the potential sitter would handle problems such as a medical emergency or the escape of your pet.

5   Expect the potential sitter to ask you if your pet's vaccinations are up-to-date, how your pet behaves when he is out among other animals and people, and what to do if the sitter must suddenly leave the job before you have returned home.

### ✳ Tip

Pet sitters should be insured for their protection and yours.

6 Once you've selected a sitter, provide him or her with the names, phone numbers and addresses of your pet's regular vet, the closest emergency veterinary hospital, a nearby friend, and the place where you can be reached.

7 Go over what and when to feed your pet, any medicines to be given, and the duration and preferred location of outings.

## Find a Day-Care Centre for Your Dog 627

If you worry about leaving your dog home alone during the day, you may want to consider enrolling him in a day-care centre for dogs, where he can socialise with four-legged friends.

⊙ Steps

1 Do a search online or in the Yellow Pages to find a service nearby.

2 Ask other dog owners you meet at the park to recommend a service they have used, or check with a local pet shop, vet or grooming parlour for references.

3 Call the animal welfare organisation in your area to see if it runs a day-care service for dogs or can direct you to one.

4 Browse the classifieds section of your local newspaper to find ads for local day-care services.

5 Contact the Animal Boarding Advisory Bureau at Blue Grass Animal Hotel on 01606 891303.

6 Visit the day-care centre you are considering before enrolling your dog. Find out what types of activities are planned for the dogs during the day.

7 Make sure your dog is old enough to attend the day-care centre you choose. Five or six months is usually the minimum age.

8 Have your dog spayed or neutered in advance to avoid pregnancy.

9 Take your dog to your vet to be sure your dog is up-to-date on vaccinations, is parasite-free and is in good health before his first day of attendance at the day-care centre.

**✻ Tips**

Dog day-care centres should be clean and odour free, and the dogs should be well supervised. Check to make sure that there are enough care-givers to provide proper supervision.

Even if you don't enrol your pet full-time, you may want your dog to attend day care if you have any maintenance people coming to your house during the day. This is also a good option to ease your mind during a particularly stressful week at work or when planning a special event at your home.

## Feed Your Dog a Balanced Diet 628

No single dietary plan can be considered ideal for every dog. Here are some general guidelines to follow that can keep your dog healthy and her appetite satisfied.

⊙ Steps

1 Be sure to choose a reputable brand of dog food. Check with your vet for recommendations.

**✻ Tips**

When switching dog foods, do it gradually over a week by increasing the ratio of new food to old food. This will help avoid digestive upsets.

2  Select a high-quality dog food that's appropriate for your dog's age, weight, activity level or size. Make sure to feed your dog dry food as well as moist canned food to help keep his teeth clean.

3  Be sure that protein ratios are appropriate for your dog's breed and age. Typically, dog food with 20 to 30 per cent protein content provides a healthy balance.

4  Avoid overfeeding, since obesity can lead to a variety of medical problems, including musculoskeletal problems, and can aggravate hip dysplasia (abnormal growth or development of the hip joint).

5  Avoid feeding your dog table scraps – it encourages begging and may not be good for her digestive system. If you must give her "people food", put the scraps in her dog bowl after the family has finished the meal. Be careful to avoid giving her onions or chocolate.

6  Feed your dog a measured amount twice daily, but keep in mind that some dogs prefer to eat one meal a day.

Consult a vet before adding vitamin and mineral supplements to your dog's diet.

Dry food is better than canned food at preventing dental tartar.

### ⚠ Warnings

Avoid over-supplementing your dog's diet with vitamins and minerals. Excess dietary supplements cause nutritional imbalance and medical disorders. Some vitamins and minerals are toxic in high dosages.

Never feed your dog chocolate. Chocolate is toxic for dogs.

## 629 | Feed Your Cat a Balanced Diet

No single dietary plan can be considered ideal for every cat. Here are some general guidelines to help keep your cat healthy and her appetite satisfied.

### ◉ Steps

1  Be sure to choose a reputable brand of cat food. Check with your vet for recommendations.

2  Feed your cat dry food as well as wet, canned food. Dry food helps keep her teeth cleaner. Read the label to be sure the nutrient level is appropriate to your cat's stage of life. Usually, cat food containing 34 to 38 per cent protein and 19 to 22 per cent fat provides a healthy balance.

3  Remember that most cats are snackers or nibblers and like to eat small amounts of dry food throughout the day.

4  Know that cats with digestive problems may require higher fibre content in their diet. Check with your vet.

5  Remember that cats begin to show their age at 8 to 10 years, with diminished abilities to smell, taste, chew and digest. Make sure an older cat has food that is highly digestible and palatable.

6  Feed your cat a small, measured amount of canned food twice a day. Leave the dry food out so that he can snack throughout the day.

### ✳ Tip

Cats with kidney or heart disease might need reduced protein, phosphorus and sodium in their diets. Purchase these foods from your vet.

### ⚠ Warnings

Never feed a cat dog food. Cats require more protein and fat in their foods.

Make sure not to overfeed your cat. Obesity in cats contributes to disease and can lead to premature ageing and early death.

## Determine if Your Cat or Dog Is Overweight | 630

Obesity in a pet can lead to health problems – and can itself be a sign of a serious medical condition. Monitor the weight of your cat or dog with this simple test.

### ⊙ Steps

1  Check that your pet's ribs are easily felt but not visibly sticking out. This indicates that your cat or dog is at a desirable weight.

2  Look at your pet from above. Some indentation between the rib cage and the hips, depicting an hourglass shape, indicates that your pet is at a desirable weight.

3  Check your pet's belly. If the belly of a cat protrudes, the cat may be overweight. (A protruding belly on a cat is called an apron.) A dog should also have a trim abdomen.

4  Feel your pet's hips. Anything more than light fleshiness indicates that your pet is above normal weight.

5  Always consult a vet before putting a pet on a diet. Your vet can recommend a special diet appropriate to your pet, and can examine your pet to rule out the possibility that a serious medical condition is causing the obesity.

### ✳ Tips

Regular exercise helps your pet lose weight.

A dog or cat's weight at 1 year of age often reflects the animal's optimal body weight, although this is not true of pets that are already obese at 1 year. A vet can provide weight guidelines.

### ⚠ Warning

Visible ribs or excessive thinness could be a sign of hyperthyroidism (overactive thyroid) In cats, especially in those over 12 years of age. Consult a vet if your pet is chronically underweight.

## Walk Your Dog | 631

Dogs that are confined to the house for long periods need relief from boredom, an outlet for their energy and a chance to explore the world.

### ⊙ Steps

1  Make sure your dog is trained for basic obedience commands, such as "Heel", so that you can keep him under control at all times.

2  Resist the urge to let your dog run wild and free on public property – keep him safe by putting him on a lead. If you're concerned about restricting him too much and your dog is well trained, consider purchasing a retractable lead.

3  Take your dog on a 1-hour walk or two 30-minute walks each day, even if you're home for part of the day and spend lots of time with him.

4  Adjust the walking distance and pace to the age and health of your dog.

5  Allow your dog time to stop and smell the ground. Dogs gather information this way – they can determine what animals have passed and what changes have occurred since the last walk.

6  Let your dog greet people and other dogs appropriately while on the walk. This will help develop his social skills.

7  Carry a pooper-scooper or small plastic bags to clean up after your dog as you go.

### ✳ Tip

Walking your dog regularly helps alleviate inappropriate behaviour at home such as barking, chewing or digging.

### ⚠ Warning

Reduce the time and distance of the walk in extremely hot or cold weather, especially if your dog is old or in poor health.

## 632 | Run With Your Dog

Dogs are great companions for runners, and they offer visible security. Vigorous exercise can also help keep your dog fit.

### ⊙ Steps

1 Check with your vet before starting your dog on an exercise programme. Make sure running is the right kind of exercise for your dog.

2 Warm up your dog. Put the animal through a few sprints to loosen up her muscles and get her heart pumping. Dogs may show signs of stiffness after the initial run, just like humans.

3 Build up slowly, and watch for signs of fatigue. If your dog lies down during a workout, end the session.

4 Keep water on hand before, during and after a workout.

5 Watch the running surface. If your dog is not accustomed to running on pavements, build up gradually.

6 Keep your dog on a lead and by your side when running.

### ⚠ Warnings

Avoid running with your dog in very hot weather. Dogs do not sweat and can easily become overheated.

Running on hot pavements can cause blisters on your dog's pads – check the pavement with your own bare hands or feet before taking the dog out in hot weather.

Take care not to overdo it. Animals don't always know when to stop, so don't let your dog run until she drops.

## 633 | Wash Your Dog

Your dog is dirty, and he stinks. Instead of making him suffer under a cold hose, give him a bath indoors.

### ⊙ Steps

1 Place a medium-sized bucket, three large towels and a hair dryer in a warm bathroom.

2 Make certain a rubber bath mat is securely in place to keep the dog from slipping in the bath.

3 Isolate the dog in the bathroom before running the water.

4 Make certain the water is comfortably warm, and fill the bath with about 8 cm (3 in) of water. Put the dog in the bath.

5 Protect your dog's eyes from the shampoo by using a lubricating eye ointment, which your vet can provide. A drop of olive or baby oil will also do.

6 Use the bucket to wet the dog from the head down towards the tail, including the undersides, being careful not to get water in his eyes.

7 Apply a small amount of dog shampoo – available at pet shops – to the top of the head. (Do not use ordinary soap, as it can dry and irritate a dog's skin.) Be extremely careful to keep it away from the eyes. Lather down to the tail, including the neck and underside fur. If using a flea shampoo, leave the lather on for the recommended time.

8 Keep a hand on your dog, because he will want to shake the lather off. Be ready to turn your head away.

9 Pull out the plug and run the water again; adjust the temperature.

### ⚠ Warnings

Trembling is not uncommon during a bath – for the dog, that is.

Your dog may snap at the hair dryer if you hold it too close to his face.

### Things You'll Need

☐ medium-sized bucket

☐ 3 large towels

☐ hair dryer

☐ rubber bath mat

☐ eye ointment

☐ dog shampoo

10  Use the bucket to carefully and completely rinse the head first, avoiding the eyes and inner ears. Work the water towards the dog's back and undersides. Use your hands to work the water through the suds.

11  Turn off the water. While your dog is still in the bath, let him shake excess water off his fur.

12  Drain the water from the bath and dry the dog with towels from head to toe. Concentrate on the areas of thickest fur and between his toes.

13  Remove your dog from the bath. Turn on the hair dryer to a medium setting, testing the heat with your fingers. Aim first for the thickest hair, running your fingers or a comb through it until it is just slightly damp. Keep the hair dryer approximately 15 cm (6 in) from the skin to prevent burning and overdrying.

## Wash Your Cat                                                      634

If your cat is infested with fleas, you'll probably want to give her a bath. Otherwise, wash your cat as you deem necessary – since cats wash themselves, they do not often need bathing.

### ◉ Steps

1  Adopt a calm, positive attitude before and during the bath – it will help ease your cat's anxiety.

2  Consider trimming your cat's nails beforehand to reduce your risk of getting scratched (see 641 "Trim Your Cat's Nails").

3  Bring your cat into the bathroom. Close the door and keep it closed until you are finished.

4  Fill the bath with enough lukewarm water to cover your cat's paws.

5  Gently set your cat in the bath.

6  Give your cat free rein in the bath using minimal restraint, but gently hold on to the back of her neck if she tries to escape.

7  Apply lubricating eye ointment (available from your vet) or a drop of baby or olive oil to your cat's eyes to prevent irritation from the shampoo.

8  Scoop water in a plastic cup, and pour it over the cat until her fur is wet, making sure to avoid her eyes.

9  Apply a regular shampoo made for cats, or a flea shampoo if needed, and rub it into the cat's fur. Use caution around the eyes.

10  Hold your cat under the tap or scoop clean water over her to rinse.

11  Quickly pat or rub your cat dry with a towel.

12  Comb through your cat's fur to spend quality time together as she dries, then give her a special treat such as catnip for a job well done.

### ✱ Tip

If your cat's fur is matted or soiled from contact with hard-to-clean substances such as oil, gum or paint, it is best to have the cat bathed by a professional groomer.

### ⚠ Warning

Be sure to remove all soap when rinsing, since cats will groom themselves and ingest anything left on their fur.

### Things You'll Need

- ❑ plastic cup
- ❑ eye ointment
- ❑ cat shampoo
- ❑ towel
- ❑ pet comb
- ❑ cat treats

## 635 | Get Persistent Smell Out of Your Pet's Fur

Did your cat or dog manage to roll in something unpleasant during a walk? Keep your pet outdoors until you get rid of any obnoxious odour with the following solution.

### ◎Steps

1   Mix 900 ml (1½ pt) hydrogen peroxide with 4 tbsp. baking soda and 1 tsp. washing-up liquid.

2   Put cotton wool balls in your pet's ears to protect the inner-ear tissue from the cleaning mixture, which could easily drip in.

3   Don rubber gloves to protect your hands during this process.

4   Start with your pet's head, taking care not to get the solution into his eyes, ears or mouth. Apply a drop of olive or baby oil to his eyes to prevent irritation.

5   Rub the mixture evenly into your pet's coat. It will probably be more pleasant to do this outdoors.

6   Rinse the coat with clean water.

7   Repeat if the smell persists.

### ✳ Tips

Tomato juice can also neutralise nasty smells. Rub it into your pet's fur, let it soak for approximately 15 minutes, then wash it off with water.

Pet shops sell a range of products for removing persistent smells from fur. Ask your vet for advice on which product works best.

## 636 | Clean Your Dog's Ears

If your dog's ears are smelly or look dirty, or if he's scratching them a lot, it may be time for a clean.

### ◎Steps

1   Use an ear wash formulated for cleaning animals' ears, as recommended by your vet.

2   Soak a cotton wool ball in the ear wash. Squeeze out the excess.

3   Place the cotton ball in your pet's outer ear and gently rub up and down.

4   Allow your pet to shake off excess moisture. This is important for preventing ear infections.

5   Soak the tip of a cotton swab in the ear wash and run it along the nooks and crannies of the outer ears, being careful never to push into the ear canal. Clean only the flaps and visible parts of the ear. Dogs' ear canals are deep and don't drain like human ears.

6   Leave cleaning down inside the ear canal to the vet.

### ✳ Tip

Some dog breeds, such as poodles, need hair removed from their ear canals to prevent infections. Consult your vet.

### ⚠ Warning

If your pet has chronic ear infections (symptoms include excessive itching, discharge, pain around the ears, redness or swelling of the ear canal, unusual tilting of the head, or bad odour), consult a vet.

## Brush Your Cat's or Dog's Teeth     **637**

Brushing your cat's or dog's teeth is simple after you've had a few practice sessions. Try to do this every day to promote healthy teeth and gums.

### ⊙ Steps

1   Ask a vet to check your pet's teeth before you start a tooth-brushing regime. If your pet has gum disease or damaged teeth, the process will be painful and he will associate pain with tooth brushing. He may even bite you. Get your cat or dog used to your looking into his mouth. After each time you do so, reward him with a treat or praise.

2   Buy a pet dental kit, including toothpaste (made for dogs and cats) and a toothbrush, at a pet shop or from your vet. Follow the kit's instructions for use.

3   Place your cat or dog on a comfortable surface while brushing his teeth.

4   In general, try to use minimal restraint on your pet while brushing – especially if it's a cat. However, it may be easier to handle an especially reluctant cat by wrapping him in a towel to keep him from scratching or trying to escape.

5   Brush your cat's or dog's teeth with a gentle, massaging motion.

6   Reward your cat or dog with a tartar-control treat after the procedure.

### ✳ Tips

Starting at age 3, take your dog or cat to the vet for annual serious tooth-cleaning sessions.

Try to brush as part of daily quality time with your pet. He will come to associate tooth brushing with affection and praise.

Research alternatives, such as a finger toothbrush, if your pet refuses to let you brush his teeth with a toothbrush. Ask your vet for suggestions.

### Things You'll Need

☐ pet dental kit

☐ tartar-control treats

---

## Prevent Bad Breath in Your Cat or Dog     **638**

Bad breath may be a sign that your cat or dog has a build up of bacterial growth in the form of plaque, or possibly a more serious condition, such as gingivitis.

### ⊙ Steps

1   Understand that brushing your cat's or dog's teeth is the best method for preventing bad breath and other dental problems (see 637 "Brush Your Cat's or Dog's Teeth").

2   Look for abscessed teeth and other dental problems while you're brushing, and have a vet properly treat any such problems.

3   Consider offering your cat or dog mouthwash; some mouthwashes made for pets claim that they can deter dental tartar build up.

4   Consider your pet's diet. Some soft canned foods are particular offenders when it comes to bad breath. Make sure your cat or dog eats dry food in addition to soft food, unless he is elderly and needs to eat soft food exclusively.

5   Be sure that your vet includes a dental examination and cleaning as part of your pet's routine examinations.

6   Consider other possible causes of bad breath – such as gastrointestinal disease – if it persists in spite of clean teeth and proper food. Bring your pet to the vet for a check-up.

### ✳ Tip

Some pet foods are designed to help prevent tartar build up and gum disease. Certain chew toys also can help prevent and remove tartar build up.

## 639 | Care for Your Cat's or Dog's Paws

Keep your pet's paws in good shape by inspecting them on a regular basis.

### ⊙ Steps

1 Trim nails as needed (see 640 "Trim Your Dog's Nails" or 641 "Trim Your Cat's Nails").

2 Check regularly between toes for burrs and other foreign bodies. They can sometimes be deeply embedded between toes.

3 Pull out any irritants you can locate, using tweezers.

4 Check for cuts on paw pads. If cuts are small, wash them gently with antibacterial soap. If they are large or bleeding excessively, contact your vet for care.

### ⚠ Warnings

Running on pavements can wear out your dog's pads – check them regularly if you run with your dog. Also, avoid running with your dog on hot pavements, since it can burn his pads.

Take your pet to the vet to be checked and treated if he's limping and excessively licking a paw.

## 640 | Trim Your Dog's Nails

Your dog's nails should just touch the ground when she walks. If her nails are clicking on the floor or getting snagged in the carpet, it's time for a pedicure.

### ⊙ Steps

1 Use trimmers designed for pets. Ask your vet or a groomer for advice about what types of nail trimmers are best for your dog and how to use them properly.

2 Make sure the trimmers are sharp.

3 Start at the tip of the nail and snip a little at a time. When you can see a little bit of moisture, stop clipping.

4 Avoid cutting into the quick, which contains nerves and blood vessels. It is painful and will bleed easily. On white nails, the quick is the pink section. Be extra careful when cutting dark nails, because the quick is difficult to see.

5 If the tip of the nail begins to bleed, apply pressure using styptic powder or a substitute such as baby powder. Avoid wiping the blood clot off the tip of the nail once the bleeding has stopped.

6 Remember to trim the dewclaw nail, on the inside of the leg. Since it doesn't touch the ground, it wears down less rapidly than the others.

7 Give your dog a treat after trimming her nails.

8 Trim your dog's nails once or twice a month. The quick will lengthen if you don't trim the nail regularly, and long nails can cause problems with traction or become ingrown.

### ✱ Tip

If you have not cut your dog's nails since she was a puppy or you're uncomfortable with the task, ask your vet or groomer to demonstrate proper nail trimming or to do it for you.

### ⚠ Warning

Never attempt to trim your dog's nails with clippers designed for use on humans.

### Things You'll Need

☐ pet nail clippers

☐ styptic powder

☐ dog treats

## Trim Your Cat's Nails — 641

If your cat has the habit of using his nails inappropriately on you or the furniture, a regular trimming can help.

### ⊙ Steps

1 Get your cat accustomed to having his feet and nails handled; whenever you're snuggling, take a moment to massage each paw.

2 Turn on a strong light. Trimming your cat's nails in good light will help you see the quick – the part of the nail containing nerves and blood vessels. Cutting into the quick is painful and will cause bleeding.

3 Have everything ready before you start. Cats don't like restraint, especially for long periods.

4 Place your cat in your lap, and gently hold one of his paws.

5 Unsheath your cat's retractable nails by placing your index finger underneath one toe and your thumb over the top of the same toe. Squeeze your fingers together gently. As you do this, you'll see the toenail protrude; it will remain extended until you release your hold.

6 Trim each nail just beyond the point where it starts to curve downwards, using trimmers specifically designed for cats.

7 Start gradually, clipping a few nails in one sitting, using positive reinforcement, such as petting or treats as you clip.

8 If bleeding occurs, apply pressure to the tip of the nail using styptic powder or a substitute such as baby powder.

9 Work up to trimming the nails on all four paws in one sitting.

### ✳ Tips

Cats usually have five nails on each front foot and four on the rear, although they can be born with extra toes. The nails on extra toes tend to become ingrown and should be trimmed more frequently.

This is often a job for two people – one to hold the cat and one to trim the nails.

Avoid punishment or negative reinforcement if your cat protests the pedicure – cats generally don't respond well to this approach. Try again when you sense that your cat might be more cooperative.

### Things You'll Need

☐ pet nail clippers

☐ styptic powder

## House-Train Your Puppy — 642

A puppy isn't born knowing that your carpet is not an acceptable place to relieve himself. Here's a relatively easy way to train him that doesn't require punishment.

### ⊙ Steps

1 Watch your puppy's behaviour while relieving himself outdoors so you can detect the warning signs and intercept him when indoors.

2 Stay outside as often as possible during nice weather so your puppy can develop a preference for eliminating outdoors. Help him develop a liking for surfaces like dirt and gravel by taking him outdoors to eliminate after eating, playing and sleeping – or, ideally, every 15 minutes.

3 When it's time, go straight to a designated area and don't leave until the puppy urinates.

4 Tuck your puppy into a cosy box in your bedroom at night. Dogs are den animals and don't like to soil the area where they sleep.

5 Carry the puppy outdoors when he becomes restless in the middle of the night, and wait until he's finished relieving himself.

### ✳ Tip

Corrections and punishments for indoor accidents will only teach your puppy not to eliminate around you (even when outdoors), but won't stop him from eliminating indoors when you're not around. If you catch the puppy in the act, say "No!" sharply and carry the puppy outside.

### ⚠ Warning

Avoid giving your dog the message that relieving himself is wrong. Don't rub his nose in the mess, and don't hit him with a newspaper.

6   Supply a litter box (filled with sand or cat litter) during the night, unless you plan on getting up every couple of hours to carry him outside. If you do want to take him outside, set your alarm if you sleep too deeply to notice that your puppy has started fidgeting.

7   Carry the puppy outside first thing in the morning so he won't soil the floor as he walks outside.

8   Be consistent with training. Consult a pet behaviourist if you have problems.

9   Reward your dog with puppy treats and praise every time he successfully eliminates outdoors.

## 643 | Train Your Dog

The key to proper training is positive reinforcement – treats and unlimited praise. Be patient and avoid harsh punishment, and you and your dog will both benefit.

### ◎ Steps

1   Enrol your dog in a basic obedience class to learn the "Heel", "Sit" and "Stay" commands.

2   When your dog is learning a command, say "Good" the instant she exhibits proper behaviour, and then follow up quickly with a reward of treats and more praise.

3   Begin increasing your expectations very slowly. For example, lengthen by a few seconds the time your dog must sit before you shower praise.

4   Reward even the slightest sign of effort your dog is making to meet your increasing expectations.

5   Move on to other commands once your dog is comfortable with "Heel", "Sit" and "Stay", and with training in general.

6   Train throughout the day, when you have free time, in a quiet area free from distractions. Limit each session to 5 to 10 minutes.

7   Train in a busier environment only after your dog understands the command entirely, but realise that you may need to start from scratch – dogs are situational learners.

8   Reduce food rewards gradually, but always give an abundance of praise.

### ✳ Tips

Check with your local animal welfare organisation or adult education institute to find out about obedience classes.

Be consistent in training – always use the same words, body language and tone of voice for the same command. You will confuse your dog otherwise.

Be patient. Your dog needs time to understand what you want from her. If she isn't responding, reconsider your approach. Most of the time it's the trainer's fault that a dog doesn't understand what's wanted.

Teach your dog a release command, such as "OK" or "Free", early on, so she will know when the task is over and it's OK to relax.

## 644 | Train Your Cat to Come When You Call

Follow these steps, and even your aloof, independent cat will come to you when he hears you say a special word.

### ◎ Steps

1   Talk to your cat – a lot. Encourage him verbally to come to you, and regularly pet him and brush him.

### ✳ Tips

Choose a dry, crunchy snack that is nutritious and also good for the teeth.

2    Choose a special dry snack that he has shown he likes – and use it only when you call him. It cannot be his regular dry food.

3    Pick a special word for his snack – such as "snack" or "dessert" – and plan to always say it in the same tone of voice.

4    Use your special word during his next snack time. In his presence, place one piece of the food in his empty dish and say the special word.

5    Say the word again after he eats the first piece. Place another piece of the food in his dish and say the special word again.

6    Walk away. If he is giving you "I am really starving" cries, say your word again and give him one more piece. Then walk out of the room.

7    Repeat the procedure in 5 minutes. Cats learn very quickly when they are motivated.

8    Follow this procedure for the next several days.

Use the special word daily, not only when it's time for a trip to the vet or when it's bath time. On those occasions, give him the snack and try to allow a few minutes before following through on your hidden motive.

### ⚠ Warning

Use your special word only when you will follow through with the snack, or you may confuse your cat.

---

## Teach Your Dog Not to Beg at the Table          **645**

Teach your dog from the very beginning that begging isn't allowed. It's much easier to prevent the habit from starting than to end it.

### ◎ Steps

1    Avoid feeding your dog at the table at all times.

2    Ignore your dog completely while you eat, to discourage begging behaviour. That means no eye contact, no talking and no reprimanding throughout the training phase.

3    Train your dog to perform a "Down, stay" and sustain it (see 643 "Train Your Dog").

4    Give your dog a feeding ball – a toy filled with food that drops out as the dog plays – while you eat. Make sure the feeding ball is suitable for the size of your dog.

5    Reward your dog with plenty of praise and affection and a treat (away from the table) after you've finished your meal.

6    Be consistent in your training. Giving in now and then will only confuse your dog.

### ✱ Tip

If you can't resist giving your dog table scraps, keep him in the other room while you eat and give him the scraps later in his food bowl.

---

## Stop Your Dog's Excessive Barking          **646**

Barking is a perfectly natural behaviour in dogs, but that's not a good enough explanation for angry neighbours in the middle of the night. Here are a few hints for turning down the volume.

### ◎ Steps

1    Try to determine why your dog barks – eliminating the cause will increase your chances of success.

### ✱ Tips

Some breeds tend to bark more than others. Check with other owners to find out if your dog's barking habits are normal.

2   Place your dog's favourite treat within reach.

3   Praise the dog for barking once he starts by saying "Good boy" and then "What's the matter?"

4   Tell the dog, "Be quiet".

5   Wave the treat in front of your dog's nose. Most dogs will instantly quiet down, because they will be concentrating on smelling and attempting to lick the treat, rather than barking.

6   Keep praising the dog. Tell the dog that he is a good dog for being quiet.

7   Let the dog have the treat after 3 seconds of quiet time.

8   Wave another treat in front of your dog if he starts to bark again. This time, try not to let your dog have the treat until 5 seconds of quiet time have elapsed. Your dog should learn that after each successful quiet-time interval, he will be rewarded.

9   Scold your dog every time he makes a mistake. If the dog barks, even for just an instant, as you're waving the treat in front of his nose, say "Be quiet", in a louder voice. Then reward the dog immediately after he stops barking.

10   Increase the quiet-time intervals by 3 seconds each time: from 3 seconds to 6 seconds to 9 seconds and so on. It is possible to continue to a couple of minutes of quiet time during the first session, which would mean significant progress in curbing your dog's barking habit.

It takes time to get your dog to break the habit of excessive barking. Remain calm and patient, and eventually he will bark only when it's appropriate.

If you have trouble getting your dog to stop barking, consult a vet trained in behavioural problems.

## 647 | Prevent Your Dog From Chewing on Furniture

It's common for dogs under two years old to chew on everything from your best shoes to your windowsill. Here's how to show your growing dog that there are better things to chew on.

### ⊙ Steps

1   Determine whether the chewing stems from teething, curiosity, boredom or a behavioural disorder. Discuss these options with your vet or an animal-behaviour specialist.

2   Give a teething puppy a teething ring or a chew bone to chew on.

3   Watch your puppy constantly. Use a baby gate to keep him in the same room as you, or train your puppy by puting him in his box with toys for short periods when you're unable to supervise.

4   Divert your puppy's attention to something appropriate, such as a dog toy, when you catch him chewing. Have toys of soft and hard textures available, and rotate them to pre-empt boredom.

5   Set aside specific times for your puppy to interact with you: practising obedience training exercises, learning tricks, exercising and going on outdoor adventures.

6   Exercise your puppy, and play with him using toys. If he's tired, he won't have the energy to chew.

### ✱ Tips

Use chew toys designed for dogs. They are inexpensive and safe and will teach your dog what is OK to chew on.

Some household items that are safe for your dog to play with, under your supervision, are cardboard boxes and paper bags.

### ⚠ Warning

Obedience training by itself won't change behavioural disorders. You may need to correct the underlying problem with the help of an animal-behaviour specialist.

7   Establish a routine with an adult dog, which should include feeding schedules, elimination times and exercise periods he can count on. Adult dogs usually chew out of boredom or frustration.

8   Avoid punishing your dog for chewing, as chewing is a natural behaviour in dogs. It will just make him feel conflicted and anxious.

9   Consult a vet who specialises in animal behaviour if you suspect a behavioural disorder. Common motivations for chewing include separation anxiety, phobia, or a desire to escape or seek attention.

## Things You'll Need

- ❏ teething ring or chew bone
- ❏ baby gate
- ❏ dog crate
- ❏ chew toys

---

## Stop Your Cat From Scratching Furniture          648

Cats scratch to mark their territory, sharpen their nails and stretch their muscles. Here's how to help your cat curb the urge (or at least redirect it away from the sofa).

### ◎ Steps

1   Provide scratching posts and place them in locations where your cat likes to linger – by a sunny window, for instance.

2   Keep in mind that individual cats like different textures (cardboard, wood or rugs) and post orientations (horizontal or vertical). Experiment with different types of posts to find the best ones for your cat.

3   Encourage kittens to use posts, and reward them with food and praise.

4   Consider giving your cat extra attention when he stirs from a nap, and then placing him near the scratching post, since many cats scratch when waking up.

5   Avoid punishing your cat if he scratches an inappropriate area. Punishment teaches the cat not to scratch in your presence, but it won't deter a cat from scratching when you're not around.

6   Avoid letting your cat scratch an old sofa, even if you plan to get rid of it soon – this will only encourage him to scratch the new sofa as well.

### ✳ Tip

Using unpleasant-tasting substances doesn't help, since scratching does not involve the taste buds.

### ⚠ Warnings

Scratching is a natural behaviour, so blocking the cat's access to one area will simply encourage him to scratch elsewhere.

Consult your vet about alternative treatment options before you give up. Destructive behaviour is a leading reason why people surrender their cats to animal shelters.

---

## Stop Your Dog From Digging Up the Lawn          649

Digging can be either a characteristic of your dog's breed or evidence of separation anxiety or a desire to escape.

### ◎ Steps

1   Avoid punishing your dog for digging – this only teaches her not to dig in your presence. She may resume digging when you're not around.

2   Take her on walks. Dogs often dig to expend energy, and walking is a less destructive way to accomplish this.

3   Put up a fence to keep your dog out of areas – like your well-manicured lawn – where you don't want her to dig.

4   Confine your dog in a dog run with toys, shade and water.

### ✳ Tips

Digging is often a result of boredom, so keep your dog occupied with other activities.

5   Keep your dog's sleeping area shaded in hot weather, and supply a paddling pool if it's hot outside. Dogs often dig in search of a cool place to lie down.

6   Turn on the sprinklers or spray your dog with a hose each time she starts digging – this may discourage her from digging if she doesn't like water sprayed on her.

Give your dog her own place to dig – a sandbox or dirt area – and encourage digging in only that spot by hiding treats for her to find. This allows your dog to enjoy the natural behaviour of digging without ruining your garden.

---

## 650 | Approach an Unfamiliar Dog

Attacks by dogs can be fatal. Teach your child to be careful when approaching an unfamiliar dog, and take the same precautions yourself.

### ⊙ Steps

1   Never approach a dog that is chained, tied, enclosed in a pen, behind a fence or in a car. Also don't touch or disturb a dog that appears to be sleeping or is unaware of your presence.

2   Recognise signs of aggressiveness such as barking, growling, snarling with teeth bared, holding the ears erect or tight against the head, holding the tail up stiffly, keeping the legs rigid or bristling the hair. Keep your distance from a dog exhibiting any of these signs, even if the dog is wagging his tail. If the dog advances, move away slowly, in a sideways direction; do not turn and run. Say "No" or "Stay" in a firm voice.

3   To be on the safe side, only approach a dog that is with his owner and on a lead. Make sure the owner approves and invites you to approach and pet the dog.

4   Squat or crouch in front of the dog and allow him to approach you before attempting to pet him. Avoid staring directly into the dog's eyes, as this may be seen as a challenge.

5   Avoid reaching out to touch the dog, even if he appears to be friendly, as the dog may interpret this as a threat.

6   Do not tease or make any sudden movements or loud noises as you approach the dog. This may excite him and cause him to attack.

7   Let the dog keep any items that are in his possession – food, toys, chew bones and so on.

8   Offer a treat to the dog once contact is made, provided the owner says it's OK to do so.

### ⚠ Warnings

Remember that children comprise a high percentage of dog-bite victims, so always take extra precautions when children are present around puppies or dogs.

Never approach stray dogs or dogs who are not within sight of their owners.

## Break Up a Dog or Cat Fight
**651**

Breaking up a fight between two dogs or two cats can be dangerous and challenging. Depending on your size and abilities, you have a few options to choose from.

### ⊙ Steps

1  Avoid hitting the dogs or cats or getting your hands anywhere near their mouths. Hitting could make the situation worse and could cause the attack to be redirected towards you.

2  Enlist another person and separate two dogs by grabbing their hind legs and walking them backwards like wheelbarrows. Secure the dogs away from each other before releasing them. This is not for cats.

3  Spray the aggressor with a water hose. If this doesn't make a difference, aim for the nostrils.

4  Hold a broom between the dogs or cats to separate them.

5  Use a noisemaking device such as an air horn to drive the animals apart, and be prepared to move away quickly or defend yourself.

### ✳ Tip

Consider keeping your cat inside. Abscesses resulting from cat fights can pose serious health risks and are expensive to treat.

### ⚠ Warning

Most cases of feline immunodeficiency virus (FIV) are spread through bites – such as in a cat fight.

---

## Help Your Pet Cope With Loud Noises
**652**

Fear of loud noises is a common behavioural disorder in pets. The symptoms range from mild (trembling) to extreme (panic attacks, destructive behaviour, running away).

### ⊙ Steps

1  Be aware that controlling reactions to loud noises may require the help of a vet or trainer using medication or behavioural modification.

2  Desensitise or countercondition your pet through repeated exposure to sounds. Start with a greatly reduced volume, and gradually intensify the sounds over time. This may result in controlling the problem.

3  Invest in nature recordings with sounds of thunder or pounding rain to help your pet get used to these sounds.

4  Keep your pet company if there is potential for exposure to loud noises.

5  Bring your pet inside if loud noises are likely. Do not leave a pet in a run or cage or tied with a rope, chain or cable.

6  When loud noises occur, confine the pet in familiar surroundings that are insulated from sound, are dimly lit and present no opportunity for escape. A basement or a room without windows is ideal.

7  Play soft music or videos, or leave the television on during a loud storm or noisy event. This may calm or distract your pet.

8  Find a suitable boarding facility at especially high-risk times, such as Guy Fawkes night.

9  Avoid punishing a pet to suppress a fearful response to loud noises.

### ✳ Tips

Pets can sense your anxiety, so stay calm. Try not to overreact; your reaction could cause the condition to worsen.

Tranquilisation may be required. Use only drugs developed especially for animals – not people – as prescribed by a vet.

## 653 Treat Your Dog's Separation Anxiety

Barking, whining, escaping, destructive behaviour or, in severe cases, self-mutilation can be your dog's way of expressing anxiety over your absence.

### ⊙ Steps

1 Consult your vet to get a correct diagnosis of separation anxiety. Your vet will help you with treatment or refer you to an animal behaviourist who can prescribe effective drug therapies to alleviate your dog's anxieties.

2 Practise leaving your dog alone for short periods of time. Pick up your keys and leave for 1 minute.

3 Gradually increase the amount of time you stay away. This will accustom your dog to your absence.

4 Avoid overly emotional good-byes and greetings. Instead, pat your dog on the head and offer a quick goodbye or hello.

5 Keep your dog confined in a safe area while you are away. Be sure to leave a bowl of water and plenty of chew toys.

6 Exercise your dog for an hour each day in places other than your garden or home. This helps your dog feel comfortable in other locations and allows her to let off steam.

7 Praise your dog often to build self-confidence, rather than punishing her for exhibiting frightened behaviours. Punishment only increases anxiety and makes the situation worse.

### ⚠ Warning

The first time you administer medication to control separation anxiety, stay with and watch your dog carefully in case she has an adverse reaction. Take her to the vet if you witness odd behaviour, as the dosage may need adjustment.

## 654 Protect Dogs and Cats From Household Dangers

Accidents such as falling, being dropped or crushed, or ingesting a foreign body are the leading causes of injury for dogs and cats in the home. Here are some simple precautions.

### ⊙ Steps

1 Keep your cat or dog away from toxic plants. Toxic plants commonly found around the house include laburnum, mistletoe, philodendron, dieffenbachia and caladium. Talk to your local nursery about which toxic outdoor plants are common in your area.

2 Keep objects that are small enough to be swallowed away from your cat or dog. A small ball or loose string is easy to swallow and may cause bowel obstruction.

3 Store toxic chemicals, as well as dangerously sharp objects and utensils (knives, razors and scissors), in closed containers inside cupboards and cabinets.

4 Avoid confining your cat or dog in areas where cleaning products and other chemicals are stored.

### ✱ Tip

Animal behaviourists compare cats and dogs to children when it comes to understanding and avoiding hazards. Be vigilant in protecting your pet.

5  Clean up any spilled chemicals thoroughly – especially antifreeze – before letting your pet into the area where a spill has occurred (see 663 "Detect Antifreeze Poisoning in Your Pet").

6  Keep chocolate in areas where your dog cannot reach it. Chocolate is toxic to dogs.

7  Secure electrical cords behind appliances, hidden from your pet's view, and tape them to the wall if necessary. Discourage your pet from chewing on them by spraying the cords with lemon juice or other unpleasant flavours (see 655 "Prevent Your Pet From Chewing on Electrical Cords").

8  Check and repair any damaged fencing, gates, doors or windows where your cat or dog might escape.

9  Be cautious – watch for your cat or dog as you drive in and out of your garage to make sure you don't run over her or get her caught in the garage door.

10 Keep medicines and vitamins out of your pet's reach, and never give her medication labelled for people unless directed by your vet. For example, acetaminophen is toxic for cats, and ibuprofen can cause kidney failure in dogs.

## Prevent Your Pet From Chewing on Electrical Cords      655

Chewing on electrical cords can burn or shock your pet, causing respiratory problems, cardiac arrest and even death. His sharp teeth and inquisitive nature can put him at high risk.

### ⊙ Steps

1  Tape cords to the wall with electrical tape to help prevent your pet from gaining access to them.

2  Stow excess lengths of cord behind furniture or appliances, hidden from your pet's view. Cats are attracted to dangling cords and may think they are toys.

3  Block access to visible cords by wrapping flexible safety cable (available at hardware shops) around them.

4  Place contact paper, sticky side up, in the general area of electrical cords to discourage your pet from approaching them.

5  Apply unpleasant-tasting substances to exposed cords. These could include hot-pepper sauce, menthol, toothpaste, mouthwash or lemon juice. Experiment with different flavours, since pets' taste aversions vary.

6  Have favourite toys available to distract your pet from the cords, and rotate toys every few days to prevent boredom.

7  Keep your pet out of any room with exposed electrical cords until your furry friend loses interest in chewing on them.

### ⚠ Warning

Electrical-cord injuries are most common in puppies and kittens, especially when they are first adopted, so be extra vigilant with the young ones when you bring them home for the first time.

### Things You'll Need

- ❏ electrical tape
- ❏ flexible safety cable
- ❏ contact paper
- ❏ hot-pepper sauce, menthol, toothpaste, mouthwash or lemon juice
- ❏ pet toys

##  656 Give Pet Medicine

If you've never administered medication to your pet, ask your vet for a hands-on demonstration; also ask about any danger in handling the medication if you are pregnant. When you give a pet medicine, keep other pets or unfamiliar people out of the room, and stroke and praise your pet before and after the procedure. Before administering medicine to an animal with a dropper, practise using lukewarm water.

### To a bird by dropper

1 Close all doors and windows and remove any other pets before you open the cage.

2 Fill the dropper with the prescribed dose of medication and place it within easy reach.

3 Try giving the medicine with a dropper while the bird is on a perch.

4 If this doesn't work, capture the bird and hold him gently in your hand or wrapped in a towel, head exposed and tilted upward.

5 Gently but firmly restrain his wings and legs in your grasp to prevent injury or escape.

6 Place the dropper at the corner of his beak and slowly dispense by squeezing the bulb.

7 Allow the medication to trickle down between the upper and lower beak.

8 Release the bird if he struggles intensely.

### To a cat by dropper

1 Place your cat on a flat surface such as a table, facing the same way as you are.

2 Fill the dropper with the prescribed dose.

3 Stand along the cat's left side (your right).

4 Grasp his head with your left hand, holding the mouth closed by placing your thumb on the bridge of the nose and your fingers under the lower jaw.

5 Tilt the head upward at a 30-degree angle.

6 Pick up the dropper with your right hand and insert it between the lips and teeth at the corner of the mouth on the right side.

7 Slide the dropper to the back of the cheek pouch and deposit the medication there.

8 Loosen your grasp on the head, but do not let go. Tilt the cat's nose down at an angle of about 30 degrees to make him swallow.

### To a dog by dropper

1 Place your dog in a sitting position – or if she's small, in your lap.

2 Fill the dropper with the prescribed dose.

3 Grasp the muzzle gently with your left hand, fingers under the lower jaw, thumb on the bridge of the nose.

4 Tilt the nose upward at a 30-degree angle.

5 Pick up the dropper in your right hand and insert it into the corner of the mouth, between the lips and teeth, on the right side of the dog's muzzle.

6 Gently slide the dropper between the lips and teeth.

7 Squeeze the bulb to deposit the medication at the back of the cheek pouch.

8 Release the muzzle to let the dog swallow.

### To a cat, dog, or horse by pill

1 Give your pet a treat without medication to whet her appetite. Offer cats a lump of butter. For dogs, consider a bite size portion of meat, cheese or peanut butter. Give horses grain with treacle.

2 For cats or dogs or dogs, break the pill into small pieces if necessary, and enclose it completely within the meat, cheese, peanut butter or lump of butter.

3 For horses, grind up the pill and add it to the grain with plenty of treacle to hold the mix together.

4 Be sure the treat is large enough to cover the pill or pieces of the pill, but not so large that your pet will chew, discover the medicine and spit it out.

## Pack a First Aid Kit for Your Pet 657

Keep a first aid kit for your pet accessible at home or in your car when travelling. Gathering the necessary items ahead of time could help save your pet's life in an emergency.

### ⊙ Steps

1   Get a durable, waterproof (or at least water-resistant) container that opens and closes easily yet securely. It should be large enough to hold the items mentioned below.

2   Start off with bandage material, such as gauze pads or cotton gauze, and adhesive tape or masking tape.

3   Add hydrogen peroxide and antibacterial ointment or cream.

4   Include diarrhoea medication, but seek your vet's approval before using it. Check expiration dates and replace as needed.

5   Add a pair of scissors, plus tweezers or forceps.

6   Include a few eyedroppers for dispensing liquid medication (see 656 "Give Veterinary Medicine") or for cleaning superficial wounds.

7   Be sure to include syrup of ipecac, to induce vomiting in the event your pet is poisoned. Consult your vet before inducing vomiting.

8   Find activated charcoal at any health food shop. This remedy is good for poisoning or diarrhoea and controls flatulence resulting from any stomach or intestinal upset.

9   Store blankets in the kit to keep your pet warm in extreme conditions.

10  When travelling, call ahead to your destination to see if there are any particular dangers, such as snakes, poisonous plants or extreme heat, that you will need to consider when packing your first aid kit.

11  Include the phone numbers of your pet's regular vet and of a nearby emergency veterinary hospital.

### ⚠ Warnings

Muzzle an injured dog if possible, since overly stressed dogs are more likely to bite.

Never give your cat aspirin or acetaminophen. It is extremely toxic to cats. Avoid giving ibuprofen to dogs, as it can cause kidney failure.

### Things You'll Need

- ☐ waterproof container
- ☐ bandages
- ☐ hydrogen peroxide and antibacterials
- ☐ diarrhoea medication
- ☐ scissors and tweezers
- ☐ eyedroppers
- ☐ syrup of ipecac
- ☐ activated charcoal
- ☐ blankets

## Get Rid of Fleas 658

Fleas can transmit disease and tapeworm. Keeping your pet and his environment clean is the single most important part of a successful flea-control programme.

### ⊙ Steps

1   Understand the life of the flea. An adult female can lay one egg per hour for every hour of her life (usually three months). Fleas thrive in heat and humidity and are most active in summer and autumn.

2   Help prevent fleas indoors by vacuuming your home thoroughly and frequently, paying close attention to corners, cracks and crevices. Dispose of vacuum cleaner bags conscientiously, as adult fleas can escape.

3   Remove fleas from your pet using a fine-toothed comb, and drop the fleas into soapy water to drown them.

### ✱ Tips

Be diligent in your exterminating efforts. A flea pupa while in the cocoon is impervious to treatment and can live for eight months without feeding.

Vets are sceptical of homemade flea remedies such as garlic, vinegar, vitamin C and kelp.

4   Wash pet bedding in hot, soapy water weekly; this is the most likely site for flea eggs and larvae.

5   Prune foliage and keep grass trimmed short to increase sunlight, as flea larvae cannot survive in hot, dry areas. Remove piles of debris in areas close to your home.

6   Bathe pets weekly if possible. If bathing is not an option, speak to your vet about appropriate alternatives.

7   Watch your pet for signs of flea trouble: excessive scratching and biting, especially around the tail and lower back; "flea debris" (black, granular dried blood) and fleas themselves on the skin; and possibly raw patches where the animal has been biting and scratching himself.

8   Talk to your vet about various treatments for your flea-plagued pet: a flea adulticide applied monthly to the skin; a monthly pill that prevents fleas from reproducing but doesn't kill adult fleas; and multipurpose products that prevent flea reproduction and control heartworms, hook-worms, whipworms and roundworms. Also consider flea collars and flea powders.

9   Look into chemical flea-treatment products to apply by hand around the environment in spray or powder form. Ask your vet for a recommendation on the best product and how to use it.

Call on a professional exterminator for severe indoor and outdoor infestations.

## ⚠ Warnings

Be very careful with all insecticides to be used on pets or around your home. Read directions carefully.

Never apply a flea product to a cat or kitten unless it is labelled as safe for cats. Cats are very sensitive to insecticides.

Ingesting fleas could give your pet tapeworm (see 660 "Prevent Worms in Cats and Dogs").

---

## 659 | Remove Ticks From Pets

Ticks thrive in woody, grassy and brushy areas and carry diseases such as Lyme disease. That's why it's essential to keep them off your pet.

### ⊙ Steps

1   Check your pet for ticks daily if he spends a lot of time outdoors, especially if you live in an area known for ticks.

2   Put on latex gloves to avoid direct contact with the tick and contaminated skin, as diseases can be transmitted from tick to pet to human.

3   Feel your pet all over, especially around the neck, head and ears. If you encounter a lump like a small pea, move the fur on your pet to see if you have found a tick.

4   Look to see if a tick is protruding from the skin. Ticks are tiny black, brown, reddish or tan disklike arachnids (having eight legs), about the size of the head of a pin. If they have attached themselves to their host (your pet), then they can swell up to the size of a grape in some cases.

5   Put your pet in a comfortable position. Ask a friend or family member for help in distracting your pet.

6   Grasp the tick with tweezers as close to your pet's skin as possible; make sure not to pinch your pet's skin.

7   Pull the tick out using a straight, steady pulling motion. Be gentle; pulling too hard on the tick can cause its head to remain lodged in your pet's skin, which can lead to inflammation and secondary infection.

### ✳ Tips

Consider using a flea and tick shampoo if you find several ticks in your search.

Obtain a tick collar from your vet. Also ask about anti-tick products that you can apply to your pet's skin.

### ⚠ Warning

Contact your vet if you suspect that your pet has been infected with Lyme disease. The most common symptoms are a rash (visible if you part the hair), followed by recurring joint pain (which the pet may manifest by limping).

8   Dispose of the tick by throwing it into a fire, or by squishing it in a tissue using the tweezers and then flushing it down the toilet. Do not squash it with your foot or your bare hands.

9   Apply antiseptic ointment to the bite.

10   Remove and wash the gloves, and wash your hands thoroughly.

11   Clean the tweezers with hot water or isopropyl alcohol or by holding them over a flame.

## Things You'll Need

- ☐ latex gloves
- ☐ tweezers
- ☐ antiseptic ointment
- ☐ isopropyl alcohol

---

## Prevent Worms in Cats and Dogs     660

Roundworms, hookworms and tapeworms are some of the common parasites that can infest your pet. They can cause diarrhoea, weight loss or vomiting.

### ⊙ Steps

1   Get puppies and kittens tested as early as three weeks after birth. They will often already be infested with worms and will need to be treated.

2   Take your pet in for an annual examination. Ask your vet to recommend broad-spectrum preventive products. The newest products protect against roundworms, heartworms, ticks and fleas.

3   Control fleas (see 658 "Get Rid of Fleas"). Fleas can transmit tapeworm if your pet ingests them.

4   Avoid exposing your pet to stray animals or wildlife, as they are often carriers for fleas and other parasites. Dog parks that are not well maintained are a common source of parasites.

5   Prevent your pet from eating animal carcasses, such as those of birds, rabbits and rodents. Carcasses can carry immature worms that can then mature after your pet has ingested them.

6   Prevent your dog from eating faeces – his own or that of other dogs and other animals. Contact with faecal material from another animal is the most common way for a dog to get intestinal parasites.

7   Take precautions when travelling with your pet. Before you go, check with your travel agent or vet about risks at your destination.

8   Inspect your pet's anus and faeces to spot signs of tapeworms. Tapeworm segments are small, white and flat, resembling grains of rice.

9   Have a stool specimen checked by your vet to be certain that your pet remains parasite-free.

### ✳ Tips

Parasite types vary, depending on locale and whether the animal is an indoor or outdoor pet

Infestations can be asymptomatic until triggered by stress.

### ⚠ Warnings

Avoid over-the-counter and home remedies. These are generally less effective and can also be dangerous.

Contact your vet immediately if your pet shows any signs of illness (vomiting, diarrhoea, tremors or poor coordination) after administration of worm medication.

## 661 | Care for a Dog Who Has Allergies

Canine allergies are a lot like human allergies – dogs can react to allergens in the air, in food or on their skin. Learn to recognise canine allergy symptoms, then provide relief.

### ⊙ Steps

1 Look for allergy symptoms in your dog. The most common signs of an allergy to inhalants or fleas are frequent itching, chewing and biting, especially on the tail, the stomach and the insides of the hind legs, as well as licking and chewing the paws. Inhaled allergens can also result in sneezing, coughing and watery eyes. Vomiting, itching and diarrhoea can be symptoms of food allergies. Hives and rashes can be symptoms of various types of allergies.

2 Consider the season: Allergies to airborne mould and pollen erupt in the spring and autumn. Flea allergies are most prominent during the flea season, which is summer in most areas but can range from early spring to late autumn.

3 Take your dog to a vet if you observe any of the above symptoms, especially vomiting or diarrhoea, as they could be caused by a more serious underlying medical condition.

4 If you suspect an allergy to food, realise that typical canine food allergens include maize, beef, dairy products, wheat and soybeans – ingredients in most pet foods.

5 Talk to your vet about putting your dog on a special restricted diet to determine which food she is reacting to. Follow the vet's guidelines to gradually introduce other foods into the diet until the allergen is found. Your vet may also recommend food-allergy tests to find the allergen.

6 If you suspect an allergy to inhalants, vacuum and dust frequently. Culprits include dust, mould spores and pollen grains.

7 Treat your dog to a cool bath, and shampoo or rinse with aloe vera or oatmeal to help soothe itchy skin. Your vet may also recommend medicated shampoos, antihistamines or other drugs to keep the itching at bay while the skin heals and contact with the allergen is diminished.

8 Check your dog for fleas, as your dog could be suffering from fleabite dermatitis (an allergy to a flea's saliva). Careful grooming and frequent examinations for fleas and flea droppings can help alleviate this allergy. Ask your vet about flea products such as sprays, shampoos, topical ointments and pills. Again, an oatmeal or aloe vera bath can help soothe the itching.

9 Consider the possibility of contact allergies, realising that the symptoms will be limited to areas of contact. Some dogs are allergic to bedding (wool is one possible offender), grass or plastic food bowls. If your dog has acne on his chin and uses a plastic feeding bowl, try switching to a steel, glass or ceramic feeding bowl.

10 Talk to your vet about a referral to a veterinary dermatologist if your dog is not responding to recommended treatments.

### ✱ Tips

Frequent baths (once or twice a week) can help eliminate many skin problems suffered by dogs (see 633 "Wash Your Dog").

It only takes one or two flea bites to set off a dog's allergies to fleas.

Certain dog breeds, such as golden retrievers, are more prone to allergies than others. If buying a pedigree dog, ask the owner whether the parents have allergies, since allergies can be inherited.

### ⚠ Warnings

Bring your dog to the vet when the itching first manifests itself, to avoid the possibility of skin infections caused by excess chewing and scratching.

Never apply flea products to irritated or broken skin; the chemicals could further irritate and injure the skin.

## Detect Skin Cancer in Your Pet                    662

Early detection of skin cancer in your pet is the key to successful treatment. Here is how to spot the disease in the initial stages of development.

### ⊙Steps

1 Examine your pet monthly, at a minimum. Check for tumours; areas of colour change; or scaly, crusty lesions.

2 Use your fingers to separate the hair, and look closely at the skin.

3 Take note of any new growths, as well as any changes in the colour or size of existing growths. If you find changes, continue to observe the growths and call your vet for advice.

4 Be concerned if you find tumours that bleed easily or any areas that refuse to heal.

5 Pay attention if your pet is licking at one area continually. Examine that area closely.

6 Call your vet at once if you notice a swelling in your pet's breast tissue or discharge from a nipple. Check under his tail for any suspicious lumps or areas of discoloration.

7 Look closely at your cat's eyelids and lips and inside his mouth for irregular areas or colour changes. If your cat's nose or ears are white, check them closely for scaly, bumpy or reddened areas.

8 Check your pet's mouth. Look for masses or tissue that seems different from surrounding areas.

9 Bathe, groom and massage your pet frequently; this will help you to detect any small changes as you feel for unusual masses or other suspicious areas. Fingers can often find things that are camouflaged by fur.

10 Report all things that are not normal to your vet right away.

### ✱Tips

Dogs frequently develop soft masses under the skin, called "lipomas". Your vet should quickly be able to tell this from skin cancer.

Orange tabby cats often develop smooth dark spots on their lips and eyelids as they age; these are not cancerous.

Chronic infections from cat-fight wounds that will not heal may resemble skin cancer.

### ⚠Warnings

Delay in treatment of skin cancer can result in serious harm to your pet's health.

A long, thick coat may obscure tumours that would otherwise be seen easily.

## Detect Antifreeze Poisoning in Your Pet          663

The taste and smell of antifreeze are attractive to animals, and ingesting it can be deadly. Here's how to spot possible ingestion so you can seek help immediately.

### ⊙Steps

1 Prevent antifreeze poisoning by keeping antifreeze away from animals, including antifreeze puddles that sometimes form under cars.

2 Take your pet to the vet immediately if you catch him drinking antifreeze or think he has done so.

3 Visit the vet immediately as well if you notice signs of ingestion such as stupor, swaying, weaving, listlessness, frequent urination, excessive thirst or vomiting.

### ⚠Warnings

An animal must be taken to the vet within 12 hours of ingesting antifreeze. After 12 to 24 hours, kidney failure will occur, followed eventually by death.

In freezing weather, the only water that's not frozen may contain antifreeze, so don't allow your pet to drink from puddles.

4   Understand that in the second stage of poisoning, the liver will metabolise ethylene glycol into more toxic substances.

5   Consider using new, safer propylene glycol antifreeze, which is less hazardous to animals.

---

## 664 Take Your Pet's Temperature

Take your pet's temperature when she is healthy so that you'll recognise when her temperature is above normal in the future.

### ⊙ Steps

1   Use a rectal thermometer specific to your animal's size. These are available at many pet shops. Human thermometers also work.

2   Sterilise the thermometer by dipping it in surgical spirit.

3   Allow it to dry, then apply Vaseline or a similar lubricant to the tip.

4   Allow your pet to stand, or lay her on her side, and gently hold her down.

5   Shake the thermometer until it reads below 37.7°C (100°F).

6   Insert the thermometer three-quarters of the way into the rectum and wait 1 to 3 minutes. Your pet may respond to this uncomfortable procedure by scratching or snapping. As you proceed, gently stroke her and talk in a gentle, soothing tone. If this doesn't work, try again later – most pets eventually allow their temperature to be taken.

7   Take the thermometer out and read it.

8   Wipe or rinse the thermometer after use, and then sterilise it by dipping it in surgical spirit.

9   Reward your pet with a treat.

### ✱ Tips

Digital thermometers designed for humans work well on pets. They can be used orally or anally and deliver a reading in seconds.

The average temperature for a dog or cat is 38.1 to 39.2°C (100.5 to 102.5°F).

### ⚠ Warning

Do not try to take a bird's temperature using these instructions.

### Things You'll Need

❑ pet thermometer

❑ Vaseline

❑ surgical spirit

❑ pet treat

---

## 665 Determine if Your Dog Needs Medical Care

Since your dog can't talk, you'll need to watch carefully for signs of illness. Spotting the symptoms early can dramatically affect the outcome – and expense – of treatment.

### ⊙ Steps

1   Learn your dog's daily routine. Observe her activities – such as her eating and drinking habits and her patterns of urination and defecation – closely, so you can quickly detect variations from her normal behaviour.

2   Learn to do simple things like monitoring her heart and respiratory rates and taking her temperature (see 664 "Take Your Pet's Temperature"). Normal temperature for a dog is 38.05 to 39.17°C (100.5 to 102.5°F).

3   Watch for symptoms such as persistent vomiting, retching or gagging; diarrhoea; or straining to defecate or urinate. These can signify serious medical problems. Call your vet immediately.

### ✱ Tips

Listlessness and refusal to eat or drink are usually the first symptoms of illness. Hot weather causes dogs to become inactive and eat less, but they will also drink more.

Ask any children in your household if they think the dog is ill. They often see things that busy adults overlook.

4   Notice lethargy or weakness, a reluctance to eat or drink, or persistent coughing or sneezing, coupled with a change of behaviour. These are sure signs that your dog needs medical attention.

5   Be aware that excessive drooling and shaking or generalised tremors, convulsions, seizures or laboured respiration can indicate poisoning. Call your vet immediately.

6   Try not to confuse normal behavioural changes and mood swings, which can be caused by alterations in your daily routine or variations in household activities, with true signs of illness.

⚠ **Warning**

Take action as soon as you notice a problem. Delays in calling your vet will often result in prolonged treatment, increased stress on you and your dog, increased expense and possibly the loss of your pet.

## Determine if Your Cat Needs Medical Care                666

Disguising symptoms of illness is one of your cat's specialities, so he may have been sick for days before you notice. Here's how to tell if something's wrong.

### ◉ Steps

1   Watch your cat closely. Become familiar with his normal habits and patterns of activity, such as eating, sleeping and defecating. The slightest variation may indicate the beginning of illness or disease.

2   Prepare yourself to do simple things like monitor his heart and respiratory rate and take his temperature. Normal is 38.1 to 39.2°C (100.5 to 102.5°F).

3   Groom him daily, checking for masses, swellings and sensitive areas.

4   Understand that lethargy, refusal of food or water, and reluctance to play are often the first symptoms of illness. Sick cats dehydrate quickly, so prompt response is essential.

5   Be aware that even the slightest elevation in temperature will account for his listlessness.

6   Notice any symptoms, such as sneezing, runny eyes or nose, or laboured breathing, that may indicate respiratory illness, and call the vet for advice.

7   Remember that coughing or hacking could simply mean that your cat has a hairball. But if these symptoms persist, call his doctor.

8   Know that straining to urinate, especially in male cats, is considered a sign of urinary-tract obstruction. Get medical help immediately, as this can be life-threatening.

9   Be aware that violent retching, attempting to vomit or unusual panting are symptoms of serious illness or pain in cats, so call your vet immediately.

10  Call your vet as soon as you think your cat is ill. Delaying the call often leads to greater risk for the cat, prolonged recovery and higher costs.

✱ **Tips**

Cats are finicky eaters, so refusal to eat a new food may not indicate that your cat is ill.

Ask any children in your household if they think the cat is ill. They often see things that busy adults overlook.

⚠ **Warning**

Use caution when handling a sick cat. He may react suddenly and bite or scratch when he would not normally do so.

## 667 | Calm a Pet's Fear of Visiting the Vet

A fearful or aggressive pet is difficult for veterinary staff to examine. If your pet has an extreme aversion to visiting the vet, help her get acquainted with that environment.

### ⊙ Steps

1   Visit the veterinary hospital or office with your pet once a week until your pet is habituated.

2   Take treats and have the staff give them to your pet. Make it a fun experience, and then take your pet and leave.

3   Use a gradual approach if your pet is already fearful and won't accept treats. For example, play with her on the front lawn of your vet's office and make her feel comfortable. Over a period of a few weeks, gradually bring her to the front door and progress to standing in the waiting room and visiting with the staff.

4   Give treats for calm behaviour.

5   Attempt to get your pet acquainted with a single staff member so she has a friend – pets, like people, get along with some individuals better than others.

### ✳ Tips

Ask your vet if a previsit tranquiliser might be the best solution.

If your pet is fearful and an examination is essential, give her to the staff and leave. Sometimes pets do much better when alone with the vet. Animals sense your anxiety.

## 668 | Find Your Lost Pet

If your pet is missing, don't give up hope. Take the following measures to recover your furry or feathered friend and bring him back home.

### ⊙ Steps

1   Organise a search party. Travel on bikes, on foot and by car and search the area.

2   Walk slowly and call your pet's name. Listen for any response – a miaow, bark or chirp. He may be hiding, afraid to come out in the open.

3   Make familiar sounds likely to attract your pet: shake a box of his favourite dry food, whistle or open a can of wet food.

4   File a lost-pet report with all animal-control agencies, newspaper lost-and-found departments, and animal shelters in the surrounding area.

5   Call your local veterinary and emergency clinics to see if someone has presented your pet for treatment.

6   Search your neighbourhood thoroughly late at night. Look closely under cars and around rubbish bins.

7   Make flyers that include the date of loss, the pet's name, a description, any unique markings, a picture and your phone number.

8   Put the flyers up around your neighbourhood and at shopping centres, veterinary clinics, pet shops and anywhere else you can think of – including your old neighbourhood if you've recently moved.

### ✳ Tips

To help prevent your pet from becoming lost in the first place, equip him with tags and a microchip. A microchip is a tiny identification chip injected under the skin. It is read with a special scanner that animal welfare organisations, vets and agencies have, and it contains information that can help these organisations find you.

If your pet is small, check open vents and crawl spaces and listen for noises. Sometimes pets venture into small spaces and get stuck between walls or in vents.

9   Check the "found" section of your local newspaper daily, and be sure to pay a visit to your local animal shelter and animal welfare organisation – don't rely on a phone call.

10  Place familiar-smelling items such as T-shirts you've worn and not washed in a cardboard box, and then place the box in your garden, as far away from the house as possible. Regularly check it late at night and early in the morning.

## Slow the Ageing of Your Dog                                    669

Dogs age more quickly than people, so start working to keep your dog young when you adopt her. Paying close attention to a few details may add years to her active life.

### ⊙ Steps

1   Get your dog annual health checks, and follow the vet's advice on preventive health-care measures. Preventing disease while maintaining optimal health is the first step towards a long, healthy life.

2   Spay or neuter your dog as soon as possible. Having puppies, especially repeated litters, is stressful and will contribute to premature ageing.

3   Food high-quality food designed for the life stage of your dog. Your dog's nutritional requirements will change throughout her life.

4   Talk to your vet about adding vitamin and mineral supplements, including antioxidants, and extra fibre to your dog's diet.

5   Exercise your dog daily. Playing, running or swimming will help prevent obesity and keep her active well into old age.

6   Groom and bathe your dog regularly, paying particular attention to her ears and skin. Chronic infections and inflammation are stressful and speed the ageing process.

7   Have your dog's teeth cleaned professionally. Good dental health is a key component of longevity.

8   Provide adequate shelter and bedding, especially during inclement weather. Sleeping on cold, hard surfaces such as concrete will promote joint disease, stiffness and ageing.

9   Avoid subjecting your dog to environmental stresses such as second-hand smoke, harassment by other animals, noise or crowding.

10  Shower your dog with love and attention. Keeping her feeling young at heart will promote a strong desire to stay active so she can join you in all activities.

11  Look for signs of arthritis – stiffened joints and limping – early on to get proper pain medication to help your dog avoid unnecessary suffering.

### ✳ Tips

Find a vet with a special interest in ageing who keeps abreast of advancements in this rapidly developing area of pet care.

Research this subject on your own. Experts' understanding of the ageing process is changing rapidly, and knowledge gained about humans is often applicable to animals.

Mental fitness is important in delaying ageing in dogs, just as in people, so challenge your dog with commands and have her do tricks even as she ages.

### ⚠ Warnings

Consult your vet, and use caution and common sense, when tempted to try supplements or "miracle cure" products that promise unrealistic results.

Also consult your vet before offering your elderly dog pain medications. Some products that humans consume safely – such as ibuprofen – are poisonous to dogs.

## 670 | Slow the Ageing of Your Cat

Cats may not have nine lives, but they can live longer than many people think – 18 to 20 years is common. Here's how to keep your cat purring into advanced old age.

### ◉ Steps

1   Take your cat to the vet at least once a year for a complete physical examination, and follow your vet's advice regarding preventive health-care measures. Preventing disease and maintaining optimum health are the first steps towards a long, healthy life.

2   Spay or neuter your cat as soon as possible. Having kittens, especially repeated litters, is stressful and will contribute to premature ageing.

3   Keep your cat inside at all times to reduce the risk of accidents, injuries from fights or disease.

4   Feed your cat high-quality food designed to meet the specific nutritional requirements during all stages of his life.

5   Prevent obesity at all costs by controlling your cat's diet and engaging him in play activities.

6   Talk to your vet about adding vitamin and mineral supplements, antioxidants and extra fibre to your cat's diet.

7   Have your cat's teeth cleaned professionally. Good dental health will add years to his life.

8   Groom your cat daily, checking for abnormalities, and seek medical help promptly when you discover anything suspicious (see 662 "Detect Skin Cancer in Your Pet").

9   Make sure no harmful chemicals such as pesticides or household cleaners find their way onto your cat's fur, since cats groom themselves with their tongues constantly. Even small amounts of harmful chemicals on their bodies can have adverse effects if consumed over many years.

10   Protect your cat from environmental dangers such as household cleaners and second-hand smoke.

11   Help your cat avoid the stress of harassment from other animals by providing a quiet place for undisturbed catnaps.

12   Provide your older cat with a heat source such as a heating pad set on low, since cats more than 12 years old require extra heat. You'll notice a difference in his attitude and activity level.

13   Give your cat daily full-body massages and lots of love. Despite their aloof demeanour, cats thrive on affection.

### ✳ Tips

Find a vet with a special interest in ageing who keeps abreast of advancements in this rapidly developing area of pet care.

Research this subject on your own. Experts' understanding of the ageing process is changing rapidly, and knowledge gained about humans is often applicable to animals.

### ⚠ Warning

Call your vet before giving your cat any product not specifically approved for cats. Some products, such as acetaminophen, commonly consumed safely by people or dogs, are poisonous to cats.

## Teach Your Parrot to Talk

### 671

As satisfied bird owners can attest, teaching a parrot to talk takes patience but is well worth the effort.

### ⊙ Steps

1 Begin teaching your parrot to talk when she is 4 to 6 months old at the latest. Try a simple "Good morning" to your bird at the start of each day. Keep in mind that some parrots will pick up words sooner than others.

2 Hold the bird in front of your mouth when you teach her, so that you have her attention.

3 Repeat words or phrases, such as family members' names and common expressions. Be sure to show lots of excitement in your voice. Your parrot will gradually begin to repeat after you.

4 Repeat certain words or phrases every time you do something, such as "Up" when you lift your bird up, to teach her to associate a certain movement with certain words.

5 Reward with treats when your parrot mimics you.

6 Consider playing recordings of words you want her to learn for up to 15 minutes at a time – longer than that can cause boredom.

### ✱ Tips

Don't let your bird hear sounds or words you don't want her to mimic. Discourage unwanted utterances by simply ignoring them.

Some experts believe that parrot owners should teach their birds to talk before teaching them to whistle, as whistling can interfere with learning words.

Mynah birds and certain types of parakeets can also learn to repeat words.

## Trim Your Bird's Wings

### 672

Trimming a bird's wings allows him to flutter to the ground safely – but not fly out the window.

### ⊙ Steps

1 Have a vet show you how much to trim the first time, and take notes so you'll know how to trim the feathers on your own. The amount to trim depends on the strength and body weight of the bird.

2 Have someone assist you in restraining the bird.

3 Examine all feathers of the wing.

4 Look for emerging feathers, which have blood in the shafts (see Tips). These feathers should never be cut.

5 Locate the primary feathers on each wing. These feathers start at the leading edge of the wing and are followed by secondary and tertiary groups of feathers.

6 Use scissors to cut the primary feathers on each wing, just behind the protective coverts (small feathers) overlying the flight feathers. You may want to cut just one or two feathers a day until you see a sufficient reduction in flying ability.

7 If you cut or damage a blood feather, pluck it out at the base with tweezers or needle-nose pliers to stop the blood loss.

8 Be sure to clip both wings evenly, as clipping only one may leave the bird unbalanced.

### ✱ Tips

Newly emerging feathers, called "blood feathers", have soft, dark shafts that contain a nourishing blood supply. When the feather is completely grown in, the blood supply is closed off and the shaft turns hard and whitish. These are the feathers you can trim.

Having wings clipped is painless for the bird, much like having your hair or fingernails cut.

### ⚠ Warning

Cutting secondary feathers may cause the bird to fall straight down rather than flutter to the floor.

## 673 | Care for Your Rabbit

Rabbits need affection from their owners and can become wonderful pets if properly socialised. You can even house-train them
like cats. Follow these guidelines for a happy, healthy bunny.

### ⊙ Steps

1   Have your rabbit examined by a vet when you first get him, and continue
with regular check-ups as recommended.

2   Keep your rabbit in an indoor cage with walls and ceiling composed of
stainless steel bars. At least part of the floor should be a flat surface
rather than wire mesh to prevent foot injury. The cage should have
930 sq cm (1 sq ft) for every half kilo (pound) of rabbit. Line the cage
with newspapers and wood chips.

3   Make sure to keep the cage in a cool environment, as rabbits are very
sensitive to hot temperatures. If you live in a hot climate and keep your
rabbit in a hutch outdoors (instead of in an indoor cage), provide shade
and ice packs to help prevent heatstroke – frozen 2-l (3½pt) bottles make
good ice packs.

4   Provide fresh water daily in a water bottle that attaches to the cage, and
clean the water bottle once a week.

5   Give your rabbit 110–170 g (4–6 oz) of rabbit feed (depending on his size
and age) once a day, and keep a salt block in the cage.

6   Provide chew toys designed specifically for rabbits to keep his teeth
worn down. Rabbits' front teeth (incisors) grow continuously.

7   Have your rabbit spayed or neutered, even if he lives alone. This will
promote well-being, reduce aggressiveness and prevent some common
health problems.

8   Note that you can house-train a rabbit and allow him to roam indoors.
Begin by placing a cat litter box in the cage where your rabbit usually
relieves himself. Once he learns to use it, you can leave the cage open
and place an additional, larger litter box elsewhere in the house. The
cage can serve as the rabbit's nest, where he sleeps and eats, as well
as his primary spot for relieving himself.

9   Place a few handfuls of hay in your rabbit's litter box. Rabbits like to
munch on the hay and use the litter box at the same time. This will
encourage your rabbit to use his litter box more often.

10  Trim your rabbit's nails regularly, just as you would trim a cat's nails (see
641 "Trim Your Cat's Nails").

11  Clean your rabbit's cage at least once a week and replace the lining.

### ✱ Tips

Pick up your rabbit by placing
one hand under his chest and the
other under his hind legs. Then,
gently hold your rabbit at your
chest with one hand under his
belly and the other under his
neck. If your rabbit starts squirm-
ing, drop to one knee so he won't
fall very far if you lose your grip.

Rabbits are available in regular
and dwarf sizes, and with erect
or lop ears.

### ⚠ Warning

Rabbits love to chew on just
about anything. Keep them away
from electrical wires and both
indoor and outdoor plants (see
655 "Prevent Your Pet From
Chewing on Electrical Cords").

### Things You'll Need

☐ cage

☐ water bottle

☐ rabbit pellets

☐ salt block

☐ chew toys

☐ hay

## Care for Your Hamster

Hamsters are perfect first pets for youngsters and can live for two to five years. They fit in the palm of your hand, they're lovable and cuddly, and caring for them is easy and inexpensive.

### ◎ Steps

1 Buy a hamster that is between 4 and 7 weeks old. They're easier to tame when they're young.

2 Keep the cage away from draughts and direct sunlight.

3 Cover the cage floor with a thick layer of bedding. Wood shavings are best, because they are absorbent and non-toxic. Keep the bedding warm and dry – moisture can cause fatal infections.

4 Keep a filled, clean water bottle attached to the side of the cage.

5 Provide plenty of chew toys. Hamsters love the cardboard tubes found inside rolls of toilet paper and paper towels. Attach hamster wood chews to the side of the cage.

6 Make a small box for your hamster to sleep in. Cut a 5-cm (2-in) doorway into a closed box. Place the box in a far corner of the cage. The hamster will fill the box with bedding and chewed-up pieces of cardboard from the toilet paper tubes and will use the box as a bedroom. He will not urinate in the box, so you can use it for many months before replacing it.

7 Feed your hamster a commercially prepared hamster-food mix once or twice a day. Supply a small amount of fresh fruits and vegetables year-round. When you introduce new foods, initially feed small portions so his system can get used to them.

8 Exercise your hamster by putting an exercise wheel in his cage. Let him exercise outside his cage inside a specially designed plastic hamster ball, available at pet shops. Close the doors to your bedroom, take him out of his cage, and let him run around in the hamster ball.

9 Wash your hamster's cage at least once a week. Remove the hamster and dip the cage in water that has a few drops of household disinfectant added to it.

10 Remove any uneaten fruits and vegetables after a few days. Fresh foods that turn mouldy can make your hamster sick.

11 Don't bathe your hamster. Hamsters clean themselves. If you think your hamster smells bad, the odour is probably coming from dirty bedding. Clean the hamster cage more often.

12 Always be careful when handling hamsters. Although normally they bite only when they are frightened, they do have very sharp front teeth.

13 Take your hamster with you or find someone to take care of him if you are going on holiday for more than three days.

### ✻ Tips

If you put your hamster in a plastic exercise ball, be sure to keep the ball away from steps. Falling down a flight of stairs can result in serious injury.

Hamsters are active at night. The best time to clean the cage or exercise the hamster is in the evening or morning, rather than at midday when the hamster prefers to rest undisturbed.

Care and housing requirements for rodents vary. If you plan to acquire a gerbil or guinea pig, a vet who specialises in "pocket pets" can provide more detailed information.

### ⚠ Warnings

Consult a vet promptly if your hamster needs medical care, since hamsters die quickly.

Hamsters can catch the human cold virus, so avoid contact if you are sick.

### Things You'll Need

- ☐ hamster cage
- ☐ wood shavings
- ☐ water bottle
- ☐ chew toys
- ☐ small box
- ☐ commercially prepared hamster-food mix
- ☐ exercise wheel
- ☐ plastic hamster ball
- ☐ household disinfectant

## 675 | Care for Your Guinea Pig

Originating from the grasslands of South America, guinea pigs are naturally sociable, unaggressive and affectionate animals that make excellent family pets.

### ⊙ Steps

1 Obtain a pair of guinea pigs – one guinea pig on its own will suffer from loneliness and boredom.

2 Introduce yourself to the guinea pigs by holding out food to them in the palm of your hand and talking to them quietly. Gradually accustom them to being handled.

3 Buy the largest hutch that you can afford, to give the guinea pigs plenty of room for exercise.

4 Cover the floor of the hutch with a layer of sawdust and place some hay or other suitable bedding material at one end of the hutch to create a sleeping area.

5 Provide the guinea pigs with fresh food and water every day. Use a bottle, rather than a bowl, for the water.

6 Feed the guinea pigs with a dried food mix from a pet food supplier, but supplement their diet with some fresh fruit, vegetables such as broccoli or cauliflower, and hay.

7 Tidy the guinea pigs' hutch every day, removing soiled bedding or sawdust and scrubbing the inside of the water bottle before refilling it with fresh water. Give the hutch a thorough clean once a week.

8 Allow your guinea pigs to romp around in the house or in a secured run in the garden at least once a day.

9 Check the guinea pigs' teeth and nails regularly to see whether they are becoming overgrown. If the teeth and nails seem too long, take the guinea pigs to a vet.

10 Monitor the guinea pigs' health daily, looking out for warning signs such as a dull coat, loss of appetite, or discharges from the eyes or nose.

### ✳ Tips

Guinea pigs like being handled, but they can easily be hurt if you drop them from a height. To avoid this risk, sit on the floor when handling your pets.

For your pair of guinea pigs, choose two females or a neutered male and female. A pair of males may fight one another.

### Things You'll Need

❑ hutch

❑ dried guinea pig food

❑ water bottle

❑ feeding bowl

❑ sawdust

❑ hay or similar bedding material

## 676 | Care for Your Ferret

Ferrets are ultradian animals – they have short bursts of activity separated by hours of rest. They can adapt their schedules to yours so they'll be awake and ready to play when you are.

### ⊙ Steps

1 Feed your ferret a high-quality ferret or kitten food that's high in protein (34 to 38 per cent) and fat (19 to 22 per cent) but low in fibre. Make this readily available throughout the day, as ferrets digest food quickly and eat 7 to 10 meals a day. Avoid giving your ferret any moist, canned cat food, which can contribute to dental-tartar formation.

### ⚠ Warning

Ferrets can catch colds from people, so stay away from your ferret if you are feeling ill.

2 Offer treats such as meats, starches, vegetables and fruits. Give no more than 1 tsp. a day, and mash or chop food into small pieces to make it easier for him to consume. Examples are bits of mashed banana, pieces of seedless melon, green peas and chopped cucumber.

3 Provide a cage that's equipped with a water bottle and lined with newspaper on top of linoleum. Make sure the cage is large enough for exercise. For one or two ferrets, the cage should measure 45 by 80 by 90 cm (18 by 30 by 36 in) and contain at least two levels. Keep your ferret in his cage unless supervised.

4 Place a litter box inside the cage filled with kitty litter. A ferret will learn to use the litter box to relieve himself, much like a cat. If he does not work it out himself, encourage him to use the litter box by placing him there when you suspect he needs to go.

5 Give your ferret 2 hours of playtime and exercise outside the cage each day. Be sure to ferret-proof your home by removing hazardous products before allowing him to roam the house. If you take your ferret outside, always keep him on a lead made for small animals.

6 Protect your ferret from extreme weather and temperatures, especially direct sunlight and heat – anything over 26°C (80°F) can be harmful.

7 Have a ferret-savvy vet vaccinate your ferret for rabies and canine distemper. Also, remember that ferrets can get fleas, heartworm and intestinal parasites. Consult a vet for preventative measures and treatment (see 658 "Get Rid of Fleas" and 660 "Prevent Worms in Cats and Dogs").

8 Spay or neuter your pet ferret. This is especially critical for females, as female ferrets are induced ovulators (they ovulate when bred). If she is not bred when in heat, she can die from anaemia.

9 Give your ferret toys such as tennis balls, cardboard boxes and cat toys. Make sure none of your ferret toys have small, removable parts, as your ferret can ingest these and develop an obstruction in the digestive tract.

10 Pick up your ferret from behind. Use one hand to support his chest and the other to support his hips.

## Things You'll Need

- ☐ ferret or kitten food
- ☐ treats
- ☐ cage
- ☐ water bottle
- ☐ litter box
- ☐ small-animal lead
- ☐ toys

## Care for Your Snake 677

Snakes have bcome increasingly popular as pets, partly because they are seen as low-maintenance. But don't embark on snake ownership without proper preparation and equipment.

### ⊙ Steps

1 Choose which type of snake will suit you as a pet. Check in a detailed reference source or with an experienced pet supplier to identify the varying needs and characteristics of different species

2 If you don't want to buy a purpose-built cage, obtain an aquarium tank and cover it with a pegboard top. Alternatively, take a plastic storage box and cut ventilation holes in it. The cage should provide a minimum

### ✱ Tips

If your snake is refusing its food, it may be because the snake is too cool. Check that the temperature in its cage is correct.

Reduce the temperature in the cage by a few degrees at night, of 0.5 sq m (5 sq ft) of space for each 1 m (3 ft) of snake – so a 1 sq m (10 sq ft) cage for a 2 m (6½ ft) long snake.

3   Place an empty cereal box in the cage – this will provide the snake with somewhere to hide. Also put a water bowl in the cage.

4   Cover the floor of the cage with newspaper. This will aid cleaning.

5   Heat the cage to the appropriate temperature for the type of snake, which will generally be between 26 and 31°C (78 and 87°F). Attach a thermometer to the cage so that you can check this.

6   Do not heat all of the cage evenly. Provide a temperature gradient – warmer and cooler spots – so that the snake has a choice and can suit its needs by shifting around.

7   Clean the cage regularly – at least every fortnight – because the build-up of droppings can lead to disease. Use a detergent and a disinfectant, but avoid products containing phenol or coal tar.

8   Feed your snake every week or 10 days if it is a fully-grown adult, more often if it is still growing. Although snakes can survive for much longer periods than this without food, they are healthier if fed smaller amounts regularly than larger amounts at longer intervals.

9   Check in a reference book or with an expert to determine the natural diet of the species of snake that you own. Always try to provide the snake with its natural food. Observe the snake feeding to see whether it prefers its food alive or dead.

10  Keep a record of the times when you feed your snake. This will help you keep track of its feeding schedule.

11  If your snake fails to shed its skin completely (a process that should take place every one to three months), soak the snake for about an hour in a container half filled with warm water. Then gently peel the old skin off.

12  Snakes can suffer from a variety of parasites and ailments, so locate a vet with plenty of experience in dealing with reptiles to treat your pet when this becomes necessary.

to imitate the day-night cycle of temperature the snake would find in its natural environment.

⚠ **Warning**

Do not use wire mesh to cage the snake. The animal will hurt itself rubbing against the wire.

**Things You'll Need**

☐ a purpose-built cage or secure alternative

☐ heat source

☐ thermometer

☐ water bowl

☐ suitable food, often live animals such as mice

---

## 678  Care for Your Tortoise

Tortoises, the land-based relatives of turtles and terrapins, are docile pets especially suitable for children, but they will only flourish if you provide them with a suitable environment.

### ◉ Steps

1   If you start with a baby tortoise, you will need to keep it in a purpose-built vivarium, with a heater to maintain the temperature at between 20 and 30°C (68 and 86°F) and a full-spectrum fluorescent light.

2   Most tortoises kept as pets in the UK are from the Mediterranean and, as adults, can live outside in a sheltered garden from about April to October. But bring them inside during the day when the weather is bad and on chilly spring or autumn nights.

3   To help your tortoise cope with British temperatures, bathe it for 5 to 10 minutes in a warm, shallow bath at the start of the day.

✱ **Tip**

Have your tortoise microchipped. Even with vigilant owners, tortoises are easily lost. A microchip makes it more likely your tortoise will be returned.

⚠ **Warning**

Tortoises frequently encounter health problems. They should be checked by a vet at least twice a year, in the spring and autumn.

4  Ensure that your garden is safe for the tortoise by keeping it free of slug pellets or weed killers. Also search carefully for any gaps in fencing through which the tortoise might escape.

5  A garden-dwelling tortoise will forage for grasses and weeds, but you can add to its diet with shop-bought green vegetables and small amounts of root vegetables and fruit.

6  To counter possible vitamin or calcium deficiency in a young tortoise, buy a food supplement from a pet shop or vet.

7  Prepare for your tortoise's winter hibernation by half-filling a box with shredded newspaper and place it in a shed or garage. The box must have ventilation holes, but keep out mice or rats by covering the holes with wire mesh.

8  During hibernation, keep the temperature in the box between 4 and 9°C (40 and 48°F); monitor it regularly with a thermometer.

9  Weigh your tortoise regularly during hibernation. If it starts to lose weight rapidly, bring it out of hibernation and have it checked by a vet.

10 To help the tortoise emerge gently from hibernation, from late January begin to bathe it every day for about 30 minutes in warm, shallow water. Keep the tortoise in a vivarium until the weather is warm enough again for it to be allowed outside in the spring.

The import and sale of some species of tortoise is now banned under CITES (the Convention on International Trade in Endangered Species). Take advice from a vet or reputable pet shop.

### Things You'll Need

- [ ] vivarium
- [ ] full-spectrum light (for baby tortoises)
- [ ] hibernation box
- [ ] thermometer

---

## Care for Your Fish                                    679

Fish need an optimal environment. These general guidelines apply to most freshwater fish in pet shops but not to saltwater or tropical fish, which have different requirements.

### ⊙ Steps

1  Start off with healthy fish. View every fish in the tank before you purchase one. They should move about the tank with purpose and not display any signs of sickness, such as cloudy eyes or slimy-looking bodies.

2  Keep new fish in a quarantine tank with the same water quality as the main tank. They should stay there for at least two weeks (preferably three) before you introduce them to the new tank. When you start getting impatient, think about how much trouble it would be to treat the entire population for infection instead of just one fish.

3  Place the tank against an inside wall – away from windows, doors and heating systems – to prevent draughts and sudden temperature changes.

4  Maintain the water quality. Test the ammonia, nitrite and pH levels regularly with a special kit. Chemical imbalances are a leading cause of sickness in fish. Once the water quality is acceptable, use a special filtered siphon to change 20 per cent of the water every 10 days. A pet shop that sells fish should also sell test kits and siphons.

5  Provide your fish with a diet of commercially prepared fish food. Store it in a cool, dry place for no more than a few months.

6  Remove waste and uneaten food with a net every other day. Rinse the net thoroughly before and after use to avoid the potential spread of infection.

### ✳ Tip

Make sure your tank is large enough – about 194 sq cm (30 sq in) of surface area per 2.5 cm (1 in) of fish. Increase the size of the tank by 50 to 100 per cent before adding more fish.

### ⚠ Warnings

Mixing faster and stronger fish with slower, weaker ones is a bad idea. The slower fish will not get enough to eat, and the others will be overfed.

Discuss what types of fish are compatible in a tank and which to keep separate – some species can be very territorial and will kill other fish.

### Things You'll Need

- [ ] two fish tanks (one for quarantine) ➤

7   Keep a canopy or hood over the tank at all times. Some fish are jumpers.

8   Don't let your fish get stressed by poor water conditions, drastic lighting changes or constant activity outside the tank. These things will lower their resistance to disease.

☐ fish food

☐ fish net

---

## 680  Wash Your Goldfish's Bowl

**Because goldfish are a cold-water species, they don't need a heated tank. If you're one of those people who love the classic look of a fishbowl, read on.**

### ⊙ Steps

1   Plan on cleaning out your fishbowl every two weeks, if not weekly.

2   Catch your fish with a small net and place it in a smaller secondary bowl full of room-temperature water from the original bowl.

3   Empty the primary fishbowl into the sink. Catch any rocks or other objects in a strainer as you pour the water out.

4   Rinse the bowl thoroughly with hot water, scrubbing the sides with a paper towel, if needed.

5   Pour out the dirty water, and repeat with more hot water. This will help kill germs and bacteria.

6   Clean your bowl using a chemical cleaner designed specifically for goldfish bowls. Never use soap or detergent when washing a fishbowl.

7   Rinse the bowl out thoroughly with cold water.

8   Run cold water over the objects in the strainer (gravel, plastic plants) until they are clean. Return them to the bowl.

9   Refill the bowl and let the new water sit for 24 hours to allow the chlorine in the tap water to evaporate and to bring the water to room temperature.

10  Return your fish to the primary bowl.

### ✱ Tip

Transfer the fish quickly from one bowl to another. A fish out of water can suffocate and die within minutes.

### ⚠ Warning

Ask at the aquarium shop about special chemical cleaners designed to safely clean your bowl in the event that your fish has died and bowl sterilisation is necessary.

---

## 681  Feed Your Goldfish

**Keeping goldfish properly fed is easy when you do it right.**

### ⊙ Steps

1   Purchase the right kind of food for your fish. Goldfish need protein and a wide range of vitamins and carbohydrates, so choose a nutrient-rich food specifically for goldfish. Use either flake-form or floating pellets. Ask at the aquarium shop for food recommendations for the specific type of goldfish you own.

2   Consider occasionally offering snacks, such as leafy vegetables (lettuce and spinach) or live food (brine shrimp and mosquito larvae), for variety.

### ✱ Tip

Buy a holiday food block if you are going to be away from the tank for more than a weekend.

### ⚠ Warning

Overfeeding pollutes the tank, endangering the fishes' lives.

---

3   Feed your fish once a day by adding one small pinch of food to the tank at a time. In general, provide as much food as the fish will consume in 2 minutes. (Vary this accordingly for larger fish.) Remember to offer just a tiny amount in each pinch.

4   Remove excess food with a net after the feeding session, to avoid polluting the water.

5   Consider using a feeding ring, which attaches to the side of the tank and allows better control, thus reducing the risk of overfeeding your fish.

**Things You'll Need**

☐ goldfish food

☐ fishnet

☐ feeding ring

---

## Help Your Child Cope With the Death of a Pet           682

The loss of a family pet can be a child's first experience with death. Helping children cope with grief will help them understand a very painful aspect of life and begin the healing process.

### ☉ Steps

1   Talk about the pet's health and any decisions to be made prior to the animal's death, if possible.

2   Respond to your children honestly and age-appropriately. While young children will not understand the concept of death, they will feel a tremendous loss. Older children may want to discuss the decline of the pet's health, plans for the body and the concept of death itself.

3   Avoid the commonly used phrase "putting to sleep". This phrase can confuse young children, and even scare them as they prepare to go to bed at night.

4   Try to explain the concept of "dog years" or whatever is applicable to the species of your family pet. But make it clear that Mum and Dad live in "people years" and are not going anywhere.

5   Ask your vet to answer any medical questions for your children. Older children may have questions about euthanasia – how it is done, what the pet will feel, what equipment is used and what happens to the animal's body.

6   Say goodbye to the pet in a ceremony to make it official. Bury it in a special place (a pet cemetery is an option) so your children can remember the pet whenever they visit this spot.

7   Memorialise your pet in a way that is unique to your family. Plant a tree in your pet's favourite spot in the garden, write down thoughts about fun times spent with the pet, draw pictures, or hang a favourite photo of the pet in your home for all of the family to share.

8   Show your own grief. Children will grow to understand their own feelings better if they see that their sadness is shared by other family members.

9   Encourage children to talk about their feelings, memories of the pet and favourite times spent together.

10  Share the loss with your children's teachers to explain any changes in behaviour and to add further support.

**❋ Tips**

Many books are available for different ages about dealing with the death of a family pet. Reading such a book with your child may help him talk about feelings of loss.

When the family is ready, think about adopting another pet. After a period of mourning, this addition to the family will bring a new set of experiences and will not take anything away from your child's memories of his previous loving companion.

## 683 | Write an Invitation

**Your invitation sets the tone for your party – take time to think about what you want it to communicate.**

### ⊙ Steps

1 Decide on the tone, voice and level of formality you're going to use, based on the event itself. This will dictate whether you handwrite the cards or have them printed, and whether you choose a pre-printed or personalised invitation.

2 Consider making a theme invitation – using such items as travel postcards, photographs and envelopes studded with confetti – for a casual, festive occasion.

3 Choose the type of card you want, and order or buy a few more than you think you'll need. This will permit you to add some guests to your list at the last minute, if necessary.

4 Determine the wording based on the level of formality. For example, a formal invitation might say, "Dr and Mrs Stanley request the pleasure of your company," whereas a more casual note might say, "Please join us."

5 Include the names of the host and/or hostess, as well as the place, time, date and purpose of the party, even if it's a simple get-together. Make sure to add RSVP information.

6 Include a respond-by date in a formal invitation so you can get an accurate head count in time to adjust the amount of food, number of place settings and room size. For a wedding, charity function or other formal event, consider including a response card and a stamped, self-addressed envelope inside the big envelope.

7 Post invitations three weeks before most events, four weeks before a formal affair. For events held during the Christmas season send invitations around the end of November.

### ✻ Tips

Use precisely the kind of RSVP method that best serves the occasion: a response card for a head count, a telephone number for expediency, or an e-mail address if you know that the invitees have computers.

Large dinner parties, receptions and weddings call for written invitations.

Count out those who don't reply, but be prepared for a few who haven't replied to show up.

Printing invitations costs much more but is worthwhile if you are planning a formal or large event.

## 684 | Reply to a Written Invitation

**Replying to an invitation properly demonstrates your good manners, and it is also a mark of respect and consideration for your host.**

### ⊙ Steps

1 Read the invitation carefully. Often it gives a hint as to a preferred mode of reply.

2 If a response card with envelope is provided, fill it out and send it off in a timely manner. If the invitation gives a phone number, call as soon as you know whether you will attend.

3 Use your personal headed stationery or a blank card to respond to a formal invitation that doesn't come with a response card. Write some variation of the following: "Joseph Mackenzie and guest, Rachel

### ✻ Tip

RSVP is an abbreviation for the French phrase *répondez s'il vous plaît,* which means "please reply".

### ⚠ Warning

If you don't reply – unless specifically instructed not to – your host's horrified face shouldn't surprise you when you make an appearance anyway.

Helfond, accept with pleasure the invitation to dine with the Bletchley-Smythes on 28 October 2003."

4   If you cannot attend, send your regrets: "I regret that I will not be attending the dinner party, as I will be away."

5   Post the reply in time to assure that you are giving your host at least one week's notice.

## Buy a Wedding Present                                                    685

Wish the lucky pair well with a heartfelt and useful gift.

### ⊙ Steps

1   If the couple has a wedding list registered at a department store, the details may be enclosed with your wedding invitation. If they're not, phone a member of the wedding party to find out.

2   Search the wedding list, making sure you have the full names of both bride and groom, as well as the wedding date, to make the search easier. The list should provide an updated list of gifts the couple hasn't yet received.

3   Select a gift from the list that's within your price range, even if that means you can only buy one cup and saucer.

4   Ask for the present to be gift-wrapped.

5   Address the gifts to the bride before the wedding, and to both the bride and groom afterwards.

6   Arrange to have your gift sent in advance of the wedding instead of bringing it to the wedding; this is much easier for the wedding party. Most department stores will post your gift for you, especially if you order it online or by telephone.

7   If you prefer to give money instead of a gift, present it on the day of the ceremony. Make a cheque payable to both the bride and groom.

### ✳ Tips

As a rule of thumb, select a gift from the list since the couple has expressly requested these items. Refrain from buying a print by your favourite artist or an antique cake platter you love unless you are absolutely positive the couple will also love it.

Consider purchasing a large gift with a group of friends.

Shop early when buying a gift from the list. You'll have a wider choice in your price range.

### ⚠ Warning

Avoid monogramming your gift. The couple can't return or exchange a monogrammed gift, and you may not know what names the couple will choose.

## Be a Proper Wedding Guest                                                686

Bear in mind these quick pointers for being a perfect wedding guest, and you'll help the wedding day go smoothly for the bride and groom.

### ⊙ Steps

1   Make your hotel and plane reservations early, especially if you receive a "save the date" notice.

2   Purchase your wedding present early, and use the list. It is designed to make your life – and the lives of the bride and groom – easier.

3   Reply as soon as possible after you get the invitation. Bring a guest only if you receive an invitation addressed to you and a guest.

### ✳ Tips

If you have questions about attire, whether you can bring children to the ceremony, or other logistics, call the best man or maid of honour, who is often much more accessible than the bride or groom.

Bear in mind that the bride and groom want to see and talk to

4   Dress appropriately. If the invitation says black tie, men should wear dinner jackets and women should wear formal dresses. If you are unsure of the dress code, you're safer erring on the side of dressing up too much.

5   Bring children only if the invitation expressly mentions them. Weddings are formal events and typically not appropriate for little ones.

6   Arrive 15 minutes before the ceremony begins. Tradition dictates that friends and family of the bride sit on the left and friends and family of the groom sit on the right. Typically, an usher will lead you to your seat.

7   Wait in the receiving line, if there is one, to congratulate the newlywed couple and their parents after the ceremony. Keep your greeting upbeat and brief.

8   Remain quiet and attentive during toasts at the reception, and while the couple cuts the wedding cake.

9   Wait for the bride and groom to have their first dance before you hit the dance floor. Then get up, dance and enjoy the party; the couple will be pleased to see all their guests having a good time.

10  Avoid engaging the bride or groom in conversation for too long – they have many guests to greet, and a honeymoon suite awaits them.

every guest, so don't feel disappointed if you don't get to chat with them for long.

Post your present ahead of time to make it easier for the bride and groom. If instead you bring it with you, take it to the reception and place it on the gift table.

---

## 687  Be a Proper Guest at a Party

A good guest responds promptly to the invitation, arrives fashionably late, is cheerful and friendly, and isn't the last one to go home.

### ⊙ Steps

1   Reply to the invitation in a timely manner. Use the method indicated: phone, post or e-mail.

2   Bring a friend only if you receive an invitation for you and a guest. Your hosts may have a food, budget or space limitation.

3   Go with the spirit of the party. If it's for a special occasion, such as a housewarming, bring a gift. If it's dressy, wear your glad rags. Costume required? Dig into your wardrobe and get creative.

4   Prepare. Read up on current events; think of a few good stories; recall a few films, books or plays. Try hard not to be shy or moody – for your host's sake, if not your own.

5   Arrive reasonably close to the starting time. The starting time for a cocktail party tends to be looser than it is for a dinner party, which requires punctuality. Fashionably late means no more than 30 minutes past the indicated time.

6   Seek out your host or hostess and say hello as soon as you arrive.

7   Make an effort to mix and mingle cheerfully. Don't just hide in a corner chatting with people you already know.

8   Know your alcohol limits and don't exceed them. Take into consideration your energy level, food intake and drink size. Nothing's ruder than ruining a party with inappropriate behaviour.

### ✱ Tips

If you know your hosts, you might call and ask about the dress code, if the invitation doesn't make it clear. Or ask another guest who's attending.

Unless it's clear that this is not necessary, bring something to drink, whether or not it's alcoholic.

### ⚠ Warning

Never arrive early; your hosts may not be ready to receive guests.

9   Treat your host's home as you would your own – no wet glasses on the furniture, no cigarettes ground out in the plants, no cocktail sticks on the floor. Don't smoke without asking permission.

10  Leave at a reasonable hour. Some hosts close the bar half an hour before they want the party to end. Take a hint when others start slipping on their coats.

11  Find your hosts to say thank you and good night personally. It's also thoughtful to call the next day and let your host know how much you enjoyed the event.

## Introduce People                                                    688

Want to meet new people and improve your social graces? Here's how to make proper introductions at parties, dinners and other social situations.

### ⊕ Steps

1   Introduce individuals to each other using both first and last names.

2   If you're introducing someone who has a title – a doctor, for example – include the title as well as the first and last names in the introduction.

3   Introduce the younger or less prominent person to the older or more prominent person, regardless of the sex of the individuals. (However, if a considerable age difference lies between the two, it is far more courteous to make introductions in deference to age, regardless of social rank.) For example: "Arthur Dent, I'd like you to meet Dr Gertrude Smith."

4   If the person you are introducing has a specific relationship to you, make the relationship clear by adding a phrase such as "my boss", "my wife" or "my uncle". In the case of unmarried couples who are living together, "companion" and "partner" are good choices.

5   Use your spouse's first and last name if he or she has a different last name than you. Include the phrase "my wife" or "my husband".

6   Introduce an individual to the group first, then the group to the individual. For example: "Dr Brown, I'd like you to meet my friends Kim Howe, Simon Campbell and Michael Vince. Everyone, this is Dr Kurt Brown."

### ❋ Tips

If you've forgotten a name, you'll seem impolite if you try to ignore the need for the introduction. It's less awkward (and better manners) to apologise and acknowledge that the name has escaped you.

If your host neglects to introduce you to other guests, feel free to introduce yourself, but make your relationship to the host clear in your introduction.

## Shake Hands                                                         689

Historically used to show that both people were unarmed, the handshake today is a critical gauge of confidence, trust, sophistication and mood.

### ◎ Steps

1   Extend your right hand to meet the other person's right hand.

2   Point your thumb upwards towards the other person's arm and extend your arm at a slight downward angle.

### ❋ Tip

A two-handed handshake is not for first meetings. It is a sign of real affection, and you should reserve it for friends and intimates.

3   Wrap your hand around the other person's hand when your thumb joints come together.

4   Grasp the hand firmly and squeeze gently once. Remember that limp handshakes are a big turnoff, as are bone-crushing grasps.

5   Hold the handshake for two to three seconds.

6   Pump your hand up and down a few times to convey sincerity. (This gesture is optional.)

⚠ **Warning**

Handshakes are not appropriate in all cultures. Investigate local customs if you will be visiting a foreign country.

---

## 690 | Remember Names

The ability to remember the names of people you meet will always serve you well in social situations.

### ⊙ Steps

1   Pay attention when you are introduced to someone. A few minutes after you meet the person, say his or her name to yourself again. If you have forgotten it, talk to the person again and ask for the name.

2   Write down the new name three times while picturing the person's face; do this as soon as possible after meeting someone.

3   Ask how to spell a difficult name, or glance at the spelling on the person's business card, if it's offered. If you know the spelling of a word and can picture it in your mind, you'll remember it better.

4   Connect a name to a common word you will remember. For example, the name Salazar could sound like "salamander", "bazaar" or "sell a jar".

5   Make a connection to the person's hobby or employment. "Bill the pill" might help you remember the name of a pharmacist, for example.

**✳ Tip**

Writing down new names is generally a very successful memorising technique that doesn't require a lot of work.

---

## 691 | Propose a Toast

A few carefully selected words can add a personal touch to any social gathering. People make toasts over festive drinks, such as champagne or sparkling wine.

### ⊙ Steps

1   Let the host or hostess make the first toast at a dinner party. If she or he does not do so, initiate a toast after the plates from the main course are cleared.

2   Make certain that everyone, no matter what he or she is drinking, has a full glass to raise.

3   Stand up and tap your glass to get everyone's attention.

4   For a formal occasion, have everyone (except for the person you are toasting) stand up. If it is less formal, guests may remain seated.

5   Direct your toast towards the host or hostess or the guest of honour. Speak loudly and slowly so that everyone can hear you.

**✳ Tips**

If you know ahead of time that you will be giving a toast, write down some thoughts on note cards and practise delivering the toast before the big event.

Remember that the toast puts the spotlight on the person being honoured, not on you.

If you are the recipient of a toast, remain seated and refrain from drinking when everyone drinks to you.

**How to Do (Just About) Everything**

6   Keep it brief, sincere and to the point; choose simple but substantial words to convey your feelings. Some of the best toasts are just a single sentence or two.

7   If you are feeling more creative, you can begin with an appropriate quotation, a poem or an amusing anecdote.

8   Consider mentioning an unusually brave, heroic, romantic or awesome act performed by the person you are honouring.

9   Weave humour into your toast, but don't embarrass the person you are honouring. If the assembled group is close-knit, it's all right to refer to shared experiences, but don't make the toast a private joke between you and a few of the people present.

10  When you have finished your toast, lift your glass to the recipient and lead the group in drinking to that person.

## ⚠ Warning

Make sure your toast is appropriate for everyone at the event. For example, a best man's speech at a wedding ceremony shouldn't refer to stag night escapades.

---

## Leave a Party Graciously                                                      692

Arriving at the party is the easy part. When you are ready to leave, exercise tact and always thank the host or hostess before you depart.

### ⊙ Steps

1   Wait until the host is not in conversation or caught in the middle of cooking or serving duties.

2   Express your gratitude for the invitation, and compliment the host on one particular aspect of the party.

3   Make a tentative reference to the next time you will see each other. For example, saying "We should get together for drinks soon" takes the emphasis off your departure.

4   Acknowledge everyone in the room, if possible. If the party is too large to permit this, express a parting gesture to those guests with whom you spent time talking.

5   Make your parting words short and sweet in an attempt to let everyone else get back to the festivities.

### ✳ Tips

Avoid long and effusive apologies. Others will look upon your departure negatively if you insist on apologising for it.

If the party invitation included an ending time, don't stay too long after the time indicated.

---

## Write a Thank-You Note                                                        693

You can fill even short thank-you notes with appreciation and meaning. And remember, "better late than never" applies – the recipient will always enjoy your thanks.

### ⊙ Steps

1   Mention the gift, favour or party you attended.

2   Talk about the appropriateness of the gift or favour: "Your baby-sitting for my children has truly been a lifesaver in these difficult times." (You can describe a gift that didn't quite suit your taste as "a conversation piece" or "unique").

### ✳ Tips

Many people consider it unnecessary to write thank-you notes for gifts given in person, with the exception of wedding gifts, as long as you thank the giver verbally. But when in doubt, a written note is always a good idea.

3   Tie the appropriateness of the gift to the person who gave it to you: "You've always understood my taste in clothes."

4   Talk about how you plan to use the gift (or substitute this step for step 2): "I have a picture of my parents that would look perfect in your frame." If you received a gift of money, mention how you will spend it.

5   Add a small personal note to update the giver about your life: "I have completely recovered from my cold and plan to hit the slopes again as soon as I can."

6   Consider sending a token of appreciation along with your note if you're thanking someone for a good deed. Possibilities include flowers, chocolate or an invitation to lunch (your treat).

A newly married couple should write individual, handwritten notes to all gift givers, and post these within three months of the wedding (at the very latest).

Send a thank-you note for birthday and holiday gifts within three days of when you receive them.

---

## 694 | Tie a Tie

Once you've mastered the technique, you won't need a mirror to look dapper in your favourite tie. These instructions will teach you how to tie a four-in-hand knot.

### ⊙ Steps

1   Lift up the collar of your shirt and put the tie around the back of your neck. The wide end should hang down about twice as low as the thin end; it can hang closer to your right or left hand, depending on what's most comfortable for you.

2   Wrap the wide end around the thin end twice, a few inches below your neck. The wide end should go over the thin end at first.

3   After wrapping the wide end around the second time, push it through the back of the V shape made by the partially formed knot.

4   Tuck the wide end through the front loop of the knot.

5   Gently pull down on both the thin and wide ends below the knot until it is tight.

6   Hold the thin end and slide the knot up to your neck.

7   If the thin end hangs below the wide end, untie the tie and begin again, with the wide end hanging lower than it did the first time.

8   If the wide end hangs too low, untie the tie and begin again, with the wide end hanging higher than it did the first time.

9   Flip your collar back down once you and your tie look dapper.

### ✳ Tip

When untying a tie, follow the directions in reverse rather than just pulling the narrow end through the knot. Otherwise, you may distort the shape of the tie.

# ✓ 695 Dress to Flatter Your Figure

Not all of us are able – or willing – to spend hours in the gym in quest of a perfect body, so it's good to know that there are much less painful ways to hide flaws and enhance attributes. Here's how to meet a few common fashion challenges.

## Minimise a large bottom

- Wear wide-leg trousers. Steer clear of back pockets or any detailing around the buttocks. Opt for styles that hang full from the middle of the bottom. Front pleats and pockets will help balance your silhouette.

- Choose full or A-line skirts that hang loosely.

- Pair a short jacket with a long skirt and a long jacket with a shorter skirt.

- Select jackets that are slightly fitted and taper gently.

- Wear "empire" dresses for evening. Avoid clingy bias-cut styles.

- Attract admirers' eyes to your upper body. Wear brightly coloured or patterned tops and consider neckline accessories.

- Wear slimming dark colours such as navy, dark brown, charcoal and black.

## Minimise a large stomach

- Direct attention towards your upper body. Accessorise your neckline or choose tops with detailing above the breasts.

- Choose trousers with a narrow or tapered leg. Leggings and stirrup trousers are great if they are not too tight.

- Select skirts that do not gather at the waist. Straight skirts will narrow your silhouette.

- Wear tunic-style tops and jumpers, and square jackets that cover the stomach.

- Look for sheath dresses that create a column from your shoulders to your lower leg.

- Avoid belted or drawstring looks, which draw attention to your waist.

- Choose trousers with details around the turn-ups to draw attention down your leg and away from your stomach.

## Make breasts appear larger

- Stand up straight.

- Buy a padded push-up bra.

- Insert foam pads into your bra. Place them in special pockets built into the bra, or place them in the cup under the breast.

- Apply blusher, a shade darker than your skin tone, between the breasts to suggest shadows and cleavage.

- Remember that too much padding or blusher can be obvious. Try to go for a subtle, subliminal effect.

- Wear a tight Lycra top over your bra and under your shirt to add an extra layer.

- Choose clothing material that hugs and draws attention to the bustline.

## Appear more slender

- Choose clothing all in one colour to give yourself a long, lean look.

- Wear black, which looks slimming.

- Avoid shapeless clothing. Loose clothes often make you appear wider or heavier.

- Choose softly tailored – not tight – pieces, which define but don't constrain.

- Steer clear of horizontal stripes, which make you appear wider.

- Consider vertical stripes, which make you look longer and leaner.

- Wear blocks of colour that draw the eye away from less-than-perfect areas.

- Wear shoulder pads and wide necklines.

- Choose trousers with narrow or tapered legs.

reference

## 696 | Buy a Perfect Little Black Dress

Every woman needs a little black dress. It's the one garment you can always slip on when you aren't sure what to wear for the evening, but you need to look fabulous.

### ⊙ Steps

1 Think about your body type. If you need to wear a bra when you go out for the evening, you may not be comfortable in halters, backless numbers and sheer shoulders. But remember that there are plenty of other ways to look sexy.

2 Identify your key assets. Is your back worth showing off? Want to expose a little shoulder? Is the low-cut look for you? Do your legs deserve the spotlight?

3 Find a dress that's comfortable. Eliminate any dress that makes it hard to walk, sit or dance.

4 Choose a well-constructed dress of a good fabric – a light wool or silk crepe is best – with a lining. The lining will smooth your figure so the shell hangs neatly.

5 Follow the 3:1 ratio – three parts conservative to one part racy. Choose a little black dress that's plain except for that one saucy feature: crisscross straps in back; a daring neckline; a deep slit in the side, back or front.

6 Accessorise for understated drama: fishnet stockings, a bold bracelet, a choker, or leopard pumps with a matching bag.

**✱ Tip**

Surprisingly, some well-made spaghetti-strap dresses work well even if you're on the busty side – they offer a good way to show a little skin without feeling too exposed.

## 697 | Buy a Man's Business Suit

Everyday business attire may have become more casual, but the suit is still the anchor of any man's formal wardrobe. Start with a classic navy suit and move on to grey, pinstripe or camel.

### ⊙ Steps

1 Choose a jacket style. The two-button, single-breasted jacket is a popular style, but three- or four-button jackets are also available. Keep in mind that fashions change for men's clothing, just as they do for women's. Only thin men should wear formal double-breasted jackets, which add bulk to the figure. These should be kept buttoned at all times, as the jacket hangs awkwardly otherwise.

2 Select a fabric colour and pattern. If you opt for a patterned fabric, check to see that patterns line up at shoulder and lapel seams.

3 Choose a fabric. High-quality worsted wool is the most seasonally versatile. Cotton and linen are good for summer wear. Avoid blends that are made with too much polyester, as they don't breathe well and may look cheap.

4 Crumple the fabric to make sure it bounces back instead of wrinkling, unless you've chosen a fabric that's meant to wrinkle, such as linen.

**✱ Tips**

Tall men should emphasise horizontal lines and avoid pinstripes. Double-breasted suits often flatter tall, thin men. Short men should consider single-breasted, shorter jackets in pinstripes or dark solids. Heavier men should also opt for pinstripes and avoid double-breasted suits.

When you buy a suit off the rack, you may have to take whichever trousers come with the jacket. If this is the case, the jacket style, which is more noticeable, should take precedence over the style of trousers. Keep in mind that turn-ups can be added to or removed from most pairs of trousers.

5   Select a trouser style. Pleats make trousers dressy and provide room for movement, while flat-front trousers are slimming. Turn-ups are formal, add weight to the suit and can make the legs seem shorter; trousers without turn-ups elongate the legs and are more informal.

6   Test the jacket for fit. Make sure the collar lies flat against the back of your neck and shows a 6-mm (¼-in) rim of shirt collar. Shoulders should be lightly padded and neither too boxy nor too sloped. Sleeves should reveal 6 to 12 mm (¼ to ½ in) of shirt cuff and fall 13 cm (5 in) above the tip of your thumb.

7   Button the jacket and sit down to verify that it is comfortable and doesn't bunch up.

8   Make sure the trousers sit on the waist, not hips, and drape over and break slightly at the tops of your shoes. Check that your socks aren't visible when you walk.

Buying a jacket and trousers separately will give you more style choices, and is a good approach if you need a special fit (if you have a large chest and a small waist, for example). It may be difficult to match the garments, though.

---

## Hire a Dinner Jacket                                          698

A dinner jacket is usual for a number of formal occasions, such as the opening night at the opera and, increasingly, for a trip down the aisle, although a morning suit is still the traditional choice.

### ◎ Steps

1   Check the phone book for local hire shops. When hiring for wedding attendants, look for shops that have lots of branches or shops that will fit a dinner jacket based on measurements, to help ensure a consistent look.

2   Visit your chosen shop four to eight weeks prior to the event to have your measurements taken. Good sales assistants measure around your chest (both including and excluding the width of your arms); your naked waist at belt height; your hip girth, including your seat; your neck circumference; and your sleeve length from the centre of your back.

3   Consider cuts that complement your build and accommodate the formality of the occasion. In contrast to the rule for business suits, double-breasted dinner jackets and those with wider lapels look great on a broad-chested, heavier-set man. A cropped jacket will elongate the height of a shorter man.

4   Prepare to pay around £100 for hiring a dinner suit, depending on how much is included (for example, whether you get trousers, a bow tie, a shirt and a cummerbund as well as your dinner jacket). You usually leave a deposit when you have your measurements taken, and pay the balance before leaving with dinner jacket in hand.

5   Schedule a final fitting one week before the event. Ask whether the hire cost includes alterations – you may need a lift in the sleeve or a tuck in the waist to be dancing through the wee hours comfortably and in style.

6   Ask the sales assistant for tips on how to get dressed in a dinner suit. You may find it fiddly with the cufflinks, cummerbund and bow tie if you do not understand how to put them together.

### ❋ Tips

There are a number of different types of formal wear available for different occasions. Your local hire shop should be able to advise you on these.

Plan ahead to ensure the proper fit and best selection. Use establishments that offer an in-store inventory. Should you have any last-minute changes or needs, they can offer you an alternative.

### ⚠ Warnings

If you're coordinating the hiring for formal wear as the best man, don't expect everyone to remember all the dates and details about their rentals. It's a good idea to confirm that they've hit all the deadlines for measurement submission and have made appointments for fittings.

If the shop you're using doesn't have lots of branches, encourage out-of-town members of the wedding party to have measurements taken locally at a hire shop or by a tailor, then send the figures on to the shop providing all the formal wear. Self-measurements can be very inaccurate.

7   Plan to return your dinner jacket the day after your event, although some shops may give you a few additional days. You are seldom required to dry-clean the dinner jacket, but damages and excessively late returns will add to your final bill.

---

## 699 | Dress for a Cocktail Party – Men

Cocktail parties give you a chance to mingle among friends, acquaintances, and current and potential business associates. Look sharp and dress appropriately for the occasion.

### ⊙ Steps

1   Consider the type of invitation. If it came by phone or e-mail, chances are the party is casual. If you received a formal invitation, and especially if the event benefits a charity or association, consider it a dressier affair.

2   Think about the season. Wear lighter-weight fabrics and brighter colours for spring and summer get-togethers. Stick to dark, muted tones in heavier fabrics for autumn and winter gatherings.

3   Dress up casual business attire for a more formal after-work cocktail party. Add a blazer to khaki trousers and a button-down shirt, or pair a sports jacket with black jeans and a black turtleneck. Switch sandals or trainers for dark leather loafers or lace-up shoes.

4   Treat cocktail parties on weekend afternoons less formally than those scheduled in the evening. Go dressy business casual for a more formal late-afternoon gathering; opt for a suit in the evening. For a less formal event, wear a nice casual outfit in the afternoon and dressier business casual clothes in the evening.

### ✳ Tips

Trainers and sports socks are inappropriate for a cocktail party. Shorts are also not advisable, even on summer afternoons. Opt for lightweight trousers in cotton or linen instead.

Check a formal invitation for terms like "semi-formal" or "black-tie optional". If you see these, a suit and tie is your best option.

Coordinate your outfit with your date's.

---

## 700 | Dress for a Cocktail Party – Women

Cocktail parties are the perfect occasion for the famous little black dress (see 696 "Buy a Perfect Little Black Dress"). Whatever your attire, keep it dressy and elegant, but not too formal.

### ⊙ Steps

1   Think about your invitation. If it came by phone or e-mail, chances are it's a more casual affair. If you received a formal invitation, and especially if the event benefits a charity or association, consider it a dressier affair.

2   Choose dress and skirt lengths from mini to just above the ankles. Save anything resembling a full-length sequined gown for a different occasion.

3   Choose fabric according to the season. Wool and wool blends are perfect for autumn and winter; satin, silk, rayon and fine-gauge knits are great for the spring and summer. These materials can be dressed up or down with jewellery, handbags, shoes, shawls and hairstyles.

### ✳ Tips

Colours such as grey, crimson, black, dark brown and dark blue flatter for evening, autumn and winter events. During the summer and spring, consider florals and seasonal shades like light pink, sky blue, pale green, pale yellow and other pastels.

Choose a dress that flatters your figure – don't squeeze into a dress that's too tight or low-cut.

4   Attend a more formal after-work party in a business suit, or if you wear more casual clothes to work, bring an outfit to change into. A black wool dress with stockings and slip-on shoes is a simple solution for autumn or winter. Pair a strapless or spaghetti-strap dress with an embroidered cardigan and slingbacks or strappy sandals for a spring or summer event.

5   Head to a more casual after-work gathering in a dressy-casual outfit. Pair a wool skirt with a fitted turtleneck and flat leather shoes for winter parties. Consider a fine-knit twinset, slim satin trousers and low-heeled backless shoes in the summer.

6   Wear a printed A-line sundress to a cocktail party on a weekend after-noon. A party scheduled for a weekend evening warrants a more flirty or elegant ensemble. Pair a colourful satin or silk empire-waist dress with a velvet or silk shawl.

7   Accessorise. Show off your gold charm bracelet or favourite pair of dangling earrings. Match hair adornments and a handbag to the motif, material or colours in your outfit.

## Dress Business Casual – Men                701

Many businesses allow somewhat casual attire at least once a week, but dress codes vary. Here are some guidelines for dress-ing business casual, which is a notch below business formal.

### ☉ Steps

1   Ask your human resources department for official guidelines. Business casual means different things at different companies. At a large corpora-tion, it may mean a sports jacket with a tie; at a smaller company, it may mean khaki trousers and a polo shirt.

2   Before you go casual, check your business diary to make sure you don't have any meetings that require formal business attire.

3   Select clean, pressed and wrinkle-free clothes. Your outfit should com-municate professionalism.

4   Wear a collared shirt with a waistcoat. You can break up the ordinary cotton shirt monotony by wearing a linen or flannel shirt or one with a band collar. Knitted shirts and polo shirts are also generally acceptable. A casual sports jacket is appropriate.

5   Wear chinos, or khaki, corduroy or other non-denim trousers. Check your company's policy before you decide to wear jeans to work.

6   Be sure to wear a belt, and have it match the colour of your shoes.

7   Wear socks that match the colour of your trousers – leave white socks in your gym bag.

8   Choose oxfords, slip-ons, or rubber-soled leather shoes or boots for casual day. Wingtips are often too formal. Worn-out shoes, sandals or trainers won't do.

### ✳ Tips

Observe what others are wearing to get an idea of what is accept-able, if your company has no written guidelines.

Your casual-day outfit should be formal enough that you can throw on a sports jacket and meet a client.

### ⚠ Warning

Casual days generally do not include the option of not shaving.

## 702 | Dress Business Casual – Women

Women can often get away with a wider range of attire than men. Let comfort and professionalism guide you when you're dressing for business casual occasions.

### Steps

1 Ask your human resources department for official guidelines. Business casual means different things at different companies. At a large corporation, it may mean trousers or a business skirt; at a smaller company, it may mean a cotton jumper and a floral skirt.

2 Before you go casual, check your business diary to make sure you don't have any meetings that require formal business attire.

3 Select clean, wrinkle-free clothes.

4 Wear a good-quality blouse or knitted top. Include a casual jacket or cardigan if appropriate.

5 Don pressed khakis or other slacks, or a dress or skirt. If a dress is sleeveless, wear a blazer or cardigan over it. Check your company's policy before you decide to wear jeans to work.

6 Wear shoes that are comfortable and appropriate for your outfit. Funky platform trainers or strappy sandals might be formal enough for some companies; however, it's more typical to wear closed-toed leather shoes. Avoid worn-out shoes.

7 Keep the make-up light. Let your natural beauty shine through.

8 Accessorise with a silk scarf or classic bracelet to give your casual outfit a polished look.

**❋ Tips**

A basic pair of black trousers is a must for any work wardrobe.

Business casual attire is more formal than weekend wear. Faded T-shirts, shorts, torn clothing and risqué attire are not appropriate.

## 703 | Choose a High-Quality Garment

Check the quality of clothes before you spend your hard-earned money. The following is a quick rundown on the particulars of good craftsmanship.

### Steps

**Fabric and Stitching**

1 Inspect fabrics to make sure patterns line up at the seams – especially at the shoulders, collar and sewn-on (patch) pockets.

2 Hold fabric up to the light and make sure the weave is tight, even and uniform, with no loose or undone threads. If the fabric has beads or sequins, make sure they're securely attached.

3 Check the grain of the fabric. The vertical grain should run straight up and down the garment, and the horizontal grain should run at a 90-degree angle to this line.

4 Crumple heavier fabric, such as wool, to see if it bounces back, either immediately or in several minutes, indicating resistance to wrinkling.

**⚠ Warning**

Take note of stains on a garment, particularly lipstick and other make-up marks around the neck area. If you notice a stain and still want to buy the item, find out if the store will dry-clean it, or ask for a discount. Alternatively, find out if you can get a refund if you can't remove the stain at home.

5   Verify that all stitches are secure and straight. You should see about 8 to 12 stitches per 2.5 cm (1 in).

6   Examine hems, which should be nearly invisible. Hemmed bottoms should hang straight and not curl or pucker.

## Other Details

1   Compare fabric lengths: fold trousers, shirts, skirts and other garments in half lengthwise to ensure that the right and left sides are symmetrical. Check that the right and left sides of the collar are equal in shape, size and positioning.

2   Confirm that patch pockets lie perfectly flat against the cloth, with no space between the pocket and the front of the garment. While holding the garment upright, make sure that the pocket doesn't hang away from the front.

3   Hold up clothing to ensure that the lining follows the cut of the garment, falls smoothly and does not extend below the hemline. In general, women's trousers are fully lined, while men's trousers are lined only in front to just below the knees.

4   Verify that buttons and buttonholes are sewn tightly, with no unravelled thread. In general, the more buttons a shirt has, the higher quality it is; spare buttons are an added plus.

5   Try on a shirt before buying it. Button it fully, making sure that buttons are placed well so that the shirt doesn't gape open across the chest.

6   Pull zips up and down a few times to make sure that they run smoothly and don't snag.

---

## Choose High-Quality Shoes   704

You don't have to spend a fortune to buy well-made shoes that fit comfortably – you just need to know what to look for.

### ⊙ Steps

#### Ensuring Fit

1   Ask a sales assistant to measure both your feet, as right and left foot sizes often differ slightly.

2   Try on shoes with socks of appropriate thickness – pop socks, thin socks or athletic socks, depending on the type of shoe you're thinking of buying.

3   Press on the shoe to locate your longest toe. You should feel at most a thumb's width between your longest toe and the end of the shoe.

4   Walk several paces with the shoes on and feel how they fit around your heels, insteps, balls and toes.

5   Make sure the shoe doesn't scrape against your anklebone.

6   Keep in mind that shoes should feel comfortable from the start; don't rely too much on "breaking them in" over time, despite what the sales assistant may say.

### ✱ Tips

When deciding on shoe size, consider the shoe material's ability to stretch. For example, calfskin stretches more than manufactured materials.

Shop for shoes in the late afternoon rather than the morning. Your feet may swell slightly over the course of the day.

Determining where the shoe is made can help you assess quality: Italian materials, design and assembly, for example, often indicate a shoe of high quality.

## Ensuring Quality

1 Examine the sole to make sure it is firmly attached to the shoe. Keep in mind that some soles are cemented to the upper shoe and others are stitched. Either type is acceptable, and some shoes (mainly men's shoes and trainers) will be both cemented and stitched.

2 Check the heel. High-quality dress shoes have leather heels, sometimes with a layer of rubber or nylon on the back edge of the heel. Heels on high-heeled shoes for women are usually made of plastic and covered with leather. The higher the price, the higher quality the plastic.

3 Inspect the shoe's interior. Leather interiors absorb foot moisture best. Good-quality shoes are fully lined from front to back.

4 Consider the shoe material. Shoes with an oiled, natural finish are durable, while patent- and polished-leather shoes resist dirt. Suede shoes stain easily and need to be sprayed with a protectant.

5 Examine buckles and any adornments on the shoe. They should be securely attached and reinforced with even, smooth double stitching.

## ⚠ Warning

You should not find bits of glue anywhere on the shoe. This is especially true for trainers.

---

## 705 | Buy a Diamond

Choosing a diamond involves more than a casual trip to the jewellers. Armed with the proper knowledge, you can make an informed decision and a wise investment.

### ⊙ Steps

1 Decide how much you can spend. If you are buying an engagement ring, the general rule is two months' salary, but the sky's the limit if you're in pursuit of the perfect stone.

2 Choose the shape of diamond you prefer. Although the round, or brilliant, cut is most popular, diamonds come in many cuts, including oval, square or even heart-shaped.

3 Inspect the diamond's clarity (the degree of transparency). A "flawless" diamond, free from all inclusions or blemishes, is very rare. Other diamonds are rated on a clarity scale that grades diamonds from "flawless" to "obvious inclusions" – the higher the diamond's rating on this scale, the greater its value.

4 Examine the diamond's colour. Although you may not generally think of diamonds as having colour, some have a yellow, grey or brown cast. Pure, colourless diamonds are at the top of the colour scale. Diamonds are also available in "fancy" colours such as red, blue or purple. These diamonds are rare and more expensive than the normal clear to yellow variety.

5 Examine the diamond's cut, which is crucial to the brilliance of the stone and a major factor in its value. A well-cut diamond reflects and disperses light in beautiful ways, thanks to qualities such as symmetry and depth (the bottom of the diamond shouldn't be too shallow or too deep). Diamonds are graded according to the cut quality, and this grade should carry a great deal of weight in your decision.

6 Determine the weight, which is measured in carats. The greater the carat weight, the more valuable the diamond. Keep in mind that since larger

### ✳ Tips

Enquire about a certificate from the Gemological Institute of America (GIA). The GIA, the largest impartial diamond-grading authority in the world, issues a grading report and details the diamond's specifications after examining it.

A nicked and scratched stone is almost certainly fake, but only a jeweller can detect some fakes. Have a questionable stone professionally appraised.

Buy from a jeweller who will guide you through the process. A good jeweller will help you assess how much you can spend, show you a wide selection of diamonds, and explain what to look for.

Buying a loose diamond gives you the option of designing a setting around the stone.

If you buy a ring band, opt for platinum or white gold: metals other than yellow or rose gold enhance the brilliance of the diamond due to their colour.

stones are more rare, two $\frac{1}{2}$-carat diamonds are less expensive than a single 1-carat diamond.

7  Compare several diamonds side by side and get a good idea of what you can find in your price range. No two diamonds are alike, so examine all of them carefully for their unique qualities.

8  Make your final decision based on which diamond offers the best combination of the four C's: clarity, colour, cut and carat. Ignore any of these attributes, and you jeopardise your chances of getting the best diamond for your money.

⚠ **Warning**

Don't try to get the largest possible diamond for your money. This can mean overlooking quality in favour of size and ending up with an inferior stone. Balancing all factors is the best approach to choosing a quality diamond.

---

## Buy Pearls　　　　706

Versatile and classic, pearls are a worthwhile investment that can soften a business suit or add more elegance to a dress. Here's what to look for.

### ⊙ Steps

#### General Considerations

1  Decide whether you want natural, cultured or imitation pearls. Keep in mind that imitation pearls are costume jewellery and are of very little value; natural pearls are almost impossible to buy and often aren't as high in quality as cultured pearls.

2  Choose a pearl shape: round, symmetrical or baroque and/or irregular. Sphere-like round pearls are the most expensive and highly prized. Symmetrical pearls, such as those shaped like teardrops, should be evenly shaped.

3  Consider pearl size, the most important factor in price. The larger the pearl, the more it will cost.

4  Decide if you want a double-strand necklace of smaller pearls (cheaper) or a single strand of larger pearls (more expensive).

5  Place pearls directly under a light on a flat, white surface in order to inspect them.

6  Inspect each pearl for lustre. Lustrous pearls have a shiny surface, good contrast between light and dark areas, and strong, crisp reflections. Avoid pearls that resemble dull, cloudy white beads.

7  Look at the pearl's "orient", a play of iridescent rainbow colours – characteristic of high-quality pearls.

8  Examine pearl colour, which can be white, yellow, black, grey or various other colours. Ask whether the colour is natural or dyed; the latter is less expensive. More exotic natural colours are more expensive.

9  Inspect the pearl's "overtone", a tint secondary to the main body colour. Pinkish overtones can increase pearl price, while green or blue tints may lower the price.

10 Verify the pearl's cleanliness by checking that it has minimal surface blemishes such as nicks, cracks, pits or discoloration.

↑ ↑ ↑

✱ **Tips**

Natural pearls, which are rare and valuable, form when oysters reflexively coat a foreign particle with nacre. Cultured pearls start off with an artificially implanted bead nucleus that triggers the same response in the oyster. Imitation pearls are composed of glass or plastic.

The only certain way to distinguish between a natural and a cultured pearl is to have the pearl X-rayed.

If you're buying a pearl necklace, it should have a knot between each pearl to hold the necklace together in case the string breaks.

Compare a pearl with others in the same strand. Verify that pearls within a strand match in colour, tint and size. Comparing one strand of pearls with another might help you assess lustre and colour more accurately.

⚠ **Warning**

Pearls offered at unbelievably low prices are probably fake.

11  Turn the pearl in your hands to examine it from all angles. Colour, shape, smoothness and lustre all may vary within a single pearl. Roll a strand of pearls on a flat surface to test them for roundness – round pearls roll more smoothly and evenly.

## Distinguishing Real Pearls From Imitations

1  Run the pearl lightly along the biting edge of your front teeth. A real pearl will feel slightly gritty or sandy, whereas a fake pearl will feel smooth. This is a standard test for authenticity that most sellers will allow, as long as you ask first.

2  Look at and feel the pearl. Absolutely flawless-looking pearls, as well as those that feel unusually light when you bounce them in your hands, are probably fake.

3  Examine the pearl under a 10x magnifier (a loupe). Imitation pearls appear grainy.

---

## 707 | Clean Jewellery

Before cleaning your jewellery, examine it carefully to make sure that all settings, clasps and prongs are secure. Once you've done that, you're ready to proceed.

### ⊙ Steps

### Gold, Platinum and Gemstones

1  Use a non-abrasive jewellery cleaner, which you can purchase at a local jewellers. Or use a cleaning solution of mild soap and water.

2  Dip the jewellery in the cleaner or cleaning solution.

3  Rinse in warm running water.

4  Buff dry with a soft, lint-free cloth until it's shiny.

### Silver

1  Clean the silver with a non-abrasive silver polish.

2  Apply the polish with a soft cloth, gently working it into stains.

3  Wipe away excess polish and buff the jewellery with a soft, lint-free cloth until it's shiny.

4  Keep in mind that frequently wearing silver jewellery can keep it from becoming tarnished.

### ✱ Tips

Store jewellery carefully to avoid damage. Sturdy cases with partitioned, soft interiors protect and organise items.

Jewellers recommend having jewellery professionally cleaned at least once a year.

### ⚠ Warnings

Do not use jewellery cleaner on pearls and porous stones, such as emeralds, rubies, lapis lazuli, coral and turquoise. Wipe them clean with a soft, damp cloth or have them cleaned professionally. Consult a jeweller when in doubt about a particular stone.

Exposure to perfume, cosmetics or perspiration can stain gemstones.

## ✓ 708 Buy a Gemstone

When you're shopping for jewellery set with precious or semi-precious stones, it pays to buy from a reputable and trusted jeweller. Here are a few guidelines for judging quality; also see 705 "Buy a Diamond" and 706 "Buy Pearls".

| | CUT OR SHAPE | COLOUR | CLARITY | ADDITIONAL NOTES |
|---|---|---|---|---|
| Amethyst | Comes in a variety of cuts. | Deeper purple stones are more valuable. | Look for perfect clarity with no visible flaws. | The regal purple colour is purported to ward off drunkenness and is prized in the crowns of royalty. |
| Aquamarine | Comes in a variety of cuts. | Dark blue stones are more valuable; those with green less so. | Make sure the gem is free of flaws or inclusions. | Said to be a favourite of mermaids and a protection against evil, fear and marital discord. |
| Emerald | The rectangular step-cut – or "emerald cut" – is most popular. | Colour should be a deep, vivid green. | Although perfect clarity makes an emerald exceptionally valuable, some inclusions may be acceptable as long as they are not so deep as to weaken the stone. | The emerald is a symbol of love, rebirth and youth. |
| Garnet | Many garnets are quite small, but larger ones can be cut in a variety of shapes, including hearts. | The rarest and most valuable are of the green demantoid variety. Pink and red rhodolite garnets are among the most popular. | The light should reflect evenly off the surface. Check for obvious flaws and inclusions. | Most garnets are reasonably priced. They are said to protect travellers from harm and sleepers from nightmares. |
| Ruby | Rubies are usually cut in an oval shape; other shapes are available. | The best stones are pure red with a fiery intensity. The centre of the stone should not appear dark. | You will see no inclusions in a perfect, transparent ruby. The star-shaped highlights of star rubies result from tiny inclusions. | Because large rubies are so scarce, you may not be able to find a stone larger than five carats. |
| Sapphire | Oval shapes are popular, but sapphires come in a variety of cuts. | The most valuable sapphires are deep, pure royal blue, although sapphires come in a range of colours. Valuable "colour-change" stones have different hues in natural and artificial light. | Hold the stone face up and be sure the light reflects evenly. There should be no scratches, and the centre of the stone should not appear dark. | Sapphires can be heated to give them a better colour and clarity. It is estimated that more than 90 percent of those on the market have undergone this process, which does not affect value. |
| Topaz | Topaz can be cut into a variety of shapes. | The rarest topaz is light pink or red. Other colours include yellow, brown, green, blue and peach. | Be sure the stone has no visible flaws or inclusions. It should reflect light evenly when held face up and should not show any scratches. | Clear topaz can also be irradiated to become blue. Topaz treated this way is more affordable than the rare blue topaz found in nature. |
| Turquoise | Turquoise can be cut into a variety of shapes. | The most valuable turquoise is pure blue without any greenish cast. The presence of veins is a matter of personal taste. | Check the condition of the stone. It should have no chips or fractures. | Turquoise is fairly soft, so it often is coated with acrylic resin to make it more resilient. |

chart

---

## 709 | Sew On a Button

Don't let that shirt or jumper that has lost a button gather dust in the fix-it pile; a few minutes of handiwork with a needle and thread can put it back in your regular rotation.

### ⊙ Steps

1   Select a button if you don't have the original. Look inside the seam or lining for the extra button that manufacturers sometimes include, or buy one that closely matches the size and colour of the other buttons.

2   Choose thread that matches either the thread colour used on the other buttons, the colour of the button or the colour of the material.

3   Cut a piece of thread about 45 cm (½ yd) long.

4   Thread the needle, feeding the thread through the eyehole. Moisten the thread with your tongue first to stiffen it and make this easier.

5   Move the needle to the middle of the thread and fold the thread in half. Tie a knot at the end of the thread, where both ends meet. Tie another knot so that you've double-secured the end. You're ready to sew.

6   Place the button on top of the material where you intend to sew it into place. You can put a match or toothpick between the button and the material to give the thread the necessary slack.

7   Push the needle up from under the material through one of the holes on the button. Pull the thread all the way through until you've anchored the knot against the material.

8   Push the needle down through the next hole on the button and through the material.

9   Repeat steps 7 and 8 three times, going up through the material and then down through the button and material, so that you've secured each hole with multiple strands.

10  End with the needle on the material side. Stitch through the material only and up again, forming a knot against the material with the needle and thread. Do this twice, forming two knots against the material to ensure that your button will stay secure. Snip off the remaining thread.

### ✱ Tip

Your button may have two or four buttonholes, or it may be the kind of button you attach from underneath via a shank – you follow approximately the same steps in either case. For four-hole buttons, you can crisscross the thread to form an X on the top of the button, or you can go straight across the top of the button to form two lines. Use whichever pattern matches the thread on the other buttons.

### Things You'll Need

❑ button

❑ thread

❑ scissors

❑ needle

---

## 710 | Darn a Sock

You can use the darning technique to repair small holes in socks and other clothing. With a darning needle and yarn, you'll form a network of stitches across the gap.

### ⊙ Steps

1   Find thread or yarn that matches the sock in colour and texture; you can use embroidery floss (a type of thread) to repair a crew sock, while wool yarn is appropriate for a wool sock. Choose a darning needle as well.

2   Place a lightbulb in the sock and position the hole over the lightbulb. Your needle will glide smoothly over the bulb's surface, making your stitching go faster.

### ✱ Tips

Use a darning needle for your repairs. The eye of this needle is large enough to accommodate a thicker yarn.

Sew a running stitch by bringing the needle up through the fabric, then down again, then up again. Space stitches evenly.

3   Thread the darning needle with the yarn or thread and leave the end unknotted. The darning process should create a tight weave that makes knots unnecessary.

4   Start your work on either side of the hole. Take several small vertical running stitches in the intact fabric of the sock, about 1 cm (1/2 in) to the left or right of the hole. Turn the sock upside down and make another row of stitches next to the first.

5   Increase the number of running stitches you make as you come closer to the hole. When you reach the point at which the hole begins, your stitching line should extend from 1 cm (1/2 in) above the hole to 1 cm (1/2 in) below it.

6   Continue making vertical running stitches. When your stitching reaches the hole, take your thread or yarn over the hole and into the fabric on the other side, forming what resembles a vertical bridge over the hole. Stitching should extend 1 cm (1/2 in) beyond the hole at both the top and bottom edges.

7   Cut the thread end once you have covered the hole with vertical threads and extended the stitching 1 cm (1/2 in) past it so that both sides of the hole look identical.

8   Thread your darning needle and begin your work 1 cm (1/2 in) from either side of the hole at either the top or bottom. Take the threaded needle and weave it under and over the vertical threads that cover the hole (as well as the vertical threads that lie within 1 cm/1/2 in of the hole).

9   Turn the sock upside down once you reach the opposite end of the hole, and weave another yarn strand next to the first. Continue stitching back and forth until you've completely filled the hole. Trim excess thread.

Lay both your running-stitch lines and crosswise threads as close together as possible to create a tight weave.

You can replace the lightbulb with another round, smooth object of similar dimensions, such as a hard plastic ball.

## Things You'll Need

❏ thread, yarn or embroidery floss

❏ lightbulb

❏ darning needle

❏ scissors

---

# Hem Trousers                                                 711

Whether you're tailoring new clothes or adapting hand-me-downs, you'll want to get the hem right.

## ⊙ Steps

1   Select thread that matches the colour and thickness of the thread used in the original hem.

2   Use small scissors or a seam ripper to undo the existing hem carefully.

3   Try on the trousers and fold each trouser leg inwards to the length that looks correct for the new hem. Pin it in place.

4   Take off the trousers, turn them inside out, and use a tape measure or ruler to determine the length of the fabric folded inwards to form the new hem length. Use this measurement as your gauge for folding the trouser legs all the way around.

5   Measure and pin the new hem length into place on both legs according to the measurement you just made.

6   Iron the edge of the new hem on both legs to create a good crease. (If you want to hide the unfinished edge of the fabric to prevent fraying, fold it approximately 5 mm/1/4 in towards the inside of the trouser leg and iron it in place.)

## ✳ Tips

Try on trousers with the appropriate shoes and hem accordingly.

With lined trousers, the lining is typically hemmed slightly shorter than the trousers.

## Things You'll Need

❏ thread

❏ pins

❏ tape measure or ruler

❏ small scissors or a seam ripper

❏ needle

❏ iron and ironing board

7　Try on your trousers after you have pinned and ironed the new hem, to ensure that both legs match in length. If the original trouser length was excessive, you may need to trim some fabric before securing the hem.

8　Sew the hem into place by hand, lightly catching a few threads on the inside of the garment to avoid having the stitches show on the outside, and forming one line equidistant from the edge of the leg.

## 712 | Iron Trousers

**Almost all trousers, aside from jeans, require ironing.**

### ⊙ Steps

1　Turn the trousers inside out. Look for the tag that gives ironing and fabric information for the garment.

2　Choose the heat setting on your iron appropriate for that fabric. Linen and 100 per cent cotton take a high setting; wools and cotton blends call for medium heat; polyester, rayon, nylon, silk, acetate and acrylic all require a low heat setting.

3　Fill the iron with distilled (de-ionised) water if you will be using the steam setting on cotton or linen.

4　Test the iron on a small area to make sure you don't have the setting too high – this can damage or discolour the fabric.

5　With the trousers still inside out, iron the waistband, pockets (on both sides), fly area, seams and hems, in that order.

6　Turn the trousers right side out and pull the waistband over the pointed end of the board. Iron the waistband area and any pleats along the front of the trousers below the waistband.

7　Lay the trousers lengthwise along the ironing board with both legs together and carefully line up any pre-existing creases.

8　Take the hem of the top trouser leg and bring it towards the waistband, folding the top leg away from the bottom leg. Iron the inside (hem to crotch) of the lower leg. Turn the trousers over and repeat for the other leg.

9　Smooth out both legs carefully and iron the outside of the top leg. Give extra attention to turn-ups, if the trousers have them.

10　Turn the trousers over and iron the outside of the other leg.

11　Hang warm trousers immediately to avoid wrinkling. Fold them through a suit hanger to avoid crushing them in a trousers hanger.

### ✱ Tips

The material in many suits can become shiny with too much ironing. You can avoid this by placing a clean cotton cloth over the area before ironing it.

Avoid spot-cleaning trousers just before ironing. Any wet spots may become permanent stains if ironed.

### ⚠ Warning

Irons are very hot and heavy; avoid ironing when small children are near, and never leave a hot iron unattended.

## Iron a Shirt    `713`

Even so-called no-iron shirts often require ironing – but if you learn to do it yourself, you'll save enough on laundry bills to buy several more.

### ⊙ Steps

1 Locate the tag on your shirt that indicates the materials that were used in the garment.

2 Plug in the iron and set the dial to the recommended setting for that fabric. Linen and 100 per cent cotton take a high setting; wools and cotton blends call for medium heat; polyester, rayon, nylon, silk, acetate and acrylic all require a low heat setting.

3 Fill the iron with distilled (de-ionised) water if you will be using the steam setting on cotton or linen.

4 Test the iron on a small area to make sure you don't have the setting too high – this can damage or discolour the fabric.

5 Iron the back of the collar first, then the front, taking care to iron in from the edges a little at a time to avoid creases.

6 Open the cuffs fully. Iron inside first, then outside.

7 Iron the sleeves after smoothing them flat to avoid creases. Do the sleeve backs first, the fronts second.

8 Hang the shirt over the board so that you can extend one front panel of the shirt flat (with the collar at the narrower end of the board). Iron from shoulder to shirt-tail.

9 Rotate the shirt over the board so that you iron the back next, and the other front panel last.

### ✱ Tips

Hang your warm shirt on a hanger immediately to avoid rewrinkling it.

If you'll be wearing a buttoned jacket all day and are short of time, you need only iron the collar, sleeves and top of the front. If you'll be wearing a jumper all day, iron only the collar.

### ⚠ Warning

Irons are very hot and heavy; avoid ironing when small children are near, and never leave a hot iron unattended.

## Prepare Your Clothes for Dry-Cleaning    `714`

Distressed about the stain you found on your favourite silk blouse? You can take several steps to ensure that your dry-cleaner gets the best results possible.

### ⊙ Steps

1 Keep care tags or labels on garments.

2 Do not wash, dry or iron in stains if you know you are going to take the item to the cleaners anyway.

3 Avoid pre-treating stains, especially those on delicate fabrics and on clothes that are dry-clean only. You'll get best results when you leave these stains untouched and bring the item in immediately.

4 Include a note that explains the source of the stain and how long it's been there. Better yet, explain this to the cleaner personally.

5 Empty pockets of make-up, change and other items at home.

### ✱ Tips

Dry-cleaners are professionals, but some stains lie beyond even their cleaning capabilities.

Fabrics that generally require dry-cleaning include silk, wool, linen and rayon.

6   Notify dry-cleaners ahead of time of any pre-existing tears or damage. Otherwise, they might not clean your garment for fear you'll think they caused the damage.

## 715  Do the Washing

Has a parent, spouse or someone else decided that it's time you did your own washing? You'll soon discover it's really simple to clean your own clothes.

### ◎ Steps

1   Sort your clothes according to the washing instructions on their labels. Make separate piles for whites, bright colours and darks. If you mix whites with colours in the wash, the colours may bleed onto and ruin your whites. Also separate clothes that tend to produce fluff (towels, sweatshirts, chenille and flannel) from clothes that tend to attract fluff (corduroy, velvets and permanent-press clothes).

2   As you sort, close zips to prevent snagging, and empty pockets (you don't want soggy shreds of tissues all over your clothes!).

3   Pre-treat heavy stains with laundry detergent or stain remover, heeding instructions on the product label.

4   Put your clothes in the washing machine and close the door.

5   Use the measuring cap of the detergent bottle or the cup found in detergent boxes to measure according to the manufacturer's instructions.

6   Pour the detergent into the dispenser. Add liquid fabric softener, if desired, according to the product instructions.

7   Select the correct wash cycle. Consult your washing machine's instruction manual or the detergent container for recommendations. In general, use cold water to protect colours and darks from bleeding or fading, and to avoid shrinkage. Use warm or hot water for durable fabrics like cotton (make sure they're pre-shrunk), and to ensure that your whites stay white. Make sure that you use a gentle cycle for sheer or delicate fabrics.

8   If you need to add bleach, pour it into the bleach dispenser.

9   Turn on the machine and let it do its dirty work.

10  Once the cycle is complete, turn off the washing machine and take out your clothes. Hang them to dry on a clotheshorse or on a washing line if the weather is fine. If you have a tumble drier, put the clothes (and an anti-static sheet, if desired) in the drier. Do not place delicates (such as bras and certain woollens) in a tumble drier. Check the washing instructions on the clothes if in doubt. Remove any fluff from the drier's lint filter and then turn on the drier.

11  Once the clothes are dry, remove them from the drier, clotheshorse or washing line and fold them.

### ✱ Tips

If you stuff too many clothes into the washing machine, it won't clean them very well.

Handle bleach carefully. Avoid splashing it directly onto clothes or yourself.

### ⚠ Warning

Remember that you should typically dry-clean some fabrics – silk, wool, linen and rayon, for example. You should hand-wash lingerie in the sink to preserve delicate lace and other elements.

### Things You'll Need

☐ stain remover

☐ laundry detergent

☐ fabric softener

☐ bleach

☐ anti-static sheets

**716 Remove Stains From Clothing**

The first step in removing a stain is to know what caused it. There are several basic categories of stains, each requiring a different treatment. Use the reference below to guide you in identifying and treating the stain. Once you've run the stain through the wash, make sure it's completely gone before throwing the garment in a tumble dryer; otherwise the heat could set it permanently. If you are at all in doubt about how to treat a stain, take the stained article to a dry-cleaner for professional advice.

### Protein stains

Caused by protein foods such as meats, milk and eggs, as well as by blood, urine, faeces, grass and perspiration.

- If a urine stain is still wet, cover it with salt until all the liquid is absorbed. Rinse. If the stain remains, use white vinegar or hydrogen peroxide.

- Soak the garment before washing, using a biological pre-soak product. Make sure you follow the instructions on the product label.

- Wash in cold water if you are dealing with blood stains.

- Do not use bleach to treat protein stains.

### Grease stains

Caused by cooking oil, butter, margarine, mayonnaise, motor oil and cosmetics.

- Use a pre-wash stain remover as soon as possible after the stain occurs.

- If you're using a spray or liquid pre-treatment product, launder the garment as usual immediately after treating it.

- If you're using a stick or gel product, let the garment sit for as long as a week before laundering.

- If the stain remains, pre-treat and launder again.

### Tannin stains

Caused by coffee, tea, ketchup, juice, wine, chocolate and soft drinks.

- If you can treat a red wine stain immediately after a spill, cover the spot with salt to absorb the liquid. Then soak it in cold water.

- If you have a chocolate stain, use an enzyme treatment before washing.

- Use bleach if that's safe for the fabric. If it's not, soak in a detergent and wash as soon as possible to make sure the stain is completely removed.

- Check that the stain is gone; if not, repeat the treatment.

### Miscellaneous stains

- To remove mustard, treat with a pre-wash stain remover, then use bleach, if that's safe for the fabric. Then wash.

- If you're removing chewing gum, rub it with ice to harden it. Then scrape off as much as possible with a blunt knife. Treat with stain remover and wash.

- For ink stains, apply methylated spirits to the stain using a clean cotton bud. Wash the fabric as usual.

- To remove nail polish, use nail polish remover; rinse, then launder. If the fabric is acetate or triacetate, treat with glycerin, then take to a dry-cleaner.

reference

## 717 Wash a Cashmere Jumper

Instead of sending your cashmere jumper to the dry-cleaners, wash it! Many people don't realise that cashmere can be hand-washed, and that such care will prolong the life of the garment.

### ⊙ Steps

1 Buy a detergent specifically intended for delicate garments.

2 Fill your sink or basin with lukewarm or cool water, depending on the garment's washing instructions. Add the recommended amount of detergent to the basin.

3 Briskly run your hand through the water to distribute the detergent and generate suds.

4 Submerge the jumper and gently squeeze the suds through it.

5 Let it soak for 20 minutes.

6 Drain the sink and rinse your jumper with lukewarm water until the water rinses clear.

7 Gently press water out of the jumper and place it lengthwise on a clean, dry bath towel.

8 Roll up the towel. Press with your palms to squeeze out excess water.

9 Remove the jumper from the towel and smooth it out so it is back in its original shape.

10 Lay the jumper flat on a dry towel and let it air-dry, or use a drying rack if you have one.

### ✱ Tip

Dry-cleaning cashmere is also a viable option. However, as cashmere is a delicate fibre, excess chemical treatments may shorten your jumper's life.

### ⚠ Warnings

Wringing out your jumper may pull it out of shape.

Sunlight can fade your jumper, and other heat sources may wear fibres prematurely. It's better to let your jumper dry naturally indoors, away from sunny windows and heat vents.

### Things You'll Need

☐ detergent for delicate items

☐ towel

## 718 Shine Shoes

Want to keep your shoes looking as good as new? Learn how to shine them like a pro.

### ⊙ Steps

1 Clean dust and dirt from the surface of your shoes or boots with a shoeshine brush or damp cloth.

2 Select a wax or cream shoe polish that matches the leather's colour.

3 Use a shoe-polish brush (a small, soft brush that's distinct from the large, bristly shoeshine brush) to apply a conservative amount of polish to the surface of the leather. Brush in circular motions until the leather has a dull coating. Get into tight spots using an old soft-bristled toothbrush.

4 Wait up to 15 minutes, or until the polish completely or nearly dries, depending on the instructions for the polish.

5 Brush the shoes or boots with a shoeshine brush.

6 Buff them to a gleaming shine with a clean cotton cloth, such as an old sock or T-shirt.

### ✱ Tips

Don't polish suede or patent leather.

"Instant" shoe polishes generally do not last and can harm shoe leather.

Don't attempt to change the colour of leather with polish. Have a shoemaker dye the shoes.

## Clean Trainers 719

Being busy is no excuse for having dirty, smelly trainers. These instructions work for trainers of various materials.

### ⊙ Steps

1   Prepare a solution of water and a neutral cleaner (such as washing-up liquid or another mild product).

2   Remove laces and inserts and rinse the shoes with water inside and out.

3   Use a soft brush and the cleaning solution to scrub every part of both shoes, including liners and insoles.

4   Remove scuff marks with a white nylon-backed scrub pad.

5   Rinse the shoes thoroughly with water.

6   Stuff the shoes with paper (not newspaper – the ink will run and make a mess) to absorb excess water and to help the shoes keep their shape. Allow them to drip-dry.

7   Wash the laces in a load of washing. Allow the inserts to air out, and apply baking soda to them if they're smelly.

8   Replace the inserts and laces after the shoes dry completely.

9   Apply white cream shoe polish to white leather parts and black polish to black leather parts.

### ✳ Tips

Many shops selling trainers carry special shoe-cleaning kits for use with specific brands and models.

If your trainers will stand up to the cycle, run them through your washing machine to get them clean.

### Things You'll Need

❑ washing-up liquid or other mild cleaner

❑ soft brush

❑ white nylon-backed scrub pads

❑ paper

❑ white or black cream shoe polish

## Prevent Shoe Odour 720

Bacteria, which thrive in moist, dark areas, cause foot odour. It is essential to keep your feet and shoes clean and aired out to prevent shoe odour from occurring.

### ⊙ Steps

1   Wash your feet thoroughly with antibacterial soap, and scrub between your toes. Dry your feet completely after washing.

2   Apply antiperspirants to your feet to control moisture if your feet sweat excessively. Use antiperspirants specifically designed for feet rather than underarm products. You can also apply antibacterial gels to your feet to control bacterial growth, or antifungal powder to prevent athlete's foot.

3   Wear absorbent socks, such as cotton, and avoid nylon socks, which don't absorb sweat very well. Change socks once or twice a day if your feet sweat a lot.

4   Wear shoes that breathe, such as sandals or shoes made from mesh and canvas. Allowing your feet to air out reduces bacterial growth.

5   Avoid wearing shoes two days in a row – let them air out for 24 hours between uses.

6   Remove the insoles and allow them to air out for 24 hours after an excessively sweaty day, or if your shoes get wet.

### ✳ Tips

If fashion dictates that you wear your shoes without socks, shake in a bit of talcum powder to absorb sweat.

If your shoes ever get drenched on a rainy day, let them dry completely before wearing them again.

### Things You'll Need

❑ antibacterial soap

❑ foot antiperspirant

❑ antibacterial gel

❑ antifungal powder

❑ absorbent socks

7   Wash your shoes, if appropriate, making sure to dry them thoroughly. If your shoes are not washable, replace the insoles every few months or even more frequently, and put baking powder in them to absorb odours. You can also try special odour-reducing sprays and inserts.

8   If you have a severe problem with foot odour, consult a doctor to get prescription medicine that controls bacterial growth and perspiration.

## 721 | Control Perspiration

Perspiration, or sweating, is your body's way of regulating its temperature and responding to stress. But it can also lead to foul odours and damp clothing.

### ⊙ Steps

1   Use a product that contains both deodorant and antiperspirant. The deodorant only helps control odours, whereas the antiperspirant helps block sweat.

2   Sprinkle talcum powder or cornstarch in problem areas to absorb moisture.

3   Dress in layers so you can control your temperature, thereby reducing your body's need to sweat. Wear a white or light-coloured hat to reflect sunlight on hot days, since your head is an important temperature-control point on the body.

4   Wear natural fabrics such as wool, silk and cotton that allow air to circulate around your body easily.

5   Drink plenty of fluids and stay fit. Fluids and a fit body help regulate your temperature and reduce sweating.

6   Relax as much as possible using regulated breathing, yoga or meditation. This can reduce stress, a perspiration trigger.

### ✱ Tip

Cotton socks and foot antiperspirants can minimise foot sweat. (see 720 "Prevent Shoe Odour"). Cotton panties help to prevent sweating, too.

### ⚠ Warning

If you perspire even when you're relaxed and the temperature is cool, see your doctor – it could be a sign of an underlying health problem.

## 722 | Find the Perfect Fit in a Bra

Whether you choose a bra to enhance, minimise, support or show off your bust, fit is crucial – it's the key to keeping you comfortable and supporting your breasts properly.

### ⊙ Steps

1   Use a tape measure to measure around your bare ribcage, just beneath your naked breasts. Add either 4 or 5 inches to this number to bring it up to an even-numbered measurement. This number indicates the band size most appropriate for your figure.

2   Measure the widest part of your bust, sliding the tape around the middle of your back. Hold the tape as level as possible to ensure accuracy.

3   Note the difference between the two measurements. Use the following as a guide, and try on a range of sizes above and below your measurement: if your bust measurement is up to ½ inch larger than your band

### ✱ Tips

Remember that all bras are not made equal. Experiment to find the brand or style that best suits your figure.

Wash bras by hand, or in a washing machine in a mesh bag on the delicate cycle. Avoid shrinkage and prolong life by hanging bras to air-dry instead of putting them in a tumble dryer.

size, then your cup size is an AA. A measurement of ½ inch to 1 inch more than the band size indicates an A cup, 1 to 2 inches indicates a B cup, 2 to 3 inches indicates a C cup, 3 to 4 inches indicates a D cup, and 4 to 5 inches indicates a DD or E cup.

4 Select a range of bras according to your band and cup size.

5 Try on a bra. Place your hands through the straps and bend over to allow your breasts to fall into the cups. The cups should contain your breasts – unless you're trying a plunge or an enhancing bra – and should centre your nipple in the fullest part.

6 Close the bra using the middle hook. Look for a band that fits snugly but doesn't cut into your ribcage. If it's too tight, try adjusting the hook closure before proceeding to a larger size.

7 Adjust the straps so the band fits comfortably under the breasts and around the ribcage. If the bra seems to slip forwards, if you find yourself pulling up on the straps, or if it feels as if your breasts are falling out of the bottom of the cups, the band size is too big.

8 Check the fabric or bridge between your breasts. This should lie flat on the breastbone. If it sticks up or stabs your breastbone uncomfortably, try a larger cup size. If it puckers, try a smaller size.

9 Move up a cup size if your breasts bulge from the bra. Move down a size if you notice wrinkles in the cup material.

---

## Choose a Flattering Swimsuit                    723

A flattering swimsuit makes the most of the proportions of a woman's figure. It's all about a careful mixing of colour, print, and the right lines and silhouette.

### ⊙ Steps

1 Use blocks of colour to divert attention from wide hips or a belly bulge. Wear one-piece suits with a dark-coloured, solid lower half and a lighter-coloured or printed bodice.

2 Choose suits with at least 15 per cent spandex to minimise flabby areas. If you have wide hips, opt for styles that cut across the hips rather than hanging below them.

3 Enhance a small chest with a lightly padded halter top or a demi cut with an underwire; the demi cut resembles a bra, but it's not a full cup. Also look for suits that offer texture, like ruffles or smocking, and material with a small print – these are guaranteed to deflect attention from your bust.

4 Minimise a full chest with a dark, monochromatic bodice that has a high or square-cut neck. Make sure the suit offers your bust ample support to resist drooping or sagging, and choose a wider-cut bottom to balance your overall look.

5 Elongate a petite frame with a one-piece suit that has thin vertical stripes. Lend short legs length with a suit cut high on the hip.

6 Give a square or boyish figure the appearance of a waist with a one-piece, or a bikini with the top shaped like a vest, that has a darker colour

### ✱ Tips

Nowadays, you can essentially create your own two-piece suit. Look for companies that offer a variety of mix-and-match, co-ordinated tops and bottoms.

Wear your swimsuit with a long sleeveless blouse, print sarong or wraparound skirt if the thought of walking around in your swimsuit makes you uncomfortable.

### ⚠ Warning

You generally can't return bathing suits. Check restrictions prior to purchase.

from the crotch to the middle ribs and a lighter colour over the chest. Consider a "skort" – a combination of shorts and skirt – to conceal and divert attention away from a too-round bottom.

7   If you have toned legs and sexy shoulders, flaunt them in a string bikini or cut-out one-piece swimsuit.

---

## 724 Choose Sunglasses

Sunglasses not only look fashionable, but they also help protect your eyes from the harmful rays of the sun.

### ⊙ Steps

1   Check labels to make sure the sunglasses provide 100 per cent UVA and UVB protection.

2   Look for sunglasses that filter out at least some blue light, which can damage the retina and lead to macular degeneration (vision loss from degeneration in parts of the eye). To make sure, try wearing them outside; a blue sky should appear grey with these on. Also ask about polarisation, a type of filtering that helps reduce glare.

3   Choose a lens colour based on your preferences and comfort level. Grey doesn't affect colour perception; orange-brown lenses are a good choice for those with macular degeneration, since they filter out UV and blue light rays for maximum retinal protection; green lenses distort colour less than other shades, such as red or yellow.

4   Opt for lightweight, plastic, shatterproof sunglasses if you're going to be wearing them when playing sports.

5   Purchase sun goggles for total protection of your eyes. These cover a large area and include side shields. As an added bonus, they also fit over prescription glasses.

### ✻ Tips

A darker lens does not necessarily indicate better protection, and lighter-tinted lenses offer better visibility. Check labels to find sunglasses that provide the best protection possible.

To insure against mislabelling, you may want to purchase a UV card, a credit card–size device for testing sunglasses. Contact an optometrist, or look for the product online.

For added eye protection, wear a hat with at least a 8-cm (3-in) brim.

---

## 725 Choose Flattering Eyeglass Frames

Glasses these days have a dual purpose: they improve your vision, and they serve as a fashion accessory that can enhance, rather than detract from, your looks.

### ⊙ Steps

1   Pull your hair back in a ponytail (if necessary) and inspect your face shape in front of the mirror.

2   Keep in mind that oval faces are egg-shaped and balanced on top and bottom, and can support any type of frame.

3   Make a long, thin face seem wider and shorter with larger frames in round or triangular shapes. Or try a wide, rectangular shape. Frames that have colour, width or embellishment near the sides will also broaden your face.

### ✻ Tips

Make sure that your eyes are positioned in the middle of the lens. If your eyes are close-set, avoid large frames.

Your eyebrows should align with the top bar of your glasses.

Avoid wearing frames that have shapes similar to your face, as a general rule. In other words, don't wear round frames if you

4   Try round frames made of thin metal to soften the angular look of a square face, which has a wide forehead and cheeks, and an angular chin.

5   Remember that round faces are fuller, with a gentle chin, wide cheeks and small cheekbones. Avoid round frames, which make the face look larger; wear boxy or rectangular ones instead. Dark frames can weigh down your face, making it appear heavier.

6   Balance a heart-shaped face, which has a wide forehead that angles down to a small chin, with frames that are wider at the bottom than at the top.

7   Flatter a diamond-shaped face, which has a narrow forehead, wide temples and an angular chin, by wearing small frames in geometric or oval shapes to minimise the horizontal distance between your temples.

8   Choose smaller frames if you have facial hair such as a beard. Large frames will further mask your features.

9   Stick with small frames if you have a small head. Make sure your glasses aren't any wider than the widest part of your face.

10  Select large frames that fit comfortably if you have a large head. Avoid glasses that appear to squeeze your face or temples.

have a round face. Rather, choose frames in a different cut from your face shape.

---

## Choose a Hairstylist                                726

Finding a good hairstylist may take some searching, but it's worth the time investment to locate the right one for your look and hair.

### ⊙ Steps

1   Ask your friends and acquaintances about their stylists. If you see someone on the street who has a haircut you admire, don't hesitate to ask for the stylist's name – most will be flattered and only too happy to tell you.

2   Pick a salon with a good reputation and ask for a stylist who specialises in your type of hair, or choose one based on what you've heard.

3   Schedule a consultation, for which the salon shouldn't charge you.

4   Make sure the salon looks clean and orderly.

5   Find out as much as you can about that particular stylist – how long he or she has been in business and what products he or she prefers.

6   Enquire about the beauty school the stylist attended if you wish, but keep in mind that the work is more important than where he or she studied.

7   Evaluate the stylist's own hair to see if it's chic and healthy-looking.

8   Note whether the stylist asks appropriate questions about your hair history and how much time you're willing to spend styling your hair.

9   Consider asking for a new haircut, if you're a risk-taker, and letting the stylist do his or her best work.

### ✳ Tips

Plan ahead – a skilled stylist may book several weeks in advance.

If you're looking for a stylist to do your wedding, he or she will most likely charge for a consultation because your hair requires complete styling at that time so you can see how it will look on your wedding day. This amount is like a down payment that the stylist will subtract from the bill for the big day.

## 727 Choose a Flattering Hairstyle

If you are a woman who knows what she wants, you will make the job of the hairstylist easier. Use these guidelines to help the stylist create the look that's best for you.

### ⊙ Steps

1 Tie your hair back, if necessary, and examine your face shape in front of a mirror. Decide if your face is oval, long, square, round or heart-shaped.

2 Show off an oval face – egg-shaped and balanced on top and bottom, and widely considered ideal. Since any type of hairstyle flatters this face, explore a variety of looks.

3 Make a long face look shorter with hair that sits above the shoulders. Long layers work well, as does a fringe. Since a centre parting elongates the face, use a side parting instead.

4 Choose curvy hairstyles to soften your face if it's square, with a wide forehead, wide cheeks and an angular chin. Wearing layers around your jawline frames your face and can mask a strong, angled chin. Avoid sharp, straight lines.

5 Elongate a round face – full, with a small chin, wide cheeks and small cheekbones – with longer hair that extends below your chin. Layers on top add volume and height; layers around the cheeks narrow your face. Avoid a fringe and chin-length styles.

6 A heart-shaped face has a wide forehead that angles down to a small chin. Try shoulder-length hair, adding layers from the chin down. Curl or flip out these layers to create a fuller bottom that balances your small chin. A chin-length bob also works well. Avoid any look that adds fullness to the top and tapers down to wisps on the bottom.

### ✻ Tips

In addition to face shape, consider your hair texture when deciding on a hairstyle. A long hairstyle can render fine hair flat and difficult to manage. A shorter cut adds more body. Wavy hair looks nice in chunky layers, and thick hair is suited to soft, textured layers.

Although most hairstylists learn the above guidelines, some do not choose hairstyles this way. Ask during the consultation if your hairstylist will help you choose a style based on your face shape.

## 728 Blow-Dry Hair Straight

Want to calm the frizzies or straighten your curls for a day? All you need is a round brush, a blow drier, some hair products and about 30 minutes.

### ⊙ Steps

1 Towel-dry your just-washed hair.

2 Apply a heat protectant to your hair, paying special attention to the ends.

3 Place a 10p-sized dollop of straightening balm in your palm. Rub your palms together to distribute the product in your hands, then massage it evenly throughout your hair.

4 Comb through your hair with your fingers while gently blow-drying it on a low setting. This removes excess water.

5 Pull your hair into three sections, two at the sides and one at the back. Clip the two sides up.

6 Select a small portion of the hair from the unclipped section.

### ✻ Tips

Always point the dryer down as you are blow-drying the hair; blowing hair upward can make it frizzy.

Tame flyaway hair with an anti-frizz serum or pomade. Place a few drops in your hand, rub gently to distribute it, then apply it to your hair according to the product instructions.

7   Using a thick, round brush and beginning at the roots, gently pull the brush through the hair to the ends while you blow-dry it. Pull the hair away from your head, stretching and straightening it as you go.

8   First pull the brush through the underside of your hair so that you expose it directly to the heat of the dryer. Once that area is mostly dry, switch to the top of the hair.

9   Keep the tension consistent and evenly distribute heat over the section of hair you're working on. This ensures uniform hair texture and prevents overdrying of certain areas.

10  Continue with the other sections of damp hair.

## Things You'll Need

❑ towel

❑ heat protectant

❑ straightening balm

❑ hair dryer

❑ hair clips

❑ round brush

---

# Make Dreadlocks                                729

Dreadlocks, or dreads, are a cool hairstyle for some, a spiritual pursuit or political statement for others. If you have the right kind of hair, these steps will put a new twist into your locks.

## ◉ Steps

1   Consider that dreads work best on those with curly or very kinky hair. If you have thin, straight or wavy hair, you may want to give yourself a home perm with very thin rods. The perm will impart the needed texture.

2   Stop using conditioner a week to ten days before you begin the process. Rinse your hair with a vinegar-and-water solution the day you plan to start making your dreads. This solution – about 1 tbsp. vinegar mixed with 1 l (1³/₄ pt) water – will remove any residue or build-up that may impede the process.

3   Begin with dry hair. Take a portion of hair about 2.5 cm (1 in) square at the roots. Twist the hair tightly.

4   Pin the rest of your hair back with hair clips or put it in a rubber band so you can concentrate on one portion at a time. Comb the section of twisted hair, beginning at the root and moving to the ends and then back to the scalp again. People with a great deal of texture in their hair might find that their hair stays in that tangled position after twisting and some combing, while those with less texture will have to comb quite a bit.

5   Add a dab of dread styling wax, beeswax or pomade to each section after combing, then retwist it. Wax will mould your dreads and help each lock stay twisted.

6   Secure the end of each dread with a rubber band, leaving some hair poking out. This step holds the twist and eventually gives your locks rounded ends.

7   Complete the twisting process on your entire head. Depending on your lifestyle or time frame, you might twist a few portions a day or your entire head in one sitting. Enlist the help of friends to get to the back parts of your head.

8   Twist, comb and wax on a regular basis to get your dreads to hold their shape. Remember that this hairstyle requires a lot of maintenance, so work on it while you watch television, while you listen to music or whenever you have a free moment.

## ✳ Tips

Look for a fine-tooth metal comb or back comb. With the amount of combing you'll need to do, plastic combs may not hold up under the pressure.

Hair wax or beeswax helps secure your dreads, but it may also dry out your hair and scalp and attract dust and dirt. Look for styling waxes or pomades specifically made for dreads.

Wait a few weeks after the initial process before washing your hair.

Avoid towels, hair bands and bandanas made out of materials that shed: terry cloth, flannel or combed cotton. They will leave little particles embedded in your dreads.

## Things You'll Need

❑ 1 tbsp. vinegar

❑ hair clips or rubber bands

❑ fine-tooth metal comb or back comb

❑ dread styling wax, beeswax or pomade

9   Exercise patience. A full head of dreadlocks takes time and commitment. They will not appear overnight. In fact, it might take a few months until you're satisfied with your entire head.

---

## 730  Conceal Hair Loss

Both men and women can be subject to hair loss. Although you can't do much to prevent it, you *can* take steps to hide it.

### ⊙ Steps

1   Consult with your doctor or a dermatologist before considering any method to conceal hair loss.

2   Think about wearing a hat or bandana, when appropriate, or even a toupee or hairpiece. You can get a hairpiece made to fit your remaining hair or bald head and wear it even during swimming and other athletic activities. However, in addition to the initial cost of the hairpiece, you often have to pay for a plan, which involves payments for maintaining hairpieces over the years.

3   Conceal thinning hair with hair weaves or extensions, available for people of all ethnicities. See your hairstylist for more information.

4   Try one of the products that help to regrow hair. Two popular ones are minoxidil topical (Regaine), available over the counter, and finasteride (Propecia), available on prescription. Results vary widely for Regaine, which you apply to the scalp, and Propecia, which is an oral medication.

5   Consider hair transplants. This surgical procedure takes healthy hair from one part of your head and transplants it to a bald area. Keep in mind that a qualified dermatologist experienced in this area must perform the procedure.

6   Investigate other forms of surgery, such as scalp reduction, which involves removing the bald part of your scalp and pulling the remaining portions together, and flap surgery, which involves pulling a receding hairline forwards.

### ✱ Tips

Aside from the products mentioned, no creams, lotions, herbs or other over-the-counter products have been proved to increase hair growth or reduce hair loss.

Avoid hair transplants in the early stages of baldness – you may look unnatural if you lose more hair down the line.

### ⚠ Warning

Always follow your doctor's advice concerning medication and surgery. Inform your doctor about any medication you take regularly, and find out about side effects and interactions.

---

## 731  Dye Away the Greys

If you're not ready to accept greying hair, consider colouring it to hang on to your natural shade.

### ⊙ Steps

1   Consult your hairstylist and discuss your plans to colour your hair. Get suggestions for at-home products, natural vs. chemical treatments, and after-treatment hair care.

2   Consider how much of your hair is grey.

### ✱ Tip

Going to a salon is easier, but it costs a lot more than doing it yourself.

**How to Do *(Just About)* Everything**

3   Use a semi-permanent dye if your hair is close to 20 per cent grey. Colour will begin to fade after about 6 to12 washings, so hair will require frequent recolouring if you shampoo daily.

4   Opt for longer-lasting semi-permanent colours if you're up to 50 per cent grey; they'll last for approximately 24 to 28 washes.

5   Use a permanent dye if most of your locks have made the change. To test the colour, cut off strands of hair from the back of your neck to get a lock about 5 mm (¼ in) wide and 25 mm (1 in) long, and bind one end with tape. Mix together a small amount of the hair-colour solution according to the instructions and place the hair in it. Check the hair after the least amount of time recommended. Keep checking until it has reached the desired colour, and then note how long this took.

6   Look for colours that closely match the natural shade of your hair. Consider a shade darker than your natural colour if you're mostly grey, as the colour may appear a shade lighter than indicated, and may fade in the sun. Touch up roots as needed, and dye again by the third month.

7   Begin your transition on a Saturday morning, if possible, so you have time to adjust to your new look before heading back to work, and so that co-workers won't notice an abrupt change as readily. Give yourself plenty of time to complete the process, as it may seem awkward at first.

8   Spread an old towel over the bathroom counter and put on an old T-shirt. Wearing fitted rubber gloves, begin your colour process. Follow the directions exactly as indicated in the colouring kit.

9   Set the timer and enjoy a book or magazine while you wait. Rinse as indicated in the product instructions.

⚠ **Warnings**

Some colour-enhancing products may irritate the scalp, so test new hair products by applying them to a small patch of skin on the back of your neck.

If you're pregnant, get your doctor's OK before proceeding with any hair-colour treatment.

If you have applied henna to your hair, remember that you cannot perm it or use a chemical colour over it.

Avoid chlorine and salt water for a few days after colouring your hair, since it may alter the colour.

Avoid getting solution into your eyes at all costs. Rinse well with tepid water and get medical help should this occur.

## Make Colour Last Between Dye Jobs    732

Maintaining the colour is an ongoing enterprise for people who dye their hair. Here's how to make your colour last longer – and how to cover up those troublesome roots.

### ☉ Steps

1   Opt for a colour-boosting shampoo and conditioner every other day until you achieve the colour you want, and then stop. Your salon will have good choices, or you can try a chemist, which may sell discounted products. Ask your hairstylist to recommend a brand.

2   Use a colour-safe shampoo and conditioner when you wash your hair, once you've achieved the colour you want with colour-boosting shampoo and conditioner. You can buy all of these at beauty stores or chemists.

3   Think about a hair sunscreen, which can protect your hair colour from fading. Look for it in spray-on hair protectants.

4   Try smoothing your hair back with gel – this darkens the hair so colours blend together – and using a headband to conceal roots.

⚠ **Warnings**

Some colour-enhancing products can irritate the scalp, so test all new hair products by applying them to a small patch of skin on the back of your neck.

If you're pregnant, get your doctor's OK before proceeding with any hair-colour treatment.

Avoid chlorine and salt water for a few days after colouring your hair, since it may alter the colour.

## 733 Trim a Moustache

There are many ways to groom a moustache. Decide how you want yours to look before following these instructions.

### ◉ Steps

1 Wet your moustache slightly.

2 Use a fine-tooth moustache comb to brush the hair down.

3 Clip the hair on your moustache's outer edges with a pair of thin scissors. Remember to clip conservatively.

4 Snip across the bottom of the moustache.

5 Trim the body of the moustache to achieve the desired evenness and bushiness, and to clip errant hairs.

6 Touch up the top of the moustache with a razor until you have the desired line. If you have an unusual moustache, such as a pencil or handlebar moustache, use the razor more or less as appropriate. Take care not to shave off the top of the moustache accidentally.

7 Comb again with the moustache comb.

### ✱ Tips

Work carefully. Clipping even a small amount of hair can change the appearance of a moustache greatly.

A beard trimmer is an excellent tool for reducing the bushiness.

For fancier styles, use moustache wax to shape or groom.

## 734 Trim the Back of Your Neck

You can solve one of life's irritating little problems with a few quick strokes of a razor.

### ◉ Steps

1 Loosen your collar or remove your shirt.

2 If you're using an electric trimmer, set it on its closest setting and turn it on. If you're using a razor, apply a small amount of shaving cream to the back of your neck.

3 Begin trimming, using two mirrors if possible. Working in vertical lines, run the trimmer up the back of your neck from the base to the hairline. If you're using a razor, shave down in short strokes from the hairline to the base of the neck.

4 Even out the hairline as necessary.

5 Wipe off the shaving cream or brush off the clippings.

### ✱ Tips

Remember to shave all the way around to the area of the neck behind the ears.

Consider enlisting a friend to help you.

## Shave Your Face

Shaving makes a man look well groomed, and is also a terrific way for an older man to trim a few years off his age. Here's how to do it correctly using a razor blade.

### ◉ Steps

1   Select a razor with a sharp blade; blunt blades can cause nicks and cuts.

2   Wet your face with warm water. You may want to hold a hot flannel to your face for a few moments to open the pores and soften the hair. This will also remove excess oil, which could interfere with the closeness of your shave.

3   Fill the washbasin halfway with water.

4   Make sure you have a sharp blade. Replace the used blade in your usual razor if it's blunt.

5   Squirt a dollop of shaving cream or other lubricant into your hand and apply it to your beard with an upward circular motion. The amount you use may vary depending on the thickness of your beard, but you should cover the area uniformly. Or lather up shaving soap with a wet shaving brush and apply it liberally.

6   Shave downwards, the way your whiskers grow, from your sideburns towards your jaw using long, even strokes. Apply light but firm pressure, pulling your skin taut before each stroke.

7   Rinse your razor with warm water after every stroke or two to keep it from getting clogged with hair.

8   Shave the area around your chin. Shave upwards as necessary to make the area smooth. When shaving under your chin, pull the razor from your throat area towards your chin.

9   Shave your upper lip, keeping the skin tight by stretching your lip down over your front teeth.

10  Wash off any excess shaving cream and examine your face for straggling hairs. Check the edge of your jaw, around your ears, and near your lips and nostrils for missed hairs. Go back with the razor to shave anything you missed.

11  If you cut yourself, dab the wound with a styptic pencil. It will sting slightly, but the bleeding will stop. A touch of toilet tissue can also help. Apply some aloe vera to the wound after the bleeding has stopped.

12  Reapply the hot flannel to help soothe your open pores if your skin is feeling irritated.

13  Drain and wash out the basin and rinse your face with cold water.

### ✱ Tips

An electric shaver does not give as close a shave as a razor blade. However, some men prefer electric shavers since no lathering is required.

Wait at least 15 to 20 minutes after you get up in the morning before you shave. This will allow any puffiness in your face to subside, making shaving easier.

Shave the areas of thickest growth (usually the chin and upper lip) last so your shaving lubricant has more time to soften the hair.

### ⚠ Warnings

Dull blades can irritate your skin and cause shaving mishaps.

Women should never shave facial hair, as it will grow back stubbly and not soft (see 737 "Get Rid of Unwanted Hair").

### Things You'll Need

❑ hot flannel

❑ razor

❑ shaving cream or shaving soap

❑ styptic pencil

## 736 | Shave Your Legs

Many women dread the return of summer, when their leg-shaving skills (or lack thereof) are put on display. Below are some helpful shaving tips to get you through the season nick-free.

### ⊙ Steps

1  Shave in a warm shower or bath, if possible.

2  Wait a few minutes before starting to let the leg hair soften. If you take only showers, wait until the end of the shower to shave.

3  Sit on the ledge in your shower, if possible. If your shower has no place to sit, raise one leg against the wall of the shower and balance carefully.

4  Apply a small amount of shaving cream, rubbing it into a thick lather and spreading it over your leg. Avoid using soap in place of shaving cream, as it will dry out your skin.

5  Place the razor at the base of your ankle and pull gently up over your entire leg. If you experience severe razor burn, try shaving in the same direction as the hair growth. You may not get as clean a shave, but you'll avoid raising red bumps.

6  Rinse the blade between every stroke, and be sure to keep the razor wet while you're shaving.

7  Shave the entire leg until you've removed all the shaving cream.

8  Rinse.

9  Repeat for the other leg.

10 Pat dry and moisturise.

### ✳ Tip

Having your legs waxed at a salon is a nice alternative that also reduces overall hair growth. One drawback is that you'll have to wait for the hair to grow out before you can wax again – this can take six to eight weeks.

### ⚠ Warnings

Blunt blades can cause razor burn on sensitive skin.

Shaving areas where bone is close to the skin surface, such as ankles and knees, can result in painful cuts and nicks. If you cut your leg while shaving, get out of the bath quickly, as the hot water will increase blood flow. Dab the wound lightly with a styptic pencil. It will sting slightly, but the bleeding will stop. A touch of toilet tissue can also do the trick.

## 737 | Get Rid of Unwanted Hair

Sick to death of the moustache shadow under your ladylike nose? Want your legs to feel silky smooth for that special someone? You have options.

### ⊙ Steps

1  Consider bleaching. Although this does not get rid of unwanted hair, it does lighten hair to a soft blond hue, rendering moustaches almost invisible. Some women also bleach the hair on their arms.

2  Try depilatories – cream-based products you apply on top of unwanted hair. Depilatories, popular for the bikini area, come with specific instructions for how long to leave the cream on. When you rinse away the depilatory, the unwanted hair should wash away with the cream. However, results vary widely.

3  Use that old standby – shaving. It's fast and easy, but the hair grows back quickly. Women should never shave a moustache, as it will grow back stubbly and not soft.

### ✳ Tips

Use sunscreen on skin you've treated with a depilatory cream.

Keep in mind that stubble cannot be waxed or sugared.

4   Consider plucking, which is effective for small patches of hair. Keep in mind that repeated tweezing of the same hairs over the years can damage the hair roots enough to result in permanent hair removal, so be careful when tweezing eyebrows – if styles change, you may not get your old brows back.

5   Evaluate waxing – especially popular for eyebrows and the bikini area. A mixture of hot oil, rosin and paraffin is spread over unwanted hair. Once the wax cools, it's ripped off, along with the unwanted hairs. Though this method can be uncomfortable, the advantage is that the hair doesn't return for several weeks.

6   Investigate sugaring, a technique devised by the ancient Egyptians that uses all-natural ingredients. A paste of sugar and water is applied over unwanted hair. When the sugar mix dries, it's yanked off, along with the hair. As with waxing, the advantage is that the hair doesn't return for several weeks; the discomfort is similar to that of pulling off a plaster with hair underneath.

7   Look into electrolysis, which involves removal of each hair with an electric current and a fine needle. You must continue electrolysis for several months or even years to remove all unwanted hair, and the process can be quite painful.

8   Investigate laser removal of unwanted hair. The light emitted from the laser vaporises the pigment located in the hair follicles, destroying or disabling several hair follicles at a time. However, it may not result in permanent hair removal.

---

## Prevent Hangnails    738

When your nail cuticles become dry or rough, painful and unsightly hangnails often form. Pamper your nails to keep them healthy and free of hangnails.

### ⊙ Steps

1   Give yourself regular manicures: clean and trim your nails, brush your nails with a manicure brush, and push back cuticles with a cuticle stick. This removes excess skin that may later form hangnails.

2   Use a cuticle moisturiser as needed throughout the day to keep your nails and cuticles moisturised and strong. Try an exfoliating lotion if your skin is particularly dry or roughened.

3   Wear rubber gloves when washing dishes or doing housework. Hot water and various cleaning agents can dry out your hands and encourage hangnails. If possible, avoid soaking nails and cuticles in water, as this can weaken them.

4   Don canvas gloves when gardening or doing other tasks that can roughen and dry out your hands, causing cuticles and nails to crack.

5   Fight the urge to bite fingernails or hangnails. Such habits can aggravate the nail area and cause hangnails to bleed.

### ✳ Tips

If you have extremely dry or rough hands, try applying moisturiser at night, then donning cotton gloves when you sleep.

Cut hangnails as soon as you see them.

### Things You'll Need

❑ manicure scissors or nail clippers

❑ manicure brush

❑ cuticle stick

❑ cuticle moisturiser

❑ exfoliating lotion

❑ gloves (rubber, canvas, cotton)

---

### 739 | Pluck Your Eyebrows

Tweezing your eyebrows is the most dramatic way to change your face without make-up or surgery. It can make your eyes look larger and give your face a clean, polished look.

#### ◉ Steps

1 Sit near a window to get the best light.

2 Wash the area thoroughly so it's not oily.

3 Decide what shape you want for your eyebrows. Styles change: it may help to flip through fashion magazines for ideas.

4 Draw a brow line on your eyebrow with an eyebrow pencil to serve as a guide. Follow the brow's natural line by conforming to the curve of your upper eyelid.

5 Pull the skin at the outer end of the eyebrow taut against the brow bone, and use the brow bone as an additional guide.

6 Use a pair of angled eyebrow tweezers to pluck the hairs below the brow; never shape your brow by plucking above it. Pluck only one hair at a time.

7 Start plucking in the middle of the eyebrow and pluck towards the outer end; then go back to the middle and pluck towards the nose. Your brows should extend a little beyond each corner of your eye.

8 Use a cotton wool ball or pad soaked in pure tea tree oil or witch hazel to soothe your plucked brows.

#### ✱ Tips

Consider having your brows waxed once professionally to get exactly the shape you want. You can then pluck the strays as they grow in.

Habitual plucking may make some hairs stop growing permanently, so pluck with caution.

#### Things You'll Need

❑ eyebrow pencil

❑ eyebrow tweezers

❑ cotton wool balls or pads

❑ pure tea tree oil or witch hazel

---

### 740 | Alleviate Puffy Eyes

Late nights, allergies, high salt intake or general stress can cause the unsightly phenomenon of puffy eyes. Try any or all of these remedies.

#### ◉ Steps

1 Splash your entire face with the coldest water you can stand immediately after you wake up. Use either cold tap water or a mixture of cold water and ice cubes in a large bowl or tub. Splash your face for up to five minutes, if possible.

2 Prepare two tea bags by soaking them in water, wringing them out and chilling them in the refrigerator or freezer. Once they are chilled, lie down and place the bags on closed eyelids for five to ten minutes.

3 Cut two slices off a cold cucumber, each approximately 1 cm (½ in) thick. Place a slice on each eyelid for five minutes.

4 Drink lots of water. Puffy eyes often indicate water retention, which you can alleviate by drinking plenty of liquids; this flushes excess salt from your system.

5 Use an aloe vera-based eye-soothing gel or cream.

#### ✱ Tip

Remove contact lenses each night before bed to avoid puffiness caused by lens irritation and drying.

#### ⚠ Warnings

Don't use a haemorrhoid cream near the eye area – it's unsafe and won't diminish puffiness.

If the problem persists, see your doctor. You may be reacting to dust, pets, medication or other irritants, or you may have an underlying medical condition.

## Apply Make-Up

Try to follow the same basic routine whenever you apply your make-up. Experiment to find out what works best for you.

### ⊙ Steps

1. Wash your face and apply moisturiser (see 751 "Care for Dry Skin" or 752 "Care for Oily Skin" if your skin is dry or oily).

2. Apply a concealer that is one shade lighter than your foundation. Dot it on over any blemishes or under-eye circles and blend with your finger-tips or a make-up sponge. If your concealer tends to cake, apply eye cream first.

3. Choose foundation that matches your skin tone exactly. Apply it in dots over the central part of your face, then blend it out with a make-up sponge or your fingertips until it covers your entire face (see 742 "Choose Foundation").

4. Use a loose or pressed powder to keep foundation and concealer on longer. Use pressed powder to touch up when you're away from home.

5. Do your eyebrows next. Use powdered eyebrow shadow on brows instead of pencil, which can often look unnatural. Apply it with a hard, slanted brush.

6. Choose three colours of eye shadow: light, medium and dark. Use the dark only to line your upper eyelid, in a fairly thin line along the upper lashes. Use the medium shade for the crease and the lightest shade for the area under the eyebrow. There are many variations on eye shadow application techniques (see 744 "Apply Eye Shadow" for more ideas).

7. Apply eyeliner. Use a cake eyeliner with a damp, thin liner brush, or an eyeliner pencil, and line the lower lid below the lashes. Line only the outer two-thirds of the lower lid, or all the way across if you're trying to achieve a darker look. Line all the way across the upper lid (just above the lash line and as close to the lashes as possible), or start the line where your lashes begin (see 745 "Apply Eyeliner").

8. Apply mascara to upper and lower lashes, in two thin coats to avoid clumpiness. Choose brown mascara if your colouring is fair; black or brown-black works well for darker colouring. Or try a coloured mascara such as navy or plum for fun, but don't go too bright if you want to be taken seriously (see 746 "Apply Mascara").

9. Smile to find the apples of your cheeks, and apply blusher to the apples or below, whichever you prefer. If you have to blend in blusher, it's too bright.

10. Choose a lipstick colour that's suited to your skin tone and that's perfect for your day look. You can mix colours and textures to suit your moods and your outfits (see 748 "Choose a Lipstick Colour").

11. Line your lips *after* applying lipstick, not before. Avoid combining very dark lip liner and pale lipstick.

### ✴ Tips

Choose brighter or darker tones for a stronger look.

Clean make-up brushes by gently washing them in warm water and mild shampoo. Air-dry them overnight.

Don't skimp on make-up tools. High-quality tools make applica-tion easier and faster.

If you decide to curl your eye-lashes, do this just before apply-ing mascara – never after. Insert your eyelashes into the curler, squeeze just once, and hold for a few seconds.

### ⚠ Warning

Bacteria can grow in older cos-metics, which can lead to infec-tions. Be on the safe side: throw out anything that's seems old, especially mascara, and avoid sharing products with others.

### Things You'll Need

- ❑ concealer
- ❑ foundation
- ❑ loose or pressed powder
- ❑ eyebrow shadow
- ❑ light, medium and dark eye shadow
- ❑ eyeliner
- ❑ mascara
- ❑ blusher
- ❑ lipstick
- ❑ lip liner

## 742 | Choose Foundation

To even out your skin's appearance and create the illusion of flawless skin, head to the cosmetics counter. The right foundation can do wonders.

### ◎ Steps

1 Consider your skin type. If you have oily skin, stick with an oil-free formula. If you have drier skin, select a creamier formula that offers moisturising benefits.

2 Decide what type of look you'd like to achieve. Foundations can offer sheer to heavy coverage and finishes that range from satiny to matt.

3 Test the colours of your preferred formula on your jawline, which offers the truest facial colouring. Any foundation will look slightly darker in the bottle, so keep this in mind when assessing your options.

4 Blend in the foundation gently with a make-up sponge. The foundation should disappear into your skin. If you find you're between shades, blend two colours together, or keep looking for a brand that offers the perfect shade.

5 Bring a hand mirror along so you can view your options in natural light.

6 Look for yellow-toned foundation or tinted moisturiser if you're white or Asian; if you have an olive complexion, opt for foundation or tinted moisturisers with yellow-orange undertones. If you are black, it's a good idea to use light, medium and dark shades of foundation to allow for different gradations of colour on different parts of your face.

7 Remember that you have plenty of options to choose from, so if you don't find a good colour match, keep looking.

### ✱ Tips

For sheer, no-nonsense coverage, consider using a tinted moisturiser.

Look for the many extras some foundation formulas offer, such as sunscreen or ingredients that hide fine lines.

### Things You'll Need

❑ foundation

❑ make-up sponge

❑ hand mirror

## 743 | Conceal Freckles

If you're absolutely certain you don't love your unique distinguishing marks, experiment with these tips and techniques.

### ◎ Steps

1 Try over-the-counter skin-bleaching agents to lighten your freckles, but know that you can't erase them entirely.

2 Apply tinted moisturiser or foundation, if you prefer light coverage, in a shade slightly darker than your natural skin tone to blend in and downplay your freckles.

3 Cover yourself in sunblock with an SPF rating of 15 or higher every time you go outside, even in cloudy or overcast weather. As your skin tans, so do your freckles. Self-tanners will make your skin appear darker, but they will also darken your freckles.

4 Talk to a dermatologist if you want to try stronger measures intended to eliminate freckles. Ask about the pros and cons of acid or chemical peels, lasers and various bleaching agents available only on prescription.

### ✱ Tips

Protect your skin from sun to avoid a new crop of freckles. Freckles are inherited; limiting your sun exposure is the only way to prevent them. That's why you probably don't have any freckles on your bottom.

Learn the difference between moles and freckles, and keep an eye on the growth and shape of moles. Let your doctor know about any significant changes.

## Apply Eye Shadow 744

Sweep a touch of shadow over your lids to accent your eyes. There are many good techniques for applying eye shadow; here's one that works well.

### ⊚ Steps

#### Application on Entire Lid

1 Prime the eyelids by dusting them with a small amount of loose powder.

2 Select a light base eye shadow. Using an eye shadow brush, sweep it across your entire lid, from brow to lash line.

3 Use a medium-toned shade to cover your lower lids.

4 Contour the crease of your eyelid with a dark shade, using a smaller eye shadow brush. This colour can also work as an eyeliner (see the next section for instructions).

5 Blend shadow by stroking the lid gently with an eye shadow brush. Don't use your finger – you could wipe off the eye shadow entirely.

6 Use a cosmetic puff and a little pressed powder to tone down heavy eye shadow. Shake any excess powder off the puff, then press it gently on your lid.

#### Eye Shadow to Line the Eyes

1 Choose a medium or dark eye shadow colour to line your eyes.

2 Use a small, flat, angled brush for the application.

3 Stroke the brush over the eye shadow.

4 Start at the inside edge of your upper lid. Angle the brush so that the longest tip follows the shorter end as the brush moves across your lash line. Bring the brush to the outer corner of the eye.

5 Create a more dramatic line by wetting the brush before stroking it through the shadow. Mist a small amount of water onto the brush, or dab it into a few drops of water and proceed with the line. The shadow may feel wet as you draw your line, but it will dry quickly.

### ✱ Tips

Before applying shadow with the brush, always tap any excess off the brush so you don't scatter loose powder on your face.

Apply eye shadow before putting on eyeliner and mascara.

### ⚠ Warnings

Don't share eye make-up or tools – you can unknowingly transfer eye infections such as conjunctivitis.

If you get eye shadow in your eyes, flush them gently with tepid water.

### Things You'll Need

❑ loose powder

❑ light, medium and dark eye shadow

❑ eye shadow brushes

❑ eyeliner brush

❑ powder puff

❑ pressed powder

## Apply Eyeliner 745

Shape and define your eyes with eyeliner after you've applied eye shadow and before applying mascara. Whether you choose a soft line or a dramatic stroke, eyeliner draws attention.

### ⊚ Steps

1 Choose an eyeliner appropriate for your eye colour. Brown, navy and charcoal accent light eyes well, while brown and plum shades flatter brown eyes. Make sure your liner complements the colour of your eye shadow.

### ✱ Tips

You may find eyeliner, particularly the liquid version, difficult and messy the first few times. Practise and have patience.

2   Consider the type of look you're after. Pencil eyeliner gives your eyes soft definition, while liquid versions offer precision and drama. You can also moisten dark eye shadow and apply it with a small, flat brush.

3   Prepare a cake liner or a dark eye shadow by applying a small amount of water to your brush. Or, if you're using a pencil eyeliner, ensure that you've sharpened the pencil adequately.

4   Move the wet brush gently through your cake liner or dark shadow. Hold the brush or pencil as you would hold a pen.

5   Tilt your head back slightly and bring your eyes to a half-open state. This creates a good angle for application, while allowing you to see what you're doing.

6   Draw a line across the upper lid just above the lashes, from the inside corner to the outside corner of the eye. If you're using liquid liner, allow it to dry before opening your eyes all the way, or the colour may transfer into the crease of your eye.

7   If you used a brush or a pencil, soften the look by gently smudging the line with your brush, a cotton bud or your finger.

8   Line the lower lids. Moving from the outside edge inwards, draw a line on the outer two-thirds of the lid or more, depending on the look you're going for. Your line should be slightly thicker at the outside corner, becoming thinner as it moves in towards your nose. Using your brush or pencil, lightly stroke the area. If using a liquid liner, apply it in one smooth stroke. Apply less colour so your eyes don't appear panda-like.

Wash brushes regularly with make-up remover or a mild shampoo.

## ⚠ Warning

Lining the inside of the lower lid is not recommended – it may cause eye infections, and it greatly increases the risk of getting make-up in your eye.

## Things You'll Need

❑ eyeliner

❑ eyeliner brush

❑ cotton buds

---

## 746 | Apply Mascara

Mascara – one of the most popular beauty items – defines and brings colour to the lashes, and highlights and dramatises eyes. Different formulas can enhance your lashes in different ways.

### ⊙ Steps

1   Consider the types of mascara and select one appropriate for your lashes and the occasion. You have a choice of lengthening, thickening, long-wearing, conditioning and waterproof formulas, among others. For day, you might decide to add length, while a night on the town may require a long-wearing or thickening formula.

2   Select a colour. If you have blond or red lashes, opt for brown mascara. Darker-lashed women can consider brown for a casual look, and black or brown-black for more pronounced or dramatic lashes.

3   Curl your lashes with an eyelash curler, if desired, and apply all other eye make-up prior to your mascara.

4   Remove the wand from the tube in one pull. Pumping the mascara will push air into the tube, potentially drying out the formula and introducing bacteria into it.

5   Begin with the underside of your upper lashes, moving the brush slowly upwards towards the tips of your lashes. Always hold the wand parallel

### ✳ Tips

Contact lens wearers should stick to waterproof mascara formulas, as they break down more slowly, minimising the chance of any flakes getting into the eyes.

Always remove eye make-up thoroughly before going to bed. This will keep lashes healthier and prevent any mascara from getting into your eyes during the night.

Apply mascara after eye shadow and eyeliner.

to your eyelid. Roll the brush slowly on the upward stroke to promote separation of the lashes.

6 Allow the first coat of mascara to dry before applying the second coat in the same manner.

7 Use an eyelash comb to separate the wet lashes. Also blot the lashes with tissue paper if necessary to remove excess mascara.

8 Use less mascara for the lower lashes. Begin where the lashes meet the rim of the lower eyelid, and gently stroke downwards.

9 Remove any stray mascara around the eye with a cotton bud dipped in a small amount of eye make-up remover.

### Things You'll Need

- ❏ mascara
- ❏ eyelash curler
- ❏ eyelash comb
- ❏ cotton buds
- ❏ eye make-up remover

---

## Use False Eyelashes 747

Go for glamour with false eyelashes. Whether you apply a few singles to create a subtle change or full lashes for optimal drama, practise first – this is a tricky manoeuvre.

### ⊙ Steps

1 Decide what look you're seeking. A full set of false eyelashes adds high drama to your evening appearance or returns the eyelashes that may have disappeared due to illness. Little clumps of fake lashes on the outside corners of your eyes create a subtle, sophisticated glamour.

2 Choose a colour that complements the occasion. For evening, stick to black (or dark brown if you have pale lashes), which adds drama without requiring mascara. In the daytime, go dark brown (light brown or blond if you have pale lashes) for a natural look.

3 Check their length. Full lashes should follow the natural line of your own lashes. Trim them with sharp scissors to accommodate your needs.

4 Begin with clean eyes, free of make-up or debris.

5 Hold the lashes in your hand and apply a very thin line of glue or adhesive along the base; let it sit for 1 minute. Begin with a minimal amount of glue, adding more if needed.

6 Look into a mirror, either on the wall or placed on a countertop. Apply the false lashes above your eyelashes, as close to your lash line as possible, following its natural curve.

7 Adjust the lashes with your fingertips, tweezers or a toothpick.

8 If you're using lash clumps, place them at the outside corners of your upper lashes (one or two per eye should suffice). Adjust their position with a toothpick, fingers or tweezers.

9 Apply eye make-up. You may find your new lashes dramatic enough without mascara, so take a good look in the mirror first.

10 Practise a few times before your debut. This is a challenging beauty trick to master, but a dress rehearsal should make for a smash opening.

### ✳ Tips

Remove false eyelashes before you go to bed, using a warm compress or make-up remover. Never pull the lashes from your lids, as you may pull your own lashes out or rip your skin.

After wearing full lashes, soak them in eyelash-cleaning solution until the next time you wear them.

### ⚠ Warning

Never apply glue directly to your eyelids; it may get into your eyes, or you may glue your eye shut.

### Things You'll Need

- ❏ false eyelashes
- ❏ eyelash glue or adhesive
- ❏ mirror
- ❏ tweezers or a toothpick

## 748 | Choose a Lipstick Colour

Lipstick can be subtle, glamorous or flirty, adding the final touch to your day or evening make-up.

### ⊙ Steps

1   Choose a colour that complements the natural shade of your lips and skin. Plums, wines and deep reds flatter a dark skin tone, while light-brown beiges with pink or orange undertones complement a lighter skin tone. Olive skin looks good with brownish reds, light browns and raisin shades of lipstick.

2   Keep colours lighter for daytime and darker for night. Matt and cream finishes offer a subtler daytime look, while a high-gloss finish adds glamour for the evening. A sheer, natural-looking colour with a little shine also works well for daytime.

3   Experiment. Head to your local department store and ask a make-up artist to test different shades on your lips. Whenever possible, check in natural light to see how the colour really looks with your complexion.

4   Create your own shade by combining colours. If the shades you find don't completely satisfy you, mix your own colour. The easiest way to do this is by applying each colour to your lips with a lip brush, then blending with the brush on your lips.

5   Opt for a lip liner that is a shade darker than your lipstick and in the same colour family.

6   Line lips *after* applying lipstick, not before. That way you won't end up with a dark circle of lip liner after your lipstick has worn off.

### ✳ Tips

Try a coloured gloss or lip tint for a sheer hint of lip colour.

Buy the colours that look good on you – not the ones that look good in the tube.

Deep or bold lip colour complements light eye make-up, while light or nude lipstick flatters heavy eye make-up.

### Things You'll Need

❑ lipstick

❑ lip liner

## 749 | Apply Make-up to Achieve a Natural Look

This system of applying make-up for a natural look is fast and easy when you get the hang of it.

### ⊙ Steps

1   Understand that a "natural" look is one that uses colours that are right for your skin tone. How much you use, and where, depends on your personal style.

2   Make sure your concealer is yellow in tone since it mutes imperfections without adding colour, giving your skin a natural look.

3   Apply foundation that matches your skin tone. The right foundation will seem to disappear on your face. If you are black, it's a good idea to have light, medium and dark shades of your foundation to allow for different gradations of colour on different parts of your face.

4   Apply eye make-up in earthy tones – beige, brown, gold or plum for eye shadows and brown and charcoal grey for eyeliner and mascara. Skip liner or shadow entirely if you want to keep make-up light.

5   Choose a blusher colour that is close to the colour of your cheeks after you've exercised.

### ✳ Tips

Apply make-up in the order described in 741 "Apply Make-Up", and remember to clean and moisturise your face first.

Choose brighter or darker tones for a stronger, more made-up look.

Intensify your natural make-up for evening. Instead of brown, for example, go for charcoal around the eyes. Apply blusher with a brighter colour over your usual one. Make lips brighter, darker or more shimmery.

6   Select lipstick that matches your skin tone. Try on colours when you are not wearing any other make-up. The lipstick colour should not stand out too much.

7   Blend make-up well. For foundation, blend out to your hair and jawline with a make-up sponge until the foundation vanishes. Blend eye shadow by stroking your lid gently with a clean brush. Don't use your finger – you could wipe off the shadow entirely

8   Make sure to check your make-up – particularly the foundation – in daylight before you go out because natural light helps you spot heavy, unnatural make-up application.

9   Enhance contrast between eyes and lips when intensifying natural make-up for the evening. For example, if you opt for a strong mouth, do softer eyes, or vice versa. You run the risk of looking overdone and unnatural if you opt for heavy make-up on both your eyes and mouth.

## Remove Make-Up Thoroughly                                    750

Although you may be tempted to hop directly into bed after a long night out, discipline yourself to remove make-up first so your skin can breathe and regenerate while you sleep.

### ⊙ Steps

1   Pull your hair away from your face with a headband, if necessary, or secure it in a hair clip or ponytail holder.

2   Begin with your eye make-up. Moisten a cotton wool ball or pad with eye make-up remover and take off all traces of make-up by gently wiping each eye until the make-up dissolves.

3   Select a skin cleanser suitable for your skin type that can also remove make-up. Some soaps and cleansers don't thoroughly cleanse your skin of make-up. Check the packaging to see if the product is designed for make-up removal, or ask a make-up sales assistant for advice.

4   Splash your face with lukewarm water, the best temperature for lathering up and facilitating the breakdown of make-up.

5   Place a dollop of cleanser in the centre of one hand and rub your hands together to generate lather. Add water if necessary.

6   Apply the lather to your entire face and rub gently, concentrating on the places where you applied make-up.

7   Spend about a minute retracing your path to ensure that you've cleaned all areas.

8   Rinse your face multiple times to ensure the removal of the cleanser and make-up residue.

9   Pat your face dry with a towel.

### ✳ Tip

If your preferred skin cleanser does not break down make-up, wash your face first with a make-up remover that suits your skin type.

### ⚠ Warning

Avoid washing off eye make-up with cleanser, as it's too harsh and drying for this delicate area.

### Things You'll Need

❑ headband, hair clip or ponytail holder

❑ cotton wool balls or pads

❑ skin cleanser

❑ eye make-up remover

❑ make-up remover

## 751 Care for Dry Skin

Only a lucky few have "normal" skin; the rest of us have a dry, oily or combination variety. If dryness is your problem, read on.

### ◎ Steps

1   Remember the basics: drink at least eight glasses of water a day to keep your skin well hydrated; eat a high-quality diet rich in fruits and vegetables; and limit sun exposure.

2   Wash your face no more than twice a day with a gentle cleanser formulated for dry skin. Washing more often can dry your skin.

3   Take short baths or showers and use warm rather than hot water. Try to limit showers and baths to one per day. Use soap only where you need it, such as on your underarms and groin.

4   Add a few teaspoons of olive oil or lavender-scented oil to your bath.

5   Pat your skin dry after washing. Avoid rubbing yourself dry with a towel, which can whisk away essential oils needed for moisture.

6   Apply moisturiser while your skin is still damp. Heed the advice of many experts in choosing a moisturiser – less is more when it comes to the ingredient list.

7   Understand that moisturisers contain barriers, which keep water on the skin, and water binders, which whisk moisture from the inner layer of skin to the top layer. Look for ingredients such as glycerin, alpha hydroxy acids, urea and lactic acids (binders), combined with petrolatum, lanolin or silicone derivatives (barriers). You have a choice of hundreds of products. A dermatologist or other skin care expert may be able to advise you on your specific needs, but trial and error will probably be your best bet in finding the product that's right for you.

8   Aim for a comfortable level of humidity in your home or office. Too much heat or too much air-conditioning can rob your skin of moisture.

### ✱ Tips

Consult an allergist to find out if an allergic reaction might be causing your dry skin.

Avoid caffeine and alcohol, which cause dehydration.

Steer clear of added fragrance, preservatives and botanicals, which may irritate already dry skin.

### ⚠ Warning

Check with a doctor if you have irritated, red or scaly skin. You could have a serious condition requiring medical treatment.

## 752 Care for Oily Skin

Do you have overproductive sebaceous glands, which are responsible for oily skin? The following steps can minimise the negative effects.

### ◎ Steps

1   Stick with the basics: the experts suggest cleansing your face two or three times daily with good old soap and water. Pack a pre-moistened cleansing pad if you won't be around a wash basin throughout the day.

2   Understand that dermatologists often disagree on which types of soaps or cleansers to use – but all agree that once you find a product that works well for your skin, you should continue using it.

3   Follow the recommendations of dermatologists and shower or bathe in tepid rather than steaming-hot water. Hot water can strip your skin of needed moisture, while cold water can shock your skin.

### ⚠ Warning

A spotty skin may indicate that you have acne or another skin condition. See your doctor for medical advice and guidance.

4   Avoid using cleansers that tend to overdry skin. This paradoxically causes your skin to produce even more oil than usual.

5   Use only non-comedogenic moisturisers and sunscreen products – this means they're oil-free and won't clog pores.

6   Talk to your doctor about a class of drugs called retinoids, which reduce production in oil glands and shrink their size.

7   Keep in mind that oil glands are very sensitive – stimuli such as hormones, heat and (some say) fatty food can trigger them.

8   Remember that your efforts to keep your oily skin clear can only go so far, as some studies indicate that oily skin is hereditary.

---

## Treat Pimples 753

Although many people suffer from this condition only during the teenage years, pimples can occur throughout adulthood, depending on your hormonal activity, heredity and hygiene.

### ⊙ Steps

1   Resist the urge to attack when these plugged sebaceous glands pop up. In other words, don't pop your pimples – this can cause infections and even scarring.

2   Keep in mind that a combination of hormonal activity, a build-up of bacteria and the shedding of dead skin cells causes pimples. Do what you can to prevent them by establishing a skin-care routine appropriate for your skin type.

3   Have patience. It could take up to one month for a blemish to disappear completely. The less you poke at it, the better.

4   Buy an antibacterial, oil-free concealer that can blend the redness of the pimple into your own skin colour. Green shades tend to offset redness the best. (This might not be an option for those who don't wear make-up.)

5   Try a facial mud mask. This may shrink a pimple.

6   Realise that despite the happy teenagers in the commercials, medication that you apply directly to pimples doesn't do much more than dry out the top layer of skin covering the pimples. These products don't provide a long-term cure.

7   If you are going to break the rules by "extracting the blemish" – beautician-speak for popping your pimple – wash your hands, then lightly squeeze the top of the pimple with a tissue or cotton bud. Clean the area thoroughly when you've finished. If nothing happens, leave the pimple alone until it's ready to pop.

### ✳ Tip

If you're desperate (you get an unsightly blemish two days before your wedding, perhaps), consult a dermatologist about receiving a shot of cortisone to eliminate a pimple.

### ⚠ Warnings

Pimples can indicate the presence of acne, a chronic skin disease. If you have recurring pimples, talk to a doctor or dermatologist about acne medication. You may be prescribed antibiotics, certain brands of birth control pills, or even Roaccutane for severe acne.

Consider carefully before using Roaccutane. Although this is the only truly long-term solution for severe acne, it can have serious side effects and is known to cause serious birth defects when taken during pregnancy. Sexually active women who use Roaccutane should use two forms of birth control.

## 754 | Brush Your Teeth

We do it every day without thinking too much, but here are some important points to remember when brushing your teeth.

### ◎ Steps

1   Squeeze some toothpaste onto a soft-bristled toothbrush. Your toothpaste should contain fluoride.

2   Use short, back-and-forth brushing motions to clean the outside and inside surfaces of the teeth, as well as the chewing surfaces. Follow with up-and-down motions to clean the inside surfaces of the front teeth.

3   Brush along the gum line. This is extremely important, as gum disease starts here. Brush gently to avoid damaging your gums.

4   Make sure to brush your back molars, where bacteria like to hide.

5   Brush your tongue to remove bacteria that cause bad breath.

6   Spit out the toothpaste and rinse your mouth with water or mouthwash.

7   Try to floss at least once a day, since most adult cavities occur between teeth. The most important time to floss is before going to bed. Floss before or after you brush – either is fine. Guide the floss between the teeth and use it to gently rub the side of each tooth.

### ✱ Tips

Brush at least twice a day – or better yet, after each meal. Visit your dentist every six months to have your teeth cleaned.

Replace your toothbrush every three to four months, or sooner if the bristles become worn, splayed or frayed.

### Things You'll Need

❑ toothbrush

❑ toothpaste with fluoride

❑ dental floss

## 755 | Treat Bad Breath

The main cause of bad breath is a build-up of food particles in the mouth and the bacteria that result.

### ◎ Steps

1   Visit your dentist at least every six months for cleanings and check-ups to keep your mouth free of plaque build-up and other problems that may lead to bad breath.

2   Watch your consumption of foods such as alcohol, coffee (both caffeinated and decaffeinated), dense proteins (such as those found in dairy and meat products), garlic and onions, and sugars. These are all bad-breath offenders.

3   Try to breathe through your nose. Breathing through your mouth can lead to having a dry mouth, which creates a breeding ground for odour-causing bacteria.

4   Keep a regular log of your eating habits and any medication, as these can cause bad breath. Share the log with your dentist.

5   Brush your teeth and tongue twice a day to remove food particles and plaque, and floss between teeth once a day, preferably in the evening after you eat.

6   Try using a fluoride mouth rinse with antiseptic ingredients and a pleasant mint flavour. This helps to protect your teeth, and the flavour masks odour problems.

### ✱ Tips

Keep mints and gum on hand (or better yet, a toothbrush and toothpaste) for meals that include ingredients such as garlic and onions.

If bad breath persists, check with your dentist – this may indicate other health problems.

If you wear removable dentures, take them out at night and clean them before putting them in again.

### ⚠ Warning

Smokers often suffer from bad breath and other mouth-related problems.

7 Consider internal breath fresheners – such as over-the-counter pills you take before or after a meal to aid the prevention of malodorous breath – or go the natural route and munch on some parsley after a meal.

## Whiten Your Teeth 756

Tobacco, coffee, cavities, ageing and drugs can stain teeth. Treatment for discoloured teeth depends on the magnitude of the stain; remedies appear here in order of increasing intensity.

### ⊙ Steps

1 Brush and floss regularly to reduce or prevent stains.

2 Try whitening toothpastes. Although heavily advertised, these only partially whiten teeth and don't provide a complete remedy. Ask your dentist to recommend one. Very few whitening toothpastes have undergone any type of clinical trial, and ones that are too abrasive can damage tooth or make them very sensitive.

3 Get regular dental cleanings, which remove many food and tobacco stains. No amount of cleaning will remove the severe staining left by tetracycline or systemic disease because these pigments lie inside the tooth; you'll have to take more aggressive measures against those.

4 Consider the two options – in-surgery and at-home treatments – for bleaching your teeth. A dentist performs in-surgery treatments by coating the teeth with a bleaching agent, then using periodic flashes of light to activate the solution. Treatments last 30 to 60 minutes, and the complete procedure often requires several appointments. In at-home treatments, patients wear a mouth guard fitted with bleaching gel two hours a day for two weeks, depending on the severity of staining.

5 Think about getting veneers, which are custom-made shells bonded to the teeth with resins. This procedure often requires removing a small amount of tooth structure and is the most invasive – as well as the most expensive – treatment option.

### ✱ Tips

No bleaching method can permanently whiten tooth, and all require repeated treatments – especially if the factor that caused the staining still exists.

All of the bleaching mechanisms described here can cause tooth sensitivity, usually temporary (lasting up to several weeks).

### ⚠ Warnings

Never try to remove or scrape off stains with your fingernails or other sharp objects.

## 757 | Stock an Emergency Supply of Medicine and First Aid

When an injury occurs, having medical materials within easy reach can help minimise bleeding, swelling and trauma. That's why every home should possess a well-stocked first aid kit.

### ⊙ Steps

1. Buy a plastic storage container that is shoe box size or larger – an art-supplies container with big handles or a fishing-tackle box will work nicely. Think of this container as the "safe box" for your emergency supplies.

2. Gather materials necessary to treat cuts and lacerations: sterile plain and non-stick gauze pads in a variety of sizes, bandages, soft bandage wraps and a pair of latex gloves for the care of fresh bleeding wounds (caution: some people are allergic to latex).

3. Be sure to pack soap to clean wounds. Soap containing chlorhexidine makes a good antiseptic. If no family members are allergic to iodine, consider including products containing povidone-iodine, such as Betadine. Use Betadine swabs to clean difficult-to-reach areas and Betadine pads for small scrapes.

4. Include at least two sizes of bandage tape, and an elasticised wrap to hold gauze pads or other dressings in place.

5. Place analgesic/antihistamine cream in the kit.

6. Add a bottle of syrup of ipecac if you have children, so you can induce vomiting in case someone swallows poison. Do not use ipecac until you have confirmed the need with your doctor or a hospital.

7. Consider keeping an aqueous epinephrine solution kit (called an EpiPen) in the box if anyone in the family is allergic to bees or wasps. You will need a prescription for the kit. Review how to use the kit with everyone who might need to know.

8. Put a good pair of tweezers and a pair of sharp scissors in the kit. The tweezers are great for removing gravel from scraped knees, as well as splinters and pieces of glass. The sharp scissors can quickly cut away a trouser leg from a lacerated thigh.

9. Include a bottle of sterile eye-irrigating solution.

10. Put a torch with fresh batteries in the kit, and be sure to check the batteries every few months. Good light is vital for detecting foreign bodies in the eyes, mouth and ears, and in assessing the depth and severity of wounds.

11. Keep a first aid manual inside the kit. Review the manual every six months so you'll remember what to do in an emergency.

12. Enrol in a CPR and a first aid class for optimal emergency preparedness. These are available at most adult education institutes.

### ✱ Tip

Add a flannel and towel (in a sterile plastic bag) to your kit when you travel. Most wounds can be cleaned effectively with soap and clean water, as long as the flannel and towel are also clean.

### ⚠ Warnings

Inspect your kit once a year and replace any expired medication.

Keep first aid kits in a cool, dark place, out of reach of children.

### Things You'll Need

- ☐ plastic storage container
- ☐ sterile plain gauze pads
- ☐ sterile non-stick gauze pads
- ☐ bandages and bandage tape
- ☐ soft bandage wrap and elasticised bandage wrap
- ☐ latex gloves
- ☐ Betadine swabs and pads
- ☐ soap with chlorhexidine
- ☐ analgesic/antihistamine cream
- ☐ syrup of ipecac
- ☐ epinephrine kit (EpiPen)
- ☐ tweezers and sharp scissors
- ☐ sterile eye-irrigating solution
- ☐ torch and batteries
- ☐ first aid manual

## Deal With Wasp or Bee Stings                758

Thousands of people every year are stung by wasps or bees. Fortunately the effects are only serious in a tiny number of cases, and appropriate first aid can reduce the pain endured.

### ⊙ Steps

1   If the casualty has received a large number of stings or is showing signs of a severe reaction or anaphylactic shock (see 771 "Recognise Signs of a Medical Emergency"), go immediately to the nearest hospital's accident and emergency department.

2   Remove the sting by scraping the skin in the opposite direction to the sting's direction of entry. Use a blunt knife, a pair of tweezers, or even your fingernails. Do not attempt to pluck the sting out by gripping it with the tweezers or between your fingernails, as this may squeeze the poison sac in the sting, releasing the rest of the poison into the body.

3   Wash the site of the sting with soap and water.

4   If the casualty is in pain, apply an ice pack for 10 or 15 minutes to reduce pain and swelling. Alternatively, apply vinegar to the site of a wasp sting, or bicarbonate of soda to counter the effects of a bee sting.

5   If the sting is to the mouth or throat, give the casualty an ice cube to suck or cold water to rinse their mouth. Monitor any swelling in the mouth or throat carefully. If it appears worrying, take the casualty to your local hospital's accident and emergency department.

6   Take a painkiller or antihistamine if necessary to reduce the level of pain and swelling.

**✳ Tip**

If you know that you are allergic to insect stings, obtain an appropriate treatment kit at a chemist and carry it with you at all times.

## Avoid and Treat Sunburn                759

Like any kind of burns, sunburn is a potentially serious condition and needs to be treated properly. Of course, the best advice is to avoid burning in the first place.

### ⊙ Steps

1   Take sensible measures to limit your exposure to the sun's ultraviolet rays (see 806 "Protect Your Skin from the Sun").

2   When applying sunblock, take special care to protect areas of your skin that might be particularly prone to burning. If you change your style of swimwear, note whether you are uncovering areas not previously exposed to sunlight – these could be vulnerable. Remember to protect the soles of your feet which may be exposed when sunbathing.

3   Check repeatedly for any reddening of the skin when you are out in the sun. If reddening appears, you are suffering over-exposure and should cover yourself immediately. The full effects of sunburn will take between two and six hours to emerge.

4   Rest in a cool shady place and apply calamine lotion to soothe the burned skin. Note that after-sun products designed to moisturise your skin are not of any significant use in the case of burns.

**✳ Tip**

A common cause of sunburn is failure to apply enough sunblock, or to reapply it often enough. Buy two tubes of cheap sunblock instead of one more expensive product, and use lavishly.

**⚠ Warning**

Harmful UV radiation can pass through cloud cover. You can suffer sunburn even in overcast weather, especially if you are high up on mountains.

5   Take a painkiller if the discomfort of the sunburn seems likely to stop you having a good night's sleep.

6   If the burning is severe, seek medical treatment. Also seek treatment urgently if you show symptoms of sunstroke, such as vomiting and fever.

7   Avoid exposure to sunlight for at least 48 hours after being burned.

**Things You'll Need**

☐ sunblock

☐ calamine lotion

☐ painkiller

---

## 760 | Help Prevent Altitude Sickness

When you rapidly ascend above 2,440 m (8,000 ft), you run the risk of not being able to adjust to the lower oxygen level.

### ⊙ Steps

1   Ascend slowly to give your body time to adjust gradually to the lower oxygen concentration in the air. A good rule of thumb is to ascend no more than 455 m (1,500 ft) per day, with plenty of rest in between.

2   Drink water as you climb, to maintain proper hydration.

3   Fill up on carbohydrates, with only enough proteins and fats to meet essential nutritional needs.

4   Take it easy when first reaching higher altitudes. Over-exertion can make you more susceptible to acute mountain sickness.

5   Avoid alcohol and caffeine, which cause dehydration, and smoking and sedatives.

6   Before you go on your trip, ask your doctor about any medication that can be prescribed to help your body acclimatise. Some research suggests that ginkgo biloba can help protect against altitude sickness.

### ✳ Tip

You'll know that you're drinking enough water if your urine is clear (not yellow) and copious.

### ⚠ Warning

If someone is showing signs of altitude illness – dizziness, apathy, loss of appetite, headache, confusion, lethargy, nausea, vomiting, or difficulties with breathing, walking or sleeping – descend until the symptoms subside. Seek medical attention if the symptoms fail to subside. Severe altitude illness can be fatal if left untreated.

---

## 761 | Help Prevent Heat-Related Illness

A summer's day can be deadly to someone who is unable to cool down as a result of heat, dehydration or over-exertion.

### ⊙ Steps

1   Identify climatic conditions in which heat-related illnesses are likely: temperatures of 32°C (90°F) or higher, and high relative humidity.

2   Get plenty of sleep and eat fruits and vegetables high in potassium to help your body adjust to the heat.

3   Keep cool: stay out of the sun if you can; seek shade or air-conditioned buildings; wear sunscreen, a hat, sunglasses and baggy clothing that breathes well; schedule demanding activities for cooler parts of the day.

4   Limit physical exertion. If you're dripping with perspiration, this may be a sign that your sweat is not evaporating sufficiently to cool your skin.

5   If you can't avoid physical activities in the heat of the day, allow your

### ✳ Tips

Thirst is not a reliable indicator of heat stress. Follow the advice in step 6 and note that dark or scant urine indicates that your body needs more fluids.

Children, the elderly and people with endocrine or skin diseases are especially susceptible to heat-related illnesses.

body to acclimatise by spending an hour or so doing physical activities in the heat over a period of ten days. Increase the amount of time gradually to allow your body to adjust to the heat.

6 Stay hydrated. Drink a minimum of 3 l (5 pt) of fluid per day and increase this to 4 or 5 l (7 or 8 pt) if you will be exerting yourself. If you will be exercising vigorously or sweating a lot, water alone is not enough. You'll need a sports drink with electrolytes – about 1 l (1³/₄ pt) for every hour of exercise.

7 Avoid amphetamines, antihistamines, antidepressants or other drugs that affect your body's basic functions.

## ⚠ Warning

If someone is exhibiting signs of a heat illness (muscle cramping, tiredness, a headache, dizziness, nausea or heavy perspiration), get him or her to a cooler place immediately. If a person exhibits vomiting, diarrhoea, confusion or disorientation, hot and red or cool and clammy skin, elevated body temperature, an increased heart or respiratory rate, or seizures, seek medical help immediately. Heatstroke is potentially fatal.

---

## Prevent Frostbite                               762

When it's cold enough (0°C/32°F or below), skin can freeze, resulting in frostbite. Not only painful, frostbite can cause the loss of fingers and toes, or even limbs.

### ⊙ Steps

1 Recognise that by venturing out into the cold, you are risking frostbite. Wind and wetness will drain your body of heat – especially your frostbite-prone extremities – with astonishing speed. Stay mindful of the risk.

2 Keep a close eye on the weather wherever you go into the wilderness, and adjust your plans as necessary to avoid the risk of frostbite. Frostbite can strike in any season, especially at high altitudes.

3 Bring along warm clothing when going outdoors: an inner wicking layer, a middle insulating layer and an outer wind- and water-resistant layer for both your upper and lower body. Be sure you also have gloves or mittens (mittens are better), a hat, and wool or thick fleecy socks.

4 Make sure you have clothing that will not lose its insulating properties when wet. The primary offender is cotton; wool is much better, as are many kinds of synthetic fleece.

5 Stay hydrated. Dehydration is a predisposing condition for frostbite and hypothermia.

6 Eat plenty of food, especially carbohydrates, which are quick to digest and easy for your metabolism to turn into heat. Eat small amounts frequently rather than large amounts infrequently.

7 Set a reasonable pace when engaging in vigorous activities. Exhaustion can make treatment and even recognition of frostbite more difficult.

8 Stop and warm your feet or hands if they start to feel numb; this is an early warning of frostbite.

9 Turn back and seek shelter if the weather turns nasty, especially if you encounter snow, rain and/or strong winds.

### ✳ Tip

When layering your clothing, make sure each layer is roomier than the layer underneath to allow for some insulating air between layers.

### ⚠ Warnings

Avoid tight-fitting clothing – including footwear – that might impair circulation.

Avoid alcohol, which could contribute to dehydration and impair judgement, as well as caffeine and nicotine, which constrict blood vessels and therefore reduce the blood supply to extremities.

## 763 | Prevent Seasickness

The sea's repetitive motions can overstimulate the inner ear, causing nausea and vomiting. Here are some tried-and-tested preventative measures.

### ⊙ Steps

1  Talk to your doctor about prescription medicines, or ask a chemist about over-the-counter medication.

2  Try an anti-seasickness wristband, which stimulates the median nerve in your wrist, a well-known acupuncture point.

3  Try eating ginger 12 to 24 hours before your trip. Take it as a supplement, following directions on the package, or talk to a nutritionist at your local health food store. Some sources recommend putting powdered ginger into muesli or sprinkling it on top of toast. Snacking on ginger biscuits several hours before your trip may also help.

4  Drink plenty of water before your trip. Good hydration helps prevent seasickness. But once on board, avoid foods and fluids until you're sure you won't get seasick. Avoid all alcoholic beverages; alcohol can not only add to your tipsy feeling but promote dehydration.

5  Eat oatmeal or crusty bread an hour before setting off. Some experts say that having food in your stomach can reduce seasickness.

6  Position yourself where the least motion is felt, usually in the centre of the deck, and avoid going below deck, as the fumes and stuffy air will not help your nausea.

7  Suck on lemon drops – or your favourite hard sweets – as soon as the boat begins moving. Besides tasting good, these tart treats may help to keep your nausea in check.

8  Take deep breaths and stare out into the distance. Focus on the horizon, not on waves or moving objects.

### ✱ Tip

For many people, the most effective preventive medication is scopolamine, available on prescription.

### Things You'll Need

- ☐ anti-seasickness medication
- ☐ anti-seasickness wristband
- ☐ ginger or ginger biscuits
- ☐ lemon drops

## 764 | Stop a Nosebleed

Nosebleeds are caused by broken blood vessels inside the nose and are especially common in children. They usually go away on their own but will stop more quickly with help.

### ⊙ Steps

1  Pinch your nose between your thumb and forefinger, and apply moderate pressure by squeezing against the nasal septum – the midsection of your nose – for 15 minutes.

2  Lean your head forwards, not backwards, so that the blood does not trickle down your throat. This will prevent a feeling of gagging.

3  Breathe through your mouth.

4  Apply a cold, soft compress around your nose as you continue to pinch it between your fingers.

### ✱ Tips

Anterior (in the front) nosebleeds are the everyday kind. Posterior (in the back) nosebleeds involve heavy bleeding from deep within the nose and are much more difficult to stop. Posterior nosebleeds occur most often in the elderly.

5   Once bleeding has stopped, elevate your head above your heart when you are lying in bed or on the sofa. This helps alleviate nasal pressure.

6   Turn on a cool vaporiser to moisten mucus membranes, which will help prevent the nosebleed from recurring.

7   Apply a small amount of petroleum jelly to the inside of the nostrils to moisten the passages and prevent the nosebleed from recurring. Use your fingertip.

8   Avoid blowing your nose for 24 hours, and when you do blow it again, blow gently.

9   Avoid lifting heavy objects or engaging in other strenuous activities after a nosebleed. This can produce momentary surges in blood pressure that could cause the nose to bleed again.

Keep your child's fingernails trimmed if she likes to poke around in her nose.

## ⚠ Warning

Seek medical care if your nose continues bleeding after 20 minutes, if the bleeding worsens rather than improves, or if you have specific medical conditions or concerns.

---

# Care for Minor Cuts and Abrasions                    765

Treating a cut right away reduces the chance of infection.

## ◎ Steps

1   Wash your hands before and after tending a wound.

2   Rinse the wound with clean water. Flush out all dirt and debris.

3   Using clean gauze, put pressure on the wound to stop any bleeding.

4   Clean the area around the injury with soap and water or Betadine, but avoid getting any solution inside the wound.

5   Leave the wound open to the air unless there is a chance that you'll be exposing it to dirt or infection. In that case, bandage the wound loosely, allowing air to get in.

6   If the wound edges are open, use a butterfly bandage – a butterfly-shaped bandage that brings the edges of the wound together and reduces scarring – to close straight, clean, superficial wounds.

7   Call your doctor if you detect signs of infection, which include redness, warmth, redness up the arm, or oozing or drainage from the wound.

## ⚠ Warning

See a doctor if the wound is deep, won't stop bleeding or has edges that won't come together. Animal bites, human bites and deep wounds should be evaluated by a doctor in case antibiotics are needed. Also see a doctor if the wound is very dirty and it has been more than ten years since your last tetanus injection.

## Things You'll Need

☐ soap or Betadine

☐ gauze

☐ bandages

---

# Remove a Splinter                    766

Splinters can cause pain, swelling and possibly infection if they're not removed promptly.

## ◎ Steps

1   Try to "milk" out the splinter by gently squeezing your fingertips over or on each side of it. If this doesn't work, try the following steps.

2   If you're worried about causing pain, rub the splinter site with a numbing teething gel or ice before removing the splinter. Keep in mind, however, that chilling the area may cause the splinter to retract from the top of the skin and may make its removal more challenging.

## ✳ Tips

Soak the infected area in warm water to soften the skin if you have trouble getting access to the splinter.

Most splinters eventually work themselves out on their own.

3   Clean a needle, a pair of tweezers and a small pair of nail clippers with isopropyl alcohol or Betadine solution and let it air-dry. Be sure to swab the pinching surfaces of the tweezers and the cutting edges of the nail clippers.

4   Use soap and water, or Betadine, to wash the skin where the splinter has lodged.

5   With the tip of the needle, make a small hole in the skin above the splinter. Once you have access to the splinter, gently try to squeeze it through the hole. If necessary, increase the size of the hole with the needle. Use your tweezers to pull out the splinter as soon as you can get hold of it.

6   If you're not able to open a path for the splinter with the needle, use the nail clippers very carefully to cut away the skin above the splinter.

7   Wipe the site with isopropyl alcohol or Betadine when you've removed the splinter.

8   Apply an antibiotic ointment to the site.

## ⚠ Warnings

Do not dig at a splinter for longer than five minutes. If you're unable to remove it within that time, leave it alone, or see a doctor if you feel you are at risk of infection. Too much poking and prodding will lead to tissue damage.

Be sure you are up to date with your tetanus injections. Once you've had your initial injection, you need to get a booster every ten years. If a splinter comes in contact with earth or animal dung before it punctures your skin, it could be carrying the bacterium that causes tetanus.

---

## 767 | Check a Wound for Infection

Even cleaned and dressed wounds are by nature contaminated and may still become infected. Check daily for infection to minimise tissue damage and health risk.

### ⊙ Steps

1   Protect yourself. Scrub your hands thoroughly with soap and water, and put on latex gloves to prevent the spread of infectious disease.

2   Remove the bandage and dressing from the wound. Dispose of them immediately, handling them only with latex gloves or tweezers. The best means of disposal is burning, but wrapping them in plastic and throwing them away in the trash can is suitable for most situations.

3   Check the wound for any pus, swelling, redness or faint red lines radiating from the wound.

4   Feel the area surrounding the wound for any heat.

5   Ask the injured person if he or she has experienced any pain or chills.

6   Look for swelling or tenderness in the lymph nodes, located under the armpits, in the groin and neck areas, and behind the ears.

7   Take the person's temperature. Consider a temperature higher than 37.7°C (100°F) a possible sign of infection.

8   Contact your doctor immediately if you observe any fever, chills, swelling of the lymph nodes, or red lines radiating from the wound, or if you are in any doubt whatsoever.

9   Gently draw a circle with a pen around any reddening of the skin to help monitor whether the infection is spreading.

10  When you finish examining the wound, apply a fresh dressing and bandage the wound.

## ⚠ Warnings

If you see signs of infection or have questions or concerns, contact your doctor.

Infectious diseases such as AIDS and hepatitis are transmitted via the exchange of bodily fluids. Protect yourself by wearing latex gloves, and use responsible means of disposing of used bandages and gauze.

Tweezers and any implements used to check a wound should be disinfected by soaking in isopropyl alcohol immediately after use.

Some people are allergic to latex gloves. Use latex gloves only if you know you are not allergic to them.

## Soothe a Burnt Tongue 768

That soup just smelled too good to wait for it to cool, didn't it? Now it's time to give your burnt tongue about 24 hours to heal.

### ⊙ Steps

1 Remember that the surfaces of your mouth and tongue are mucus membranes, and as such, they heal faster than other areas of your body. So even though your tongue may really hurt, be comforted in knowing that by tomorrow, the burn should be gone.

2 Cool your tongue with a frozen dessert such as ice cream or sorbet. Let the treat linger on top of your tongue before you swallow it. For severe burns, frozen foods can be left on top of the tongue for three to four minutes, until the tongue becomes slightly numb and the pain is dulled.

3 Suck on an ice cube. Don't bite down on the cube, though, because it can crack your teeth.

4 Inhale air through your mouth, across and over your tongue. The cool breeze will help relieve some of the sting.

5 Suck on a cough drop containing phenol, which helps numb the tongue's surface.

6 Talk to your doctor about prescription medication that you could apply to your tongue to numb it and completely relieve the pain.

7 Avoid using mouthwash or harsh toothpaste until the burn heals.

8 Do not eat oranges, pineapple and other acidic foods until your tongue stops hurting.

### ⚠ Warning

Contact a doctor if you have suffered a serious burn – blistering or severe pain – to your tongue.

## Make a Sling 769

A sling is used to support an injured arm, wrist or hand. Making a proper sling requires a bandage, but if you don't have one, available articles of clothing can offer an alternative.

### ⊙ Steps

1 Make a triangular bandage, if you do not have one ready-made, by taking a piece of material at least 1 m (3 ft) square and cutting it in half diagonally from corner to corner.

2 Sit the injured person down and have them support their damaged arm with their other hand, so the forearm is across their chest with the hand slightly higher than the elbow.

3 Slide one tip of the triangular bandage upwards between the patient's chest and their injured arm.

4 Pull the bandage up, over the shoulder of the sound arm, and around the neck, so that the tip is pointing downwards on the injured side.

### ✳ Tips

Always stand on the injured side of the casualty when you apply a sling. Then you will be better able to help support the injured arm while making the sling.

You can improvise a sling using a scarf, a belt, a tie or even a pair of tights, looped under the injured arm and tied around the patient's neck. Alternatively, if the casualty is wearing a coat, pin the sleeve, with the injured arm inside, to the front of the coat.

5   Take hold of the lower end of the bandage and fold it up over the injured forearm and hand, leaving only the fingertips showing.

6   Tie the ends of the bandage together in the hollow of the collarbone.

7   Check that the sling is not inhibiting circulation in the injured arm. To do this, press one of the patient's fingernails with your thumb until the nail turns white. Then release the pressure. The nail should become pink again. If it does not, adjust the sling until circulation is restored.

8   Place some soft padding under the knot if it is pressing uncomfortably on the patient's skin.

## 770 | Treat Food Poisoning

Symptoms of food poisoning may include vomiting, diarrhoea, fever or abdominal cramps. They usually begin 3 to 36 hours after eating tainted food, and can last from 12 hours to several days.

### ⊙ Steps

1   Consult your doctor if the symptoms are severe or if you have severe abdominal pain. You may be suffering from something more serious than food poisoning.

2   Sip clear fluids. Dehydration is the primary concern when experiencing vomiting or diarrhoea.

3   Take small amounts of fluid frequently. Electrolyte replacements (such as sports drinks) are your best options. You can also sip flat ginger ale, which may help settle your stomach.

4   Suck on an ice cube if nothing else stays down.

5   Introduce food slowly after vomiting stops.

6   Eat bland, easily digestible foods such as water biscuits if you are still having diarrhoea. Bananas, apple sauce, rice and toast are good.

7   Avoid milk, fatty foods, high fibre and caffeine for a few days until you are feeling better – these foods are harder to digest.

8   Limit your time in the sun, as this may dehydrate you further.

9   Gradually resume your normal diet once symptoms subside.

10  Contact your doctor if symptoms fail to subside in 24 hours.

### ✳ Tip

You can use over-the-counter medicine to control vomiting or diarrhoea, but it is usually better not to use anything for at least the first six to eight hours. The bacteria or virus causing the problem will pass from your body faster if you don't try to slow it down.

# ✓ 771 Recognise Signs of a Medical Emergency

Urgent medical attention is required for a number of medical conditions, including those whose common signs and symptoms are listed below. Call a doctor or visit the nearest hospital's accident and emergency department immediately if any of these occur, even if you are not entirely sure that it is an emergency.

## Appendicitis

❏ Is the patient between the ages of 10 and 30? The condition is most common in this age group but can occur at any age.

❏ Is there pain and/or tenderness in the navel area that moves towards the lower right of the abdomen over the course of a few hours?

❏ Does the patient describe the pain as severe and sharp, and worsening with any movement?

❏ Is there a fever? This may be a sign of inflammation and infection, a possible sign of appendicitis.

❏ Is the patient experiencing signs of nausea, vomiting or loss of appetite?

❏ Did the patient take any pain medicine that may mask the symptoms of appendicitis?

## Anaphylactic shock

❏ Has the patient been exposed within the last two hours to a common allergen, such as an insect sting, nuts, peanuts, seeds, legumes, eggs or shellfish? A person may be allergic to any of these even if he or she has been exposed to them before without problems.

❏ Does the patient report tingling in the mouth and tongue and/or throbbing ears?

❏ Does the patient appear uneasy or agitated?

❏ Does the patient's skin appear flushed and feel itchy, and are hives appearing on the skin or swellings becoming evident on the eyes, lips or tongue?

❏ Is the patient sneezing, coughing, wheezing or having difficulty breathing?

❏ Is the patient vomiting or experiencing abdominal cramps or diarrhoea?

## Heart attack

❏ Is there crushing pain, pressure or squeezing in the centre of the chest that lasts for more than a few minutes?

❏ Does the pain spread to the jaw, neck, shoulders, back or arms (often the left arm)?

❏ Is there any nausea, sweating, dizziness or shortness of breath in combination with chest pain?

❏ Is the person over 50 and experiencing indigestion or heartburn that does not respond to over-the-counter medication?

❏ Is there a combination of these symptoms?

## Stroke

❏ Is there any numbness or weakness on one side of the body such as in one arm or leg, or on one side of the face?

❏ Is the person having problems such as difficulty speaking or a loss of speech altogether?

❏ Are there any vision problems such as double vision or loss of vision, especially if this occurs in just one eye?

❏ Is there any sign of sudden, severe, unexplained headaches, dizziness, loss of coordination or balance, or sudden falling without apparent cause?

checklist

## 772 | Get the Medical Care You Need

To get the best out of the increasingly complex health system in Britain today, you need to evaluate all your options and make the right choices at each step along the path to treatment.

### ⊙Steps

1   Check out private medical insurance (PMI) while you are well. Once you are ill, no insurance is going to cover treatment of your condition.

2   Obtain details of at least three PMI policies for comparison. Assess whether any of the schemes available is affordable and suits your needs.

3   Be aware of other options that may be more suitable for you. Much cheaper hospital cash plans can provide help with medical expenses. Or you may choose to rely on the NHS, but resort to self-pay treatment when necessary to avoid waiting lists.

4   When you are unwell, make a list of your symptoms and of questions you want to ask your GP before you go for your appointment.

5   Ask your doctor about different treatment options and their likely cost if you choose to pay. He should help you assess how far paying would speed up seeing a consultant, having tests done and obtaining treatment.

6   If you are paying to see a consultant, establish how much it is going to cost when you make the initial appointment. If the charge seems excessive, ask your doctor to refer you to another consultant.

7   Prepare a list of questions before you see a consultant. If the consultant is proposing to operate on you, ask how many operations of a similar kind he or she has performed and what has been the failure rate.

8   If you have PMI, obtain written authorisation from the insurer before you go ahead with the treatment.

9   If you have opted for self-payment, shop around different hospital groups to see which offers the most affordable deal.

10  If you are an NHS patient, seek out the hospital with the shortest waiting list. Contact the College of Health (020 8983 1225) for information.

### ✱ Tip

If you are paying for surgery, go for an all-in fixed-price package. Otherwise you may find costs escalating alarmingly, especially if it turns out that you require a lengthy stay in hospital.

### ⚠ Warning

Private medical insurance policies always have a long list of exclusions – medical procedures or conditions that the policy does not cover. Always check the small print carefully before signing up for PMI, and double-check with the insurer to be certain you are covered before commiitting yourself to a course of treatment.

## 773 | Know When to Call a Doctor if Your Child Is Sick

It's sometimes hard to know when your child needs a doctor. Here are some general guidelines to help you decide – but remember that if in doubt, it's always safest to call the doctor.

### ⊙Steps

1   Take his temperature. High fevers can lead to seizures in children who are prone to them. If your child has a very high temperature (greater than 39.4°C/103°F measured by an oral thermometer), is lethargic, is very irritable or refuses to eat, or if he doesn't respond to fever-reducing medication, contact a doctor.

### ✱ Tips

Put together a first aid kit with supplies you may need for your child (see 757 "Stock an Emergency Supply of Medicine and First Aid") .

2   Check his breathing. If your child is having respiratory difficulties such as wheezing or rapid breathing, get him to a doctor immediately. This is especially important if your child is asthmatic.

3   Consider allergies. If your child has one or more severe food or environmental allergies, seek treatment immediately when you know or suspect that he has been exposed.

4   Go to a doctor if your child falls or bumps her head hard enough to lose consciousness – even a mild concussion can be dangerous. An inability to remember the events surrounding the injury may also indicate a concussion. Look for confusion and drowsiness as warning signs of more serious problems.

5   Talk to your child. If she is unresponsive or semi-conscious, or has trouble focusing her eyes, get medical help immediately or call 999.

6   Seek help for cuts if you have trouble stopping the bleeding, or if the cut is deep and severe enough to require stitches.

7   Call the doctor if your child is vomiting frequently or has severe diarrhoea. The doctor will be able to tell you how to monitor your child for dehydration, and will let you know whether to visit the surgery.

8   Call NHS Direct (0845 4647) if you think your child has ingested anything toxic. A nurse will be able to tell you what to do and whether the situation is a medical emergency

9   Seek medical attention if your child complains of a severe headache, especially if it's accompanied by a stiff neck and a fever – these symptoms sometimes signal meningitis.

10  Whenever in doubt, call your doctor, or call 999 in an emergency. It's always better to be on the safe side.

Keep emergency numbers, including the number for NHS Direct (0845 4647), next to the phone.

⚠ **Warnings**

If your child is asthmatic, be sure to have a spare inhaler where you can find it immediately, as children often misplace inhalers.

If you think your child has taken poison, do not induce vomiting unless your doctor or the nurse at NHS Direct tells you to.

If your child requires regular medication for any condition, always replace it well before it runs out or reaches its expiration date. This includes having an aqueous epinephrine kit if your child has a history of allergies and there is the possibility of a severe reaction that could lead to anaphylactic shock.

---

## Care for a Sinus Headache 774

A sinus headache is a symptom of inflamed, congested sinuses. To get rid of your headache, you must reduce the inflammation in your sinuses. Learning the cause will make it easier to treat.

◉ **Steps**

1   Take paracetamol, aspirin (if older than 18) or ibuprofen for pain relief.

2   Apply warm compresses to the site of your pain four times a day.

3   Call your doctor if the drainage from your nose is discoloured. Clear or slightly white mucus is acceptable. Yellow, rust-coloured or green drainage indicates a serious infection and is cause for concern.

4   Use extra pillows to elevate your head, which will allow your sinuses to drain.

5   Try using a nasal spray or a decongestant. Depending on the cause of your sinusitis, over-the-counter decongestants may offer some relief. Do not use nasal sprays for more than a few days because they can become addictive. If sinusitis persists, see a doctor.

6   Avoid allergens if you suspect your sinusitis is allergy-related.

✽ **Tip**

Blow your nose with your mouth slightly open and blow through both your nostrils. This helps to equalise the pressure in your sinuses. Avoid blowing too hard.

⚠ **Warnings**

Call your doctor if you have persistent fever, ringing in your ears, eye drainage or facial swelling associated with your sinus headache.

7   Stay away from cigarette smoke, which can aggravate sinuses.

8   Keep your distance from people with colds and flu. Your body is already compromised and fighting off an inflammatory process.

9   Eat properly to help increase your body's resistance to disease.

10  Get plenty of rest. Catnaps can do a lot to lessen the severity of a sinus headache. Stress and fatigue may aggravate it.

11  Try increasing the humidity in your room. Use a humidifier, or take a hot bath or shower. Boil a pan of water, take it off the hob, drape a towel over your head and the pan, and inhale the steam for ten minutes, four times a day. Keep your face at least 45 cm (18 in) away from the pan to avoid burning yourself.

12  Increase your fluid intake. This encourages your sinuses to drain by hydrating your body. Hot (non-caffeinated) tea is especially good because the steam loosens congestion in your sinuses.

Never take more than the suggested dosage of over-the-counter painkillers.

Do not give aspirin to children under 18 years of age.

---

## 775 | Care for a Migraine

Migraine attacks can last for hours or days. Treatment for severe, chronic headaches begins by finding the cause, if possible. Don't accept unrelenting pain; treatments are available.

### ⊙ Steps

1   Talk to your doctor about your symptoms so he or she can make a proper diagnosis and rule out the possibility of an underlying disease. Look for signs of migraine such as throbbing pain, often on one side of the head, and nausea. These symptoms may be preceded by visual disturbances such as flickering lights.

2   Ask your doctor which type of prescription migraine medication is right for your type of headache. Many of these can effectively relieve a migraine if taken early on.

3   Lie in a darkened, quiet, odour-free room and apply cold compresses to the temples, eyes and eye sockets. This may curb a full-blown migraine.

4   Compress and release the artery running along the side of your temple with your fingers.

5   Quell the queasiness with a prescription anti-nausea medication.

6   Avoid any foods that might trigger a migraine. Common foods are preserved meats, shellfish, nuts, mature cheese, yogurt, alcohol (especially red wine), MSG, chocolate, artificial sweeteners and certain fruits. If you eat a food for the first time and get a migraine two hours later, it's probably best to stay away from this food.

7   Try drinking coffee. For some people suffering from caffeine withdrawal, caffeine helps relieve symptoms.

8   Ask your doctor if a preventive medication would be appropriate for you.

### ✱ Tips

These severe headaches can affect anyone, but most sufferers are women, and migraines often occur around the time of their menstrual periods.

The treatment of migraines is often accomplished through prescription drug therapy, which is relatively safe and effective. It's best to avoid narcotics, as addiction can be a problem.

### ⚠ Warning

Headaches that require medical attention include those that are of sudden onset or extremely painful, persistent or increasing in severity, increased by exertion or coughing, accompanied by fever or altered mental status, or unresponsive to treatment.

# Avoid a Hangover 776

The best way to avoid a hangover, of course, is never to drink at all. But if abstinence is not a part of your plans, check out these proven techniques.

## ⊙ Steps

1   Eat before you drink. Starchy carbohydrates such as bread and pasta will slow the absorption of alcohol.

2   Avoid very sweet drinks that disguise their alcohol content, and avoid mixing different types of alcohol.

3   Drink water in between alcoholic drinks to prevent dehydration.

4   Eat hearty food while you are drinking.

5   Drink another glass of water when you get home.

### ✳ Tip

If you get a really bad hangover, keep track of what you had to drink the night before and avoid it next time.

### ⚠ Warning

Avoid aspirin or ibuprofen if you have stomach ulcers or gastritis.

# Care for a Hangover 777

The headache, nausea, thirst and fatigue you feel are all symptoms of dehydration. Follow these steps to eliminate those symptoms and get back to feeling your best.

## ⊙ Steps

1   Drink water as soon as you get up in the morning to rehydrate yourself. If possible, have a sports drink. The electrolytes and nutrients in a sports drink can replenish your body's depleted reserves.

2   Drink even more water if you plan to have coffee. Caffeine is a mild diuretic and can contribute to dehydration.

3   Stick to liquids that are at room temperature. Drinks that are excessively hot or cold will be even more of a shock to your struggling stomach.

4   Take an over-the-counter pain reliever such as aspirin or ibuprofen to relieve a pounding headache or body aches.

5   Eat easily digestible foods when you're ready. Fresh fruit, toast and water-based soups are all easy on the stomach. Harder-to-digest foods, such as eggs and milk, can cause stomach problems.

6   Relax, rest or go back to bed. Allow some time for your body to feel positive effects from your treatments.

### ✳ Tip

Take preventative measures beforehand: drink responsibly and in moderation. If you've drunk in excess and suspect you'll be hung over the next morning, drink a few glasses of water just before you go to bed.

### ⚠ Warnings

Do not take a paracetamol-based painkiller to relieve symptoms. Combining paracetamol and alcohol can damage your liver. Consider ibuprofen instead.

If you are an excessive drinker, use caution when taking any over-the-counter painkillers.

## 778 Care for a Stye

A stye is a bacterial infection that occurs inside an oil gland on your eyelid. Styes are usually benign and almost never cause damage to the eye or to vision.

### ⊙ Steps

1 Wash your hands with soap and water before touching the eye area.

2 Soak a clean flannel in warm or hot water.

3 Wring it out and place it directly on the affected eyelid. Make sure to keep the eye closed.

4 Keep the flannel on the eyelid for about ten minutes.

5 Repeat this three to four times a day for best results.

6 Continue the warm soaks until the stye comes to a head and drains.

7 Do not touch or squeeze the stye. This can cause the infection to spread.

8 See your doctor if the stye is still there after two days of self-care, if you have any eye pain, if the stye appears to be getting larger and spreading over the eyelid, or if you have questions or concerns.

### ✱ Tip

Most styes heal on their own. Antibiotics are usually only necessary if a stye is extremely large or does not respond to treatment. Occasionally, styes may need to be lanced and drained by a doctor. Do not attempt to do this on your own.

## 779 Care for Conjunctivitis

Conjunctivitis, or pinkeye, is an inflammation of the membrane that lines your eyeball and eyelid. It can be caused by a foreign body, an allergic reaction or a bacterial or viral infection.

### ⊙ Steps

1 Determine if you have one or more of the following conjunctivitis symptoms: red, watery eyes; itching; sensitivity to light; or eye discharge that might be crusty around the eyelashes.

2 Wash your hands before touching the eye area.

3 Clean the eye area with a clean flannel dampened with warm water.

4 Use a cool compress to relieve itching.

5 Wash any clothing, towels and bedding touched by the infected eye; bacterial and viral infections are very contagious.

6 Avoid wearing contact lenses until the infection clears up.

7 Note any yellow or greenish discharge from the eye. If this occurs or if only one eye is affected, it is more likely to be a bacterial infection than a viral infection or an allergy – consult your doctor for treatment.

### ✱ Tip

There is no over-the-counter medicine specifically for conjunctivitis. If the problem is caused by bacteria, you'll need to see a doctor for treatment. Viruses need to run their course. If the conjunctivitis is caused by an allergy, get rid of the allergen or see your doctor for allergy relief.

## Care for a Black Eye 780

A black eye is caused by bleeding under the skin around the eye, usually from a blow or other trauma. Take these steps to minimise the swelling and discomfort and to speed recovery.

### ⊙ Steps

1　Check the eyelid carefully for lacerations. If the lid has been cut, a doctor may need to repair it with a few fine sutures.

2　Place an ice pack or cold compress over the injury for ten minutes every hour for the first day. Never put ice directly on your skin. Always use an ice pack or wrap a cloth around the ice. Ice helps constrict blood vessels and localise bleeding.

3　On the second and third days, apply a heating pad or warm, moist compresses to the injury for 10 to 20 minutes each hour or two. Heat applied 24 to 48 hours after the injury will help your body absorb the excess blood around delicate eye tissue.

4　Sleep with your head elevated on two pillows. This helps to reduce swelling of the eyelids.

5　Talk to your doctor about taking aspirin, ibuprofen or paracetamol for discomfort if you are an adult. Children should not take aspirin.

6　Wear dark glasses, especially in well-lit areas, to reduce eyestrain as the black eye is healing.

### ✳ Tips

The eyeball, the bones around the eye and the eye muscles may all be affected by trauma to the eye.

Blood may drain into the eyelid, making it difficult to open. Blood may also drain into the cheek.

The tissue around the eye will remain bruised for two to three weeks.

See your doctor if your black eye causes you any special concerns.

### ⚠ Warning

If you experience double vision or any decrease in vision, see a doctor immediately.

## Care for a Toothache 781

Toothache symptoms include throbbing pain around a certain tooth, sensitivity to hot or cold, and discomfort when chewing. Causes vary from cavities and gum disease to cracked teeth and exposed roots.

### ⊙ Steps

1　Clean your mouth by rinsing it with warm water.

2　Floss gently around the sensitive tooth to dislodge any food particles.

3　Try placing an ice pack on your jaw to soothe the pain.

4　Use over-the-counter painkillers such as aspirin (for adults only) or ibu-profen to relieve the pain, or talk to a pharmacist about topical analgesic ointments.

5　Call your dentist if you have a fever or if the pain worsens, is recurrent or lasts for more than a few hours. Your dentist will ask you questions to determine the urgency of your need for treatment.

6　Prevent future toothaches with good oral hygiene. Brush twice a day with a fluoride toothpaste, floss once daily and see your dentist for check-ups every six months.

### ✳ Tip

Some people find relief by chewing on cloves – if you can't find a clove, look for oil of cloves as the main ingredient in a pain reliever.

### ⚠ Warning

Never put aspirin or other painkillers directly on or around the sore tooth unless they are specifically designed to be used this way; some products can burn your mouth.

## 782 Avoid a Cold

The common cold is caused by any one of more than 200 virus-es. Symptoms can include a fever, watery eyes, nasal conges-tion, a runny nose, sneezing, a sore throat and a cough.

### ⦿ Steps

1 Wash your hands often. Cold viruses can be transmitted by handshakes and by touching contaminated objects such as doorknobs.

2 Keep your hands away from your eyes, nose and mouth.

3 Avoid people who are coughing and/or sneezing.

4 Get plenty of rest to help strengthen your immune system.

5 Maintain a healthy diet and get an adequate amount of exercise.

6 Drink plenty of fluids.

7 Consider taking one 500 mg tablet of vitamin C twice a day. Some scientists believe this can help boost your immune system, although there is no hard data to support this.

### ✱ Tips

Some studies have shown that the herbal supplement echinacea may be effective at fighting cold symptoms when taken during the first few days of illness – but not prior to exposure. However, there is no scientific data that supports the effectiveness of echinacea.

You may be more susceptible to colds when you are under stress, during your menstrual period, or when you are old – times when your immune system is weakened.

## 783 Care for a Cold

The common cold is an upper respiratory infection involving the nose, throat and surrounding air passages. There is no quick cure, but these measures should help to hasten your recovery.

### ⦿ Steps

1 Eat chicken soup. It contains an amino acid called cysteine, which thins mucus and breaks up congestion. Plus, the steam from the soup helps open up air passages.

2 Gargle at the first sign of a scratchy throat with either mouthwash or ½ tsp. of salt dissolved in 225 ml (8 fl oz) warm water.

3 Stay warm. Getting chilled compromises your immune system.

4 Take aspirin, paracetamol or ibuprofen to reduce fever and inflammation if you are an adult. Give children paracetamol or ibuprofen. Determine the dose according to the child's age and weight.

5 Drink hot beverages and take hot showers. Steam helps open up nasal passages and reduces congestion.

6 Drink a lot of liquid, enough so that your urine turns clear. Yellow urine means your urine is fairly concentrated. Clear urine means your body is well hydrated.

7 Use cough syrup sparingly. Coughing is one of the ways the body gets rid of mucus.

8 Suck on a throat lozenge for relief from a sore throat. Choose a menthol-, phenol- or benzocaine-based lozenge; these are the ones that will help to numb the throat. They also help open up nasal passages.

### ✱ Tips

Antibiotics are effective only against bacteria, so they won't work against cold viruses.

Be careful not to overmedicate yourself with over-the-counter drugs. Some cough syrups have multiple ingredients that counteract each other.

### ⚠ Warning

Contact your doctor if your symp-toms become severe, if your fever fails to go down, if you have diffi-culty breathing, if you develop a serious cough, or if you have specific medical conditions or concerns.

9   Put an extra pillow under your head when you sleep to help your nasal passages drain.

10  Rest. If you have a bad cold, one of the best ways to treat it is to take a few days off and sleep.

## Prevent the Flu                                                        784

Maintaining a healthy immune system is your best bet for avoiding the flu (short for influenza). Here are some simple ways to support your system through the flu season.

### ⊙ Steps

1   Avoid sharing drinking and eating utensils with people who are sick.

2   Wash your hands before eating – it really does help keep germs away.

3   Increase your vitamin C intake – which may boost your immune system – by eating ample amounts of fresh fruits and vegetables. Oranges, tomatoes and broccoli are good choices.

4   Drink at least eight glasses of water a day. Herbal teas and diluted fruit juices are good options for increasing your water intake.

5   Get enough sleep. Most people need at least seven to eight hours a night for optimal rest.

6   Manage your stress. Chronic stress can weaken the immune system.

7   Take a multivitamin every day to make sure you are getting enough vitamins and minerals.

8   Exercise regularly – it's been shown to reduce the occurrence of colds and flu.

### ✻ Tips

Flu injections are available and particularly recommended for high-risk groups, such as those with immune disorders and anyone over the age of 65.

Some studies have shown that the herbal supplement echinacea may be effective at fighting flu symptoms when taken during the first few days of illness – but not prior to exposure. However, there is no scientific data that supports the effectiveness of echinacea.

Too much vitamin C can cause diarrhoea and gastric discomfort. Avoid taking more than 500 mg of vitamin C twice a day.

## Fight the Flu                                                          785

Influenza can incubate in your body for up to three days. When it hits, be prepared.

### ⊙ Steps

1   See your doctor: there are effective prescription drugs that can treat flu if taken within 48 hours of the onset of symptoms.

2   Sleep as much as you need to; let your body be your guide.

3   Stay hydrated by drinking plenty of water – at least eight glasses a day. If you don't feel like having plain water, add freshly squeezed lemon juice to water or drink diluted fruit juice.

4   If you are having nausea and/or vomiting, avoid solid foods until the vomiting stops and you are able to hold down clear fluids.

5   Start off with chicken or vegetable broth and dry crackers once you feel like eating. These are both easy to digest.

### ⚠ Warning

The flu is caused by a virus and cannot be cured with antibiotics. But if you are still sick three to five days after its onset, or if you become very sick very quickly, see a doctor. It's possible to have a bacterial infection along with a viral one, or to have an extremely virulent case of the flu.

6   Drink tea or herbal tea with honey. It is very soothing to a sore throat.

7   Take ibuprofen, aspirin or paracetamol for fever, aches and pains if you are an adult. Give children paracetamol or ibuprofen, not aspirin.

8   Use a humidifier or vaporiser if the air is dry. It will help break up mucus.

9   Choose an appropriate over-the-counter cough syrup based on your symptoms. Keep in mind that multiple-ingredient medicines may contain ingredients that counteract each other.

## 786  Take a Temperature Orally

An oral thermometer is one of the best at-home diagnostic tools available. Most medical thermometers nowadays are digital, but here's how to use a glass one.

### ⊙ Steps

1   Clean a glass thermometer with isopropyl alcohol before using it, then rinse or dip the tip in some cool water or wipe it with a tissue to remove the taste of the alcohol.

2   Shake down the thermometer, holding it firmly by the end opposite the metal bulb and snapping your wrist in a downward motion, until the mercury line is below 35.8°C (96.6°F).

3   Slide the tip of the thermometer under one side of the tongue, well into the back of the mouth.

4   Close your lips around the thermometer – don't clench a glass thermometer with your teeth. Breathe through your nose, with mouth closed.

5   Leave the thermometer under your tongue for three full minutes, or as directed by the instructions on the original packaging.

6   Remove the thermometer and hold it under a bright light so you can see how high the mercury has risen. An arrow will indicate the point for a normal temperature reading, which is 37°C (98.6°F).

### ✱ Tips

Use a thermometer specifically designed for taking an oral temperature. Do not use the same thermometer for oral and rectal temperatures. A rectal thermometer has an end that's more stout and stumpy.

For an oral temperature to be accurate, the person must not have had anything hot or cold to eat or drink for at least ten minutes prior to inserting the thermometer in the mouth.

### ⚠ Warnings

Never heat a thermometer, either under hot water or by placing it on a hot surface.

Discard a broken thermometer immediately.

## 787  Help Reduce a Fever

A fever is a sign that your body is attempting to fight an infection. Help your body fight the fever in the following ways.

### ⊙ Steps

1   Get plenty of rest.

2   Drink plenty of fluids. Suck on an ice cube or flavoured ice, or drink iced fruit juice or chilled clear broth.

3   Dress lightly and keep the room temperature between 21 and 23°C (70 and 74°F). Use a blanket if you feel cold.

### ✱ Tips

A fever of 39.4°C (103°F) is not unusual in a young child. For adults, a fever higher than 38.3°C (101°F) or a fever that is greater than 38.3°C (101°F) at its onset is cause for medical attention.

4   Take anti-fever medicines only when necessary. For children under 18 years old, use paracetamol or ibuprofen. For adults, use paracetamol, aspirin or ibuprofen.

5   Give a child a lukewarm sponge bath for a temperature higher than 38.8°C (102°F), but wait 30 minutes if you have given her paracetamol. Wipe the child with a lukewarm flannel or place her in a lukewarm bath for 20 minutes, then dry her thoroughly and check her temperature. If it is lower than 38.8°C (102°F), don't continue with the lukewarm baths. If the child is shivering, warm up the water by a few degrees for the next bath.

6   Know your medicines. Some drug allergies cause fevers. If you suspect that one of your prescription medicines may be causing a fever, talk to your doctor or pharmacist.

7   Spread lip balm or Vaseline over the lips during the fever and for several days thereafter, since lips often crack and split during a fever.

Ice packs can be placed in the groin and armpit areas when an adult has a very high fever, but consult your doctor first.

## ⚠ Warnings

Call your doctor or the hospital if a high fever is accompanied by a stiff neck, difficulty breathing, confusion, lethargy, delirium or convulsions, or a cough with coloured sputum.

Never use alcohol for a rubdown. The fumes are toxic, and alcohol is absorbed through the skin. Use lukewarm water.

---

## Relieve a Sore Throat                                        788

Sore throats can be caused by bacteria or a virus and often accompany an illness such as a cold or flu. Most require no medical intervention and will go away in two or three days.

### ⊙ Steps

1   Consider the cause: a bug that's going around the office, enthusiastic cheering, or perhaps something more serious, such as a throat infection.

2   Take an analgesic to reduce inflammation – aspirin, paracetamol or ibuprofen for an adult, or paracetamol or ibuprofen for children – as recommended by your doctor.

3   Suck on throat lozenges if you are an adult – especially those containing menthol, benzocaine or phenol, which numb the throat. Children should suck on cough drops or hard sweets.

4   Gargle with mint mouthwash or salt water (see 789 "Gargle").

5   Spray a throat spray containing numbing agents into the back of your throat, if you are an adult.

6   Brush your tongue. Sometimes, removing the build-up on your tongue can lessen the soreness in your throat.

7   Rinse your toothbrush in mouthwash between brushings to kill bacteria.

8   Drink ice-cold beverages. Try filling a glass half-full of crushed ice; then pour fruit juice over the ice. Let it sit for ten minutes, insert a straw and suck slowly, letting the juice rest a minute on the back of your throat.

9   Add moisture to your environment with a humidifier or vaporiser, or sit in a steamy shower or bath.

10  Eat soft or liquid foods, especially sorbets and chicken broth.

11  Avoid cigarette smoke and other airborne irritants.

### ✳ Tip

Ask your chemist to recommend a good lozenge or throat spray.

### ⚠ Warnings

For a severe sore throat accompanied by fever, difficulty swallowing or breathing, a red rash, or coughing up of brown sputum, see your doctor or go immediately to the nearest hospital's accident and emergency department.

Contact a doctor if you have a sore throat that keeps you from being able to swallow.

Check young children for dribbling. Dribbling indicates trouble swallowing, which can lead to difficulty in breathing and requires immediate medical attention.

---

## 789 | Gargle

Gargling is a great way to kill bacteria in your mouth. It also helps to give you fresher breath.

### ⊙ Steps

1 Buy mint-flavoured mouthwash, the flavour that's usually preferable for someone feeling ill. Opt for other flavours or salt water if you like.

2 Pour the mouthwash into a clean glass or paper cup. If you pour it into the cup attached to the top, you'll run the risk of contamination, especially if you share the bottle with others. If you prefer to gargle with salt water, dissolve 1/2 tsp. in 225 ml (8 fl oz) of warm water.

3 Slide the mouthwash quickly over your tongue.

4 Throw your head back and stop the mouthwash right before it hits your epiglottis (the cartilaginous flap in the back of your throat). You'll know the mouthwash is resting in the right spot if you feel as if you're going to gag or swallow.

5 Make the mouthwash bubble and gurgle for at least 45 seconds. Pull your tongue back a little and blow air through your throat slowly. Be sure to keep your head way back, and remember to keep the mouthwash right in front of your epiglottis. That's where the germs are sitting, far back and out of sight. Try not to swallow any of the mouthwash.

6 Drop your head back down and spit the mouthwash out.

7 Repeat.

### ⚠ Warning

For children under eight, check with your paediatrician. Children who are too young to understand how to gargle should not be given mouthwash – there's a good chance they'll swallow it. Mouthwash isn't lethal, but don't let children swallow a lot of it.

---

## 790 | Blow Your Nose

It's best to follow a few basic guidelines for blowing your nose – especially when you're ill.

### ⊙ Steps

1 Use tissues instead of cloth handkerchiefs. Germs thrive in dark, moist environments. Wadded-up hankies are a perfect breeding ground for them.

2 Avoid blowing your nose too hard. Too much pressure will force infectious drainage into your ears and sinuses.

3 Press one finger over one nostril.

4 Blow gently through the open nostril.

5 Repeat on the opposite side.

6 Use tissues once, then throw them away.

7 Wash your hands. Germs will be on your fingers after you've handled your nose and your tissue. Don't spread the germs to other people or back to yourself.

### ✳ Tip

You'll feel most congested in the morning, after lying flat in bed all night. Wait to start blowing your nose until you've been sitting upright at least five or ten minutes.

## Sneeze Properly 791

Sneezing on or near someone is perhaps one of the easiest ways to pass around a cold. Here's how to minimise the spread of germs when you sneeze.

### ⊙Steps

1   Be prepared. If you have a cold, make sure you have lots of tissues.

2   Turn away from other people when you feel a sneeze coming on.

3   Use sturdy, fresh tissues to avoid getting the mucus on your hands.

4   If there are no tissues available, sneeze into your arm or elbow rather than your bare hands. This will help prevent the spread of germs.

5   Wash your hands after wiping or blowing your nose.

6   Avoid suppressing a sneeze. It can damage your ears.

7   Avoid holding your nose when you sneeze. That can also damage your ears.

**✱ Tip**

When you start to sneeze, don't hold it back. Let the air explode out into a tissue. Trying to suppress a powerful sneeze can cause your inner ears to pop or can spray bacteria into your sinuses and ears.

## Evaluate Your Sneeze 792

A reflex of the nasal passages, sneezing is one way the body rids itself of irritants. It's hard to know what a sneeze means, but there are some deductions you can make.

### ⊙Steps

1   Evaluate the force of your sneeze. A weak sneeze indicates that a tiny bit of irritant may be tickling you. A strong sneeze means a big irritant.

2   Examine your tissue for discharge. Did you expel anything when you sneezed? If not, the sneeze was probably caused by an environmental irritant or bright light, which stimulates the optic nerve.

3   Look at the colour and consistency of the discharge if you did expel. Green, yellow, rust-coloured, or thick, globby nasal discharge indicates infection. Clear discharge can mean an allergy or the beginning of a cold or flu. Runny, watery discharge points to allergies or a cold draining.

4   Consider frequency. Repeated short, weak sneezes without significant discharge indicate allergies. Off-and-on sneezing, along with a handkerchief full of white or coloured discharge, means you're fighting an infection.

5   Check the pollen and mould spore count. If those levels are high, your sneezes may be allergy induced.

6   Think back on what you did earlier in the day. Clean the house? Mow the grass? Paint furniture? Frequent sneezing after doing certain chores indicates allergies.

7   Check your temperature. A fever in the presence of frequent sneezing indicates an upper respiratory infection or flu.

8   Consider whether you might be pregnant. Unexplained sneezing has been associated with the hormonal changes in pregnancy.

**✱ Tip**

Sometimes people sneeze for no discernible reason. However, consistent sneezing may be a sign of an allergic reaction to an unknown trigger.

## 793 | Ease a Cough

Coughing is a useful protective mechanism because it helps remove mucus and infectious agents from your respiratory system. Treatment that completely suppresses it could do more harm than good. Still, it's sometimes necessary to calm a cough, especially so you can sleep.

### ⊙ Steps

1 Determine the cause. Since a cough is not an illness but a symptom, it's important to figure out what is causing your cough in order to ease it.

2 Eliminate smoking. Many coughs are caused by irritants to the respiratory system such as cigarette smoke.

3 Remove chemical irritants you may be inhaling.

4 Use a vaporiser or humidifier. Moist air can help relieve a dry cough and break up thick mucus.

5 Drink plenty of liquids, especially clear fluids such as water. This will help relieve a dry throat and also liquefy mucus.

6 Sip hot liquids such as broth or tea. Tea with honey can soothe a tickle in the throat.

7 Use an antihistamine or an alternative method if your cough is caused by allergies.

8 Suck on lozenges, cough drops or other throat soothers.

9 Use an expectorant cough medicine if you have thick mucus that you cannot get up. An expectorant thins mucus, making it easier to cough up and get out of your respiratory airways. Carefully follow label directions.

10 Decrease the activity of a cough with an antitussive cough medicine. An antitussive reduces the frequency of a cough. Use it only at night to help you sleep. It is important not to use antitussives around the clock because a cough helps clear your airways. Carefully follow label directions.

### ⚠ Warnings

See a doctor if your cough lasts for more than a week; if you are producing yellow, green, pink, blood-tinged or rust-coloured mucus; or if your cough is exhausting, persistent and/or accompanied by any of the following symptoms: a fever of 38.3°C (101°F) or higher, chest pains, wheezing, shortness of breath or weight loss.

Any smoker whose cough changes should contact a doctor. as this may be an early sign of lung cancer.

## 794 | Fight Allergies

The best way to fight allergies and their symptoms, including stuffy nose, watery eyes, sinus pressure or rashes, is to figure out the cause and avoid it as best you can.

### ⊙ Steps

1 Get tested for allergies by your doctor, or use the process of elimination to pinpoint your triggers. The most common allergens are pollen, mould, dust mites, animals, medication and certain foods.

2 Identify the allergen(s) as specifically as possible.

3 Keep your windows closed and stay indoors as much as you can if seasonal pollen is a problem. Consider a ventilation or filtration system for your home.

### ✳ Tip

A saline-solution nose spray can help loosen secretions. It is not a drug and can be used as often as needed. You can make your own by adding ¼ tsp. salt to 225 ml (8 fl oz) warm water.

4    Seal your mattress, pillows and comforters in allergen-proof covers. Dust mites, a common allergen, live in bedding.

5    Sleep on a latex mattress (as long as you're not allergic to latex). Dust mites can't survive in latex mattresses.

6    Install a dehumidifier in your home if you live in a humid climate. Dust mites, mould and mildew all thrive in humid environments.

7    Use an extractor fan in the bathroom or keep the window open.

8    Buy a vacuum cleaner with a HEPA filter and use it often.

9    Avoid wall-to-wall carpeting. It is virtually impossible to remove dust mites from carpeting.

10   Eliminate certain foods from your diet if you suspect they are causing allergy symptoms. Learn alternative cooking techniques if you are allergic to common foods such as wheat, corn or milk.

### ⚠ Warning

Read over-the-counter antihistamine labels carefully. Many make you drowsy. Avoid alcohol when taking them.

---

## Help Control Asthma Symptoms     795

Although there's no cure for asthma, there are many things you can do to manage your asthma and keep symptoms to a minimum. Avoiding triggers and modifying your lifestyle will help.

### ⊙ Steps

1    Follow your doctor's medical advice, and don't discontinue any medication on your own. Undergo allergy tests as recommended by your doctor and comply with the follow-up treatment.

2    Keep a notebook and write down what you were doing right before you developed asthma symptoms, no matter how mild they were, each time they occur. Look for a pattern.

3    Stay away from any external trigger or allergy that your observations uncover or that tests reveal, whether that means dust that gets stirred up from cleaning, animal hair you're exposed to when riding a horse, or even your bedding if you find you can't breathe upon waking.

4    Avoid cigarette smoke, petrol and paint fumes, perfume, aftershave, cold air and pollution, including smoke from a wood fire. These are all irritants to someone with asthma.

5    Do your best to prevent colds. Stay away from anyone with an upper respiratory infection. Many patients say their symptoms started after a cold.

6    Control stress. Muscle tension and shallow breathing encourage asthma attacks. Practise relaxation techniques. Take yoga classes. Participate in activities that help you relax.

7    Drink a moderate amount of caffeinated coffee, tea or cola, unless otherwise ordered by your doctor. Caffeine, related to theophylline, is mildly therapeutic for asthma. However, too much caffeine can aggravate it.

8    Take prescribed asthma medication, both oral and inhalant, as recommended by your doctor. Bronchodilators and other drugs prescribed by your doctor relax smooth bronchial muscle tissue, decrease inflammation and help keep airways open.

### ✳ Tips

Get a flu injection if you have asthma.

Talk to your doctor about getting a peak flow meter, which can help you monitor your asthma.

For more information about asthma, including breathing exercises, call the National Asthma Campaign helpline (08457 010203), or log onto their website www.asthma.org.uk.

9   Exercise regularly per your doctor's recommendation. Proper use of prescription medication can decrease or eliminate asthma that is induced by exercise.

10  Learn how to breathe from your diaphragm and purse-lip breathe whenever your breathing feels laboured, tight or fast, or when you feel stressed. To breathe from your diaphragm, lie down or sit in front of a mirror. Put one hand on your stomach, the other on your chest. Take a deep breath through your nose. Your stomach should rise under your hand each time you breathe; your chest should not rise. To purse-lip breathe, close your mouth and inhale through your nose. Purse your lips as if you're going to blow out a candle. Exhale slowly with as little force as possible. Your exhale should last twice as long as your inhale. Don't hold your breath between inhalation and exhalation.

## 796 | Reduce Snoring

**Snoring can be a real problem. Airway blockages that cause snoring often come from relaxed muscles in the back of the throat, or from stuffy nasal passages.**

### ⊙ Steps

1   Don't drink alcohol before going to bed. It can increase muscle relaxation, which may make snoring more likely.

2   Avoid muscle relaxants and sleeping pills.

3   Sew or tape a tennis ball to the back of your pyjamas or nightdress. Snorers are more likely to snore when lying on their backs. The ball will make this position uncomfortable and force you to roll over onto your side.

4   To prevent snoring while lying on your back, elevate your upper body 30 degrees using a foam wedge.

5   Talk to your doctor about taking an antihistamine if your snoring is caused by a cold or allergy.

6   Give up smoking. Experts believe cigarette smoking disturbs sleep and increases the likelihood of snoring.

7   Lose weight; this helps reduce the size of the palate.

8   Offer your partner earplugs if your snoring keeps him or her awake.

9   See a dentist for information about an anti-snoring dental device, which prevents the lower jaw from falling back while you're sleeping.

10  Ask your doctor about being referred to an ear, nose and throat specialist for possible surgery or treatment. There are a variety of techniques that can help reduce snoring.

### ⚠ Warning

Heavy snoring can be a symptom of sleep apnea, a sleep disorder that has been linked to serious health problems. If you snore heavily and often feel drowsy or fatigued despite sleeping all night, consult a doctor.

## Care for Swimmer's Ear

**797**

When water gets in the ear, it can carry bacteria or a fungus and cause an outer-ear infection. Swimmer's ear usually clears up after a few days, with medication.

### ⊙ Steps

1   To help clear up a mild infection, use a mixture of equal parts isopropyl alcohol and white vinegar in the ear canal after swimming or showering. Tip your head to one side so the affected ear faces the ceiling, place a few drops of the mixture in your ear using a medicine dropper, then tip your head the other way to let the mixture drain out.

2   Take aspirin (adults only), ibuprofen or paracetamol every four to six hours for any symptoms of a mild infection, such as discomfort or fever.

3   Apply mild heat, using a hot water bottle or a heating pad, to help reduce any pain.

4   Contact your doctor if your condition doesn't improve in 24 hours, the glands in your neck become swollen, your ears begin to drain a milky fluid, or you experience dizziness or ringing in your ears.

### ✳ Tips

Symptoms include itching, discomfort and swelling of the outer ear canal, which is usually tender to the touch.

During the healing process, keep water out of your ears. Clean them by wrapping your finger in a soft cloth and gently wiping the outer ear area. Avoid using instruments or cotton buds to remove earwax.

### ⚠ Warning

Don't put any drops in your ear if you suspect a perforated eardrum.

## Get Rid of Hiccups

**798**

The cause and function of these abrupt diaphragmatic contractions have always baffled medical practitioners, but a few home remedies can help get rid of them.

### ⊙ Steps

1   Swallow 1 tsp white granulated sugar, dry. A study found that this stopped hiccups immediately in 19 out of 20 people. Repeat up to three more times at two-minute intervals if necessary.

2   Gulp down a glass of water if the sugar doesn't work.

3   Eat a piece of dry bread slowly.

4   Breathe in and out of a paper bag. Do not use a plastic bag under any circumstances, and don't do this longer than one minute.

5   Gargle with water (see 789 "Gargle").

6   Repeat the above steps until your hiccups stop.

### ✳ Tip

Hiccups can be brought on by eating too fast and subsequently swallowing a lot of air, or by drinking too much alcohol.

### ⚠ Warning

See a doctor if you have severe pain, if your hiccups last longer than a day (or three hours in the case of a small child), or if they started after you took prescription medication.

## 799 | Reduce Excess Wind

Although it can be annoying and embarrassing, excess wind usually doesn't indicate a serious medical condition.

### ⊙ Steps

1 Slow down when you eat. The more slowly you eat, the less air you will swallow along with your food.

2 Watch your intake of wind-producing foods such as beans, cabbage, onions, brussels sprouts, wheat and wheat bran.

3 Keep a list of your food intake and note when you have wind. If you notice that wind and certain foods seem to go together, cut down on or eliminate those foods from your diet.

4 Find out if you are lactose intolerant. If you are, milk and dairy products can cause wind as well as general stomach discomfort.

5 Take supplements to aid in lactose digestion if you are lactose intolerant but want to eat dairy products.

6 Introduce high-fibre foods into your diet gradually. A sudden change from a low-fibre diet to a high-fibre diet can cause wind.

7 Reduce your consumption of high-fat foods.

8 Avoid or cut down on the use of sugar substitutes. People can't absorb them, which can cause wind.

9 Ask your pharmacist for advice on over-the-counter medication to combat wind.

10 Add Japanese kombu, a sea vegetable, to the water when you cook beans to make them more digestible and neutralise their wind-producing effect.

### ✱ Tip

If you are lactose intolerant, consider buying lactose-free milk.

## 800 | Treat Diarrhoea

Diarrhoea is characterised by excess water in the stool and can be quite debilitating. The cause varies from tainted food or a virus to severe anxiety. These steps can help you cope.

### ⊙ Steps

1 Rest to give your body time to recover.

2 Avoid milk products because temporary lactose intolerance is common after an insult to the intestine.

3 Wash your hands after every bowel movement to reduce the chance of transmitting the pathogen to someone else.

4 Consider your diet. Some people believe bananas help to form stools in children. Consider a "BRAT" diet: bananas, rice, apple sauce and toast. But use them sparingly and cautiously so as not to aggravate the problem.

### ✱ Tip

Check your medicines: products containing magnesium may cause diarrhoea.

### ⚠ Warning

The elderly and children can quickly become dehydrated, which can turn an intestinal illness into a systemic emergency. Replace fluids by drinking water, an electrolyte replacement drink or juice if tolerable.

5   Withhold food for 24 hours in moderate to severe cases, allowing only lukewarm clear liquids. As stools begin to form, slowly add soft foods.

6   Visit your doctor if the diarrhoea is painful, is severe, contains blood or is accompanied by a high fever. Also, see or call a doctor immediately if you are taking antibiotic or prescription drugs.

7   Ask your pharmacist about any anti-diarrhoeal medication you're considering to make sure that it does not interact with any medication you are already taking.

## Treat Constipation                                       801

If you move your bowels only once every three or four days, feel bloated, or pass small, hard stools, you may be constipated. Changing some of your daily habits may help.

### ⊙ Steps

I   Drink lots of liquid every day. Eight glasses of water is recommended. When the intestines lack proper hydration, stools can turn hard and dry and become much more difficult to pass.

2   Add several servings of fibrous whole grains, fruits (such as prunes or prune juice) and vegetables to your diet every day – or opt for a fibre supplement. Fibre adds bulk to the intestines and creates well-formed stools that are easier to pass.

3   Drink hot water, tea or coffee. Hot beverages, especially those containing caffeine, may help stimulate the bowels.

4   Incorporate a regular exercise regimen into your lifestyle. Digestion is enhanced when the abdominal muscles are used. The contraction and relaxation of the muscles help the intestines to move stools more effectively through the digestive tract. Aerobic exercise such as jogging, tennis and brisk walking are especially helpful.

5   Check the medication you're taking. Antacids (particularly those containing calcium) and iron supplements can cause constipation, as can some other over-the-counter and prescription drugs, especially pain relievers that contain narcotics.

6   Keep in mind that constipation can be caused by digestive disorders such as irritable bowel syndrome, colon cancer, colitis, Crohn's disease or diverticulitis. Stress, pregnancy and even a new routine can temporarily cause a slowdown in the bowels.

7   Take a laxative if constipation continues, but avoid regular usage.

8   If you have a fever, severe abdominal pain, continuous vomiting, prolonged bloating, very thin stools, blood in your stools or frequent bouts of constipation, see a doctor.

### ❋ Tip

There is no evidence that constipation need occur with ageing. If you do have a problem as you grow older, add more fibre, fluids and exercise to your daily regimen.

### ⚠ Warning

Use enemas with extreme caution. They are a temporary solution, and frequent use may lead to dependency. Never give an enema to a child unless instructed to do so by a paediatrician.

## 802 | Care for Haemorrhoids

Haemorrhoids, or piles, develop when anal and rectal veins become swollen because of straining or prolonged sitting. They may cause inflammation, pain or rectal bleeding. Haemorrhoids can be internal, external or both.

### ◎ Steps

1 Apply a cold compress directly on the haemorrhoid to help ease the pain.

2 Avoid straining when you have a bowel movement.

3 Wipe with moistened toilet paper, a baby wipe or a pad soaked with witch hazel after a bowel movement. Commercial haemorrhoid-relief pads are commonly soaked with witch hazel.

4 Clean the area well with warm water several times a day. A hand-held showerhead or a bidet works well.

5 Soak in a hot bath every day. Avoid bath salts, which may be irritating.

6 Increase your fibre intake. Eat fresh vegetables, whole grains and beans. Fibre helps your regularity and forms stools that are large and soft, which makes them easier to pass.

7 Drink at least eight glasses of water a day. This will keep stools loose and easier to pass.

8 Get regular exercise. Walking three times a week, for 30 minutes each time, will aid your digestion and make moving your bowels less difficult.

9 When lifting heavy objects, use proper body mechanics to avoid putting excessive strain on the lower body. Avoid sitting or standing for long periods of time.

10 Use over-the-counter haemorrhoid medication as directed on a short-term basis. Those containing corticosteroids are especially helpful in reducing anal pain. Check with a pharmacist to make sure the medication does not cause problems with any other medication you are taking.

### ✳ Tip

In very rare cases, haemorrhoids may need to be treated surgically, either through injection sclerotherapy (which causes the vein to shrink), rubber-band ligation or haemorrhoidectomy. Consult your doctor to find out more about these treatments.

### ⚠ Warnings

Never assume that rectal bleeding is caused by haemorrhoids. It could be caused by colon cancer.

Prolonged use of over-the-counter haemorrhoid medication can lead to inflammation and scarring of the rectal tissue.

## 803 | Care for a Bruise

A bruise occurs when blood vessels rupture from a blow. It usually disappears in three days to two weeks with no special care, but you can reduce the swelling, coloration and duration.

### ◎ Steps

1 Rest the bruised area. This permits the blood to clot more quickly, which limits the spread of blood beneath the skin.

2 Apply a cold compress to the bruise – 20 minutes on, 20 minutes off – as often as you can for the first day or two. The cold will constrict blood vessels and help keep the bruise from spreading. Never apply ice directly to the skin. Always use an ice pack or a cold compress.

### ✳ Tips

Once blood vessels under the skin rupture, the area swells and oxygen is cut off. When the haemoglobin has less oxygen, the blood turns blue – hence the black and blue colour of a bruise. When haemoglobin begins to break down, the bruise looks yellowish-green.

3   Avoid aspirin until the bruise has started to heal. Aspirin is an anticoagu-
lant, which prevents blood from clotting as quickly. Blood that does not
clot spreads more extensively underneath the skin.

4   Take paracetamol for pain. This does not affect clotting.

5   Apply a warm, wet compress after the first 48 hours to reduce pain and
swelling. Heat is recommended once the blood has stopped spreading
around the bruise. Heat dilates blood vessels, which will help speed the
sweeping away of blood cells from around the ruptured vessels.

It's best not to wrap a bruise;
the bruise needs room to swell.
Elastic bandages can cause
constriction that slows healing.

## ⚠ Warning

See your doctor if you find
yourself bruising for no apparent
reason.

---

## Recognise the Signs of Arthritis                    804

The most common form of arthritis is osteoarthritis, a degeneration of the joints. Rheumatoid arthritis is an autoimmune
disease in which joints become inflamed.

### ◉ Steps

1   Notice whether exercise causes an intensified ache in your joints. This is
the first telltale sign of arthritis.

2   Take note if you experience stiffness in one or more joints in the morning
that typically subsides after 15 to 30 minutes of movement. This may be
an early sign.

3   Evaluate your afflicted joint for range of motion. Does the joint creak or
cause you pain when you bend it to its normal limits? This may be a sign
of arthritis.

4   Is your skin pulled taut over a joint due to swelling? Is the taut skin
shiny? These symptoms are indicative of joint swelling due to either
osteoarthritis or rheumatoid arthritis (though they can also be signs of
gout or an infection).

5   Test your afflicted joint for temperature. For instance, test your right knee
joint by placing one hand on your right knee and one on your left knee,
and feel for a temperature difference between the two. Hot joints can be
a sign of rheumatoid arthritis, gout or joint infection. Cold, bone-hard
joints are apt to be a sign of osteoarthritis.

6   Notice whether the joint pain is associated with fever or noticeable
swelling. These are signs of rheumatoid arthritis or joint infection.

7   Pay attention if your joints have a gritty sensation, such that they seem
to crackle and make noise when moving. In osteoarthritis, irritated carti-
lage and bones rub together, making a grating sound.

8   Check the location of the painful joints – are they located symmetrically?
For instance, if you have joint inflammation in some of the fingers of your
right hand, do you feel joint pain in the corresponding fingers of your left
hand? This is characteristic of rheumatoid arthritis.

9   Visit your doctor for advice and possible treatment if you suspect that
you have arthritis.

### ✱ Tips

Researchers have recently discovered a faulty gene that causes one type of osteoarthritis.
Obesity also predisposes a person to osteoarthritis. The causes
of other types of osteoarthritis
are unknown.

For more information about
arthritis, contact Arthritis Care on
020 7380 6500 or log onto their
website www.arthritiscare.org.uk.

## 805 | Use Crutches

Using crutches often appears easier than it actually is. Get proper instruction from your doctor or physiotherapist and remember the following pointers.

### ⊙ Steps

1 Make sure the crutches fit properly. Your shoulders should lean forwards slightly and your wrists and elbows should be bent.

2 Check that the padding is not worn or torn.

3 Walk by placing both crutches in front of you. Shift your weight and your healthy leg forwards.

4 Keep your steps small. They should be no longer than 45 cm (1½ ft).

5 Rest as needed. Crutches can irritate your armpits.

6 Try not to lean on your crutches. Sit down or lean against a wall.

7 Avoid stairs whenever possible. Use ramps and lifts when available.

8 Call ahead when you're going to a new building or area, and find out about disabled access. Try to avoid places where you will have to climb long staircases, or that have staircases without railings.

9 Move slowly, especially if you are climbing stairs. Don't hurry and risk further injury.

10 Opening a door takes a little bit of skill. Make sure the door will clear your feet when you open it. Support yourself on one crutch and open the door with the other hand. Hold both crutches as the door opens, and place the tip of one crutch against the door to keep it open. Then go through the door.

11 Use the crutches as prescribed. If they are really uncomfortable, you may not be using them properly or they may not be the right size.

### ⚠ Warning

Speak with your doctor or a physiotherapist about the proper use of crutches, especially if you may be using them for a long time. They can be tricky to manipulate on stairs and in wet, icy or uneven conditions. Improper use can cause further injury.

## 806 | Protect Your Skin From the Sun

To minimise skin damage from the sun, follow these guidelines, based on the recommendations of the American Cancer Society and the Centres for Disease Control and Prevention.

### ⊙ Steps

1 Long-term exposure to the sun's ultraviolet (UV) rays can damage your skin. To protect it, stay out of the sun between 10 am and 4 pm, when the rays are at their strongest. And remember that clouds don't block UV rays.

2 Seek shade when you're outdoors.

3 Wear a hat, preferably with a 10-cm (4-in) brim all around, to cover your face, neck and ears effectively.

### ✳ Tip

Some clothing manufacturers offer SPF ratings for clothing.

### ⚠ Warnings

Sunscreen is not recommended for children under six months old. Cover them with a hat, shirt and trousers, and keep them in the shade.

4 Wear long sleeves and long trousers, making sure they're made of tightly woven fabrics.

5 Use sunscreen with a sun protection factor (SPF) of at least 15 every day to help protect against incidental sun exposure; reapply it after swimming or sweating.

6 Keep in mind that a typical T-shirt has a lower SPF than recommended for wearing in the sun, so you'll still need to apply sunscreen to areas the T-shirt covers.

7 Be aware that ultraviolet rays generally reflect off water, sand, snow and any light-coloured surface, such as concrete; be diligent in applying sunscreen when you're around these surfaces.

8 Remember that some ultraviolet radiation will penetrate water and windows, so you always need protection.

9 Avoid indoor sunlamps and tanning beds, since they can be more harmful to your skin than the sun.

Frequent sunburns or lifelong sun exposure can increase your risk of getting skin cancer and speed your skin's ageing process. Protect your skin diligently.

## Things You'll Need

☐ broad-brimmed hat

☐ long-sleeved shirt and trousers

☐ sunscreen

---

# Examine a Mole                                                807

Keeping watch on moles can help you detect the early stages of the form of skin cancer known as melanoma. Here's what to look for as you examine yourself or someone else.

## ⊙ Steps

1 Look for asymmetry. See whether the shape or colour of one half of the mole does not match the other.

2 Note any irregular borders, such as blurred edges.

3 Examine the mole to see whether its colour is no longer uniform.

4 Be alert to any increases in the size of your mole, especially if its diameter is greater than 6 mm (¼ in).

5 Check for any spread of pigment from your mole to the skin in the surrounding area.

6 Note any redness in your mole, as well as changes in the surface, such as crusting or oozing.

7 Be alert to any changes in the sensation of your mole, such as pain or itchiness.

8 If you discover any of the above changes or any other unusual characteristics in your mole, see your doctor.

## ✱ Tips

Examine your body regularly to become familiar with the size, shape and colour of your moles, blemishes and birthmarks. This can help you be alert to changes that might indicate melanoma growths.

Ask your doctor if you should have regular examinations by a dermatologist, especially if you spend a lot of time in the sun or have fair skin or a family history of skin cancer (see 814 "Keep on Top of Physical Examinations"). The doctor can make a body map of your moles, blemishes and birthmarks, thereby tracking any unusual growth or changes.

## ✓ 808 Treat or Avoid Injuries Caused by Exotic Wildlife

Holidays to exotic destinations can be a rewarding experience, but they also bring the risk of encounters with creatures that can inflict harmful bites or stings. Injuries from venomous snakes, scorpions and spiders may need urgent care, and even mosquitoes can cause serious problems as carriers of malaria and other diseases in the tropics.

### Snakebite

- Seek medical help immediately. Remain calm and lie quietly until you can see a doctor.

- Remove watches and jewellery in anticipation of swelling.

- Wash the area with soap and water and keep it below heart level.

- Wrap a bandage snugly several inches above (not on) the bite if the snake has bitten an arm or leg. Immobilise the area – use a splint if at all possible.

- Don't use a tourniquet, apply ice or heat, cut the wound or try to suck out the venom. Avoid alcohol and medication.

- Take small sips of water to maintain hydration if possible.

### Mosquito bites

- If the country you are visiting is in the tropics, begin a course of anti-malaria drugs at least two weeks before you travel.

- Soak ankle bands in a solution of water and insect repellant before you travel. Wear these for some protection against bites.

- Wear long sleeves and long trousers in the tropics after dark. Use an insect-repellent slow-burner or spray in bedrooms. If possible, sleep under a fine-mesh net.

- Treat mosquito bites by washing the affected area and applying a soothing cream such as calamine lotion.

- If you experience flu-like symptoms such as fever and a headache within two weeks of returning, go to a doctor for a check-up, as you could be suffering from malaria.

### Poisonous spider bite

- Note that people often aren't aware that a spider has bitten them until these signs and symptoms appear: stinging or pain at the site of the bite, a blister that will often grow in size and rupture, and possibly nausea, vomiting, fever and chills.

- Clean the bite with soap and water. Do not attempt to lance the bite or extract the venom.

- Apply an ice pack to the area of the bite.

- Take a painkiller, such as ibuprofen, to obtain some relief from the symptoms.

- If a blister forms, then pops, carefully clean and dress the wound to prevent infection.

- See a doctor immediately for treatment to minimise tissue damage.

### Scorpion sting

- Look for the signs and symptoms of a scorpion sting: burning pain, swelling or numbness at the site of the sting.

- Seek medical attention immediately to receive an antivenin and be monitored for signs and symptoms of severe poisoning: muscle spasms, stomach pain, convulsions, impaired vision or speech, nausea, vomiting, difficulty breathing, impaired circulation, or coma.

- Remain calm to slow circulation, and keep the wounded area below heart level.

- Clean the sting with soap and water (gently – it may be painful), then apply an ice pack to the site.

- Immobilise the stung extremity with a sling if possible.

# Care for a Blister                                    809

Friction, minor injuries, pressure and sunburn can all cause blisters. If you can prevent a blister from getting infected, it will usually go away within a few days.

## ⊙ Steps

1   Clean the skin around the blister.

2   Place a ring doughnut-shaped piece of moleskin over the blister. This will keep pressure off it.

3   Try to avoid popping the blister unless it's in an especially awkward place, such as the bottom of your foot. The blister provides a sterile environment for the skin underneath. Breaking it makes the area more susceptible to infection.

4   If you need to pop the blister, use sterile implements, puncture it in a few places at its base and drain the fluid.

5   If you need to puncture it or if it breaks on its own, clean the area with soap and water or Betadine.

6   Avoid peeling any skin off the blister; this can lead to an infection and delay healing.

7   Cover the exposed blister with dry sterile gauze.

8   Change the gauze regularly and watch for signs of infection, such as pus or redness.

### ✳ Tips

Prevention is always the best remedy (see 907 "Avoid Getting Blisters While Hiking").

If an infection from a blister doesn't clear up quickly, your doctor may want to prescribe an antibiotic.

### Things You'll Need

❏ moleskin

❏ soap or Betadine

❏ gauze

---

# Care for a Boil                                     810

A boil is a skin infection, most often caused by the bacteria *Staphylococcus aureus*. It gets into a hair follicle and pus forms, causing the surrounding skin to rise and swell.

## ⊙ Steps

1   Avoid squeezing a boil, as this may spread the infection.

2   Allow the boil to come to a head and open on its own. Applying a warm compress two or three times a day will speed up this process.

3   Keep the area very clean, especially after the boil has begun to drain.

4   Apply a saline solution once the boil has opened. Mix 1 tsp table salt with 225 ml (8 fl oz) hot water. Wet a flannel in the solution and apply it to the boil. This can help dry it out and reduce the amount of pus.

### ⚠ Warning

Most boils will heal without help. See a doctor if the area becomes increasingly red and inflamed, if you have a fever, or if the boil does not go away after two weeks.

## 811 | Care for Mouth Ulcers

These painful sores inside the mouth may be triggered by stress, injury, nutritional deficiencies, menstruation or genetic factors. They usually clear up in one to two weeks.

### ⊙ Steps

1 Avoid hot and spicy foods, which can irritate mouth ulcers.

2 Brush your teeth with a soft-bristled toothbrush to lessen aggravation.

3 Apply crushed ice or an over-the-counter oral anaesthetic to the sore to numb the pain.

4 Practise good oral hygiene. Rinse with mouthwash or salt water, and try brushing with a toothpaste free of sodium laurel sulphate, which has been implicated in aggravating mouth ulcers.

5 Consult a doctor if sores persist longer than two weeks, recur more than two or three times a year, are extremely painful, or occur with other symptoms, such as fever, diarrhoea or skin rash.

6 Talk to your doctor about treating the sores with oral or topical steroids or oral antibiotics.

### Things You'll Need

- ❑ soft-bristled toothbrush
- ❑ crushed ice or anaesthetic
- ❑ mouthwash or salt water
- ❑ toothpaste without sodium laurel sulphate

## 812 | Treat Head Lice

Infestations of head lice – small insects whose eggs (nits) become attached to hair shafts – are extremely contagious and spread through shared clothing and personal contact.

### ⊙ Steps

1 Assess whether you or your child actually has lice. Symptoms include itching, swollen glands in the back of the neck, foul-smelling hair, and small, oval white or grey-white spots stuck to the hair shaft.

2 Check for live lice and nits. Work in strong light and section the hair. Use a fine-tooth comb (a pet flea comb works well) to find the insects and to comb them out if possible; or remove them using tweezers, your fingernails, or a piece of tape wrapped around your finger, sticky side up. Adult lice are reddish-brown; nits are white or clear and adhere to the hair shaft. They do not jump or fly.

3 Check everyone in the household. Lice are very contagious.

4 Wash all bedding, recently used towels and recently worn clothing in hot water, and dry them in a hot dryer. Soak all combs and brushes in hot water for at least ten minutes.

5 Treat eyelashes and eyebrows with a thick layer of petroleum jelly. Apply twice a day for eight days. Never use any chemical treatment on eyelashes or eyebrows.

6 Try using olive oil or mayonnaise on the head. There is some evidence

### ✳ Tips

If you don't have access to a washer-dryer, isolate the infected clothes and bedding in a rubbish bag for two weeks. The lice will die in this time period.

Avoid sharing hats, bicycle helmets, combs, brushes and clothing with anyone who may have lice. If you have lice, do not allow anyone to use your personal items.

Manual removal with a comb is the safest and often the most effective method of controlling lice.

Your doctor can prescribe a shampoo or cream that will kill lice or nits.

that it works by smothering the nits. Massage it into the hair and leave it in as long as possible. Manually comb out the nits after the olive oil or mayonnaise application.

7   Use a blow dryer, as heat can kill lice and nits. But exercise caution – avoid placing the dryer too close to the scalp.

8   Examine the hair daily to make sure that all nits and lice are gone. If you see more nits, it may mean that there are still lice in the hair or that reinfestation has occurred.

9   Report the presence of lice to your child's school so that staff can check for an outbreak. Some schools prefer children with a lice infection to be kept home from school. They can return after the lice have been removed or have been treated with a commercial product.

10  Check with your chemist to make sure that any product you plan to use does not contain lindane. Lindane has been associated with a number of serious medical conditions, including seizures and possibly cancer.

## ⚠ Warning

Speak with your doctor before using any chemical lice treatments if you are pregnant or nursing, or if you have allergies, asthma or other medical conditions. Never use a lice treatment on a baby unless directed by your doctor.

---

## Examine Your Breasts                                   813

The cure for breast cancer remains unknown, but research indicates that early detection from annual mammograms and monthly self-examinations can increase survival chances.

### ⊙ Steps

1   Lie down on your back and place a pillow under your right shoulder to flatten your right breast.

2   Put your right arm behind your head.

3   Place your left hand on your right breast, and press firmly with the pads of three fingers.

4   Move your hand over the area in concentric circles (starting from the perimeter and closing in on the nipple). Be sure to include the armpit, since breast tissue extends into this area.

5   Put a pillow under your left shoulder and repeat steps 2 to 4 to check your left breast with your right hand.

6   Examine your breasts in front of a mirror. Carefully note any changes in their appearance.

7   Squeeze the nipples to check for discharge.

8   Contact your doctor right away if you find any lumps, swellings, dimpling, skin irritations, distortions, scaliness, thickenings, discharge, unfamiliar retraction of the nipples or other changes.

9   Examine your breasts on a regular basis – preferably every month, about a week after your period begins. Regularity is the key. With practice, you will know how your breasts normally feel, so you can detect changes easily.

### ✱ Tips

Apply powder, lotion or oil to your breasts to make it easier to move your fingers over the surface of your skin.

For the most thorough self-examination, ask your doctor or practice nurse to teach you.

Most breast lumps are not cancerous, but they should be checked by a doctor anyway. The maxim "Better safe than sorry" is especially true when dealing with breast cancer.

The NHS recommends that women over 50 have a mammogram every three years.

Risk of breast cancer increases with age (especially over 50 years), if first-degree relatives have had breast cancer, or if you have not given birth.

## ✓ 814 Keep on Top of Physical Examinations

No matter how healthy you are (or think you are), it's a good idea to get regular check-ups. Many forms of cancer are more curable when they are detected early, and other conditions such as high blood pressure and high cholesterol can be caught before they cause life-threatening damage. Note that these are general recommendations and not endorsed by the NHS. Everyone has specific needs and risks, depending on family and medical history and risk factors, so consult your doctor for specific advice.

| PROCEDURE | FREQUENCY | WHO SHOULD HAVE IT DONE |
|---|---|---|
| Blood cholesterol | Every five years | Everyone over 18 |
| Blood pressure | Once a year | Everyone over 21 |
| Breast examination by doctor | Once a year | Women over 40; women over 35 whose mothers or sisters have had breast cancer |
| Breast self-examination | Once a month | Women 20 and older |
| Dental examination | Every six months | Everyone |
| Electrocardiogram | Once | Anyone over 40 with greater risk of heart disease |
| Eye test | Every one to two years | Everyone |
| Faecal occult-blood test | Once a year | Everyone over 50; anyone over 40 with ulcerative colitis or a relative who has had colon cancer |
| General check-up | Once a year | Everyone |
| Glaucoma | Every three to five years<br>Every one to two years | Everyone 39 to 49<br>Everyone 50 and over; everyone of African ancestry; anyone who has had a serious eye injury in the past or who is taking steroid medication |
| Height and weight | Once a year | Everyone |
| Mammogram | Every other year<br>Once a year | Women over 40<br>Women over 50 |
| Osteoporosis (bone density) | At least once | Women in early menopause; men and women with multiple risk factors for osteoporosis |
| Cervical smear | Once a year | All women after onset of sexual activity |
| Rectal examination | Once a year | Everyone over 50 |
| Skin cancer check | Once a year | Everyone, especially those at increased risk |
| Sigmoidoscopy | Every five years | Everyone over 50 |
| Testicular examination by doctor | Once a year | Men beginning in adolescence |
| Testicular self-examination | Once a month | Men beginning in adolescence |
| Tuberculin skin test | As needed | Anyone exposed to or at risk for tuberculosis |

chart

## Relieve Period Pains　　　815

Period pains are caused by the contraction of the uterus during menstruation and vary in intensity from mild to debilitating.

### ⊙Steps

1　Reduce your consumption of salt, sugar and caffeine during the week before your period to prevent period pains or reduce their severity.

2　Increase your intake of calcium-rich foods such as milk, yogurt or leafy green vegetables.

3　Keep in mind that a high-potency B-complex vitamin may help if you're susceptible to period pains. Vitamin B$_6$ is especially important, but don't take more than 100 mg per day.

4　Apply heat to your muscles when period pains occur. Take a hot bath or place a hot water bottle on your abdomen or lower back.

5　Get moving. Sitting or lying around may actually make you feel worse. Swimming and walking are good activities because they are gentle and not too stressful. Certain stretches and yoga positions will also help to relieve the pain.

6　Avoid standing for long periods if you have pain in your lower back.

7　Massage your lower back to relieve tension and pain.

8　Take ibuprofen to help relieve period pains.

9　Take a break, breathe deeply and listen to soothing music.

### ✳ Tips

If you are interested in using herbs, homeopathy or other natural remedies, consult a naturopath or a doctor who practises natural medicine.

You can buy microwaveable bean-bags which you may find more convenient and comfortable than a hot-water bottle.

### ⚠ Warning

If you are in extreme pain, have an unusually heavy flow or notice big blood clots, or if you also have other symptoms such as vomiting and fainting, consult a doctor.

## Find Out if You Are Pregnant　　　816

Thankfully, these days finding out whether you are pregnant or not can be determined very early on.

### ⊙Steps

1　Calculate when your period is due. If you have a regular cycle and you keep track of it, a late period is one of the earliest signs of pregnancy.

2　Notice any other changes in your body. Are you extremely sleepy? Are your breasts tender? Are you moody? Although sometimes subtle, these changes can be clear indicators.

3　Buy a home pregnancy test. Choose one with two tests per box so you can double-check your results.

4　Test after you miss a period, or 14 days after you think you conceived.

5　Read and follow the test instructions carefully. Some tell you to urinate in a cup; others say to urinate right onto the test stick.

6　If the test is positive, make an appointment with your doctor to confirm a pregnancy with other tests and a physical examination.

7　Retest after a few days if the test is negative and you still suspect that you're pregnant.

### ✳ Tips

Do the test first thing in the morning, when hormone concentrations are highest.

Home pregnancy tests claim to be 97 per cent accurate. When there are mistakes, they're usually false negatives; false positives are very rare.

## 817 | Deal With Morning Sickness

You will probably feel morning sickness for the first three months, but it can happen throughout the day and can last throughout your pregnancy. These steps can ease the nausea.

### ⊙ Steps

1 Try not to let yourself get hungry; an empty stomach can increase nausea.

2 Keep a supply of bland crackers handy. Have some in the morning before you get out of bed to settle your stomach.

3 Avoid high-fat foods – especially fried foods – and stay away from spicy and acidic foods.

4 Eat foods high in B vitamins, which may reduce nausea.

5 Add a bit of ginger to your diet in the form of ginger ale, ginger tea or ginger biscuits. Or use ginger in your recipes.

6 Experiment with natural remedies such as papaya enzyme, vitamin $B_6$ or an acupressure wristband.

7 Drink plenty of water between meals. Try sparkling water flavoured with a slice of lemon.

8 Take your prenatal vitamins with food. Your nausea will increase if you take them on an empty stomach.

9 Avoid taking iron supplements in the first three months of pregnancy unless you are anaemic. Iron can be hard on your stomach.

10 Utilise the fleeting moments when you feel OK to eat healthful foods and get a little exercise.

### ✱ Tips

Nausea can be a sign that everything is going well with your pregnancy. Hormonal adjustment may be what makes you feel so sick.

For most women, nausea lessens or disappears after the third month of pregnancy.

### ⚠ Warnings

Call your doctor if the nausea becomes debilitating or if you are unable to hold down any food.

If you are suddenly being sick after the third month of pregnancy and you weren't sick earlier, call your doctor.

If vomiting is accompanied by pain or fever, call your doctor immediately.

## 818 | Cope With the Menopause

If you're a woman around age 50 or have had an ovariectomy, you're most likely facing the menopause. Although some women breeze through the menopause, others experience mood changes, hot flushes, sweats or vaginal dryness.

### ⊙ Steps

1 Research as much as you can about menopause therapies, such as hormone replacement therapy, that reduce symptoms and delay changes brought on by the decline in oestrogen and progesterone production. This will help you decide which, if any, are best suited for your needs.

2 Realise that you may have headaches, perhaps even an occasional migraine. Hormonal changes, especially decreases in oestrogen levels, may cause vasoconstriction of the blood vessels in your forehead.

3 Understand that the menopause lessens the amount of elastin and collagen in the skin. Use lotions and body oils liberally to keep thinning skin supple and hydrated and to reduce the appearance of wrinkles.

### ✱ Tips

Be aware that as female hormone production declines, you are at increased risk of heart disease and osteoporosis. Get a periodic bone-density test as well as cholesterol and blood-pressure screening.

Many women have had success with homeopathy and acupuncture as alternatives to oestrogen replacement therapy. Discuss these and other options with your doctor.

Consider using hormone creams to relieve vaginal dryness.

4   Prepare yourself for night sweats – hot flushes that occur when you are sleeping. They are more common than hot flushes during the day.

5   Get enough calcium. A woman going through the menopause needs 1,200 to 1,500 mg of calcium a day, as does a postmenopausal woman on hormone replacement therapy. Women not on hormone replacement therapy need 1,500 mg of calcium per day. Discuss this with your doctor. Remember that vitamin D (or exposure to sunshine) helps your body absorb calcium.

6   Eat a diet rich in fruits and vegetables, which contain an abundance of vitamins $B_6$ and $B_{12}$, folic acid and certain antioxidants. These can help women through the menopause and ease the ageing process.

7   Talk to your doctor about eating foods high in phyto-oestrogens – soy products, flaxseed and some legumes and whole-grain foods. Intestinal bacteria can transform these foods into substances that your body can use to offset menopause-related hormonal depletions.

### ⚠ Warnings

Some menopause therapies are controversial because of potential side effects. Consult your doctor to find out about the risks.

Too much calcium may cause constipation and kidney stones.

---

## Conduct a Testicular Self-Examination                 819

A monthly testicular self-examination helps increase your chances of detecting a tumour and getting early treatment.

### ⊙ Steps

1   After a warm shower or bath, grasp one testicle with both hands. Place your middle and index fingers underneath the testicle and your thumbs on top.

2   Roll the testicle between your thumbs and fingers, feeling for any abnormal lumps. An abnormal lump will feel like a hard pea. Don't mistake the epididymis, a rope-like structure on the back and top of each testicle, for an abnormal lump.

3   Check your other testicle in the same way.

4   See your doctor immediately if you feel any lumps.

5   Repeat the self-examination once a month or as instructed by your doctor.

### ✱ Tips

An abnormal lump may also be a sign of a non-cancerous infection.

You may find that one testicle is slightly larger or hangs lower than the other. This is normal.

A testicular self-examination is not a substitute for a medical examination. Any male who has reached adolescence should have an annual testicular examination by a doctor as part of a normal check-up.

---

## Care for Groin Itch                 820

Groin itch is caused by a fungus called *Tinea cruris* that infects skin on the groin, inner thighs and sometimes the buttocks.

### ⊙ Steps

1   Apply an over-the-counter antifungal cream three times a day, or as directed in the product instructions, to get rid of the fungus. Treatment must continue for three to four weeks or the fungus will reappear.

2   For a severe or persistent infection, see your doctor and discuss the possibility of topical and/or oral antifungal medication.

### ⚠ Warning

Your symptoms should improve within seven to ten days of using antifungal creams. If they don't, see your doctor.

3   Apply an antifungal powder when chafing aggravates the condition.

4   Wear a jockstrap or an athletic support to keep your genitals away from the rest of your skin.

5   Keep the groin area clean and dry. After showering and towel drying, consider carefully drying the area completely using a hair dryer at a low setting.

6   Wear roomy cotton underwear – boxer shorts are best.

7   Wear loose-fitting clothes.

8   Remove wet swimming trunks as soon as you have finished swimming.

9   Sleep naked to let the infected area air out.

---

## 821 Treat "Crabs"

Pubic lice, which resemble tiny crabs, lay their eggs, or nits, at the base of the hair shaft, and are usually spread by physical contact, shared towels and linens, or infested toilet seats.

### ⊙ Steps

1   Treat the area with an insecticide solution formulated for pubic lice. You can purchase one over the counter or by prescription. Use according to the directions.

2   Wash in hot water all linens, bedding, towels and clothing that may have come in contact with the pubic lice. Dry them in a hot dryer.

3   Dry-clean infested items that cannot be machine washed.

4   Put non-machine-washable duvets and blankets inside a large rubbish bag and seal it tightly. Leave it sealed for at least ten days. Pubic lice can survive for only 24 to 48 hours away from the body, but nits may take longer to hatch and then die.

5   Inform your sexual partner and anyone who has shared any bedding or towels with you. They will need to be treated.

### ✳ Tips

Shaving your pubic hair is not usually necessary, and that alone will not kill the pubic lice.

"Crabs" are annoying but are generally not dangerous, and are not carriers of other sexually transmitted diseases.

### ⚠ Warning

Avoid lotions containing lindane, and make sure any prescription you are given is not for a lindane-based product. Lindane has been associated with a number of serious medical conditions, including cancer and seizures.

---

## 822 Treat Athlete's Foot

Several over-the-counter remedies can help cure athlete's foot, which is a fungal infection. Once you have successfully treated it, be diligent in preventing its return.

### ⊙ Steps

1   Apply a topical antifungal ointment two or three times a day. Reapply after showering and before going to bed. Continue for three to four weeks to avoid recurrence.

2   Dry carefully between each toe whenever your feet get wet. Consider using a hair dryer set on low to dry your feet thoroughly.

### ✳ Tip

You should begin to see improvement within seven to ten days of using over-the-counter antifungal creams. If not, see your doctor.

3   Place cotton wool balls between your toes at night if your feet perspire excessively when you sleep.

4   Avoid harsh soaps, especially deodorant soaps.

5   Sprinkle an antifungal powder into your socks and shoes whenever you plan to wear your shoes for several hours.

6   Pour a small amount of astringent onto a piece of gauze and wipe the crusty areas on your feet and between your toes. Then let the gauze sit on the crusty spots for a few minutes. The astringent will draw more moisture from your foot.

7   Wear open sandals or go barefoot as much as possible during the acute phase of athlete's foot.

8   Ask your doctor to help with athlete's foot that spreads or will not go away. Your doctor can prescribe topical or oral antifungal medication.

## Treat Corns                                           823

A corn is a callus – generally a pea-size bump – that may ache and be tender with pressure. Corns usually develop over bony prominences on the feet, especially toe joints.

### ⊙ Steps

1   Apply a lotion containing cocoa butter, vitamin E or lanolin to soften the corn. This may aid in diminishing the corn's size or eliminating it.

2   Use non-medicated corn plasters on corns to protect painful spots on the toes when you're wearing shoes. Always remove plasters carefully, so as not to damage surrounding tissue, and never wear the same plaster longer than one day.

3   Soak the affected foot in warm water for a while to soften the corn, then run a pumice stone or stick or an emery board across the corn. Pumice helps to abrade away the horny callus surface.

4   As another option, consider applying a keratolytic agent to remove horny corn tissue, choosing either a 17 per cent salicylic acid solution in collodion or 40 per cent salicylic acid plasters. Remove the agent with warm water, and blot the foot dry. Apply a 5 per cent or 10 per cent salicylic acid ointment, then place an adhesive bandage over the corn. Repeat this once or twice a week until the corn becomes loose enough to be dislodged easily.

5   Use a corn pad. Its oval opening forces a corn to bulge into the hole and displaces pressure in the area. Horseshoe-shaped corn pads are the most effective, as they protect against external pressure without creating new pressure.

6   Wear shoes with plenty of toe room – enough space so that you can wiggle your toes around freely inside.

### ⚠ Warnings

If you detect any redness around the corn, stop using any corn medication until normal colouring returns.

If the corn looks too advanced for you to deal with on your own, consult a chiropodist.

If you have certain medical conditions, such as diabetes or circulatory problems, consult your doctor before treating any foot problems yourself. If you choose to treat yourself, you may develop ulcerations or other problems.

Never try to use a razor on a corn.

## 824 Relieve Bunions

A bunion is a deformity and swelling at the base of the big toe. If a bunion is allowed to worsen, the big toe may eventually come to rest under the second toe.

### ⊙ Steps

1  Wear shoes with plenty of toe room. If your shoe is not shaped like a human foot, don't wear it.

2  Go barefoot as much as possible. This reduces pressure on the big toe.

3  Buy custom-made shoes if your doctor advises it. Shoes can be designed to help position the big toe properly.

4  Ask your doctor about special bunion pads and dressings available by prescription to protect your toes from shoe pressure. You can also buy bunion pads at a chemist.

5  Elevate your foot and ice your big toe if the bunion is red and sore. Put the ice on for 20 minutes, every hour, until the bunion feels less painful. Do not apply ice directly; always use an ice pack, ice bag or compress.

6  Ask your doctor about getting a steroid injection and local anaesthetic in your bunion to reduce inflammation. This injection is occasionally given when the bunion is causing bursitis, which is the inflammation of the bursa, or sac-like joint covering.

7  Ask your doctor about splints or digital orthotics to reposition your big toe. Orthotics are devices that act as aids in improving body mechanics.

8  Consult your doctor about bunion surgery to correct foot deformities.

### ✳ Tip

Women are much more likely than men to get bunions, due to narrow-toed shoe fashions.

### ⚠ Warnings

If you have certain medical conditions, such as diabetes or circulatory problems, consult your doctor before treating any foot problems yourself.

If severe swelling, redness, heat or pain persist for two days, or if you see a break in the skin and feel feverish, contact your doctor.

## 825 Care for Ingrown Toenails

When the skin around your toenail turns red and swollen and starts causing pain, the nail has probably grown into your toe.

### ⊙ Steps

1  Add two capfuls of povidone-iodine (Betadine) solution to 2 l (3½ pt) warm water and soak your foot for ten minutes to soften the tissues and nail.

2  Soak your toe in warm water for ten minutes each day for three days, or until the soreness is gone. After soaking, dry your foot gently and apply an adhesive bandage.

3  Insert a sliver of cotton wool (tear a small piece from a cotton wool ball) between the nail and the skin and leave it in for a few days. This will keep pressure from the nail off the toe. Remove the cotton wool as soon as the nail begins to grow out and away from the toe.

4  Wear loose shoes or go barefoot as much as possible while your toe is healing. Consider switching permanently to shoes with more toe room. Your goal is to eliminate any pressure around your toenail.

### ⚠ Warnings

If you have certain medical conditions, such as diabetes or circulatory problems, consult your doctor before treating any foot problems yourself.

If severe swelling, redness, heat or pain persist for two days, or if you see a break in the skin and feel feverish, consult a doctor.

Chronic ingrown toenails require a chiropodist's services.

5  Keep your nails trimmed straight across and not too short. If the nail is curved, it is more likely to grow under the skin.

6  See your chiropodist for chronic ingrown toenails. A chiropodist may manipulate and elevate the end of your nail to prevent pressure on soft toe tissue, or correct the problem surgically.

---

## Be an Organ Donor    826

If everyone arranged to be an organ donor, there would be enough organs for every person who needed a transplant. Donating an organ is easy.

### ⊙ Steps

1  Make sure your family and doctor understand that you want to donate your organs. If and when the time comes for your family to face these issues, you'll be unable to communicate your wishes to them, so it's important for them to know beforehand.

2  Call the Organ Donation Information Line on 0845 60 60 400. Request an organ-donor registration form, and fill it out. Alternatively, fill out a form online at www.nhsorgandonor.net.

3  Return the form. You will be placed on the NHS Organ Donor Register, a nationwide computerised list of people willing to become donors after their death.

4  Carry an organ-donor card on you at all times, as this will speed up the process of donation in the event of your death.

5  Understand that if you add your name to the Organ Donor Register, you can always remove it at a later date. Be sure to inform your family, too, if you change your mind.

**✳ Tip**

Adding your name to the NHS Organ Donor Register or carrying a donor card will not in any way affect the medical treatment you receive. Donation is considered only after two doctors have independently certified you as dead.

**⚠ Warning**

If you have a donor card but your family refuses to allow your organs to be donated, the hospital will follow the wishes of your family. So make sure your family understands what you want.

---

## Add Fruit to Your Diet    827

By adding fruit to your diet, you'll gain a rich source of nutrients and also enjoy some delicious flavours. Fruits are terrific sources of vitamins, minerals and fibre.

### ⊙ Steps

1  Make an instant breakfast by blending a frozen banana, a handful of frozen strawberries and 225 ml (8 fl oz) of milk.

2  Stir apple sauce – or sliced or shredded apples – into a bowl of hot oatmeal in the morning.

3  Choose an orange instead of crisps with lunch.

4  Add bananas to vanilla yogurt for an afternoon snack.

5  Try some less familiar fruits like guava, papaya, mangoes, star fruit or kumquats.

**✳ Tips**

Citrus fruits, berries and melons are great sources of vitamin C.

Orange-coloured fruits such as mangoes, apricots and papayas are plentiful sources of vitamin A and beta-carotene.

6   Keep dried dates or apricots in your desk for snacks.

7   Create a fruit salsa out of diced mango, red onion, diced mild or hot chillies, and coriander.

8   Serve fruit salad for dessert.

9   Aim for four or five servings of fruit every day. A serving of fruit is one medium piece (such as an apple or orange), 175 ml (6 fl oz) of juice or a small can of fruit. Fruit juice counts towards your four or five servings, but try to choose whole fruit instead, since most juices are low in fibre.

## 828  Add Vegetables to Your Diet

Mum was right when she told you to eat your greens. They are great sources of fibre, vitamins and minerals – not to mention the phytonutrients so highly touted in medical news today.

### ⊙ Steps

1   Mix carrot juice into your breakfast orange juice.

2   Add chopped broccoli or grated courgettes to an omelette.

3   Toss sliced cucumbers with seasoned rice vinegar for an instant Chinese-style salad.

4   Dip raw vegetables (cherry tomatoes, mushrooms, celery or carrots) into low-fat salad dressing or hummus.

5   Toss cooked, chilled sweetcorn (fresh or frozen) into a green salad.

6   Experiment with unusual vegetables such as kohlrabi, celeriac and Jerusalem artichokes.

7   Try oriental vegetables, such as bok choy and long beans from China, and edamame (young soybeans) and kabocha squash from Japan.

8   Spread tomato and onion salsa over grilled fish.

9   Sprinkle peeled, diced beetroot and carrots with salt, pepper and olive oil, then roast them at 220°C (425°F) for 30 minutes.

10  Mix chopped spinach, kale or other greens into a tomato sauce to serve with pasta.

11  Aim for four or five servings of vegetables a day. A serving is 110 g (4 oz) cooked vegetables (such as carrots or broccoli) or 55–85 g (2–3 oz) raw salad vegetables (lettuce or spinach, for example). Vegetable juice counts, but try to choose the whole vegetable instead, since most juices are lower in fibre.

### ✱ Tips

Buy prewashed salads to reduce salad-preparation time.

Check out the supermarket salad bar for pre-cut broccoli, cauliflower and other vegetables. Eat these raw or steamed.

## Gain Weight | 829

Gaining weight may be a cinch for most people, but for those who don't put on pounds easily, it can be a real struggle. Here's how to bulk up while maintaining a healthful lifestyle.

### ☉ Steps

1 Eat nutritious foods that are high in calories. Some examples are whole-grain breads, avocados, potatoes, kidney beans, lean red meat, poultry and fish.

2 Boost the caloric value of your meals using healthful additions. Add powdered milk to casseroles, add avocados and olives to sandwiches, add wheat germ to cereal, add chopped meat to pasta sauce, and so on.

3 Eat three meals a day and at least two snacks.

4 Increase your normal portion size. Take a second scoop of pasta, or add a banana to your oatmeal.

5 Choose higher-calorie foods when given a choice. For example, sweet corn is higher in calories than green beans.

6 Relax – excessive fidgeting and restlessness can burn up a lot of calories.

7 Add weight lifting to your exercise programme. It helps build muscle mass. Be aware, though, that this will speed up your metabolism, so you'll need to increase your calories even more.

8 Tally up your caloric intake, and compare it with the number of calories you're burning. You need to be taking in more than you use up, and you may need to ease up a little on your exercise programme.

### ✳ Tips

If you cannot seem to put on any weight, you should have a doctor rule out any physical problems, such as hormonal imbalances.

Although it seems like a logical way to bulk up, avoid adding excess fat and sweets to your diet. Too much fat is bad for your health regardless of your weight, and filling up on junk food will keep you from getting all the nutrition you need from healthier foods. Eat fats and oils in moderation; they should account for no more than 30 per cent of your total caloric intake.

### ⚠ Warning

Consult your doctor before beginning any weight-gain programme.

## Lose Weight | 830

Proper diet and exercise can aid in weight loss, as well as keep you healthy. The challenge is to follow through. Others have lost weight by following these simple guidelines – so can you.

### ☉ Steps

1 Set small, realistic goals. Some good goals are to increase your exercise or activity by ten minutes, or to cut down on unhealthy snacks or canned drinks in the afternoon.

2 Start a regular exercise programme and stick with it. Aim for a minimum of 30 minutes, three or four times a week. You'll burn more calories and get fit faster if you exercise even more – 30 to 60 minutes, five to seven times a week.

3 Sneak in extra exercise in addition to your regular programme. Park at the far end of the car park and walk; take the stairs instead of the lift.

4 Eat low-fat, high-fibre foods such as salads and vegetable pasta dishes.

5 Choose foods that you like. Learn to prepare healthful, low-calorie foods that taste good. Eating well doesn't have to mean eating dull foods.

### ✳ Tips

Lose weight with a friend, or join a support group.

Avoid vending machines by carrying around your own healthful snacks.

### ⚠ Warning

Consult your doctor before beginning any weight-loss programme.

6  Eat smaller, more frequent meals. Some experts believe that this way, your body starts to increase its metabolism so that calories are burned faster. Also, mini-meals can prevent overeating later on. Keep in mind that this may not work for everyone – and remember that snacking on crisps or doughnuts is not going to shrink your waistline. Stick to healthful, low-calorie foods.

7  Drink a minimum of eight glasses of water per day – more if you are active. Water is critical for weight loss.

8  Plan ahead. Keep the fridge stocked with healthful food, and you'll be less likely to run out for high-calorie, high-fat junk food.

9  Keep a food diary. This will help you pinpoint where you can improve your eating habits.

10  Once you discover your favourite snack time, be sure to have plenty of healthful options available.

11  Make sure you've chosen an exercise programme you enjoy, and don't rule out the unconventional – regular vigorous dancing is exercise, too. Consult a doctor to find an exercise programme that is best for you if you are extremely overweight.

12  Lose weight gradually – you are more likely to keep it off. A safe amount is 0.5 to 0.75 kg (1 to 1½ lb) per week.

## 831 Help Your Family Lose Weight

According to a recent study, people with a family history of obesity are up to 75 per cent more likely to have weight problems. Stop the trend by organising a family weight-loss plan.

### ⊙ Steps

1  Take a trip to the supermarket together. Let everyone choose his or her favourite nutritious foods, and remind one another to avoid the aisles with the junk food.

2  Share low-fat recipes and healthy cooking tips, and put these to good use by preparing meals together.

3  Serve reasonably proportioned meals on individual plates. That is, bring to the table plates that are already full, as opposed to passing around dishes from which family members can help themselves.

4  Take a walk together after dinner.

5  Turn off the television set and computer and spend time together doing more active things, such as playing football or riding bicycles around the neighbourhood.

6  Join a health club together – be sure to ask about family or group rates.

7  Indulge your family's taste for adventure by planning the next holiday around an activity that requires movement, such as hiking, skiing, cycling or canoeing.

### ✱ Tip

When talking to your children about losing weight, be sure to put the emphasis on being healthy and fit, not on looking slim. Instead of saying that it would be nice to look thin in the next school picture, remind them that a healthy diet and exercise will give them more energy and make them stronger.

### ⚠ Warning

Consult your doctor before beginning any weight-loss programme.

## Build Lean Body Mass 832

Chiselled abs, shapely legs, toned arms – these can be yours when you increase your lean body mass and decrease your body-fat percentage.

### ⊙ Steps

1  Get your body-fat percentage measured before making dietary or exercise changes; this way you'll be able to track your progress. There are many ways to measure body fat, including calipers (skin-fold pinching), underwater (hydrostatic) weighing, and bioelectrical impedance. Your doctor's surgery or your gym should be able to provide this service.

2  Strength-train to build lean body mass. Work the major muscle groups, including the quadriceps (thighs), hamstrings, gluteal muscles (buttocks), back, chest, shoulders, arms and abdominal muscles.

3  Realise there is no such thing as spot reducing. You can increase the strength and tone of a certain part of your body, but unless you shed your overall excess body fat, you won't be able to see the definition.

4  Expend more calories than you consume. Any activity, from mowing the lawn to vacuuming, burns calories and helps create a calorie deficit, resulting in fat loss. Losing fat will help reveal your hidden muscles.

5  Keep in mind that to lose ½ kg (1 lb) of fat, you have to create a calorie deficit of 3,500 calories. Reducing calorie consumption or increasing activity by 500 calories a day will result in ½ kg (1 lb) of fat loss per week.

6  Include cardiovascular training in your workout. Aerobic exercise will increase the number of calories you burn and enhance your endurance.

7  Consider working with a personal trainer to help you get started on an exercise regimen.

### ✱ Tips

Keep in mind the following body-fat percentage standards: for women, 17 to 20 per cent is considered lean, 20 to 25 per cent is normal, 26 to 30 per cent is overfat and 30 per cent or higher is obese. For men, 8 to 12 per cent is considered lean, 13 to 19 per cent is normal, 20 to 24 per cent is overfat and 25 per cent or higher is obese.

Strength training creates an after-burn effect, meaning that your metabolism continues to burn calories at a higher rate even after the exercise is over.

Dieting without strength training can leave you with a high body fat percentage. It's possible to appear thin but have a high percentage of body fat.

## Fit Exercise Into Your Busy Schedule 833

Make a commitment to exercise every day if you can. Try to get in at least 30 minutes of walking or more vigorous exercise.

### ⊙ Steps

1  Try walking, cycling or roller-blading to work. If this takes longer than your usual commute, plan ahead: pack your briefcase and lay out your clothes the night before. Keep a change of clothes at work if need be.

2  If an alternate commute is impossible, get off the bus a little earlier and walk the rest of the way, park at the far end of the car park, or take the stairs instead of the lift.

3  Make use of your lunch break. Play a quick game of squash, make a speedy gym visit, go for a jog or take a brisk walk (use some light hand weights for a bonus workout).

4  Stretch at your desk. This reduces muscle tension, gets your circulation moving and prepares you for more strenuous activity later.

### ✱ Tips

New mums can join an aerobics class specially designed for them and their babies. You can network with other mums, stay fit and keep an eye on the baby, who gets involved as part of your workout routine.

Exercise with a friend – you can motivate one another.

Carry a notebook and keep a record of your activities and their duration. Increase your daily exercise as time goes on.

5   Do some chores. Mow the lawn or rake the leaves for 20 minutes. Housework burns calories, and you have to get the work done anyway.

6   Play games with your children. Kick a football or play some hopscotch.

## 834 | Exercise at Your Office

You may not want to turn your office into a gym, but there are exercises you can do at or near your desk to boost your energy level, relieve stress and burn calories.

### ⊙ Steps

1   Try some squats. Stand in front of your chair with your feet shoulder-width apart. Bend your knees as though you're sitting on the chair, keeping your weight on your heels. When your legs are parallel with the seat of the chair, slowly rise to your original standing position.

2   Hold up the wall with wall sits. Stand with your back touching the wall. Move your feet away from the wall so that the wall is supporting the weight of your back. Bend your knees so that your legs form a 90-degree angle. Hold as long as you can.

3   Pose like a warrior – with a lunge. With your arms by your sides, take a giant step forwards with your right leg so your thigh is parallel with the floor. Pushing off the same leg, return to your starting position. Repeat with the left leg. (Travelling lunges are also an option if you have room – keep moving forwards with each lunge.)

4   Try calf raises during a coffee break. Holding on to your desk or a filing cabinet for balance, raise your heels off the floor, then lower them.

5   Peek into your neighbour's cubicle while you do toe raises. Sitting in your chair or standing, lift and lower your toes while keeping your heels on the ground, or walk around on the heels of your feet.

6   Burn that bottom with a gluteal squeeze. While sitting or standing, squeeze the muscles of your rear end. Hold, then relax.

7   Get on the floor and do some crunches. Lying on your back with your knees bent, reach for your knees, hold for two counts, then return to the floor. No need to curl all the way up – stop when your abdominal muscles are fully contracted; your shoulders will be just a few inches off the floor.

8   Do some push-ups, standing upright and pushing against a wall with your hands a little wider than shoulder-width apart, or lying face down on the ground.

9   Do some dips. Sitting on your chair, with the palms of your hands on your chair and feet on the floor, scoot your rear end off the end of the seat. Bend your elbows, lowering your body, then straighten your arms to return to the starting position.

10  Release tension with shoulder raises. Raise your shoulders up to your ears, hold, then relax.

### ✱ Tips

Doing squats will help protect your knees from future injuries. However, if you've had a knee injury in the past, check with your doctor about what exercises are appropriate for you, and go easy when trying any new exercises involving the knee.

If you're not familiar with strength-training exercises, seek the assistance of a qualified personal trainer or a physiotherapist to get you started properly.

Always warm up or begin exercising gradually.

Perform enough repetitions of each exercise to feel fatigue in the muscles being worked.

It helps to have comfortable clothes on hand or to work for a company that observes a casual dress code.

### ⚠ Warnings

Use discretion in the workplace: Do only what's appropriate for your particular work environment.

If using a chair to perform exercises, be sure to choose a sturdy, supportive one without wheels.

## Stay Motivated to Exercise

You know you should exercise, but some days it's tough to get moving. Discover what motivates you, and use these strategies to develop and maintain an active lifestyle.

### ◉ Steps

1 Determine an attainable goal, such as exercising twice during the week and once on weekends. Creating realistic goals will set you up for success. If your goal becomes too easy, you can always design a more ambitious one.

2 Devise rewards for achieving your goal. The reward can be a massage, a new workout outfit, a new CD, a session with a personal trainer or that hardcover novel you've had your eye on – whatever you really want.

3 Partner with a friend, co-worker or loved one – someone who will support you and your goals without sabotaging them.

4 Subscribe to a fitness magazine or online fitness newsletter. New tips and exercises can be inspirational and alleviate boredom.

5 Create a competition with co-workers or friends. For example, the team whose members exercise for 30 minutes, three times each week, for two months wins a prize.

6 Change into your workout clothes. Sometimes, just getting dressed is the biggest barrier.

7 Erase the concept that if you can't do at least 30 minutes you're wasting your time. Even in small doses, exercise burns calories, increases energy and improves your health.

8 Try a new sport or class. Adding variety, group support and competition can increase your likelihood of exercising.

9 Make a commitment to your dog or your neighbour's dog to go for a long walk at least twice each week.

10 Look for ways to incorporate activity into your day, even if you can't do your normal exercise routine. Take the stairs instead of the lift, go bowling instead of to the cinema, or use a push mower instead of an electric mower.

11 Sign up for a race and send in the entry fee. Whatever your activity – running, cycling, walking, swimming – there are hundreds of races offered all over the world. Pick a place you've always wanted to visit.

12 Join a gym or health club. For some, paying for a membership increases the likelihood of compliance. It also eliminates the bad-weather excuse.

### ✳ Tips

Exercise in the morning. Research shows that people who make exercise a priority first thing in the day are more likely to stick with it.

Every person goes through periods when it's very challenging to maintain an exercise programme. Acknowledge it when it happens, recognise that it's just a brief period of time, and restart your programme as soon as possible.

Choose things that motivate you – not what others want.

Remind yourself of the many health benefits of an exercise programme.

## 836 Ease Sore Muscles

You can always relieve sore, tight muscles with a massage, or by using sports creams or medicines. Before spending money, though, try these simple remedies.

### ⊙ Steps

1 Apply an ice pack for 20 minutes to any area that hurts. Repeat this every hour until the pain subsides.

2 Opt for heat if you have a chronic condition or continual episodes of pain. In these situations, heat can work better than ice (if you are not treating an acute injury). Try a heating pad, or a warm shower or bath.

3 Stretch the sore area gently to loosen up damaged muscles.

4 Walk 15 to 30 minutes at least once a day to increase circulation throughout your body. This will also help deliver much-needed oxygen to the sore muscles.

5 Drink a minimum of eight glasses of water daily – more if you're active – to hydrate your body.

6 Avoid strenuous activity as long as you're in pain.

### ✳ Tips

Be sure to warm up before exercising and stretching.

An over-the-counter non-steroidal anti-inflammatory medication, such as ibuprofen, may also reduce muscle soreness.

Avoid exercising or stretching to the point of pain.

## 837 Get a Massage

Massage has been touted as a panacea for everything from migraines to ulcers. Although the scientific proof is sparse, almost everyone agrees that a massage at the very least feels good.

### ⊙ Steps

1 Avoid eating close to the time of your massage.

2 Relax. Give yourself plenty of time to get to your massage appointment.

3 Wear clothing that you can get out of easily. If you plan to keep your clothes on, wear something like loose shorts and a jogging bra for a woman or boxer shorts for a man; these options make it easier for the massage therapist to work on you.

4 Tell the therapist if you have any health concerns, if you may be pregnant or if you have had any injuries.

5 Let the therapist know if there is any area where you do not wish to be touched, or if there is an area where you would like special work done.

6 Clear your thoughts. A massage is a time to relax, not to worry about projects at work or your bank account.

7 Breathe normally. Don't hold your breath if a sensitive spot is being worked on.

8 Try not to contract your muscles. Your body needs to be relaxed and flexible to get the best results. Imagine you are a rag doll.

### ✳ Tips

Before booking a professional massage, make sure the therapist is qualified.

If you prefer a massage therapist of a certain sex, remember to register your request when you make your appointment.

Leave on some clothing if you are uncomfortable being nude. The key is to be comfortable.

9   Report any discomfort or problems during the massage. If you feel any pain, are cold, don't like the music, and so on, tell the therapist.

10  Rise slowly after the massage is over. Get off the table gradually. Take your time, and try to maintain your state of relaxation.

11  Drink a tall glass of water after your massage.

12  Avoid driving if you are feeling spaced-out or light-headed. Wait a few minutes to get grounded.

## Give a Back Massage                                        838

Providing a little touch therapy for stress reduction is a wonderful and therapeutic gift in this era of 14-hour workdays and repetitive-stress injuries.

### ◎ Steps

1   Have the person receiving the massage lie on her tummy on a firm, comfortable surface, such as a floor mat or firm bed. Make sure you can reach her whole back without straining your own.

2   Stand or kneel by her side. Place one hand on the lower back and one hand between the shoulder blades, over the heart.

3   Warm up the back by applying thumb pressure along both sides of the spine simultaneously: start at the lower back and knead gently with your thumbs up to the neck area. This will also promote relaxation.

4   Use a smooth, delicate stroke (called "effleurage") to apply massage oil. In one long stroke, slide your palms down either side of the spine to the pelvis; scoop out around the hips and back up the sides to the shoulders. Maintain contact with the back. Glide your hands over the back to start a new area.

5   Continue up both sides of the neck to the base of the head.

6   Start at the spine and slide your palms in opposite directions outwards to the sides of the back, starting with the lower back area and moving up to the shoulders.

7   Knead the fleshy muscular areas at the top of the shoulders, the mid-back area and the buttocks to loosen tight muscles and fascia (the connective tissue).

8   Use your thumbs or fingers to apply pressure to areas that feel hard or tight, often called knots.

9   Perform clockwise circular friction with your fingertips along the muscles that are close to the spine and around the shoulder blades.

10  Rotate the arms gently, one at a time, to loosen the shoulder joints and enhance blood flow.

### ✳ Tips

The many benefits of massage include relaxation, increased body awareness, improved circulation, and improved lymphatic drainage for release of toxins.

Massage oil is typically used to decrease the friction created on the skin and to prevent the pulling of hair. The less oil, the greater the friction and the deeper the pressure.

Incorporate effleurage throughout your massage as a connective stroke to move from one area to another, to soothe an area of localised deep tissue work or to make a transition to another stroke.

Use slow movements for a soothing or calming response and fast movements for a stimulating effect.

### ⚠ Warnings

Do not put any direct pressure on the spine.

Avoid any broken skin, blisters or areas of possible infection.

## 839 Meditate

Meditation can be calming, rejuvenating and restorative. When practised regularly, it can aid in reducing stress, lowering blood pressure and increasing personal awareness.

### ◎ Steps

1 Choose a tranquil location, free of distractions.

2 Decide whether you'd like to have soothing music in the background.

3 Select a comfortable chair or place to sit, and assume a sitting position with your spine relatively straight.

4 Close your eyes.

5 Breathe in, allowing your ribcage and belly to expand as you inhale.

6 Exhale slowly.

7 Concentrate on your breathing. Be aware of each breath and the feelings of deeper relaxation.

8 Allow thoughts and feelings to enter your mind. Acknowledge them, allow them to pass, and refocus on your breathing.

9 Open your eyes after you feel more relaxed and centred.

10 Begin with five to ten minutes of meditation each day and increase to 20 minutes or more twice each day.

### ✳ Tips

There are many forms and variations of meditation. If one particular form doesn't work for you, try another.

Avoid meditating on a full stomach. The best time to meditate is just before eating.

Some studies have suggested meditation may decrease the risk of heart disease, possibly because the resulting stress relief may promote the body's self-repair system to thin the fatty build-up on artery walls. Still, meditating should never be used as a substitute for a healthful diet, exercise and proper medical care.

## 840 Fight Insomnia

Everyone has an occasional sleepless night. Life's daily stresses, major decisions and caffeine too late in the day all contribute to insomnia.

### ◎ Steps

1 Use your bed for sleeping only. Try to refrain from catching up on work or just hanging out in bed.

2 Relax by listening to soft music or a meditation tape before bedtime. Do yoga or gentle stretching.

3 Take a hot bath. Keep the lights dim.

4 Use essential oils to help you relax. Add six to eight drops of lavender or marjoram to a bath, or put four drops of oil on your pillow.

5 Snack on foods high in tryptophan, an amino acid that can help you relax. These include turkey, bananas, figs, dates, milk and tuna.

6 Try an herbal sleep remedy to help induce sleepiness. Valerian, camomile, catnip, lavender, lime flower, passionflower, hops or skullcap can be taken in tea or capsule form. The hormone melatonin can be taken as a pill or a lozenge and may promote sleep as well. Keep in mind that further research is still needed to verify the effectiveness of these alternative remedies.

### ✳ Tips

Room temperature, noise and physical ailments can all contribute to sleeplessness.

Trying too hard to fall asleep can have the reverse effect: you'll stay awake. Distract yourself by doing something else instead.

7   Get out of bed if you can't sleep. Lying in bed sleepless will only make you feel more stressed.

8   Read or perform a light chore until you start feeling sleepy. Then try to go back to sleep – or if you're feeling stressed or agitated, try some relaxation techniques.

9   Return to bed once you're feeling sleepy and relaxed.

## Break a Bad Habit                                    841

Habits such as biting your nails, downing large amounts of caffeine and even gossiping are automatic behaviours that can be changed with patience and persistence.

### ⊙ Steps

1   Decide how serious you are about breaking the habit. In addition to a strong commitment, you'll need time and energy to pay attention to your behaviour so you can change it.

2   Keep track of the behaviour. Keep a notepad or journal handy.

3   Write down when it happens (what the overall situation is when it occurs) and what you were thinking and feeling. Writing increases your awareness of when and why you have this habit.

4   Read and think about what you write down. What does this habit do for you? Is it a way to deal with feelings of boredom, anxiety, stress or anger?

5   Think of what you could do instead of the habit that would be a more positive way to deal with the feelings or situation that provoke it. Write down some simple alternative behaviours. Pick one you want to practise.

6   Try to catch yourself when you find yourself indulging in the habit, and stop yourself as soon as you can. Start the alternative behaviour you decided you wanted to do instead.

7   Aim to do this once a week at first, then increase the number of times per week over time. The more you practise a new behaviour, the more it becomes the new habit.

8   Get support from others by letting them know you are working on the habit and telling them what they can do to help.

### ✱ Tips

Be patient with yourself. Habits are so automatic and unconscious, you may not even realise you're engaging in the behaviour until you're already doing it.

Be kind to yourself. Browbeating yourself is another bad habit to be broken.

## Stop Smoking                                          842

You've probably already heard the many reasons why you should stop smoking – now check out the various ways of how to go about it.

### ⊙ Steps

1   Ask yourself why you want to stop smoking.

2   Write your answers on a piece of paper and carry it with you.

### ✱ Tips

Ask your doctor about nicotine products and other types of medication if you have tried unsuccessfully to stop in the past.

3 Whenever you feel like smoking, use your list to remind yourself of why you want to stop.

4 Fill out a "stop smoking contract". Sign it, and have a family member or friend sign it as a witness.

5 Throw away all your cigarettes, lighters and ashtrays.

6 Change your schedule to avoid circumstances in which you usually smoke. Walk around the block or chew gum when you would normally be smoking.

7 Put up no-smoking signs in your house, your work area and your car.

8 Prepare yourself to feel the urge to start smoking again. Here are four ways to deal with the urge to smoke: delaying, deep breathing, drinking water and doing something else.

9 Carry around "mouth toys" – sweets, chewing gum, straws, carrot sticks.

10 List the good things that have happened since you stopped smoking, and keep the list with you as an inspiration wherever you go. For example, you might note that your breath is fresher, you can climb the stairs without getting winded, and you've saved enough money to buy a new DVD player.

11 Reward yourself for stopping smoking; for example, you could take the money you have saved and buy yourself something nice.

Be prepared to persist despite a few relapses.

Planning meals, eating a healthful diet and staying active will help you maintain your weight.

Look for a support group or smoking-cessation class.

## ⚠ Warning

You may experience irritability, depression or a dry mouth due to nicotine withdrawal after you stop smoking. These symptoms should pass.

---

## 843 Overcome a Phobia

Overcoming a phobia entails learning how to relax and calm yourself so that you can gradually face the feared object or situation and feel less afraid.

### ⦿ Steps

1 Explore exactly what it is you are afraid of. Is there some underlying reason or past event that causes you to avoid an object or situation? Is there something you gain by avoiding it (besides avoiding the fear or anxiety)?

2 Learn how to relax and calm yourself. There are many ways to do this. Here is one method. Take a slow, deep breath into your belly to the count of six and then breathe out slowly to the count of six. Practise this daily for five minutes; increase over time to 20 minutes.

3 Make a list starting with the feared object or situation – for example, driving on motorways. Then, write down what object or situation would be slightly less anxiety-producing – for example, driving on A roads.

4 Continue making a list of items that are slightly less anxiety-producing than the previous item – for example, driving on big, busy streets, then driving on less congested streets, and so forth.

5 Get into a relaxed state using whatever method you have been practising. Starting with the least anxiety-producing item on your list (the last item), imagine yourself in that situation as vividly as possible while continuing to breathe and stay relaxed.

### ✱ Tip

Since this is quite challenging, it is often helpful to go through these steps with a psychotherapist. A therapist can teach you how to relax, help you come up with ways to challenge negative thoughts, and help you feel safer as you face your phobia.

### ⚠ Warning

Seek professional help if your phobia is interfering with your daily life or causing you significant distress.

6   Go on to the next item up. Visualise yourself in that situation while continuing to practise relaxation and calm yourself.

7   Work up the list, imagining yourself in each situation while continuing to practise remaining relaxed and calm. Only go to the next item when you can successfully stay calm imagining the previous item. If one of the items produces too much anxiety, stop the exercise and come back to it later. Start at the beginning of your list each time, and progress as far as you can. It may take you several sessions before you progress to the top of the list.

8   Write down all the thoughts you have when facing your phobia, such as "I'm going to die", "I'm going to have a heart attack" or "I can't breathe".

9   Write down alternative thoughts that would help you calm down, such as "I am not going to die", "I can breathe" or "I can relax".

10  In real life, put yourself in the least anxiety-producing situation on your list (the last item) and practise relaxing and calming yourself just as you imagined. Include telling yourself the alternative thoughts to help you calm down.

11  Work yourself up to your most feared situation or object (your phobia) while practising being relaxed and calm.

# Stop Worrying 844

The keys to worrying less are to challenge your worrisome thoughts and to calm yourself physically and emotionally.

## ⊙ Steps

1   Write down what you are worried about. Include your imagined worst-case scenarios.

2   Think about how you would handle your worst-case scenarios.

3   Decide what actions you could take that would change the situation and give you less to worry about. Then follow through on those actions.

4   Try to think logically about the worrisome thoughts that you feel you can't take any action on. Consider which of them are excessive or distorted and have very little basis in reality.

5   For each of these worrisome thoughts, write down an alternative way of looking at the problem that presents a rational challenge to your worries.

6   Try to catch yourself when you notice that you're becoming over-whelmed with worry. Stop and remind yourself of the alternative way to look at the situation.

7   Practise relaxation and stress-reduction techniques. One simple thing you can do to help quiet your mind and calm your emotions and body is to breathe in slowly and deeply to the count of six and breathe out slowly to the count of six. Do this for five minutes; gradually increase to 20 minutes over time.

8   Learn to accept what you cannot change or have no power to control in life. Read books dealing with worry, anxiety, acceptance and inner peace. Look in the psychology, self-help and spirituality sections of your bookshop or library.

## ✱ Tips

If you need to, get help from others in coming up with challenges to your worrisome thoughts. They can often present you with a different perspective on things.

Many people find spiritual teachings or belief in a higher power extremely helpful in decreasing worry and developing more trust in life.

## ⚠ Warning

Seek professional help if your worries are interfering with your daily functioning or causing you significant distress.

## 845 | Head a Football

Heading is an essential skill for a complete all-round footballer. It allows you to gain possession of the ball, pass, set up an attack, score goals, and clear the ball from in front of goal.

### ⊙ Steps

1 Arch your back as the ball approaches, with your chin inwards, neck firm and legs bent. Keep your arms out to your sides for balance and to fend off opponents.

2 Spread your feet apart, wider than shoulder width. Keep both feet on the ground (unless you need to jump to reach the ball).

3 Snap your upper body towards the ball from the waist. Drive your head and neck forward as you make contact. Keep your head and neck moving together instead of holding your neck still while your head moves.

4 Make contact with the ball squarely with your forehead. Keep your eyes open and on the ball, and keep your mouth closed. Avoid making contact with the top of your head.

5 Direct the ball down by making contact with your head slightly closer to the top of the ball.

6 Make contact slightly lower on the ball to send it upward.

7 Follow through by continuing to drive your head forward. The strength of the header comes from the waist.

### ✱ Tips

If you need to jump, then jump early, so that you have reached the highest point of your jump by the time the ball arrives.

When heading the ball to score a goal, direct the ball down to make it harder for the goalkeeper to save.

To clear the ball from in front of your own goal, direct the header upward.

### ⚠ Warning

Incorrect heading can lead to neck injury. Beginners should go slowly. Practise with a light ball, such as a beach ball or soft volleyball, and gradually move on to a regulation football.

## 846 | Make a Chip Pass

The shortest distance between you and your team-mate may be a straight line, but defenders sometimes don't cooperate. So, send a lofted ball that's easy for your team-mate to get hold of.

### ⊙ Steps

1 Understand that a "chip" is when the ball travels in a tall arc. Usually a quick kick is used to send the ball up and over a short distance, rather than in a long, soaring flight.

2 Approach the ball at a slight angle.

3 Place your non-kicking foot approximately 15 cm (6 in) to the side of the ball and slightly behind it.

4 Take a back swing with your kicking leg, keeping in mind that a shorter back swing will allow you more control and better direction.

5 Angle your toe down – imagine your foot to be like a wedge – as you make contact with the ball below its centre.

6 Lean your body back as you kick to increase the lift of the ball. The further you lean back, the greater the ball's arc.

### ✱ Tips

A proper chip should have back-spin, which makes it easy for your teammate to control. A ball spinning backward is less likely to run away from the receiver once contact is made.

If the goalkeeper has off his line to cut down the angle of your shot, chipping the ball over his head is a good technique for scoring a goal.

Be comfortable chipping with both feet, and chipping dead balls as well as moving ones.

## Cross From the Wing

One of the deadliest lines of attack in football is to outflank the opposing defence with a run down the wing – as long as you can complete the move with a telling cross for your strikers.

### ⊙ Steps

1  Control the ball as you move down the wing, eluding defenders along the way.

2  Glance to the middle of the field to see where your team-mates are making runs.

3  Decide whether to make an early cross, if an attacker is free to receive it, or carry the ball on to the goal line.

4  Use a lofted cross, if defenders block the route to your team-mates running in on goal (see the technique described in 846 "Make a Chip Pass"). Don't hit your cross too close to the goalkeeper.

### ✳ Tip

The ball will tend to swerve away from the goal if you cross with your outside foot; using your inside foot makes the ball swerve towards the goal. So if you are on the right wing and you want the ball to curve away from the goalkeeper's grasp, cross with your right foot.

## Make a Slide Tackle

A slide tackle is a sideways slide that attempts to knock the ball away from your opponent's feet. You use it as a last-ditch effort if your opponent is going to get past you.

### ⊙ Steps

1  Commit yourself to the slide, deciding whether you'll simply be kicking the ball away or trying to gain possession.

2  Slide on one side of your body.

3  Lead with one leg. If you're sliding on your left side, lead with your right leg, extending your foot toward the ball, while the left leg is bent at a 90-degree angle.

4  Be sure to slide leaning part of the way down on the side of your leg; sliding in a more upright position will allow you to spring up after the slide.

5  Make contact with the ball first. If you hit your opponent first, the referee will certainly award a freekick and may even show you a yellow card.

6  Knock the ball a long way if you're sending it out of play, or tap it more gently if you're attempting to gain possession.

7  Using your left arm and left leg, quickly rise from the ground and get back into the action.

### ✳ Tips

You'll discover that you're more comfortable sliding on a particular side of your body, but always practise using both sides.

It's a good idea to learn to slide tackle on a wet day, when the ground is soft.

### △ Warning

Bumps, scrapes and bruises are all likely when you use the slide tackle. You also risking injuring your opponent.

## 849 | Take a Long Throw-in

The long throw-in has become a formidable attacking technique in modern football. It makes a throw-in near the opposition penalty area as dangerous as a corner kick.

### ⊙ Steps

1 Grip the ball firmly in both hands. Wipe off moisture if the ball is wet so that you can grasp the ball securely.

2 Take two or three steps back from the touchline.

3 Decide to which of your team-mates you intend to reach with the ball and focus on the distance and direction required for your throw.

4 Make a short run to the touchline, to give yourself extra momentum that will propel the ball further infield.

5 Bring the ball back over your head and arch your back.

6 Ensure that both your feet are on the ground, as required by the rules. You may either have one foot in front of the either or stand square with the feet side by side.

6 Use the full power of your back and shoulders to propel the ball into its trajectory.

7 Release the ball when it is in front of your head, not from behind or over your head.

### ✳ Tip

A long throw-in requires muscle-power as well as technique. Working out to strengthen your upper back, neck and upper arms will contribute to your success with throw-ins.

## 850 | Take a Penalty

Success or failure from the penalty spot often depends on nerve as much as skill. But a solid technique will help a penalty taker resist the pressures of the situation.

### ⊙ Steps

1 Practise penalty kicks in training. Establish a routine for taking penalties that suits you, and follow that routine exactly when playing in a match.

2 Place the ball precisely on the penalty spot – otherwise the referee may intervene to place it properly and this could break your concentration.

3 Compose yourself as you step back to the start of your approach run, focussing your attention totally on the ball

4 Decide precisely where you intend the ball to go before you begin your run-up to shoot. Never change your mind during the approach run.

5 Aim to shoot into one of two bottom corners of the goal.

6 End your run-up with your non-kicking foot alongside the ball, not behind it.

6 Make sure your head and the knee of your kicking leg are over the ball. Kick firmly with a high follow through.

### ✳ Tips

Concentrate on the ball, not on the goalkeeper. If you focus your attention on the keeper, you may end up kicking the ball straight towards him.

Keep your shot on the ground. If you loft the shot, you'll probably make it easier for the goalkeeper to save, and you may blaze the ball over the crossbar.

## Run Past Defenders With the Ball                                    851

There is no surer way of unsettling defenders than to run at them with the ball. Successful dribbling requires the ability to change direction and speed almost instantaneously.

### ⊙ Steps

1  Approach the opposing defender with the ball close to your feet. Keep your legs slightly bent and your body tilted forwards so that you are leaning over the top of the ball.

2  Advance slowly at first, controlling the ball with touches from the inside and outside of both feet.

3  Feint with your body to left or right, or both alternately. This will throw the defender off balance.

4  Push the ball to one or other side of the defender, or (rarely) through his legs, and accelerate rapidly after it.

5  Once in the clear, straighten up from your crouched posture.

6  Lengthen your stride for maximum speed, pushing the ball several metres in front of you at each kick.

7  When running at speed, keep aware of the position of defenders and evade them with unexpected changes of direction.

### ✳ Tips

When you are running with the ball at speed, kick it forwards with the outside of your foot, not the inside, which will be awkward and slow you down.

Many attempts at dribbling break down because the attacker stumbles or trips over the ball. Minimise these embarrassing errors by avoiding overelaborate feinting moves.

## Score With a Swerving Free Kick                                    852

One of the most spectacular sights in football is a curling free kick hit over or around the defensive wall into the goal. So how can you learn to "bend it like Beckham"?

### ⊙ Steps

1  Place the ball and observe the angle and distance to the goal. Size up the position of the defensive wall and goalkeeper.

2  Decide exactly where you intend your shot to go – which side of the goal you are aiming at and whether you intend the ball to travel over the top or around the side of the wall.

3  Retreat a half a dozen steps to the start of your run-up. Using an angled run-up will increase the lift and spin on the kick.

4  Keep your eyes fixed on the ball as you run up to kick, and maintain your head as steady as possible.

5  Draw back your kicking leg with the foot stretched back from the ankle, so that the line from knee to toe is as straight as possible.

6  Strike the ball low down on the left or right of its centre line. The ball will swerve in the opposite direction to the side struck, so if the foot contacts the ball on the right of centre it will swerve to the left in flight.

7  Follow through so that your kicking leg swings up to waist level.

### ✳ Tips

If the shot fails to bend, this is often a sign that your follow-through is inadequate. When you complete the kick, your leg should be high and turned in the direction of the intended swerve.

Contact the ball right or left of centre, but not too far right or left. If you strike the outer edge of the ball, you will not achieve sufficient power in the shot.

## 853 | Avoid Injury at Rugby

Rugby is a sport involving not just contact but collision. With proper preparation and supervision it is safe, but without these it can become seriously bruising and even dangerous.

### ⊙ Steps

1 Exercise regularly to ensure that you are physically fit enough to withstand the strains of a rugby match. Developing strong core muscles in the back, in particular, will protect against injuries.

2 Train thoroughly to learn good technique, especially for tackling and scrums, before you begin to play competitively at any level. Many injuries result from avoidable technical errors.

3 Before playing a match, warm up for between 15 and 30 minutes, with plenty of stretches.

4 Use a mouthguard (gumshield). This will prevent damage to your teeth and give some protection against injuries to the head and jaw. Either obtain a custom-made mouthguard from your dentist or buy a "boil-and-bite" shield.

5 Protect your head with a plastic scrumcap. Wear lightweight padding on your shoulders and chest.

6 Drink plenty of liquid in the course of a match to avoid dehydration and heat stroke.

7 Follow the rules of the game scrupulously; they are designed to minimise serious injuries. In particular, never deliberately cause a scrum, ruck or maul to collapse.

6 Withdraw from the game immediately if you suffer a blow to the head that results in even momentary loss of consciousness, or in temporary mental confusion or loss of balance.

### ⚠ Warnings

Players who suffer a knock that renders them unconscious for more than 15 seconds should be taken to a hospital accident and emergency department.

If unconscious, a player should be assumed to have a serious neck or spinal injury until proven otherwise, and should be moved only with the greatest caution.

### Things You'll Need

☐ mouthguard

☐ plastic scrumcap

☐ upper body padding

## 854 | Win the Ball in a Scrum

Rugby is a team game, and it is never more so than in the scrum. A set-piece eight-a-side pushing contest, a successful scrum depends on a throughly coordinated combined effort.

### ⊙ Steps

1 Link up firmly with other players in the scrum. In the front row – with the hooker in the centre flanked by two props – the hooker should loop an arm around each prop's near shoulder, gripping their jerseys. The props each place an arm around the hooker's back.

2 The second and back row players similarly bind together, pushing with their shoulders against the thighs or buttocks of the team-mates in front of them.

3 Players in the front row crouch down, with their shoulders slightly higher than their hips and their legs bent and splayed outwards. Players in the

### ⚠ Warnings

If the scrum collapses play must stop immediately.

Poor technique in a scrum can lead to injury. Young players should carefully learn the correct body and leg positions and linkage with other players before attempting to take part in a scrum in any competitive match.

second and back row lean into the players in front, keeping a straight back and legs slightly bent, ready to push.

4 The front row focus mentally on the scrum about to engage, staring directly into the eyes of the opposing front row at close quarters.

5 Engage with the opposing players at the referee's signal, the heads of the two front rows interlocking.

6 When the scrum-half is about to feed the ball into the scrum, use a pre-arranged code so he can tell the players on his team that the ball is coming. This allows them to react a fraction faster than their opponents.

7 The scrum-half feeds the ball in at a slight angle towards his own side, to give his side's hooker a better chance of hooking it back with his foot.

8 Channel the ball back through the scrum, pushing all the while.

## Win the Ball at a Line-Out 855

The line-out is a set play that restarts the game after the ball has gone over the touchline. Winning the ball at a line-out depends on an accurate throw and a good jump to receive it

### ⊙ Steps

#### Taking the Throw

1 Agree a set of code words or numbers before the match, each one representing a particular play at the line-out.

2 Line up where the throw is to be taken. Use seven players for the line-out, with your tallest players and/or best jumpers in the second, fourth and sixth positions, counting away from the thrower.

3 The thrower calls out the code for the throw he is about to make, ensuring that all the players hear it. This should identify which player in the line-out is expected to catch the ball.

4 For an effective throw, take the ball back behind your head and throw it forward with one hand, straight down the gap between the two lines.

5 Throw the ball in such a trajectory that the player who is intended to receive it can catch the ball at the top of his jump.

#### Receiving the Throw

1 Face the ball and, starting with both feet on the ground, propel yourself upwards. Supporting player should help hold you up in the air as you make the catch.

2 Land with the ball and immediately turn away from the opposition to shelter it from them.

8 Release the ball to another member of your team.

**✤ Tip**

Vary your tactics from time to time with a quick throw-in. It is perfectly within the rules to take the throw before a line-out forms, picking out a player in a good position. Remember that the throw must still be straight – at right-angles to the touchline.

## 856 | Score With a Kick at Rugby

Both drop kicks in open play and place kicks – either penalties or conversions after a try – are a valuable source of points at rugby. Kicking requires a cool head and solid technique.

### ⊙ Steps

#### Place Kick

1 Place a kicking tee in the turf at the spot from which the kick is to be taken.

2 Position the ball on the tee. Stand it on one pointed end, leaning slightly away from you and with the seam aligned towards the goalposts.

3 Take a few steps back, sizing up the distance and direction to the goal, and noting the strength and direction of the wind, if any.

4 Stand at the beginning of your run for as along as you need to focus entirely on the kick you are about to make. Visualise the ball flying between the uprights.

5 Run up with your eyes on the ball.

6 Place your non-kicking foot alongside the ball and pull back your kicking leg in a high backlift.

7 Kick the ball with your instep, striking it at a point just above the ground.

8 Make sure that your kicking leg follows through to guarantee sufficient power in the kick.

#### Drop Kick

1 Size up the direction to the goal posts and the distance that the kick has to carry.

2 Hold the ball in both hands at waist height.

3 Position the ball vertically, with the bottom point tilted slightly towards you and the top point away.

4 Take one step forwards with your non-kicking leg.

5 Drop the ball, while simultaneously lifting and drawing back your kicking foot.

6 Swing the kicking foot forward, keeping your eye on the ball and extending your arms to the sides for balance.

7 Strike the ball with the inside of your foot a fraction of a second after it bounces.

8 Follow through for a powerful kick.

### ✳ Tips

If you are a good distance from the goal, make your kick carry further by leaning forwards into the ball as you kick.

For a higher kick travelling a shorter distance, lean back as you kick and get your foot underneath the ball.

### Thing You'll Need

☐ kicking tee

**How to Do *(Just About)* Everything**

## Tackle Effectively at Rugby                                    857

Tackling at rugby is not for the faint-hearted. But as well as the physical courage to endure a potentially bruising collision, a front-on tackle requires skilful technique and expert timing.

### ⊙ Steps

1   Make a rapid assessment of the speed at which the ball-carrying opponent is running, the direction he is following, and how far he is from your position on the field.

2   Estimate the best direction to take to close the gap between you and the ball-carrier. Move swiftly to intercept his run.

3   Focus your attention on the player's legs as you draw closer, watching for early signs of a swerve or side-step to left or right. Do not focus on the player's face or upper body, since it is relatively easy for the ball carrier to mislead you with feinting movements of the eyes or arms.

4   Concentrate totally as you enter the tackle. Mentally commit yourself fully and fearlessly to the hit.

5   Look for a moment when the ball-carrier is unbalanced, either because in mid-stride or jinking to left or right.

6   Crouch with legs bent and lean your upper body towards the ball carrier. Aim for the player with your leading shoulder.

7   Thrust with your legs, driving your shoulder into the opposition player's lower chest. Keep your head to the side of the player's body.

8   Wrap your arms around the ball-carrier's waist and the back of the upper part of his thighs.

9   Pull the back of the opponent's thighs towards yourself, while pushing with your shoulder in the opposite direction on his chest, with all the strength that you can muster.

10  Force the ball-carrier down on his back and crash on top of him.

### ✳ Tips

Hit an opponent with a tackle just as he receives a pass from a team-mate. With his attention focussed on the ball, the opponent is ill-prepared to ward off or withstand the tackle.

If you fail to complete a tackle successfully by bringing your opponent to the ground, still cling on and slow him down as best you can. This will give one of your team-mates time to arrive and finish the job.

## Choose and Care For a Cricket Bat                              858

Made of natural willow, a soft springy wood, a classic cricket bat requires careful treatment in the first few weeks after purchase to become a strong, durable piece of equipment.

### ⊙ Steps

1   Select a bat of the right size by measuring the bat against your leg. The top of the handle should be level with the top of your thigh.

2   Select a bat of suitable weight by trying out the bat with the top hand only – the left hand if you are right-handed. If you can execute strokes such as a drive and a cut one-handed, the bat is of the right weight.

3   Oil a new bat immediatey after purchase. Using a soft rag, spread a teaspoonful of oil over the face, edges, toe and back of the bat.

### ⚠ Warnings

Don't over-oil the bat. This can cause as much harm as failing to oil the bat at all.

Avoid getting oil on the handle or the splice (where the handle joins the blade of the bat).

4   Lie the bat in a horizontal position until the oil has soaked in. Repeat the oiling a second time to give full protection.

5   "Knock in" the oiled bat by striking the face and edges repeatedly with a soft mallet or an old cricket ball (one that has softened through use). Repeat the "knocking in" of the bat every day for ten days, spending about a half an hour on the process each time, steadily increasing the firmness of the blows.

7   Prepare the bat further by using it for light practice, such as giving short catches to fielders, still employing an old ball.

7   Use the bat for full practice in the nets or match play.

### Thing You'll Need

☐ cricket bat

☐ raw linseed oil

☐ soft rag

☐ mallet or old cricket ball

---

## 859 | Bowl an Out-Swinger

One of the deadliest balls in cricket is the pacy out-swinger, curving in the air away from the batsman and inviting an edge to the wicketkeeper and the slip catchers.

### ⊙ Steps

1   Rub the ball on one side repeatedly so that it has a clearly distinguished shiny side and duller side.

2   Grip the ball with your index finger and middle finger on either side of the seam at the top of the ball and with the inside of your thumb on the seam at the bottom.

3   Make sure that the shiny side of the ball is facing in the opposite direction to the way that you want the ball to swing – to your right if you are a right-handed bowler facing a right-hand batsman.

4   Run up with steady acceleration, so that you achieve your maximum speed as you plant your back foot (the right for a right-handed bowler) just behind the line of the stumps.

5   Bring your leading foot (the left for a right-handed bowler) slightly further across to the on-side than your back foot in the final stride, turning your body in the same direction.

6   Look down the wicket over your leading shoulder, concentrating on the spot where you want the ball to pitch.

7   Swing your bowling arm over as high and as straight as possible, with the seam of the ball vertical and pointing towards first slip – that is, a position slightly to the wicketkeeper's right.

8   Make your bowling arm follow through down and across your body, past your left hip, making your body pivot sharply with the motion.

### ✳ Tip

For maximum effectiveness with the out-swinger, make sure the ball pitches in line with the stumps and on a good length or well up to the batsman. If the ball is pitched short or outside the line of the stumps, swing is largely ineffective.

### ⚠ Warning

Fast or even medium-pace bowling puts considerable strain on the body. It is vital to warm up and loosen up properly before a spell of bowling.

## Bowl a Leg-Break

Australian cricketer Shane Warne has many times shown the match-winning potential of leg-break bowling. Spun with the wrist, the ball turns away from a right-handed batsman after pitching.

### ⊙ Steps

#### Spinning the Ball

1 Grip the ball loosely by the seam with your thumb, index finger, middle finger and fourth finger. Ensure that your fingers are evenly spaced along the seam.

2 Flick the ball energetically with your wrist and fingers so that it is pro-pelled out of the back of your hand – that is, past your little finger. It will spin anti-clockwise.

3 Practise this spinning action first holding the ball at waist level and toss-ing it on to the ground.

4 Practise spinning the ball with your arm held out sideways at shoulder level, with the elbow bent

5 Combine the wrist-spin flick with a high straight-arm bowling action.

#### Delivering the Ball

1 Take a run-up of six paces, beginning with your right foot.

2 Turn side-on to the batsman as you take your final stride, bending your wrist sideways so it is 'cocked' to give a powerful flick to the ball.

3 Keep the wrist bent and parallel to the ground as your bowling arm comes over.

4 Drop your left shoulder slightly as you deliver the ball with a sharp flick of the wrist and fingers.

### ✻ Tips

Aim to pitch your leg-break on the line of the leg stump, so that it spins across the wicket towards the off stump.

Constantly vary the speed and flight of your deliveries to deceive the batsman. In general, the slower the delivery and the higher its trajectory, the more the ball will turn on hitting the pitch.

## Bowl an Off-Break

The finger spin that produces a right-handed bowler's off-break cannot match wrist spin for turn off the pitch, but it has the advantage of allowing better control of length and line.

### ⊙ Steps

#### Spinning the Ball

1 Grip the ball with the seam vertical and your index finger along the side of the seam nearest to yourself. Support the ball with your thumb, mid-dle and fourth fingers evenly spread around it.

2 Spin the ball in a clockwise direction by pushing the side of your index finger vigorously against the edge of the seam. Aid this motion with a clockwise flick of your wrist.

### ✻ Tips

Aim to pitch your off-break just outside the line of the off stump, from where it should turn in to the right-handed batsman.

3   Practise this spin action with bent-arm throws against a wall or to a colleague before you try to combine it with a proper high straight-arm bowling action.

### Delivering the Ball

4   Take a run-up of six paces, starting with your right foot.

5   In the final stride, bring your leading foot slightly further across to the on-side than your back foot, turning your body in the same direction, so that you are looking down the pitch over your left shoulder.

6   Bring your bowling arm up and over, releasing the ball at the highest point you can reach with a vigorous flick of the finger and wrist.

7   Pivot as you deliver the ball, so that your right leg comes across the front of your body.

---

## 862 | Play a Forward Defensive Stroke

The forward defensive stroke is the most basic element in the batsman's armoury. The following directions are for a right-handed batsman; reverse all rights and lefts for a left-hander.

### ⊙ Steps

1   Settle into a correct stance before the bowler begins the run-up. Ensure that your feet are on either side of the crease and parallel to it, and that your left shoulder is pointing towards the bowler.

2   Keep your head upright and turned to face the bowler running in.

3   As the bowler prepares to deliver the ball, lift your bat behind you to just above the level of the top of the stumps.

4   Assess the probable trajectory of the ball as it leaves the bowler's hand, judging where it is going to pitch.

5   Step forward with your left foot, placing the foot as close to the pitch of the ball as possible. Do not move your right foot, which remains behind the crease and in contact with the ground from heel to toe.

6   Swing your bat forward under the control of your left arm and hand so that it arrives directly alongside the pad on your left leg.

7   Bend your left knee and lean forwards with your upper body so that your head is over the bat.

8   Tilt the bat forwards slightly and play the ball down into the ground in front of you..

### ✱ Tips

Make sure that your backlift is straight, so that the bat swings down the line of the ball, rather than across the line.

Do not leave any gap between your pad and the bat. The pad and bat should present a united barrier to the ball.

### ⚠ Warning

When you are playing a forward defensive stroke, a sharply lifting ball may strike you on the hand. Be sure that your wear proper cricket gloves which will protect against broken fingers.

## Play a Hook Shot **863**

The hook shot is used against a quick, short-pitched ball that is lifting towards the batsman's chest. It requires nerve and physical courage, but can offer the batsman a rich haul of runs.

### ⊙ Steps

1   Adopt the correct stance and focus your full attention on the bowler (see steps 1 to 3 in 862 "Play a Forward Defensive Stroke").

2   Spot that the ball is directed towards your body – that is, on the line of the leg stump or outside it – and is going to pitch short.

3   Lift your bat high behind you, so the toe of the bat is above shoulder height.

4   Move your back foot quickly back and across, so that it is a short distance outside and in front of the off stump.

5   Move your front foot back to line up with the other foot, swivelling your body around so that your chest is facing the ball. Your foot should be about 50 cm (20 in) apart, toes pointing straight down the pitch.

6   Swing your bat across in a wide arc in front of your chest, keeping your head steady and your eyes fixed on the ball.

7   Turn your wrists over so that the face of the bat is angled downwards as you make contact with the ball, ensuring that the shot is hit into the ground and doesn't present a catch to a fielder.

### ✳ Tip

Your head should be slightly inside the line of the ball as you play the hook shot – that is, if you are right-handed, the ball should be going to pass over your left shoulder.

### ⚠ Warning

Playing a short-pitched ball from a fast bowler, there is always a risk that you might be struck in the face or on the head. Always wear a protective helmet with a face guard when batting.

## Play a Reverse Sweep Shot **864**

The reverse sweep is a risky stroke used against a slow bowler to exploit gaps between fielders on the off side. The directions here are for a right-handed batsman.

### ⊙ Steps

1   Look around at the position of the fielders, fixing in your mind any undefended spaces on the off side which you might be able to exploit.

2   Adopt the correct stance and focus on the bowler running in to deliver the ball (see steps 1 to 3 in 861 "Play a Forward Defensive Stroke").

3   Spot that the ball is directed on the line of the leg stump or outside it, and that it is pitched up to you – you need to be able to hit it before it bounces or very shortly after the bounce.

4   Take a long stride down the wicket with your front foot. The pad on your front leg should be directly in line with the ball and your foot pointing across the ball's line of flight.

5   Bend the knee of your back leg so that the knee padding is touching the ground. Keep the toe of your back foot behind the crease.

6   Lift your bat up and to the side of your body, keeping your head still and your eyes fixed on the ball.

### ✳ Tip

Don't try to inject power into a reverse sweep, it won't work. Rely on placing the shot accurately between fielders to pick up runs.

### ⚠ Warning

The reverse sweep is a difficult shot to execute successfully. Never attempt it until you have had sufficient time at the crease to "get your eye in".

7 Swing the bat down and across, towards the ball.

8 Pull your left elbow down and twist your right wrist over so that your arms are crossed.

6 Use your right arm to control the bat as the stroke reverses, the bat now moving from left to right.

7 Guide the ball from in front of your pad into one of the gaps that you have indentified in the off-side field.

---

## 865 | Hit a Forehand in Tennis

Are your forehand ground strokes not making it over the net? Add zip to this most common of tennis shots. These directions are for right-handers; reverse them for left-handers.

### ⊙ Steps

1 Position yourself just inside the court's baseline and near the centre line.

2 Keep your feet shoulder-width apart.

3 Hold the racket at about waist level directly in front of you. Use the handshake grip, which works well for beginners. This grip is like shaking hands with the handle of your racket, while the string face is perpendicular to the court surface.

4 Bend your knees slightly. You should be able to feel some strain on the quadriceps muscles in your thighs.

5 As the ball is hit towards you, turn your shoulders to the right, pulling the racket back. Lower the racket head towards the playing surface. This should be done prior to the ball's crossing the net.

6 Pivot on your right foot. With your other foot, step forwards and across your body. Plant your left foot at a 45-degree angle, pointed towards the right net post.

7 Stop your backswing when the racket head is slightly below waist level and your arm is extended and relaxed. The racket, and your arm, should be perpendicular to the net so your arm and racket are pointing directly towards the back of the court.

8 Before the ball reaches you, pause for a moment, holding the racket in the backswing position. Think: "Bounce, step, hit".

9 Begin your swing from a position below your waist. Swing through the ball, with the contact occurring in front of your net-side hip. Try to hit the ball on the sweet spot (middle area) of the racket. This gives you a solid forehand by maximising the efficiency of the shot.

10 Finish the swing above the opposite shoulder. Think: "Start low, finish high".

11 Quickly get back into your original position for the next shot.

### ✱ Tip

Always pull the racket back as soon as the ball approaches your forehand side. Your backswing should come from the shoulders, not the arm.

### ⚠ Warning

Using a two-handed forehand is quite difficult. If you're a beginner, learn the one-handed approach for more control and power. Leave the two-handed technique for your backhand.

## Hit a Lob in Tennis 866

You hit a lob (a high, slow shot over and beyond your opponent) offensively to add surprise to your game, or when you have no alternative defensively.

### Steps

1 Assume the ready position at or near the baseline.

2 Drop your racket head lower than you would for a normal forehand.

3 Attempt to get under the ball.

4 Hit the ball at a greater angle than you would use for a normal forehand. In other words, your racket path must be more vertical than with a standard forehand.

5 Hit the ball up over your opponent's head.

6 Finish with the racket head over your back shoulder.

7 Be aware that the height of the shot depends on whether it's an offensive lob (hit with topspin) or a defensive lob (hit with underspin).

### Tips

You can hit a lob on the run, with your weight on either the front or the back foot.

Practice with a partner by lobbing the ball over the net to each other, attempting to send the ball as deep into your partner's court as possible.

## Hit a Backhand Ground Stroke in Tennis 867

The backhand ground stroke (turning 180 degrees to hit on the opposite side of your racket) is an essential tennis skill. Reverse the following alignments if you're a southpaw.

### Steps

1 Move from the ready position, pulling the racket across your body and back to the left-hand side before the ball crosses the net.

2 Keep your right hand loose on the grip.

3 Tuck the racket towards the inside of your body while dropping the racket head.

4 Step forwards with your right foot as you dip your right shoulder to the front, towards the net.

5 Swing from low to high, making contact when the ball is in front of your right hip, and finish above your right shoulder.

6 Help your playing arm during the shot by pointing the racket at the ground just before contact, then use your non-playing hand to grab the throat of the racket and pull upward after contact as you turn your shoulders.

### Tips

Take small steps to position yourself after getting to the ball.

Tightening your forearm can cause pain in the wrist and elbow. Let the racket head do the work for you.

## 868 | Hit a Slice Serve in Tennis

A slice serve is usually the first serve that tennis players learn. These instructions explain a serve for right-handed players; reverse them for left-handers.

### ◎ Steps

1 Stand 2 or 2.6 m (6 or 8 ft) to the right (or left) of the centre mark.

2 Assume the regular serve posture: standing sideways to the net, with your left foot pointing towards the right net post.

3 Keep your arms down and relaxed to begin.

4 Hold the racket at the throat with the non-hitting hand. Your hitting hand should be as loose as possible on the grip.

5 Shift about 80 per cent of your body weight to the back leg to start.

6 Toss the ball with your left hand, which remains pointing at the ball in the air. Your right arm should be bent at 90 degrees, with the racket head pointing up at the sky.

7 Bend your knees and move your body up when beginning to swing at the ball. Think: "Toss, bend".

8 Shift your weight forwards and swing the racket head aggressively up and over your right shoulder, then hit the ball out diagonally in front of you, to the left.

9 Transfer your body weight, uncoiling your upper body, and thrust upwards from the legs as you hit the ball.

10 Fold in your tossing arm quickly towards your ribs as your racket makes contact with the ball. The weight transfer carries the body forward onto the court.

11 Allow your feet to come off the ground or nearly off the ground.

### ✳ Tip

A consistent toss is essential for a consistent serve. Practise tossing the ball with your left arm. The ball should land one foot in front of you and in line with your right shoulder.

### ⚠ Warning

Swinging aggressively can lead to back, shoulder and elbow problems.

## 869 | Grip a Golf Club

Your grip can make the difference between a good golf shot and a poor one. These directions are for right-handers. Reverse them if you're left-handed.

### ◎ Steps

1 Hold the grip with your left hand at the top of the club.

2 Adjust your hand so your thumb is heading straight down the golf grip. The top of your thumb should be facing out away from your body and the club's shaft, while the remainder of your left hand wraps around it.

3 Look at your right palm and notice the small vertical crease near your wrist (this is the crease formed when your thumb folds inwards). Grip the golf club with your right hand so that this crease rests on top of your left thumb. Your hands should fit perfectly and lock together in this formation.

### ✳ Tips

Players with large hands should use an overlapping grip, with the little finger of the right hand resting between and on top of the left hand's forefinger and middle finger.

Players with smaller hands should use a 10-finger grip, with all fingers on the club, without overlapping the hands.

4    Notice the V where the thumb and finger meet. That angle should be pointing to your right shoulder.

5    Make sure your right thumb is not running straight down the club, but instead slightly to the left of the top of the grip.

Hold the club lightly with both hands. The more relaxed your grip, the straighter and farther you'll hit the ball.

## Replace the Grip on a Golf Club                                         870

A worn grip can cause your hands to slip, leading to errant shots. The daily golfer should regrip clubs two or three times a year, the weekend golfer yearly.

### ⊙ Steps

1    Pull off the old grip. Use a sharp knife to cut it off if necessary. Scrape off tape fragments with your fingers or a knife.

2    Put solvent on a rag and clean the shaft where the grip and tape used to be, then let the shaft dry for a minute.

3    Put the middle of the shaft in a vice shaft holder—a special vice adapter that is capable of holding a thin rod like a golf club. These can generally be found wherever vices are sold. Put this adapter, with your club secured inside, into the vice. Tighten the vice for a strong hold.

4    Measure where the new grip will fit: Take the new grip in one hand and hold it alongside the bare shaft of the golf club. Align the butt of the grip with the end of the shaft. With the other hand, make a pencil mark on the shaft where the opposite side of the grip ends—down towards the head of the club.

5    Strip a piece of double-sided tape from the roll (cellophane tape works fine) and place one end at your pencil mark. Gently smooth down the length as you stick the tape along the shaft to its butt end.

6    Trim the tape off the roll at the shaft's end, then carefully wrap your piece around the shaft, overlapping the tape's width as necessary.

7    Take the new grip (it will be a pliable, rubbery piece of tubing) and plug one end by placing a golf tee in the little hole at its butt. Now, pour some solvent inside the grip. (Window cleaner works well as a solvent.) Its purpose is to take the tackiness off the tape without dissolving it.

8    Place a finger or thumb over the open end of the grip, leave the tee-plug at the bottom, and shake the entire grip. This allows the solvent to spread throughout the interior of the grip.

9    Spray or pour additional solvent onto the taped portion of the shaft.

10   Pull the golf tee out of the end of the grip, then slide the grip onto the shaft, over the tape. The longer you wait, the harder it will be to slide the grip on. If it's hard to slide it on, use more solvent, either inside the grip or on the tape.

11   Remove the club from the vice shaft holder and vice.

12   Hold the club as if you were hitting a shot. Adjust the grip gently so that it's straight on the club, making sure that any pattern on the grip is not twisted around the shaft.

### ⚠ Warnings

When using a sharp knife, cut away from your body.

If solvent gets into your mouth or eyes or on your skin, flush immediately with water.

### Things You'll Need

☐ golf club grip

☐ sharp knife

☐ bench vice

☐ vice shaft holder

☐ double-sided tape

☐ solvent

13  Work your hands up and down the golf shaft, pressing the grip firmly against the club to seat the adhesive.

14  Let the grip dry for about 10 hours before using.

---

## 871 | Hit a Golf Ball

Hitting a golf ball is easy, but hitting the ball where you want it to go takes a lot of practice. These instructions were written with right-handed hitters in mind; reverse them for left-handers.

### ⊙ Steps

1  Stand behind the ball and pick out your target far up the fairway or driving range.

2  Check you are gripping the club properly.

3  Stand facing the ball with both feet together, about three-quarters of an arm's length away from the ball. Your left shoulder will be towards the target.

4  Take a tiny step towards your target (to the left) with your left foot, and take a normal step backwards (away from the ball) with your right foot. Your feet should now be shoulder-width apart.

5  Place your hands in a position known as the forward press. Viewed from above, this moves your hands slightly to the left of the ball. This angles the club forward (viewed from behind you, the shaft is now tilted to the left), flattening its already angled hitting face.

6  Pull the club to your right (straight back from the golf ball) to the top of the backswing. The club should be parallel to the ground, and back over your shoulder.

7  Without pausing at the top of the backswing, immediately swing the golf club back down along the same path.

8  Keep your head down and strike the ball. Allow the club to follow through until it touches your back.

9  Watch the ball travel towards the target.

### ✱ Tips

Don't be afraid to hit down on the ball and create a divot (a chunk taken out of the turf). Many people only catch the top of the ball, causing it to skip off down the fairway; this is because they do not dig deep enough. Replace the divot after your shot.

Remember that the harder you hit down, the higher it will go.

### ⚠ Warnings

Swinging the club too hard and too fast may cause back pain from all the furious twisting motion.

Make sure nobody is standing close to you when you swing a golf club.

---

## 872 | Read a Putt

Reading a putt requires a player to look at the green from all directions to determine how hard to hit the ball, and to compensate for the slope and any passing breeze.

### ⊙ Steps

1  Stand halfway between your ball and the hole to get a better idea of the slope of the green. This will help determine how fast or slow the putt should be.

2  Walk directly behind the hole and look back at your ball.

### ✱ Tip

Think about your putt while other group members are putting, to speed up the play.

How to Do *(Just About)* Everything

3 Read the slope of the green and determine whether it is straight or angled more to the right or left.

4 Return to your ball and stand behind it. Read the slope of the green once more to see if it looks the same as it did from the other side of the hole.

5 Choose your putting path based on your study of the green.

6 Pick a spot on the green about 15 cm (6 in) in front of your ball, along your chosen putting path. This spot can be a dark area of the green or a taller blade of grass.

7 Keep your eye on the spot and stand up. This tactic allows you to lock in your putting path even as your perspective changes.

8 Approach the golf ball and take a practice stroke, putting at the air between your feet and the ball.

9 Place the putter behind the ball and putt the ball into the hole.

### ⚠ Warning

Avoid stepping in other putting paths while reading your putt.

---

## Calculate Your Golf Handicap    873

Your handicap measures how well you'd stand up to a scratch golfer on any given course and allows golfers of different abilities to compete fairly.

### ◉ Steps

1 Take the scores from the last five rounds (18 holes each) you played.

2 For each of these scores look up the rating and slope for the course you played. This information is usually printed on the scorecard, although you can also get the rating and slope by calling the course.

3 Subtract the course rating from the score you earned on that course.

4 Multiply that number by 113. The resulting number is the differential.

5 Take the lowest of your five differentials and multiply it by 0.96, and you have your handicap.

### ✱ Tips

If you have seven or eight scores to use instead of five, average your two lowest differentials and then multiply by 0.96. If you have nine scores, average the three lowest differentials and multiply the result by 0.96.

Once you have 20 or more scores, use the most recent 20 scores and average the 10 lowest differentials; multiply the result by 0.96 to get your handicap.

---

## Begin a Running Programme    874

Running will improve your stamina, help you control your weight and improve your general health. Here's how to get started.

### ◉ Steps

1 Jog before you run. Every running programme, no matter what level, has some jogging.

2 Begin at a conversational pace – one that allows you to talk comfortably without being winded.

3 Mix running with walking, if necessary. As you progress, increase the amount of running and decrease the walking.

### ✱ Tip

Find a partner or group. This will strengthen your commitment to a running programme.

4   Be patient with your initial aches and lack of stamina. Understand that although the heart and lungs grow strong quickly with exercise, muscles and joints take longer.

5   Increase your running time or distance by no more than 10 per cent each week to minimise the risk of injuries.

6   Build up your running to at least 20 to 30 minutes three times a week, done at a moderate level of intensity. Studies have shown that this is a sufficient amount of exercise for basic cardiovascular fitness. Running more than this amount is done for reasons beyond basic fitness.

7   Use the first month to learn about yourself. Pay close attention to your body; learn to read its signals of fatigue and stress, and when you can push beyond them.

### ⚠ Warning

Have a physical examination and consult your doctor about your basic health and fitness before beginning a running programme.

---

## 875 | Run a Marathon

You've been training for months, and the big race is finally here. For peak performance, heed the following suggestions.

### ◎ Steps

1   Position yourself at the starting line according to your predicted pace.

2   Start slowly – this is the key to finishing in good form. Check your time at the 2-mile marker. If you're going faster than your target pace, then slow down.

3   Avoid attacking hills too aggressively. You'll need to conserve energy for the rest of the course.

4   Drink water or sports drinks at every rest station, even if you don't think you're thirsty.

5   Resist the urge to pick up your pace between miles 4 and 10; stay relaxed, calm and focussed. Breathe rhythmically and pretend this is a practice run.

6   Towards the middle and end of the race, pour water over your head at each station, in addition to drinking it.

7   Carry power gels or other sports foods, or get them at rest stations if offered; eat what has worked for you in your practice runs.

8   Try to maintain your pace between mile 10 and mile 20 of the marathon. If you've gone through the first 10 miles too quickly, don't try to keep up your pace. A common error is to run too fast for the first 20 miles.

9   Shake out your arms and change your form for a few strides to provide relief between mile 14 and mile 20 of the race.

10  Draw willpower from the runners around you—concentrate on passing them or following one.

11  Slow down and visualise the finish if you hit the wall at mile 20. Think in terms of how much time is left, and approach the remaining distance as a 10-km race.

### ✳ Tip

Understand that there's no shame in walking and no shame in dropping out if you can't continue. Listen to your body.

### ⚠ Warnings

Never attempt a marathon without proper training; this event is incredibly hard on the body. A good training programme will help prevent injury.

Do not attempt to run a marathon if you have sustained an injury during training.

12  Gather your remaining strength for a final push during the last 2 miles; use the sight of the finish line and the crowd's cheers to overcome fatigue and discouragement.

13  Stay loose as you approach the finish. Keep your knees up and your arms moving. Run hard at least a dozen strides beyond the finish line, to keep yourself from slowing before you cross it.

14  Congratulate yourself—you deserve it!

## Cycle Up Hills                                                        876

Climbing hills on a bike can be quite daunting. Focus on your technique, however, and you can make it a lot less painful.

### ⊙ Steps

1  Consider your equipment. Having toe clips, or clipless pedals, will make you much more efficient on hills. It also helps to have a clean drive train (your chain, sprockets and gears) and to make sure your tyres are inflated to the proper pressure.

2  Be sure your seat is adjusted properly for your height. To check, sit on the seat with your right foot on the pedal. Turn the pedal to its lowest point. Your leg should now be almost fully extended.

3  Select the proper gear for the hill. Find a gear that allows you to maintain your proper spin. In cycling, "spin" is defined as your optimum rate of revolutions—the point between cranking your pedals too fast (not enough resistance) or too slow (too much resistance).

4  Watch the gradient and feel for subtle changes in the pedals' resistance. You may need to shift often to stay in the groove.

5  Stay relaxed. If you tense up, it will make getting up the hill all the more difficult. Keep your arms loose and don't hold the bars in a tight grip.

6  Sit back on the seat and pedal smoothly. Try not to favour one leg over the other.

7  Stand up on the pedals from time to time. This allows you to switch muscle groups and stretch out a bit.

8  Concentrate on exhaling. Breathe all the way out and let your lungs fill back up on their own.

9  Power over the crest of the hill. Many riders start to ease up before they get to the top. Keep the power turned on, and you will have a smoother transition into the flat or downhill.

### ⚠ Warning

Always wear a helmet when cycling.

## 877 | Change a Flat Tyre on a Bike

Don't let a flat tyre slow down your biking fun. Pack the proper lightweight tools and an extra tube, get savvy with your wheel workings, and get back on the trail.

### ◎ Steps

#### Remove the Tyre

1 Invert the bike and remove the bicycle wheel from the frame by flipping the quick-release lever or unscrewing the bolt. Release any remaining air from the tyre.

2 Insert the thin end of a tyre lever (a plastic wedge) between the tyre and the rim.

3 Pull the lever down, and clip the hook end to the nearest spoke.

4 Move over two spokes, and repeat with a second tyre lever.

5 Move over two more spokes, and repeat with a third lever.

6 Take the first lever out, move over two spokes from the third lever, and repeat.

7 Work around one side of the wheel in this way until one side of the tyre is free.

8 When one side of the tyre is completely off the rim, pull the other side off with your hands.

#### Change the Inner Tube

9 Pull out the old tube with your hand and discard it, or save it to patch later.

10 Run a hand lightly over the inside of the tyre to find the cause of the flat, and remove it.

11 With a bicycle pump, put one or two strokes of air into the new tube.

12 Put the new tube in the tyre.

#### Remount the Tyre

13 Find the hole in the tyre rim for the inflation valve; this is the piece of metal attached to the rubber tube into which air is pumped.

14 Push the valve through the hole in the rim, and pull the tyre (with the tube inside it) over the wheel.

15 Working around the wheel with your fingers, push one side of the tyre onto the rim. The tyre's edge will seat itself along the inside edge of the wheel's rim.

16 Once one side of the tyre is on the rim, check that the tube is not pinched between the edge of the tyre and the rim. If it is, gently pull the tube out from the other side.

17 Turn the wheel around when one side is complete.

### ✳ Tips

Buy the right size tube: Mountain bike inner tubes are 66 cm (26 in) in diameter, while road bike tubes are 70 cm (27 in).

Make sure your new inner tube has the correct kind of valve. There are two kinds: A Presta, or European, valve is long and skinny and is usually found on road bikes; a Shrader, or American, valve looks like a car tyre's valve and is usually found on older bikes and on most mountain bikes.

After changing the tube, don't use the tyre levers to prise the tyre back on. This could pinch the tube and create a new hole.

Inflate the tyre slowly, watching for irregularities that might identify kinks in the tube or other problems with your installation.

### ⚠ Warning

A nail or a piece of glass may be sticking through the tyre, so proceed with caution.

### Things You'll Need

☐ 3 tyre levers

☐ inner tube

☐ bike pump

18  Push the second side of the tyre onto the rim with your thumbs. When the tyre is nearly all on the rim, it will become taut and will require a last hard push with your thumbs.

19  Inflate the tyre to its recommended pressure as printed on the side of the tyre.

## Swim the Breaststroke 878

This can be a relaxing and gliding swim stroke, or it can be a quick, intense motion if you're racing. It's accomplished by a strong, froglike kick and pull, then a long glide.

### ⊙Steps

1  Lie face down in the water with your head bent back, above the surface.

2  Keep your legs close together and pull your knees up against your chest. At the same time, hold your palms together and against your chest, as if in prayer.

3  Take a deep breath, then dip your head below the surface so the crown points straight forwards.

4  Kick out to the side and apart with your legs, spreading them wide; then quickly squeeze them together, straight out behind you. Try to imitate the way a frog kicks.

5  As you kick, extend your arms out in front of you, keeping your palms pressed together.

6  Glide for a moment, with arms extended like a spear in front, and toes pointed behind you.

7  Turn your palms outwards and pull with both hands out and around in a circular motion, until your hands end up in their original position, together against your chest.

8  Use the thrust of the outward pull with your hands to pull your head up and out of the water to take a breath.

9  As you push your hands together into their original prayer position, pull your knees up into their original position against your chest.

10  As your head goes back down, your arms should be just beginning to plunge forwards with the next kick.

**✳ Tip**

The glide is the most important aspect of this stroke. After the big kick, streamline your entire body as much as possible. Your shoulders should be almost against your ears. Glide, and then pull your head up and forwards with your stroke.

## Swim the Freestyle Stroke 879

The freestyle is known as the fastest swim stroke. Often called the "crawl", it is one of the most common swimming styles.

### ⊙Steps

1  Visualise a line running down the centre of your body from your chin to your chest. This line is the axis upon which your whole body should pivot, and it should extend in the direction in which you are swimming.

**✳ Tips**

Stretch out your stroking arms fully without ever pausing from the windmill motion.

2  Keep your legs straight but not rigid, with your toes pointed behind you. Kick up and down using your entire leg, bending your knees only slightly. Continue kicking the entire time. Your kick should not make a big splash, but rather should just churn the surface of the water.

3  Move your arms in a windmill motion opposite each other. While one arm is extended completely out, the other should be all the way back, almost against the side of your body.

4  Cup your hands and pull your extended front arm through the water beneath your body.

5  Bend this arm at the elbow and draw your fingertips along the imaginary line down the centre of your body.

6  Lift your other arm out of the water from behind you and move it all the way forward as the first arm is pulling beneath you. Bend at the elbow and drag your fingertips along the surface of the water—right past your ear—then penetrate the surface as you completely extend the arm.

7  Breathe on one side by turning your head to that side as the arm comes out of the water.

Remain horizontal in the water. A strong kick will keep your legs from sinking behind you.

As you pull your hands through the water, keep them cupped firmly but not rigidly. Fingers should be held just slightly apart.

---

## 880 | Swim the Butterfly Stroke

**This is the most strenuous swimming stroke of all and makes considerable demands on the swimmer's physical strength. But it can also be faster than any other stroke except the crawl.**

### ◉ Steps

1  Position yourself face down in the water with your legs together and your arms extended out in front of you.

2  Kick your legs up and down. First press down with your hips and upper legs, bending your legs at the knee, so that your hips are below your toes. Then raise your hips and straighten your legs, pushing your feet downwards into the water.

3  Pull both arms through the water beneath your body at the same time as you execute this powerful kicking movement. Your body will be driven forwards and upwards above the surface of the water.

4  Lift your head and take a breath as you simultaneously pull your arms out of the water and swing them forwards through the air.

5  Re-enter the water with your head and arms together, rather as if you were executing a dive.

6  Glide for a moment, while performing a smaller version of the same kick as before.

7  Repeat the full kick and simultaneous pulling motion of the arms.

**✳ Tip**

Generate the power of the kick in this stroke from your hips, not with a thrust from your knees.

The two arms should move simultaneously and symetrically throughout the execution of the butterfly stroke.

## Swim the Backstroke
**881**

The backstroke or "back crawl" is a swimming style that can be mastered reasonably easily by following the right instructions.

### ⊙ Steps

1  Float on your back with your eyes looking up to the sky or ceiling.

2  Kick your legs up and down, keeping the legs straight but not quite rigid, and the feet relaxed. Don't make a big splash with your kicks; try just to churn up the surface of the water.

3  Move your arms in a windmill motion. Raise one arm out of the water from your waist to a fully extended position behind your head, keeping the arm straight. At the same time, pull the other arm back through the water alongside your body from the extended position to your waist. This arm should be bent and the hand cupped.

4  Continue kicking your legs and windmilling your arms, with your head floating back in the water. Maintain normal breathing.

5  Lean your head back so that you can see the side of the pool as you approach the end of a length.

### ✳ Tip

Your hands should enter the water turned outwards, so that the little finger is first to strike the surface.

### ⚠ Warning

Take care not to hit your head on the side of the pool. Err on the side of caution until you have enough experience to judge the distance to the end of the lane correctly.

## Dive From a Springboard
**882**

These instructions are for the forward pike, a suitable springboard dive for relative beginners to take on.

### ⊙ Steps

1  Establish the best starting position for your dive. Walk to the end of the springboard and turn to face away from the pool. Take four natural steps and then advance a further 25 cm (10 in). This will place you on the optimal spot.

2  Turn to face the water and stand with your arms down by your sides, while you settle your mind to concentrate on the dive that you are about to make.

3  Take two steps along the board, making the first step with your stronger leg – the one you would naturally use to kick a ball. These should be normal walking steps.

4  Take a third step, this time a longer stride, while simultaneously swinging your arms upwards to about shoulder height. This should cause you to rise about 30 cm (1 ft) above the springboard.

5  Bring both feet together in the air and drop down on to the end of the board, at the same time swinging your arms back down.

6  Bend your knees as the board flexes downwards under your weight.

7  Straighten your legs, pushing the board down to its furthest limit.

8  Swing your arms up so that they are straight out and above your head as the springboard rebounds and propels you into the air.

### ✳ Tip

Don't close your eyes during a dive. Keep them open from start to finish.

### ⚠ Warning

Springboard diving is physically demanding and potentially dangerous. Never dive unsupervised and preferably seek training from a professional before you attempt this activity.

9   Bend at the hips, bringing your arms down as far towards your toes as you can, while keeping your legs straight.

10  Let your legs swing up and backwards so they are above your body.

11  Bring your hands together, with your arms stretched out in front of your head. Keep your head tucked in between your shoulders, your legs straight and toes pointed. Strike the water as near to vertical as you can.

## 883 Hit a Softball

Softball, essentially a gentler version of baseball, has become an increasingly popular participation sport in Britain. So how do you set about hitting the (in fact, not-so-soft) ball?

### ⊙ Steps

1   Hold the bat as you would the handle of an axe if you were about to chop wood. If you are a right-hander, place your left hand nearest to the knob at the end of the bat and your right hand next to it; left-handers do the reverse. The middle knuckles of the two hands should be aligned.

2   Stand side on, with your left shoulder towards the pitcher if your are right-handed. Adopt a comfortable stance, feet wide enough apart to give good balance and knees slightly bent.

3   Lift the bat so that your hands are close to your back shoulder – the one furthest from the pitcher – and the bat is pointing upwards behind you. Keep your back elbow pointing directly to the ground and your front elbow relaxed and slightly lower than the knob of the bat.

4   Keep your head straight and focus your attention on the area where you expect the pitcher to release the ball, alongside his leg.

5   Shift your weight on to your back foot as the pitcher draws his pitching arm back.

6   Take a step forwards with your front foot as the ball leaves the pitcher's hand, but do not shift your weight forwards. Keep your upper body and head steady over your back foot.

7   Read the line and flight of the ball and aim to strike it in front of your body.

8   Swing the bat, shifting the weight of your body forwards into the shot. Follow through after you hit the ball, so that your hands swing to the opposite shoulder.

### ✱ Tips

Don't hold the bat in the palms of your hands. It should rest in the middle of your fingers only.

Make sure the barrel of the bat – the part you hit with – is above your hands as you go into the swing, not pointing downwards.

### ⚠ Warning

Softball is a strenuous sport that can occasionally result in serious injury. Seek out the proper equipment and training to prepare yourself for this activity.

## Hit a Home Run in Softball

A home run is a hit that gives you time to scamper around all four bases. It depends on striking the ball with strength and speed, but also on intelligent placement of the shot.

### ◉ Steps

1 Glance around the field, ensuring that you are aware of the position of each fielder and any gaps that you might exploit between fielders. Note in particular the positions of potential catchers in the deep, if you don't want to be caught when lofting a shot over the top of the infield.

2 Adopt the correct grip on the bat and a comfortable, balanced stance (see 883 "Hit a Softball").

3 Focus on the pitcher. Take a step forwards with your front foot as the pitcher winds up to pitch, but don't shift your weight forwards.

4 Watch the ball leave the pitcher's hand.

5 Keep your head steady and your eyes fixed on the ball. Rotate your upper body as you swing the bat, pivoting on your back foot. Shift your weight from the back to the front foot as you execute the shot.

6 Follow through the swing with unbroken momentum, so that the bat ends up around the middle of your back. Remember that it is the speed of the swing and the muscle you put into it that will carry the ball into the far reaches of the park.

7 Set off to run around the bases as soon as the shot is completed. Bear in mind that fast running can make a homer out of a relatively modest hit, as long as it is well placed.

### ✳ Tips

Practise repeated rapid swings of the bat without a ball to build up your speed and refine your hitting technique.

Develop your tactical sense. It is far more productive to hit a home run when the bases are loaded – that is, when other team-mates are part of the way round. Focus maximum effort when this situation arises.

## Pitch in Softball

Being the pitcher is the most important role in any softball team. Follow these directions for a successful slow pitch, the style of delivery adopted for most softball matches.

### ◉ Steps

1 Remember that you are required to pitch the ball underarm so that it reaches the batter between shoulder and knee height. The ball must follow an arc that rises more than 1 m 80 cm (6 ft) above the ground, but no higher than 3 m 60 cm (12 ft).

2 Grip the ball with your fingers across the seam.

3 Stand with your pivot foot – the right foot if you are right-handed – in contact with the pitcher's plate.

4 Hold the ball out in front of you, palm upwards, as you focus on the delivery that you intend to make.

5 Remember that your main resource in slow pitching is the ability to vary the arc of the ball's flight. Mentally select a higher looped trajectory or a

### ✳ Tip

Practise and more practise is the key to pitching. Pitch repeatedly to the home plate without a batter, until you have learnt precisely how much momentum is required for the ball to cover the distance at the necessary height.

### ⚠ Warning

The ball can on occasion be hit back at the pitcher fast and hard. Keep your attention on the ball and be alert.

lower, flatter delivery.

6 Swing your pitching arm back and then forwards to deliver the ball. Release the ball after your hand passes your hip.

7 Consider the possibility of taking a step backwards or forwards as you deliver the ball. This is legal as long as your pivot foot stays in contact with the pitcher's plate.

8 Be alert to assume your fielding responsibilities as soon as the batter hits the ball. The pitcher has an important responsibility for backing up the fielders at the bases, including home base.

## 886 | Shoot a Free Throw in Basketball

Free throws are crucial to a team's success. Making these unguarded shots within range of the hoop often separates the winners from the losers.

### ⊙ Steps

1 Balance yourself at the free throw line. Keep your feet shoulder-width apart and parallel to one another.

2 Point both feet and square your upper body towards the basket. Position your feet just behind the line; move one of your feet back an inch or two, if that's comfortable.

3 Hold the ball by using the hand of your non-shooting arm to support and cradle it lightly. Place the middle three fingers of your shooting hand on the seams of the ball, with your thumb and palm acting as supports.

4 Keep your shooting forearm straight, and avoid tilting it to one side. Try to keep the arm that will be releasing the ball oriented towards the basket.

5 Aim for a target just above the rim, and try not to shoot the ball short. A good target is the backboard shooting square drawn above the rim.

6 Bend your knees. An accurate shot doesn't rely on arm strength; it uses leg strength to propel the shooter upward.

7 Shoot in one fluid motion, straightening your knees to strengthen the shot and your arm to provide aim. Release the ball with your fingertips. This allows you more control over your shot and a softer arc because of the backspin you create.

8 Follow through by bending your shooting hand forward, as though you were reaching for the rim.

### ✳ Tips

Practise, practise, practise.

Being comfortable with your shot can make a big difference. If you find a motion that helps, such as adding a little hop while shooting, use it.

Take your time at the line. Most players bounce the ball or spin it in their hands before setting up their free throws.

## Make a Jump Shot in Basketball 887

Don't allow tall defensive players to steal your moment of glory. Get some spring in those legs and shoot right over them.

### Steps

1 Bend your knees as you prepare to jump.

2 Spring straight up.

3 Bring the ball from your waist up to your face, then into shooting position as you jump (see 886 "Shoot a Free Throw in Basketball" for the correct shooting position).

4 Shoot the ball when you reach the top of your jump.

5 Follow through after you release the ball by bending your wrist forward in a slow wave.

### ✻ Tips

The arc of the ball from a jump shot tends to be flatter. You may have to compensate by aiming for the back of the rim instead of the front.

Use the backboard to bounce the ball off for more control of side-angle shots.

## Spin a Basketball on Your Finger 888

Spinning the ball on your fingers is a stunt which, performed with smoothness and grace, can be an eye-catching addition to your basketball repertoire.

### Steps

1 Balance the ball on the pads of the five fingers of your dominant hand.

2 Stretch out your arm until the elbow is slightly bent.

3 Twist your wrist to the left if you're holding the ball with your right hand (the right if you're using your left hand). At the same time, bend your elbow 90 degrees, causing the ball to hop to your fingertips and spin on your middle finger.

4 Expect to lose contact with the ball for a split second when the ball gains its maximum spin velocity; concentrate on returning your middle finger to the ball's centre when it drops down.

5 Continue to spin the ball by snapping your wrist and forearm together to the right (if you're using your right hand) or to the left (if you're using your left hand), then back again as in step 3.

### ✻ Tips

Snap your wrist more forcefully to achieve more spin. The more spin, the easier it is to balance the ball on your finger—it's the gyroscope effect.

For the split second that you're not in contact with the ball, don't let it get far from your hand.

## Play Beach Volleyball 889

The same rules apply to beach volleyball as to the indoor game – you've just got a ton of sand slowing you down.

### Steps

1 Bring an all-weather, outdoor volleyball and a net system of regulation size to the beach.

2 Gather a minimum of four players (two per side).

### ✻ Tips

The less advanced the participants, the more players you'll need to cover the ground and have long rallies. It's tough to get around on sand.

3   Set up your court away from sunbathers, in an area where the ball will not continually roll into the water.

4   Play games to 15 points, earning a point only when you win a rally where you serve.

5   Serve only once per turn and within the court lines (draw a line in the sand to mark these), or forfeit the ball to your opponents.

6   Hit the ball a maximum of three times before it must go over the net to your opponents.

7   Bump the ball to a setter, who sets the ball for the spiker, who spikes the ball over the net (see 890 "Bump a Volleyball"). Do this without grabbing the ball or allowing it to rest in your hands. The same person cannot contact the ball twice in a row unless the first touch is off a block at the net.

8   Avoid touching the net at all times or lose the ball, and possibly a point.

9   Rotate player positions clockwise whenever your team has won a change in possession (called a "sideout", it's when it's your turn to serve).

10  Play a set of three or five games. The team that wins the most games in the set is the winner.

Drink lots of water and wear plenty of sunscreen.

Try not to kick up too much sand if it's windy and there are people lying on the beach nearby.

## ⚠ Warning

The most important rule to enforce is keeping players away from the net—opposing players who land on, or crash into, each other at the net can cause serious injuries.

---

## 890 | Bump a Volleyball

**A volleyball player's most important skill is bumping—passing a volleyball by bouncing it off his or her extended forearms.**

### ◉ Steps

1   Remember that the first contact after a serve is normally the bump, which sets in motion the three-step volleyball attack of bump, set (snapping the ball upwards with two hands), and spike (sending the ball forwards and downwards over the net).

2   Anticipate the flight of the ball so that you can receive it in a stationary, athletic position with your knees bent, your weight forwards on the balls of your feet, and your arms extended forwards and down.

3   Hold your palms open and facing up, and then lay one hand on top of the other.

4   Fold your hands inwards until your thumbs are side by side, pointing away from your body and slightly down. The knuckles of your fingers should be facing out.

5   Bring in your elbows and lock them so that your forearms are as close to touching as possible, creating a flat platform from your elbows to the tips of your thumbs.

6   Tilt your platform towards your target.

7   Allow the ball to bounce off your forearms (rather than swinging your arms at it).

### ✱ Tips

The two keys to good, consistent bumping are using your feet to get in proper position to meet the ball, and keeping your elbows locked so that the ball hits a flat surface.

Bump-pass the ball high to a position where the setter can get to it easily.

If you're setting and are having a hard time with the traditional setting technique that uses the hands, or are dealing with a bad, low pass, use the bump to get the job done.

**How to Do (Just About) Everything**

## Stop on Inline Skates

There are two ways to stop or slow down on inline skates. Master both techniques before you take your skates out into the world.

### ⊙ Steps

#### Heel Braking

1 Skate forward with moderate speed.

2 Transfer the majority of your weight onto the skate without the heel brake.

3 Keep the other skate on the ground, but lift up on the toe. This causes the heel brake to rub on the ground and slow you down to a stop. The more pressure you put on your heel brake, the faster you'll stop.

#### Dragging a Skate

1 Skate forward at a moderate speed.

2 Transfer the majority of your weight to your left skate.

3 Lift up your right skate and hold it perpendicular to your left, which you're riding on. The right heel should be behind and almost touching the left heel, so the two skates form an L shape.

4 Drag the wheels of your right skate against the ground. This scrapes the sides of the wheels but acts as your brake.

5 Push harder on the dragging wheels to slow down faster.

6 Avoid tilting your skate too far towards the ground or you'll scrape the side of the skate as well as the wheels.

### ✳ Tips

Dragging a skate is more functional than using the heel brake, but it also wears out your wheels faster. (This can be done with either skate; just reverse the directions above to drag your left skate.)

Many skaters prefer to remove the heel brake to improve the manoeuverability of their skates, which is why the skate-dragging method of stopping evolved.

### ⚠ Warning

Always wear a helmet, wrist guards and knee pads when inline skating.

## Do an Ollie on a Skateboard

So, you think you're ground-bound on four wheels? Flip your ride into the air – a move that's known as an "ollie" – and stay aloft upon it.

### ⊙ Steps

1 Stand on the board with your rear foot placed on the tail and your front foot between the middle of your board and the front bolts (see 920 "Determine if You're a Regular or Goofy Foot").

2 Place the ball of your rear foot on the tail of the board, with your foot positioned perpendicular to the board. When you push the tail down with that foot, the ball of your front foot should feel the pressure of the end of the board rising,

3 Place your front foot across the board, with the toe pointed slightly torwards (at about a 20-degree angle to your other foot).

4 Practise pushing down as fast as you can with your back foot and putting all your weight on the tail. This is the initial motion of the trick.

### ✳ Tips

Get comfortable with the motions of this trick before actually rolling on the board. Once you feel comfortable with the basics, you will be able to adapt to moving and going up or down things.

The hardest part is the timing of when to push down on the tail, when to jump and how quickly to suck up your legs. The secret: It's all done at the same time. The faster you do it, the easier it becomes. Think about jumping off with one foot and sucking your legs up to your chest.

5  Notice that the harder you push, the more your board wants to keep going up once the tail is on the ground. You will use that motion in the next step.

6  Strike the tail on the ground and jump off the board with your rear foot as you slide your front foot up the board (so your knee moves towards your chest).

7  Drag the side of your front foot up the board as you are jumping. This will cause the board to come up with your jump. Once both feet are in the air, the board will seem to stick to them.

8  Come back down and try to land with both feet back in their original position. Or, once you're comfortable, you can use the ollie to jump obstacles, land on rails and slide, or do a hundred other tricks.

⚠ **Warning**

Because this trick requires a lot of jumping and landing, you risk injuring yourself and your board. Use caution.

## 893 | Get Fully Equipped for Ice Hockey

**Fast-moving pucks, cross-checking and body checks make injuries in ice hockey a very real concern. Protective equipment allows you to play the game more than once.**

⊙ **Steps**

1  Start with the basics: a hockey stick, hockey skates, knee pads, a protective cup and jockstrap (for both sexes), a helmet with attached mouth guard, some hockey pucks and a pair of hockey gloves.

2  Add hockey socks, a garter belt, shoulder pads, elbow pads and (optionally) a neck protector. A huge hockey jersey will go over all of this.

3  Choose a form-fitting protective girdle with a covering nylon shell. This piece will protect you from mid-thigh up to your ribs. It's belted in place.

4  Put on your jockstrap with the cup and strap, and secure the garter belt around your waist. Make sure everything is snug but not too tight.

5  Put on your knee pads. Pull your hockey socks over them and secure your socks at the top with the garter belt.

6  Pull the girdle over your other equipment. Cover it with your nylon shell. Belt it in place.

7  Tie your skates tightly. The bottoms of your knee pads should come just to the tongues of your skates.

8  Use athletic tape to secure anything that feels as though it could slip. Skates and knee pads are the most common equipment to be taped in place.

9  Pull on your shoulder and elbow pads, and cover them with your hockey jersey. Put on your helmet, neck protector and gloves, and you're ready to play.

✱ **Tips**

It's a lot of gear, so you need to decide between mobility and greater protection if you have doubts about wearing all of it. At the very least, wear your helmet; males should also wear a jockstrap and box.

All the equipment is adjustable. If it doesn't fit quite right the first time, try playing with the settings.

## Hit a Slap Shot in Ice Hockey            894

The slap shot – when the puck rises with bullet speed from the ice and shoots into the goal – is a powerful but difficult and dangerous attacking weapon.

### ⊙ Steps

1   Skate to within a reasonable shooting distance from the goal.

2   Position your body sideways to the net and in a normal passing stance: skates parallel, knees bent, back bent forward, stick extended, blade edge flat on the ice (or roller rink surface) and puck cradled in the centre of the blade.

3   Grasp your stick with hands about 30 cm (1 ft) apart, then raise it up and straight back until your bottom hand is at shoulder level.

4   Keep your bottom arm straight.

5   Shift your weight to your back foot.

6   Raise your eyes and mark the desired target (an open edge of the goal, not an opponent's helmet).

7   Bring the stick aggressively forwards by pushing strongly with the bottom hand.

8   Transfer your weight to your front foot.

9   Strike the puck on its bottom edge.

10   Follow through with the stick.

11   Adjust the stick's blade to control the height of the puck.

### ✱ Tips

The slap shot is good for dumping the puck in the upper corner of the net.

The height of the shot depends on the height of the follow-through.

A slap shot is inherently inaccurate. Practice in aiming is essential.

## Choose a Martial Art            895

Martial arts are highly regimented systems of techniques used for fighting and self-defence. Use these guidelines to find the one that's right for you.

### ⊙ Steps

1   Assess your physical condition. Do you have any limitations that might affect which martial arts style is right for you?

2   Consider whether you prefer a hard or soft style. Attacking techniques, such as punching and kicking, indicate a hard style, which tends to be physically intense. Defensive techniques, such as blocking and redirecting, indicate a soft style, which can be less physically challenging and well-suited to older students and those with physical limitations.

3   Think about your preferences for either striking or grappling techniques. Striking is attacking with fists, feet, elbows and knees. Grappling uses joint locks and throws to control an attacker.

4   Bear in mind that karate – a style originating in China and developed in Japan – is a hard, striking style that includes training with a variety of martial-arts weapons.

### ✱ Tips

Talk to students of different styles and ask what kinds of injuries are common. For example, if knees tend to get injured in a certain style, and you have bad knees, try another style.

Choosing a teacher is often more important than choosing a particular style. Observe a class at several different dojos to get a feel for the master's teaching style – some are much more formal than others.

5 Realise that tae kwon do, from Korea, is also a hard, striking style that teaches joint locks and vital-point striking.

6 Understand that kung fu (also known as wushu), a style from China, can be hard or soft, striking or grappling; more than 400 styles exist.

7 Be aware that jujitsu, from Japan, is a soft, grappling style that emphasises using the least amount of force necessary to confront and defeat an opponent.

8 Realize that judo, a style that is also from Japan, is a soft, grappling art based on jujitsu; its purpose is to use a calm and serene mind to defeat an opponent.

9 Consider the fact that aikido, another style based on jujitsu, is a soft, grappling martial art suitable for older practitioners or those with physical limitations. Though there is a good deal of tumbling involved in aikido, this martial art teaches you to fall correctly and safely. It differs from jujitsu by using weapons such as the bokken (a wooden sword) and the jo stick.

10 Bear in mind that tai chi, a style from China, is a soft, defensive style that has strong philosophical principles, stressing harmony with nature and fellow humans.

11 Scan a martial arts encyclopedia (or try an internet search engine) for a more detailed overview of martial arts styles.

12 Delve into history to understand how the different styles originated. For instance, high kicks in tae kwon do began as a way for foot soldiers to attack mounted soldiers. Jujitsu is an unarmed variation of Japanese samurai sword fighting. Does the legacy of any of the arts appeal to you more than others?

13 Watch practitioners from the various styles that interest you before making a choice. Many schools have an observation area so you can watch while a class is being taught. Ask permission first.

14 Review what you have learned and settle on the martial arts style that best suits your interests, preferences and physical abilities.

## 896 | Make a Fist in Karate

Whether you're a boxer, a martial artist or a cardio-kickboxing enthusiast, knowing how to make a proper fist will lend power to your straight punch while keeping your hand safe.

### Steps

1 Open your hand with your fingers extended and touching each other.

2 Separate the thumb from the other fingers.

3 Bend the four fingers inwards and touch the tips to the top of your palm. Don't allow the little finger to separate from the other fingers.

4 Bend your thumb and press it over your index finger. Don't allow your thumb to extend past your finger knuckles.

### ✳ Tip

Practise punching a heavy bag to make sure your striking surface is the first two knuckles of the fist.

5   Keep your wrist straight.

6   Keep your fist closed but relaxed when making contact with a target.

## Handle a Punch in Martial Arts — 897

Martial arts training stresses confidence and avoidance of panic in an attack. Here's a way to deal with physical contact without being unnerved by it.

### ⊙ Steps

1   Accept physical contact as an essential part of your martial arts training. Sparring with safety gear will help you absorb an opponent's punches as you develop your skills and confidence.

2   Practise with a partner to learn how to handle a punch. Drill on how to dodge, parry (deflect), block and counterpunch. When you do get hit, you'll know how to recover.

3   Adjust your level of contact while practising with a partner. Don't throw full-contact punches unless you're both wearing safety gear and have agreed to the escalation.

4   Remain as calm and detached as possible if you get hit. Don't panic. If you're relaxed, your body will absorb or deflect the force of the impact. Your quick recovery acts as a psychological counterpunch to the attacker.

5   Trust your skills in a real situation. Acknowledge the possibility of getting hit before the fight, and visualise the surprise of your attacker when you execute your counterpunch.

✻ **Tips**

Unlike trained fighters, most people throw weak and ineffective punches. They tend to throw a punch from the shoulder instead of using the power of the whole body by pivoting from the hips.

Remember, the principle behind self-defence is to defend yourself as quickly as possible without taking unnecessary chances.

⚠ **Warning**

Use caution. Physical contact in martial arts may result in injury.

## Paddle a Canoe — 898

Seemingly the simplest manoeuvre in canoeing, the forward paddle can take years to truly master. These instructions offer beginner's guidelines for the canoer's most essential skill.

### ⊙ Steps

1   Kneel or sit in the canoe facing forwards at either the stern or the bow, if two people are paddling. If you're canoeing solo, sit or kneel just a little rear of the middle.

2   Hold the paddle with your inside hand on top and your water-side hand 60 to 90 cm (2 to 3 ft) down – wherever feels most comfortable – with knuckles facing out.

3   Insert the blade of the paddle completely into the water with the paddle blade at a right angle to the side of the canoe, at least 60 cm (2 ft) in front of you, or as far forwards as you can reach without lunging your body forwards.

✻ **Tips**

Bent-shaft paddles are more efficient for forward paddling than straight-shaft paddles because the bend allows you to pull the paddle back farther in the water before you begin pushing water up.

After learning to paddle, next focus on steering and turning.

4    Push your top hand forwards and pull your bottom hand back, drawing the blade through the water. Keep the shaft of the paddle perpendicular to the water and the top of the paddle handle lower than eye level.

5    Pivot your shoulder to draw the blade straight back. Avoid following the curve of the canoe – the paddle's handle should always stay to your side, never crossing in front of your body.

6    Pull the blade back through the water as far as your hip – no further. After the blade reaches this point, it's actually slowing the canoe down by pushing water up and hence pushing the canoe down in the water.

7    Lift the blade out of the water and turn the blade parallel to the water (this is especially important on windy days) to carry it forward to the starting position.

8    Reinsert the blade and stroke again.

⚠ **Warning**

Avoid lurching forwards on each new paddle stroke. Not only is it bad for your back, but it also wears you out faster.

---

## 899 | Paddle a River Raft

Paddling instead of rowing is a fun way to guide a raft through whitewater rapids. These instructions are for the typical inflatable eight-person raft.

### ⊙ Steps

1    Position the paddlers evenly on both sides of the raft. Paddlers should kneel, sit on thwarts or straddle the buoyancy tubes when paddling.

2    Hold the paddle with the inside hand on the top of the paddle and the outside hand, knuckles facing out, gripping the paddle low on its stem.

3    Lean forward and insert the paddle into the water. Dip the blade completely beneath the surface. Keep the shaft of the paddle perpendicular to the water and the top of the paddle handle lower than eye level.

4    Straighten your top arm while pulling back on the paddle with your lower arm to draw it through the water. This is the standard forward paddle.

5    Reverse the forward motion to back paddle. Dip the blade and pull the upper arm back while extending your lower arm.

6    To turn the bow right, have the right side of the raft (from the paddler's perspective) paddle back while the left side paddles forward. Reverse this procedure to go left.

7    Reach out with the paddle, dip in deep and pull towards yourself to draw stroke, pulling the raft in the direction of your paddle stroke.

8    Dip the paddle in close to the raft and push away to pry stroke, or move the raft sideways away from the direction of your paddle stroke.

9    Communicate with your rafting team and work together.

✴ **Tip**

Paddling is all about teamwork. Pick a captain, the most experienced rafter, to call out directions so everyone can work together.

⚠ **Warning**

When rafting on a river, always provide personal flotation devices for everyone on board.

## Catch a Wave

The surf may be up, but you can't surf until you master this critical skill of catching and riding a wave.

### ⊙ Steps

1. Paddle out beyond the breaking waves, sit on your board facing out to sea and wait for a good wave.

2. Sit just behind the middle of your board, with the nose pointing slightly out of the water, so you can easily pivot in any direction to paddle for a wave.

3. When you see a good wave coming, swing your legs up behind you to lie down on your board, and paddle to position yourself near the peak, where the wave is highest and will break first. If you are too far out, the wave won't be ready to break, and if you are too close to shore, the wave will immediately break and thrash you.

4. After paddling into position, sit up on your board and spin it around until you point in the direction you want to go when the wave picks you up.

5. Lie down when a choice wave swells your way. Paddle in the direction the wave is moving so that it overtakes you just before it breaks.

6. Note which way the wave is breaking: from your left to the right, for example. Eventually, you'll be propelled towards the beach and will want to surf sideways away from the break.

7. Accelerate your paddling as the wave approaches, applying full power as the wave picks you up and propels you.

8. Don't stop paddling until you feel the wave completely propelling you and your board. Keep your weight as far over the nose of the board as you can without dipping it under the water.

9. Grab the rails (edges) of your board directly beneath your shoulders and push up when you are sure the wave is taking you.

10. Quickly pop up from the rails of your board, pushing the board down into the face of the wave and quickly pulling your legs up beneath you.

11. Put your left foot forwards if you're regular-footed, or place your right foot forwards if you're a goofy-foot (see 920 "Determine if You're a Regular or a Goofy Foot"). Your feet should be roughly perpendicular on the board, depending on your own comfort. Keep in mind that the positioning of your feet depends on the size and shape of your board, but the position should enable you to instantly turn and control your board.

12. Lean to your wave-side rail (in this case, the right side). You should now be zipping along, riding the perfect wave.

### ✻ Tips

Keep your eyes focused down the wave, especially as you pop to your feet. The second you lean your weight back, you'll lose the wave.

Different breaks and different types of waves have different tendencies.

Take mental notes on each wave you miss and make corrections. Then try again.

Lay your board on the sand and practise pushing up and popping to your feet. When you pop up, try to plant your feet in the riding position, so you won't have to make adjustments as you drop in. Be careful not to break your fins or get sand in your wax, however.

### ⚠ Warning

Observe the rules of surfer right-of-way, allowing other surfers to catch the wave when appropriate. If you "drop in" (catch an already breaking wave) in front of another surfer, that person will, justifiably, get very angry with you.

## 901 Bodyboard

A bodyboard (often called a boogie board) is shorter and wider than a surfboard and made of pliable foam core rather than hardened fibreglass. It's all you need to ride the waves.

### ⊙ Steps

1   Lie belly-down on your bodyboard, and position yourself beyond the breaking waves. As a wave approaches, begin kicking towards the beach so that the wave propels you instead of breaking behind you. At this point, both hands should be on the front of the board.

2   Feel the wave begin to carry you along and determine whether you are going to ride to the right or to the left along the wave's face.

3   Reposition your hands so that, if you are going left, your right hand is on the rail (the side of the board) while your left hand remains on the front, or vice versa.

4   Pull your body up over the front of your board and arch your back so that your chest is over the front of the board and your head is held high.

5   Use your outside hand to pull up on the side of the board, causing the wave-side rail of the board to dig into the face of the wave. This will prevent you from sliding down the face of the wave.

6   Release the right rail to slide down the face, and dig in again to ride up. Going up and down the face helps you build speed and control.

7   Drag your swimming fins (which are a necessity for serious bodyboarding) if you wish to slow down, but otherwise hold them up out of the water.

### ⚠ Warning

Beginning bodyboarders eat a lot of sand. If you get tossed in the waves, hold your breath until the tumbling stops, then swim ashore to rest.

## 902 Launch a Sailboard

Take that boom in your hand and harness the power of the wind. Skimming across the surface of the water with the wind in your face is exhilarating. Here's how to start.

### ⊙ Steps

1   Bring your board and rig (sail, boom and mast) to the water's edge and prepare for action by attaching the mast to the board, inserting the daggerboard (if you use one) and putting on your life vest. Wear a wet suit if the water is cold.

2   Carry the board and rig into the water as a single unit. If you are unable to carry it by yourself, ask someone for help. If you are on soft sand, you can hold the tail of the board (the end with the fin) and the mast and drag the board into the water.

3   Enter the water knee-deep, with the board floating completely in the water and the sail on the leeward (downwind) side of the board. The wind should be at your back.

4   Step up on the board, facing the rig, and place one foot on either side of the mast.

### ⚠ Warning

Always keep your rig on the leeward side of the board. Otherwise, the wind can catch it, flip the sail and mast, and smack you in the face.

5  Bend down and grasp the up-haul line. One end is attached to the boom, the other to where the mast enters the board. Hoist the rig by pulling up on the up-haul line.

6  Grab the boom with both hands.

7  Sheet in (pull the boom and sail in to catch wind), and you should be propelled forward immediately.

## Use a Snorkel                                                   903

Using a snorkel properly will give you a clear vision of what's going on under the sea without having to breathe water.

### ⊙ Steps

1  Test your mask and snorkel together to determine fit and comfort.

2  Position the small rubber strap that attaches the snorkel to your mask so that the snorkel passes just above your left ear. (If you are using a special left-handed snorkel, it will be on your right.)

3  Take a deep breath, bite down on the mouthpiece and submerge your head in the water

4  Exhale sharply once to clear any water that may be in the snorkel shaft. This is commonly called "blasting" or "purging".

5  Inhale gently at first in case there is any residual water. Blast a second time if needed, and continue to do so whenever water enters the snorkel.

6  Learn to move gently on the surface—rapid or abrupt movements can fill the snorkel with water.

7  Inhale and hold your breath, then dive to explore the underwater environment around you.

8  Ascend, make sure the snorkel end is above the surface, then purge to clear the tube of water.

9  Breathe cautiously to be sure the snorkel has cleared completely. If you don't have enough air left to purge, lift your head above the surface and take the snorkel out to breathe.

### ✱ Tips

When you're floating face down in the water in a relaxed position, the snorkel should extend vertically above your head.

It's normal for snorkels to flood with water periodically because of wave action as you move about on the surface. Practise purging your snorkel until it becomes routine.

### ⚠ Warning

If your snorkel becomes flooded too frequently, it is probably positioned incorrectly on your head, or you are snorkeling in conditions that are too rough.

## Fish for Carp                                                   904

Carp will often come right to the surface to feed early in the morning and later on in the afternoon. This is a great chance for even an inexperienced angler to hook one.

### ⊙ Steps

1  Talk to people at your local carp lake and find out when any fish seem to come to the surface to feed most confidently.

2  Wait for a still day when there is scarcely a ripple on the water for your ideal carp-fishing expedition.

### ✱ Tip

If no carp are visible, you will need to resort to fishing with your bait on the bottom or with a float.

3 Choose a 12 ft carp rod or heavy-feeder rod. Simply push the two pieces of the rod together to assemble.

4 Select a fixed-spool reel and fill it with a 10 lb line. Note that brightly coloured line is not good for this kind of fishing.

5 Select a suitable bait. Among those that work with carp are bread, sweet corn, dog biscuits and maggots.

6 Attach the kind of weighted float known as a "carp controller" to your line, plus a hook (see 905 "Tie On a Fishhook").

7 Locate the surface-feeding carp and watch them for a while, trying to learn where they go and how they feed. If you have difficulty seeing the fish because of surface glare from the water, don polarised sunglasses to cut the glare. Know that you must remain very quiet while observing the fish.

8 Cast your bait beyond the feeding fish. Then very slowly wind your bait in so that it lies among the fish.

9 Keep a close eye on your bait and, when a fish sucks it in confidently, strike, holding the rod with your right hand and reeling in with your left. Take care not to strike until the carp has engulfed your bait; know that striking too early will lose you the fish and may cause the rest of the carp to vanish.

10 Make sure that the drag on your fixed spool reel is set so that the fish can run and not break your line. Be aware that carp can run and fight very hard.

11 Play the carp until you can safely net it.

12 Gently remove the hook from the carp's mouth, photograph the fish and kindly slip it back into the water.

13 Be aware that catching a carp like this can often "spook" the rest of the fish that are feeding, but if you wait a little they will soon go back to feeding and you will be able to cast again.

### Things You'll Need

❑ 12 ft carp rod

❑ reel with 10 lb line

❑ hook

❑ bait

❑ carp controller (weighted float)

❑ net

❑ polarised sunglasses

❑ camera

---

## 905 | Tie On a Fishhook

It won't matter how many pounds your fishing line can withstand. If the hook knot is weak, you've got no fish. This simple knot looks like a tiny noose.

### ⊙ Steps

1 Ready your fishing line on the rod with any appropriate weights, spinners and other tackle.

2 Grab the fishhook along its flat plane between the thumb and index finger of your left hand.

3 Take the end of the line with your right hand. Thread 2.5 cm (1 in) of the line through the hook eye.

4 Bend back the end of the line.

5 Cross the end over the main line and pin the intersecting lines with your

### ✱ Tips

Keep the end of the line taut (both in your teeth and by pulling back on the main line) while pushing down the knot with your fingernails.

To ensure that the knot is tight, pull back on the main line while holding the hook, then push down the knot again. Repeat until pulling on the line does not loosen the knot.

right index finger and thumb. The hook should be trapped inside a loop you've created.

6 Turn the hook about five times with your left hand to make a twist in the line.

7 Feed the end of the line through the loop near the hook eye. The loop should be small now that you've twisted it down.

8 Grab the end of the line with your teeth.

9 Pull gently until the line is taut.

10 Let go of the hook with your left hand and then grab the main line above the knot.

11 Let go of the line with your right hand and pinch it above the knot between your right thumbnail and the nail of your index finger.

12 Tighten the knot by pushing it down the line towards the hook eye with your fingernails while pulling on the short end with your teeth.

13 Bite or cut off the excess line.

Don't twist the hook too many times or there will be no hole left to feed the end through.

Be sure to tighten the knot before trimming the excess line. If you trim too close and too soon, you'll pull the knot free while trying to tighten it.

# Cast a Line in Fly-Fishing                                906

In fly-fishing, casting is a back-and-forth motion of the rod and line that allows you to place your fly where you'd like. It takes a good deal of practice to get just right. This is the basic cast.

## ◉ Steps

1 Let out 8 m (26 ft) of line in front of you. Practise out of the water and without a fly on the line so that you won't have to worry about getting caught up in anything.

2 Grip your rod as if you were shaking hands with it. Set the rod's handle in your palm and close your fingers around it, keeping your thumb on top.

3 Face the direction that you want to cast, putting your weight on the balls of your feet. Keep your wrist still and stiff, don't allow it to bend. Your elbow, not your shoulder, should be your pivot point. Picture hammering a nail.

4 Think of the movement of your arm in casting as being like that of a clock's hands. If you view a fly fisherman from his or her left profile, the caster will move the rod between 11 o'clock on the forward cast and 1 o'clock on the back cast.

5 Hold the rod at 11 o'clock to begin. From the tip, the loose fly line should trace down the rod until you can grab it with your free hand. Hold and keep it above waist level.

6 Pull the rod back to 1 o'clock, release the line and wait there until the line straightens behind you. Now accelerate the rod forward to 11 o'clock and wait for the loop formed by the arcing line to straighten out.

7 Bring the fingers of your free hand towards the reel and grasp the line between your index finger and thumb.

## ✳ Tips

Consider learning how to cast on grass first. Working on concrete will ruin the protective coating on your line. If you want to practise on concrete, use a piece of junk line you don't mind ruining.

Add a piece of coloured yarn to the end of your line when practising so you can see where your fly will end up without worrying about getting an actual hook snagged on the grass.

8  Pull in your outstretched line in 15 cm (6 in) lengths so it forms a big excess loop right above the reel. You're not pulling more line off the reel or putting any back – you're simply gathering slack to ease the next cast. Pull in only as much as you need to place your cast.

9  To end casting, stop with the forward cast at 11 o'clock. All the slack you pulled in will sail out with your fly (when you have one on the line), which should land right on your target. Assuming, of course, that you've been practising.

---

## 907  Load a Backpack

A well-loaded pack takes less energy to carry than one that's off-balance. It's also much more comfortable.

### ⊙ Steps

1  Assemble all food, water, clothing and other equipment you intend to carry.

2  Small items you won't need until you pitch camp can go inside empty spaces, such as the inside of your cooking pot, to take full advantage of space.

3  Load your sleeping bag at the bottom of your pack (if you have an internal-frame pack) or tie it below (if you have an external-frame pack). You won't need it before you pitch camp, and a sleeping bag is light for its volume.

4  Pack heavy items – food, stove, fuel and water – above the sleeping bag and next to your back. Be sure that objects don't protrude into your back.

5  Keep your water bottle separate for easy access.

6  Try to keep the weight evenly distributed from side to side within the pack so that it won't be lopsided when you carry it.

7  Fill the remaining volume with clothing. The items furthest from your back should be the lightest.

### ✳ Tips

Keep only the items you need handy in the pockets or top flap of the pack. Most packs don't close very well, and a large, unstable load in the top pocket can throw you off balance.

If your pack doesn't have a special outside pocket for your water bottle, tuck a bottle underneath the top flap on its side and right up against your back.

Think "Heavy High, Light Low".

---

## 908  Avoid Getting Blisters While Hiking

There's nothing like painful blisters to ruin a walking holiday in the wilds, but you can avoid them by taking these measures.

### ⊙ Steps

1  Break in hiking shoes or boots well before your walk, wearing the same shoe-sock combination you will use in the field.

2  Wrap your blister-prone spots with athletic tape or duct tape before you start hiking, if you know you're likely to have a problem. Put the tape directly on your skin; when you're done hiking, take off your boots and pull off the tape immediately. The heat and sweat from your feet will make it easier to remove.

### ✳ Tip

Many hikers use liner socks – thin socks that absorb sweat and heat away from your feet. Regular thicker socks are worn on top of these. The liners provide a protective layer for the outer socks to rub against.

3  Soak any developing hot spot (an area that is irritated from rubbing) in cold water or air-dry it until the spot cools.

4  Apply a patch or doughnut of moleskin to the hot spot or cover it with tape. Theories about the pros and cons of patches, doughnuts and tape vary. Experiment and find what works best for you.

5  Use foot powder and change into a dry pair of socks before you put your boots or shoes back on and continue hiking.

**Things You'll Need**

❑ athletic or duct tape

❑ moleskin

❑ foot powder

❑ dry socks

---

## Relieve Yourself in the Woods                                   909

Human waste is one of the biggest problems people import to the wilderness. Going's OK – it's where you go that's important.

### ◉ Steps

1  Anticipate the need to go so you can select a good site before urgency overwhelms you.

2  Find a spot at least 60 m (200 ft) from water and 60 m (200 ft) from campsites, footpaths and other popular areas.

3  Once you find a spot, dig a hole at least 15 cm (6 in) deep.

4  Drop your drawers, squat down over the hole and go.

5  Use smooth rocks, grass, leaves or even snow in place of toilet paper if you want to go with a no-trace camping strategy. If you use toilet paper, burn it or carry it out of the woods with the rest of your belongings.

6  Fill the hole back up and use leaves, pine needles or rocks to camouflage the site.

7  If you only need to urinate, do so on sand, mineral soil or exposed rock.

**✳ Tip**

Urine burns plants, and its odour attracts animals that will destroy the site digging for the salt.

**Things You'll Need**

❑ camping trowel or shovel

❑ toilet paper

---

## Signal for Help in the Wilderness                               910

If you are far from civilisation and weather conditions get so poor that you lose your way, or if you get stranded and need help despite sunny skies, keep the following in mind.

### ◉ Steps

1  Know that any series of three signals is a universal call of distress: Three whistle blasts or three gunshots, for instance, will alert others that you need help.

2  Understand that yelling is only effective if people are nearby. The human voice doesn't carry well, so save your vocal cords and strength.

3  Find a clearing or hilltop and start three signal fires, making sure to keep them under control. Place them in triangular form (a known signal for help) and space them 15 m (50 ft) apart so that a plane can distinguish the pattern from overhead.

**⚠ Warning**

Only light fires in a genuine emergency.

**Things You'll Need**

❑ whistle

❑ waterproof matches

❑ mirror

4   Use green and wet wood to send up ample smoke during daylight; use dry material at night to make a strong, roaring blaze.

5   Spread out three sets of brightly coloured equipment – for example, a tent cloth, a tarpaulin and a blanket – in an open space to signal your distress. Again, put them in triangular form.

6   Use brightly coloured gear or dark brush or rocks to create three piles, or lay out an "SOS" or a big "X" on an open snowfield to signal aircraft rescuers in wintry conditions.

7   Use a mirror to flash a sunlight signal over long distances if you see a plane or people in the distance. (This technique won't work on cloudy days.)

## 911 | Climb Mount Everest

Everest can mercilessly test even those who respect it. Whether you choose a packaged, guided expedition or trek with friends, there are several things to keep in mind.

### ◎ Steps

1   Start training today. Take mountaineering courses that teach you about technique, equipment, routes and survival. Then begin a minimum of two to three years of regular practice climbs in high alpine terrain, including steep faces, rough rocks, night climbs, ice falls and snow climbs.

2   Get a complete physical check-up. You'll need healthy veins and arteries to pump lots of blood to your brain and muscles, as well as to warm your body. Keep your blood pressure and cholesterol down.

3   Raise the cash. You'll need plenty—even a low-budget trip will cost around £35,000, with guided package trips soaring to double this. Realise that permits are expensive; then add travel, food, equipment, oxygen, insurance and Sherpa fees. Consider looking for sponsorship deals to cover your expenses.

4   Plan a May expedition. The weather is most cooperative then – when it isn't a whiteout, with 160 km/h (100 mph) winds blowing. Six months in advance, you'll need to file for permits from the Nepalese administration, sending copies of passports and climbing letters of recommendation for your team. You'll also need to contact a trekking agency to help you with transporting your gear and to contract Sherpas to aid you on your climb. For more information, contact the Nepalese Embassy in London, or the Nepal Mountaineering Association in Kathmandu, Nepal.

5   Pack a first aid kit, medications, satellite phone, walkie-talkies, laptop computer, padlocks for bags, tents, sleeping bags, mountaineering clothing, climbing equipment and ropes, water, food, rubbish bags, sunscreen, vision protection, oxygen bottles and anything else you can fit on a yak or on your back, or that you can hire a Sherpa to carry for you. Make sure you've tested all your gear in cold, severe conditions before you pack it.

### ✱ Tips

Climb with people you know and trust, and who have extensive experience.

Ask other climbers who have tackled Everest to recommend the most skilled and reliable Sherpas.

Drink lots of purified water to stay hydrated.

### ⚠ Warnings

Stay warm, or risk losing body parts.

Climbing Mount Everest puts you at risk of severe injury, disease and possibly death from avalanche, falling rocks, crevasse falls, exhaustion, dehydration, frostbite, pneumonia, dysentery, Khumbu cough, whiteout disorientation, hypothermia, high-altitude cerebral and pulmonary edema, and other hazards.

Be prepared to call off your summit attempt due to fatigue or poor weather conditions.

6   Get yourself to Kathmandu, Nepal, where your expedition truly begins. You can fly a number of international carriers connecting through major airports; none of these flights will be direct or nonstop. Jet lag is guaranteed. Check in with the local authorities, pay your fees and organise your crew.

7   Trek from Lukla to Base Camp at 5,400 m (17,500 ft). Scale the Khumbu Icefall up to 6,100 m (20,000 ft). Rest at Camp I in the Valley of Silence. Push on to Camp II at 6,500 m (21,300 ft). Scale the Lhotse Face and climb to Camp III at 7,400 m (24,000 ft). Rest and acclimatise for the trip to Camp IV, which at 8,000 m (26,000 ft) is the only camp located in the "death zone".

8   Charge the summit when you have a weather window. Start early in the morning, before sunrise, with extra down mittens and plenty of oxygen.

9   Sit atop the 8,850 m (29,035 ft) summit and know that you are at the highest point on earth. And mentally prepare for the descent – getting down is just as dangerous.

10  Pack out all of your empty oxygen bottles and rubbish to get back your environmental deposit and leave the mountain with good karma.

## Spot Potential Avalanche Danger                   912

If you can identify the site of a recent or potential avalanche, you will reduce your chances of being caught in an extremely dangerous situation while skiing.

### ◎ Steps

1   Check the amount of recent snowfall. Heavy amounts of new snow increase the likelihood of an avalanche.

2   Pay attention to radical changes in temperature that may cause snow to melt, become heavier or change consistency. Layers of snow will settle and fracture where there is a major difference in consistency.

3   Stay away from steep slopes, where gravity will have a greater effect on the new snow.

4   Keep an eye out for fractures in the snow along the face of the slope.

5   Look in the chutes, in gullies and at the bottom of steep slopes for avalanche debris. You will see a marked difference in the snow – it looks like cottage cheese or boulders.

6   Watch the snow around you as you ski. If it comes loose and sloughs down the hill with you, then you are at risk of getting caught up in it.

### ✳ Tip

Point out areas of concern to your guide and others in your group.

### ⚠ Warning

Don't get cocky armed with this information – stay out of areas prone to avalanches.

## 913 | Walk on Snowshoes

For thousands of years, snowshoes have been used for winter transport. Today they're more popular than ever, thanks to improvements in their technology.

### ⊙ Steps

1 Dress appropriately for winter recreation.

2 Stretch your muscles for 10 to 15 minutes. Be sure to stretch at least the thighs, groin and calves.

3 Attach the snowshoes to your footwear snugly so your foot and snow-shoe move as one.

4 Keep your feet shoulder-width apart, as most snowshoes are wider than regular footwear.

5 Swing the striding foot sideways and forward, clearing your opposite ankle. Your foot will wing out in an arc pattern. Be sure to swing away from your body and far enough forward to clear the opposite snowshoe.

6 Land with the pressure focused on the ball of your foot.

7 Repeat with the opposite leg.

### ✱ Tips

Packed trails and flat slopes are the best places to learn to snowshoe.

Look back at your tracks – they should look like a zip line.

## 914 | Make a Snowplough Turn on Skis

Learning how to make a snowplough turn – also known as a wedge turn – is the first step to controlling your speed and direction on skis.

### ⊙ Steps

1 Spread your feet about shoulder-width apart.

2 Make sure your knees and ankles are slightly bent.

3 Point your toes in towards each other. This will force the tips of your skis to angle towards each other.

4 Keep your weight approximately even between both feet until you're ready to initiate a turn.

5 Increase pressure on the inside edge of the ski you want to turn. If you want to turn left, you put pressure on the right ski by pushing down with your right big toe.

6 Maintain your centre of gravity above both skis.

7 Turn the ski with your legs, hips and feet, not your upper body.

8 Allow your shoulders to face down the slope. Your shoulders and upper body should not follow the turn of your skis.

9 Ease pressure off the ski edge as you finish the turn.

10 Prepare for the next turn.

### ✱ Tips

Control your speed by making bigger turns or by making a bigger snowplough shape with your skis.

Linking one turn with another allows the skier to progress down the slope in a fluid manner. Linking turns is the ultimate goal when learning the snowplough turn.

### ⚠ Warning

Skiing is an inherently dangerous activity that can result in serious injury or death. Seek proper training and equipment.

# Make a Stem-Christie Turn on Skis

After you've mastered the snowplough turn to the right and to the left, and you've become accustomed to skiing at greater speed, the stem christie (also known as the wedge christie) is the next turn to learn.

## ◉ Steps

1  Form a snowplough (see 914 "Make a Snowplough Turn on Skis") before you begin your turn.

2  Begin increasing pressure on the inside ski that you want to use to initiate the turn – the left ski if you're turning right, or the right ski if you're turning left. Keep your focus on the downhill slope ahead and not your skis.

3  Turn right by pointing your left arm to your right ski tip while holding your arms out in front of you. Turn left by pointing your right arm to your left ski.

4  Touch the pole to the ground (on the right, for example, to turn right) a little in front of your body, and turn around the planted pole. Increase the pressure on the inside edge of the ski you want to turn. If you want to turn right, you put pressure on the left ski by pushing down with your left big toe. To turn left, do the opposite.

5  Allow the tail of your inside ski to slide down towards your outside ski as you finish the turn. This is known as matching or parallel skiing. This step is the goal of the stem-christie turn. As the hill becomes steeper and you start skiing faster, your skis will naturally want to come together through the turn.

6  Keep your hands up and in front of your body throughout the turn.

7  Finish your turn with your skis together.

## ✳ Tips

Look downhill the entire time, not at your skis.

The faster you're going, the easier it is to do a stem-christie turn.

As you become more comfortable with the stem christie, form your wedge later and later before the turn.

Increase pressure on your edges to make the turn more crisp.

## 916 | Start Out on Cross-Country Skis

The sport of cross-country skiing can take you to some of nature's most beautiful winter terrain. It is also one of the easier snow sports to learn.

### ⊙ Steps

1 Pick an easy trail to start. Flat terrain with only an occasional hill is the most suitable for beginners.

2 Put on your skis by inserting the fronts of your boots into the bindings.

3 Stick your poles in the snow at your sides and slide your skis back and forth while remaining in a stationary position. This exercise gives you a feel for your equipment.

4 Put your hands through the pole straps.

5 Put one foot in front of the other, letting the skis slide as if you were walking across an ice-skating rink.

6 Plant your poles in a rhythmic manner, placing the left one in the snow at the end of a right-foot glide and vice versa.

7 Practise until you feel comfortable enough to increase your speed and gliding distance.

### ✻ Tips

Make certain that your boots are free of snow before stepping into your bindings.

Expect to fall a few times on your first excursions – it's all part of the fun of cross-country skiing.

## 917 | Carve a Turn on a Snowboard

Carving – linking a toe-side turn with a heel-side turn – is one of the most basic manoeuvres in snowboarding and one of the most pleasant experiences on earth.

### ⊙ Steps

1 Start by making a toe-side turn. Do this by leaning forwards slightly, lifting your heels, and turning your shoulders to the right. (Reverse these directions if you ride goofy foot; see 920 "Determine if You're a Regular or Goofy Foot".)

2 Straighten up as you come to the end of your toe turn; face your shoulders straight ahead and arch your back slightly. In this position, your board should be flat on the snow, with neither edge engaged.

3 Lean forward with your knees bent, keeping your body low and flexible.

4 Make a heel-side turn: Rotate your shoulders to the left while lifting your toes and leaning back slightly.

5 Straighten up as you come to the end of your heel-side turn, and face your shoulders downhill.

6 Start your second toe-side turn. Lean forward, keep your body low and flexible (with your knees bent), and rotate your shoulders to the toe side while lifting your heels slightly.

### ✻ Tips

As you get more advanced, you can stay lower, face your shoulders downhill more and go faster. You also won't need consciously to go flat in between edges – you'll make a smooth transition.

The transition between the heel turn and the toe turn is where people often catch an edge and fall. It helps to have your weight low and slightly forwards on the board.

### ⚠ Warning

Snowboarding is an inherently dangerous activity that can result in serious injury or death. Seek proper training and equipment.

## Stop a Snowboard With Your Toes

**918**

Stopping is a basic skill you need when snowboarding, and being able to stop on either your toes or heels is essential.

### ⊙ Steps

1 Prepare for the toe-side stop as you would for a toe-side turn by lowering your weight and leaning forwards, rotating your shoulders around to the uphill side of the slope, and straightening your back as the turn ends.

2 Continue rotating uphill until the board is perpendicular to the slope instead of letting the turn flatten out to make the transition into the heel turn.

3 Hold that position perpendicular to the slope with your heels up, and let the board sideslip to scrub off speed. The faster you're going, the more you'll need to sideslip before you stop.

4 Sideslip to a full stop.

**✳ Tip**

To avoid overrotating the tail and going backwards down the slope, balance your weight evenly between your front and back legs. If you feel the tail of your board drop too far, put more weight on the back foot.

---

## Catch Air on a Snowboard

**919**

Here's the most basic way to get airborne on a snowboard – your first step towards flying the friendly skies.

### ⊙ Steps

1 Approach the bump you'll use to catch air. Keep your knees deeply bent and your upper body relaxed.

2 Compress as you reach the bump.

3 Spring up just before you reach the top of the bump.

4 Draw your legs up evenly as you leave the ground.

5 Keep your board pointed forwards, level and directly underneath you.

6 Extend your legs (back foot first If you've caught big air) as you come back down.

7 Compress again when you return to earth to absorb the landing.

**✳ Tip**

Make sure you can see the landing area so you don't run into anyone.

## 920 | Determine if You're a Regular or Goofy Foot

In snowboarding, surfing and skateboarding, you're a "regular foot" if you keep your left foot forwards, a "goofy foot" if you go right forwards. Here are three ways to tell which you are.

### ⊙ Steps

1 Put forward whichever foot makes you feel the most balanced, controlled and relaxed in that position. Generally, this will be the same for you from one board sport to another.

2 Lie on your stomach on the ground as you would on a surfboard, putting your hands under your shoulders as if you were going to do a pushup. Spring into a surfing or riding stance. Try it first with your left foot forwards and then with your right. Whichever stance feels better is probably the right one for you.

3 Have someone give you a surprise shove from behind. Not only will your friend probably enjoy this, but whichever foot you step forward with first to catch your balance is probably the foot that goes in front when you surf, skateboard or snowboard.

## 921 | Develop Good Cueing Technique at Snooker

The basics of snooker technique lie in the grip on the cue, the stance, the bridge made by the hand resting on the table, and the action with which you strike the cue ball.

### ⊙ Steps

1 Grip the cue lightly but firmly – too tight a grip might make your arm muscles tense, while too loose a grip risks your losing control of the cue while playing a shot.

2 Adopt a balanced, stable stance, with your front leg and your back leg straight. If you don't feel comfortable setting yourself for the shot, experiment with different positions of the feet until you find what works.

3 Make a bridge with the fingertips of your left hand (right hand for left-handers) resting on the baize. The bridge must provide stable support for the cue – it must not move when you play the shot.

4 Lean the cue on the bridge, forming a groove with your thumb and fingers to control it. Be aware that the cue must move smoothly and unimpeded, but be firmly enough contained to avoid any wobbling or sliding around.

5 Settle for the shot. Ensure that the line from the elbow of your cueing arm to the hand holding the cue is perpendicular – that is, the forearm is at right angles to the cue. The cueing hand, the cue ball and the object ball – the ball you intend to hit – should all lie along a straight line.

6 Ensure that your head is over the line of the cue, so that you are looking directly down the line from the cue ball to the object ball.

### ✱ Tips

Watch top snooker players on television and learn from their technique.

Test your basic cueing technique by hitting straight long pots. You will only carry off these apparently simple shots successfully if your cueing action is good.

If you want to take up snooker seriously, get the help of a coach early on, before you develop a lot of bad habits that could be hard to shake off.

7　Flick your eyes back and forth between the cue ball and the object ball. Make your last glance before playing the shot be to the object ball.

8　Move the cue forwards with a movement from your elbow. Keep the rest of your body and your head perfectly still. Do not move your arm or wrist independently – the elbow moves them.

9　Strike the cue ball with the tip of the cue and continue with the stroke in a smooth follow-through.

---

## Give the Cue Ball Spin at Snooker | 922

Cue-ball control is one of the most satisfying skills that a snooker player can develop. Learn to make the ball do what you want by applying spin in four directions.

### ⊙ Steps

1　Make the cue ball spin forwards, so that it follows through – that is, rolls as far as possible given the power of the shot. Raise the bridge, bending your fingers so that the palm of your hand is well clear of the cloth. This will raise the tip of your cue. Keeping the cue parallel to the cloth, strike the cue ball slightly above centre.

2　Make the cue ball stop quickly or screw back with back spin. Lower the bridge so that your hand is virtually flat on the cloth. This will lower the tip of the cue. Keeping the cue parallel to the cloth, strike the cue ball slightly below centre.

3　Make the cue ball curve to the left and deflect left off the cushion by striking the ball with the tip of the cue slightly right of centre. Ensure that your cue still moves straight down the line that you want the cue ball to take – don't cue across the ball towards the right-hand side.

4　Make the cue ball curve to the right and deflect right off the cushion. Follow instructions in step 3 above, but reversing the directions.

**✳ Tip**

Practise using different bridges, not only to achieve follow through or screw the ball back, but also in case you meet awkward cueing positions, for example over the top of another ball.

**⚠ Warning**

Avoid striking the cue ball too far off centre. This is the cause of many embarrassing miscues.

## 923 Buy a New Car

Choosing a car is an important decision that merits careful planning. You are likely to live with this vehicle for quite some time. These pointers will help you choose wisely.

### ⊙ Steps

1 Decide what you intend to use the car for – work; fun; weekends and evenings out; carrying things; towing a trailer; carrying more than one passenger; driving in the city, suburbs or country. Consider other factors that may be important to you, such as fuel efficiency, reliability and safety features.

2 Consider the type of fuel your chosen model uses. A diesel car will be more costly to buy than its petrol equivalent, but your fuel costs may be halved, so great savings are possible for high-mileage drivers. (Diesel cars have improved enormously over the past few years to the point where performance is usually comparable with equivalent petrol models.

3 Set a realistic budget based on what you can afford – don't forget to account for such matters as monthly payments and running costs.

4 If you're considering a trade-in, check the value of your current vehicle in publications such as *What Car?*, *Parker's Guide* or *Used Car Price Guide* – they will give you an indication of how much your car will be worth in the future. Factor your car's trade-in value into your total budget.

5 Find a model that interests you. There are plenty of monthly motoring magazines that will give you an idea of what's on the market. Look out for in-depth reviews which will give you a detailed specification as well as – in theory – an impartial point of view.

6 Look on the manufacturer's web pages or obtain a sales brochure for the model that interests you. (But be aware that these documents will be anything but impartial!)

7 Find the nearest car dealerships that sell your chosen model; check car magazines, local newspaper advertisements or a business directory. Choose a number of dealerships to visit – preferably on a weekday; remember to bring your driver's license so you can test-drive. You can also shop online (see 926 "Shop for a Car Online").

8 Locate the car that interests you. Check its price – it will usually have a sticker on windscreen.

9 Seek out a sales representative. (That shouldn't be too demanding – in practice, he'll be more than likely to pounce on you the moment you step through the front doors of the dealership.)

10 Ask to have a look inside the car. Adjust the seat and mirrors, and check leg room in each part of the car.

11 Check what the quoted price includes: the majority of new models are available with a variety of extras. Some of them – such as air conditioning or sun roof – can make a considerable difference to the overall price.

### ✳ Tips

With few exceptions, all new cars depreciate at an alarming rate – your car could be worth half what you paid for it within a year. Buying "nearly-new" is far better in terms of value for money.

You should be able to negotiate a good price on the biggest-selling models – especially from the less prestigious marques, such as Ford, Vauxhall or the cheaper Japanese brands.

Prestige models are usually produced in smaller quantities, so be aware that you could find yourself on a waiting list for the best part of a year before you take delivery of your new car.

Try to avoid setting your heart on one particular model or make. There are hundreds of excellent vehicles on the market, and becoming attached to one of them is likely to make you less hard-headed in your bargaining.

Pay attention to the customer surveys published in motoring or consumer magazines. These can give you important clues as to a car's potential reliability, or the level of service you are likely to receive from a manufacturer or dealership.

12 Ask to take a test drive. Try as many different types of road as possible – town driving is considerably different from the motorway experience. Look out for ease of steering, turning radius, braking response and acceleration. Adjust controls while you're driving to test convenience.

13 Return to the dealership. If you like the car, ask for a business card and say you will return later. Don't make an immediate decision.

14 Head to the next dealership and investigate other car models as described above. Ask dealers which car most closely resembles the one you previously test-drove, providing the make and model and explaining which features you liked. Test a number of models until you decide on a car, and compare these prices with those at other dealerships.

15 Inquire about availability and delivery time, especially if you're interested in a popular model or want special features.

16 Factor the dealership and its sales staff into your choice. A dealership with a competent service centre on site may be worth more than money in your long term.

17 Go home and think about about what you have seen. Now's the time for more research. Consider calling a non franchised car "superstore" to check out prices or special offers, or – for maximum savings – importing from mainland (see 924 "Buy a Car From a Dealer in Europe").

18 Treat marked prices as a starting point for negotiation. Make your first offer. It should be at least 10 per cent lower than what you're willing to pay, but not an insulting figure.

19 Expect the salesman to make a counter-offer. If the price is too high, say you're not able (or willing) to afford that. If you really have reached your ceiling, ask him to talk to his manager.

20 If the salesperson balks at your first offer, make a slightly higher one. Continue negotiating until you can agree on a price within your budget. If you can't agree on a price, seek out another dealer. You may be able to go back and get the first dealer to underbid the second dealer.

## Buy a Car from a Dealer in Europe
## 924

Substantial savings, perhaps as high as 20 per cent, are possible when buying a new car from mainland Europe. What's more, it isn't difficult – if you know how.

### ⊙ Steps

1 Do your basic research in the UK. Choose suitable models and test drive them before you make a move (see 923 "Buy a New Car").

2 Go to a good international newsagent and buy car magazines from the country in which you plan to make your purchase: *AZ*, *Motor Markt*, *Auto Motorrad Freizeit* and *Auto Motor und Sport* for Germany; *Auto Week* for Holland, *Coche Actual*, *Autopista* or *Top Auto* for Spain, *Irish Auto Trader* for Eire. Look for suitable dealerships. (Some overseas dealerships now advertise in the UK motoring press.)

### ✱ Tips

If time is a more of a valuable commodity to you than money then you may find buying direct from an overseas dealer to be an arduous task. Use a specialist car importer.

3  If your grasp of foreign languages is poor, try dealerships in Holland where nearly everyone seems able to speak English.

4  Call the dealer to agree pricing and availability. Overseas dealerships are likely to want higher deposits than are usual in the UK – up to 30 per cent is normal. Send your deposit (and balance) by telegraphic transfer. Your bank will advise you on how to do this.

5  Make sure that the price you pay is exclusive of local taxes; if inclusive, ensure that the dealership can provide you with the paperwork to reclaim the money.

6  The changes that should be made in order to register the car in the UK are: it must be right-hand drive rather than left-hand drive; the front lights should dip to the left not right; the speedometer must be shown in miles per hour. This needs to be incorporated in the dealer's price.

7  You may be able to save up to 50 per cent if buy a left-hand drive car and choose not to get it converted. The delivery time will also be much shorter. However, the car's resale value will be greatly reduced, and you may find it hard (or impossible) even to find a buyer.

8  Make sure that the dealer also provides you with English manufacturer's documentation.

9  To bring the car back to the UK, see 925 "Bring a Foreign-Bought Car into Britain".

10 If all of this fills you with dread, you can still save money (although not as much) by buying your car from a specialist importer. Many of these advertise in the back pages of the UK motoring press. (As always, the most reliable way of choosing is to get a personal recommendation from a satisfied customer.)

## ⚠ Warning

Don't forget to make allowances for VAT and local taxation. Subtract them from the source, but understand that you'll have to pay UK VAT (17.5 per cent) when you import your car. (In some territories you may have to pay the tax first and then reclaim it later – which will affect your cashflow.)

If a dealership goes bankrupt between taking your deposit and delivering your car you will join the queue of creditors, you are likely to come away from the experience empty handed. Although this is no different to having bought in the UK, higher deposits mean thar there is more at stake. (You may be able to protect yourself from such an occurrence by using a credit card.)

---

## 925 | Bring a Foreign-Bought Car into Britain

When you pick up your car from an overseas dealer (or private seller) it should be in a legal state to drive on a UK road. Here's what you need to do.

### ⊙ Steps

1  In the case of buying a new car from a dealership, make sure that it has been converted for use on UK roads. It should be right-hand drive, the front lights should dip to the left, and the speedometer must be shown in miles per hour. This can be done legitimately in the UK, but it's much easier to get it sorted out first. (See 924 "Buy a Car From a Dealer in Europe"). It IS legal to use a left-hand drive car in the UK, but it will result in a greatly reduced resale value. Your driving experience will also be less safe.

2  When you pick up your car it should have temporary export plates. If these are not part of the deal you'll have to pay around £150 extra to organise them. The dealer must supply you with an EU-approved "Certificate of Conformity" (or "C.O.C"). This is critical – without it you won't be able to register your car in the UK.

## ⚠ Warning

Your car will be subject to the warranties that apply in the country of origin. This may not be the three years offered as standard in the the UK.

If a car bought overseas proves to be seriously faulty, it is not covered by the UK's "Sale and Supply of Goods Act 1994" and will have to be returned to the supplying dealer in that country. However, if you buy your car from an independent importer in the UK, and that car was first registered in the UK, then it is covered by UK law.

3  Arrange import insurance covering your journey to the UK. (Since your car won't yet be registered, regular car insurance policies won't be of any use.)

4  Find the nearest ferry to your pick-up point.

5  When in the UK, you have up to thirty days to pay the VAT on your car. For more information, read VAT Notice 728, which is available from HM Customs and Excise, Vehicle Appraisal Unit, PO Box 242, Dover, Kent, CT17 9GP (telephone: 01304 224372).

6  Register your car at your nearest DVLA office. Take with you your Certificate of Conformity and a valid certificate of insurance.

## Shop for a Car Online                                926

Shopping for a new or used car over the internet can reduce the hassle of working with dealerships and provide you with detailed information about a specific car before you even leave for the showroom.

### ◉ Steps

1  Form a general picture of the kind of car you're looking for. Consider how you'll be using the car, what you're willing to spend, and which are important to you, such as fuel efficiency, reliability and safety. (See 923 "Buy a New Car".)

2  Look on the manufacturer's web pages or obtain a sales brochure for the model that interests you. (But be aware that these documents will not be impartial!)

3  Check into the resale value of your choice in publications such as *What Car?*, *Parker's Guide* or *Used Car Price Guide* – they will give you an indication of how much your car will be worth in the future.

3  Open your browser and type in the name of a manufacturer – for example, www.ford.co.uk or www.toyota.co.uk. Use a search engine if this doesn't produce what you're seeking.

4  Enter requested information when prompted. Most manufacturers' websites have detailed information on models, including available options, photos and the Recommended Retail Price.

5  Find websites containing ads for used cars, if new models are a bit out of your price range. For example, look in the business or automobile sections of popular search engines, or try search strings like "internet car dealers" and "buy a car online".

6  Look for a site that offers detailed information about each of its used-car listings. Some sites conduct inspections of used cars via independent mechanics – these are generally good places to shop. Look in the "about us" section of each site for information on its background and services. As ever, personal recommendation from a satisfied customer is always best.

### ✳ Tips

Once you decide on a car, you'll most likely be referred to a local dealer or seller, so you may not be able to find exactly what you're looking for. This is even more likely when shopping for a used car.

If you do shop online, make sure you test-drive the car before finalising the purchase.

The degree of involvement in any transaction depends on the nature of the company running the web pages. Some function as simple advertising forums, while others take a more active role in car sales.

Many such sites act mainly as a communication point between buyers and sellers, but you should be prepared to pay extra if the site provides additional services, such as inspections and warranties, or even delivery.

7 Use the internet to find independent reviews and ratings for specific cars by make, model and year. (Treat those found on sites affiliated with car companies and dealerships with suitable scepticism.)

8 Understand that many sites, whether selling new or used cars, will only put you in contact with retailers or individual sellers, leaving you to finish the deal the old-fashioned way: person to person.

9 Online car shopping is a rapidly developing area. It is possible to buy a new car at a competitive price and have it delivered to your door. You may even be able to arrange a part exchange deal, and have your old car towed away at the same time.

## 927 Inspect a Used Car Before Buying

Thinking about buying second-hand? Some people answer classified advertisements with great trepidation. Such anxiety is rarely justified, but careful inspection is critical.

### ◉ Steps

1 Look at the car's exterior. If the paint is new, ask when the car was painted. If the paint finish is slightly different in some areas it is almost certainly a post-accident repair: discover what happened – a re-spray following a major incident may conceal all manner of horrors.

2 Check bumpers and wheel arches for signs of rust, dents or body filler. Then search the rest of the vehicle for rust, remembering to scan the underside. Exterior rust may indicate more in unseen areas.

3 Inspect both sides of the car – as well as the front, rear and beneath – for any signs of more major body repair. Look for inconsistencies: Do the edges of the bonnet and door panels line up with the bumpers and other side panels? Does the frame look aligned correctly? Inconsistencies may give clues to previous accidents.

4 Open the door. Check the interior for tears in upholstery, sun damage and general appearance.

5 Check the tyres. Uneven wear may be due to incorrect alignment or bent suspension components. Be particularly wary of uneven front tyre wear.

6 Open the bonnet. Look at the engine's overall level of cleanliness. Look for rust on the exhaust manifold and oil leaks around the valve cover and head gasket.

7 Unscrew the oil cap. If there is a deposit of white "cream" underneath, it means that he car has been used largely for very short runs from cold starts, and has never warmed up properly, creating condensation which has mixed with the oil. Such engines will have a vastly reduced life expectancy than an engine run properly. Also, check the oil on the dipstick by rubbing it against your thumb (make sure the engine is cool). If you feel small particles in the oil, the engine may be worn or have other problems.

8 Start up the engine. It should start immediately.

### ✱ Tips

If the vehicle's mileage appears unusually low, have a mechanic determine whether someone has tampered with the odometer. If so, steer well clear.

For peace of mind, have the car professionally inspected. The three main organisations are the AA (telephone: 0345 500610), ABS (telephone: 0345 419926), and Green Flag/National Breakdown (telephone: 01254 355606). Inspections usually cost from £50 to £150 depending on the car. You will receive a written report afterwards.

For a cheaper alternative, call the Institute of Automotive Assessors (01543 251346). They will put you in contact with your nearest affiliated independent assessor. They usually cost around half that charged by the motoring organisations.

9    Take the car for a test drive. Check the brakes. They shouldn't squeal and should bring the car to a stop in a sufficiently short distance.

10    Test the transmission for slippage. Set the emergency brake, depress the clutch pedal and shift through the gears (if the car has a manual transmission). There shouldn't be any grinding sounds.

11    Check to make sure all of the lights (front and back) work, as well as the windscreen wipers, indicators and in-car music system.

12    Ask to see the car's service history. Look to see that the car had regular oil changes and checkups (maintenance schedules will vary by model). Also, inquire about additional work that has been done on the car and ask to see receipts.

## Buy a Used Car    928

If you're still interested in a used car after a careful inspection (see 927 "Inspect a Used Car Before Buying") it's time to begin negotiations. The best way to know what's a reasonable price is to learn about the car's condition and value.

### ⊙ Steps

1    Check publications such as *What Car?*, *Parker's Guide* or *Used Car Price Guide* for the value of that model and year of manufacture. Compare it with the asking price. If it differs by too great an amount find out why. (Low mileage and a good service history may be worth paying more for.)

2    Set yourself an upper limit – this is the figure you won't go beyond, whatever happens during negotiations.

3    Prepare to negotiate. Make a fair offer that fits your budget. It's usually a waste of time coming up with a figure that greatly undervalues the car – remember, the seller has more than probably reached his own price by following the guidelines suggested by the likes of *What Car?*, *Parker's Guide* or *Used Car Price Guide*.

4    If the offer is not accepted, try to convince him rationally why your offer is fair – point out any problems you noticed about the car. Make a second offer reflecting your argument.

5    Continue until you reach an agreement or a stalemate.

6    If you pay for the car with a building society cheque, take your pass book along – the buyer might want to see it to prove that the cheque is not a fake.

7    If you pay by a bank draft, take it along during banking hours – the seller may want to phone the issuing bank to ensure that it's genuine.

8    Take sensible security measures if you pay by cash – if you're worried about handling large quantities, take someone along with you to deter would-be muggers.

### ✳ Tips

The art of getting a good deal is in balancing how low you think the seller will go with the risk of losing out altogether. Chat before you begin to negotiate. Try to figure out the circumstances surrounding the sale. Think like a detective: if the seller's bags are packed and his furniture gone, he may be looking for an urgent sale – factor this into your offer.

## 929 Sell a Used Car

Whatever shape your car is in, you should be able to find a buyer if you follow these steps.

### ⊙ Steps

1 Check publications such as *What Car?*, *Parker's Guide* or *Used Car Price Guide* for the model and year of your car. Also, check the classified section of local newspapers to get an idea of the going rate.

2 Consider factors such as your car's condition, mileage, extras or repair work before setting your selling price.

3 A well presented car is far more likely to sell, so give it at least a wash (and maybe even a wax) before letting any would-be buyer inspect it. Make sure that you tidy up the interior: empty the rubbish, clean the upholstery and fix small problems such as broken knobs or sticking windows (see 934 "Wash a Car" and 935 "Wax a Car").

5 Advertise. The cheapest approach is to place a "For Sale" sign (including the price and a contact telephone number) in the window of your car while it's parked. You might also try putting up a card in your local newsagent – these will cost a matter of pence, or may even be free. This approach is only likely to work for the cheapest cars (below £2,000).

6 If you advertise in a newspaper or magazine make sure you choose the right one. *Loot* is good for selling budget cars (less than £10,000); use *Auto Trader* for mid-proceed vehicles; for prestige cars use specialist magazines such as *Top Marques* or *Classic Car Weekly*, or broadsheet newspapers such as the *Daily Telegraph* or *Sunday Times*.

7 Adverts that feature a photograph of your car will be more costly, but will also sell more quickly. If you take this approach, make sure you use a good-looking picture with a simple uncluttered background that will reproduce well on low-quality newsprint.

8 Describe your car accurately and simply, avoiding pointless superlatives. The critical information is the marque, model, type of vehicle (hatchback, cabriolet, etc.), year, mileage, colour and price. Mention any other features that may grab the attention of a potential buyer, such as full service history, power steering or multi-play CD system.

8 When a buyer shows interest, explain your reasons for selling the car. Point out any noteworthy features.

9 Any potential buyer will doubtless want to test drive the car. First, check that they are insured. (Many private insurance policies cover driving other cars – some sellers may have "any driver" policies covering their own cars.)

10 The buyer will almost certainly try to knock down your asking price. Never bother making a counter-offer to an insultingly low opening bid: politely decline and say you cannot accept anything so low. Lower your price only when the buyer gets closer to a price you might accept. Continue until you agree on a fair price.

11 Unless you know the buyer personally, only accept cash, a building society cheque or bank draft.as payment for the car. (See 928 "Buy a Used Car".)

### ✳ Tips

Always allow the buyer to inspect your car using an independent assessor. Be honest about both major and minor defects – rust, a bad engine, failing brakes – and subtract the cost of repairs from your asking price. Agree to meet the prospective buyer at a garage or accept a deposit of a few hundred dollars while the car is being inspected.

Write the buyer a receipt for the transaction, indicating that you are selling the vehicle "as seen", to avoid future problems.

## Check Automatic Transmission Fluid 930

Check your car's automatic transmission fluid (ATF) every month, or whenever the transmission isn't shifting smoothly.

### ⊙ Steps

1 Park your car on level ground and start the engine, leaving the gear in neutral (or "Park"). Wait for the engine to warm up. Unless your owner's manual directs otherwise, allow the engine to continue running throughout this procedure.

2 Find the ATF dipstick, located at the back of the engine – this is often shorter than the engine oil dipstick but otherwise looks similar. If you're lucky, it will be labelled.

3 Remove the dipstick completely.

4 Wipe the dipstick with a rag, replace it in the engine, push it all the way in and remove it again.

5 Look at the dipstick's tip. Observe whether there are two different full markings: one for cold readings and one for warm readings. If so, read the one for "Warm". If the fluid does not come up to the line marked "Full" add ATF.

6 Add ATF (see Tips) into the hole that the dipstick came out of. Use a funnel with a long, narrow neck. Add only a little at a time, and check the level with the dipstick as you go along. It's easy to add ATF but rather difficult to take it out if you add too much.

7 Put the dipstick all the way back in when you are finished.

### ✱ Tips

There are two types of ATF: Dexron (also called Mercron) and Type F; your owner's manual should list the type to use.

With some cars the engine should not be running while you check the fluid, so be sure to consult your owner's manual.

### ⚠ Warning

ATF doesn't get used up, so if it's low, that indicates a leak. Don't ignore leaks or drive around with low ATF – it can only lead to expensive transmission repairs.

### Things You'll Need

☐ rags

☐ automatic transmission fluid

☐ funnel with a long, narrow neck

## Check Brake Fluid 931

While checking your car's fluid levels, be sure to add brake fluid to the list. It's easy to do and only takes a moment.

### ⊙ Steps

1 Find the brake master cylinder. This is usually located under the hood on the driver's side of the car, toward the back of the engine compartment. Imagine where your brake pedal would end up if it went all the way through to the engine. The brake master cylinder is a small (about 6 by 2 inches), rectangular piece of metal with a plastic reservoir and a rubber cap on top, and small metal tubes leading from it.

2 Check your manual if you aren't sure that you've found the master cylinder. The rubber cap will usually read "Use only DOT 3 or 4 brake fluid from a sealed container".

3 Note that on most newer-model cars the reservoir is translucent and you can see the fluid level without removing the cap. There will be a "Full" line—the brake fluid should be at this line.

4 In older cars (pre-1980) the brake master cylinder reservoir may be made entirely of metal so that you must take the top off to check the fluid

### ✱ Tip

If the brake master cylinder is empty, the brake pedal will go to the floor. If this is the case, you will have to bleed the brakes in addition to adding fluid: Time to see your mechanic, who will flush and refill the braking system.

### ⚠ Warning

Brake fluid is very toxic. Keep it away from hands and eyes, and avoid spilling it on the ground or on your car's paint. Dispose of empty containers carefully.

level. The top is held on by a metal clamp—use a screwdriver to pop off the clamp and lift the lid.

5    Add brake fluid to the Full line. Use the correct brake fluid for your car: Check the rubber cap and your owner's manual to find out what grade of brake fluid your car requires. Most cars use DOT (Department of Transport) 3 or 4. If the reservoir has two parts, fill both halves.

**Things You'll Need**

❑ screwdriver

❑ brake fluid

❑ rags

## 932 | Know if Your Car Has a Fluid Leak

Except for petrol and windshield wiper solution, the fluids in your car shouldn't get used up or go anywhere. If you notice that any are low, there's a good possibility of a leak.

### ◉ Steps

1    Understand that the fluids you may have in your car are petrol, oil, coolant, brake fluid, windscreen washer fluid, gear oil, power steering fluid and automatic transmission fluid. All cars will have at least gas, oil and brake fluid. Air-cooled engines (like old VW Beetles) do not have coolant. Your model of car may or may not have power steering or automatic transmission fluid.

2    Open the hood and visually inspect the engine and engine compartment. Many leaks are easily detectable with just a simple look.

3    Note that you don't need to know the name of the fluid that's leaking or the name of the part it's leaking from to be able to find a leak.

4    Inspect underneath the engine and the car with a torch. Look for wet areas or drips clinging to the underside of the vehicle's carriage.

5    If you don't see any signs of a leak, lay down a large piece of corrugated cardboard and park your car so that the engine sits over it. With a pen, mark the position of the wheels.

6    Remove the cardboard the following morning. Note the position of any drip marks relative to the wheel markings. This information will help your mechanic diagnose the problem.

**✱ Tips**

Green or blue sticky fluid is coolant. Bluish, watery liquid is windshield wiper fluid. Honey- or dark-coloured, greasy fluid is engine oil. Honey- or dark-coloured thick fluid with a chestnut smell is gear oil. Clear or yellowish liquid with a very slippery consistency is brake fluid. Slippery reddish fluid is automatic transmission or power steering fluid.

Petrol will evaporate when it leaks out and may not leave any residue, but it's easy to smell.

**⚠ Warning**

Ignoring a leak, even if there are no noticeable symptoms, can leave you stranded and/or cost you more in repairs later.

## 933 | Change Your Motor Oil

Plan to change your motor oil every 3,000 miles or every three months. However, you may want to do it sooner if you've been driving in very hot and/or dusty conditions.

### ◉ Steps

**Getting Ready**

1    Gather the necessary tools and materials. Consult your owner's manual or an automotive-parts specialist to find out the weight of oil and type of oil filter your car needs. If you go to an auto-parts shop, first make a note of your car's year, make and model.

**✱ Tip**

Record the date and mileage after you change the oil so you will know when your car is due for another oil change. It helps to put a small sticker on your windscreen to remind you.

2   Run the car's engine for 10 minutes before you drain the oil. Warm oil drains faster than cold oil.

3   Park the car on a level surface, engage the parking brake and turn off the engine. If your car has a low ground clearance, raise it by driving it onto a ramp or by jacking it up and supporting it securely. You will need two jack stands to support the front of your car after jacking it up. Never get under a car that is supported only by a jack (see 946 "Jack Up a Car Safely").

4   Open the bonnet and place the new oil and funnel on top of the engine to ensure that you won't forget to add oil afterwards (an expensive mistake that many do-it-yourselfers make).

## Draining the Oil and Changing the Oil Filter

5   Crawl under the car once it is securely supported. Remember to use two jack stands to support the car.

6   Locate the oil drain plug on the underside of the engine, usually near the front centre of the car. Consult your owner's manual for the exact spot.

7   Place an oil drain pan under the plug and loosen the plug with a socket wrench. Remember: Turn the wrench anti-clockwise to remove the plug. Use the right size wrench or socket—and avoid using an adjustable wrench—or you risk stripping the plug's threads and rounding the plug's hex head.

8   Carefully remove the plug by hand. Be prepared for the rush of warm oil. Wear rubber gloves to remove the plug if it's hot.

9   Let the oil drain into the pan. Hold on to the plug.

10  Reposition the pan, if necessary, to catch all the dripping oil.

11  Wipe off the drain plug and the plug opening with a rag when the oil finishes draining.

12  Reinstall the plug. Begin turning it by hand to prevent cross-threading.

13  Tighten the plug with your socket wrench; be careful not to over-tighten.

14  Locate the oil filter, which is usually on one side of the engine.

15  Position the oil pan underneath the filter to catch any remaining oil.

16  Use an adjustable oil filter wrench to unscrew the oil filter. Be careful when removing this, as it is full of oil.

17  Use a rag to wipe the area where the filter mounts to the engine. Make sure the rubber seal of the old filter is not stuck to the engine.

18  Open a new quart of oil and use some to lightly coat the rubber seal of the new filter.

19  Screw the new filter into place by hand. It's usually not necessary to tighten the oil filter with the oil filter wrench, but have the wrench ready in case your grip's not strong (or large) enough.

## Adding New Oil and Cleaning Up

20  Locate the oil filler cap on top of the engine. Remove it.

21  Place the funnel in the opening and pour in the new oil. Typically, you will use 4.5 l (1 gal) to 5.5 l (1¼ gal) of oil. Check your owner's manual for the correct amount of oil.

## ⚠ Warnings

Handle hot automotive oil with extreme care.

Use extreme caution when jacking up the car. Make sure the jack stands are completely secure.

On some new vehicles, oil must be changed every three months or the guarantee will be invalidated. Check your warranty carefully.

## Things You'll Need

❑ 2 jack stands

❑ 4.5 l (1 gal) to 5.5 l (1¼ gal) motor oil

❑ small plastic funnel

❑ oil drain pan

❑ socket wrench with appropriate-size sockets

❑ rubber gloves

❑ rags

❑ adjustable oil filter wrench

❑ oil filter

❑ old plastic containers

22 Replace the cap when you're finished.

23 Run the engine for a minute, turn it off, then check the dipstick. Add more oil if necessary.

24 Check the area around the oil drain plug and the filter for leaks. Tighten the plug or oil filter if you find leakage.

25 Use rags and newspapers to wipe away excess oil.

26 Pour the used oil into a plastic container after it cools.

27 Dispose of the used oil and filters at authorised locations: Take them to either a recycling centre or an auto repair shop that can recycle for you. Don't pour oil down a drain.

## 934 | Wash a Car

The key to a successful car washing is working from top to bottom and doing one side at a time.

### ⊙ Steps

1 Choose a shady spot, preferably away from trees that are dripping sap or dropping leaves.

2 Close all car doors and windows.

3 Put one cap of car soap into a bucket and fill it three-quarters of the way with warm water. Set the bucket aside.

4 Hose any excess dirt off the car, beginning at the roof and working down to the tyres.

5 Lather a sponge or terry cloth rag in the bucket of soapy water and sponge the roof of the car. Spray off excess soap when the entire roof has been cleaned.

6 Repeat for all four sides of the car, washing one full side, including the windows, fenders and tyres, and rinsing completely before going to the next side.

7 Give the car one final rinse with the hose to get rid of any water spots when all four sides have been washed and rinsed.

8 Take a chamois leather ("shammy") or towel and dry the car thoroughly by setting the towel flat against the car's surface and dragging it along to pick up any water spots. Start at the roof and work your way down to the tyres.

9 Wash the windows with a rag soaked in plain water and dry them with a dry rag, or use window cleaner and pieces of wadded-up newspaper on both the inside and the outside of the windows.

10 Give any metal or chrome an extra rubdown to get rid of water spots.

11 Clean the interior if you have time (see 936 "Clean a Car's Interior").

### ✳ Tips

Wear old clothes for this task.

Soap dries fast. Wash one side at a time to keep the soap from drying on your car's paint. Otherwise, you'll have to re-wash to get the dried soap off.

Wet and wring out your chamois leather before you dry; it will be more absorbent.

### Things You'll Need

❑ car soap

❑ large bucket

❑ sponge or travelling rags

❑ chamois leather or towel

❑ window cleaner and newspaper (optional)

## Wax a Car

Although nothing beats a professional valet service using an electric buffer, following these steps every few months will protect your car's paint finish and keep it looking good.

### ⊙ Steps

1 Wash and dry your car thoroughly before waxing.

2 Remember that some waxes contain abrasives. This can damage clear-coat and lacquer finishes, and may be harmful to dark-coloured paint jobs. When in doubt, use a non-abrasive wax.

3 Park the car in a cool, shady spot. If you don't have access to a shady spot, wax one section at a time so the sun doesn't bake the wax onto your car. Avoid waxing if it's very hot or very cold outside.

4 Dip a damp wax sponge into the car wax, getting a dollop on your sponge the size of a 10 pence piece.

5 Rub the wax onto the car using small circles. Avoid getting wax into seams and jambs – if this happens, use an old, very soft toothbrush to remove it.

6 Working on a section at a time, cover the car's entire surface, remembering the path you took. By the time you have finished, the wax will be ready to remove.

7 Using soft towels, wipe off the wax in the same order in which it was applied.

8 Shake out the towel or cloth as you work, in order to avoid wax build-up and streaking.

9 Leaning as close to the surface of your car as you can, look down the sides and across the front, back and roof to spot any residual wax.

10 Use a soft cloth to polish the car's entire surface.

11 Wash your used towels, cloths and pads with liquid fabric softener to keep them from scratching your car the next time you use them.

### ✱ Tips

Professionals differ on which car wax is best, but most agree that the more expensive carnauba is superior to other inexpensive varieties – it seals better, and is easier to apply and buff.

As a rule, the easier the wax is to work with, the more often you'll have to apply it.

Don't leave wax on your car for more than 2 hours or it will be very difficult to remove. Excess wax left on the car can damage the paint, especially if the car is exposed to direct sunlight.

### Things You'll Need

❏ car wax

❏ wax sponge

❏ soft toothbrush

❏ towels

## Clean a Car's Interior

You can cut down on the cost of a professional valet service by getting out the vacuum cleaner and a few household products.

### ⊙ Steps

1 Remove the floor mats from the car. Shake them to remove any debris sticking to them.

2 Using the hose attachment, vacuum all seat cushions, paying special attention to the crevices where cushions meet. Be sure to vacuum the bottom and back of the seats. Check beneath seats for coins and rubbish before vacuuming.

### ✱ Tips

Vacuum the seats first, then do the floors.

Car-interior and vinyl protectants are made to protect against sun damage and cracking. Carefully read the instructions before use.

3 Vacuum the floor of the car, including the area beneath the seats, still using the hose attachment.

4 Vacuum the floor mats. When finished, give the mats a final shake to remove any remaining debris, then return them to the car.

5 If any fabric seat cushions or carpets are stained, use a damp towel to apply a small amount of carpet shampoo to the stain. Work the carpet shampoo into a light lather.

6 Sponge away the shampoo with a damp sponge and allow to air dry. Don't use carpet shampoo on leather.

7 Clean all the windows using a window cleaner and newspaper.

8 Vacuum or wipe debris from the dashboard and doors.

9 Spray a small amount of car-interior or vinyl protectant on a towel or rag. With the moistened rag, gently wipe the dashboard, door handles and all vinyl parts.

10 Allow to air dry.

**Things You'll Need**

❏ vacuum cleaner

❏ carpet shampoo

❏ window cleaner and newspaper

❏ car-interior or vinyl protectants

❏ rags and towels

## 937 | Remove Bumper Stickers

You bought a used car and were lucky enough to inherit all sorts of fascinating bumper stickers. Here's how you can remove those tacky, sticky proclamations.

### ⊙ Steps

1 Spray the sticker with a lubricant such as WD-40, and try to peel it off. If this doesn't work, proceed to step 2.

2 Soften the adhesive with heat from a hair-dryer.

3 Start to peel off a corner of the sticker while continuing to apply heat, or gently scrape off the sticker with a rubber spatula (or a putty knife with its metal blade wrapped in duct tape). Do not use a razor blade; it can scratch paint and bumpers.

4 Wipe the remains of the sticker away with a soft, lint-free rag dampened with surgical spirit.

5 Buff the bumper or panel with a polishing compound and a fresh coat of wax to complete the job.

**Things You'll Need**

❏ lubricant

❏ hair- dryer

❏ rubber spatula or putty knife (wrapped in duct tape)

❏ surgical spirit

❏ car polish

❏ rags

## Replace Windscreen Wiper Blades | 938

Windscreen wiper blades are usually packaged with the rubber wiper as well as its support structure. Follow these steps to replace this entire piece, referred to here as the "wiper blade".

### ⊙ Steps

1  Go to a car supplies shop or any other place that sells windscreen wipers (many large supermarkets sell car spares). Not all wipers fit all cars, so look up your vehicle's make and model in the reference chart where the wipers are sold.

2  Open the package containing the new windscreen wiper blade. The package should include several different styles of blade attachment – the small plastic piece that secures the new blade to the wiper arm.

3  Examine the existing attachment (where the arm and the blade meet), then find a new one in your package that matches it.

4  Grasp the windscreen wiper arm and pull up, away from the car. The blade and arm should now be sticking out perpendicular to the window.

5  Remove the windscreen wiper blade from the arm at the attachment. There will usually be a small tab you can depress with a screwdriver that will allow you to pull the blade from the arm. Some attachments have a small metal bump and two tabs on either side; you depress the tabs and pull hard to remove the blade. Some just snap onto the blade.

6  Remove the old attachment from the wiper blade and replace it with the new one.

7  Install the blade onto the windscreen wiper arm.

8  Test by turning on the wipers. If the blades slip, turn off the wipers and seat the attachments more firmly.

### ✱ Tips

Replace your wiper blades when they are no longer clearing the windshield efficiently in normal rainy conditions.

Changing wiper blades for the first time can be extremely frustrating. Relax! When you've done it once, you'll be able to do it again in a matter of minutes.

### ⚠ Warning

Do not let the windscreen wiper arm snap back against the windscreen when there is no blade attached – this can crack the windscreen.

## Replace a Tail, Brake or Reverse Light | 939

Replacing a bulb on your car is almost as easy as replacing a light bulb at home. Perform this simple maintenance and avoid getting pulled up by the police for having a missing brake light.

### ⊙ Steps

1  Determine how the bulb is accessed: On some models the lens (the red or white plastic part over the light) must be unscrewed from the outside, and on others the bulb is accessible only from inside the boot. If there are no screws on the lens, you can assume that the bulb must be replaced from inside. Usually there will be a plastic cover that must be removed in order to access the bulb; there may be tabs, screws or small knobs that hold this plastic cover in place.

2  Unscrew the lens on the outside, or take off the plastic cover from inside the boot, to reveal the bulb.

3  Remove the bulb. You'll have to push in and turn at the same time.

### ⚠ Warning

In theory, you can be prosecuted for driving a car with faulty lights. In practice, the police are likely to give you the benefit of the doubt on condition that you get it fixed straight away.

4   Take the bulb with you to the shop to help you find an exact duplicate.

5   Clean the connection with a wire brush and/or wipe it clean with a rag if there's any corrosion.

6   Install the new bulb in the empty socket. Again, you'll have to push in and turn simultaneously. Line up the tiny raised bumps on the base of the bulb in order to screw it in.

7   Replace the lens or the plastic cover.

8   Test your work by stepping on the brakes and turning on the headlights while a friend watches the new bulb to make sure it lights up.

## 940 | Spend Less on Car Fuel

**With the high price of petrol and diesel, why spend more than necessary? Here are a few simple tips to help you save money.**

### ⊙ Steps

1   Check to make sure you're not carrying any extra or unnecessary weight in the boot, back seat or roof rack.

2   Use cruise control (if you have it) on the highway.

3   Turn off the engine instead of idling when you plan to be waiting for more than 3 or 4 minutes.

4   Avoid sprint starts and speeding from one stop sign to the next. Accelerate slowly.

5   If your car runs on petrol, use only high-octane fuel (the expensive one at the pump) if your engine is "pinking". (This is a rattling noise from the engine, mostly heard on acceleration and when driving uphill.)

6   Keep all the tyres properly inflated. The recommended tyre pressure is listed in the vehicle's manual, embossed on the side of the tyre, and often on a sticker on the driver's-side doorjamb. When in doubt, 14.5 kg per 6.5 sq cm (32 psi) is a good average until other sources can be consulted. Low air pressure will result in poor mileage.

7   Follow a maintenance schedule. Most cars need a tune-up every year or 10,000 miles, whichever comes first. Older cars need to be serviced more frequently. A car in need of a tune-up may exhibit poor mileage as a symptom.

8   Change the air filter every 6,000 miles.

9   Don't exceed 70 mph on motorways – the faster you drive, the more fuel your car will use. (And it's also against the law.)

10  Shut off the air conditioning when you don't absolutely need it.

11  Keep the clutch properly adjusted. A slipping clutch uses extra fuel.

### ✳ Tip

Pay attention to how much fuel your car is using. Some problems manifest themselves in reduced mileage without any noticeable driving symptoms. Visit a garage if you notice any major changes in mileage.

# ✓ 941 Maintain Your Car Regularly

You can extend the life of your car if you keep up with the checks recommended by the manufacturer and your mechanic. Use this calendar as a guide. It assumes that you drive 15,000 miles a year; if you drive more miles or on rough and dusty roads, perform these checks and services more frequently.

### Once a month

- Check oil, coolant, brake fluid and power steering fluid levels.
- Check the clutch reservoir and add brake fluid if low.
- Check the automatic transmission fluid.
- Check the windscreen-washer fluid reservoir.
- Check the belts for proper tension, cracks and age.
- Check the hoses for leakage, cracks or other signs of age.
- Visually inspect the engine for any leaks.
- Look under the car for any indication of leaks from the engine.
- Check the tyre pressure on all the tyres.
- Check the tyre pressure in the spare tyre.
- Visually inspect the tyres for uneven wear, nails or other sharp objects lodged in the tread.
- Check the dashboard lights for proper operation.
- Start the engine and listen with the bonnet up. After doing this a few times, you will learn what sounds "normal" for your car.

### Once a year

- Schedule a full service, if due.
- Flush the cooling system and replace the coolant.
- Replace the windscreen wiper blades.
- Have the battery serviced and load-tested to check its ability to hold a charge. If it is more than 4½ years old, replace it
- Check the tyre pressure for all four tyres and the spare.
- Check the lights, heater and defroster.
- Remind yourself to keep the fuel tank as full as possible to prevent moisture from freezing in the fuel lines.
- Get a brake check.
- Check the fluids under the bonnet and replenish as necessary. Change the oil and oil filter if it's been 3,000 miles since the last oil change.
- Assemble an emergency winter kit for the boot: blanket, extra boots and gloves, ice scraper, small shovel, torch and cat litter (for traction when stuck in snow).
- Replace the air filter.

### Every two years

- Replace the fuel filter.
- Change the spark plugs (unless they're platinum, in which case you have 30,000 more miles to go). Also replace spark plug wires as needed.
- Replace the distributor cap and rotor if your car has them.
- Change the points and condenser if your car was built before 1978.
- Check the ignition timing and adjust as needed.
- Adjust the valves as needed (unless your car has hydraulic valves). Replace the valve-cover gasket if you see oil on top of your engine.
- Check the belts. Replace if worn.
- Adjust the clutch if you have a manual gearbox.
- Service the battery.
- Replace the PCV (positive crankcase ventilation) valve.

calendar

## 942 | Keep Your Battery Alive

A little maintenance will keep your battery charged through the cold months as well as the warmer ones.

### ⊙ Steps

1 If your battery is more than four years old, replace it.

2 Ask your mechanic to perform a "load test" on your battery. This tests whether the battery is capable of generating sufficient charge on below-freezing days. If it fails the test, replace the battery.

3 Clean the battery terminals if they are encrusted with deposits. Use a wire brush dipped in baking soda and water to clean them of corrosion and ensure that the deposits do not block the flow of electrical current.

4 Check to make sure the water level in the battery hasn't dropped. You can do this on conventional batteries by popping off the plastic cover and checking to see that the water inside reaches the plastic filler necks. Add distilled water if necessary. Maintenance-free batteries, however, generally have an indicator light that goes black when the battery needs service; take these types to a mechanic for service.

5 Check the tightness of the battery cable ends. A loose connection can prevent your car from starting and acts just like a dead battery. If you can move the battery cable ends that are attached to the battery terminals at all, they are too loose.

6 Check that the battery is securely fastened in the battery tray. A loose battery that is allowed to shift around can cause damage if it is able to tip over under the hood. Excessive vibration will also shorten the life of your battery.

7 If you live in an especially cold part of the country, consider investing in an engine or battery heater – this can reduce the power that's needed to start your car.

### ✱ Tips

In severe cases, the battery may need to be recharged with a battery charger.

Your car may not be starting because other components in the charging system are failing, or because of a bad starter motor.

### ⚠ Warnings

Improper recharging may ruin the battery as well as damaging other electrical accessories in your car. It should always be carried out slowly.

Keep open flames away from your battery – the chemicals inside it are combustible.

Battery acid is highly corrosive. When adding distilled water to the battery, take care that acid doesn't splatter on your skin or clothes.

### Things You'll Need

❑ baking soda

❑ wire brush

## 943 | Interpret Tyre Wear

Tyre wear can provide clues to your car's steering, suspension and tyre pressure. Regular checks can also help you prevent flat tyres or a dangerous puncture.

### ⊙ Steps

1 Check your tyres out of doors where the lighting is good. Visually inspect all four tyres.

2 Remember that under normal driving conditions, all four tyres should wear evenly.

3 Check for even tread wear by using a tread-depth gauge, which costs less than £15. The depth of the tread (the grooves in the tyre) should be even all over.

4 Let some air out of your tyres if there is wear down the middle and not on the sides. It means there's too much air in them.

### ✱ Tips

Depending on the type of tyre, the car and what kind of driving you do, tyres need to be replaced every 40,000 miles.

Have a servicing professional examine your tyres if you're not sure that they need replacing. For an unbiased opinion, get this done by someone who does not sell tyres.

5   Add air to tyres with wear on both the inside and outside edges, which means there's not enough air in them.

6   If your tyres are worn more on one side than the other, pay a visit to an alignment shop for a front-end or four-wheel alignment

7   Run your hand lightly over the tread surface of each tyre. If the treads feel bumpy or scalloped – even if the tread is still deep – you may need new shock absorbers or struts. (Some cars have shocks, some have struts and some have a combination – struts in front, shocks in back.)

8   Check the tyre pressure in all four tyres – and the spare tyre – at least once every month. The recommended tyre pressure will be listed in your vehicle's instruction manual, stamped on the side of the tyre, and often printed on a sticker on the driver's-side doorjamb. When in doubt, a figure of 14.5 kg per 6.5 sq cm (32 pd per sq in) is a safe average to use until other sources can be consulted.

Get a front-end or four-wheel alignment if you are involved in an accident – even just a minor bumper scrape. If anything is out of alignment, it will affect your tyres' wear.

## ⚠ Warning

Driving on tyres that are bald or badly worn greatly increases your chance of a puncture, and is especially dangerous when the roads are wet or slick. Don't put off buying new tyres when you need them – not when your safety is at stake.

## Things You'll Need

❏ tread-depth gauge

❏ tyre-pressure gauge

---

# Buy Car Tyres                                    944

Here's how to properly re-outfit your set of wheels.

## ⊙ Steps

1   Think about how and where you drive. Tyre engineers design product lines for specific purposes, such as comfort, durability, sporty handling, or traction in rain and snow. But choosing one virtue usually means giving up a little of the others.

2   Consider an all-season tyre. It's a reasonable compromise for most drivers – that's why car manufacturers usually provide them as original equipment on new cars.

3   Know your current tyre. In general, it's best to replace your tyres with those of the same brand, design and size, all of which you'll find printed on your tyres.

4   Decide where to buy your new tyres. In addition to car dealerships, tyre shops and garages and petrol stations, they can now also be bought at discount shops or ordered over the phone or the internet. Prices and service vary, so shop around if you can.

5   Have a mechanic or tyre dealer perform the installation. Special machines are needed to slip your new tyres over the car's wheels.

6   Keep tyre wear even by rotating your tyres as the manufacturer suggests – new cars are sensitive to tyres with differing degrees of wear. Keeping tyre wear even means your tyres will all need replacing at the same time, so monitor tread depth to help you budget ahead for the expense.

##  Tip

If you buy your tyres from a tyre centre, make sure the price quoted includes installation as well as wheel balancing. Also be aware that getting new tyres doesn't necessarily mean that you need a wheel alignment, which some tyre dealers will offer as part of a purchase package. Check the uniformity of wear on your current tyres to judge for yourself (see 943 "Interpret Tyre Wear").

## 945 Change a Flat Tyre

If you drive a car, you should know how to change a flat tyre – whether or not you have a mobile phone or membership of a roadside service.

### ⊙ Steps

1 Park the car on a level area and apply the handbrake. Place manual transmission cars in gear. Make sure you have pulled off the road. Turn the engine off and put on the hazard warning lights. You may want to open the bonnet to indicate to other drivers that you have stopped to make some repairs.

2 Place a wheel chock or a large stone behind (if facing uphill) or in front (if facing downhill) the diagonally opposing wheel to prevent the car from rolling. Do this even on a slight incline. Get out the spare, a lug nut wrench (tyre iron) and the car jack.

3 Remove the hubcap, if necessary.

4 Loosen the lug nuts – these hold the wheel in place – before jacking up the car. Place one end of the lug nut wrench over a lug nut. If necessary, use a hollow pipe for leverage by slipping it over the end of the lug nut wrench. Turn the wrench anticlockwise to loosen the lug nut. Loosen the lug nuts in a star pattern – first loosen one a few turns, then loosen the one opposite. Work across the tyre until all the lug nuts are loose and unscrewed slightly.

5 Carefully jack up the car (see 946 "Jack Up a Car Safely"). Check your owner's manual for the correct and safe place to put the jack. Jack the car up a little higher than is necessary to remove the old wheel so there is room to put on the fully inflated spare.

6 Remove the lug nuts all the way and set them aside in a place where you won't lose them and they won't roll away. The wheel with the flat tyre should be hanging from the threaded studs now.

7 Remove the flat tyre and set it aside.

8 Lift the spare wheel onto the wheel studs. If you're confused about which is the right way to put the new wheel on, check for the valve where you add air – it always faces out.

9 Replace the lug nuts. Tighten them in the same way you loosened them: Give each nut a few turns, first one, then the one opposite, working around the wheel in a star pattern. Try not to tighten adjacent nuts consecutively.

10 Slowly lower the jack and remove it.

11 Tighten the lug nuts again – as much as you can.

12 Put the hubcap back on.

### ✱ Tips

To avoid back strain, use your knees when pulling on the wrench and pipe. To avoid bruised knuckles, pull rather than push when removing lug nuts.

If a lug nut sticks, squirt lubricant around its base and wait a moment, then try again.

Check out all your tyre-changing equipment at home before you need it on the road.

Many people carry flat spare tyres. Check yours once a month.

### ⚠ Warnings

Cars can slip off jacks. Never get underneath a car with only a tyre-changing jack holding it up –.put a jack stand in place first.

Mind your hands when you remove a flat. Strands of steel sticking out of the back of a bald tyre can cut you.

### Things You'll Need

❏ wheel chock

❏ spare wheel

❏ lug nut wrench

❏ car jack

❏ hollow pipe

❏ lubricant

## Jack Up a Car Safely 946

Everyone should know how to use the jack that comes with their car. Try this at home so that if you ever get a flat, you won't have to learn by the side of the road.

### ⊙ Steps

1 Park the car on level ground and engage the handbrake. Leave manual cars in first gear or reverse; put automatics in "Park".

2 Place a chock or a brick behind or in front of (depending on the road's incline) the wheel diagonally opposite one being jacked up.

3 Place the jack under the car's frame nearest the wheel to be jacked up. There's a thin lip that runs along the side of your car – this is where the jack should go. Your owner's manual will have a picture of the safest place to put the jack. Bumper jacks will attach to slots in the front or rear bumper (on older cars).

4 When the jack is in place, insert the handle according to the directions on the jack, and turn or ratchet the handle to make the jack rise. If it lowers or cannot turn, rotate the handle the other way.

5 Raise the jack high enough to either replace a flat tyre or place the car on a jack stand (a sturdy temporary stand at a fixed height). If you're changing a flat tyre, remember to leave extra room – the spare tyre should (in theory) be fully inflated.

6 Lower the jack when you're finished. Be cautious and go slowly. If you've used a jack stand, before lowering the jack you will need to raise the car slightly to pull the stand from its place.

**✷ Tip**

Make sure everyone is out of the car before jacking it up.

**⚠ Warnings**

Never get under a car that's supported only by a jack. Use jack stands if the car will be off the ground for any length of time, if you plan to get underneath it, or if you'll be working on the car.

Don't jack up a car unless you're on a very firm surface. Soft shoulders or very hot, soft asphalt may not support the jack.

**Things You'll Need**

❑ wheel chock

❑ car jack

❑ jack stands

## Repair a Scratch on a Car 947

Small scratches can be touched up by hand. Larger ones may require the use of paint sprayers and professional help.

### ⊙ Steps

1 Determine whether your car's paint is enamelled (see the Warning); if it isn't, proceed.

2 Obtain body compound and primer paint. Primer is usually in spray-can form, comes in several colours and is generally labelled for automobile use. It's best to pick a light primer colour that your touch-up paint will cover easily in one coat.

3 Wash the scratch and surrounding area with a mild detergent. This removes any wax or coatings that would otherwise affect the new paint you'll apply.

4 Sand along the scratch with fine-grained sandpaper, being sure to sand away any rust that has accumulated.

5 Blow away all dust from the sanding, or use a soft brush.

6 Use masking tape and newspaper to isolate the scratch, leaving about a half-inch of working room around the scratch.

 **✷ Tip**

If your car has a very long scratch – across the bonnet or along an entire door – it may look better if you have the entire panel repainted in a paint shop.

**⚠ Warning**

Some newer-vehicle paint jobs are enamelled and will not mix well with lacquer-based primer paint.

7   Using a putty knife, apply body compound to a scratch that cuts deep into the metal. The knife should be made of plastic to avoid adding more scratches.

8   Let the body compound harden according to label instructions.

9   Sand the body compound flat.

10  Blow or brush away all dust.

11  Spray a small amount of primer paint to cover the scratch. Let the area dry overnight.

12  Identify the touch-up paint colour you need by consulting the car's manufacturer. You should be able to buy a small bottle of touch-up paint from an auto spares shop.

14  Use the touch-up's applicator brush to paint the primed area.

15  Let it dry overnight.

### Things You'll Need

☐ primer paint

☐ mild detergent

☐ fine-grained sandpaper

☐ soft brush (optional)

☐ plastic putty knife

☐ body compound

☐ touch-up paint

---

## 948  Find a Good Mechanic

Finding a suitable garage is like choosing any other small business. Look for quality, value and service.

### ⊙ Steps

1   As always, the most reliable way of choosing is to ask trusted friends for their recommendations.

2   Talk to people who have cars similar to yours.

3   Check if the garage is a member of a recognised body (such as the Retail Motor Industry Federation or Institute of the Motor Industry) or listed by the local Trading Standards Office.

4   Ensure that the garage mechanics are qualified, and familiar with your car's make and model. Look for evidence of qualifications, such as certificates on display. (Alternatively, you could ask the manager to outline qualifications expected of his staff.)

5   Find out what the garage hours are. Will it be open when you get off work? Is the garage near the bus or train? Will you get a loan car while your car is being worked on?

6   Check that the price of the work being done includes the costs of service, parts, labour and VAT – you should know exactly what you are paying for. Insist that no additional work will be undertaken without your prior permission.

7   Ensure that you receive an itemised report with a verbal explanation of the work undertaken and/or recommended.

### ✳ Tips

Don't wait until your car needs major repairs or a tow to find a good mechanic. Take your car into the garage for small stuff like oil changes and brake checks to get a feel for the place and develop a relationship.

Don't choose a garage based solely on price. The least expensive repair shop might not be the best place to take your car. At the same time, the most expensive (usually the dealership) may not give you the best service or quality.

8  Ensure that the name of the mechanic that works on your car is shown on your invoice and ask to speak to him or her specifically, if you have any concerns or require explanations.

9  Ensure that you receive a guarantee. Make sure you know what it covers Check how long the guarantee will be valid.

## Deal With a Bad Repair                                    949

A bad repair isn't always the result of negligence – sometimes it's just an honest mistake. Give the mechanic the benefit of the doubt, but stand your ground.

### ⊙ Steps

1  Ask the mechanic for a list of what was fixed and how before you leave the garage.

2  Go on a test drive before paying for major repairs.

3  Check the warranty on the work before you leave. Find out if it covers both parts and labour.

4  Bring the car back to the garage immediately if things are not right after you leave.

5  Ask to speak to the same mechanic who worked on the car. Explain the problem calmly: "I just went a mile from the garage and the brakes are still squealing. Something is still wrong".

6  Offer to take a ride in the car with the mechanic.

7  Request new replacement parts if new parts have been installed. Ideally, you should ask for the old parts back before the job is started; if you ask afterward, they might not be available.

8  Ask to speak to the garage manager if the mechanic will not check the problem immediately.

9  Tell the garage manager, as specifically as you can, the problem with the car. Say that you require that the car be fixed immediately. Remain calm. Assume that the manager will correct the problem. Tell him or her that you know the garage's reputation is on the line and are sure he or she will want to take care of the problem right away.

10  Inform the manager that you are cancelling the repair payment if he or she has refused to admit the car immediately. Leave the garage.

11  Consider going to another garage for a second opinion. However, be aware that if you choose to go to another garage, the original one may not honour the repair warranty, while the second garage may not want to deal with the problem if someone else has already worked on the car.

12  If you are still unhappy with the situation, consult your local Citizen's Advice Bureau. They will advise you on a suitable course of action.

### ✳ Tips

Describe the problem precisely. "The steering is still too loose" is better than "Something's still not right".

Getting angry will not get you what you want. Be reasonable, and the mechanic probably will be also.

Don't leave the garage until you either get what you want or are convinced that you will never get satisfaction, and so cancel your payment.

### ⚠ Warnings

Don't anger anyone who still has your car or keys.

A garage may well have the right to withhold your car until the repair charges are paid, especially if the charges are in dispute between the mechanic and the vehicle's owner.

# ✓ 950 Diagnose Car Trouble

If your car is giving you trouble, you may save time and money if you can accurately describe the problem to your mechanic. You may even be able to solve some problems yourself. Here is a guide to the signs of common automotive disorders.

## Brake problem

☐ Is the brake light on? Check the brake fluid.

☐ Is there a scraping or squealing noise that goes away when you step on the brake? The brake pads are worn.

☐ Do you hear a grinding, metal-against-metal sound when braking? Your brake pads or shoes are completely worn away.

☐ Does the brake pedal feel soft, or get harder and higher when you pump it? There may be air bubbles in the brake lines.

☐ Does the brake pedal slowly sink? You could need a new master cylinder.

☐ Does the car pull to one side when you brake? You may have insufficient hydraulic pressure, or one brake may be sticking.

## Manual transmission problem

☐ Can you feel any free play (or slack) when you first put your foot lightly on the clutch pedal? If so, your clutch needs adjusting.

☐ Does the engine sound like it's revving when you accelerate or start moving from a stop? The clutch may be worn.

☐ Does the clutch pedal feel stiff and require more force to depress it? You may need to replace the clutch cable.

☐ With the engine running in fourth gear, the hand brake set and the clutch pedal depressed, can you slowly let up on the clutch while stepping on the gas pedal? If you are able to completely release the clutch pedal without the engine stalling (or the car moving), you need a new clutch.

## Overheating car

☐ Is the coolant level low at the radiator overflow or coolant reservoir tank? Add more coolant if necessary.

☐ When the engine is cold, uncap the radiator and look inside. Is it empty? If so, fill with antifreeze or water and replace the cap.

☐ Do you see greenish or bluish slippery, sweet-smelling fluid around the radiator and under the car? Inspect the radiator and hoses for a coolant leak.

☐ Are the lower and upper radiator hoses securely clamped to the radiator and leak-free? If not, tighten and replace.

☐ Is a fan belt loose or an electric fan malfunctioning? Either can cause overheating.

☐ Is the water pump belt loose or the pump broken? These can cause overheating.

## Alignment problem

☐ Rest your hands very lightly on the steering wheel while driving. Does the car go in a straight line without drifting?

☐ If the car drifts, look for uneven tyre wear. Is the tread worn unevenly on one side (inner or outer)? If so, you probably need an alignment adjustment. Is it worn straight down the middle? Over-inflation is the cause. Is there wear down both the inside and outside? The cause is under-inflation. Add air to tyres as needed. Test-drive again to see if the car still drifts.

☐ Pay special attention to your car's alignment after an accident. Even a minor bump can cause problems.

☐ Though most cars typically require only a front-wheel alignment, some cars require four-wheel alignment (front and back).

## Change Gear Smoothly

If you grind from one gear to the next as you change down too quickly, or ride the clutch at the lights to set off quickly, then you'll damage the gearbox or wear out the clutch before you need to. Here's some advice on changing gears smoothly whatever the situation.

### ◉ Steps

1. If the car is parked on a steep hill and you've left it in gear to make sure it cannot roll away, press down on the clutch pedal and then move the gearstick into the neutral position.

2. Start the car.

3. Keeping the clutch pedal down, put the car into first gear by moving the gearstick to the top-left position.

4. Apply the foot brake and release the handbrake.

5. Release the foot brake when you're ready to start moving.

6. Begin to release the clutch pedal slowly; when you hear or feel the engine begin to slow down, slowly press down on the accelerator pedal as you continue to release the clutch. The car will start to move forward.

7. Accelerate until the car has reached about 3,000 rpm, then take your foot off the accelerator pedal, press down on the clutch, and pull the gearstick directly down through neutral to second gear. Be sure to pull the gearstick down until it cannot go any further.

8. Release the clutch gently, simultaneously pressing down gently on the accelerator pedal.

9. Repeat the shifting process each time you reach 3,000 rpm until you're driving at the appropriate speed for the gear.

10. Shift down by releasing the accelerator when you want to decrease your speed. Press down on the clutch and move the gearstick through neutral into the next lowest gear. Never move from fourth gear to second in one movement – you will damage the clutch. Once you are in the lower gear, release the clutch slowly, braking as you do so.

11. Stop the car by shifting down to second gear and applying the brakes. Depress the clutch just before the car stops. Don't shift down into first. Move the gearstick into neutral, release the clutch and put the handbrake on. Do not be tempted to sit at traffic lights in first gear with the clutch out and your foot on the brake as you wait for the lights to turn green. Your left foot inevitably relaxes a little, allowing the plates of the clutch to rub together slightly, wearing them down.

12. Shift down through the gears quickly to help slow the car if you are coming down a hill and your brakes are not very good. Press down on the accelerator a little as you shift the gear into neutral on its way from a higher to a lower gear. This helps to increase the speed of the lower gear, enabling it to mesh with the higher, preventing the car from lurching.

13. Drive in reverse by following the same steps you would for starting in first gear. The reverse gear engages more quickly than first gear, so make sure that you release the clutch slowly and begin to depress the accelerator as soon as the car begins to move.

### ✱ Tips

If you park your car on a steep incline, put it in gear. That way, it won't start rolling down the hill if the brakes aren't too good.

You'll know you're in the right gear for your speed if the engine runs smoothly. If it's coughing and sputtering, shift to a lower gear. If the engine noise is too high-pitched, shift up to the next gear.

Reverse is the lowest gear – lower than first. So, if you need to drive up a particularly steep hill and the car is loaded, you could try driving up the hill backwards in the last resort.

### ⚠ Warning

Frequent jerking, stalling, grinding and lurching can wear out the clutch assembly. Be kind to your car.

So that you don't accidentally shift into reverse while moving forward, gearsticks require either a simultaneous upward pull or downward push when moving into gear. If you've just bought or hired a car that is unfamiliar to you, make sure you know where reverse is before you start driving.

## 952 | Parallel Park

Practise with no obstacles first, then with plenty of space between vehicles. Take it slowly and you'll develop the skill and confidence to parallel park.

### ⊙ Steps

1   Use your indicators to signal the direction of the parking spot.

2   If the space is not yet vacant but the car in it is about to leave, wait behind the spot.

3   When the space is vacant, pull ahead of it until you have pulled up beside the car parked in front of the space. Your rear bumper should be even with that car's rear bumper with no more than an arm's length of road between you.

4   Put the car in reverse. Begin to back slowly; as soon as the car starts moving, turn the wheel as far as it will go towards the kerb.

5   Back slowly into the space.

6   When the back of your car's front door is even with the rear bumper of the car beside you, begin turning the wheel away from the kerb.

7   Continue turning the wheel away from the curb and backing slowly into the space.

8   Straighten out the wheel, then pull forward or back in the space as needed to centre yourself between the cars in front of and behind you. Your car should be around 15 to 20 cm (6 to 8 in) from the kerb when you are parked.

### ✱ Tips

Go slowly.

If you aren't sure whether you'll fit in the space, pull up beside it and size it up first.

If it's a tight fit, get a passenger or a pedestrian to guide you from the pavement.

## 953 | Jump-Start a Car

Knowing how to jump-start a car with a dead battery can keep an inconvenience from becoming a crisis. If you are unsure about how to use jump-leads, ask for help.

### ⊙ Steps

1   Read your owner's manual, as it will describe any peculiarities involved in jump-starting your vehicle.

2   Pull a car with a charged battery next to the car with the dead battery, situating the two batteries as close together as you can without allowing the two cars to touch.

3   Turn off both engines, pull out the keys, put both cars in first gear (or in "Park" for automatics), put the handbrakes on and open the bonnets.

4   Attach a red-handled/positive jump-lead clamp to the positive terminal (the one with the plus sign) of the charged battery.

5   Connect the other red-handled clamp to the positive terminal of the dead battery.

### ✱ Tip

Some new cars have special jump-start lugs for batteries that are otherwise inaccessible. Your owner's manual will describe these.

### ⚠ Warnings

The current from a car battery is dangerous whether or not the engine is running. Do not touch the metal ends of the jump-leads with your hands, nor touch them to each other.

6 Attach the neighbouring black/negative cable to the car with the dead battery. Clamp it somewhere where the current can flow to earth, such as a bolt or bracket on the engine. You can also attach it to any unpainted metal part of the vehicle's frame.

7 Earth the other black/negative cable on the charging car, as described in the previous step. Be careful, as a small spark may be produced.

8 Attempt to start the car that has the dead battery.

9 Re-adjust the red/positive clamp on the dead car if there is no response; try re-clamping it to the terminal or turning it for a better connection. Keep trying to start the dead car.

10 Once the dead car is running, remove the clamps one at a time in reverse order.

11 Allow the jump-started car to run for half an hour in order to charge the battery. It will charge whether driving or idling.

Many people jump-start a battery from a car with the engine running. However, it is safer to shut the engines off.

Be sure to remove and attach clamps one at a time to reduce the risk of shock. One trick is to work with one hand behind your back so that you don't inadvertently clasp both clamps at the same time.

## Create an Emergency Road Kit                          954

Having an emergency road kit may mean the difference between waiting for hours for a breakdown truck and being able to make your way to your destination.

### ⊙Steps

1 Get a cardboard or plastic box to keep everything in so it doesn't roll around in the boot.

2 Buy or assemble a first aid kit (see 757 "Stock an Emergency Supply of Medicine and First Aid").

3 Join a roadside emergency service, such as the AA or RAC.

4 Gather all the necessary equipment to change a tyre: working jack, spare tyre (fully inflated), lug nut wrench, pipe for leverage (see 945 "Change a Flat Tyre"). Most of this should already be stored in the car's boot, so leave them where they are to conserve room in your box.

5 Include a torch with fresh batteries and triangle reflectors.

6 Purchase all the necessary fluids: oil, brake fluid, power-steering fluid (if applicable), automatic transmission fluid (if applicable), water and antifreeze. Add rags and a funnel.

7 Add an assortment of screwdrivers, pliers, an adjustable wrench (only to be used in an emergency – adjustable wrenches can easily damage bolt heads) and jump-leads.

8 Include a pair of gloves, duct tape, a blanket and spare fuses. If you have the room, make yourself a disaster kit, too – include bottled drinking water, emergency food, matches, radio, walking shoes and extra clothing.

### Things You'll Need

- [ ] box
- [ ] first aid kit
- [ ] jack
- [ ] spare tyre
- [ ] lug nut wrench and pipe
- [ ] torch and batteries
- [ ] reflectors
- [ ] fluids (such as oil and brake fluid)
- [ ] water
- [ ] rags and funnel
- [ ] screwdrivers, pliers and wrenches
- [ ] jump-leads
- [ ] gloves
- [ ] duct tape
- [ ] blanket
- [ ] spare fuses
- [ ] disaster kit

## 955 | Belt Up a Small Child

Without a properly installed safety seat even the most minor of road accidents can be fatal to a baby or small child. Minimise the risk by following these guidelines.

### ⊙ Steps

1 In 1989 it became UK law for children under 14 to wear seatbelts in the rear seats of cars where seat belts were fitted. Make sure that your car has a seatbelt (lap belt and shoulder belt) for every child you intend transporting.

2 Read the instructions for your vehicle's seatbelt system. Ensure that any child seat you consider will fit your model of car. Incorrect or badly fitting child seats can be dangerous. Only buy seats that display the British Standard Kitemark or European Regulations Mark (EUR 44.03).

3 Babies should be transported in a rear-facing infant car seat. This should incorporate an integral harness – the complete unit is held in place by the car's lap and diagonal seat belt. They can be used both in the front or rear seats – but never in the front of a car with an airbag fitted.

4 Install a larger "toddler" seat for children who are at least 1 year old. Always carefully follow the instructions accompanying your child's safety seat. (Be guided by the size and weight of your child rather than just their age.)

5 Set up a booster seat for older children (between 4 and 8 years old). This raises the child so that the vehicle's standard lap and shoulder belts can fit snugly.

6 Even after careful installation, check each time you buckle up to make sure that straps are not twisted, buckles are fully locked and your child is restrained securely.

7 Never buy a second-hand child restraint unless you know its history and – above all – have the fitting instructions.

### ⚠ Warning

Always put a rear-facing infant seat in the rear of the car if a front passenger airbag is fitted.

Never buy a used seat or carrier if you suspect it has been in an accident, or if it is damaged in any way – you could be placing your child in danger.

### Things You'll Need

☐ rear-facing infant seat

☐ toddler seat

☐ booster seat

## 956 | Remove Ice From Your Windscreen

You walk outside to discover a sheet of ice covering your windscreen, and you're already late for work. Here's how to clear things up quickly and get on your way.

### ⊙ Steps

1 Start your car engine.

2 Turn the heat level to high and the defroster fan level to low. This low setting is extremely important – you don't want to crack the windscreen by heating it too quickly.

3 Apply a de-icing spray to your windscreen. Home remedies include the following mixtures: 50 per cent water and 50 per cent ethyl alcohol, or 50 per cent water and 50 per cent vinegar.

### ✱ Tip

Leave windscreen wipers in mid-sweep when you park your car at night, and it'll be easier to remove ice the next day.

### ⚠ Warning

Don't use hot water to melt the ice – it can crack the glass.

4   Scrape the ice from your windscreen, using shallow downward strokes to avoid scratching the glass. A plastic spatula or old credit card can do the trick if you don't have an ice scraper.

5   Work your way to the centre of the windscreen. If the ice is particularly thick, start by scratching a small square in one corner and then work your way across the windscreen.

## Things You'll Need

❑ de-icing spray (or ethyl alcohol or vinegar)

❑ ice scraper, plastic spatula or credit card

---

## Drive Safely in Winter Conditions 957

Winter driving can be tough on cars and their owners. Yet motorists can survive the most difficult circumstances by taking these measures.

### ⊙ Steps

1   Make certain your battery is holding an adequate charge, since batteries are less efficient – and engines more demanding – in cold conditions. Your mechanic can use a load testing meter to simulate the effects of cold-weather starting and determine whether the battery is adequately charged.

2   Regularly check tyre pressure in freezing weather. Tyres lose roughly 0.5 kg per 6.5 sq cm (1 psi) of pressure with each 6°C (10°F) drop in temperature. Never reduce tyre pressure in an effort to increase traction in snow, ice or mud.

3   Make sure your windscreen wipers and defroster are in good repair and that your windscreen washer is filled with antifreeze washer fluid. Keep snow and ice from accumulating on windshields, windows, rear-view mirrors and headlights (see 956 "Remove Ice From Your Windscreen").

4   Pay particular attention to the antifreeze content of your cooling system. Check your owner's handbook for information on the recommended antifreeze to use.

5   Although it's tempting to neglect a dirty vehicle because it will probably rain or snow again anyway, road salt, slush and grime are particularly brutal to your car's finish. To minimise rust and paint damage, regular washings and waxes are necessary. Full- or self-service car washes make the task much more tolerable in cold weather.

6   Brake, accelerate and turn slowly. Keep plenty of distance between cars. You never know when you will hit an icy spot.

7   Pump the brakes slowly and gently if your car hasn't got ABS. If you start to skid, take your foot off the accelerator and brake pedals, then shift into neutral. If your rear wheels are skidding, turn smoothly in the direction you want to go. If the front wheels are skidding, avoid steering until the car slows enough for the tyres to regain traction.

### ✳ Tip

Keeping your battery's terminals free of corrosion can augment its performance, and a load test by a mechanic will determine if it holds enough charge for winter starts.

### ⚠ Warnings

When road ice begins to melt, the thin layer of water on top can make it even more slippery than when conditions are colder.

Beware of dark patches on the road; these may be covered with "black ice" and are extremely slippery.

Do not warm up your car in a closed space. Carbon monoxide is odourless and can be fatal.

### Things You'll Need

❑ strong battery

❑ proper tyres

❑ tyre gauge

❑ antifreeze washer fluid

## 958 | Create Your Own Package Holiday Using the Internet

The internet has opened up a world of possibilities for travellers. It offers direct access to hundreds of travel companies and makes it easy to shop around and get the best deal.

### ⊙ Steps

1 Do an internet search for your desired destination combined with the type of accommodation you would ideally like (such as cottage, villa, hotel).

2 Search also for the tourist office that is local to your destination (start with the tourist office for the country or region and narrow it down). Tourist office websites often have comprehensive listings and links. You may wish to send off for brochures either by e-mail or by phone and post to make your final selection.

3 Check transport to your destination. There are countless websites for air (scheduled and charter), train and ferry tickets, or you can arrange car hire over the web (and obtain route planning maps). Compare prices and travel times and decide on the best means of travel.

4 When you know when and how you want to reach your destination and where you want to stay, start making your booking, only confirming when all the pieces of your package are in place.

5 Send your payment over the internet if the site offers secure payment. Most sites also offer more traditional means of payment.

### ✱ Tip

Don't forget to organise your own travel insurance.

### ⚠ Warning

Check the credentials of a company before booking with with them. Reputable companies in the UK travel industry will be members of professional and regulatory bodies such as ATOL and ABTA.

## 959 | Buy Cheap Air Tickets

With a little forethought and some flexibility, you can reach your favourite destinations without breaking the bank.

### ⊙ Steps

1 Keep yourself updated on airfare wars by watching the news and reading the newspaper. Look for limited-time promotional fares from major airlines and airline companies just starting up.

2 Be flexible in scheduling your flight. Tuesdays, Wednesdays and Saturdays are typically the cheapest days to fly; late-night flights ("red-eyes"), very early morning flights and flights with at least one stop tend to be discounted as well.

3 Ask the airline if it offers travel packages to save money in other areas. For instance, is a hire car or hotel room available at a discount along with the air ticket?

4 Find out whether the stated fare is the cheapest, and enquire about other options when speaking to the airline reservations service. If you're using the internet, check more than one website and compare rates.

### ✱ Tips

Note strict refund and exchange policies on tickets bought through name-your-price sites.

Once you've shopped around, consult a travel agent to find out if he or she can ferret out a cheaper ticket.

See also 960 "Make the Most of Your Frequent-Flier Miles".

If you will be visiting different countries on the same trip, you can save by asking the agent to arrange flights in which you arrive in one city but depart from another.

5   Enquire about stand-by fares if you're flying off-season. High season is a bad time to fly stand-by because most airlines overbook flights, making it difficult to find a spare seat.

6   Purchase tickets through consolidators (or "bucket shops"), who buy blocks of tickets and sell them at a discount to help an airline fill up all available seats.

7   Book early. You can purchase advance-ticket discounts by reserving 21 days ahead; book even earlier for holiday flights, especially in November and December. Keep in mind that holiday "blackout periods" may prevent you from using frequent-flier miles.

8   Stay with the same airline during your entire trip to receive round-trip or connecting fare discounts.

Ask about student and pensioner discounts.

### ⚠ Warning

Consolidators may delay in delivering your tickets, don't allow refunds or exchanges, and don't take reservations. To protect yourself, purchase through a travel agent, pay by credit card, and consider buying travel-cancellation insurance.

---

## Make the Most of Your Frequent-Flier Miles     `960`

Flying can earn you frequent-flier miles, as can putting purchases on a credit card with an airline tie in. After all that spending, don't waste those precious miles – learn the tricks for using them.

### ⊙ Steps

1   Choose one frequent-flier programme and concentrate on maximising your benefits within that programme.

2   Know and use the frequent-flier programme's partners, who may range from florists to telephone companies to hotels.

3   Consult the programme's newsletter frequently for updates on new partners and promotions. If you don't receive the newsletter by post, call and request a subscription, or check online for newsletter postings.

4   Keep track of your miles. Work towards attaining elite status if you are a high-frequency traveller, or a free trip if you are a leisure traveller.

5   Save your free miles for flights that are usually expensive.

6   Check your statements carefully, and keep your travel receipts in case the airline forgets to credit your account properly.

### ✱ Tip

Purchase tickets using frequent-flier miles as early as possible – even a year in advance if you can. These tickets get snapped up quickly.

---

## Choose a Good Seat on an Aeroplane     `961`

Where should you sit on an aeroplane if you're prone to motion sickness? If you have a connecting flight? If you're travelling with kids? Ask an airline agent about reserving the right seat for you.

### ⊙ Steps

1   Request bulkhead seats – those behind the dividing walls of a plane – or a seat by one of the emergency exits if you want more leg room.

2   Choose an aisle seat for easier access to the overhead storage compartment and lavatories, as well as for faster disembarking.

### ✱ Tips

If you're travelling with a companion, reserve the aisle and window seat of a three-seat row. Because middle seats are the last to be sold, you have a good chance of having an extra seat.

3   Consider sitting near the lavatories if you are travelling with children.

4   Opt for the back of the plane if you want to spread out; there are usually fewer people in the back.

5   Sit towards the front if you want to get off the plane faster, which could be important if you're trying to make a tight connection. The front of the plane also tends to be a quieter ride.

6   Choose a seat toward the wings, which are the stability point for the plane, if motion sickness is a potential problem.

7   Sit near the galleys if you want early snack, drink or meal service.

Join a frequent-flier programme to increase your chances of getting a good seat on the plane.

## ⚠ Warning

Exit-door seats must be filled by passengers willing and able to help people in an emergency situation and may not be available for reservation. Check with your airline agent.

## 962  Choose a Cruise

Cruise lines, one of the fastest-growing segments of the travel industry, offer a wide variety of interesting destinations and activities for all ages.

### ◉ Steps

1   Deal with a cruise-only travel agent or an online agency that specialises in cruise holidays. They are more likely to have access to special offers and cruise deals.

2   Decide where and when you want to cruise and the port you want to embark from. There are Caribbean and Asian sailings nearly year-round. Most cruises in Europe take place only in the summer, as do Alaskan cruises. Trips through the Panama Canal take place in spring and autumn.

3   Decide who will be joining you on the cruise. Families have different needs and entertainment requirements to single travellers or couples.

4   Outline the activities that appeal to you: ports of call, shore excursions, on-board facilities and amenities.

5   Decide if you have a preference about ship size. Large ships have more entertainment choices, while small ships have a more personal approach to service.

6   Determine your budget. Cruise lines give discounts for early bookings. You can also affect your costs by altering cruise dates, the length of your cruise and the region you sail to.

7   Ask about the typical age group of those sailing on a particular line or ship. This can help you determine whether you'll be compatible with your fellow passengers.

8   Choose the level of formality you prefer. Some ships demand formal or business attire at certain dinners. Other ships cater to holiday-makers who want to wear only casual clothing.

### ✱ Tips

Be aware that port fees are often not included in advertised prices. They can add significantly to your cruise costs.

Budget for tips to waiters, room stewards and service personnel on board. Ships often have suggested amounts, depending on the length of the cruise.

Travel light. Getting on and off ships is not as easy as picking up your luggage at the airport.

Bring along toiletries, film and sunscreen. They can be quite expensive on board.

## Apply for a Passport for You and Your Children   963

If you're going on a foreign trip, it's best to apply for your passport at least four weeks before you plan to leave, to allow time for processing and any possible complications.

### ⊙ Steps

1 Pick up a passport application form at a post office.

2 Download an application from the UK Passport Service website (www.passport.gov.uk) if you cannot find one locally, or apply online.

3 Get two identical passport pictures at a photo booth or photographers. Make sure the photos are 45 x 35 mm ($1^3/_4$ x $1^1/_3$ in) – many photo services will tell you if they are passport approved. Colour or black-and-white is acceptable, but the picture must have a light background and your face must be fully visible, though spectacles are allowed. For a first passport, one of the photos must be countersigned by a professional person to confirm the likeness.

4 Fill out the passport application form in black ink and attach photos where requested.

5 Provide the documents needed to prove your eligibility for the passport – usually a birth or adoption certificate, which must be an original.

7 Enclose the appropriate fee for the passport. You can send the passport application by post using a prepaid envelope. Alternatively use the "Check & Send" service available from some post offices and High Street partners, which, for £5, checks the form is correctly filled in and all the documents enclosed, then sends it to the regional office. Expect to wait two to three weeks for your passport. If you need it more quickly, you can request a faster service of a week or same day by making an appointment at a Passport Office and paying an additional fee.

### ✱ Tips

Get multiple application forms in case you make a mistake.

Carry a photocopy of your passport in a safe place; if you lose your passport, you'll be able to replace it more quickly.

Some foreign countries don't require a passport for entry. Check with your passport office or with the embassy of the country you plan to visit.

### ⚠ Warning

If your passport is more than 10 years old, you need a new one. For children under 16 the passport is valid for 5 years initially and can then be extended.

### Things You'll Need

❑ passport application form

❑ passport photographs

❑ birth certificate

## Apply for a Travel Visa   964

Many foreign countries require a visa in addition to your passport. You can apply for a visa at the nearest embassy or consulate of each country you plan to visit.

### ⊙ Steps

1 Call the embassy or consulate of the first country you intend to visit and ask for immigration services. Most consulates in the UK are in London.

2 Ask if you need a visa to visit the country.

3 Request an application form if a visa is required, or download the form if it is available online.

4 Fill out the application form. Describe the estimated length and nature of your visit where indicated. Enclose required documents.

5 Make a copy of your application to keep for your records.

### ✱ Tips

You may need to send passport photos with your application. For long, multicountry trips, you may want to have 10 or more photos taken at once for convenience.

If you are visiting a number of countries that need visas, you might want to use a reputable visa application service. For a fee, they make the applications and chase them, then return your passport complete with visas.

6   Attach any required fee and photos, and return the original application to the embassy or consulate. Be sure to submit it early, since processing can take several weeks. For urgent applications you may be able to get same-day service by visiting the embassy in person.

7   Repeat the application process for other countries as needed.

**⚠ Warning**

Leave plenty of time for your application to be processed, as complications are common.

---

## 965   Exchange Currency

When you're travelling abroad, banks and legal money changers offer the best rates when you need to exchange one currency for another.

### ◉ Steps

1   Look in the business section of the local newspaper for the current exchange rates.

2   Find a legal money changer (a well-known bureau de change or an American Express Travel Service, for example) or bank, which offers better rates than an airport or hotel. If you withdraw money from an ATM, you'll receive the bank's exchange rate, but may incur transaction fees.

3   Show the cashier your passport.

4   Use your own calculator to ensure the accuracy of the exchange.

5   Sign the release form.

6   Count the money before you leave the desk, and take your time.

7   Get a receipt. Customs officials won't ask to see it, but it's always a good insurance policy to have one when you've exchanged money.

### ✱ Tips

Exchange a small amount of money before you leave for your trip. Exchange rates at the airport where you're going may be OK, but it's best to have a choice.

When you use traveller's cheques, a commission is taken out per cheque. Exchange larger denominations when possible.

Money changers don't exchange coins, so spend your loose change before you return.

### Things You'll Need

❑ calculator

❑ passport

---

## 966   Prepare Your Car for a Long Journey

Whether you're heading for the hills or the beach, it's crucial that your car is in good working order. There's nothing worse than having a holiday ruined by car trouble.

### ◉ Steps

1   Make an appointment with your garage at least a few weeks before your journey to do a pre-trip inspection. Bring a checklist of things to ask your mechanic to review.

2   Check all fluids.

3   Check belts and hoses.

4   Look for any leaks.

5   Check and fill all tyres, including the spare tyre, and make sure they're in good condition.

6   Perform a four-wheel brake check (if not done in the last six months).

### ✱ Tips

These steps are in addition to routine maintenance; see 941 "Maintain Your Car Regularly".

Don't wait until the day before you plan to leave to make any big repairs or get a tune-up.

A pre-trip inspection like the one suggested here should take no more than 1 to 1½ hours.

7 Check the condition of the exhaust system.

8 Flush the cooling system (if not done in the last year).

9 Pressure-check the cooling system to inspect for leaks.

10 Load-test the battery to test its ability to hold a charge.

11 Check the alternator output to make sure that the charging system is working well.

12 Replace the spark plug wires if they are more than two years old.

## ⚠ Warning

More than half the cars that break down and get towed into garages are there for repairs that could have been prevented by regular maintenance.

---

## Pack a Suitcase     967

Packing a suitcase is a strategic exercise in maximising space and minimising creases. You may already have a favourite packing system, but read on for more suggestions.

### ⊙ Steps

#### Pack Clothing

1 Remember this order of operations: shirts at the bottom, then dresses (if applicable), then trousers

2 Stack tops, unfolded, by placing crease-prone tops towards the bottom of a pile and less easily creased ones towards the top.

3 Fold the sleeves in towards the shirts' torsos.

4 Fold the shirts in half from the bottom. You now have a rectangular bundle of shirts; place it in your suitcase.

5 Drape long dresses in the suitcase so that the ends hang over the sides.

6 Place trousers and skirts on a flat surface; fold each in half lengthways.

7 Stack trousers and skirts on top of one another, with easily creased ones at the bottom and sturdier ones, such as jeans, on top. Fold the stack over, so that its length is halved.

8 Place your stack of trousers and skirts on top of the dresses, then fold the ends of the dresses over the trousers and skirts.

#### Pack Accessories

1 Roll ties loosely.

2 Stuff socks in shoes. Pack underwear in mesh laundry bags or side pockets to save space.

3 Arrange each pair of shoes so that the heel of one aligns with the toe of the other.

4 Wrap pairs of shoes in separate plastic bags, and place them along the border of your suitcase.

5 Protect clothes from leaks by placing toiletries in a plastic bag.

6 Pack essential toiletries in a carry-on bag. Include your toothbrush, toothpaste, makeup, medication and other important items.

### ✱ Tips

Pack items snugly, leaving little room for them to shift. Consider surrounding them with a plastic dry-cleaning bag to minimise creases; use a suit carrier for suits or dresses.

Pack an easily flattened extra bag, such as a lightweight holdall, for carrying purchases you make on your trip.

Label both the outside and inside of your suitcase with your name, address and phone number. Remove old baggage claim stickers.

Travel light. Check with your airline regarding restrictions on size, weight and number of pieces of luggage allowed.

### ⚠ Warning

Avoid packing money, jewellery, travel documents, medication, keys and other valuables in your suitcase. Carry these items with you.

## 968 Avoid Overpacking

Moderation is key when packing for any trip. A good rule of thumb is to pack approximately half of what you initially think you're going to need.

### ⊙ Steps

1 Know your itinerary. If you know about the dressy events, casual evenings and business days you have in store, you can plan accordingly and avoid bringing unnecessary outfits.

2 Research the weather at your destination. If dry weather is expected, take a risk and skip the umbrella; if nighttime temperatures are known to plummet, pack layers for warmth.

3 Plan your clothes around one main coordinating colour. Black and khaki are good, neutral "foundation" colours that you can dress up, dress down, add colour to and accessorise for different events and different days. Consider bringing dark colours and prints that don't show the dirt.

4 Choose clothes for lightness and washability. Select several light layers that pack down easily and dry quickly, should you need to do hotel-room washing. Avoid bulky items like sweaters and heavy coats if you can be comfortable in two to three interchangeable layers.

5 Pack a couple of favourite scarves or belts for variety.

6 Pack a bum bag or small backpack for day trips. If you're planning to shop, pack a lightweight holdall.

7 Wear your bulkiest outfit while travelling to save space in your luggage.

### ✱ Tips

Even if travelling for several months, you should never need more than five or six days' worth of clothing.

Check with your airline regarding restrictions on size, weight and number of luggage pieces allowed.

For more comfortable travelling, each bag should weigh no more than 9 kg (20 lb) when fully packed.

## 969 Travel Crease-Free

To avoid looking creased and crinkled while you're on the road, buy and pack clothes in fabrics that resist crumpling – or that at least look good even when they're a bit rumpled.

### ⊙ Steps

1 Buy fabrics in wool or silk. These natural fibres have some elasticity, which keeps them from crinkling.

2 Buy synthetic fabrics or clothes that contain blends of synthetic and natural fibres. These fibres make clothing less crease-prone, more durable and easier to care for.

3 Opt for linen, which creases easily but "falls out" nicely and carries off the crumpled-casual look well.

4 Choose knits instead of weaves. Knitwear – which includes cable, ribbed, tricot and jersey knits – creases less than woven fabrics.

5 Pack intelligently. Make use of flat suitcase pockets and special packing accessories that hold clothes in place, and don't overstuff your bags. Consider rolling knitwear, denims and linens to avoid harsh fold lines.

6 Unpack your bags upon arrival.

### ✱ Tips

Synthetics include nylon, polyester, microfibres, spandex, acrylic and acetate.

Cotton, like linen, is a natural fibre that creases easily (although the crumpled cotton look isn't generally in vogue). If you arrive at your destination with a few creases, hang up the clothes in the hotel bathroom while you run a steamy shower – harsh creases will fall out.

## ✓ 970 Pack for Your Destination

Besides your regular clothes and toiletries, you'll need to include articles appropriate to your particular holiday plans. Use the checklist below as your guide to four popular types of travel excursions.

### Beach

- ❑ bathing suit
- ❑ sandals
- ❑ sunscreen and lip balm
- ❑ aloe vera gel for sunburn
- ❑ hat with a wide brim to protect your face
- ❑ sunglasses with adequate UV protection
- ❑ large towel, thin enough to fit into your beach bag
- ❑ refillable water bottle
- ❑ beach toys that fit easily into a bag, such as inflatable balls and Frisbees
- ❑ long-sleeved overshirt
- ❑ thin pair of long trousers
- ❑ long dress for cover-up
- ❑ reading material

### Ski slopes

- ❑ thermals or undergarments made from polypropylene or a similar synthetic fibre
- ❑ polonecks and light sweaters
- ❑ heavy-duty ski jacket
- ❑ thin fleece jacket
- ❑ ski hat
- ❑ waterproof trousers
- ❑ goggles or sunglasses with adequate UV protection
- ❑ scarf
- ❑ gloves or mittens
- ❑ earmuffs or headband
- ❑ sunblock and lip balm
- ❑ several pairs of wool and liner socks
- ❑ refillable water bottle

### Boat

- ❑ jacket
- ❑ rain jacket or foul-weather gear
- ❑ wool socks
- ❑ waterproof shoes with non-slip soles
- ❑ gloves
- ❑ hat
- ❑ sunglasses
- ❑ sunscreen and lip balm
- ❑ binoculars
- ❑ still or video camera in waterproof bag
- ❑ seasickness medication (check with your doctor)
- ❑ life jackets
- ❑ navigation charts and guidebooks

### Outdoor activities

- ❑ sports bra
- ❑ three or four pairs of easy-to-wash trousers
- ❑ poloneck or other warm shirt
- ❑ warm jacket
- ❑ vest
- ❑ rain jacket
- ❑ thick wool socks
- ❑ broken-in boots
- ❑ hat
- ❑ gloves
- ❑ sunglasses and sunhat
- ❑ sunscreen and lip balm
- ❑ maps and guidebooks

checklist

## 971 Clean Clothes While Travelling

Most of us take clean clothes for granted – until we travel. The following steps will help you launder clothes efficiently while on the road.

### ⊙ Steps

1 Pick clothes for your trip that are easy to wash. Buy as many drip-dry garments as you can.

2 Buy a universal sink plug and a mesh bag for laundry. Three metres (10 ft) of string or a small elastic bungee cord make a line for drying.

3 Fill the sink with water and put in your clothes.

4 Work up a lather using shampoo, a bar of soap or, at a pinch, laundry detergent, which requires more rinsing than the other two.

5 Wring out clothes. If there's a dry, clean towel in your room, roll it up with your hard-to-dry wet stuff to expedite the drying process. Twist or sit on the clothes while they're rolled.

6 Hang clothes near a vent, air-conditioning unit or window, or in sunlight.

7 Put any undried clothes in your mesh bag when checking out. In dry, warm weather, you can keep this bag exposed to the air while travelling.

### ✳ Tips

Keep your body clean with showers, antiperspirant and powder, and your clothes will stay cleaner on the inside.

You can get clothes professionally laundered almost anywhere in the world, but the cost varies greatly. Hotels charge the most.

### Things You'll Need

❑ sink stopper

❑ mesh laundry bag

❑ string or small elastic bungee cord

## 972 Make a Hotel Reservation

Comfortable and convenient places to stay – whether in a large hotel or a small bed-and-breakfast – will make your trip more pleasant. Here's how to arrange them without using a travel agent.

### ⊙ Steps

1 Buy a travel guide to your destination, especially if you're not familiar with the area. Read up on accommodation options and areas where places to stay are plentiful.

2 Plan your arrival and departure dates. If possible, choose off-season dates when you may be able to save money on accommodation.

3 Choose the area you want to stay in. This generally depends on where you will be doing business or on the recreational or cultural sights you want to see.

4 Find two or three hotels in your price range that appeal to you.

5 Call each hotel. Tell them the dates you will be lodging there and your room requirements, and ask for the room rate. Ask about family packages where kids stay for free or at a substantial discount, and about special deals that give you a discount on surrounding attractions.

6 Find out what other services are included in the room rate. Is a hot breakfast included? Afternoon tea?

### ✳ Tips

You can also request a guide to places to stay from the tourist office of the area you'll be visiting. Remember, though, that you may get more honest appraisals from an independent guidebook, from friends' recommendations or from various websites.

If you are arriving at a local airport, ask if the hotel provides free transport from the airport to the hotel.

Ask about other extras that may be important to you: fridge, hair dryer, iron, gym, on-site restaurant, swimming pool, video, film rental, wheelchair access, pet-friendly facilities.

7   Ask about any special rates that are available. For example, if you stay 4 nights during the low season, are you entitled to a special long weekend rate? If you adjust your dates slightly, can you get a better deal? Be sure the adjustment will be reflected in the final room rate.

8   Compare room rates and services and book one of the hotels. Be sure to specify a smoking or non-smoking room.

9   Reserve the room with your credit card. This will generally hold the room for you no matter what time you arrive.

⚠ **Warning**

Check the hotel's cancellation policy. These differ from hotel to hotel, but if you cancel without letting the hotel know within the specified time, you may have to pay for a night's accommodation.

## Get a Hotel-Room Upgrade                                    973

Sometimes upgrading your hotel room is possible, and sometimes it's not. Your chances depend on a combination of the available space, your arrival time and luck.

◉**Steps**

1   Establish loyalty by always choosing the same hotel in cities you visit often. Being friendly with the reception staff never hurts.

2   Ask about freebies and other special deals when you book your reservation. If you don't ask, you usually don't get.

3   Join frequent-visitor programmes at the chain hotels you visit. Your points earn upgrades and free stays along with other perks.

4   Organise reunions, meetings or conferences at your favourite hotel. Lots of hotels say thanks with credit for upgrades or free nights, either at the time of the event or at a later date.

5   Trade airline frequent-flier points for upgrades at participating hotels. But weigh this option carefully – it's rarely the most cost-effective way to spend frequent-flier points.

6   Be vocal. If the room you were assigned isn't satisfactory – dirty, noisy or lacking the view you were promised – ask for an upgrade.

7   Offer to be appeased. If the staff makes a mistake that causes a delay or distress – say they misplace your luggage or, in a worst-case scenario, fail to make your room safe – make it known that an upgrade will help you forget all about the bad experience.

8   Take a chance on luck. Once in a while, you'll be in the right place at the right time. Budget rooms sometimes get overbooked, and the lucky guest who gets bumped up to the executive floor could turn out to be you.

✳ **Tip**

Friendliness and charm may help encourage a hotel receptionist to go the extra mile for you.

## 974 | Overcome Your Fear of Flying

Studies have found that millions of people have a fear of flying, despite the enormous odds against a mishap. There are several ways to conquer your fears and make air travel more endurable.

### ⊙ Steps

1   Accept that it is unlikely you can conquer your fear of flying without help.

2   Get counselling or join a group. Since fear of flying is such a common phobia, many excellent clinics are available to help you. Look in the Yellow Pages under "Clinics" or "Psychologists".

3   Read a book. Countless books are devoted to overcoming the fear of flying. Most include instructions on special breathing and relaxation methods and other helpful techniques.

4   Buy a tape. Some fear-of-flying programmes are on tape so you can listen to instructions for relaxation and breathing.

5   Have confidence that you can succeed. Even the most serious fears about flying can be conquered with proper treatment and hard work.

6   Ask your doctor for a prescription drug to relax you when you must fly, if all else fails. Keep in mind, however, that most professionals believe you can conquer this fear without medication.

### ✳ Tip

Symptoms often associated with fear of flying include anxiety attacks, heart palpitations, dizziness, a feeling of suffocation, sweating, nausea and shaking. These are symptoms of anxiety and are not medically dangerous.

### ⚠ Warning

Avoid using alcohol as a way to relax yourself, as it may impair sleep and cause dehydration. Never drink alcohol if you are also taking tranquilisers or other prescription drugs.

## 975 | Prevent Jet Lag

Jet lag doesn't have to ruin the first few days of your trip abroad. A few simple tips will help keep it in check.

### ⊙ Steps

1   Start shifting your sleep-wake cycle to match that of your destination several days before departure, changing at the rate of one hour per day.

2   Begin adjusting to the time zone of your destination by resetting your watch at the beginning of your flight.

3   Sleep on the plane when it is night-time at your destination. Earplugs, headphones and an eye mask can help diminish noise and light.

4   Stay awake on the plane when it is daytime at your destination. Read a thriller with the light on and the window shade open, or walk around.

5   Drink plenty of water. The air on planes is extremely dry, and dehydration can worsen the effects of jet lag.

6   Avoid alcohol and caffeine while flying. They increase dehydration.

7   Exercise as much as you can on the flight during waking hours: stretch, walk down the aisles and do leg lifts (see 978 "Exercise on a Plane").

### Things You'll Need

❑ earplugs

❑ headphones

❑ eye mask

## Treat Jet Lag

**976**

Flying across numerous time zones can affect travellers for days. Try the following tips to speed up the adjustment process.

### ⊙Steps

#### Daytime Arrival

1  Reset your watch to local time if you haven't done so already.

2  Eat a protein-packed breakfast, such as an omelette, which will help you stay awake.

3  Soak up natural sunlight to cue your body that it is time to be awake. Or spend your first day in well-lit places.

4  Get some exercise, but don't overdo it; a good option is a gentle walk outside during the day to get fresh air and keep your body moving.

5  Take a short nap if you are really weary, but do so before 2 pm and sleep for no longer than an hour.

6  Go to bed at a reasonable time. Even if you feel like dropping off at 5 pm, try to hold out until at least 8 or 9 pm so that you won't wake up too early the next morning.

#### Nighttime Arrival

1  Eat a high-carbohydrate meal, such as pasta, to help make you drowsy.

2  Plan to go to bed at the local bedtime, even if you aren't sleepy.

3  Think about other ways to induce sleep; a hot bath with lavender oil, a cup of chamomile tea or a massage. Keep lights dim.

4  Avoid sleeping late, even if you did not sleep well.

### ✱ Tip

Make sure your hotel room is not too hot. You'll get the best night's sleep in a cool (but not cold) room.

### ⚠ Warnings

Avoid drinking alcohol to help you sleep. It will interfere with your body's natural sleep patterns. Also avoid drinking a lot of caffeinated drinks to keep yourself awake during the day. These will dehydrate you and make you more tired when they wear off.

Avoid driving, especially in an unfamiliar place, if you are over-tired. If you must drive while weary, be very careful. Keep the window open and make frequent stops to keep sleepiness at bay.

## Kill Time in an Airport

**977**

Waiting long hours at an airport can be boring and frustrating. Why not improve your mood by seeking out the attractions the airport has to offer?

### ⊙Steps

1  Dissolve stress and increase energy by exercising in the airport gym. A growing number of airports now contain workout areas.

2  Power-walk around the entire airport if there is no gym. Store luggage in terminal lockers, lace up the walking shoes and get the blood pumping.

3  Surf the internet and answer e-mail at an internet kiosk to make the time fly. Keep in mind that you'll be charged for the time you spend online.

4  Purchase souvenirs and presents for friends and family at the airport's gift shops and retail outlets.

5  Get your shoes polished. Many larger airports feature hallway shine specialists to buff and polish your shoes.

### ⚠ Warning

Keep your eye on a clock at all times, and check the departure screens regularly to ensure that you do not miss your flight.

6   Enjoy a drink in the airport bar if there is one. In some airports the day's big sporting event will probably be blaring on the television.

7   Bring a good book or a stack of your favourite magazines. Airport time can constitute some of the most peaceful reading time you will ever get.

---

## 978 | Exercise on a Plane

Combat poor circulation, swelling, sore joints and lethargy on cramped flights by doing a short exercise routine. At the very least, you'll entertain your fellow passengers.

### ⊙ Steps

1   Squeeze a tennis ball, a squash ball or even a pair of socks with your hands until they're tired.

2   Keep the balls of your feet planted and raise your legs using your calf muscles. If this is too easy, place your hand luggage on your knees. Continue until tired.

3   Plant your heels firmly and raise your toes as high as possible. Hold for five seconds, and relax. Repeat until tired.

4   Place your hands on your armrests and raise your knees slowly (together is harder than one at a time) towards your chin. Lower them slowly. Repeat until tired.

5   Cross your legs. Rotate the dangling foot in as wide a circle as possible. Continue until tired.

6   Stretch your neck by keeping your chin close to your throat and tilting your head forwards. Roll your head from one shoulder to the other, but avoid rotating it backwards.

7   Flex your trapezius muscles by doing shoulder hunches. Lower your shoulders, and then raise them up towards your ears into a shrug. Hold for five seconds. Continue until tired.

8   Arch your torso gently backwards and forwards like a cat.

9   Flex your gluteus muscles and hold for as long as possible. Squeezing your rear like this may occasion strange glances, but these muscles are the biggest in the human body and need to be exercised, too.

### ✱ Tip

When aisles are relatively empty and the seatbelt sign is off, walk around, stretch and do lunges. To lunge, take a big step (about half your height) and gently lower yourself as far as you can while keeping the torso upright and back leg straight. Return to a standing position by stepping either forward with the rear foot or backward with the front foot. Repeat. Once you become skilled, you'll be able to work up a sweat (and an audience) lunging to the toilet and back.

---

## 979 | Eat Healthily on a Plane

With a little foresight and know-how, you can actually get a healthy – and edible – meal in the sky.

### ⊙ Steps

1   Call your airline at least 24 hours before you fly and order a special-diet meal at no extra cost. Vegetarian, Hindu, kosher, low-salt and sugar-free options are usually available. A special-diet meal doesn't guarantee that the food will be good, but at least you'll get some special preparation.

### ✱ Tip

Culinary possibilities open up on long international flights with major carriers. Call in advance and ask what special meals are available – you may be pleasantly surprised.

2  Pack a meal, if you have the time. Bring food that travels well and that requires no cutting, messiness or permanent containers. Steer clear of foods that will bother other passengers, such as items with too much crunch or odour.

3  Bring an energy bar or some other meal replacement in case the in-flight meal is inedible or your flight is delayed.

4  Eat in the airport if you don't want to entrust your airline with your culinary fate. Large airports have the usual variety of fast-food franchises, so pick what you know to be the most nourishing.

5  Follow any alcohol or caffeine consumption with plenty of water to avoid becoming dehydrated.

⚠ **Warnings**

Avoiding MSG (monosodium glutamate) is tricky. You can speak to your airline, but don't expect a promise that MSG will be absent from your food. Consider bringing your own meal if you are sensitive to MSG.

Be wary of vegetarian breakfasts if you want something filling – you might get just a banana or juice.

# Sleep on a Plane                                     980

Sleeping through the night or even taking a power nap on a plane can be tricky. But with the proper preparations, a satisfactory snooze is possible for almost everyone.

## ◉ Steps

1  Reserve your seat in advance. Window seats give you a wall to lean on, and your neighbour won't need to disturb you on the way to the lavatory.

2  Buy and pack in your hand luggage the following: travel pillow and eye mask, earplugs, comfortable clothing, slippers and bottled water.

3  Make sure that your body will be tired for the flight: before your departure avoid sleeping in, napping or consuming caffeine, and try to get some exercise.

4  Grab a pillow and blanket as soon as you get on the plane. Remember, your seat is reserved, but blankets may not be.

5  Scan the cabin for better seats once the flight is under way. A row of empty seats with movable armrests is the best situation for sleeping on a plane – aside from first class.

6  Adjust your seat for maximum comfort. If you can't put it back far enough, try putting a pillow or blanket behind your lower back to make you more reclined.

7  Ask what time the in-flight meal will be served. Falling asleep is easier on a full stomach.

8  Tell your neighbour that you plan to sleep. The purpose is twofold: he or she will leave you alone, and can discourage the flight attendants from disturbing you while you sleep.

✳ **Tip**

Most travel shops carry a variety of pillows designed for sleeping in an upright position. Budget travellers find the inflatable U-shaped vinyl pillows satisfactory and compact.

⚠ **Warning**

Consult your doctor before taking any variety of sleeping pill.

**Things You'll Need**

❑ travel pillow

❑ eye mask

❑ earplugs

❑ bottled water

## ✓ 981 Use Essential Phrases in Foreign Languages

When you're in a country whose language you don't speak, a few key phrases can get you a long way. This table lists useful expressions in 15 foreign languages, along with the pronunciation (in brackets) where helpful. For languages that do not use the Roman alphabet or have a standardised transliteration, only the pronunciation is listed.

| LANGUAGE | HELLO | GOODBYE | PLEASE | THANK YOU | I WOULD LIKE | DO YOU SPEAK ENGLISH? |
|---|---|---|---|---|---|---|
| Arabic | mar-ha-ba | ma'a el-sa-la-ma | min fad-lak | shoo kran | o-reed | Let ka-lam In-glee-zi? |
| Chinese (Mandarin) | ni hao | zai jian | qing (ching) | xie xie (shieh shieh) | wo yao (woh yau) | Ni hui jiang ying yu ma? |
| Danish | hej (high) | farvel (far-VEL) | vaer så venlig (vaer SA VEN-lee) | tak (tahk) | jeg vil gerne (yigh veel GEHR-nor) | Taler de engelsk? (TA-ler dee EHN-gerlsk?) |
| French | bonjour (bohn-ZHOOR) | au revoir (oh ruh-VWAR) | s'il vous plaît (see voo PLAY) | merci (mehr-SEE) | je voudrais (zhuh voo-DRAY) | Parlez-vous anglais? (PAHR-lay voo ahn-GLAY?) |
| German | guten Tag (GOOT-en TAK) | auf Wieder-sehen (owf VEED-uh-zain) | bitte (BIT-uh) | danke (DAHNK-uh) | Ich möchte (ikh MURKH-tuh) | Sprechen Sie Englisch? (SHPREKH-en zee ENG-lish?) |
| Greek | kherete (KHE-re-te) | andio (an-DEE-o) | parakalo (pah-rah-kah-LOH) | efkahreesto (eff-khah-rees-TOH) | tha I'thela (thah EE-the-la) | Milate Agglika? (Me-LAH-teh eye-lee-KAH?) |
| Hebrew | sha-LOM | sha-LOM | ba-va-ka-SHA | to-DA | a-NEE row-TSEH (if you're male); a-NEE-row-TSAH (if you're female) | At-a me-da-BER Ang-LIT? (to a male); at me-da-BER-et Ang-LIT? (to a female) |
| Hindi | namaste (na-MAS-tay) | namaste (na-MAS-tay) | KRIP-ya | dhan-ya-VAAD | mai cha-HA-ta hoon (if you're male); mai cha-HA-ti hoon (if you're female) | K'ya ap koh ungrazi hay? (Kya aap ko an-GREE-zi aa-TI hai?) |
| Italian | ciao (chow) | ciao (chow) | per favore (pehr fa-VOR-ay) | grazie (GRATS-ee-ay) | vorrei (vohr-RAY) | Parla inglese? (PAHR-la een-GLAY-zay?) |
| Japanese | konnichi wa | sayōnara | onegaishimasu | arigatō | kudasai | Eigo o hanashimasu ka? |
| Polish | dzień dobry (jane DOUGH-bray) | do widzenia (dough ve-ZEN-ya) | prosze (PRO-shoa) | dziekuje (jen-KU-yeow) | poprosze (po-PRO-shoa) | Czy mowisz po angielsku? (che MOVE-ish poe an-GELL-sku?) |
| Portuguese | olá (oh-LA) | adeus (ah-DAY-oosh) | por favor (por fah-VOR) | obrigado (oh-bree-GA-doo) if you're male; obrigada (oh-bree-GA-dah) if you're female | queria (KREE-ah) | Fala ingés? (FA-lah in-GLESH?) |
| Russian | preev-YET | duh svi-DAR-nya | pah-ZAHL-sta | spa-SEE-ba | ya khah-TYEL-bi | VWEE guh-vah-RYEE-tya Pahn-GLEE-ski? |
| Spanish | hola (OH-la) | adiós (ah-dee-OS) | por favor (por fah-VOR) | gracias (GRA-see-as) | quisiera (kee-see-YARE-uh) | Habla inglés? (A-bla een-GLACE?) |
| Swahili | JAM-bo | kwa-HE-ri | ta-fa-DHA-li | a-SAN-te | nin-ge-PEN-da | U-na-SE-ma kiin-ge-re-za? |

## Learn Key Foreign Phrases Without a Phrase Book | 982

You don't need a phrase book to learn a few key words in the local language where you're travelling. A little effort will make your travel easier and your hosts feel appreciated.

### ⊙ Steps

1 Set a reasonable goal about what you would like to learn, and stick with it. This can be as simple as learning a few basic greetings, polite terms of address, or how to order your favourite dish in a restaurant.

2 Pay attention to how others greet one another or part from one another; learning proper greetings and goodbyes will always engender goodwill.

3 Find yourself a few good "teachers" – a hotel receptionist, a waiter in a restaurant, a taxi driver. This doesn't have to be someone you will spend a great deal of time with, just someone who appreciates your curiosity about the language and with whom you can comfortably interact about day-to-day needs.

4 Ask how to say a few words that will help introduce you to the language's sounds. You don't need a common language to do this; pointing and gesturing will do just fine. Learning how to say your teacher's name, the name of the town you're visiting, or the numbers one to five is a good place to start.

5 Jot down words as you learn them, making up your own phonetic system that will help you remember how they sound. Have your teacher pronounce the word while you write it down the way you think it sounds.

6 Repeat new words or phrases to your teacher immediately after she says them. Ask her to say the word again. Repeat it, making adjustments in your pronunciation as you notice differences.

7 Keep a running list of new words, and review it several times throughout the day. The key to learning vocabulary in a foreign language is review.

8 Try using your new words or phrases with locals other than your teacher. Ask them to repeat the words you have learned, so you can get used to hearing the ways other people pronounce them.

**❉ Tip**

Keep your sense of humour. Trying to speak a foreign language often feels silly, embarrassing or frustrating at first, but be persistent – the payoff is worth it.

## Avoid Traveller's Diarrhoea | 983

When visiting areas with poor sanitation, avoid traveller's diarrhoea by taking extra precautions with water and food.

### ⊙ Steps

1 Consider the following safe to drink: commercially bottled water with an unbroken seal, canned or bottled carbonated drinks, hot drinks made with vigorously boiled water, and wine and beer in their original containers.

2 Check seals on water bottles carefully; if the seal has been tampered with, the bottle may have been refilled with tap water.

3 Wipe off the lip of any bottle or can before drinking or pouring from it.

**❉ Tips**

Traveller's diarrhoea, which is usually caused by consuming faeces-contaminated water or food, may clear up by itself. But if it is very watery and lasts for several days, or if you are vomiting and have a fever, seek medical care; it may be a sign of a more serious infection.

4   Consider non-disposable glasses and cups unsanitary; drink from original containers and use straws, or carry your own cups.

5   Boil untreated water to purify it. Use both a filter and iodine tablets if bottled or boiled water is not available.

6   Avoid ice, fruit juice and any drinks made with tap water, such as mixed drinks or lemonade.

7   Brush your teeth with bottled water, and make sure to rinse your toothbrush with bottled water. Try not to swallow water when taking a shower.

8   Avoid any foods that may be rinsed in water, including salads, raw fruits and raw vegetables. Also stay away from dairy products if there's a question about pasteurisation.

9   Eat meat, poultry and fish only if they are well-cooked, and make sure that cooked food is served hot. Some fish from contaminated waters may be toxic even after cooking; if there is any doubt, do without.

If you choose to eat raw fruits and vegetables, peel them.

For boiling water, consider purchasing an immersion coil. If you are travelling to a foreign country, you may also need to purchase a plug adapter and current converter.

## 984 | Get Post on the Road

**Most foreign post offices will allow travellers to receive mail via the Poste Restante service; all it takes is a little planning.**

### ◉ Steps

1   Distribute envelopes to family and friends marked "Poste Restante" and addressed to the main post office in major destination towns on your itinerary.

2   Provide family and friends with a copy of your itinerary and the dates by which they should send post so that it gets to you in time.

3   Ask family and friends to send all correspondence to your destination towns at least two weeks prior to your arrival. This will help ensure that the mail arrives by the time you do.

4   Note the hours of the local post office. Many post offices in foreign countries close for a few hours in the middle of the afternoon.

5   Bring your passport with you when you go to the post office to collect your post. You may have to check back every few days until your correspondence arrives.

### ✳ Tip

Look for American Express locations in the area. You can also ask people to send you mail there, provided that you hold an American Express card or traveller's cheques.

## 985 | Get E-mail on the Road

**E-mail is a worldwide amenity these days. A few simple steps will make communicating from afar as easy as a mouse click, even when you've left the laptop at home.**

### ◉ Steps

1   Sign up for a free internet-based e-mail account.

2   Give family and friends your new address, to prevent an empty inbox during your trip.

### ✳ Tip

Before your trip, scan your passport and e-mail it to yourself. If you lose your passport abroad, print it out from e-mail at an internet station.

3   Write down your e-mail password, and keep it in a safe and accessible place. Better yet, just memorise it.

4   Enter the e-mail addresses of family and friends in your e-mail address book before you leave for your trip.

5   Mark all listings for internet cafés, universities and libraries in your travel guide. Most of these locations will offer internet service for a nominal fee. Internet cafés typically abound near tourist spots and youth hostels.

6   Check airports each time you arrive at a new destination for internet-access kiosks.

⚠ **Warning**

Make sure that your e-mail environment is safe. Lurkers may try to access information about you by watching you type your password or by reading your e-mail messages over your shoulder. When you've finished checking your e-mail, be sure to log off the website.

## Pay Bills During an Extended Absence　986

It's important to find someone who is organised and trustworthy to assist you in paying bills while you're away. Your credit rating depends on it.

### ◉ Steps

1   Call all credit-card companies, insurance companies and other creditors that bill you monthly. Have all bills forwarded to a trusted family member or friend during your absence.

2   Make a list for your family member or friend of all creditors who must be paid monthly.

3   Make sure that your current account has sufficient funds. Write one cheque to each creditor for each month that you'll be away. Post-date all cheques accordingly, and leave them with your temporary bill payer. Supply envelopes and postage as an extra courtesy.

4   Log all postdated cheques in your chequebook so that you can check it against your statement later.

5   Call all creditors once you return to have your address reinstated.

✳ **Tips**

Ask your temporary bill payer to keep all bill receipts for your records.

If you are not paid directly into your bank account, arrange for someone to deposit your earnings during your absence.

⚠ **Warning**

Make sure that all cheques are thoroughly filled out, except for the amount. Blank cheques are an invitation to fraud.

## Travel Alone　987

Travelling alone can open you up to unique personal experiences in new places. Take full advantage of these opportunities while maintaining your safety.

### ◉ Steps

#### Get Comfortable on Your Own

1   Follow some of the routines you have at home: drink a cup of coffee in the morning, take an afternoon jog, visit the market in the evening.

2   Create a temporary home, if you are staying more than a couple of days, by decorating your room with familiar objects, such as pictures, candles and flowers.

✳ **Tips**

Before your trip, get used to the idea of being alone. Go to see a film or dine out alone.

To deter male attention, a woman should consider wearing a ring on her left ring finger, whether married or not. A whistle on a chain around the neck is also a wise idea – and don't be afraid to make a noise if you're in trouble.

3   Go to a restaurant and bring a book, journal or materials for writing letters. You might also bring a guidebook or map to help plan the next part of your trip.

4   Become a regular: visit one shop consistently or have breakfast at the same café each morning, and get to know the people who work there. They can give you helpful advice about the area and, when you need it, provide assistance, which can be especially important in an emergency.

5   Meet other travellers through classes or tour groups. They can share travel tips with you and even become temporary travel companions.

## Practise Personal Safety

1   Consider learning basic self-defence. For instance, by striking the eyes, nose, throat, groin or knees, you can disable an assailant (see 895 "Choose a Martial Art").

2   Research your destination so you'll know what to expect in terms of attitudes toward foreigners and, if you're female, women.

3   Request a room that isn't on the ground floor, which can offer easy access through a window.

4   Avoid opening your door to people who are unknown to you or who do not identify themselves.

5   Become familiar with the people at your hotel's reception desk, and inform them of your comings and goings. Give them emergency numbers of family or friends.

6   Get to know the area where you'll be staying, and trust your intuition; avoid places that look risky.

7   Dress like a local resident, or at least try to look inconspicuous in your dress and behaviour.

8   Walk with confidence. If you're feeling nervous, seek out a fellow traveller as a temporary companion or stay close to another pedestrian so that you don't appear to be alone.

9   Stay sober, or at least know your limits when drinking.

⚠ **Warnings**

Be somewhat cautious when meeting new people. Ask lots of questions and get to know people first before you tell them that you're travelling alone. You don't want to become a target for others to take advantage of you.

If you run into trouble in a foreign country, contact your country's embassy or the closest consulate as soon as possible.

If you are harassed, be clear and firm in your rebuff and get away from the harasser as quickly as possible. Seek out the police or other authorities if necessary.

---

## 988 | Choose a Travelling Companion

There's no single "right" way to travel – it depends on the individuals involved. What is certain is that two people with different expectations travelling together is a recipe for trouble.

### ⊙ Steps

1   Talk in great detail about goals and expectations for the trip before agreeing to travel with someone. Why are you going? What do you most want to get from the trip? What will you regret not having done? Be completely open and honest with the other person and encourage him or her to do the same.

2   Consider generating a set of questions to discuss with any potential travelling companion. Encourage your potential companion to create their

 **Tip**

Be patient and persistent in looking for a companion. Better yet, make your trip a challenge to overcome any fear of being alone. Don't settle on someone only because you're afraid of travelling alone (see 987 "Travel Alone").

own list of questions – the topics that concern you both may themselves be revealing.

3   Discuss your budget in detail. Consider not just how much money you have for the trip, but also how and where you want to spend it.

4   Come up with a tentative itinerary that includes locations you plan to visit, length of stay in each place, expected travel times from one place to another, and time spent together and separately.

5   Talk about your respective travel styles. Determine whether each of you is a morning or night person, how much shopping you each like to do, how spontaneous you like to be, whether or not you smoke or drink, and how much you expect to immerse yourself in local culture.

6   Consider getting assistance from an organisation that specialises in matching travel partners, if you don't know a family member or friend with whom you would be willing to travel. An internet search on "partner travel" or "travel companion exchange" should get you pointed in the right direction.

## Make a Long Car Journey With a Baby                    989

Even very young babies can safely go on long trips – in fact, children are at their most "portable" during the first year of life. Here are some tips to help you take your baby on the road.

### Steps

1   Plan frequent stops for feeding or nappy changing. Babies can get cramped and uncomfortable when they are in car seats for long periods of time.

2   Bring toys that you can attach to the car seat. Clips for attaching dummies work well, even if your baby doesn't use a dummy.

3   Try to travel during times when your baby is likely to be asleep. You can even travel at night, as long as the driver is well-rested and alert.

4   Pack some restful music – perhaps some soothing children's music – to help keep everyone calm even during fussy times.

5   Try to travel during the cooler parts of the day, and protect your child from heat and glare by bringing an adjustable sunshade that you can move to different windows as the sun moves.

6   Pack lots of plastic bags to hold dirty nappies, used baby wipes, soiled clothes or rubbish.

7   Bring an insulated cool bag if you're bottle-feeding, or take along prepared single servings of formula to use while you're on the road.

### ✱ Tip

Keep an eye on your baby as you drive with a small adjustable mirror clipped on to your rear-view mirror.

### ⚠ Warning

Never take your baby out of his car seat in a moving vehicle.

### Things You'll Need

❏ infant car seat

❏ baby toys

❏ dummy clips

❏ music tapes

❏ car sunshade

❏ plastic bags

❏ cool bag

## 990 | Make a Long Car Journey With a Toddler

Making a long journey with a restless toddler can be a challenge, but there are many ways to make the time go faster and keep everyone happy for at least most of the trip.

### ⊙ Steps

1 Follow the seatbelt/car-seat rule: the car doesn't move until everyone is securely strapped in, and the car stops if anyone gets unstrapped.

2 If your child naps, try to travel during the time he or she is most likely to fall asleep. You can even travel at night, as long as the driver is alert.

3 Make regular stops at service stations or safe laybys. Service stations and some laybys have a grassy area where kids can run and stretch their legs.

4 Pack cool drinks and healthy finger foods; avoid sticky or moist foods that can ruin your car's interior. Dry cereal and crackers, along with a spill-proof cup of milk, juice or water, can keep a toddler busy for a while.

5 Try to play car games that involve looking out of the window. This makes it less likely that your child will get carsick, and helps to distract him or her from the reality of being stuck in a car seat.

6 Bring a portable potty, and consider bringing along some pull-ups for extra insurance if your child is toilet training.

7 Pack a selection of quiet toys for the trip to keep the child busy without driving the adults crazy.

8 Bring lots of good sing-along children's music tapes, which will help everyone pass the time.

### ✳ Tips

Even if your car has tinted windows, an adjustable sunshade can help to keep your toddler cool and comfortable.

If your child tends to drop his or her cup, consider attaching it to the car seat with a dummy clip or a short piece of string.

### ⚠ Warning

Give your child lots of fluids, as long car trips can be dehydrating.

### Things You'll Need

❑ car seat

❑ drinks and snacks

❑ portable potty or pull-ups (if applicable)

❑ toys

❑ children's music tapes

❑ car sunshade

## 991 | Fly With a Baby

Planning ahead can make a world of difference in maintaining your sanity when you're travelling the friendly skies with your adorable little one.

### ⊙ Steps

1 Book a non-stop flight during off-peak hours, and hope for empty seats.

2 Book in advance, if possible, and select the seats you want. Where there are three-seated rows, you can often request a window seat and an aisle seat and then have one seat for your supplies.

3 Check with the airline about what you can bring on the plane. If the flight is not full, you can often bring an airline-approved car seat on board even if you didn't buy an extra ticket. Also, most airlines will allow you to check-in a fold-up stroller at the gate.

4 Enquire about services and amenities when you book the flight. Does the airline provide a Moses basket? Does it provide special food for babies?

### ✳ Tips

Do a nappy change in an airport changing room before boarding.

Children under two fly for free but sit on your lap. Consider buying a ticket for your baby. It's safer to bring a child's car seat on board.

5   Consider taking a night flight if it's a long flight. Although you may not get a good night's sleep, it may be easier for your baby to travel at night and avoid dramatic changes in routine.

6   Try to fly with another adult, who can offer an extra pair of hands and provide additional ideas for entertaining the baby.

7   Bring food, bottles and new toys as well as old favourites. Also bring an extra pair of baby clothes and plenty of nappies. Being stranded in a plane with a baby in wet clothes or nappies does not bode well for anyone on the plane.

8   Travel equipped with medical records and your doctor's phone number if your baby takes medication.

9   Board early. If you're choosing seats, try to sit near other families. In addition to the distraction other children can provide, another family may tolerate your child's temper tantrum better than most other travellers.

10  Offer your baby a bottle, cup or breast on the ascent and descent. Swallowing helps eliminate any discomfort from changing air pressure.

## ⚠ Warning

If your child has a cold or any upper-respiratory symptoms prior to the flight, check with a doctor about whether to fly at all.

## Things You'll Need

- ❑ food
- ❑ bottles
- ❑ baby toys
- ❑ change of baby clothes
- ❑ nappies
- ❑ medical records and doctor's phone number

## Fly With a Toddler                                992

You don't have to stay at home just because you have a toddler. It's possible to go anywhere you like – even on long aeroplane trips – with some careful preparation.

### ⊙ Steps

1   Schedule a night flight, if possible, so that your little one is likely to sleep for at least part of the time.

2   Pack a change of clothes, or dress your child in layers that can be easily removed in case of spills.

3   Consider boarding early. If your child is mellow and sleepy, it's a great idea, but if he or she is wide awake and excited, it might be better to delay boarding as long as possible.

4   Keep in mind that only certain car seats are airline-approved. Be prepared to check-in your car seat as baggage if necessary.

5   Bring a selection of healthy, non-perishable snacks and a drink in a spill-proof cup. In-flight food services aren't designed with hungry, impatient toddlers in mind.

6   Prepare a surprise pack of small new toys, picture books and other tiny treats. Bring them out one treat at a time, whenever your child begins to get restless.

7   Remember that anti-nausea medications are a good idea if your child has a sensitive stomach. They also cause drowsiness.

8   Bring a collapsible push-chair or backpack for carrying your child to use in the airport, especially if you have a connecting flight to catch. If it doesn't fit in the overhead lockers, a flight attendant will check it in for you. Airports are big and can be very tiring for little feet.

## ✱ Tip

Do a nappy change in an airport changing room before boarding.

## ⚠ Warning

Turbulence can be dangerous for people who aren't strapped in, and walking or running in the aisles can also be disruptive.

## Things You'll Need

- ❑ change of clothes
- ❑ car seat
- ❑ snacks and drinks
- ❑ spillproof cup
- ❑ books and toys
- ❑ collapsible push-chair or backpack

## 993 | Quickly Childproof the Grandparents' House

Grandma and Grandpa's can be a worrying place when break-able or dangerous objects are within your child's reach. Here are some quick ways to help make the house child-friendly.

### ◎ Steps

1  Call first. Remind Grandma and Grandpa to move treasured figurines out of reach of little hands, preferably before your child sees them and wants to play with them.

2  Pack safety items you may need, such as simple push-in plug covers, twist-ties to secure blind cords, or removable edge/corner guards for tables and low shelves.

3  Quickly tour the area your child will be in, preferably on your hands and knees. This will allow you to see possible hazards from his or her level.

4  Check cupboards and drawers, and remove dangerous objects like pens, lighters and matches. Remember to look under beds as well.

5  Move houseplants out of reach. Not only can some be toxic, but they also provide a great opportunity for your child to make a mess or injure him- or herself with a falling pot.

6  Make sure that bags containing medication are out of reach. Grandparents often replace childproof caps with caps that are easier for them to remove.

7  Lower the toilet lid and close the bathroom door. You'll reduce the risk of drowning and eliminate the opportunity for your child to lock him- or herself in the bathroom.

8  Ask if outside doors and doors to other rooms within the house can be closed, and ideally locked. This makes it much easier to keep track of your child if he or she tends to wander.

9  Bring toys and books from home, making your child less likely to get into other things.

10  Be cautious with pets that may not be used to children and their quick, unpredictable movements.

11  Supervise! There's no substitute for the watchful eye of an adult.

### ✱ Tip

If your child will be sleeping in a big bed, bring a portable guard-rail, or pull a couple of high-backed chairs next to the bed so that he or she can't fall out.

### ⚠ Warnings

If your child has food allergies, remind grandparents ahead of time, and suggest a list of appropriate snacks. Allergy attacks are common when children eat unfamiliar foods.

Ask Grandma and Grandpa not to leave out bowls of nuts or sweets, which could pose a choking hazard.

Watch out for dangling blind and curtain cords; ask if you can tie them out of reach with a twist-tie or piece of string.

### Things You'll Need

❏ plug covers

❏ twist-ties

❏ removable edge/corner guards

## 994 | Plan a Round-the-World Trip

A round-the-world trip is many people's dream, whether they are on a gap year or well into retirement. Plan carefully for the trip of a lifetime.

### ◎ Steps

1  Give yourself time to research your trip and your route before you set off.

2  Know yourself. Do you thrive on sponaneity or surprises or do you like to have a good idea of what's coming next? The answer will affect how you

### ✱ Tips

Be realistic about your budget. Your ticket is the major expense, but ensure you have enough funds for the rest of the trip, too.

**How to Do (Just About) Everything**

plan your trip. If you like order and organisation, you can plan a detailed schedule. Otherwise, you might be better off with a few key stops and time inbetween to wander off and explore.

3 List your must-see places and decide how long you would like in each.

4 Research the weather in the places you want to go, but don't get obsessed with it. You're not likely to be able to go to each place at the best time of year, but you can plan to avoid monsoons or deep winters.

5 Start to put together an itinerary. Decide whether you want to travel westwards or eastwards. Some websites offer a planning service.

6 Look into different flight deals. Some round-the-world tickets are offered by single airlines, and some by groups of airlines. All have different restrictions such as whether you can backtrack or how many stopovers you can have. You might have to accept some limits to get a cheaper deal.

7 Firm up your route to match the ticket deal you have chosen.

If you can only travel at a certain time of year, consider planning your trip around the places that are best during those months. Otherwise you may end up at your dream destination but at the worst time to see it.

Travel light, taking clothes with more than one use, such as trainers that can be rugged in the hills and the cities or thermal tops that are warm yet also light and easy to wash.

Keep up to date with world events in case they affect your route. No matter how much planning you've done, stay flexible.

## Time Your Trip to Sydney 995

Sydney is a great destination year-round. It's a cosmopolitan, fun loving city offering beaches, museums and galleries and plenty of open green spaces.

### ⊙ Steps

1 Decide when you want to visit. Seasons are the opposite of those in the northern hemisphere. Summer is from December to February and winter is from June to August. The average winter low is about 16°C (61°F) and the average summer high is about 26°C (79°F).

2 Book well ahead if you want to come for Christmas. December is peak season for getting to Sydney, with air tickets at their most expensive. It's a great time to visit, though, with barbecues on the beach and, through-out January, the Sydney festival, which ends with Australia Day on 26 January, and the Tall Ships race in Sydney Harbour.

3 Visit at the end of summer and start of autumn to see and participate in two of Sydney's major community events: the Gay and Lesbian Mardi Gras in February and March, and the St Patrick's Day parade on 17 March (or the previous Sunday).

4 Don't miss the Sydney Film Festival (in mid-June) if you like movies. More active visitors can watch or join in the City to Surf race on the second Sunday in August.

5 Join in with a national obsession and come for the rugby. In September there are both Rugby League and Rugby Union finals. Book early.

### ✱ Tips

At any time of year, you won't want to miss major sights like the Sydney Opera House, the Royal Botanic Gardens and the Art Gallery of New South Wales. For harbourside colour, shops and restaurants, visit The Rocks, and for speciality galleries and boutiques in small-scale streets of Victorian houses, visit the suburb of Paddington.

The Sydney Tower in the city centre offers amazing views over the city and beyond.

**996 Tip for Service When Travelling**

Tipping is de rigueur in most of the world, but the methods and percentages vary. In some countries, a service charge is added to restaurant or hotel bills in lieu of gratuities. In many others, waiting staff rely on tips to bring their wage up to a decent level. The following are suggested guidelines only. Consult an up-to-date travel guide for more information about local customs.

chart

| COUNTRY | SUGGESTED TIP | NOTES |
|---------|---------------|-------|
| Australia | Optional | Tipping is not usual in Australia, but a small tip for good service by waiters, hotel porters and taxi drivers is appreciated. |
| Canada | 10–20% | Tipping is usual and expected in restaurants and bars, for taxis and for food delivery. |
| China | None | Tipping is not usual in China. |
| Egypt | Variable | Tips are expected by waiters, hotel staff, tour guides, drivers (but not taxi drivers). Tip generously if you have had good service. |
| France | 15–20% | The 15% service charge is usually included in the price in restaurants. Many people leave another 5% or so on top. |
| Germany | Variable | Service charge is included in restaurant bills but small tips on top are appreciated. Give taxi drivers a 10% tip. |
| Hong Kong | 10–15% | Most restaurants add about 10% to a bill and you are expected to add another 5% or so on top. |
| India | Variable | About 10% is added to the bill in tourist hotels and restaurants. Drivers and tour guides will expect a tip; if they have been especially helpful or spent a long time with you, tip generously. |
| Ireland | 10–12.5% | Tipping is usual in restaurants and for taxis, but not in hotels. Restaurants sometimes include a service charge in the bill. |
| Italy | Up to 15% | Service of 15% is sometimes included in restaurant bills. If not, leave a tip of 10% or so. Some family restaurants do not expect a tip. Tip taxi drivers and hotel porters if they have been helpful. |
| Japan | None | Service charges are included in restaurant and hotel bills; tipping is not necessary and may even cause offence. |
| Mexico | Variable | Expected by taxi drivers, waiters, food delivery services and hotel staff. |
| New Zealand | Optional | Tipping is not usual in New Zealand, but is becoming more common in larger cities where you can tip 5–10% of a restaurant bill. |
| Thailand | Optional | Not usual except in upmarket hotels. |
| United Kingdom | 10–15% | Usual for restaurants, although some include service in the bill, especially for larger parties. Taxi drivers expect a similar tip. |
| United States | 15 to 20% | Essential for waiters and cocktail waiters, taxi drivers and hotel room service. Also tip a couple of dollars to hotel maids and bellhops. |

## Time Your Trip to Thailand — 997

With its amazing mix of frenetic urban life, awe-inspiring temples and laid-back beaches, Thailand offers an unparalleled range of experiences for the visitor.

### ⊙ Steps

1 Visit in the cool season of November to February, when there is less rain than at other times and it is not too hot, with an average temperature of about 27°C (80°F). The climate varies hugely around the country, and it's often better in the south in March to May, when the north is steaming hot – up to 33°C (91°F). The monsoon is from June to October.

2 The peak months for tourism are December and August – prices may be higher and it will certainly be more crowded.

3 Thai New Year is celebrated with the Songkran Festival in mid-April. A family affair, it involves bathing Buddhas and generally throwing water around in the streets – prepare to get soaked.

4 Rice festivals are important in rural life. In mid-May the Ploughing Ceremony marks the start of the rice planting. Between September and May there are local celebrations for the rice harvest.

5 After the rainy season (usually in November) comes the lovely Loi Krathong Festival in which hundreds of candle-lit floats shaped as flowers are sent along the waterways for good luck.

6 Shoppers might like to visit Bangkok between mid-November and mid-December when shops hold a Grand Sale with up to 80 per cent off everything. But within this period avoid the King's Birthday, 5 December, when the city is heaving with celebrating crowds.

### ✳ Tips

In Bangkok don't miss Wat Phra Kaew and the Grand Palace, and Wat Traimit (the Temple of the Golden Buddha). Jim Thompson's House is a peaceful collection of Thai art and architecture.

Beyond the capital, head for the second city of Chiang Mai in the north, and the Ayuthaya complex of temples and ruins, also north of Bangkok.

The most renowned islands are Ko Samui and Phuket.

### ⚠ Warning

Avoid the borders with Burma and Cambodia, where there may be bandits who pose a risk to travellers and others.

## Time Your Trip to New York City — 998

What other city has the audacity to style itself "the capital of the world"? New York is a city of superlatives, a kaleidoscope of famous buildings, museums and colourful neighbourhoods.

### ⊙ Steps

1 Remember that late spring and early autumn bring the best weather to New York. Summers are often sweltering and humid, while snowfall and freezing temperatures are common during winter. The average July high is 29°C (84°F); the average January low is -3°C (26°F).

2 If food is your passion, don your trousers with the elastic waistband in mid-May and eat your fill of exotic fare at the International Food Fair on Ninth Avenue.

3 Listen to the greatest musicians in jazz at the JVC Jazz Festival during the second half of June. About 300 artists play 40 venues in and around the city.

4 Celebrate the end of summer by joining the million-plus people who participate in the Caribbean Day parade on Labor Day, in Brooklyn.

### ✳ Tips

New York is in a perpetual state of tourist high season. You stand the best chance of finding lower hotel rates and airfares from January to March, although even during these months it's difficult.

To find out what cultural events are going on, check out listings in *The Village Voice* weekly newspaper or the weekly magazines *New York* or *The New Yorker*.

5   Catch the latest arrivals to the silver screen at the New York Film Festival, held at Lincoln Center from late September to early October.

6   Cheer on runners at the New York City Marathon in early November. It's the largest in the United States and one of the most prestigious events of its kind worldwide. Two million cheering spectators line the course, along with 40-plus musical bands.

7   If you can bear the cold weather, experience the Christmas season New York–style by ice-skating in Rockefeller Plaza and by shopping among show-stopping window displays along Fifth Avenue and the designer boutiques along Madison Avenue.

8   Find out in advance about special exhibitions that may be coming to New York's world-class museums, which include the Metropolitan Museum of Art (the Met), the American Museum of Natural History, the Guggenheim Museum and the Museum of Modern Art (MOMA).

9   For good deals on tickets to Broadway and off-Broadway shows, stop by the TKTS (cut-price tickets) booth at the northern end of Times Square before afternoon or evening performances.

No matter when you visit, make sure to ascend the Empire State Building and the Statue of Liberty, which afford great views of New York City but usually involve queuing. When you need to regain your sanity, take a day-time stroll in Central Park.

## ⚠ Warning

While recent years have definitely seen a decline in crime, visitors should nonetheless observe the precautions they would in any large city, keeping personal valuables well secured and avoiding secluded or unsavoury-seeming areas after dark.

---

## 999 Time Your Trip to San Francisco

Scenic, colourful and tolerant, San Francisco offers something for everyone. Its location between the ocean and the bay makes the weather as unusual as the city itself.

### ⊙ Steps

1   For the best weather, visit in May, September or October, but remember that gorgeous weather is possible any day of the year. The climate can change dramatically from moment to moment, and it even varies from neighbourhood to neighbourhood. June, July and August are often cold and foggy, suitable only if you're trying to escape from somewhere hot.

2   Take in the Chinese New Year Festival and Parade in late January or early February. The parade is one of the biggest nighttime illuminated processions in the country, and features floats, Chinese acrobats, a 60 m (200 ft) long dragon and lion dancers.

3   Check out the San Francisco Flower and Garden Show in mid-March to see how the visions of Bay Area landscapers reach fruition. Attend free seminars on various aspects of gardening.

4   Learn about Japanese culture – martial arts, tea ceremonies and singular food – at the Cherry Blossom Festival in late April.

5   If you are a film buff, don't miss the San Francisco International Film Festival, which runs from mid-April into early May. Well-respected throughout the world, the festival screens a variety of films, puts on gala opening and closing nights, and includes lots of glitzy parties for attendees and stars.

6   Jog from San Francisco Bay across the city to the Pacific Ocean. The Bay to Breakers, on the third Sunday in May, is a race with so many thousands of eccentrics that it feels more like a parade.

### ✳ Tip

No matter what time of year you visit, make sure to take in a panoramic view of this spectacular city. Drive or walk up to Twin Peaks, a small double-tipped mountain sitting in the middle of San Francisco. Other good places from which to admire city views are the top of the Mark Hopkins Hotel on Nob Hill, Coit Tower in North Beach and the Golden Gate Bridge, which you can walk across.

7   Fly your rainbow in June, the month San Francisco's gay community celebrates its freedom. There's a film festival, Gay Pride Week and a Gay Freedom Day parade.

8   Hit the North Beach Festival in June if you are a big fan of Italian and/or Beat culture. You can hear everything from opera to poetry readings and feast upon some of the city's best Italian cuisine.

9   Attend the San Francisco Blues Festival in late September. Always extremely popular, and a San Francisco favourite for almost 30 years, the festival includes world-class blues headliners playing at Fort Mason's Great Meadow.

10  Take your favourite chocoholic to the Ghirardelli Square Chocolate Festival, held in early September at the landmark Fisherman's Wharf headquarters of the famed local chocolate company. Sample all kinds of yummy treats like chocolate cheesecake and chocolate-covered strawberries.

11  Check out the fun at Fleet Week, a salute to sailors and the sea held in early October. You can watch the parade of ships, see Blue Angels air shows, tour ships or mingle with sailors to your heart's content.

## ⚠ Warnings

Summer is the season when travellers might wish to avoid San Francisco. Attractions are overrun by tourists, prices are higher, and the weather is often cold and foggy.

Rainy weather and poor visibility can cause significant delays at San Francisco International Airport. Find out if your airline flies into Oakland Airport just across the bay, which is often a better alternative.

# Time Your Trip to Tokyo    `1000`

Tokyo is so built-up and energetic, it makes New York feel like a lazy Sunday in the suburbs. Despite this intensity the Japanese are hospitable and helpful to strangers. Crime is extremely rare.

## ◉ Steps

1   Enjoy Tokyo's fairly temperate climate, which has four distinct seasons. Winter brings cold, sunny weather and the occasional snowfall. Spring and autumn are usually pleasant. June and early July are often rainy. Summer is hot and humid. The average July high is 27°C (80°F), and the average January low is 2°C (35°F).

2   Visit during April to pack numerous cultural events into one trip. The Buddha's birthday is celebrated nationwide on 8 April, and the cherry blossom season (Sakura Matsuri) is appreciated at parks around Tokyo during the same month.

3   Take the train to the medieval capital of Kamakura for a spectacular festival honouring heroes of the Middle Ages; it's held at the Tsurugaoka Hachimangu Shrine on the second to the third Sunday in April. Head to Kanayama Shrine in the city of Kawasaki in mid-April for the Jibeta Matsuri, a festival and parade praising the wonders of fertility.

4   Watch nearly naked giants wrestle. Most sumo matches in Tokyo are held in January, May and September, although you can see them on TV almost year-round.

## ✳ Tip

No matter when you go to Tokyo, make sure to visit the grand old Tokyo National Museum to learn about all aspects of Japanese civilisation through thousands of artifacts. Attend a performance of kabuki, ornate and easy-to-follow stage plays that have historically been the favourite form of entertainment in Japan. Asakusa (old Tokyo), the Tsukiji Fish Market and Roppongi, Tokyo's club district, are other popular destinations.

## ⚠ Warning

Tokyo is the world's most expensive destination, estimated to be at least 60 per cent more costly than New York.

## 1001 Use eHow

eHow.com is the website where you can find out how to do just about everything – and purchase the products and services you need to do it. Here's how to get the most from our site.

### ⦿ Steps

1   Go online, type "www.ehow.com" in your browser's web-address field and press Enter or Return. Welcome to our home page!

2   Search for a how-to (what we call an "eHow") by typing a question – such as "How do I water a lawn?" – in the search field at the top of the page. Click "Do it" to search our database of eHows.

3   Or browse through our eHow centres, such as Home & Garden. You'll find these listed on our home page, and you can also find them via colour-coded navigation tabs that are visible on every page.

4   Read the eHow on the topic you've chosen. Note that some eHows also include video instructions.

5   As you're reading, check out tips contributed by other eHow users. (See "Ask Someone on a Date" or "Boil an Egg" for hundreds of enlightening examples.) If it's something you know how to do well, why not contribute your own tip?

6   Look for the handy shopping list that accompanies each eHow, and notice the featured books and tools. Just click on whatever you need to buy in order to get things done – or visit the eHow shop. The products you choose to buy travel with you in a virtual shopping cart as you go through the site.

7   Probe further into the eHow universe by clicking on Related eHows. Or explore other websites associated with your topic by clicking on one or more Related Sites.

8   Share favourite eHows with friends and family using our E-mail to a Friend feature. You can send any eHow – with a special message of your own – to anyone you want.

9   While you're online, sign up for our award-winning newsletter and be kept up to date on the latest eHow happenings.

10  Personalise your view of the eHow site by creating a My eHow page, for your favourite eHows, important reminders and any other goodies you choose to put there.

11  Put information in the palm of your hand by downloading any eHow to your personal device – for instant reference wherever you need it.

12  Take advantage of the time you've freed up by using our site to do the things you love. Or try something new and different: Start a business, paddle a canoe, win a sandcastle competition, plan a salsa party, redecorate your living room – or any of thousands of other things – using eHow's step-by-step instructions.

### ✳ Tips

If you don't have the time or desire to do a task, we can still assist you in getting the job done. Look for the Who Can Help You With This section to find people and services that can help you complete just about any task.

Check out our site regularly for new and timely features. For example, our seasonal centres come to life at holiday time to help you enjoy the festivities in new and creative ways. And the eHow shop will help make holiday shopping a breeze.

Share with us what you think of our site or this book. E-mail us directly at feedback@ehow.com.

### ⚠ Warning

eHow can be highly addictive. People come to our site to find out how to do one task and end up learning a lot of other things along the way. Visit eHow.com only if you're prepared to learn more – and do more – than you ever thought you could.

## Contributor Credits

eHow would like to thank all of the writers, consultants and experts who helped make this book possible, especially the following:

Allan Abbott, MD
Jill Adler, MD
Steve Adler, MD
Ankush Agarwal
David Algeo
Paul Auerbach, MD
Gloria Averbuch
Sam Ayoubpour
Steve Baker
Sally Ann Barnes
Patrick Barrett
Jennie Basarich
Susan Batten, DMD
Shelly Bellamy
Bryant Benson
Quita Bingham
Grant Bixby
Richard Booth
Anita F. Bott
Julia Bourland
Renee Branski
Karen Bridgers
Mike Brigante
Bobbi Brown
Terry Burrows
Teresa Cameron
June Campbell
Sandy Carlson
Joyce Chan, RN
Paul Chartrand
Jo Ann Cichewicz
Danny Clark
Lon Clark
Daniel Collado, DDS
Paula Criss
Greg Crouch
Laurie Daniel
Stephanie Daniels
Justin Davidson
Gail Davis, RN, IBCLC
Sanna James Delmonico, MS, RD
Annette Doherty, MPT
Pat Doherty
Ivan Donohue
Antonia Ehlers
Rob Einaudi
Lisa Ellis
Catten Ely
Sherri Eng
Melanie Feinberg
Jim Finnerty
Gary Fluitt
Veronica Lorson Fowler
Pam Gelman
Henry Gilbey
Sarah Golden

Jason Graff
Reg Grant
Stephanie Green
Beth Haiken
Kim Haworth
Rob Heidger
David Henry
John Henshell
Maria Hess
Peter Hingston
Daria Hutchinson
Alan Isabelle
Lea Jacobson
Robert Janis
James Jenson
Allison Johnson
Robin Jones
Marie Kare
Angella Kay
Dong Ho Kim, DDS
Eugene Kim, MD
Jane Kim
Jack Kolodny
Bill Kramer
Carl LaFong
Jane Laing
Angela LaVelle
Margie Levinson
Danielle Lewis
David Lignell
Cindy Lin
Karen Lipker
Kim Llauget
Kai Llauget-Kurnik
Zen McCann
Paul McGrath
Tim McNell
Doug McPherson
William Merrimack
Julie Metzler
Ronald Bruce Meyer
Sonia Michaels
Ryan Modjeski
Mary Ann Mohanraj
Candace Murphy
Shannon Murphy
Theresa Musser, DVM
Nathan Meyers
Nellie Neal
Roxanne Nelson, RN
Ellie Newman
Nolo.com
Andrew Nunn
Deborah Oksenberg, MD
Ben Olsen
Derek O'Neil

Ricardo Ortega
Jennifer Overhulse-King
Jason Patent
Jeff Peacock
Eve Pearlman
Larry Peetz, DVM
Thomas Penberthy
Annette Pennock
Christine Perez
Craig Perfect
Colette Plum
Joe Putnam
Janine Queller
Nik Remer
Gail M. Rickards
Bethallyn Black Rogers
Michelle Rogers
Sumit Sablok
Matt Samelson
Scott Samelson
Fred Sandsmark
Susan Sawyer
Helene Schneider, MA, MFT
Barry Schwartz
Larry Sebon
Brette Sember
Pamela Shaffer
Jane Simmonds
Valerie Singer
Kristin Steele
Catherine Stone
John Swartzberg, MD, FACP
Suzanne Sweers
Elvis Terrler
Ted Thomaidis
Doug Tinker
Jeff Tinker
Ryan Tinker
Patrick Towle
Jacqueline Tresl, RN
Ray Vandermay
Joseph Vause
Regina Vause
Kate Vause-Miller
Mary Vinnedge
Ren Volpe
Sharon Wagner
Lance Walheim
Kevin Walsh
Vicki Webster
Susan Wiedmann
Thatcher Wine
Marty Wingate
Sharron Wood
Ileana Zapatero, MD
Morgan Zeitler

## ACKNOWLEDGEMENTS

I thank every person who has helped us create both a phenomenal company and our first book: our employees, investors, partners and clients, and most of all, the millions of eHow.com users.

On a personal note, my deepest, heartfelt gratitude to my mum; my ex-husband, Jeff; my siblings, Noah and Erin; my mentors; and my dear friends for their endless enthusiasm, patience, honesty and loving support. With you, I can do just about everything!

And finally, thank you for reading our book. Please make sure to visit us soon at www.ehow.com.

Courtney Rosen

**How to Do** *(Just About)* **Everything**